For too long students of Scripture have jumped historically from the fall of Jerusalem to the birth of Jesus, skipping some of the key moments in the redemptive story and the key theological role that these wrongly named "intertestamental" years and texts play in biblical theology. George Athas invites us into this era and its literature, showing how the communities of the Second Temple as well as enduring exile continue the history of redemption that emerges with the same community gathered around the temple in the Gospels and Acts. Historically accurate, carefully presented, *Bridging the Testaments* is an extremely helpful invitation to what is for many unfortunately the "dark ages" of Jewish and biblical history.

— MARK J. BODA, professor of Old Testament,
McMaster Divinity College

In his volume *Bridging the Testaments*, Athas exposes the political, cultural, religious, economic, and social realities of the Second Temple period. Through a serious inquiry into biblical and extrabiblical literature written in Hebrew, Aramaic, Persian, Greek, and Latin, the author counters the notions that there was a cessation of Jewish literature that led to a silent intertestamental period. Athas provides an exhaustive description of major events under Persian, Hellenistic, Hasmonean, and Roman rules between 597 BC and 4 BC. As stated by the author, "these centuries are laden with fascinating twists and turns, close calls, and a cast of enthralling characters." This masterpiece bridges the gap between the worlds of the Old and New Testaments and paints a clear picture of Second Temple Judaism during the centuries that precede the advent of the Messiah. Highly recommended.

—HÉLÈNE DALLAIRE, Earl S. Kalland professor of
Old Testament and Semitic languages and chair of
Old Testament department, Denver Seminary

This is a winsomely written yet carefully nuanced account of the historical landscape of Judea in the Second Temple period. It is unburdened by excessive footnotes, yet clearly informed by extensive research. Athas helps us hear how passages both from the Jewish Scriptures and extrabiblical texts spoke to people in their lived contexts during this period—and makes some provocative suggestions for how several Old Testament texts are actually *part* of the bridge between the testaments. I highly recommend this book to those looking for a solid immersion into the story of the deceptively blank page that separates Malachi from Matthew.

—DAVID A. DESILVA, trustees' distinguished professor of
New Testament and Greek, Ashland Theological Seminary

George Athas has done us a great service in writing *Bridging the Testaments*. This is an outstanding book—it is interesting, well-written, erudite, and relevant for anyone seeking to understand either the postexilic period or the social, historical, and religious background for the New Testament. Providing more information and going more in depth than most other New Testament background studies, this volume will serve as a valuable textbook for any college or graduate class seeking to understand the intertestamental period and its impact on the New Testament. Furthermore, even if it is not required for class, it is a great read.

—J. DANIEL HAYS, senior professor of Old Testament, Southwestern Baptist Theological Seminary

Taking a traditional critical viewpoint, Athas provides a useful synthesis of the biblical texts and the extrabiblical sources to weave together an important review of these diverse elements. The work is worthy of consideration as a means to understand the complex picture of these centuries.

—RICHARD S. HESS, distinguished professor of Old Testament and Semitic languages, Denver Seminary

With great detail, nuance, and insight, George Athas walks the reader through a remarkable expanse of history and the way it affected the growth and reception of Scripture. He shows how the texts transmitted within the Bible provide ways to cope with world-changing events carrying great theological relevance both for modern readers and for the ancient communities who experienced them. This book contributes enormously to a thoughtful engagement of the biblical tradition as a cornerstone of the human reckoning with history.

—MARK LEUCHTER, professor of ancient Judaism, Temple University

Even Old and New Testament experts often ignore or don't pay sufficient attention to the period *between* the Testaments. George Athas provides a detailed yet accessible account of this fascinating period that helps us understand the biblical material more fully. His presentation of the Persian, Greek, and Roman periods with a focus on Judah is riveting and insightful. I recommend this book to all who are interested in biblical history and theology.

—TREMPER LONGMAN III, distinguished scholar and professor emeritus of biblical studies, Westmont College

Bridging the Testaments is an absolutely wonderful volume! Professor George Athas covers this crucial period so very well—this volume is thorough, carefully documented, very well written, and provides everything that students of Scripture should know about this pivotal period. I highly recommend it for scholars and students alike.

—CHRISTOPHER ROLLSTON, professor of Northwest Semitic languages and literature, George Washington University

Sooner or later all students of the Bible must consider the relationship between what we call the Old and the New Testaments. The relationship is complex, rich, and important. There is continuity (the God of Israel is the God and Father of Jesus) and discontinuity (there *is* something "new" about the New Testament). All this may be profitably explored from various angles. In this impressive and stimulating volume George Athas explores chiefly the *historical* connections between the Testaments. How did the "world" of the Old Testament become the "world" of the New? Dr. Athas dispels popular misunderstandings (for example, that there were 400 years of prophetic "silence" between the Testaments) and introduces readers to outstanding characters and world-changing events unfamiliar to most of us. Some of his suggestions will raise further questions for readers, but all will benefit from Dr. Athas's deep grasp of his subject. The careful reading of this book will enrich the reader's understanding of the message of the New Testament that has turned the world upside down.

—JOHN WOODHOUSE, former principal of Moore Theological College

In this extremely useful volume, George Athas provides an accessible, highly readable, and comprehensive guide to the crucial period covering the end of the Old Testament era up to the beginning of the New Testament. In a remarkable achievement, Athas successfully weaves the interpretation of biblical books dealing with that later period and essential elements of New Testament background into the broader tapestry of world history of the centuries that saw the rise and fall of the Persian and Hellenistic kingdoms and the rise of Rome. This is a book that will engage both scholars and students, while providing an essential reference work for years to come.

—IAN YOUNG, professor of biblical studies, Australian Catholic University

BRIDGING THE TESTAMENTS

BRIDGING THE TESTAMENTS

THE HISTORY AND THEOLOGY OF GOD'S PEOPLE
IN THE SECOND TEMPLE PERIOD

GEORGE ATHAS

ZONDERVAN ACADEMIC

Bridging the Testaments
Copyright © 2023 by George Athas

Published in Grand Rapids, Michigan, by Zondervan. Zondervan is a registered trademark of The Zondervan Corporation, L.L.C., a wholly owned subsidiary of HarperCollins Christian Publishing, Inc.

Requests for information should be addressed to customercare@harpercollins.com.

Zondervan titles may be purchased in bulk for educational, business, fundraising, or sales promotional use. For information, please email SpecialMarkets@Zondervan.com.

ISBN 978-0-310-16176-9 (audio Part 1)
ISBN 978-0-310-16177-6 (audio Part 2)

Library of Congress Cataloging-in-Publication Data

Names: Athas, George, author.
Title: Bridging the Testaments : the history and theology of God's people in the Second Temple period / George Athas.
Description: Grand Rapids : Zondervan, 2023. | Includes index.
Identifiers: LCCN 2023015841 (print) | LCCN 2023015842 (ebook) | ISBN 9780310520948 (hardcover) | ISBN 9780310520955 (ebook)
Subjects: LCSH: Judaism--History--Post-exilic period, 586 B.C.-210 A.D. | BISAC: RELIGION / Biblical Studies / Old Testament / General | HISTORY / Ancient / General
Classification: LCC BM176 .A885 2023 (print) | LCC BM176 (ebook) | DDC 296.09/014--dc23/eng/20230525
LC record available at https://lccn.loc.gov/2023015841
LC ebook record available at https://lccn.loc.gov/2023015842

Unless otherwise indicated, Scripture quotations are those of the author.

Any internet addresses (websites, blogs, etc.) and telephone numbers in this book are offered as a resource. They are not intended in any way to be or imply an endorsement by Zondervan, nor does Zondervan vouch for the content of these sites and numbers for the life of this book.

All rights reserved. No part of this publication may be reproduced, stored in a retrieval system, or transmitted in any form or by any means—electronic, mechanical, photocopy, recording, or any other—except for brief quotations in printed reviews, without the prior permission of the publisher.

All maps © 2023 by Zondervan. All rights reserved. Additional data provided by George Athas.

Cover design: Thinkpen Design
Cover image: © Look and Learn / Bridgeman Images
Interior design: Kait Lamphere

Printed in the United States of America

*For my students past, present, and future,
and most especially for the students who
have sat in my Zechariah class.*

CONTENTS

Detailed Contents xiii
Acknowledgments xxi
Abbreviations xxiii
Table 1: Brief Timeline of Events (597–4 BC) xxix
Table 2: The High Priests of Jerusalem xxxii
Table 3: Rulers of the Persian Empire xxxiv
Table 4: Attested Governors of Persian Yehud (Judah) xxxv
Table 5: Attested Governors of Persian Samaria xxxvi
Table 6: Jerusalem under the Control of the Diadochi xxxvii
Table 7: Rulers of the Ptolemaic Kingdom (Egypt) xxxviii
Table 8: Rulers of the Seleucid Kingdom (Syria) xxxix
Table 9: The Zadokites and Tobiads xli
Table 10: The Hasmonean Dynasty xlii
Table 11: Sabbatical Years xliii
Introduction 1
    Estranged Testaments 1
    Bridging the Testaments 14
    The Grand Sweep 16

PART 1: THE PERSIAN ERA (539–331 BC)

1.1 The Return to Jerusalem (539–515 BC) 25
1.2 Religion in the Persian Empire 33
1.3 From Zerubbabel to Ezra (515–458 BC) 41
1.4 Ezra, Nehemiah, and the Samarians 46
1.5 The Late Fifth Century BC 73
1.6 The Shifting "Compass" of the Fourth Century BC 88
1.7 An Israelite Coalition 96
1.8 The Chronicler 131
1.9 Conclusion 144

PART 2: THE HELLENISTIC ERA (331–167 BC)

- 2.1 Uniting Greece ... 149
- 2.2 Alexander and the Fall of the Persian Empire ... 153
- 2.3 Priestly Power and Davidic Hope under Greek Rule ... 173
- 2.4 Hellenism ... 181
- 2.5 The Wars of the *Diadochi* ... 191
- 2.6 Ptolemaic Rule ... 195
- 2.7 The Rising Importance of Rome ... 264
- 2.8 Seleucid Rule ... 270
- 2.9 Conclusion ... 304

PART 3: THE HASMONEAN ERA (167–63 BC)

- 3.1 Introduction ... 309
- 3.2 The Road to Revolt ... 313
- 3.3 Resistance Literature ... 340
- 3.4 The Maccabean Revolt ... 349
- 3.5 Aftermath of Revolt ... 370
- 3.6 The Reassertion of Seleucid Sovereignty ... 401
- 3.7 Jewish Independence ... 426
- 3.8 Conclusion ... 498

PART 4: THE ROMAN ERA (63–4 BC)

- 4.1 Roman Conquest ... 505
- 4.2 The Development of Judaism ... 517
- 4.3 Roman Hegemony ... 529
- 4.4 Parthian Hegemony ... 563
- 4.5 The Augustan-Herodian Era ... 573
- Epilogue ... 609

- Ancient Texts Index ... 615
- Subject Index ... 627
- Author Index ... 637

DETAILED CONTENTS

Acknowledgments xxi
Abbreviations xxiii
Table 1: Brief Timeline of Events (597–4 BC) xxix
Table 2: The High Priests of Jerusalem xxxii
Table 3: Rulers of the Persian Empire xxxiv
Table 4: Attested Governors of Persian Yehud (Judah) xxxv
Table 5: Attested Governors of Persian Samaria xxxvi
Table 6: Jerusalem under the Control of the Diadochi xxxvii
Table 7: Rulers of the Ptolemaic Kingdom (Egypt) xxxviii
Table 8: Rulers of the Seleucid Kingdom (Syria) xxxix
Table 9: The Zadokites and Tobiads xli
Table 10: The Hasmonean Dynasty xlii
Table 11: Sabbatical Years xliii
Introduction 1
   Estranged Testaments 1
      Perceiving the Problem 1
      The New Testament View 4
      The Suppression of Prophecy 6
      Dealing with the Problem 11
   Bridging the Testaments 14
      Questions and Aims 14
      Structure and Style 15
   The Grand Sweep 16

PART 1: THE PERSIAN ERA (539–331 BC)

1.1 The Return to Jerusalem (539–515 BC) 25
   1.1.1   The Rise of Cyrus 25
   1.1.2   Pioneers in Jerusalem 27

1.2 Religion in the Persian Empire 33
   1.2.1   Yahwism and Ancient Near Eastern Religion 33

	1.2.2	Yahwistic Communities	35
	1.2.3	Yahwism under Persian Imperial Religion	36
1.3	From Zerubbabel to Ezra (515–458 BC)	41
	1.3.1	Governors and High Priests	41
	1.3.2	Jerusalem	43
	1.3.3	The Reign of Darius I (522–486 BC)	44
	1.3.4	The Reign of Xerxes I (486–465 BC)	45
1.4	Ezra, Nehemiah, and the Samarians	46
	1.4.1	The Revolt of Inarus (460–454 BC)	46
	1.4.2	The Mission of Ezra	48
	1.4.3	The Results of Ezra's Reforms	51
	1.4.4	The Revolt of Megabyzus and the Walls of Jerusalem	54
	1.4.5	The Samarian Temple on Mount Gerizim	57
	1.4.6	Jerusalem, Mount Gerizim, and Israelite Identity	62
	1.4.7	Governor Nehemiah	64
1.5	The Late Fifth Century BC	73
	1.5.1	From Artaxerxes I to Darius II (424–404 BC)	73
	1.5.2	Judah after Nehemiah	75
	1.5.3	The Yahwists at Elephantine	78
	1.5.4	The Judean Diaspora	85
1.6	The Shifting "Compass" of the Fourth Century BC	88
	1.6.1	Artaxerxes II and the Loss of Egypt	88
	1.6.2	A New Mediterranean "Pole" and Reorientation in the Levant	89
	1.6.3	Weakening Persian Power in Trans-Euphrates	92
	1.6.4	The Accession of Artaxerxes III	95
1.7	An Israelite Coalition	96
	1.7.1	The Tennes Revolt (351–345 BC)	96
	1.7.2	The Power Vacuum in the Southern Levant	98
	1.7.3	Unification and the Manasseh Affair	102
	1.7.4	Theology and Scribal Culture	119
	1.7.5	The Reassertion of Persian Power	122
	1.7.6	From Artaxerxes III to Darius III	128

1.8	The Chronicler		131
	1.8.1	A Manifesto of Israelite Identity	131
	1.8.2	Davidic Dynasty	132
	1.8.3	The Jerusalem Temple	137
	1.8.4	Ancestry	139
	1.8.5	The Land	140
	1.8.6	Torah	141
1.9	Conclusion		144

PART 2: THE HELLENISTIC ERA (331–167 BC)

2.1	Uniting Greece		149
	2.1.1	Philip II of Macedon (359–336 BC)	149
	2.1.2	The Accession of Alexander III	151
2.2	Alexander and the Fall of the Persian Empire		153
	2.2.1	The Liberation of the Greek Cities	153
	2.2.2	The Battle of Issus (333 BC)	154
	2.2.3	Conquest of Trans-Euphrates and Egypt	155
	2.2.4	Samaria and the Andromachus Affair	161
	2.2.5	The Battle of Gaugamela (331 BC)	162
	2.2.6	The End of Persia	163
	2.2.7	The Death of Alexander	167
	2.2.8	Alexander in the Book of Daniel	170
2.3	Priestly Power and Davidic Hope under Greek Rule		173
	2.3.1	Judah under Alexander	173
	2.3.2	The Expropriation of Davidic Theology	174
	2.3.3	Prophecy in Judah	177
2.4	Hellenism		181
	2.4.1	Greek Religion and Culture	181
	2.4.2	Greek Ethics and Philosophy	184
	2.4.3	The Development of Jewish Apocalyptic Thought	187
2.5	The Wars of the *Diadochi*		191
	2.5.1	Ptolemy I and Seleucus I	191

| | | 2.5.2 | Vying for Empire .... 191 |

- 2.6 Ptolemaic Rule 195
  - 2.6.1 The Siege of Jerusalem (301 BC) 195
  - 2.6.2 The High Priest Hezekiah 204
  - 2.6.3 The House of David in Egypt 210
  - 2.6.4 The Book of the Twelve Prophets 211
  - 2.6.5 Ptolemaic Administration and Influence 215
  - 2.6.6 Governance of the Jewish People 219
  - 2.6.7 The Allure of Alexandria 220
  - 2.6.8 The Last of the *Diadochi* 224
  - 2.6.9 First Syrian War 225
  - 2.6.10 The Septuagint 226
  - 2.6.11 Prayer Houses: The Beginnings of the Synagogue 228
  - 2.6.12 The Ptolemaic Economy 230
  - 2.6.13 Excursus: Economics and the Gospel 233
  - 2.6.14 Second Syrian War (261–253 BC) 234
  - 2.6.15 Third Syrian War (246–241 BC) 236
  - 2.6.16 Onias II, Joseph Tobias, and the Pessimism of Qoheleth 237
  - 2.6.17 Fourth Syrian War (219–217 BC) and the Siege of Jerusalem .. 248
  - 2.6.18 Antiochus III and the Jews in Asia Minor 251
  - 2.6.19 Discontent in Judea under Ptolemy IV (217–204 BC) 253
  - 2.6.20 Death of Ptolemy IV (204 BC) 262

- 2.7 The Rising Importance of Rome 264
  - 2.7.1 The Dawn of Rome 264
  - 2.7.2 Rome and Carthage 266

- 2.8 Seleucid Rule 270
  - 2.8.1 Fifth Syrian War (202–195 BC) 270
  - 2.8.2 Judea under Antiochus III 276
  - 2.8.3 The Book of Tobit 278
  - 2.8.4 Simon II and the Jerusalem Temple 280
  - 2.8.5 Jewish Moderates, Progressives, and Conservatives 281
  - 2.8.6 Antiochus III and Rome 288
  - 2.8.7 The Wisdom of Ben Sira 291
  - 2.8.8 Seleucus IV and the Heliodorus Affair 296

- 2.9 Conclusion 304

PART 3: THE HASMONEAN ERA (167–63 BC)

- 3.1 Introduction 309
    - 3.1.1 Sources for the Hasmonean Era 309

- 3.2 The Road to Revolt..313
    - 3.2.1 The High Priest Jason and the Cultural Divide (175–171 BC) 313
    - 3.2.2 The High Priesthood of Menelaus......................318
    - 3.2.3 Crisis in the High Priesthood (171–170 BC) 320
    - 3.2.4 Sixth Syrian War (170–167 BC)...........................324
    - 3.2.5 The Abomination of Desolation (167 BC) 329
    - 3.2.6 Excursus: The Olivet Discourse 337
    - 3.2.7 The Period of Persecution (167–164 BC)............338

- 3.3 Resistance Literature..340
    - 3.3.1 Song of Songs...340
    - 3.3.2 The Book of Daniel...344

- 3.4 The Maccabean Revolt...349
    - 3.4.1 The Outbreak of Revolt 349
    - 3.4.2 Early Maccabean Successes 353
    - 3.4.3 The Battle of Emmaus (165 BC) 356
    - 3.4.4 Negotiations with the Seleucids 358
    - 3.4.5 The Death of Antiochus IV (164 BC) 359
    - 3.4.6 The Rededication of the Temple 360
    - 3.4.7 Daniel and the End of the Antiochene Persecution...........362
    - 3.4.8 The Long-Term Theological Ramifications of Rededication 366

- 3.5 Aftermath of Revolt 370
    - 3.5.1 The New Status Quo..370
    - 3.5.2 Regional Conflict (163/2 BC) 371
    - 3.5.3 The Dilemma of the High Priesthood 374
    - 3.5.4 The "Teacher of Righteousness" and the Calendar Controversy..376
    - 3.5.5 Onias IV and the Temple of Leontopolis............384
    - 3.5.6 Excursus: The Early Church and the Temple 388
    - 3.5.7 The Accession of Demetrius I............................390

| | | 3.5.8 | The Zadokite Crisis..................................390 |
| | | 3.5.9 | Judas Maccabeus as High Priest.......................394 |

3.6	The Reassertion of Seleucid Sovereignty...........................401
	3.6.1	Jewish Sects under the Seleucids.....................401
	3.6.2	The Waning Maccabean Cause 404
	3.6.3	The Second Tenure of Alcimus........................405
	3.6.4	Return of the Hasmoneans 408
	3.6.5	Seleucid Civil War and the Rise of Jonathan Apphus.......410
	3.6.6	Jonathan Apphus and International Affairs (152–142 BC)....................................413

3.7	Jewish Independence..426
	3.7.1	The Client State of Judea............................426
	3.7.2	Simon Thassi as High Priest (142–134 BC)...............430
	3.7.3	John Hyrcanus I and the Siege of Jerusalem (134/3 BC)....433
	3.7.4	John Hyrcanus I in the Shadow of the Seleucids 438
	3.7.5	Judea and International Developments (133–123 BC)......440
	3.7.6	"John the High Priest and the Community of the Jews".....445
	3.7.7	The Conquests of John Hyrcanus I....................450
	3.7.8	Judas Aristobulus I (104 BC): Priest and King............458
	3.7.9	The Early Reign of Alexander Jannaeus.................461
	3.7.10	Alexander Jannaeus and the Jewish Civil War 469
	3.7.11	Theological Responses to Alexander Jannaeus............476
	3.7.12	The Latter Reign of Alexander Jannaeus................480
	3.7.13	Queen Salome Alexandra............................483
	3.7.14	Rome, Pontus, Armenia, and the End of the Seleucid Kingdom..486
	3.7.15	Tigranes II and the Jewish State.......................489
	3.7.16	The Death of Salome Alexandra 490
	3.7.17	The Fraternal Civil War (67–63 BC)....................491

3.8 Conclusion 498

PART 4: THE ROMAN ERA (63–4 BC)

4.1	Roman Conquest..505
	4.1.1	Pompey the Great...................................505
	4.1.2	The Roman Conquest of Jerusalem (63 BC).............507

	4.1.3	The Client State of Judea 511
	4.1.4	Theological Responses to the Roman Conquest 513

4.2 The Development of Judaism 517
- 4.2.1 The Pharisees, Schools, and Synagogues 517
- 4.2.2 Canons of Scripture 522
- 4.2.3 Hillel the Elder 524
- 4.2.4 Godfearers and Converts 527

4.3 Roman Hegemony 529
- 4.3.1 Pompey's Return to Rome 529
- 4.3.2 The First Triumvirate 530
- 4.3.3 The Uprisings of Alexander II and Aristobulus II 531
- 4.3.4 Judea and the Campaign of Crassus 536
- 4.3.5 The Road to Roman Civil War 538
- 4.3.6 The Fate of Aristobulus II and Alexander II 542
- 4.3.7 Conclusion of the Roman Civil War 543
- 4.3.8 Julius Caesar in Egypt 546
- 4.3.9 Jews and the Caesarean Settlement 547
- 4.3.10 The Developing Dynasty of Antipater 551
- 4.3.11 Julius Caesar: Master of Rome 554
- 4.3.12 The Demise of Antipater 559
- 4.3.13 The Second Triumvirate 560

4.4 Parthian Hegemony 563
- 4.4.1 Herod and Mark Antony 563
- 4.4.2 Mark Antony and Cleopatra 564
- 4.4.3 Mattathias Antigonus II and the Parthian Invasion 564
- 4.4.4 The Flight of Herod 567
- 4.4.5 The Return of Herod 568
- 4.4.6 Herod's Siege of Jerusalem (37 BC) 571

4.5 The Augustan-Herodian Era 573
- 4.5.1 Herod and the High Priesthood 573
- 4.5.2 The End of the Second Triumvirate 577
- 4.5.3 The Victory of Octavian (31 BC) 578
- 4.5.4 Emperor Caesar Augustus: The Establishment of the Roman Principate 581
- 4.5.5 Herod the King and Builder 582

	4.5.6	Herod and the Jerusalem Temple	586
	4.5.7	Herod and His Family	591
	4.5.8	The Eagle Affair (4 BC)	599
	4.5.9	The Death of Herod	602
	4.5.10	The Aftermath of Herod's Death	603

Epilogue..609

Ancient Texts Index..615
Subject Index..627
Author Index..637

ACKNOWLEDGMENTS

This volume had its inception in the Zechariah class I have taught at Moore Theological College since 2007. The research for those classes revealed to me just how unknown the postexilic period was for so many and how few resources there were for students covering the whole period. While there were a host of specialized studies on certain aspects of the history or theology of this period, there was no adequate one-stop shop that I could recommend to students. And so the idea for this work was born. I wrote this book primarily for those students, but I am also deeply indebted to them for engaging with the ideas and helping to shape the current work. Learning in community is a great privilege.

I am also grateful to several people for their support and assistance in helping this volume come to fruition. The staff of the Donald Robinson Library at Moore Theological College are a stellar bunch of people who continue to make the library one of the best resources for biblical studies in the world. Particular thanks go to the research support officer, Rod Benson. I am grateful also to those who read parts of this work, provided valuable feedback on it, acted as a sounding board, or provided encouragement: Douglas Fyfe, Jordan Peterson, Lee Won Il, Jason Matthews, Ross Ciano, Peter Kerr, Marshall Ballantine-Jones, Jordan Pickering, Sigrid Holscher, Kamina Wüst, Gary Rendsburg, Mark Leuchter, John Dickson, Margaret Mowczko, Debra Snoddy, and Constantine Campbell. A special mention must, of course, go to Katya Covrett of Zondervan Academic, who believed in this project and exercised a heroic amount of patience and good humor as it grew far bigger than either of us imagined. Her guidance helped "tame the beast" and "clarify the Nectanebos." Thanks also to Nancy Erickson for her precision as a copy editor and expertise as a scholar. Finally, I must thank my wife, Koula, my daughters, Hosanna and Josephine, and my wider family in Australia and Greece for their unstinting support, especially through some most trying times.

Δόξα τῷ θεῷ.

ABBREVIATIONS

TECHNICAL

Akk.	Akkadian
Aram.	Aramaic
Arab.	Arabic
Eg.	Egyptian
Gk.	Greek
Heb.	Hebrew
Lat.	Latin
LXX	Septuagint
MT	Masoretic Text
pl.	plural
sg.	singular

DEUTEROCANONICAL WORKS AND SEPTUAGINT

Esd	Esdras
Jdt	Judith
Macc	Maccabees
Sir	Sirach
Wis	Wisdom of Solomon

OLD TESTAMENT PSEUDEPIGRAPHA

En.	Enoch
Jub.	Jubilees
Let. Aris.	Letter of Aristeas
Pss. Sol.	Psalms of Solomon
T. Jud.	Testament of Judah
T. Levi	Testament of Levi

DEAD SEA SCROLLS AND RELATED TEXTS

CD	Cairo Genizah copy of the Damascus Document
Q	Qumran
p	pesher

MISHNAH, TALMUD, AND RELATED LITERATURE

ʾAvot	Avot
b.	Babylonian Talmud
B. Bat.	Bava Batra
Ber.	Berakhot
Gen. Rab.	Genesis Rabbah
Giṭ.	Gittin
Ḥag.	Hagigah
Ḥul.	Hullin
Ketub.	Ketubbot
Naz.	Nazir
m.	Mishnah
Parah	Parah
Pesaḥ.	Pesahim
Qidd.	Qiddushin
Sanh.	Sanhedrin
Šabb.	Shabbat
Šeb.	Sheviʿit
Soṭah	Sotah
t.	Tosefta
Taʿan.	Taʿanit
Yad.	Yadayim
Yebam.	Yevamot
Yoma	Yoma
y.	Jerusalem Talmud

CLASSICAL SOURCES

Appian

Bell. civ.	*Bella civilia*
M.W.	*Mithridatic Wars*
S.W.	*Syrian Wars*

Arrian
Anab. . . . . *Anabasis*

Caesar
Alex. . . . . *Alexandrian Wars*
Civ. . . . . *Civil War*

Cicero
Rab. Perd. . . . . *Pro Rabirio Perduellionis Reo*
Sest. . . . . *Pro Sestius*
Ver. . . . . *In Verrem*

Curtius
Hist. . . . . *Histories*

Dio Cassius
Hist. rom. . . . . *Historiae romanae*

Diodorus Siculus
Bib. hist. . . . . *Bibliotheca historica*

Herodotus
Hist. . . . . *Histories*

Josephus
Ag. Ap. . . . . *Against Apion*
Ant. . . . . *Jewish Antiquities*
J.W. . . . . *Jewish War*

Justin
Epit. . . . . *Epitome of the Philippic History of Pompeius Trogus*

Justin Martyr
Trypho . . . . *Dialogue with Trypho*

Livy
Ab urbe cond. . . . . . *Ab urbe condita*
Per. . . . . *Periochae* (summary of *Ab urbe condita*)

Memnon
Hist. Her.......... *History of Heracleia*

Orosius
Hist. Ag........... *History Against the Pagans*

Ovid
Metam............ *Metamorphoses*

Pausanias
Descr............. *Description of Greece*

Philo
Mos.............. *De Vita Mosis* I, II

Pliny the Elder
Nat.............. *Natural History*

Plutarch
Anab............. *Anabasis*
Alex.............. *Alexander*
Ant............... *Antonius*
Brut.............. *Brutus*
Caes.............. *Caesar*
Crass............. *Crassus*
Luc............... *Lucullus*
Pomp............. *Pompeius*
Sull............... *Sulla*

Polybius
Hist............... *Histories*

Suetonius
Aug............... *Divus Augustus*
Caes.............. *Caesar*
Claud............. *Divus Claudius*

Thucydides
P.W.............. *History of the Peloponnesian War*

Xenophon
Anab. . . . . *Anabasis*
Hell. . . . . *Hellenica*

SECONDARY LITERATURE

ABD . . . . *Anchor Bible Dictionary.* Edited by David Noel Freedman. 6 vols. New York: Doubleday, 1992
AHB . . . . *Ancient History Bulletin*
AJN . . . . *American Journal of Numismatics*
AL . . . . André Lemaire, *Nouvelles Inscriptions Araméennes d'Idumée. Supplément à Transeuphratène. Tome 2: Collections Mousaïeff, Jeselsohn, Welch et divers.* Leuven: Peeters, 2002
Arch. Intern. Med. Archives of Internal Medicine
AREPS . . . . *Annual Review of Earth and Planetary Sciences*
BAGRW . . . . *Barrington Atlas of the Greek and Roman World.* Edited by Richard J. A. Talbert. Princeton: Princeton University Press, 2000
BASOR . . . . *Bulletin of the American Schools of Oriental Research*
BDAG . . . . Danker, Frederick W., Walter Bauer, William F. Arndt, and F. Wilbur Gingrich. *Greek-English Lexicon of the New Testament and Other Early Christian Literature.* 3rd rev. ed. Chicago: University of Chicago Press, 2000
BJRL . . . . *Bulletin of the John Rylands University Library of Manchester*
CIIP . . . . *Corpus Inscriptionum Iudaeae/Palestinae: A Multi-Lingual Corpus of the Inscriptions from Alexander to Muhammad. Vol. 1, Part 1: Jerusalem.* Edited by Hannah M. Cotton et al. Berlin: de Gruyter, 2010–
CIJ . . . . *Corpus Inscriptionum Judaicarum.* Edited by Jean-Baptiste Frey. 2 volumes. Rome: Pontifical Biblical Institute, 1936–1952
CPJ . . . . *Corpus Papyrorum Judaicarum.* Edited by Victor A. Tcherikover. 3 vols. Cambridge: Harvard University Press, 1957–1964
DJD . . . . Discoveries in the Judaean Desert
DSD . . . . *Dead Sea Discoveries*
HALOT . . . . *The Hebrew and Aramaic Lexicon of the Old Testament.* Ludwig Koehler, Walter Baumgartner, and Johann J.

	Stamm. Translated and edited under the supervision of Mervyn E. J. Richardson. Leiden: Brill, 2001
HUCA	*Hebrew Union College Annual*
IEJ	*Israel Exploration Journal*
INJ	*Israel Numismatic Journal*
INR	*Israel Numismatic Research*
JAJ	*Journal of Ancient Judaism*
JBL	*Journal of Biblical Literature*
JEMAHS	*Journal of Eastern Mediterranean Archaeology and Heritage Studies*
JGR	*Journal of Geophysical Research*
JIE	*Jewish Inscriptions of Graeco-Roman Egypt*. Edited by William Horbury and David Noy. Cambridge: Cambridge University Press, 2007
JJS	*Journal of Jewish Studies*
JQR	*Jewish Quarterly Review*
JRA	*Journal of Roman Archaeology*
JTS	*Journal of Theological Studies*
LHBOTS	The Library of Hebrew Bible/Old Testament Studies
NEA	*Near Eastern Archaeology*
PE	*The Persian Empire: A Corpus of Sources from the Achaemenid Period*. Amélie Kuhrt. London: Routledge, 2007
PEQ	*Palestine Exploration Quarterly*
PNAS	*Proceedings of the National Academy of Sciences*
SEG	Supplementum epigraphicum graecum
SIG	*Sylloge Inscriptionum Graecarum*. Edited by Wilhelm Dittenberger. 4 vols. 3rd ed. Leipzig: Hirzel, 1915–1924
TAD	*Textbook of Aramaic Documents from Egypt*. Bezalel Porten and Ada Yardeni. Jerusalem: Hebrew University, 1986
TAHNDT	*Textbook of Aramaic, Hebrew and Nabataean Documentary Texts from the Judaean Desert and Related Material*. Ada Yardeni. 2 vols. Jerusalem: Hebrew University, 2000
TAO	*Textbook of Aramaic Ostraca from Idumea*. Bezalel Porten and Ada Yardeni. 4 vols. Winona Lake, IN: Eisenbrauns, 2004
WBC	Word Biblical Commentary
WD	Wadi Daliyeh artefact
WDSP	Wadi Daliyeh Samaritan Papyrus

TABLE 1: BRIEF TIMELINE OF EVENTS (597–4 BC)

All dates are BC.

Date	Event(s)
597	King Jehoiachin surrenders to the Babylonians and is exiled to Babylon, along with many elite Judeans.
586	Nebuchadnezzar destroys Jerusalem, including the temple.
539	Cyrus defeats the Babylonians, bringing their Babylonian Empire to an end, and inaugurating the Persian Empire
538	Cyrus allows exiled people to return to their homelands
ca. 525	Judeans begin to return from Babylon to Jerusalem
520	Zerubbabel begins to rebuild the temple in Jerusalem
515	Dedication of the temple of Yahweh in Jerusalem
458	Ezra initiates reforms, which see the Torah become the standard cultural text of all Yahwists (Judeans, Samarians)
ca. 450	Jerusalem's walls and temple are damaged in a regional revolt
ca. 447	The Samarians build a temple to Yahweh on Mt Gerizim under their governor, Sanballat I.
444	Nehemiah becomes Governor of Judah and restores the walls and temple in Jerusalem
351	Persians are defeated in Egypt, and lose control of Syria-Palestine.
350	Sanballat II, Governor of Samaria, tries to reunite all Israel under his leadership. A schism develops in the priesthood in Jerusalem. The attempted reunification is denounced by Malachi.
345	The Persians re-establish control of Judea and Samaria
333–323	Alexander the Great conquers the Persian Empire (including Judea), before dying unexpectedly.

Date	Event(s)
323–301	Alexander's successors fight for control over Syria Palestine.
301	Ptolemy I conquers Jerusalem and deports many Jews to Alexandria, including Davidic descendants.
301–198	Judea is under the control of the Ptolemaic Kingdom of Egypt.
220s	Ecclesiastes written by a Davidic descendant
198	Seleucids win control of Syria-Palestine
175	The legitimate High Priest Onias III is removed in favour of his brother, Jason, who buys the position from the Seleucids.
172	Menelaus buys High Priesthood from the Seleucids
171	Onias III is assassinated in Syria (Dan 9:26)
167	Seleucids enact a massacre in Jerusalem. Antiochus IV Epiphanes abolishes the distinction between Jews and Gentiles, and rebadges the Jerusalem temple as a temple to Zeus. The royal Seleucid cult is established in the temple (the "abomination of desolation"). The Maccabean Revolt begins.
164/3	The Maccabees win back control of the Jerusalem temple, and institute the festival of Hanukkah.
162	The Maccabees are ejected from Jerusalem by the Seleucids. Massacre of the *Hasidim* (early Essenes) by the High Priest Alcimus.
161	Judas Maccabeus takes back control of the Jerusalem temple and becomes High Priest.
160	Death of Judas Maccabeus in battle against the Seleucids. The Seleucids regain sovereignty of Jerusalem.
142	Jewish Independence achieved under the High Priest Simon Thassi. Beginning of the Hasmonean Dynasty.
133	Jerusalem besieged and conquered by the Seleucids, Jewish Independence comes to an end.
129	Jews regain independence under High Priest John Hyrcanus I.
110	John Hyrcanus I conquers the Samaritans and destroys the Samaritan temple on Mt Gerizim
104	High Priest Antigonus I declares himself King of the Jews
104–76	Reign of King Alexander Janneus. Persecution of Pharisees.

TABLE 1: BRIEF TIMELINE OF EVENTS (597–4 BC)

Date	Event(s)
76–69	Reign of Queen Alexandra Salome. Pharisees given wide civic power.
69–63	Fraternal Civil War between John Hyrcanus II and Aristobulus II.
63	Pompey conquers Jerusalem. The Jews lose their independence.
40–37	The Parthians invade Syria-Palestine. Antigonus II becomes King of the Jews under Parthian sovereignty. The Romans declare Herod King of the Jews, and he successfully fights Antigonus II for the throne.
37–4	Reign of Herod
7	Herod grows paranoid of two of his sons by his Hasmonean wife, and has them executed. Birth of Jesus (ca. 7)
4	Death of Herod

TABLE 2: THE HIGH PRIESTS OF JERUSALEM

All dates are BC.

The dates in office, lifespan, and ages of the high priests are given where they can be reasonably estimated. High priests are shown only up to the turn of the era (1 BC).

☐ Zadokite Line   ◼ Hasmonean Line   ☐ Other

Dates in Office	High Priest	Lifespan (Age During Office)
ca.525–ca.490	Joshua ben-Jehozadak	ca.555–ca.490 (33–66 years old)
ca.490–ca.460	Joiakim ben-Joshua	ca.530–ca.460 (40–70 years old)
ca.460–ca.432	Eliashib ben-Joiakim	ca.505–ca.432 (45–73 years old)
ca.432–ca.412	Joiada ben-Eliashib	ca.480–ca.412 (48–68 years old)
ca.412–ca.369	Johanan ben-Joiada	ca.445–ca.369 (33–76 years old)
ca.369–ca.329	Jaddua ben-Johanan	ca.410–ca.329 (41–81 years old)
ca.329–301	Hezekiah ben-Jaddua	367–>301 (38–>66 years old)
301–ca.279	Onias I ben-Hezekiah	ca.340–ca.279 (39–61 years old)
ca.279–ca.275	Simon I ben-Onias I	ca.315–ca.275 (36–40 years old)
ca.275–ca.260	Eleazar ben-Onias I	ca.310–ca.260 (35–50 years old)
ca.260–ca.255	Manasseh ben-Hezekiah	ca.335–ca.255 (75–80 years old)
ca.255–ca.219	Onias II ben-Simon I	ca.287–ca.219 (32–67 years old)
ca.219–ca.185	Simon II (the Just) ben-Onias II	ca.260–ca.185 (41–75 years old)
ca.185–175	Onias III ben-Simon II	ca.225–171 (40–50 years old)
175–172	Jason (Jesus) ben-Simon II	ca.222–>167 (47–50 years old)
172–162	Menelaus	?
162	Alcimus	ca.227–152 (65 years old)

TABLE 2: THE HIGH PRIESTS OF JERUSALEM

Dates in Office	High Priest	Lifespan (Age During Office)
162–160	Judas Maccabeus ben-Mattathias	ca.200–160 (38–40 years old)
160–152	Alcimus (restored)	ca.227–152 (67–75 years old)
152–143	Jonathan Apphus ben-Mattathias	ca.194–143 (42–51 years old)
142–134	Simon (III) Thassi ben-Mattathias	ca.203–134 (61–69 years old)
134–104	John Hyrcanus I ben-Simon (III) Thassi	ca.162–104 (28–58 years old)
104	Aristobulus I ben-John Hyrcanus I	ca.133–104 (29 years old)
104–76	Alexander Jannaeus ben-John Hyrcanus I	128–76 (24–51 years old)
76–67	John Hyrcanus II ben-Alexander Jannaeus	103–31 (27–36 years old)
67–63	Aristobulus II ben-Alexander Jannaeus	c.101–49 (34–38 years old)
63–40	John Hyrcanus II ben-Alexander Jannaeus (restored)	103–31 (40–63 years old)
40–37	Mattathias Antigonus II ben-Aristobulus II	ca.75–37 (35–38 years old)
37–35	Hananel (Ananelus)	?
35	Jonathan Aristobulus III ben-Alexander II	53–35 (18 years old)
35–30	Hananel (restored)	?
30–23	Jesus ben-Phiabi	?
23–5	Simon ben-Boethus	?
5–4	Matthias ben-Theophilus	?
4	Joazar ben-Simon ben-Boethus	?
4–3	Eleazar ben-Simon ben-Boethus	?
3–?	Jesus ben-Sie	?

TABLE 3: RULERS OF THE PERSIAN EMPIRE

All dates are BC.

559–530	Cyrus II
530–522	Cambyses
522	Bardiya*
522–486	Darius I
486–465	Xerxes I
465–424	Artaxerxes I
424	Xerxes II
424–423	Sogdianus
423–404	Darius II Ochus
404–358	Artaxerxes II Arsaces
358–338	Artaxerxes III Ochus
338–336	Artaxerxes IV Arses
336–330	Darius III Codomanus

* Reign Disputed

TABLE 4: ATTESTED GOVERNORS OF PERSIAN YEHUD (JUDAH)

All dates are BC.

ca.525–519	Zerubbabel
519–ca.516	Joshua the High Priest (as caretaker)
ca.516–ca.510	Zerubbabel (restored)
ca.510–ca.500	Elnathan
ca.500–ca.485	Ahiab/Ahzai
ca.485–ca.470	Jehoezer
ca.470–ca.455	Uriah
ca.455–ca.445	Hananah
445–ca.420	Nehemiah
ca.420–ca.385	Bagohi
ca.385–ca.370	Johanan the High Priest (as caretaker)
ca.370–345	Hezekiah
345–332	Jaddua the High Priest (as ethnarch)

TABLE 5: ATTESTED GOVERNORS OF PERSIAN SAMARIA

All dates are BC. Following each name in parentheses are approximate dates for the person's lifetime and approximate age while in office.

Before 448	Unknown
ca.448–ca.406	Sanballat I (488–406: aged 40–82)
ca.406–ca.385	Delaiah ben-Sanballat I (465–385: aged 59–80)
ca.385–ca.353	*Hananiah ben-Delaiah (435–353: aged 50–82)
ca.353–ca.345	Sanballat II ben-Hananiah (410–343: aged 57–67)
ca.345–331	Jeshua ben-Sanballat II (385–331: aged 40–54)

*It is possible that Hananiah was preceded by Shelemiah ben-Sanballat I, in which case Hananiah should be relabelled as "ben-Shelemiah."

TABLE 6: JERUSALEM UNDER THE CONTROL OF THE *DIADOCHI*

All dates are BC.

323–319	Laomedon (Satrapy of Syria)
319–316	Antigonus Monophthalmus ("One-Eyed")
316–315	Ptolemy I
315–312	Antigonus Monophthalmus ("One-Eyed")
312–311	Ptolemy I
311–305	Antigonus Monophthalmus ("One-Eyed")
301–	Ptolemy I

TABLE 7: RULERS OF THE PTOLEMAIC KINGDOM (EGYPT)

All dates are BC.

305–283	Ptolemy I Soter ("Savior")
283–246	Ptolemy II Philadelphus ("Sibling Lover")
246–222	Ptolemy III Euergetes ("Benefactor")
222–204	Ptolemy IV Philopator ("Father Lover")
204–180	Ptolemy V Epiphanes ("God Made Manifest")
180–168	Ptolemy VI Philometor ("Mother Lover")
168–167	Coregency: Ptolemy VI, Cleopatra II, Ptolemy VIII Physcon ("Fatso")
167–145	Coregency: Ptolemy VI and Cleopatra II
145–131	Ptolemy VIII Physcon ("Fatso")
131–128	Cleopatra II
128–116	Ptolemy VIII Physcon ("Fatso")
116–107	Coregency: Cleopatra III and Ptolemy IX Lathyrus ("Chickpea")
107–101	Coregency: Cleopatra III and Ptolemy X Alexander I
101–88	Ptolemy X Alexander I and Berenice III
88–81	Ptolemy IX Lathyrus ("Chickpea")
81–80	Berenice III
80	Ptolemy XI Alexander II
80–58	Ptolemy XII Auletes ("Flautist")
58–57	Berenice IV and Cleopatra V Tryphaena
57–55	Berenice IV
55–51	Ptolemy XII Auletes ("Flautist")
51–47	Coregency: Ptolemy XIII and Cleopatra VII
47–44	Coregency: Ptolemy XIV and Cleopatra VII
44–30	Cleopatra VII

TABLE 8: RULERS OF THE SELEUCID KINGDOM (SYRIA)

All dates are BC.

305–281	Seleucus I Nicator ("Conqueror")
281–261	Antiochus I Soter ("Savior")
261–246	Antiochus II Theos ("God")
246–225	Seleucus II Callinicus ("Good Conqueror")
225–223	Seleucus III Keraunos ("Thunderbolt")
223–187	Antiochus III the Great
187–175	Seleucus IV Philopator ("Father Lover") [son of Antiochus III]
175–164	Antiochus IV Epiphanes ("God Made Manifest") [son of Antiochus III]
164–161	Antiochus V Eupator ("Goodfather") [son of Antiochus IV]
161–150	Demetrius I Soter ("Savior") [son of Seleucus IV]
152–145	Alexander I Balas [alleged son of Antiochus IV]
145–139	Demetrius II Nicator ("Conqueror") [son of Demetrius I]
144–138	Diodotus Tryphon, on behalf of Antiochus VI Dionysus [son of Alexander I Balas]
142–138	Diodotus Tryphon
138–129	Antiochus VII Sidetes [son of Demetrius I]
129–126	Demetrius II Nicator ("Conqueror") [son of Demetrius I]
128–123	Alexander II Zabinas ("Bought") [alleged son of Alexander Balas]
126	Seleucus V [son of Demetrius II]
126–97	Antiochus VIII Grypus ("Hooknose") [son of Demetrius II]
114–95	Antiochus IX Cyzicenus [son of Antiochus VII]
95	Seleucus VI [son of Antiochus VIII]

95–88	Antiochus X Eusebes ("Pious") [son of Antiochus IX]
95–93	Antiochus XI [son of Antiochus VIII]
95–75	Philip I [son of Antiochus VIII]
95–87	Demetrius III Eukairos ("Opportunist") [son of Antiochus VIII]
88–70	Cleopatra Selene and Antiochus XIII Asiaticus [son of Antiochus X]
87–86	Antiochus XII Dionysus [son of Antiochus VIII]
75–70	*Tigranes II of Armenia*
*70–64	*Antiochus XIII Asiaticus [son of Antiochus X]
*65–64	*Philip II [son of Philip I]

*Claimed rule, but reality of reign is questionable.

TABLE 9: THE ZADOKITES AND TOBIADS

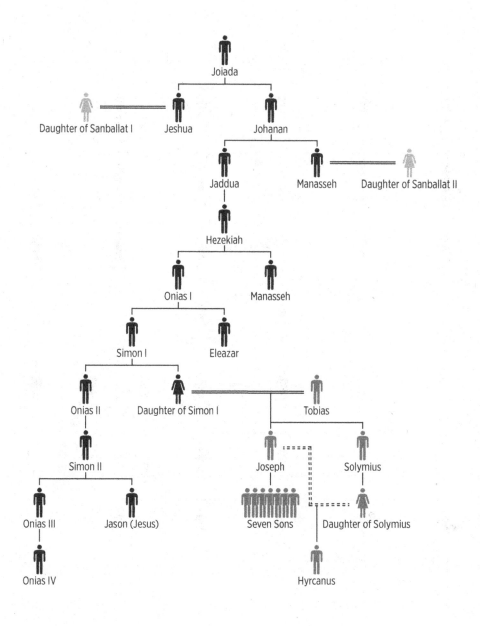

TABLE 10: THE HASMONEAN DYNASTY

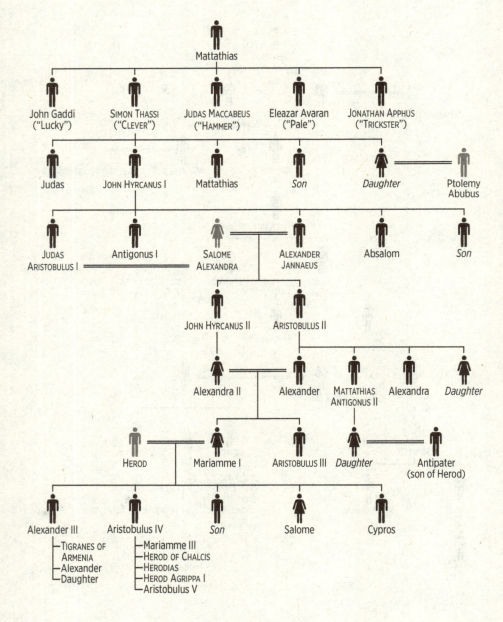

TABLE 11: SABBATICAL YEARS

Sabbatical years are attested from 163/2 BC onwards. It is unknown whether the system was in use before this, but it is likely. On the assumption that it was in use, the Sabbatical Years are listed from the beginning of Seleucid rule over Judea (198 BC), which coincides with a Sabbatical Year. All dates are BC.

198/7	128/7	58/7
191/0	121/0	51/0
184/3	114/3	44/3
177/6	107/6	37/6
170/69	100/99	30/29
163/2	93/2	23/2
156/5	86/5	16/5
149/8	79/8	9/8
142/1	72/1	2/1
135/4	65/4	

INTRODUCTION

ESTRANGED TESTAMENTS
Perceiving the Problem

When I ask people about what happened in the five centuries before Jesus, I tend to encounter three types of answers. The first is the classic Protestant answer. It states that there was a Maccabean Revolt but that most of this period was essentially one of silence in which prophecy ceased. Respondents usually refer to these centuries as the intertestamental period in which some Jewish literature was written, but none of it was inspired Scripture. It was, rather, apocryphal literature of dubious theological quality, though few can explain why. The second answer is what I call the series trailer response, which gives short scene grabs from the period. Respondents mention that the Israelites returned to the land from exile in Babylon, they rebuilt the temple, Nehemiah built a wall (though why is not altogether clear), then along came the Romans, Herod, and John the Baptist. The third answer is what I term the black hole response. It sees these centuries as a complete unknown and of little interest because no biblical literature was written in the period, making it largely unimportant.

All these responses are disheartening and impoverish biblical studies and theology by estranging the Old and New Testaments from each other. All too often there is an implicit assumption that the Old Testament is simply a literary preface to the New Testament; that its essential purpose was to provide a set of predictions that Jesus would fulfil to prove that he was the messiah; or that it was a bag of allegories supplying some moral parallels to the New Testament. This, however, misunderstands the nature of prophecy and undermines the conviction borne out in the pages of both Testaments: that God developed an ongoing, dynamic relationship with his covenant people Israel and that this relationship was not put on hold for several centuries during the postexilic era (or Second Temple period). To underscore the problem, while I was writing this book and discussing it with various people, they would often mistakenly refer to it as *Between the Testaments* rather than *Bridging the Testaments*.

At the heart of the Christian faith lies a conviction about the person and work of Jesus, buttressed by the scriptural authority of the Old and New Testaments. Jesus is understood to have been Israel's messiah who fulfilled the

Old Testament (or Hebrew Bible) by bringing to completion God's revelation and plan of salvation, which had already begun with Israel. This message is encapsulated in the New Testament. Yet the three types of responses above all unwittingly detach the two Testaments from each other. By interposing a so-called intertestamental period with centuries of apparent prophetic silence or deepest darkest ignorance, the two Testaments are prized apart and separated by a historical and theological chasm. This disconnection results in a subconscious reconfiguring of the significance of both Testaments and how they relate. Lip service is, of course, still paid to the notion that the Old Testament is fulfilled in the New, but what this means is redefined, and theological inconsistencies enter the fray. People will claim that during the postexilic era God was still in covenant relationship with his people and still at work in history to bring about the fulfilment of his purposes, and yet they will damagingly and illogically also maintain that there was a hiatus for most of this period in which God practically fell off the airwaves or went on leave for a few centuries.

Further historical and theological dissonance results. For example, the kingdom of Israel is identified as an ethnic-based, territorial state in the Old Testament, but somehow this is set aside for an ethereal kingdom of God that is spiritual and entirely lacking in ethnic, territorial, or political dimensions. Similarly, the Davidic king of the Old Testament is someone who wields civic and military power, yet Jesus is held up as a purely spiritual messiah who is uninterested in civic and military power. We read the New Testament and shake our heads disapprovingly at those who wanted a political messiah to rescue them from the Romans but will heartily read the Psalms that plead for God to remember his promises to deliver his people from foreign oppression. We encounter the pivotal importance of the land of Israel under the terms of the national covenant but do not understand how Jesus himself relates to the land. We read the canonical books that decry the flaws and failings of the establishment and yet argue that the establishment preserved these very books as Scripture. We state that God's word was authoritative and binding from the moment of delivery while also arguing that there had to be considerable time before books could achieve canonical status, and at the same time we claim that God's word often related only to people and events centuries after their delivery. We assume prophecy had ceased centuries before Jesus and yet find that Simeon and Anna were prophets when Jesus was born.

Then there are the large trajectory questions that few of us pose, or if we do, do not know how to answer. For instance, how is it that the Davidic dynasty rules Israel and Judah and its scion, Zerubbabel, leads the community after the exile, but by the first century the Davidic descendants are just tradesmen in a tiny Galilean village? How does Israel go from being ruled by Davidic kings to being dominated by priests? How do we go from Judean exiles returning to Jerusalem to having Pharisees, Sadducees, Essenes, and a Sanhedrin? Why is it that the temple is so important to the pioneers who returned to Jerusalem from exile, and yet Jesus wants to tear the temple down? Why is it so crucial that Jesus set his face towards Jerusalem? Is Jesus's pedigree as a "son of David" an optional extra, and if not, why not? How did the canon actually develop, and how does it relate to the historical progress of God's covenant people? Is the redaction of Scripture a suspect notion, or was it an attendant feature of God's ongoing dealings with his people? If the Torah demands the unity of all Israel and the prophets desire the restoration of all Israel, why is Nehemiah so determined to exclude the Samarians, and why are we generally uninterested in them, apart from one good one, one leper, and one questionable woman at a well? Why is the national covenant adamant that Israel keeps away from the nations, and yet the New Testament wholeheartedly embraces the inclusion of gentiles as gentiles within the people of God? Why is the Old Testament so focused on life in the land in the here and now, and yet the New Testament is so big on an eschatological day of judgment and resurrection?

In addition, there are countless other detail questions. What was Ezra doing with the Law—wasn't it there already? Why did Nehemiah build a wall? Why are there so many laborious genealogies in 1 Chronicles? Why did the Jews never get a Davidic king in the postexilic era, and did it matter anyway? Why do the Samarians go from being polytheistic in the early fifth century BC to devotees of Torah alone by the end of that same century? Why did Jews and Samaritans have such antipathy towards each other? Where does the notion of resurrection come from? What exactly is apocalyptic literature, and how does it work? Who were the Maccabees, and did they do the right thing in rebelling? How did the Greeks affect the Jews? How did the Jews come to be ruled by the Romans? What are the Dead Sea Scrolls all about? Why did no one have any qualms about pronouncing the name of Yahweh at an early stage of history, but by the time of the New Testament it had essentially become taboo? How did the Jewish community in Alexandria begin and develop, such that it was necessary to produce a Greek translation of the Hebrew Scriptures? How did the Jewish diaspora develop, and what are we to make of it if the traditional covenantal land was so important? What are the apocryphal and pseudepigraphal books, how are they important, and why also are they theologically suspect? Why did Herod rebuild the temple? Who were the Herodians?

Finally, there are numerous erroneous or misguided notions about this period. For example, it is usually stated that thousands of Judeans left exile in

Babylonia and returned to Judah in the second year of Cyrus (538 BC), when in fact just a few hundred Judeans accompanied Zerubbabel to Jerusalem some years after Cyrus died (ca. 525 BC). Ezra is often touted as establishing the Torah within Judah alone, when he was in fact trying to unite all Yahwists under a single cultural standard. The marriage reforms of both Ezra and Nehemiah are usually seen as protecting Judah from their Samarian neighbors to the north when they were actually about protecting the primacy of Jerusalem and the integrity of all Israel when a rival temple had been built at Mount Gerizim. Malachi is usually placed within this same context (mid-fifth century BC), when he was in fact dealing with an attempt to unite Israel a century later. Hellenism is frequently equated with Greek ideals and Greek influence imposed from above. More accurately, Hellenism was about the organic combination of Greek and Eastern cultures, producing a new hybrid culture that Judaism welcomed. The critical question was what proportion of Greek and Eastern culture could coinhere within Judaism. It is commonly held that the Maccabean Revolt, which broke out in 167 BC, was mainly directed against outside Greek influence and Seleucid rule, when it was actually more an internal Jewish conflict about controlling the complexion of Hellenistic Judaism, with political ramifications for the relationship between the Jews and the Seleucid authorities. It is also erroneously stated that the Jews gained independence under the Maccabees in 164 BC, when in fact their "victory" in 164 BC was just a temporary foot in the political door. Jewish independence was not achieved until 142 BC. The Romans tend to be seen in monochrome fashion as brutal oppressors of the Jews, but they were initially friends and allies of the Jews. Lastly, it is often touted that the Sadducees only believed in the Law and not the Prophets. In fact, they held both in esteem but believed in the primacy of the written Law, especially in opposition to Pharisaic notions of an Oral Law.

The New Testament View

Many of these dissonant situations and questions arise from the fact that we have unwittingly estranged the New Testament from the Old Testament by inserting a so-called intertestamental period between them, which we mistakenly fill with blaring prophetic silence. This damages the historical and theological trajectories that lead from the Old Testament to the New Testament and undermines our approach to them both. What's more, it's plainly unbiblical.

Jesus did not believe that God had stopped sending prophets or interacting with his covenant people for several centuries. On the contrary, Matthew's

Gospel has Jesus state that "all the prophets and the Law prophesied until John [the Baptist]" (Matt 11:13). The fact that the prophets are placed ahead of the Law and John is counted as one of them means that Jesus was not referring to the books of the canon but rather to the historical phenomenon of prophets. He saw a crescendo of sorts with the advent of John the Baptist (Matt 11:12) but never suggested that there was a cessation or pause of prophets before him (cf. Matt 10:41).

The writer to the Hebrews affirms the same thing in the opening of his treatise: "In various times and in various ways of the past, God spoke to our fathers through the prophets, but on the last of these days he spoke to us by the Son" (Heb 1:1–2a). Here the writer looks back on God's dealings with his covenant people. He implies that the revelation that came through Jesus ("the Son") was part and parcel of God's previous dealings, even as Jesus was the ultimate revelation of that long history. There is a sense of variety and antiquity to the prophetic activity but never a sense of hiatus, for the writer maintains that it was "on the last of these days" that God spoke through Christ. In other words, the writer can identify the endpoint of these prophetic dealings, but he never suggests that there was a pause prior to it. In the rest of his treatise, he will go on to liken Israel's entire historical journey with God to the journey of the Israelites through the desert under the prophetic leadership of Moses (Heb 3:1–4:11). He sees Jesus as the ultimate destination—the "promised land" of revelation—but he does not argue for any hiatus along the way. On the contrary, he urges his Jewish readers not to fall short of this ultimate rest in Christ, as the Israelites whose bodies fell in the desert. For him, apostolic faith was of a piece with Israelite-Jewish faith and its logical endpoint.[1]

The New Testament, therefore, implies God's ongoing work with and within his covenant people Israel throughout all five centuries before Jesus. This must lead us to a historical and theological reevaluation of these centuries. As we do, we will find confirmation of the New Testament's claims. Prophets were indeed active throughout this time, both biblical and nonbiblical literature was being written, and significant theological developments were occurring that would have a crucial influence upon the people and events of the first century. Indeed, if we do not comprehend the colossal contribution of these centuries to the trajectory of history and theology, we risk undervaluing or even misunderstanding the New Testament and its momentous revelation.

---

1. George Athas, "Reflections on Scripture: Using the Distinction between Jews and Gentiles as an Exegetical Key," in *Donald Robinson Selected Works: Appreciation*, ed. Peter G. Bolt and Mark D. Thompson (Camperdown/Newtown, NSW: Australian Church Record/Moore College, 2008), 127–28.

If we are to build our theology on rock, rather than sand, we must take stock of the five centuries leading up to Jesus.

The Suppression of Prophecy

Where, then, does this notion that prophecy ceased centuries before Jesus come from? The seed of the idea goes back to the second century BC, but it did not fully germinate until centuries later. The author of 1 Maccabees believed that true prophets had not appeared among the people since well before the death of Judas Maccabeus in 160 BC (1 Macc 9:27). He was referring to prophetic figures, not just prophetic writings. Even then, he viewed this as simply an absence of prophets rather than a cessation of prophecy as a phenomenon. When the Jewish nation gained independence in 142 BC, the constitutional document defining the powers of the Hasmoneans invested them with power "until a reliable prophet should arise" (1 Macc 14:41; cf. 4:46). The author of 1 Maccabees who preserves this decree was also decidedly pro-Hasmonean and therefore censorious of anything that might be critical of them. Yet he could not omit this particular detail. While the Hasmoneans were content to believe that prophecy had ceased, since it was politically expedient for them that no prophet arise to gainsay their power, other quarters of Judaism still fully believed that prophecy was ongoing and that the Hasmoneans could not be the ultimate form of restoration for the Jewish nation. It served those in power, however, to suppress the spirit of prophecy. In the first instance, this took the form of producing authoritative literature to justify that power (even if we today might question that literature). After this, John Hyrcanus I claimed to have the gift of prophecy (*J.W.* 1.68–69). Through these means, the Hasmoneans and their supporters expropriated the prophetic impulse and made it a tool of the Hasmonean establishment. But thereafter, this prophetic impulse was suppressed so as to give the impression that the final prophetic word had been spoken and that prophecy had ceased altogether. The implication was that the Hasmoneans and their supporters had become the ultimate fulfilment of God's purposes for his covenant people—ideas that, as we will see, most other Jews simply did not believe.

This suppression of prophecy was eventually taken up by other groups who came to be part of the Jewish establishment and is alluded to in the New Testament. When Jesus talks about John the Baptist, he states that violent people have tried to lay hold of the kingdom of heaven, by which he means that those in power had tried to suppress the kingdom (Matt 11:12–13). Luke has Stephen, the first Christian martyr, express a similar sentiment when he aims a stinging charge at the Jewish Sanhedrin:

> You stiff-necked people, uncircumcised in heart and ears! You always resist the Holy Spirit. You are just like your ancestors. Which of the prophets did your ancestors not persecute? They also killed the ones who foretold the coming of the Righteous One, whose betrayers and murderers you have now become—you who received the Law through the agency of angels and yet have not kept it. (Acts 7:51–53)

In the first century, the Sanhedrin was dominated by Sadducees, who had been historically aligned with the Hasmoneans and held the key positions of power, and Pharisees, who had been given civic power in the first century BC. In accusing them of resisting the Holy Spirit, as their forebears had done, Stephen does not imply that they failed to find personal salvation in Jesus. Rather, he accuses them of suppressing prophecy, with the execution of Jesus being the epitome of this. He goes on to accuse the Sanhedrin of not even being faithful to the Torah, which they prized so highly and which the Pharisees claimed was given via angels. The insinuation is that the Holy Spirit, which had inspired the Torah, was the very same spirit who had been prophetically active down to the time of Jesus but whom the Jewish leaders were now railing against. One wonders what words Stephen would have for modern readers who perpetuate the notion of prophetic silence.

There was a widespread belief in Judaism that God had not fallen silent or stopped guiding his covenant people, even if members of the establishment believed (or needed to believe) that he had. Many Jews, including the early Christians, expected prophetic figures to arise who would proclaim the word of God, interpret the times, and perform significant signs. And indeed, they did. In Wisdom of Solomon (first century BC), wisdom is said to raise prophets in every generation (Wis 7:27). We do not know the names of all the prophetic figures who arose during these centuries, but that is only to be expected. After all, we do not know the names of the Chronicler, the compiler of the Book of the Twelve Prophets, or the composer of the Song of the Songs. Furthermore, we know of prophetic figures in biblical literature without having any literature from their hand, such as Ahijah of Shiloh, Jehu ben-Hanani, Elijah, Elisha, and Uriah ben-Shemaiah. By a similar token, we have no writings from Judas the Essene (*Ant.* 13.311–13; *J.W.* 1.78–80), who prophesied the death of Antigonus in 104 BC (see 3.7.8 below); or from Onias the Circle-Drawer, an Elijah-like prophet from Galilee, who prayed for rain to break a drought in 65 BC but who was murdered the following year for failing to take sides in a Hasmonean civil war (see 3.7.17 below). Indeed, if prophecy was suppressed it is unsurprising that we do not know the names of more prophetic figures, let alone if their prophecies were ever recorded.

The Gospels portray people expecting prophetic figures (Matt 10:41) and identify Zacharias (Luke 1:67), Simeon (Luke 2:25–35), Anna (Luke 2:36–38), John the Baptist (Matt 14:5; Mark 6:15; Luke 7:26; 20:6), and Jesus (Mark 8:28; Luke 7:16; 24:19; John 4:19) among them. Anna, in particular, due to her elderly age, likely had a prophetic ministry for much of the first century BC. The early church also had prophetic figures (Acts 11:27; 13:1; 15:32; 21:9–10; Rev 18:20). The inclination of the establishment to suppress prophecy is exemplified when Jesus challenged the chief priests and elders in the temple on the prophetic status of John the Baptist. The priests and elders refused to acknowledge John's prophetic credentials, since he criticized them, and yet Jesus and the wider populace esteemed John "as a prophet" (Matt 21:21–27; Mark 11:27–33; Luke 20:1–8). The implication is that John was the "reliable prophet" who would arise to herald a new age (cf. 1 Macc 14:41). He did this by critiquing the establishment, calling for societal change, and pointing to a greater one who would come after him in fiery judgment and the prophetic Holy Spirit. But for this, John was brutally suppressed by the establishment and executed. Jesus's exchange with the priests and elders over John's prophetic status was no mere academic riddle but a politically charged challenge for them to recognize that he, Jesus, was the one who would come after John and fulfil prophetic expectation. But just days later, Jesus was arrested and tried by the leading priests, predominantly Sadducees who believed that prophecy had functionally ceased. They assaulted him and mocked him by goading him to prophesy (Mark 14:65; cf. Matt 26:67–68; Luke 22:63–64). The following morning, they successfully endeavored to have him crucified.

The Essenes believed in the ongoing role of prophecy. In addition to Judas the Essene, Josephus mentions the curious figure of Menahem the Essene, who predicted the rise of Herod (*Ant.* 15.373–78). The War Scroll, probably written in the late first century BC, says of God, "By the hands of your anointed ones, seers of the appointed things, you have told us about the e[nds] of the wars of your hands" (1QM 11:7–8). These "anointed ones" or "seers" were prophetic figures within the Essene community, and their prophetic role included forecasting eschatological events and interpreting the words of previous prophets, exemplified by the *pesharim* (interpretive commentaries) that the sect produced. While we might not view their works as authoritative, that they produced them shows again that the prophetic impulse was perceived to be active.

At the end of the first century, Josephus played a significant role in furthering the idea that prophecy ceased, though he himself never expressly stated the idea in his writings. In *Against Apion* he claimed that the history of the Jews written after Artaxerxes I was not of the same authority as that produced before because there had not been "a precise succession of prophets" (*Ag. Ap.* 1.41). Josephus's wording expresses belief in a paucity of prophets rather than the cessation of prophecy altogether. His enumeration of Jewish Scriptures includes texts written after the reign of Artaxerxes I (*Ag. Ap.* 1.40), though he may not have known this. By his day, the hyper-literalism of the Pharisees, of whom Josephus claimed to have been a member (though his claim is dubious), had reached such a level that a hermeneutical reflex assigning authorship to early named prophets became widespread. Even late anonymous prophecy was attributed to earlier prophets on the basis of hyper-literal interpretations of scrolls.² It was the same impulse that led the Pharisees to assign the Oral Law, developed in the second century BC at the very earliest, to Moses. This reassigned late biblical literature to earlier times, thereby depopulating the later period of inspired works.

Even so, Josephus's description of the Hasmonean ruler, John Hyrcanus I, as a paragon of prophecy proves that he did not believe prophecy had disappeared altogether (*J.W.* 1.68–69). He even portrayed himself as possessing a prophetic gift (*J.W.* 3.399–408). He also referred to written oracles predicting the destruction of Jerusalem and its temple. These oracles might or might not be equated with the writings of the Essenes, but their tenor is certainly similar to them (cf. War Scroll [1QM]). He also mentions writings held in the temple pertaining to someone from Judea rising to leadership of the whole world (*J.W.* 6.310–15). Josephus interpreted this in a convoluted way to

---

2. For example, Isa 40–66, which has an exilic and postexilic milieu, was attributed entirely to Isaiah of Jerusalem in the eighth–seventh centuries BC. Similarly, most of the material in Zech 9–14, which comes from the late Persian and early Hellenistic eras, was entirely attributed to the prophet Zechariah from the late sixth century BC. The preservation of anonymous prophecy on the same scrolls as the writings of named prophets from the past no doubt aided in this identification. But such was the emphasis on named prophets from the past that it eclipsed any concern for the original contexts of late prophecies. In assigning late dates to this literature, I am not suggesting that prediction could not occur. Rather, I am suggesting that the situation into which the literature spoke did not exist in the days of the prophet assigned by the Pharisees and tradition as the author. This makes it puzzling as to why revelations about later contexts would be made to authors so far removed from them. To insist on earlier dates suggests that God imparted these prophecies to contexts in which they were largely, if not completely, irrelevant. This compromises the notion of a God who communicates comprehensibly and reveals himself in a way that invites appropriate response. In other words, it suggests that God's word was, at least initially, irrelevant and potentially incomprehensible. To draw an analogy, it is akin to suggesting that John Calvin urged his students in Geneva to resist communism and the Soviet Union. How could Calvin's students respond to this? How could God hold them accountable for failing to respond rightly? Yet prophecy is given for eliciting responses, which is why dating these prophetic works is not so much "late" as "contextual." The Pharisees were the ones who first retrofitted later texts to earlier authors, as part of the impulse to assign their Oral Law to Moses. This hyper-literal and hyper-legal hermeneutic changed prophecy from being current divine comment about human affairs to being merely about predicting the future.

indicate the rise of Vespasian, but one can easily see an intersection with the son of man in Daniel 7:13–14 and the Christian belief in the cosmic supremacy of Jesus (cf. Matt 28:18; Col 1:15–20; Eph 1:10). Josephus mentioned other prophetic figures throughout his works (*J.W.* 2.261–262; 6.285–286; *Ant.* 1.240; 13.311–13; 20.97, 169), though he viewed most as necessarily false prophets because they opposed the Romans to whom he had defected. Even if we might question whether such figures were true prophets, the fact that they arose, had influence, and even wrote oracles demonstrates that there was a widespread notion that prophecy was not dead. It was the same attitude that the early church had.

In the second century, the Christian apologist Justin Martyr expressed the view that prophecy continued right up until Jesus's resurrection, whence the gift was taken from the Jews and bestowed upon Christians (*Trypho* 87). Despite his supersessionist tendency and somewhat anti-Semitic tone, Justin's view that prophecy never ceased before Christ reflects the view of the New Testament writers. His rhetoric implies that his interlocutor, Trypho the Jew, conceded that prophecy had ceased among the Jews and used that as the basis for denying the possibility of Jesus being a prophet or that there were prophets in the early church. What we cannot tell from Justin's rhetoric is when exactly Trypho dated the cessation of prophecy within Judaism.

It is not until the compilation of rabbinic literature that we find express claims of prophecy ceasing. The Talmud proclaims the end of prophecy with Haggai, Zechariah, and Malachi, with a divine voice as a mere echo being given on the rarest occasion thereafter. Only Hillel the Elder, whose life overlapped with that of Jesus, was deemed worthy of being called a prophet after this time, and yet rabbinic literature states that Hillel was not actually a prophet because his generation was deemed unworthy (b. Sotah 48b; b. Sanh. 11a; b. Yoma 9b)—an unusual notion, since prophets were traditionally seen as calling unworthy people to repentance. There is here a subtle change in which prophecy had shifted from being divine comment upon human affairs (past, present, or future) and the shaping of the human response to mere prediction bestowed upon worthy adherents (cf. Greek notions associated with oracles, such as that at Delphi). When read alongside the New Testament and the rhetoric of Justin Martyr, the implication is that rabbinic Judaism argued for the cessation of prophecy with Malachi in order to validate their hyper-literal hermeneutic, uphold claims of the antiquity of their Oral Law, redefine prophecy as prediction, and deny Christian claims that Jesus was a prophetic figure who called the Jewish nation to repentance. It also denied the phenomenon of prophets in the early church, that the destruction of the temple had verified Jesus's message, and that the documents that eventually made up the New Testament were divinely inspired.³

The notion of a four-hundred-year silence before John the Baptist, therefore, has little scriptural or historical warrant. It certainly does not accord with the undeniable production of canonical scriptural texts after the fifth century BC, not to mention the proliferation of works that did not make it into the canon or the rise of prophetic figures within Judaism throughout these centuries. The notion even appears to post-date Justin Martyr in the mid-second century. Indeed, this curious supposition sits somewhere between Josephus's view that prophetic authority ebbed after Artaxerxes I and the later rabbis' claim that it ceased altogether with Malachi. The rabbinic claim arose partly as a refutation of the early Christian claim that revelation had not ceased but had continued and reached its culmination in Jesus and the first generation of the church. In this case, the persistent Christian claim of a four-hundred-year prophetic silence is ironically predicated on an anti-Christian polemic and might have proliferated through the church's preservation of Josephus's works beyond the second century.⁴

Dealing with the Problem

Part of the reason for a Christian readiness to accept the notion of a prophetic cessation before Jesus stems, counterintuitively, from the Christian dependence upon Scripture. Being removed from the people and events mentioned in biblical literature, Christians rely upon the inspired Scriptures to convey those persons and events to them and to understand the revelation of God contained in them. Christ himself was the completion of that revelation, and the Bible is the ultimate authority within the Christian church. The sufficiency of Scripture for knowledge of God and salvation is based on its supreme authority as God-breathed (cf. 2 Tim 3:16; 2 Pet 1:21), and nothing else comes close to it. But the canon is a literary collection. It is a witness to history, but it is not the history itself, let alone the totality of history. Yet Christians tend to impose the shape of the canon, with its discrete canonical sections, onto history, thus creating a discrete Old Testament period and a discrete New Testament period, with a gap between them filled with the mortar

---

3. This is the theory of Ephraim E. Urbach in "When Did Prophecy Cease?" *Tarbiz* 17.1 (1945): 1–11. Justin Martyr's notion that prophecy was taken away as a divine punishment is also entertained in rabbinic literature, but it was certainly not present in the earliest generations of the church, which was dominated by Jewish people. See Frederick E. Greenspahn, "Why Prophecy Ceased," *JBL* 108.1 (1989): 37–49.

4. Jews did not preserve Josephus's works since they deemed him a traitor during the Jewish Revolt. It was Christians who preserved his works.

of a so-called intertestamental period. The very terminology we use shows this. But the canon and history do not share the exact same shape, even though they are related. This fact is shown in the New Testament itself, in Paul's claim that God sent his Son, born under the law, to redeem those under the law (Gal 4:4). To put it starkly, the Gospels describe persons and events who are still technically in the Old Testament period.

This, along with the fact that so much literature was written within Second Temple Judaism and yet so little of it became canonical, sparks a tendency to not require engagement with any of the non-canonical literature or the contexts in which they arose. These fall into the void of the so-called intertestamental period. The damage done to understanding the grand work of God in history is akin to ripping out four hundred pages of a novel just before the climactic resolution of the story. Engagement with the history of this period and its literature does not compromise the supremacy and sufficiency of Scripture. On the contrary, it enhances it. Prophecy in itself is a "theological interpretation of history,"[5] which involves both divine comment on human affairs (past, present, or future) and the human response to the divine comment. After all, prophecy is not mere pronouncement but is given to elicit a response from those to whom it is aimed. If we eschew understanding the human affairs addressed by the prophetic voice, we risk misunderstanding the voice itself.

Unfortunately, biblical scholars rarely venture outside the pages of canonical literature in their endeavor to understand it and the world in which it arose. There is a pragmatic consideration here: it is very difficult to master the many disparate fields it takes to come to grips with this literature and its contexts, and so biblical scholars tend to specialize. However, an unwanted fruit of this tendency is that the canonical literature gets treated as though it were hermetically sealed from the rest of the reality in which it arose. If Christians believe that God did indeed interact with real people in real times in real places, just as the writer to the Hebrews believed, then it must serve Christians well to investigate those people, times, and places.

There is, therefore, benefit in a large-scale analysis that integrates an understanding of how the biblical literature of the Second Temple period arose, what it meant in its original context, what the covenant people of God experienced in this period, and how the Old Testament leads into the New. It is

---

5. Hervé Gonzalez, "No Prophetic Texts from the Hellenistic Period? Methodological, Philological and Historical Observations on the Writing of Prophecy in Early Hellenistic Judea," in *Times of Transition: Judea in the Early Hellenistic Period*, ed. Sylvie Honigman, Christophe Nihan, and Oded Lipschits, Mosaics 1 (Tel Aviv: Institute of Archaeology, Tel Aviv University, 2021), 305.

a daunting task that involves the close reading of biblical and nonbiblical literature; interpretation and evaluation of sources written in Hebrew, Aramaic, Persian, Greek, and Latin; consideration of political, cultural, religious, economic, and social history across five centuries; appraisal of archaeological excavations and artefacts they unearth; sensitivity to theological and philosophical developments among Jews, Samaritans, Persians, Greeks, and Romans; and doing all this with an eye on discerning the trajectories between the old covenant and the new. Daunting though it may be, it can be done. Indeed, if there is no such thing as an intertestamental period, then it is vital that we bridge the Testaments so that we may recover the trajectories that join them and see with greater clarity just what it means to claim that, when the fulness of time came, God sent his Son, born of a woman, born under the law—that is, the old covenant—to redeem those under the Law, so that they might receive the adoption as sons (cf. Gal 4:4).

Furthermore, we will understand better the nature of the new revelation that occurs in Jesus and the New Testament. We will understand the idea that God progressively revealed himself and his purposes to his people through the ages and that the pages of Scripture are a very complex witness to this. It is sometimes difficult for us as modern readers to discern the development of theological ideas within biblical texts. The tendency of many modern readers is to see such ideas as perennially present throughout biblical revelation. For example, the concept of a coming kingdom of God or a day of eschatological judgment are read back into the Old Testament and assumed to have always been there rather than formulated in response to the historical circumstances that God's covenant people experienced. For some modern readers, there is an inherent bias against the idea of late theological developments, as though such an idea implies the deficiency of the texts and necessitates their rejection, or alternatively that it implies earlier revelation was incorrect. Such responses fail to understand the implications of God pursuing a relationship with his covenant people. Relationships are by nature dynamic, not static. We should, therefore, expect theological development to have occurred, but it is important to understand the contexts in which it occurred so that it might be understood correctly.

Unfortunately, the assumption that prophecy fell silent in the fifth century BC is often accompanied by a further assumption that the biblical documents were essentially systematic theological formulations. Neither assumption has any foundation. Jews throughout these centuries believed that God was still speaking to them because his relationship with them had not stagnated into a static form. Rather, there was more yet to come, so God continued to relate to his people dynamically; his story was not yet finished. Consequently, theological development should be expected in this framework, viewing the Old Testament books as unfolding revelations whose story was still unfinished. Earlier revelation was true but incomplete; partial but not deficient or incorrect.

Furthermore, while the biblical documents are theological in nature and systematic theologians rightly develop theological systems from them, this does not mean the biblical documents were themselves systematic theologies. This would be like mistaking a cluster of grapes for a bottle of wine. Rather, the biblical documents were the products of contextually bound people who were just as much products of their environment as we are of ours today. This does not preclude such concepts as divine inspiration but rather implies that God worked through complex historical circumstances to relate to his people in their circumstances. To put it another way, the biblical documents have an original context, so they should be read in light of that context. If we fail to see the progression of theological development through these eras, we fail to understand the significance of the biblical documents themselves, which were written to shape responses to historical and cultural challenges. That is, we will not do justice to the prophetic and revelatory nature of biblical literature or to our understanding of what it meant to be God's covenant people in the ancient world. Such a failure inevitably impoverishes theological endeavor by decontextualizing it—consigning it to a cell that imprisons theology by isolating it from the real world. Since biblical literature was written precisely to say something meaningful about the real world, the irony is indeed tragic.

BRIDGING THE TESTAMENTS
Questions and Aims

Before we begin the detailed work of bridging the Testaments, it is worth giving a quick overview of the journey we will take. In general, I follow a chronological model that asks two broad questions:

1. What happened historically to the covenant people of God between their return from exile in the late sixth century BC and the death of Herod in 4 BC?
2. What theological developments arose out of this history?

Underlying these two broad questions are a series of supporting subquestions. For example, in asking what happened historically to God's people, we must inevitably ask how they were affected by the larger political currents of their day. As we will see, telling the story of "Israel" in these five centuries necessarily involves dipping into the stories of Persia, Syria, Egypt, Asia Minor, Greece, and Rome. If we do not make these connections, we hermetically seal the experience of "Israel" off from the real world. Similarly, in asking what theological developments arose, we are also asking how Jews interacted with the culture and thought of their neighbors. As we will see, this means considering the political, social, and philosophical milieu of various people. When we begin our story, the Jews are a people facing Mesopotamia, while speaking and writing in Hebrew and Aramaic. At the end of the story, they are a people facing Rome, while reading Hebrew and speaking Aramaic and Greek.

Structure and Style

The book is divided chronologically into four main parts:

1. The Persian Era (539–331 BC)
2. The Hellenistic Era (331–167 BC)
3. The Hasmonean Era (167–63 BC)
4. The Roman Era (63–4 BC)

In some cases, the transition between these four eras is gradual, making the ordering of material somewhat difficult. For example, the Hasmoneans gained independence in 142 BC, but their roots go back to the Maccabean Revolt of 167 BC, when the Jews were under Seleucid Rule. Because the Hasmoneans were so important for Jewish history, I have opted to begin the Hasmonean era from 167 BC, even though technically this was still part of Seleucid Rule in the Hellenistic era. One could also argue that the whole Hasmonean era was just a part of the Hellenistic era. But I have chosen these four broad political horizons for their use in conveying the major political influences upon God's covenant people. Each part is related to the others, and there are several subsections within each part.

Occasionally, one might think that I have brought too much detail to bear on these questions. To some extent, I sympathize with such a response. I think of my students who ask me every year for that one go-to reference that gives a quick snapshot of the entire period. But my aim here is to give an integrative account of these centuries that provides some depth of analysis as well as breadth of coverage. The quick snapshot approach too often fails to make the necessary connections I wish to illuminate here. I have my students predominantly in mind, who have always been grateful that I have taken the time to initiate them into the depth and breadth of the period.

Furthermore, I want to capture something of the thrill of this period. These centuries are laden with fascinating twists and turns, close calls, and a cast of enthralling characters, in addition to the theological value that we derive from studying them. To that end, I have often translated names and nicknames rather than simply transliterating them into English. This conveys something of the real flesh and blood people who feature in this history. I also opt for designations that are more familiar to readers. Thus, I tend to follow Latinized names, as opposed to Hellenized names (e.g., "Alexander" rather than "Alexandros"). I also tend to give full names at the outset of sections, and whenever I deem them appropriate to remind people or to distinguish them from others (e.g., frequently "Onias III," and not just "Onias").

There is some debate as to whether one should refer to "Judeans" or "Jews" and "Samarians" or "Samaritans." I have opted to use "Judeans" and "Samarians" for the Persian era, but "Jews" and "Samaritans" thereafter. The reason for this is that, during the Persian era, the Judeans and Samarians had many dealings with each other in a way that evokes the older traditions of the kingdoms of Judah and Israel. "Jews" and "Samaritans," on the other hand, tends to evoke the situation of conflict between the two communities, which resulted in a permanent estrangement from the very end of the Persian era onwards. These are also the terms more recognizable to readers of the Greek New Testament, and therefore I employ them from the ascendancy of the Greek kingdoms onwards. The terms "Jews" and "Jewish," therefore, appear in material relating to the Hellenistic era onwards. I identify the Andromachus Affair (331 BC), which brought the governing Sanballat dynasty of Samaria to an end, as the tipping point for moving from "Samarians" to "Samaritans."

Since my aim is to bridge the Testaments, I will often trace a trajectory directly from the topic under discussion to the New Testament. I hope that these trajectories will help to reinforce the idea that when we understand the historical and theological developments of these centuries, we enhance our understanding and appreciation of the New Testament.

Finally, all translations of ancient texts, including biblical texts, are my own, unless otherwise indicated.

THE GRAND SWEEP

The five centuries between the return of Judean exiles to Jerusalem (520s BC) and the death of Herod (4 BC) witnessed a series of tectonic historical shifts and momentous theological developments within the covenant nation of Israel. At the beginning of this period, the political, cultural, and economic pole of the Near East was situated in Mesopotamia. Over these centuries, however, this pole moved west to the Mediterranean, and on the eve of the birth of Jesus was firmly located in Rome. Theologically, this period began with the hope of restoring a nascent Davidic kingdom under Zerubbabel, but as the centuries went by this hope became more remote, posing a series of major theological challenges. On the eve of Jesus's birth, Israel was split broadly into the Jewish and Samaritan communities, dispersed across the Roman Empire, and fragmented into competing factions and beliefs in Judea. There was no united front but rather a people being pulled forcefully towards opposite extremes.

At the heart of the Jewish nation lay the institution of the temple. As "the Sprig" (Zech 3:8; 6:12), Zerubbabel had initiated its construction in Jerusalem in 520 BC as the first step towards restoring the lost Davidic kingdom—a state that would aspire to incorporate both Judah and the remnants of the Northern Kingdom of Israel. This Davidic, pan-Israelite agenda was the expression of hopes arising from the classic notions of a national covenant, as inculcated by the canon of the Torah, and a Davidic covenant, as inculcated by the canon of the Prophets (and later by the works of the Writings, also). As a permanent cultic center, the Jerusalem temple tied both these covenants together as a place of worship (cf. the tabernacle in the Torah) and a symbol of the permanent covenant between Yahweh and David.

Yet, throughout the Persian and early Hellenistic eras, the Jerusalem temple struggled as an institution. The authority of the Davidic dynasty in postexilic Jerusalem peaked with its first figurehead, Zerubbabel, and waned thereafter, so that the dream of rebuilding a Davidic state became more unlikely with the passage of time. From ca. 447 BC, the Jerusalem temple was overshadowed by the Yahwistic temple built atop Mount Gerizim by Sanballat I, governor of Samaria.[6] This rivalry, coupled with political weakness in Jerusalem, drove the Judean establishment to writing as its primary form of resistance. The pan-Israelite agenda was adopted by the Samarian community, mainly through the establishment of the Torah as the standard for all Yahwists under Ezra. The Samarian governor, Sanballat II, even worked towards reunifying Israel under Samarian leadership during a hiatus in Persian sovereignty (351–345 BC). This unification was vehemently opposed by those adhering to the primacy of Jerusalem. For those committed to the Davidic covenant,

---

6. "Yahwism" refers to any of the ancient religions or cults that worshipped Yahweh (the national God of Israel) as either its sole or primary deity. Thus, Judaism and Samaritanism were both "Yahwistic" religions.

Israel had to be led by a Davidic descendant in Jerusalem. But there were currents already at work to make the establishment in Jerusalem the preserve of the priesthood, which had risen to prominence as the Davidic dynasty waned. Although Sanballat II's bid to unify Israel ultimately failed, the establishment in Jerusalem moved increasingly into the sphere of the priests so that, as the Greek dynasties became ascendant in the Near East, Judah became a society led exclusively by priests, backed by the Greek authorities. While the Davidic descendants could be traced down to ca. 300 BC, they had lost much of their prestige and were already on the way to becoming mere plebeians.

As the Davidic descendants were jostled off the political platform, the priesthood in Jerusalem expropriated the Zion theology of Davidic hope and emptied it of its native royal content. In time, "Zion" no longer stood for God's commitment to the Davidic dynasty, encapsulated in the temple, as it had in prophetic literature, but rather for the temple as a cultic institution only—that is, an arena of purely priestly activity and significance. Ben Sira's depiction of the high priest Simon II as the temple builder *par excellence* shows this expropriation had occurred by the early second century BC. This was a major challenge to Davidic loyalists who maintained that Israel was at its core a Davidic estate. That is, they believed that Israel's identity was anchored in the fact that Yahweh had himself entered the Davidic dynasty as its father figure and that he ruled the nation through his son, the Davidic heir, as stipulated in the canon of the Prophets (cf. 2 Sam 7:11–14). This was the essential character of the "kingdom of God" they were waiting for. The repudiation of this character and the redefinition of the "kingdom of God" as solely a "kingdom of priests" raised questions about the character of God, his commitment to past prophetic promises, and the future direction of the nation.

The expropriation of Zion theology by the priests also led to the eventual repudiation of prophecy as an ongoing phenomenon since the priests in power needed only the canon of the Law to legitimize their priestly authority. This did not amount to a rejection of the canon of the Prophets, for Jerusalem's primacy depended on prophetic traditions. Rather, the prophetic traditions (and associated literature, such as the Psalms) were simply reinterpreted through the lens of expropriated (priestly) Zion theology. While there was an element within Judaism that never abandoned the royal content of Zion theology and clung to the prophetic hope that a Davidic kingdom would be restored, the priestly expropriation of Zion theology, coupled with the growing political authority of the priesthood, moved Davidic loyalists to the margins of Jewish society. Nonetheless, these Davidic loyalists, among other groups, still believed that God was continuing to reveal his purposes to the Jewish nation and working towards the restoration of the kingdom of God as a Davidic estate. Thus, they continued to believe that prophecy was still active, and this became a feature of their anti-establishment thinking, which persisted into the first century.

Greek influence saw the adaptation of classic Israelite or Judean ideas into Jewish thought, which appropriated Greek categories for expressing itself. This spawned such ideas as an eschatological day of judgment, resurrection, and apocalyptic philosophy. These were not innovations cut out of whole new cloth but rather the weaving of classic Israelite/Judean threads on a new conceptual loom. Hellenism, as this has come to be known, combined the Greek culture and thought of the conquerors with the local culture and thought of the conquered. It fostered the ongoing writing of Hellenistic Jewish literature and the development of various schools of thought within Judaism much the same way that Greek thought spawned various philosophical schools. This, in turn, was propelled by the initially favorable disposition of the Seleucids towards Jerusalem. Indeed, during the early decades of Seleucid sovereignty (198–180 BC) Jerusalem became a major urban center for the first time since its destruction by the Babylonians in 586 BC.

However, with the development of various schools of thought came conceptual, cultural, and political competition within Judaism. A battle ensued as to whether Judaism would move closer to the liberal Greek ideals of its overlords or remain within the conservative ideals of classic, biblical thought. This battle pulled Judaism in opposing directions, producing groups with extreme and conflicting agendas. For example, there were highly progressive elements, mostly within the upper echelons of society, who embraced Greek culture and wished to align Jewish religion with Greek religion. One difficulty with this was that Jewish religion was highly centralized and monotheistic, whereas Greek religion was decentralized and polytheistic. Even if Yahweh could in some way be mapped onto Zeus, this progressive agenda was bound to produce conflict or else utterly transform Judaism into something that was no longer discernible as Jewish. It would, in other words, dissolve the holiness that defined the distinct identity of the Jewish nation according to Torah and blend Jews indistinguishably into the people of the wider Hellenistic world. On the other hand, there was the reactionary agenda of those who wished to move Judaism in the opposite direction. This involved severing a major artery of Greek influence and not only maintaining Jewish holiness but even enhancing it with additional ultraconservative traditions and regulations. The problem with this fundamentalist impulse was that Hellenism had become an organic part of Jewish thinking and could not be surgically removed without transforming Judaism into something else entirely. Ironically, then, the radical agendas of both extremes in this intra-Jewish tension ultimately amounted to a reinvention of Judaism (cf. Matt 16:6, 11–12; Mark 8:15).

This tension became a battle royale when Antiochus IV Epiphanes revoked the distinct ethnic status of the Jews within his Seleucid kingdom, effectively decreeing in favor of the radically progressive agenda (167 BC). The Maccabean Revolt ensued, which initially sought to roll back Antiochus's decree but eventually developed into a movement to take back control of all Jewish political structures and ultimately rid Judea of Seleucid sovereignty completely. The Maccabean movement started off as a band of disparate guerrillas but soon became a kind of fundamentalist terrorist group under the leadership of Judas Maccabeus. While Judas and his brothers took up the sword in opposition to the Seleucids and the progressive Jewish hierarchy they empowered, others opted for quiet resistance through continued Torah observance and hope in the intervention of God. Their objective was the same as the Maccabees: resistance of oppressive foreign power and the establishment of a Torah-observant society in Judea. Their means of achieving this, however, was vastly different: they embraced the possibility of martyrdom or withdrew into monastic seclusion.

The Maccabean movement was almost snuffed out entirely at the death of Judas Maccabeus in 160 BC. However, Judas's brother, Jonathan Apphus, transformed it into a more mainstream political movement that repudiated extremism. He was able to win concessions by playing rival claimants to the Seleucid throne off each other, even gaining firm control of the high priesthood in Jerusalem. Jonathan thereby permanently replaced the defunct Zadokite line of priests with a new Hasmonean priesthood. In 142 BC, the Jews gained independence under his last surviving brother, Simon Thassi, who established Judea as a hierocracy under the priestly Hasmonean dynasty.

Yet those committed to the classic prophetic promises of Israel's restoration could not assent to the Hasmonean dynasty as the ultimate form of Jewish independence. Davidic loyalists, Essenes, and Pharisees all believed that restoration had not been fully achieved and therefore argued that the Hasmoneans could only ever be an interim solution, pending God's further work within his covenant people. This belief was written into the constitutional document that empowered Simon Thassi and his Hasmonean dynasty by leaving room for a future reliable prophet to arise and take the Jewish nation in a new direction. For Davidic loyalists and some Pharisees, this could only be towards a new Davidic messiah. For the Essenes, it involved the re-establishment of the Zadokite priesthood. But for the Hasmoneans and their supporters, such expectations of further change were vain and ethereal and led them ultimately to decry the ongoing phenomenon of prophecy.

In 110 BC John Hyrcanus I conquered the Samaritan community and destroyed its temple on Mount Gerizim. While this eradicated a rival institution to the temple in Jerusalem and brought the Samaritans within the same political structure as the Jews, it also sealed the permanent enmity between the Samaritan and Jewish communities. The political unity of the Samaritans and the Jews at this point underscored just how far from actual unity and reconciliation, as envisioned by the prophets, the nation truly was.

Soon after the destruction of the Mount Gerizim temple, the Hasmonean hierocracy was converted into a Hasmonean kingdom under Aristobulus I (104 BC), though it was his brother, Alexander Jannaeus, who consolidated the kingdom more definitively. He combined the priestly and royal roles, though in reality it was the royal role that now took precedence. Hasmonean kingship was, therefore, very much about a "kingdom of priests" (Exod 19:6), or rather the "kingdom of a high priest." Ironically, the Hasmoneans transformed Judea into a classic Hellenistic kingdom with progressive ideals—the kind of entity their Maccabean forebears had battled against. This created consternation in many quarters of Judaism, including among the Pharisees. They opposed Alexander Jannaeus, and he unleashed a ferocious persecution upon them. But the Pharisees gained political power after Alexander Jannaeus's death, when Queen Salome Alexandra promoted them to key positions of influence.

Davidic loyalists could never see the legitimacy of a Jewish king who was not a Davidic descendant. For them, the Hasmoneans had hijacked God's prophetic promises and reverted to an aberrant form of the Mosaic notion of a kingdom of priests (cf. Exod 19:6), now narrowly defined as a Hasmonean dynasty. This illegitimately insinuated that God had changed his character and will as revealed through the prophets. But Davidic loyalists did not repudiate Torah, nor did they look towards the Pharisaic solution of developing an Oral Law as the way forward. Rather, they continued to believe in God's ongoing revelation, hoping for the advent of a prophet who would guide the nation in a new direction and for a messiah from the line of David to fulfil God's purposes by dealing definitively with the problems of sin, death, incompetence, and the nations.

Rome's eastward expansion continued while the Hasmoneans ruled, reaching a critical moment when Pompey conquered Jerusalem in 63 BC. Judea lost its status as an independent kingdom and became instead a client hierocracy within the orbit of Roman influence. Many Jews began to experience extreme social and economic hardship. Judea was then affected by the civil and political maelstrom that broke out after the assassination of Julius Caesar in 44 BC, as well as the clash between Rome and the Parthians. Throughout this time, the family of Antipater, who had served the Hasmoneans, emerged as the family within Judea most trusted by the Romans. In 40 BC, the Roman Senate designated Antipater's son, Herod, as king of the Jews in place of the last reigning Hasmonean, Mattathias Antigonus II. In 37 BC Herod established his undisputed sovereignty over Judea.

Herod's rule was not the longed-for kingdom of God under a Davidic descendant. Nevertheless, he appropriated Davidic ideology, casting himself in the mold of David and Solomon as a means of legitimizing his novel dynasty. This was seen chiefly in his grand renovation of the Jerusalem temple, which became the largest sacred complex in the Greco-Roman world, and his expansion of Jewish territory. Herod also grafted the remnants of the Hasmoneans into his dynasty as a way of bolstering his royal claims. He purged the Jewish aristocracy and created a new Herodian elite beholden to him, which included his right to appoint the high priest at will. In this new order, the Sadducees were restored to political pre-eminence at the expense of the Pharisees. While the Herodians moved the Jewish nation closer to Rome, charting a course that was open to cultural adaptation, the Pharisees were moving the lower echelons of society in the opposite direction. They sought a fundamentalism committed to cultural and religious values that were even more conservative than the biblical traditions. The development of Jewish schools and synagogues within Judea was part of their populist agenda and became the primary means by which they disseminated their ultraconservative Oral Law. It is ironic, therefore, that both the Pharisees and Herodians would eventually team up in opposing Jesus (Matt 22:15–16; Mark 3:6; 12:13)—a sign of just how significant a threat both parties perceived Jesus's moderate approach to be to their respective extreme agendas.

Even though Herod was a client king with nominal independence, he integrated Judea into the Roman Empire at a critical time when Rome itself underwent a momentous transformation from Old Republic to Principate under Augustus. While Jews were still culturally and religiously distinct from other peoples in the Roman Empire, with special concessions granted to them, Herod created a political platform that made them subjects of Rome through his own person. This situation, however, did not meet with universal acceptance, for it implied that Caesar Augustus was lord—not Yahweh. On the eve of Jesus's birth, then, the Jewish nation was subject to Augustus's lordship, straining under the tension of ideological extremes pulling it in opposite directions and living with fervent prophetic expectation for God to enact change and fulfil his promises.

PART 1
THE PERSIAN ERA (539–331 BC)

1.1 THE RETURN TO JERUSALEM (539–515 BC)

1.1.1 THE RISE OF CYRUS

On 29 October, 539 BC, Cyrus, king of Persia, walked unopposed through the gates of Babylon and took possession of the greatest imperial city in the world. The Babylonian Empire had fallen. Two weeks earlier, he had defeated the unpopular Babylonian king, Nabonidus, in battle, leaving the imperial city open for capture. Prior to Cyrus, the Persians were an insignificant people who had only recently made the transition from nomadic to settled life in the mountains of what is today southwestern Iran. Yet within the space of eleven years (550–539 BC), Cyrus carved out an enormous empire along the frontiers of Babylon before striking at the heart of Babylon itself. The mountain dwellers of Persia surprisingly now possessed the biggest empire the world had ever seen.

The Persian conquest of Babylon represented a seismic socio-political change in the ancient Near East. Both the Assyrian and Babylonian Empires, which preceded Persia, had been built on policies of brutalization. Their kings intimidated smaller states into submission and dismantled them if they were opposed. A key method of such dismantling was forcible migration in which communities were uprooted from their homelands and settled in other territories. This attempted to annihilate the community's identity and make them dependent on their conquerors. Although the Persians were not averse to using brute force, their policies were generally more beneficent than their imperial predecessors. Rather than suppress the cultural identity of subject communities and their ties to their homelands, the Persians promoted them. This was, in part, necessitated by demographic realities. Both Assyria and Babylon were heavily populated, with the Euphrates and Tigris Rivers providing the lifeblood of their sophisticated cultures. By contrast, the mountain-dwelling Persians were fewer in number and less able to press their culture onto their more populous subjects. The Persians, therefore, took a more symbiotic approach to their imperialism so that their empire became truly multicultural.

Cyrus initiated this by permitting some conquered communities to collect the statues of their gods from the temple of Marduk in Babylon and return them to their temples in their respective homelands (538 BC). The temple of Marduk housed the paraphernalia of many such conquered gods. Nabonidus had also brought many more idols into Marduk's sanctuary in a bid to gain divine protection for Babylon against Cyrus. It evidently failed, and the attempt was lampooned in Isaiah 44:9–20. Cyrus's initial decree, preserved in the Cyrus Cylinder, related only to certain communities east and north of Babylon, but he issued a similar decree of repatriation for Judeans and the temple of Yahweh in Jerusalem (2 Chr 36:22–23; Ezra 1:1–4).

The Babylonians had deported numerous Judeans in 597 BC after Judah's king, Jehoiachin, surrendered during a siege. Judah rebelled again a decade later, and the Babylonians destroyed Jerusalem, razed its temple, removed the Davidic dynasty from power, and wiped out much of the remaining population. Meanwhile, the surviving Judean deportees lived in various settlements around Babylonia, including at one place named Judah Town (Akk. *al yahudu*), from which numerous archival documents give us a glimpse into the daily lives of exiled Judeans and their neighbors. By the time Cyrus took Babylon in 539 BC, Judeans had been living in these settlements for three generations. As is usually the case with migrants, the later generations born in Babylonia knew of their roots in Judah but saw Babylonia as their home. So, when Cyrus permitted Judeans to collect the vessels of Yahweh's temple and return to Jerusalem, few answered the call. Only the most ardent of devotees considered such a costly and perilous endeavor.

The few who went were led by Zerubbabel, the grandson of Jehoiachin and scion ("Sprig") of the Davidic dynasty, and Joshua, the high priest.[1] They most likely did not depart from Babylon as soon as Cyrus issued his decree in 538 BC. The endeavor required considerable planning, finance, and a campaign of sorts to gather a viable quorum with the requisite skills to rebuild and start an entire community anew. In fact, indications are that they only arrived in Jerusalem about thirteen years later in ca. 525 BC.[2]

In the meantime, Cyrus died in 530 BC, and his son, Cambyses, succeeded

---

1. Ezra 1:8–11 says the temple vessels were given to Sheshbazzar, "the leader for Judah." It is often thought that he took the vessels back to Jerusalem, but Ezra 1:11 is better understood as saying that he had the vessels taken to Jerusalem with those who returned, implying that he himself did not return. This reading helps demystify the confusion over Sheshbazzar's role, especially in relation to Zerubbabel.

2. Ezra 4:5, which mentions opposition that discouraged Judeans from building the temple, may imply the returnees arrived in Jerusalem before the death of Cyrus in 530 BC, but not necessarily. Such opposition may also be explained as occurring in Babylonia, causing the delay of the return throughout the reign of Cyrus. See also George Athas, "The Failure of Davidic Hope? Configuring Theodicy in the Book of the Twelve in Support of a Davidic Kingdom," in *Theodicy and Hope in the Book of the Twelve*, ed. George Athas et al., LHBOTS 705 (London: T&T Clark, 2021), 230–33.

him. Though disparaged as a madman by some ancient sources, Cambyses was evidently a competent ruler, as he managed to conquer most of Egypt between 525 and 522 BC. By adding this most lucrative of countries to the Persian realm, Cambyses pushed the empire's frontiers well beyond Judah, providing enough security for the intrepid few among the Judeans to make good their return.

1.1.2 PIONEERS IN JERUSALEM

The pioneering community in Jerusalem faced several challenges. Archaeology informs us that they numbered no more than about a thousand people.[3] There were the challenges of maintaining an adequate workforce, acquiring resources, feeding a community, and dealing with suspicion and hostility from neighboring communities. Nonetheless, under Zerubbabel's leadership, they re-settled Jerusalem and prepared to build Yahweh's temple.

This was significant for two reasons. First, as the house of Yahweh, the temple was the hub of Judean religion. Without it, Judean identity was necessarily impaired. Second, the temple was the physical symbol of Yahweh's permanent covenant with the Davidic dynasty (cf. 2 Sam 7:11–16).[4] It was not just a religious building but a political monument. It was the prerogative of the Davidic heir(s) to build and maintain Yahweh's temple, and this is what Zerubbabel intended to do. In so doing, he would be reinstating the Davidic covenant and sowing the seed for a future independent kingdom of Judah. As long as Persia ruled Judah, the dream of a restored Davidic kingdom could never be completed. But few imagined the Persians were there to stay long term, for they were not a traditional superpower. Most saw them simply as the ones who brought down the Babylonian Empire, much like the Medes, who had helped bring down Assyria before being swallowed up by Cyrus themselves. Persian rule was a mere novelty. How long could it possibly last?

That question became focused in 522 BC as crisis struck the Persian Empire. On his way back from Egypt, Cambyses was thrown from his horse

---

3. Cf. Oded Lipschits, "Achaemenid Imperial Policy, Settlement Processes in Palestine, and the Status of Jerusalem in the Middle of the Fifth Century B.C.E.," in *Judah and the Judeans in the Persian Period*, ed. Oded Lipschits and Manfred Oeming (Winona Lake, IN: Eisenbrauns, 2006), 30–34. The figure of 42,360 people in Ezra 2:64 is most likely a cumulative number of those who migrated to Judah between the initial return (ca. 525 BC) and the governorship of Nehemiah (458–ca. 433 BC) or perhaps even later (the genealogies of Neh 12 go down to the end of the Persian era). There is no reason to assume that all those listed in Ezra 2:2 formed a single wave of migration.

4. This is the primary difference between the portable tabernacle and the permanent structure of the temple.

and died, leaving no son to succeed him. Exactly what happened after his death is a matter of dispute. Cambyses's younger brother, Bardiya, may have taken the reins of government, though he might have assumed control earlier in a bid to overthrow Cambyses. Alternatively, if Darius is to be believed, a Median priest ("mage") named Gaumata led a coup by assassinating Bardiya. Whatever the circumstances, the Persian Empire was left without a legitimate king, and confusion reigned instead. Ironically, the multiculturalism that the Persians had championed now backfired as people groups across the empire, emboldened by their sense of renewed identity, declared their independence. This was not so much rebellion against Persia as balkanization after the perceived collapse of the Persian Empire. There were at least sixteen such independence movements around the "empire" between 522 and 520 BC, including within Persia itself, testifying to the overwhelming sense that the Persian Empire had crumbled as many had expected.

It was at precisely this time that Zerubbabel began to build Yahweh's temple in Jerusalem (Ezra 3:6, 8; Hag 1:13–15). This was a bold political move as it signaled his intention to revive the Davidic throne in Jerusalem. He probably was not thinking of active rebellion against Persia. Like other local dynasts, he was trying to secure his control over a small fragment (little more than a city-state) of an empire that was breaking apart. In a climate of political chaos (cf. Hag 2:20–23), Zerubbabel was being an opportunist.

Yet, no sooner had Zerubbabel begun the temple construction than the Persians came back from the brink to recover control of their realm under the leadership of Darius. As he boasts in his famous Behistun Inscription, Darius successfully curtailed all "revolts" across the Persian domains. In Jerusalem, Persian officials arrived and questioned the legitimacy of Zerubbabel's projects (Ezra 5:3–4), perceiving the construction of the temple as an act of insurrection against Persian rule. Their arrival was a considerable setback for any notions of autonomy. Zerubbabel appealed to Cyrus's decree from eighteen years earlier (Ezra 5:13–15) as authorization for the construction. Yet Cyrus had been dead for a decade now. Accordingly, the Persians launched an investigation to search the royal archives in Babylon for the purported authorization (Ezra 5:17).

There are three possibilities for what happened to Zerubbabel at this juncture. The first is that nothing happened at all—he remained head of the pioneers in Jerusalem with Persian authorization. However, this goes against the grain of Darius's brutal interventions elsewhere. It also fails to account for the political significance of the temple construction, the threat that Persian intervention represented, and the rise of the high priest Joshua to the position of community head and temple builder (Zech 3:1–10; 6:9–15). The second option is that the Persians executed Zerubbabel for insurrection. While this fits more closely with Darius's mode of operation, it means that Cyrus's authorization of the temple construction and Zerubbabel's apparent presence at its dedication are both complete fabrications. A more plausible scenario is that the Persians removed Zerubbabel from leadership but did not execute him. Rather, they held Zerubbabel in custody pending the search for Cyrus's authorization of the temple construction. This makes much more sense of the rhetoric in Zechariah's vision and its epilogue (Zech 1–6), which imply that the temple project had been thrown into jeopardy, that Zerubbabel was conspicuously absent, and that Zechariah pinned his prophetic credentials on Zerubbabel's return to complete the construction (Zech 4:9). As unlikely as Zerubbabel's return might have seemed, this was consonant with the hope that the Davidic "Sprig" (Heb. *tsemah*, often translated "Branch") would return, and that this was in keeping with Yahweh's passionate zeal for "Zion"—that is, the re-establishment of the Davidic dynasty.[5]

The return of Zerubbabel to Jerusalem was by no means guaranteed. Darius treated perceived rebels with startling cruelty, usually impaling them before their own people. There must have been grave fears for Zerubbabel's life. With his absence, the meager Jerusalem community faced an uncertain future. The pioneers had thrown in their lot with the Davidic "Sprig," giving up settled lives in Babylonia to lay the foundations of the temple amongst the ruins of Jerusalem. Now that seemed to have come to naught. Was it even worth building the Davidic temple anymore? The answer came from the prophet Zechariah, who urged the community to continue the temple construction by commissioning the high priest Joshua to function as acting "Sprig" in Zerubbabel's absence. In this way, the community kept Davidic expectation alive in the hope that the actual "Sprig" would indeed return (Zech 3:8; 4:8; 6:9–15). Leadership over the community thus passed to Joshua.

Though the Persians searched the archives in Babylon (Ezra 6:1), Cyrus's authorization for the Jerusalem temple was eventually found in distant Ecbatana (Ezra 6:2). The discovery forced Darius into endorsing the temple's construction, for he was keen to be recognized as the heir of Cyrus's legacy and hence the rightful restorer of the Persian Empire (Ezra 6:3–12). To go against Cyrus's express wishes was to undermine his own legitimacy. He therefore released Zerubbabel and permitted him to return to Jerusalem to finish the construction. Against all odds, Zechariah's prophecies were validated, and Jerusalem's "king" returned to Zion:

---

5. Athas, "The Failure of Davidic Hope?," 226–41.

> ⁹Celebrate heartily, Daughter Zion!
> Shout out, Daughter Jerusalem!
> Look, your king comes to you.
> He is exonerated and liberated,
> humbled but riding on a donkey,
> on a colt, the offspring of asses.
> ¹²Return to the stronghold, prisoners of hope.
> This very day, I tell you,
> I bring you back a second time. (Zech 9:9, 12)[6]

The temple of Yahweh was completed and dedicated in February–March of 515 BC (Ezra 6:14–15). The pioneering community fell into line with Persian sovereignty, seeing it as divinely mandated (cf. Isa 45:1–6), and the prophecies of Haggai and Zechariah were accordingly timestamped by the year of Darius's reign (Hag 1:1, 15; 2:10; Zech 1:1, 7; 7:1).

Four major developments came from these critical years following Cambyses's death. First, despite the series of "revolts" across the empire, the Persians regained their grip on power under the impressive leadership of Darius (522–486 BC). He was a clever military strategist and capable administrator. He reorganized the empire into twenty-three satrapies administered by satraps and officials who were directly responsible to him.[7] He developed an intricate system of spies and informants known as "the eyes and ears of the king" (cf. Zech 3:9; 4:10), as well as an efficient "postal" system that ensured quick communication throughout the empire. Furthermore, he introduced a coinage system (the "daric"), which helped regulate trade and give cohesion to the empire's economy. It also enabled methodical taxation and increased government revenue. Thus, under Darius's dynamic leadership, the Persian Empire stabilized and grew. The Persians were here to stay after all.

Second, the system of satrapies created autonomous units across the empire. This promoted a sense of identity within subject communities, just as Cyrus had initiated with his policy of repatriation. Yet, through the satrapal system, it was the Persian king who guaranteed these local identities, and this stimulated a sense of loyalty to him. This colonial multiculturalism sought to

---

6. Though the original core of this oracle (Zech 9:1–16) comes from Zechariah's time, it has been reworked in light of later events (see 2.2.3). Its final form portrays the return of an unnamed messianic king. However, the passive participle "liberated" (Heb. *nosha'*) and the allusion to a second return hint at its original application to Zerubbabel.

7. The satrapal system pre-dates Darius, but he revamped its lines of responsibility and injected new personnel.

give subject communities a stake in the empire while bridling any notions of their independence.

Third, the promotion of the high priest Joshua to leadership over the Jerusalem community gave the Judean priests more political power than they had ever enjoyed before, and it came at the expense of the Davidic royal family. Though Joshua filled a leadership vacuum in Zerubbabel's absence, the priesthood had for the first time tasted civic authority, and it was a taste they would long savor.

Finally, Zerubbabel's extraordinary survival ensured that hopes for the restoration of a Davidic kingdom did not die. However, his taming by Darius and the promotion of the high priest considerably weakened the authority that the Davidic line possessed. After Zerubbabel, the Davidic family began to lose its grip on power within the community. As far as we know, none of Zerubbabel's sons ever held office, which may have been a deliberate restriction that the Persians imposed. A later governor of the community, Elnathan, was either married to Zerubbabel's daughter, Shelomith, or was her son.[8] In either case, Elnathan's tenure demonstrates the movement of power away from the primary Davidic line, despite the enduring significance of the family. We know the names of Zerubbabel's direct descendants for several subsequent generations (1 Chr 3:19–24), but none seems to have held office. Hopes for restoring a Davidic kingdom thus became less realistic as time wore on.

These developments effectively tranquilized the aspirations of the fledgling Jerusalem community, even though prophetic pronouncements about the restoration of Davidic rule over a reunited Israelite kingdom were still preserved and cherished. In daily life, the priests soon eclipsed the Davidic family in practical importance. This initiated the process that would, centuries later, see the temple emptied of its Davidic symbolism and viewed as purely a cultic installation run by the priestly caste under the authority of a foreign king (see 2.3.2 below). Davidic hope began to wane in quarters of Jerusalem society and slowly became mere lip service to a once glorious past.

---

8. A seal bearing the name of Shelomith names her as "wife" or "mother" of "Elnathan the Gover[nor]." The relevant Hebrew word (*'mt*) probably means "concubine" or "wife" (Heb. *'amat*) but could mean "mother" (Heb. *'immat*; cf. Ezek 16:44). The fact that she possessed her own seal demonstrates her importance and justifies her identification with the daughter of Zerubbabel (1 Chr 3:19). See Jeremiah W. Cataldo, *A Theocratic Yehud? Issues of Government in a Persian Province*, LHBOTS 498 (New York & London: T&T Clark, 2009), 91.

32 THE PERSIAN ERA (539–331 BC)

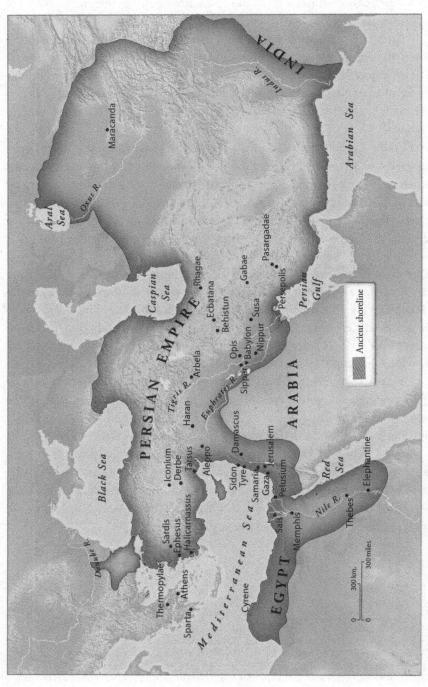

The Persian Empire during the reign of Darius I.

1.2 RELIGION IN THE PERSIAN EMPIRE

1.2.1 YAHWISM AND ANCIENT NEAR EASTERN RELIGION

For centuries before Cyrus, the ancient Near East was characterized by henotheistic religious practices. Henotheism was the focus of worship of a single deity, who ruled over a particular land and the people within it, but unlike monotheism it did not preclude the existence of other deities. Thus, the Edomites and their land were associated with the deity Qos, who was, in fact, the Edomite guise of Yahweh;[1] the Moabites had Chemosh; the Ammonites had Molech (perhaps a guise of Chemosh); the Arameans had Baal Hadad; the Assyrians had Ashur; and the Babylonians had Marduk. If one crossed a border into the territory of another people group, one was stepping into the domain of another deity who would expect appropriate honor.[2] This explains why wars in the ancient Near East were not just viewed as human conflicts but as clashes of the gods.

Yahweh was the patron deity in Israel and Judah. He was seen to be in covenant with his people to whom he had granted his land and in which they were his tenants. As his property on his land, they were required to observe his laws and customs. Failure to do so would result in their eviction. The oft-cited motto, "God's people in God's place under God's rule," is a modern-day appropriation of this henotheistic ideal. There was, therefore, a tight nexus between deity, land, and people. Like all their neighbors, the Israelites and Judeans also worshipped auxiliary deities, such as the "Queen of Heaven" (Jer 7:18; 44:17–19), most likely a goddess perceived as Yahweh's consort. The recognition of such deities flew in the face of the beliefs held by the biblical writers, but theirs was a minority view throughout the time of Israel and Judah's native monarchies.

When Cyrus took Babylon, he appealed to a mandate from Marduk, the patron deity of Babylon, for his seizure of the city and subsequent policies. Henotheism explains why he permitted the repatriation of the gods and their

---

1. Cf. Thomas Römer, *The Invention of God,* trans. Raymond Geuss (Cambridge, MA: Harvard University Press, 2015), 68–70.
2. An analogy for ancient henotheism is the way we use modern currency in different countries today, irrespective of a person's own origins or citizenship.

associated people groups—a policy from which the pioneers of the Jerusalem community benefitted. The land of Judah and Samaria/Israel belonged to Yahweh, and his people belonged there. As long as they remained outside the land, their worship of Yahweh was impaired.

Yet the period of exile had demonstrated a crucial notion to faithful Judean devotees of Yahweh. Although they were now outside his land, Yahweh had not completely abandoned them. The prophet Ezekiel, for example, received divine revelations on Babylonian soil. Another anonymous prophet viewed Nabonidus's attempts to get the gods to close ranks against Cyrus in Babylon as a laughable failure (Isa 41:22–29; 44:9–20). Yahweh was ultimately behind the unexpected rise of Cyrus (Isa 44:24–45:7). All this demonstrated clearly to them that, unlike the gods of the nations who were mere blocks of stone and wood, Yahweh was a dynamic deity who directed the course of history. He was potent within the borders of his land and beyond them. While the seeds of such overt monotheistic thinking lay in earlier forms of Yahwism, particularly as it was advocated by the biblical prophets, it was not until the exile that it began to receive clear elucidation. Such thinking promoted exclusive Yahwism, which both excluded the worship of other gods and denied their existence. Over the coming centuries, Judaism would develop its staunch monotheistic flavor in the context of Persian imperialism, which viewed the world not merely as disparate territories and peoples but as a single, collective empire.

Despite this, the nexus between Yahweh, his people, and the land was never broken. Many Judeans may have come to see Yahweh as sovereign over the whole world, but he was still first and foremost the God of Israel. Although they were under Persian hegemony, Yahweh was their true head of state. It was not enough to acknowledge Yahweh in Babylonia; they had to return to Yahweh's land and re-establish his society there. Furthermore, through the Davidic covenant, Yahweh had entered the Davidic dynasty itself as the dynastic father, ruling through his son, the Davidic king (2 Sam 7:12–16). Yahweh desired to dwell in Zion, originally the name of the fortress captured by David in which David took up residence and to which he brought the ark of the covenant (2 Sam 5:7, 9; 6:16–17). The ruling dynasty was, therefore, not a negotiable facet of Judean life but a necessity of Yahwistic worship. The fall of Jerusalem in 586 BC and the concomitant cessation of Davidic rule had been a major theological crisis in the exilic period (cf. Ps 89). The return of Zerubbabel went a long way to addressing this, but the subsequent marginalization of Zerubbabel and his descendants created an anomalous situation. Members of the Davidic royal family were present in their traditional royal capital, but they were not in power. Instead, they were subjects of a foreign empire. Moreover, as archaeological investigations show and Zechariah 5:5–11 implies,[3] syncretistic practices still pervaded the Jerusalem community after the pioneers returned from Babylonia and threatened to change the complexion of the community.

1.2.2 YAHWISTIC COMMUNITIES

Once the temple in Jerusalem was completed (515 BC), there were five identifiable groups associated with the worship of Yahweh in the Persian Empire.

First, there was the Judean diaspora in Babylonia. A good portion of the original deportees had been from the upper echelons of Judean society (e.g., royal descendants, government officials, priests, landholders). Many, therefore, were probably quite patriotic. This group viewed themselves as the true remnant of Israel, having experienced the purging punishment of exile. They were also primarily responsible for the preservation and perpetuation of earlier biblical traditions.

Second, there was the Jerusalem community. Since its pioneers had come from Babylonia to re-establish Judean society, they too viewed themselves as part of the faithful remnant of Israel and brought the biblical traditions with them. Led initially by Zerubbabel and the high priest Joshua, and including the likes of Haggai and Zechariah, they represented the most ardent of Yahwists who initially had a specific Davidic agenda. Over time, however, the priests came to dominate the leadership of the community.

Third, there were the Samarians, the descendants of the old Northern Kingdom of Israel who resided in the Samarian highlands. The Assyrians had provincialized this territory when they destroyed Israel in 723 BC and renamed the province after the former Israelite capital, Samaria. The Assyrians deported the Israelite elite and imported the elite of other lands into Samaria, but most Israelites remained in the land. Thus, most sites in Samaria show evidence of continued settlement. The Samarians revered Yahweh as their patron deity (cf. 2 Kgs 17:24–28; Ezra 4:2) but worshipped other gods too, making their brand of Yahwism syncretistic. The region was relatively stable and grew steadily in the face of Judah's demise under the Babylonians. When Jerusalem ceased to be a major cultic center after 586 BC, Samaria emerged as the territorial heartland of Yahwism and continued to be so for centuries.

---

3. This passage presents the need to remove syncretistic practices, typified by the figurine of a woman in a basket, from the Jerusalem community. Yet such figurines persisted in Jerusalem for multiple generations. See Izaak J. de Hulster, *Figurines in Achaemenid Period Yehud: Jerusalem's History of Religion and Coroplastics in the Monotheism Debate*, Orientalische Religionen in der Antike 26 (Tübingen: Mohr Siebeck, 2017).

Fourth, there were the "people of the land." These were the few native Judeans who had not been deported to Babylonia and who worked the land of Judah in sparse rural pockets. Without Jerusalem, they naturally gravitated towards the region of Benjamin on the periphery of Samarian territory, where the administrative center of Mizpah was located.[4] They carried on a syncretistic form of Yahwism, like the Samarians, so the religious practices of the two groups overlapped considerably. And yet these "people of the land" (Zech 7:5) shared an ethnic heritage with the Jerusalem community, which was seeking to rebuild its shared historic center at Jerusalem. Some of the "people of the land" might have been in favor of reinstating the Davidic family locally out of loyalty to their heritage, but this also implied the need to pay tithes to the Jerusalem temple. Their syncretism would also have been a source of tension with exclusive Yahwists in Jerusalem.

Finally, there was the diaspora community in Egypt, which had been living there since ca. 600 BC. These Yahwists tended to be syncretistic. Some of them had come from Judah and settled in Lower Egypt (Jer 44:1), while another group traced its heritage back to the Northern Kingdom of Israel. That group had initially migrated to Syria but eventually settled at Elephantine, an island of the Nile in Upper Egypt, where it formed a military enclave.[5] Here its members erected a temple to Yahweh. Some of this community's correspondence with Persian officials and personalities in Samaria and Jerusalem has survived from the late fifth century BC (the Elephantine Papyri), as well as some earlier notes written on ostraca (see 1.5.3 below).[6]

1.2.3 YAHWISM UNDER PERSIAN IMPERIAL RELIGION

As evidenced by the Cyrus Cylinder, Cyrus was a consenting henotheist who acknowledged the patron gods of the various peoples in his newly minted empire. His son, Cambyses, seems to have followed suit, evidenced by his adoption of Egyptian practices in Egypt after conquering most of the country between 525 and 522 BC.

---

4. Nitsan Shalom et al., "Judah in the Early Hellenistic Period: An Archaeological Perspective," in Honigman, Nihan, and Lipschits, *Times of Transition*, 73.

5. Porten suggests that the diaspora community at Elephantine was established as a military colony in ca. 650 BC during the long reign of Manasseh. See Bezalel Porten, *Archives from Elephantine: The Life of an Ancient Jewish Military Colony* (Berkeley: University of California Press, 1968), 119–20, 299. However, van der Toorn demonstrates that a community of Samarians probably founded the enclave in ca. 600 BC. See Karel van der Toorn, *Becoming Diaspora Jews: Behind the Story of Elephantine*, Anchor Yale Bible Reference Library (New Haven: Yale University Press, 2019). See 1.5.3 below.

6. John Curtis and Nigel Tallis, eds., *Forgotten Empire: The World of Ancient Persia* (Berkeley: University of California Press, 2005), 198–99, figs. 312, 313.

With Darius, however, a shift began. As the relief at Behistun illustrates, Darius was an adherent of the traditional Persian religion, Zoroastrianism. Its founder, Zoroaster (or Zarathustra), is shrouded in mystery, as no firm historical facts about him are known. Zoroastrianism proposed that there was one supreme deity, Ahura Mazda ("Supreme Lord"). Darius being an ardent devotee of Ahura Mazda does not mean that Cyrus and Cambyses were not—only that they were more concerned with establishing their power in the various countries of the empire, such that their henotheism left its greatest mark on the historical record. Darius's seizure of the throne between 522 and 518 BC marks a new religious era in the ancient Near East. His records show that he viewed Ahura Mazda as his imperial patron deity and other gods as low subordinates or false gods.[7] Ahura Mazda was seen as the supreme god of all heaven who had granted Darius supreme sovereignty over all the earth. This divine mandate to universal rule bestowed upon Darius such titles as "Great King" and "King of Kings," the latter of which would be adopted centuries later to describe the regnant Christ (1 Tim 6:15; Rev 17:14; 19:16).

The prominence of Ahura Mazda from Darius's reign onwards led to various local deities throughout the ancient Near East being associated with the Supreme Lord as either local manifestations of him or as his subordinates. Thus, the henotheistic approach to religion, by which each people group had their own patron deity, began slowly to transform into a kind of compatibilism. The process was complex and took centuries but saw religion become more integrated through much of the Persian Empire. Indeed, it was often in the interest of smaller people groups to equate their own patron deity with Ahura Mazda in order to gain official government recognition and backing.[8]

This religious belief found a significant parallel with the growing understanding of Yahweh among Judeans. They too were coming to view their patron God as the supreme deity of all the earth. To the Persians, this made Yahweh compatible with Ahura Mazda. We see a hint of this in Malachi's reference to the nations offering incense and sacrifice to Yahweh, who is described with Persian terminology as a "Great King" (Mal 1:14).[9] This probably alludes to Persian patronage of the Jerusalem temple and the ready compatibility the Persians saw between Ahura Mazda and Yahweh. Some Judeans might even

---

7. This repudiation of other gods can be seen in the texts and records of Darius's heir, Xerxes I.

8. This is perhaps what the Yahwists at Elephantine did in order to rebuild their temple. See Thomas M. Bolin, "The Temple of יהו at Elephantine and Persian Religious Policy," in *The Triumph of Elohim: From Yahwisms to Judaisms*, ed. Diana Vikander Edelman (Grand Rapids: Eerdmans, 1995), 127–42.

9. English versions tend to translate this verse as a prediction with future tense verbs. However, the Hebrew text uses participles and verbless clauses, suggesting current activity.

have equated Yahweh with Ahura Mazda, but there were still Judeans who maintained the distinct particularity of Yahweh as the God of Israel.

Yet, even if many did not equate Yahweh with Ahura Mazda, a conceptual and terminological development occurred as Yahwists began adopting Persian terms and concepts to describe Yahweh. In a purely henotheistic environment, referring to "God" was ambiguous for it required the subsequent question, "Which one?" As such, when talking about the divine, people always named the specific deity they were talking about. Once the Persians enthroned Ahura Mazda over their empire, "God" became the generic term for the one supreme deity, regardless of whom various people groups thought that was. This kind of terminology was completely compatible with how exclusive Yahwism viewed Yahweh as the only true God. In the Persian era, therefore, it became common to stop using the name "Yahweh" and to refer to him simply as "God," "the God of the heavens," "Heaven," or "the Lord." These were all terms the Persians employed for Ahura Mazda. Judeans even adopted some of Ahura Mazda's imagery, such as the "sun of righteousness rising with healing in its wings" (Mal 4:2[3:20 MT]), which borrowed from visual representations of Ahura Mazda's glory as a winged sun disc.[10] Again, this does not mean that all Judeans equated Yahweh with Ahura Mazda. Yahweh's particularity was always prized by exclusive Yahwists. Nonetheless, to refer to Yahweh as "God," "Lord" or one of the other associated titles became a way of affirming Yahwistic monotheism, while referring to Yahweh by name could perhaps be interpreted as leaving the door open to the existence of other gods.[11] This trend is notable in postexilic biblical literature as the name "Yahweh" gradually fell out of common usage. By the time the Greek translation of the Torah began in the 260s BC, "Lord" (Gk. *kyrios*) had become the standard cipher for "Yahweh" and thus replaced the divine name in the Septuagint.

This attitude provided the climate in which a more spiritual and ethereal view of religion developed. Before the Persian era, most people did not think of the gods as existing in another realm. Rather, the gods were part of the one universal reality. They possessed supernatural powers, but they were still within the universe. They resided in the divine court of the sky and frequented specific locations on earth, which were deemed sacred by their presence. But from

---

10. Cf. the depiction of Ahura Mazda on Darius I's Behistun Inscription and the obverse of several Persian coins. See Curtis and Tallis, *Forgotten Empire*, 204–5, figs. 348–351.

11. This situation is analogous to how Christians, Jews, and Muslims talk about "God" with each other today. The terminology reflects a particular agreement about a solitary deity, even though there are insuperable differences in understanding his identity, character, and attributes.

the Persian era on, "God" came to be seen as a spiritual being who was separate from the one universal reality.[12]

One of the major theological breakthroughs this engendered in Yahwism was the realization of God's transcendence and aseity—his ontological otherness to the universe and his non-contingent being. We can see this in the development of creation motifs in biblical literature. Before the Persian era, creation was depicted as Yahweh doing mortal combat with the sea monster of chaos, variably called Rahab or Leviathan, and making the world out of its carcass—an Israelite version of the creation motifs apparent also in other ancient Near Eastern cultures. For example, Psalm 89, composed shortly after the fall of Jerusalem in 586 BC, associated the foundation of the world with Yahweh crushing the Rahab (Ps 89:10–12; cf. Ps 74:12–17; Job 26:12–13). This developed in the exilic period, as we see a new creation account involving God making a stage of muddy soil, from which he molds a man and in which he plants a garden (Gen 2:4–8). God is still within the singular universe in this account, as he walks in the garden (Gen 3:8) and later descends from his court in the sky to look at the tower of Babel (Gen 11:5–7).[13] But when we turn to Genesis 1, which was composed during the Persian era,[14] we encounter a transcendent God who is ontologically distinct from creation. This revolutionary concept is articulated in the grand opening statement, "In the beginning, God created the heavens and the earth" (Gen 1:1). This God does not exist within a larger reality—he is pure being. There is no challenge to this God. He does not share existence or compete with it or within it. He serenely creates reality *de novo* and *ex nihilo* by speaking, making, separating, and ordering. It implies not just his uniqueness and sovereignty over created reality but his ontological otherness to it—an ethereal and transcendent being who exists independently of the universal reality. In many ways, these ideas were similar to those espoused by the early Greek philosopher Xenophanes (ca. 570–478 BC), who theorized that a perfect deity must exist as a distinct being outside perceived reality but from whom all perceived reality derived. It is doubtful that Xenophanes influenced

---

12. This was not the same as the later notion of "the Good" in Platonic thought, for that ideal was impersonal. Nonetheless, both the Persian belief in a "God of the Heavens" and the Platonic ideal of "the Good" shared a sense of ultimate reality being located in a transcendent realm with few able to comprehend it adequately.

13. The exilic date of this creation account derives from its Babylon-centric viewpoint and reference to the Etemenanki temple (the tower of Babel). Before the Babylonian exile of the sixth century BC, Judeans had no direct experience of either.

14. Jan Bremmer, *Greek Religion and Culture, the Bible and the Ancient Near East*, Jerusalem Studies in Religion and Culture, 8 (Leiden: Brill, 2008), 339–45.

the biblical writers, but it is no accident that such ideas developed in parallel when the Persians forged their empire.

The seeds of this theological development are to be found in the prior concepts of Yahweh's power, supremacy, holiness, and creativity. But Persian conceptuality provided the impetus for graduating these to the notions of Yahweh's transcendence and aseity. This does not mean the earlier creation motifs were somehow faulty or unorthodox. They were simply primitive and nascent, representing a more childlike stage of theological revelation, which was perfectly suited to a primitive and conceptually nascent environment. It was revelation accommodated to human understanding in an early context—an idea that would later be seen as evidence of God's grace. But the sense that God was in dynamic relationship with his covenant people, working towards a greater purpose, implied the need for theological growth—an awakening to ever greater theological reality and a maturing in the way this was articulated. In time, it would prepare Judaism to adopt Platonic and Aristotelian metaphysical categories for its theological expression, viewing mundane reality as connected to and shaped by an overarching spiritual reality (see 2.4). Beyond that, it would lead to the key Christian doctrine of the incarnation—that Jesus was not merely a theophany of a deity within the one universal reality but the incarnation of the non-contingent God who exists outside the universe; who became flesh, uniting divinity and humanity in his person, and thus enabled the salvation of creation and the participation of human beings in the divine nature itself (John 1:14; 2 Pet 1:4).

1.3 FROM ZERUBBABEL TO EZRA (515–458 BC)

1.3.1 GOVERNORS AND HIGH PRIESTS

Few details are known of the Jerusalem community between the dedication of the temple in 515 BC and Ezra's arrival in Jerusalem in 458 BC. The books of Ezra and Nehemiah give scant details of this time, leaving us to rely largely on what we can discern from Isaiah 56–59, Zechariah, and archaeology.[1] Two particularly important artefactual sources are the disparate collection of inscribed seals and bullae from Jerusalem bearing the names and titles of prominent people, as well as stamped jar handles from Jerusalem and Ramat Raḥel, which once stored grain, wine, and olive oil for trade and the payment of taxes. From these, we can determine the names of Judah's governors.

The first of these is Governor Elnathan, whose seal carries the Aramaic inscription, "Belonging to Elnathan the Governor."[2] The precise dates of Elnathan's tenure are unknown, but since he was the husband (or son) of Shelomith, the daughter of Zerubbabel, whose seal has also come to light,[3] it is plausible to suggest that he succeeded Zerubbabel in office. Two other figures are specifically named as governor on stamped jar handles. These are Ahiab (or Ahzai) and Jehoezer, but precise dates for them are not known.[4] Plausible arguments can also be made that two others mentioned on stamped handles, Uriah and Hananah, were also governors of Judah in the first half of the fifth century BC.[5]

---

1. Malachi is often added to the mix of evidence for this period, but as will be seen (1.7) it belongs to the mid-fourth century BC. Isaiah 56–66 is usually seen as a unit, but 60–66 have a Hellenistic provenance.

2. Nahman Avigad, *Bullae and Seals from a Post-Exilic Judean Archive*, trans. R. Grafman (Jerusalem: Institute of Archaeology, The Hebrew University of Jerusalem, 1976), 5–7, 17.

3. Avigad, *Bullae and Seals from a Post-Exilic Judean Archive*, 11–13; Cataldo, *A Theocratic Yehud?*, 91.

4. Oded Lipschits and David S. Vanderhooft, *The Yehud Stamp Impressions: A Corpus of Inscribed Impressions from the Persian and Hellenistic Periods in Judah* (Winona Lake, IN: Eisenbrauns, 2011), 83–106, 192–201. There is uncertainty about whether to read the first seal as "Ahiab" or "Ahzai" (short for "Ahaziah").

5. For a brief discussion of the evidence for all these governing figures, see Avigad, *Bullae and Seals from a Post-Exilic Judean Archive*; Ephraim Stern, *The Assyrian, Babylonian, and Persian Periods, 732–332 B.C.E.*, vol. 2 of *Archaeology of the Land of the Bible*, Anchor Yale Bible Reference Library (New

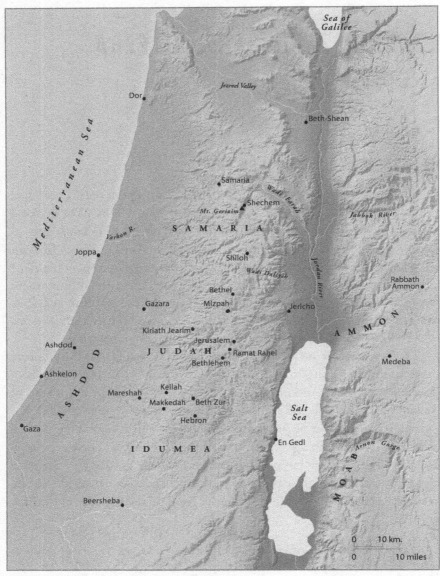

Yehud (Judah) and Samaria under the Persians.

York: Doubleday, 2001), 548–50; Lisbeth S. Fried, *The Priest and the Great King: Temple-Palace Relations in the Persian Empire*, Biblical and Judaic Studies 10 (Winona Lake, IN: Eisenbrauns, 2004), 184–85. Meyers and Meyers, Cataldo, and Lee assign a chronological order and tentative dates to the governors, but while plausible we cannot be confident that they are correct. See Carol L. Meyers and Eric M. Meyers, *Haggai, Zechariah 1–8: A New Translation with Introduction and Commentary*, Anchor Bible (New York: Doubleday, 1987), 14; Cataldo, *A Theocratic Yehud?*, 90; Suk Yee Lee, *An Intertextual Analysis of Zechariah 9–10: The Earlier Restoration Expectations of Second Zechariah*, LHBOTS 599 (London: T&T Clark, 2015), 45.

In the fifty-seven years between the temple's dedication (515 BC) and the arrival of Ezra in Jerusalem (458 BC), only three men occupied the high priesthood in Jerusalem. The first was Joshua ben-Jehozadak, who came to Jerusalem with Zerubbabel and who functioned as acting "Sprig" in Zerubbabel's brief absence (Zech 6:9–15). He was succeeded by his son, Joiakim (Neh 12:10), whom Josephus deduces came to office in the time of Xerxes I (after 486 BC) and was a contemporary of Ezra (*Ant.* 11.120–121). Joiakim's son, Eliashib, then succeeded him (Neh 12:10). Though there are some difficulties in the chronology, he is most likely the same priest who was a contemporary of Nehemiah (Neh 3:1, 20–21; 13:4–5). Eliashib was quite elderly during Nehemiah's governorship, and his son, Joiada, became high priest before Nehemiah began his second stint in Jerusalem (ca. 429 BC; Neh 13:28). There is some debate about whether others, such as Ezra, might have served as high priest,[6] but this is unlikely.[7] Ezra's position was imperial, not cultic, and his mandate spanned the region of Trans-Euphrates.

1.3.2 JERUSALEM

Archaeological excavations reveal that Jerusalem continued to be a meager settlement of between 500 to 3,000 people, with a key Persian administrative center 4 kilometers to the south at Ramat Raḥel. Yet the temple still grew in importance, as did Jerusalem's sway over the surrounding district from which it drew its tithes. This included the "people of the land," as well as towns on the southern fringe of Samaria's zone of influence, such as Bethel (cf. Zech 7:2). This also probably brought Jerusalem into contact with the Idumeans (i.e., Edomites) who had occupied southern Judah after the fall of Jerusalem in 586 BC. Some Judeans who returned from exile also settled across the Jordan in the traditional territory of the Moabites and Ammonites. The coastal plain continued to be settled by the descendants of the Philistines and Phoenicians.

These interactions brought challenges, forcing the Jerusalem community to evaluate its identity. It was part of a single empire with these people groups, but whether Jerusalem should seek closer relations with them or maintain its own distinctive identity was an open question. Persian benefaction allowed for local distinctions on the proviso that they did not undermine the empire's cohesion.

---

6. Klaus Koch, "Ezra and Meremoth: Remarks on the History of the High Priesthood," in *Sha'arei Talmon: Studies in the Bible, Qumran, and the Ancient Near East Presented to Shemaryahu Talmon*, ed. Michael Fishbane, Emmanuel Tov, and Weston W. Fields (Winona Lake, IN: Eisenbrauns, 1992), 105–10.

7. Cf. James C. VanderKam, *From Joshua to Caiaphas: High Priests After the Exile* (Minneapolis: Fortress, 2004), 46–47.

Yet relations with Samaria, with whom Jerusalem shared so much heritage, were not straightforward. They worshipped the same deity but with divergent conceptions and agendas. And since the Samarians worshipped a range of additional deities, was there room for fraternization or even compromise? What would this do to the long-term hopes for a Davidic kingdom based in Jerusalem? Would it change the nature of worship in Jerusalem? What were the economic repercussions? Samaria had been relatively stable for centuries and was now the dominant hub of Yahwistic worship, even with its syncretism. The pioneers who had returned to Jerusalem viewed themselves as the legitimate remnant of the kingdom of Israel with a divine commission to restore what their ancestors had lost. The questions of how Yahweh should be worshipped and which community owned the legacy of Israel were very real. How Jerusalem could negotiate relations with its neighbors while continuing to forge its own identity and survive as an urban center under Persian colonial oversight was a politically delicate endeavor.

The prophet of Isaiah 56–59 was open to the inclusion of Jerusalem's neighbors but without compromising either the exclusivity of Yahweh or the primacy of Jerusalem. On those bases, he believed that the priests in Jerusalem were doing a poor job. They were compromising their cultic duties, adopting syncretistic practices, and exploiting the vulnerable, all of which were seen as the reason for Jerusalem's perpetual struggle. With its Davidic aspirations thinning, the identity of the Jerusalem community became porous, and they found themselves being influenced more than they were influencing. The kind of Yahwism prevalent in Samaria was winning out.

1.3.3 THE REIGN OF DARIUS I (522–486 BC)

After Darius secured power, the Persian Empire solidified on the political landscape. In 512 BC, he led an exploratory expedition across the Hellespont and staked a claim on Thrace. This signaled to the Aegean world that Persia was looking to expand into Europe and even incorporate the city-states of the Greek mainland into its empire. It had already subsumed the Greek cities in Ionia along the Aegean shore of Asia Minor. But in 499 BC, the Greek cities of Ionia rebelled, sponsored by the cities of the Greek mainland across the Aegean. Darius successfully quelled the rebellions, but they motivated him to bring the Greek mainland under his control.

In 490 BC Darius sent his armies and navy to the Greek mainland. They were, however, thwarted by the Athenians at the Battle of Marathon. This was the first real defeat that Darius suffered. Enraged by this, he immediately began preparations to expand his forces and arm them for a second invasion. However,

Egypt took advantage of this moment of weakness and rebelled against him in 486 BC, opening a second front. By this time, Darius's health was ailing, and he died in October that year before he could attend to the rebellion.

Darius's reign was probably the apogee of the Persian Empire. He had seized the empire just when it appeared to have crumbled. Yet his military prowess and organizational skills kept it together, and by the time he died in 486 BC, it had become a solid edifice. Even though rebellions were common, the structures he had set up were adequate for dealing with them. Marathon, therefore, was by no means a mortal blow to the empire, but it did create cracks, as it gave impetus to further rebellions within the empire, particularly in Egypt. Events there also had an impact on nearby Judah, which was part of the staging ground for imperial forces heading to Egypt.

1.3.4 THE REIGN OF XERXES I (486–465 BC)

Xerxes inherited the throne from his father, Darius, and swiftly put down the rebellion in Egypt. He also ruthlessly quashed a rebellion in Babylon, going so far as to destroy the famed statue of Marduk in Babylon. Buoyed by his successes, he resumed his father's expansionist policies, undertaking more pressing incursions into the Greek peninsula. In 480 BC, with a huge force that included contingents from Judah, Xerxes outflanked the heroic Greek resistance at Thermopylae and sacked Athens. He was, however, checked by the defeat of his navy at the Battle of Salamis, and the remainder of his army suffered defeat at Plataea the following year. Thus, despite his early triumphs, Xerxes was unable to fulfil his father's ambition of subjugating the Greek mainland.

A long-term implication of this was the fanning of Greek antipathy towards Persia, which would smolder for another century and a half until the rise of Alexander the Great. In the shorter term, it became evident that Persia could be resisted. From the reign of Xerxes onwards, therefore, Persia constantly had to deal with significant challenges to its dominion. The Greeks took the offensive with the formation of the Athenian-led Delian League to combat Persia and wrest all Greek cities in Asia Minor from their control. In 466 BC, they dealt a demoralizing blow to the Persians at the Battle of the Eurymedon River in southern Asia Minor, which pushed the Persians back. The Greeks had successfully diminished Persia's empire.

Persia's vulnerability struck home the following year when a powerful court official assassinated Xerxes. The crown prince, Darius, did not succeed him, for he too was murdered, probably by the same official. It was Darius's younger brother, Artaxerxes, who then took the throne in 465 BC.

1.4 EZRA, NEHEMIAH, AND THE SAMARIANS

1.4.1 THE REVOLT OF INARUS (460–454 BC)

When Artaxerxes I (465–424 BC) came to the throne, the Persian Empire was on the back foot. He first had to address dynastic struggles to secure his throne[1] before he could turn his attention to the western fringes of the empire where trouble was brewing.

The success of the Greeks during the reign of Xerxes gave momentum to an anti-Persian feeling in Egypt. As one of the old superpowers and geographically isolated, Egypt often sought to regain its own sovereignty. The Greeks galvanized this into spurts of opposition to the Persians. The result for Persia was a delicate balancing act. To keep Egypt with all its rich resources within its sphere, the Persians had to allow Egyptians considerable cultural freedom. Darius had initiated precisely this policy to help quell rebellion in Egypt after Cambyses's death. In ca. 520 BC, he had commissioned an Egyptian noble named Udjahorresnet to ensure the continuation of Egyptian laws and culture under the aegis of Persian authority. Darius tried to ensure that Persia was viewed as enhancing Egyptian traditions, not smothering them. While this went a long way towards stabilizing Egyptian life, it did not quell completely the Egyptian desire for native rule.

In 460 BC an armed uprising broke out in the Nile Delta under Inarus, a pharaonic descendant. Inarus's grandfather, Psamtik III, had been the last native Egyptian pharaoh (Twenty-Sixth Dynasty), whom Cambyses had overthrown in 525 BC. Inarus's father, Psamtik IV, was probably the instigator of the rebellion against Darius in 486 BC. Like Zerubbabel, Inarus was the scion of a disempowered dynasty. Persian rule was for him a personal affront, and he now sought to take back what he felt rightfully belonged to him. He had been operating out of Libya and the western Delta and now found ready allies in the Athenians, who were keen to bolster anti-Persian activity on another front.

---

1. Pierre Briant, *From Cyrus to Alexander: A History of the Persian Empire*, trans. Peter T. Daniels (Winona Lake, IN: Eisenbrauns, 2002), 570.

With the aid of Athenian infantry and ships, Inarus attacked and killed the Persian satrap, Achaemenes, a brother of Xerxes, and pushed the Persians out of the Delta (Thucydides, *P.W.* 1.108; Diodorus Siculus, *Bib. hist.* 11.71.3–6).[2] But Inarus's campaign stalled when he began to besiege Memphis in Lower Egypt. This allowed Persian forces in Upper Egypt to remain unmolested, and the locals there continued living under Persian imperial sponsorship. Egyptians had by now lived under Persian rule for three generations, and some had fought in the imperial army or served in the tiers of Persian government. By contrast, the Athenians fighting alongside Inarus were viewed as a foreign invading force. If Artaxerxes could promote himself as the guarantor of Egyptian culture, he could bind Egypt more closely to himself and smother Inarus's revolt while it was limited to Lower Egypt.

Artaxerxes put his brother-in-law, Megabyzus, the satrap of Trans-Euphrates, in command of the operation.[3] The army gathered on the coastal plain of Palestine, meaning there were almost certainly Samarians and Judeans among its troops. The Persian fleet was also sent to attack through the Nile. In 456 BC the Persian campaign began. Megabyzus broke Inarus's blockade of Memphis and eventually trapped him and the Athenians on an island of the Nile. In 454 BC they surrendered to him. Megabyzus came to terms with the Athenians and permitted them to return home, but he had Inarus executed. Inarus's son, Thannyras, however, was released and permitted to retain some sway over the western Nile Delta as a petty client. While these seem significant concessions, they were politically astute as they cast the Persians as the best protectors of the peace and of native Egyptian culture. The strategy worked well, for Egypt was relatively peaceful for the remainder of Artaxerxes's reign.[4]

Inarus's revolt demonstrated the delicate cultural balance that the Persians had to maintain as a colonial power over a multicultural empire. Local populations did not automatically accept Persian rule. But native Persians were few in number and could not simply flood the territories of their empire with colonizing settlers who would impose Persian culture on their subjects. *Lebensraum* was not the mandate for the Persian Empire. The mere fact that the lingua franca of the empire was Aramaic, rather than Persian, exemplifies this. The best way for the Persians to maintain their empire was to confine the

---

2. Ctesias portrays Achaemenes as Artaxerxes's brother (*Persica* 38) rather than uncle, but this is chronologically impossible, as Achaemenes had been satrap of Egypt since Xerxes had quelled rebellion in Egypt in 484 BC. Achaemenes was brother of the king, but that king was Xerxes, not Artaxerxes.

3. Megabyzus was aided by Artabazus, satrap of Phrygia, but he was by now an old man.

4. The revolt of Amyrtaeus in the years immediately after Inarus's subjugation appears to be the only exception, but this was dealt with quickly.

power of local dynasts while also being active sponsors of local cultures. This involved both military strength, cultural sensitivity, and social cohesion. The reliefs decorating Darius's Apadana palace in Persepolis epitomize the principle artistically. They portray Persian officials gently guiding representatives of the empire's various ethnic groups by the hand into the presence of the Great King[5]—images that would convince the Greeks that the Persians were effeminate. It was rule by benefaction, backed by a multi-ethnic army drawn from all subject peoples. The Athenians, who lay outside the empire, tried to exploit this benefaction by drumming up rebellion, chiefly demonstrated by the Ionian Revolt (499–494 BC) and Inarus's Revolt (460–454 BC). Nonetheless, Artaxerxes had successfully showed himself as benefactor through both military strength and cultural sensitivity.

1.4.2 THE MISSION OF EZRA

The mission of Ezra needs to be understood in the light of Artaxerxes's efforts to tackle Inarus's revolt and the deployment of a cultural benefaction strategy. Judah, which the Persians knew as Yehud, was a small, rural province within the satrapy of Trans-Euphrates, which encompassed all the territories from the Euphrates to the border of Egypt. It was one of the most ethnically diverse satrapies of the entire empire, presenting a considerable challenge for cultural benefaction.

When Inarus took the Nile Delta in 460 BC, Judah, along with the neighboring provinces, found itself on the edge of an active theater of war. To tackle the revolt, Artaxerxes needed to secure the highways through the Levant for travel, supply, and communication during the campaign, as well the subsequent flow of tribute and trade if the campaign succeeded. He could also ill afford to have Greek city-states open a new front behind his forces after they had deployed to Egypt. The Athenians had proved how effective their navy could be at Salamis (480 BC), the Eurymedon River (466 BC), and now with Inarus in Lower Egypt. With so much of Persia's Phoenician-based fleet committed to Egypt, the Levantine coast was exposed. Still smarting from the sack of Athens in 480 BC, the Athenians needed little coaxing to wreak havoc upon their Persian foes. Thus, in Trans-Euphrates Artaxerxes embarked on a concerted program of military reinforcement and cultural benefaction, which promoted the integrity of its communities, loyalty to Persian governance, and safeguarded against Greek interference.

---

5. Curtis and Tallis, *Forgotten Empire*, fig. 20.

As part of this program, Artaxerxes built a series of forts along the road networks of Judah.[6] The garrisons he stationed in them were a visible military presence to deter unrest and secure the highways for logistical purposes. In this way, Artaxerxes emulated Darius's Royal Road, which linked Sardis with Susa via a series of garrisons and which provided the king with speedy communication and intelligence. The renovation of the main administrative center at Ramat Raḥel, just south of Jerusalem, occurred at this time. A Persian "paradise" (botanical garden) was built around the site to showcase Persian majesty.[7] It boasted an impressive water feature, local trees, and varieties of exotic trees from all over the empire, such as citrons from India, walnuts from Media, and cedars from Lebanon.[8]

Artaxerxes's second initiative was to dispatch a Judean priest, Ezra ben-Seraiah, to Jerusalem in 458 BC to create cohesion among the locals. From the biblical perspective, Ezra's mission was about establishing the law (Torah) in the land. As such, he worked to reform the temple cult and eradicate syncretism. He augmented the temple in Jerusalem with new personnel, as well as materials provided by the Persians. He also oversaw social reforms in which the men of Judah agreed to divorce their foreign wives to preserve the purity of the worshipping community (see 1.4.3 below). From a Persian imperial perspective, Ezra's mission was about cultural benefaction in a vulnerable area of the empire. Sponsoring local identity and culture promoted the cohesion of the region and bolstered Persian sovereignty.[9] By heading up this program, Ezra was cast in the same role as Udjahorresnet, whom Cambyses and Darius employed to good effect in Egypt. Like Udjahorresnet, Ezra was a priest as well as a loyal public servant of the empire. His interests aligned with the agenda of Artaxerxes, making him the right man for the job in Artaxerxes's eyes.

---

6. Fantalkin and Tal argue that the network of forts is best dated to ca. 400 BC as part of the Persian attempt to counter the secession of Egypt from the empire. See Alexander Fantalkin and Oren Tal, "Judah and Its Neighbors in the Fourth Century B.C.E.: A Time of Major Transformations," in *From Judah to Judaea: Socio-Economic Struc Tures and Processes in the Persian Period*, ed. Johannes Unsok Ro, Hebrew Bible Monographs 43 (Sheffield: Sheffield Phoenix Press, 2013), 165–70. However, this is unlikely, as the Egyptians were able to capture much of the coastal plain after their independence from Persia. The relevant sites also show evidence of temporary abandonment, which makes sense of the constant struggle between Persia and Egypt for control of the region throughout the fourth century BC. It is more likely that the fortification system was developed in response to Inarus's Revolt while Persia still had control of the Levant.

7. The term "paradise" comes from the Hebrew word *pardes*, which is itself a Persian loanword for a royal botanical park. Nehemiah 2:8 refers to the *pardes* near Jerusalem, which should be equated with Ramat Raḥel.

8. Oded Lipschits et al., *What Are the Stones Whispering? Ramat Raḥel: 3000 Years of Forgotten History* (Winona Lake, IN: Eisenbrauns, 2017), 98–112.

9. Peter Frei and Klaus Koch, *Reichsidee Und Reichsorganisation Im Perserreich*, 2nd ed., Orbis Biblicus et Orientalis 55 (Göttingen: Vanderhoeck & Ruprecht, 1996), 8–61.

Furthermore, in commissioning Ezra, Artaxerxes was attempting to placate his own deity, Ahura Mazda. Artaxerxes's decree, written in Aramaic, implored his officials to aid Ezra's mission "with diligence" (Ezra 7:23), using a Persian loanword (*'adrazda'*) that indicated religious devotion associated with Ahura Mazda.[10] In other words, Artaxerxes identified his sponsorship of Ezra's work to promote the law of "the God of heaven" as an act of piety towards Ahura Mazda, which would guarantee divine favor upon himself and his sons. This shows how the Persian regime saw Yahwistic religion as compatible with their own Zoroastrian beliefs. For Ezra, this was probably a matter of pragmatics; he may not personally have held to such compatibilism, but as long as the Persians did, Yahwism stood to benefit.

Ezra's base for operation was Jerusalem, but his royal mandate extended "to all the people of Trans-Euphrates—all who know the laws of your God" (Ezra 7:25). He thus had authority to implement the king's cultural benefaction strategy amongst all Yahwists in the satrapy, including Samaria, Idumea, and Ammon (cf. Ezra 8:36). This made Artaxerxes's strategy a regional endeavor to shore up the loyalty and cohesion of all the satrapy's southern provinces.

Four significant factors were at work in this arrangement. First, Ezra was not dispatched to Jerusalem as the governor of Judah. On the contrary, he was distinguished from the governors of the region (Ezra 8:36). So, while he was based in Jerusalem where Yahweh's temple stood, his mandate was not limited to Judah. His authority was priestly and thus supra-provincial. This helped promote the authority of Jerusalem's priests and integrate the Yahwists of Trans-Euphrates more closely, at the same time continuing the marginalization of Davidic descendants.

Second, while unofficial Yahwistic shrines probably existed throughout the region, Jerusalem had the only official Yahwistic house of sacrifice (cf. Ezra 6:3). From the Persian perspective, therefore, it made sense to concentrate Yahwism on Jerusalem where the infrastructure already existed.

Third, despite Jerusalem's cultic importance, Samaria was still the dominant Yahwistic hub in terms of population. Based on archaeological surveys, the population of Judah in the mid-fifth century BC was no more than 30,000 people,[11] while the province of Samaria had at least 80,000 inhabitants.[12]

---

10. Fried, *The Priest and the Great King*, 223.
11. Oded Lipschits, *The Fall and Rise of Jerusalem: Judah under Babylonian Rule* (Winona Lake, IN: Eisenbrauns, 2005), 270–71.
12. Zertal estimated the population of the area of Manasseh at 42,000, but this did not include the heavily populated areas of Ephraim. See Gary N. Knoppers, *Jews and Samaritans: The Origins and History of Their Early Relations* (Oxford: Oxford University Press, 2013), 108–9.

Being more developed and with easier access to the coast, Samaria also had economic contacts with the Aegean, making it more susceptible to Greek influence. Samaria's loyalty was, therefore, a more pressing concern to Artaxerxes than Judah's.

Fourth, Ezra and his entourage offered sacrifices to Yahweh in Jerusalem, including "twelve bulls for all of Israel" (Ezra 8:35) There was evidently a sense that the Israelite nation as a whole, though spread across distinct provinces, was being represented as a single people in Jerusalem. Even more importantly, this identity of the single people was premised on a historic exodus from Egypt. At the time of Inarus's Revolt, this was ideologically potent, as it encouraged dissociation from Egyptian dynasts and concentration on the land of Canaan.

1.4.3 THE RESULTS OF EZRA'S REFORMS

Implementing the Torah as the cultural standard had a radical effect on the region. First, it reformed worship in Jerusalem and curbed syncretistic Yahwism. Isaiah 56–59 shows the Jerusalem community after the rebuilding of the temple grappling with the worship of other deities. But after Ezra this no longer occurred to the same degree. Both the biblical and archaeological records attest to the curbing of syncretistic practices, including in Samaria.[13] It would be some time before syncretism died out completely, but monotheism gained considerable momentum in the Levant from this time. Although Persian law still prevailed as official imperial law, the Torah became the key cultural document for regulating a pan-Israelite identity under one deity. This was a powerful idea that would exert great influence for the next century.

Second, the books of the Pentateuch effectively solidified into their final form at this time. By gaining imperial sanction as a cultural standard, they became the Torah—an official canon.[14] By the time of Nehemiah's governorship (445–ca. 425 BC), the Torah could be read aloud to official assemblies of the people (Neh 7:73b–9:5), followed by confessions outlining the basic narrative of the Pentateuch (Neh 9:6–37) and binding pledges to uphold it as law (Neh 9:38–10:39). Once a Samarian temple was constructed on Mount Gerizim (see 1.4.5 below), pro-Gerizim statements made their way into the Torah held in Samaria, forming what has come to be known as the Samaritan

---

13. Syncretistic Yahwism continued unabated among the Yahwists at Elephantine in Egypt.
14. This does not mean the books of the Pentateuch did not exist before this time or lacked authority. Attributions of authority generally precede canonization, which represents the setting of a fixed collection of authoritative documents.

Pentateuch. These additions were theologically significant but not numerous. Thus, the text of the Torah on the whole remained quite stable from this time.

Third, through marriage reforms Ezra successfully tied the exclusive worship of Yahweh to the land. Ezra 10 describes the marriage reforms in Judah by which Judean men divorced their foreign wives and the children they had fathered by them. Failure to divorce foreign wives resulted in the forfeiture of property (Ezra 10:8). Nehemiah 13:26, which represents a later repeat of the reform, provides the example of Solomon as the rationale for these reforms. Solomon's multiple marriages to foreign women had brought the worship of foreign gods into Israel, and this provoked divine wrath against the nation. To avoid divine wrath, the foreign gods had to go, which meant their devotees—in this case, foreign women—had to go also.[15] The forfeiture of property for noncompliance was not merely a legal deterrent but an ideological confirmation that the land itself belonged to Yahweh and Yahweh alone. Family life and lines of inheritance, therefore, had to reflect Yahweh's exclusive claim over the land and the people within it. Only those with an ancestral claim to the land and who were committed to exclusive Yahwism, therefore, could own land. This was nothing short of a reinstitution of Israel's national covenant with Yahweh. Interestingly, the account of the marriage reforms in Ezra only mentions their implementation in Judah and Benjamin (Ezra 10:7, 9). This might imply that the neighboring provinces failed to implement the reforms, but it could also be that the book is simply silent about them because of its Judean focus.

Fourth, as a result of Ezra's reforms Judah and its cultic center in Jerusalem came to represent the local ideal of what the Persians wanted from the region, especially since it bordered an active theater of war. To the Persians it became an ideal local outpost of the worship of the one supreme deity, which was entirely compatible with their Zoroastrian religion. Indeed, Ezra's imperial mandate, which identified him as "Ezra the priest, teacher of the law of the God of heaven" (Ezra 7:12), echoes Persian ideals. Ezra's personal purpose was to establish Yahwistic monotheism as the unchallenged religion of the region, but this aligned with Artaxerxes's religious outlook and his purpose of consolidating his control over the region at a fragile time. A productive synergy was thus achieved. Ezra succeeded in enshrining monotheistic Yahwism as the

---

15. It is often touted that Ezra's reforms primarily focused on Judean men divorcing women associated with the Israelites of the land (e.g., Samarians) as a way of distinguishing those within Israel who had been part of the exilic community in Babylon from those who had not. For example, see Joseph Blenkinsopp, *Judaism: The First Phase. The Place of Ezra and Nehemiah in the Origins of Judaism* (Grand Rapids: Eerdmans, 2009), 63–71. However, a closer reading of the text reveals this not to be the case.

culture and religion of the land, and Artaxerxes succeeded in producing a loyal region whose ideals resembled that of the Persian people themselves.

Despite the successes of Ezra's mission, it also created a political-theological dilemma. The Torah advocated but one solitary place at which to worship Yahweh (Deut 12), but it did not name where that place was. Where exactly Yahwists worshipped was of little concern to Artaxerxes, so long as he had a set of loyal provinces. Since Jerusalem had an existing temple, it fulfilled the criterion of Torah and thus attained special privilege. Yet Jerusalem was associated with the ancient Davidic dynasty, while the Samarians were descendants of the Northern Kingdom of Israel, which denied all traditional Davidic claims. Imperial sanction of the Jerusalem temple forced Samarians to worship at a Davidic shrine. It also created an awkward situation for Idumeans to the Judeans' south. By centering the religious aspect of his cultural benefaction strategy on Jerusalem, Artaxerxes had created some potential long-term problems.

In this regard, we notice that among Ezra's retinue accompanying him from Babylonia to Jerusalem was Hattush, a Davidic descendant (Ezra 8:2).[16] From a Persian perspective, Hattush's association with Ezra showed both deference to the Davidic family and its domestication, similar to the situation of Thannyras, son of Inarus (see 1.4.1 above). But Hattush's association with Ezra and the continued presence of the Davidic family in Jerusalem would not have been missed on Samarians now forced to worship there.

The long-term implications are seen in the act of communal repentance that Ezra led in the temple. "Because of our sins" he stated, "we, our kings, and our priests have been subjected to the sword and captivity, to pillage and humiliation at the hand of foreign kings, as it is today" (Ezra 9:7). This was an implicit acknowledgement that native kingship was one of the fundamental markers of Israelite identity, and this was stated on the campus of the monument to the Davidic dynasty. This came with the admission that God had shown Israel "kindness in the sight of the kings of Persia" (Ezra 9:9), thereby recognizing Artaxerxes's cultural benefaction, but this did not repudiate the marker of native (Davidic) kingship.

Further fueling this narrative was the Prophetic History of Israel—the books of Joshua, Judges, Samuel, and Kings—which recounted the narrative

---

16. A certain Hattush is also mentioned as a descendant of Zerubbabel in 1 Chr 3:22, but the Chronicler's presentation of the Davidic genealogy means that this Hattush belongs to a later time than the one associated with Ezra. Another Hattush is mentioned in Neh 12:2, but he is listed as a priest or Levite, not a Davidide. From Ezra 8:2, then, it seems that not all Davidic descendants had returned to Jerusalem with Zerubbabel.

of David and his dynasty's rule over the nation. This Prophetic History was still being preserved by scribes and priests in the temple, who were brokers of Judean, and now pan-Israelite, identity and tradition. This Prophetic History soon attained nascent canonical status along with the prophetic books of Isaiah, Jeremiah, and Ezekiel. This represented a second canonical collection—the Prophets—appended to the canon of the Law but nonetheless distinct from it.[17] It was the Torah only that had become the cultural "law" of all Yahwists; the Davidic traditions had not, but they were still being promulgated in Jerusalem. The Persians did not empower the Davidic family, but they did force all Yahwists to worship at the Davidic temple. Artaxerxes's cultural benefaction strategy secured the short-term integrity of the region under Persian sovereignty, but it also sowed seeds of discord that would, in time, germinate into ideological conflict.

1.4.4 THE REVOLT OF MEGABYZUS AND THE WALLS OF JERUSALEM

Zechariah 2:1–5[2:5–10 MT] implies that the pioneers in Zerubbabel's day had attempted to rebuild Jerusalem's walls but abandoned the effort following Zerubbabel's arrest. Yet, Ezra praises God for the patronage of the Persian kings, which had allowed for the rebuilding of the temple and for giving a "wall in Judah and Jerusalem" (Ezra 9:9). This odd expression probably refers to the fortification network that Artaxerxes commissioned and indicates that, as part of this fortification network, the walls of Jerusalem were also to be rebuilt.

Yet the effort did not go smoothly. Ezra 4:7–16 quotes a letter sent by officials in Samaria to Artaxerxes complaining of attempts by rogue officials to rebuild the walls of Jerusalem. Given the place of this excerpt in the flow of Ezra, it is tempting to see the reference to Artaxerxes as erroneous and instead read the incident as the pioneers' attempt to rebuild the wall early in Darius's reign. However, the references to Artaxerxes are persistent, and the chronological leaps in Ezra 1–5 are clearly marked. The complaint about the rebuilding of Jerusalem's walls in Ezra 4:7–16, then, should be read as a "flash forward" to Ezra's day.

The letter argues that the unnamed officials whom Artaxerxes had commissioned (perhaps Ezra and his retinue) were engaging in sedition by

---

17. When the Book of the Twelve Prophets (Hosea–Malachi) was added to this canonical collection is uncertain. There are elements of the book that reflect a Hellenistic milieu, but it is not clear whether this represents redaction after its inclusion in the canonical collection or continued development before its final inclusion in the canonical collection in the Hellenistic era.

rebuilding Jerusalem's walls (Ezra 4:12). Since the fortification of Jerusalem was part of Artaxerxes's strategy for the region, the accusation initially seems misguided. And yet, the letter urges Artaxerxes to consult the royal archives to determine the precedent of previous attempts to rebuild Jerusalem's walls. At the very least, such an investigation would turn up Zerubbabel's aborted attempt to rebuild the walls (Zech 2:1–5[2:5–10 MT]), which coincided with the empire-wide "rebellions" after the death of Cambyses (see 1.1.2 above). A complaint lodged with Xerxes (Ezra 4:6) presumably presented another similar precedent. But if Artaxerxes had authorized the incorporation of Jerusalem into the province's defensive network, why did Samarian officials complain after the work began?

The answer lies in the revolt of the satrap, Megabyzus. After quashing Inarus's revolt in Egypt, Megabyzus staved off Athenian aid to another Egyptian rebel, Amyrtaeus, who had continued fighting in the Delta marshes. He was then involved in defeating Greek forces in Cyprus (451 BC).[18] The Greek physician-cum-historian Ctesias[19] then relates that Megabyzus rebelled against Artaxerxes (*Persica* 48–42). Ctesias is notoriously unreliable at times, and there are fanciful features in his account. Yet there are elements that do ring true, which allow us to piece together a plausible reconstruction.

Megabyzus's insubordination probably stemmed from how successful he was. He had triumphed against Inarus, coordinated a victorious campaign on land and sea, secured the integrity of Egypt, and neutralized the Athenians in the Mediterranean, after which he still had an enormous force at his disposal in his own satrapy of Trans-Euphrates. In many ways, he had emulated Cambyses's achievement in conquering Egypt, plus he had checked the Athenians, while Artaxerxes, competent but still relatively young, remained in his palace. He may have felt his success, seniority, current position, and resources justified the exercise of greater power and accordingly redirected taxes and tribute to himself. If he had Greek mercenaries in his army, as Ctesias suggests, there may have been a real danger that he could defect to the Greeks. One wonders whether the Athenians even bribed Megabyzus into rebellion.[20] In any case, Artaxerxes dispatched an army on two separate occasions to deal with Megabyzus, and both failed to tame him.

---

18. The chronology of events here is notorious to reconstruct because of conflicting information from Thucydides (*P.W.* 1.108–12).

19. Ctesias's original work, *Persica*, is no longer extant, but the portions pertinent to our considerations come from excerpts given by the Byzantine Patriarch of Constantinople, Photius.

20. Artaxerxes had employed this tactic just after Inarus's revolt began, when he had tried to induce the Spartans to invade Athens, to compel Inarus's Athenian allies to return and defend their homeland. However, the tactic did not work.

Exactly how Jerusalem featured in Megabyzus's revolt is unknown. It is unclear whether Ezra or other leaders in Jerusalem took initiative in siding with Megabyzus, or whether Megabyzus intimidated them into it. Either way, others perceived Jerusalem as party to the rebellion. The account of Ezra 4:7–23 suggests that officials claiming loyalty to Artaxerxes saw the building of Jerusalem's walls, which Artaxerxes had sanctioned, as now compromising the king's interests. These Samarian officials may well have been prompted by resentment at being forced to worship in Jerusalem and now jumped at the chance to discredit it. Either way, their efforts worked. At their request, Artaxerxes ordered an archival search, which convinced him that a fortified Jerusalem was a dangerous prospect. His reply to the letter of the Samarian officials acknowledged that "Jerusalem has had powerful kings ruling over the whole of Trans-Euphrates, and taxes, tribute and duty were paid to them" (Ezra 4:20)—a statement that might allude to the scope of Megabyzus's revolt. Consequently, the king ordered the building activity in Jerusalem to be stopped with the use of "force and army" (Ezra 4:23).

Although Ctesias's account indicates that Megabyzus repelled Artaxerxes's attempts to bring him to heel, Nehemiah 1:1–3 relates that "Jerusalem's wall was breached, and its gates burned with fire." This was not a reference to the Babylonian destruction of the city in 586 BC, as is sometimes surmised, but a new development, which came as a shock to Nehemiah in 446 BC. The damage was recently sustained and must relate to Megabyzus's revolt. Whether it was inflicted by Megabyzus or Artaxerxes's forces (cf. Ezra 4:23) is uncertain. In any case, Jerusalem was caught in the crossfire and suffered a serious setback in the years between the defeat of the Greeks in Cyprus (451 BC) and the beginning of Nehemiah's tenure as governor of Judah (445 BC).

At some point, however, Megabyzus was reconciled to his brother-in-law, Artaxerxes, and received a royal pardon. This must have occurred after the Peace of Callias in 449 BC, by which the Persians and Greeks came to terms with each other.[21] The Persians granted the Greek cities of Ionia autonomy, and the Greeks agreed not to interfere in the Persian Empire. Artaxerxes probably reached this agreement with the Greeks because, with his Phoenician-based fleet and a considerable land army under Megabyzus's control, his ability to resist another Greek attack was seriously compromised. This increases the likelihood that Megabyzus was consorting with the Greeks, but in any case, he had clearly become a significant potentate in the Mediterranean. The treaty

---

21. There was debate even in ancient times over whether the Peace of Callias was real or a fabrication of later Greek writers. There is enough warrant, however, to consider it a reality, especially as it helps explain Persian and Athenian actions in the years immediately after it.

brokered by Callias in 449 BC took the wind out of his sails. Thereafter, it was in the interests of both Artaxerxes and Megabyzus to reconcile their differences. Under the terms, Megabyzus was permitted to remain as satrap, while Artaxerxes had the integrity of his empire restored and his competent, though ambitious, brother-in-law working for him again.[22] Jerusalem, however, was in disarray and its temple seriously damaged.

1.4.5 THE SAMARIAN TEMPLE ON MOUNT GERIZIM

Josephus attributes the building of the Samarian temple on Mount Gerizim to a certain Sanballat during the time of Alexander the Great (*Ant.* 11.321–324). Archaeology, however, has proved that the Samarian temple was built in the mid-fifth century BC,[23] and there was a governor in Samaria at that time named Sanballat. This Sanballat I, mentioned multiple times in Nehemiah, founded a dynasty of governors in Samaria.

The Masoretes have pointed Nehemiah's appellation for Sanballat I as "Horonite" (Neh 2:10, 19; 13:28), implying that Sanballat was born in the Samarian town of Lower or Upper Beth Horon. But Nehemiah uses appellations in derogatory ways to imply the illegitimacy of his enemies. For example, it is evident that "Tobiah the Ammonite" (Neh 2:10) was not actually an Ammonite, for his Yahwistic name marks him as a native Israelite/Judean.[24] However, he had official authority in Ammon when he opposed Nehemiah, so Nehemiah disparages him by attaching the territorial label, "Ammonite," to him. Along these lines, it is difficult to see how coming from the heartland of Israelite territory counted against Sanballat. It is more likely that the vowels of "Horonite" should be amended to "Haranite," indicating that Sanballat's family hailed from Haran in northern Mesopotamia. Haran was a chief center of worship of the moon god, Sin, which accounts for the theophoric element in Sanballat's name (Akk. *Sin-uballit*, "may Sin give life"). It was also the city

---

22. According to Ctesias (*Persica* 43), Artaxerxes later found a trifling reason to remove Megabyzus from power.

23. Yitzhak Magen, "The Dating of the First Phase of the Samaritan Temple on Mount Gerizim in Light of the Archaeological Evidence," in *Judah and the Judeans in the Fourth Century B.C.E.*, ed. Oded Lipschits, Gary N. Knoppers, and Rainer Albertz (Winona Lake, IN: Eisenbrauns, 2007), 157–211. Eran Arie dates the foundation of the sacred precinct to 650–550 BC. See Eran Arie, "Revisiting Mount Gerizim: The Foundation of the Sacred Precinct and the Proto-Ionic Capitals," in *New Studies in the Archaeology of Jerusalem and Its Region: Collected Papers. Volume XIV*, ed. Yehiel Zelinger et al. (Jerusalem: Israel Antiquities Authority, 2021), 39–63. There might have been an earlier shrine on Gerizim, or the later builders might have employed archaic designs, but the temple itself certainly dates to the mid-fifth century BC.

24. He was also probably a descendant of the Tobiah at the time of Zerubbabel (Zech 6:9–15).

from which Abraham departed on his journey to Canaan (Gen 12:4–5), which perhaps gave Sanballat extra credibility among the people he governed. But these factors do not necessarily indicate that he himself was an ethnic Haranite any more than "Ammonite" indicates that Tobiah was an ethnic Ammonite.

Sanballat was a key figure in Yahwistic religion in Samaria (see this section below), and he gave his sons, Delaiah and Shelemiah, Yahwistic names. It is possible his family was originally Haranite and came to Samaria through deportation, voluntary migration, or governmental appointment, whereupon they adopted Yahwistic culture. More likely, however, his family was descended from the Israelite elite whom the Assyrians deported to northern Mesopotamia upon the fall of Samaria in 723 BC. Knowledge of such ancestral connections among exiled and migrating populations reached back centuries, as the example of the Yahwists at Elephantine demonstrates.[25] In this case, Sanballat was Samaria's equivalent to Zerubbabel in Judah: the scion of a long-deposed aristocracy, with a connection to a place of exile preserved in his name, returning to his ancestral homeland to build a temple. Labelling Sanballat a "Haranite," then, was akin to calling Zerubbabel a "Babylonian." Nehemiah underlines Sanballat's foreign connection to Haran, the chief center of the worship of Sin, as a means of disparaging Sanballat's concerted attempt to become a champion of Yahwism within Israel's traditional territory.

Sanballat was still alive in 407 BC, though by that time he had delegated authority to his sons, Delaiah and Shelemiah.[26] His longevity suggests that he came to office in his thirties, shortly before Nehemiah became governor of Judah in 445 BC. His relative youth suggests that his credentials lay not just in his own competencies but also in noble ancestry. This would put his appointment as governor of Samaria in ca. 448 BC as part of an administrative overhaul throughout Trans-Euphrates after Megabyzus's revolt.[27] By appointing Sanballat to provincial leadership in Samaria, Artaxerxes was promoting a native aristocracy as part of his cultural benefaction strategy in the region. It was a significant concession to Samarians after they had been forced to worship at the Davidic temple in Jerusalem, which now lay derelict. In this way, Sanballat's rise may be seen as directly related to the plight of Jerusalem and the associated marginalization of the Davidic family.

After Megabyzus's revolt, Jerusalem's position as the Levant's official

---

25. In the fifth century BC, the Yahwists at Elephantine in Egypt could recall their origins in the kingdom of Israel three centuries earlier and the time of its intervening migrations. See 1.5.3 below.

26. Sanballat is mentioned in the Elephantine papyri (*TAD* 4.7; 4.8).

27. Though Ezra 4:7–10 mentions many officials loyal to Artaxerxes, the governor of Samaria is not mentioned. Sanballat's predecessor may have been ousted by Megabyzus or removed by Artaxerxes.

center of Yahwism lay in tatters. The city had been stigmatized, its infrastructure damaged, and its population drastically reduced. As Nehemiah implies, Jerusalem and its temple had been practically abandoned (Neh 11:10–18; cf. 2:11–12, 16). It appears, therefore, that in ca. 448 BC the Jerusalem temple had virtually ceased to function.

This is where Sanballat I comes in. The Bible never overtly mentions the temple on Mount Gerizim,[28] but the archaeological record pins its construction to this very time. The political situation immediately preceding Nehemiah's governorship also provides the most appropriate conditions for the temple's construction. Nehemiah is said to have been cupbearer to Artaxerxes—an honorific, rather than menial, position. After he received news in late 446 BC that Jerusalem lay in ruins (Neh 1:1–3), he boldly requested a mandate from Artaxerxes for the city's reconstruction (Neh 2:1–8). He was motivated by the conviction that Yahweh had chosen Jerusalem as the one place in which to locate his name (Neh 1:9; cf. Deut 12). If, by this time, a rival temple was being erected on Mount Gerizim, Nehemiah would have viewed the recovery of Jerusalem's primacy as imperative. His prayer in Nehemiah 1:5–11, with its theology of divine retribution, intimated that the entire nation of Israel (not just Judah) was in peril if Jerusalem did not attain its primacy once again. Furthermore, Nehemiah viewed Sanballat as someone who did not have the welfare of all Israel in mind (Neh 2:10). This was not merely projecting a personal rivalry onto a national canvas but a conviction, framed by a theology of divine retribution, that Sanballat was putting the whole nation of Israel in jeopardy. It implies that Sanballat had done something of immense theological consequence, which risked divine wrath.

Sanballat's concerted opposition to Nehemiah was motivated by a larger politico-theological rivalry for sway over all Yahwists.[29] With the deterioration of Jerusalem's status and the dereliction of its temple, the hub of Yahwism rebounded to the more populous province of Samaria. This gave Sanballat a clear opportunity, as a temple would have granted him the sway he sought. It is even likely that Artaxerxes had appointed Sanballat as governor with express permission to build a temple to Yahweh as part of the cultural benefaction strategy. And so, Sanballat began to build a new temple on the summit of

---

28. The temple on Mount Gerizim is, however, alluded to by deliberate omission as part of a strategy of *damnatio memoriae* (cf. Zech 14:9; Mal 1:10; 2:11–13). See also 1.7 below.

29. It has been suggested that Sanballat opposed Nehemiah for creating a new provincial unit carved out of Samaria's territory. This, however, was not the case. Haggai 1:1 names Zerubbabel as governor of Judah, so the province's existence goes back at least to the early years of Darius's reign. The seals of Judean governors also bear this out (see 1.3.1).

Mount Gerizim in ca. 447 BC.[30] As far as can be ascertained, no other time in the second half of the fifth century BC presented so many intersecting political and theological factors to explain the rise of this temple, which archaeology confirms was founded at this time.

Constructing a temple on Mount Gerizim achieved several goals. First, it provided a kind of *via media* that helped to unite the region more cohesively under Artaxerxes's cultural benefaction strategy. The earlier sanction of Jerusalem had been pragmatic, for its temple already existed and had a functional priesthood. However, the ancient connection of the Jerusalem temple to the Davidic dynasty was problematic for the Samarians, who were descended from the northern Israelites and thus did not recognize Davidic claims. Similarly, the Idumeans (i.e., descendants of the Edomites) now occupied what had been the southern portion of the Davidic kingdom. They worshipped Qos, the ancient Edomite guise of Yahweh,[31] and had a modest shrine dedicated to him at the town of Makkedah.[32] The official recognition of the Jerusalem temple for all Yahwists, therefore, opened the back door to classic Davidic/Judean claims over what were now the provinces of Samaria and Idumea, in addition to Judah. It was also potentially a long-term threat to the Idumean cult of Qos.[33] The dereliction of Jerusalem's temple reduced the awkwardness both Samarians and Idumeans must have felt in having Yahweh of Jerusalem officially foisted fastidiously upon them. A Yahweh worshipped more generically on Mount Gerizim presented fewer problems all round.

Second, it consolidated the province of Samaria as the official heartland of Yahwism. Mount Gerizim was more centrally located to all Yahwists ("Israelites") in the region than Jerusalem. In that sense, building a temple on Mount Gerizim made good demographic and geographic sense.

Third, it filled the vacuum in religious leadership that Jerusalem's demise had left. Since most of the temple personnel had departed Jerusalem, many of them could find re-employment at Mount Gerizim. Thus, as priestly activity found renewed focus at Mount Gerizim, Sanballat became the patron of the Yahwistic priestly class.

---

30. This was exactly the same time that Athens, under the leadership of Pericles, began to build the Parthenon, the temple of Athena whose ruins still crown the Acropolis of Athens today.

31. Römer, *The Invention of God*, 68–70.

32. An Aramaic ostracon (AL 283) dated to the fourth century BC refers to a plot of land belonging to the "house of Yahu" in Makkedah (modern Khirbet el-Qom). It is possible that, when the ostracon was written, that temple was no longer standing and the land was a vacant lot. See André Lemaire, "New Aramaic Ostraca from Idumea and Their Historical Interpretation," in Lipschits and Oeming, *Judah and the Judeans in the Persian Period*, 416–17.

33. By way of analogy, the relation of the Idumean cult of Qos to the Judean cult of Yahweh can be likened to the modern-day relation of Roman Catholics to Protestants.

Fourth, since the Torah had been implemented as the official religious custom in the region, the temple on Mount Gerizim fulfilled the stipulation of one place of cultic worship after Jerusalem's rapid decline. According to Deuteronomy, Mount Gerizim was the place where Moses commanded the tribes of Israel to pronounce the covenantal blessings (Deut 11:29; cf. 27:12)—a command given right before the stipulation that Israel was to have only one place of worship (Deut 12). As the mountain of blessing, it was probably also the mountain on which Moses commanded Joshua to build an altar (Deut 27:4; see also this section below). This traditional significance allowed Mount Gerizim to fulfil the role of the one site for Yahwistic worship in Jerusalem's stead. The fact that the Torah kept in Jerusalem was never updated to specify Jerusalem as the one true place of worship, the way the Torah in Samaria was later updated to reflect Mount Gerizim's primacy, demonstrates that the Torah did not originally specify a location for Yahweh's singular shrine. Jerusalem's primacy was promulgated not by the Torah but by the emerging canonical collection of the Prophets. Of particular importance in this context was 2 Samuel 5–7, which stated that the northern tribes had come to David at Hebron and anointed him king over all Israel. The descendants of those northern tribes were the Samarians, and Hebron was now in Idumea. After this, David had conquered Jerusalem and transferred the ark of the covenant there before Yahweh made an eternal covenant with him. These narratives were rejected in Samaria, where the Torah alone was recognized as authoritative. But the fact that the Torah was recognized in Jerusalem too was a boon to Sanballat's strategy. A subtle emendation by Judean scribes, however, moved Joshua's altar from Mount Gerizim to the adjacent Mount Ebal (the mountain of the covenant curses [Deut 11:29]), thus erasing the memory of sacrifice being made upon Mount Gerizim and undermining the legitimacy of its temple (Deut 27:4; cf. Josh 8:30).[34]

Finally, Sanballat was a shrewd administrator. A temple within his province made him protector of the sanctuary, increased his prestige, and boosted his province's economy and his own coffers accordingly. This is not to suggest that Sanballat was motivated purely by power or greed, but the economic benefits could not have been lost on him. From a Persian perspective, the temple on Mount Gerizim made economic as well as cultural sense.

Mount Gerizim rises to an elevation of 881 meters, with a narrow valley separating it from Mount Ebal (940 meters elevation) to the north. Shechem,

---

34. One fragment among the Dead Sea Scrolls (F.154 Deut 2) preserves the reading of "Mount Gerizim" at Deut 27:4. See James H. Charlesworth, "What Is a Variant? Announcing a Dead Sea Scrolls Fragment of Deuteronomy," *Maarav* 16.2 (2009): 201–12.

which was little more than a village when the temple was built, lay in the narrow pass between the two mountains, with the city of Samaria a further 11 kilometers to the northwest. Worshippers needed to make a considerable climb from the valleys below. The sacred complex at the top measured approximately 96 × 98 meters and was surrounded by a dry-stone wall. Chambered gates in the northern, eastern, and southern walls led into an open courtyard with an altar at its center. The altar and courtyard lay directly before the sanctuary, which was approximately 40 meters long by 20 meters wide, and stood in the central western part of the complex. The sanctuary was entered on its east side, with the Holy of Holies at its western end.[35] While the configuration resembled other tripartite temple structures in the ancient Near East, it bore particular resemblance to both the Jerusalem temple in Ezekiel's day (Ezek 8–11) and his idealized temple (Ezek 40–48). This suggests that it was modeled upon Jerusalem's temple and touted as its successor.[36]

Sanballat began construction of the temple on Mount Gerizim in ca. 447 BC. The temple in Jerusalem took just over four years from the start of construction to its dedication (520–515 BC), which included the interruption when the Persians took Zerubbabel into custody. On analogy, then, the temple on Gerizim was probably nearing completion when Nehemiah arrived in 445 BC as governor of Judah.

1.4.6 JERUSALEM, MOUNT GERIZIM, AND ISRAELITE IDENTITY

As there was now an official Yahwistic temple on Mount Gerizim, and Jerusalem was in decline, the question arises as to why anyone felt the need to promote Jerusalem as a cultic center any longer. The Torah stipulated that there be one place of worship for Israel, and Mount Gerizim fulfilled that mandate. Mount Gerizim could even employ the priests and Levites who had served at Jerusalem. Three significant reasons for Jerusalem's ongoing claim, however, emerge.

First, although the Jerusalem temple was basically derelict by 445 BC, it had functioned for over seventy-five years previously and could legitimately claim historical primacy over the Samarian temple. Sanballat had therefore

---

35. The holy of holies occupied the location that is identified today as the "Twelve Stones," after a later Samaritan tradition that this was where the twelve stones symbolizing the tribes of Israel were set up (cf. Josh 4:1–9).

36. This may explain some of the older features used in its architecture, *pace* Arie, "Revisiting Mount Gerizim."

pulled off a veritable historical coup in establishing a new center on Mount Gerizim. Most Yahwists probably approved of the newer temple, since it was more accessible than Jerusalem. Yet the temple in Jerusalem was still standing, even if it was derelict.

Second, the marriage reforms that took place under Ezra's leadership tied the worship of Yahweh to the land. The Judeans had agreed to divorce their foreign wives and children, thereby removing traces of foreign gods from the land (Ezra 10; see 1.4.3 above). But it is unknown whether this had also occurred in the neighboring provinces. Syncretism almost certainly took longer to wane in more populous Samaria, even though Torah was now the official custom there too. From a Judean perspective, this compromised the Samarians' connection to the land and even risked divine retribution (cf. Neh 2:10; 13:23–31). Not everyone in Judah necessarily felt this way. Even though many Judeans divorced their foreign wives, they probably felt under duress to comply. We know that during Nehemiah's later return to Susa, some Judeans married foreign women again (Neh 13:23, 28). Most in Judah would have had Judean wives and therefore not been directly affected by the reforms. It is not inconceivable, then, that many in Judah were either completely neutral about their Samarian counterparts, sympathetic towards them, or envious of their potentially less stringent context. Nehemiah certainly encountered Judeans who opposed him or displayed Samarian sympathies (cf. Neh 6:10–13). Nonetheless, the fact that the marriage reforms had even occurred testifies to how quickly stringent exclusivist tendencies had taken root in Judah. The Samarians may have represented the geographical heartland of Yahwism, but the Judeans could claim to be its moral heartland and that they alone were legitimately tied to the land. In such a context, the Samarian temple could be viewed as a rogue institution.

Third, and perhaps most significantly, the Jerusalem temple was still the monument to the Davidic covenant, and this was still important for some Judeans. The preservation in Jerusalem of the biblical traditions about David—from the Prophetic History, the writings of the prophets, and the collation of psalms—all testifies to this. The temple on Mount Gerizim had no Davidic connection whatsoever. For Sanballat and the Samarians, this presented no issue. But if Mount Gerizim prevailed as the one place of Yahwistic worship in the Levant, hopes for the future restoration of a Davidic kingdom were in serious jeopardy. It would call into question the legitimacy of the prophetic traditions about David. According to the Davidic covenant, Yahweh promised to rule Israel permanently through the agency of David's son, whom Yahweh would adopt as his own son, thereby making God himself the father figure within Israel's ruling dynasty (2 Sam 7:11–16). This covenant meant that Israel, being the personal property of Yahweh, necessarily became the personal property of the Davidic king also. If the Samarian temple prevailed as the center of Yahwism, all such Davidic claims upon Israel would be nullified. The Samarian temple, therefore, was more than a struggle for religious power. It became a dispute over the fundamental identity of Israel, the nature of Yahwism, and the place of the Davidic dynasty. Did Yahweh make a covenant with David? Was Israel a Davidic estate? Were the prophetic traditions true and authoritative? If the answer to these questions was yes, then the one true place of worship had to be Jerusalem, where the temple was a veritable sacrament of that Davidic tradition. No other cultic site could be tolerated.

Since the temple on Mount Gerizim had no Davidic ties, Samarian tradition repudiated the prophetic traditions. Only Torah was deemed authoritative, and it was supplemented only with some traditions about Joshua, the successor to Moses. No second canon of "the Prophets" (Heb. *nebi'im*) would emerge in Samaritan theology. In Judah, by contrast, this second canonical collection became a staple of Jewish theology alongside Torah, giving rise to the hope of a future messiah who would restore Israel. A tradition of a future messiah did eventually develop in Samaritan tradition (cf. John 4:25; see 3.7.7 below), but it had nothing to do with royalty, Davidic or otherwise. Rather, it developed out of the Torah's claim that God would send a prophet like Moses (Deut 18:15) and so viewed him as a teacher of divine revelation, rather than a liberator and ruler (cf. John 1:21, 25; 6:14; 7:40).

1.4.7 GOVERNOR NEHEMIAH

Little is known of Nehemiah's heritage beyond the name of his father, Hacaliah (Neh 1:1), and that he was a Judean whose ancestors were buried in Jerusalem (Neh 2:3, 5). He had several brothers in Jerusalem (cf. Neh 1:2; 4:23; 5:10, 14; 7:2), one of whom was Hanani (the others are not named). Nehemiah's age and how he came to be the cupbearer to Artaxerxes I (Neh 1:11) are unknown. In any case, his role as cupbearer placed him in the Persian court at Susa, one of the royal capitals, far from Jerusalem.

It is tempting to surmise that Nehemiah was a Davidic descendant. It would mean that his ancestors buried in Jerusalem were none other than the Davidic kings, and interestingly, the only tombs mentioned in Nehemiah are those of the Davidic dynasty (Neh 3:16). It would also explain his fervent desire to restore Jerusalem, as well as the charge that Sanballat later aimed at him, that he was seeking to be declared king (Neh 6:6–7). However, Nehemiah only ever applied the title of "king" to Artaxerxes and refers to David as a "man of God" (Neh 12:36)—a prophetic title rather than a royal one. While we cannot preclude that he had Davidic ancestry, it is more probable that he did not.

Nehemiah's brother Hanani came with a Judean delegation to Susa in December 446 BC (Neh 1:1–2). He reported on the damage to Jerusalem, presumably during Megabyzus's revolt. Although the book of Nehemiah never mentions Sanballat's new temple at Mount Gerizim, its construction imperiled Jerusalem's future. Accordingly, Nehemiah used his personal relationship with Artaxerxes to receive an appointment as Judah's new governor with a view to repairing the damage that Jerusalem had sustained.

Nehemiah's commissioning implies that either Artaxerxes wished to replace the incumbent governor of Judah or that Judah lacked a governor at this time. Either option is plausible in the wake of Megabyzus's revolt. Nehemiah recognized, however, that he was striding into a veritable lion's den. Samarian officials had branded the efforts to rebuild Jerusalem's walls during Megabyzus's revolt as seditious (Ezra 4:7–23). With Nehemiah arriving to complete that very task, local officials would undoubtedly have viewed him with suspicion. Yet, if he possessed royal authorization, there was little they could do. The heated opposition he did face suggests the rebuilding of the walls held more explosive significance. Nehemiah was perceived as promoting Jerusalem's primacy, and this directly challenged the primacy of Sanballat's new temple on Mount Gerizim, potentially compromising Artaxerxes's cultural benefaction strategy. For Sanballat, therefore, Nehemiah's commissioning was a problem. Nehemiah also understood this and so requested royal papers to guarantee his safety among the provincial administration (Neh 2:7). Artaxerxes augmented this with an armed escort (Neh 2:9).

From Artaxerxes's perspective, any squabble between Jerusalem and Mount Gerizim over primacy was of little consequence. With Egypt now domesticated and Megabyzus reconciled to him, Artaxerxes could afford to give more leeway to locals in the southern Levant. The rivalry did not undermine his sovereignty. On the contrary, the promotion of Torah ensured the ethnos of "Israel" was still culturally recognized within the empire. Artaxerxes could also bill himself as patron of both temples, making both communities of "Israel" dependent on him. This is presumably why Nehemiah did not seek the decommissioning of Mount Gerizim, even if he personally wished for it; he could only request the rehabilitation of Jerusalem. Restoring Jerusalem, therefore, would help to bind the city once again to Artaxerxes.

Since Nehemiah could not decommission Mount Gerizim, the only way he could successfully negotiate the rehabilitation of Jerusalem was to isolate

Judah from Samaria. By moving Judah out from under Samaria's shadow, he could allow the temple in Jerusalem to function in its own right, without interference from Sanballat. He therefore concentrated on severing Judah's ties with its neighbors.

His first order of business was to rebuild Jerusalem's walls and gates, which he achieved by October 445 BC in a stunning fifty-two days (Neh 6:15). The archaeological record bears out the hurried nature of construction.[37] Excavations have shown that parts of the wall were carelessly filled, built hastily over the rubble of houses from the late monarchic era (Iron IIc), and of unequal quality, as would be expected from the multiple teams that Nehemiah employed along the wall's length.[38] The wall enclosed a narrow habitable area from the Temple Mount in the north to the Ophel and southern ridge of the old city—barely more than six acres.[39] The Mishneh quarter on the Western Hill, which had been part of the city before the Babylonian conquest in 586 BC, remained unoccupied, with its ruins a ghostly reminder of Jerusalem's brutal past.

The construction was accomplished under significant threat of violence from Sanballat, who headed up a regional bloc consisting of Tobiah, governor of Ammon, and Geshem the Arab (Neh 2:10, 19). Though Nehemiah refers to Tobiah as "the Ammonite slave" (Neh 2:10, 19; cf. 4:3), Tobiah's name demonstrates that he was a Yahwist, probably the descendant of the Tobiah who had returned from Babylon during the construction of the Jerusalem temple in ca. 520 BC (Zech 6:9, 14). The family persisted in recycling the Tobiah name through subsequent generations, holding sway over Ammon until at least 198 BC. Geshem is known from sources outside the Bible, such as the Aramaic inscription on a silver vessel that his son Qainu offered to the goddess Hanilat. The inscription identifies him as "King of Qedar," a group of pastoralist Arab tribes with roots in the Hejaz region that came to occupy the Negev steppe south of Idumea.[40] Geshem was probably a client king within the Persian Empire and may even have acted as governor of Idumea. That Sanballat was the ringleader of this bloc is seen by the fact that he is always mentioned in this coalition, while the others occasionally do not appear.

---

37. Kenneth A. Ristau, *Reconstructing Jerusalem: Persian-Period Prophetic Perspectives* (Winona Lake, IN: Eisenbrauns, 2016), 40, 63–65, n. 45.

38. Ristau, *Reconstructing Jerusalem*, 41–42.

39. Ristau, *Reconstructing Jerusalem*, 59–60, 73. For later occupation patterns, see Oded Lipschits, "Jerusalem Between Two Periods of Greatness: The Size and Status of the City in the Babylonian, Persian and Early Hellenistic Periods," in *Judah Between East and West: The Transition from Persian to Greek Rule (ca. 400–22 BCE)*, ed. Lester L. Grabbe and Oded Lipschits, Library of Second Temple Studies 75 (London: Bloomsbury, 2011), 174.

40. The Nabateans eventually replaced the Qedarites as the dominant Arab group of the region and may even have been one of the Qedarite tribes.

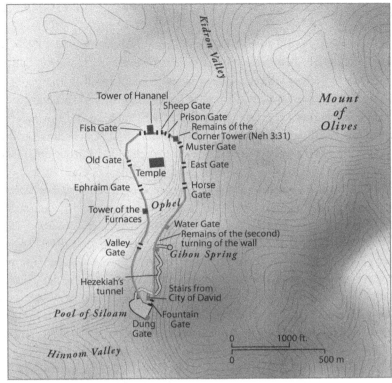

Theoretical reconstruction of the walls of Nehemiah's Jerusalem, based on archaeological excavations and biblical texts.

This coalition effectively surrounded Judah and must have proved intimidating for many of the province's inhabitants (cf. Neh 6:9). Rebuilding Jerusalem's walls would have bestowed some security, but because Jerusalem was now set in direct opposition to Mount Gerizim, it also fueled the rivalry. Some Judeans did not deem Nehemiah's goals worth the strife, especially as they apparently undermined pan-Israelite solidarity. Part of the opposition to Nehemiah on the home front came from a prophetess named Noadiah (Neh 6:14). Though ostensibly divisive and parochial, isolating Judah from Samaria was the only way Nehemiah could save Jerusalem and its temple for a future role at the center of Israelite identity. Theologically speaking, failure to preserve Jerusalem's primacy was to repudiate God's earlier prophetic revelations and to argue that he had repudiated his own promise to restore Israel under a Davidic king. This presented a fickle and unfaithful deity, and Nehemiah could brook neither. For if God had not repudiated his promises and Israel turned away from Jerusalem, as it had in the days of Jeroboam ben-Nebat (1 Kgs 12:26–33; 13:33–34), then the nation was doomed all over again.

The Davidic significance of the Jerusalem temple comes out subtly in the book of Nehemiah. Just before the city gates were finally installed, Sanballat sent a letter to Nehemiah stating that it was evident to all in the region that Nehemiah was planning to declare himself king in Judah (Neh 6:6–7). Sanballat threatened to inform Artaxerxes if Nehemiah did not meet with local leaders to discuss the political situation. Sanballat's threat would have carried no weight if there were no element of truth to his accusation. The connection between Jerusalem, its temple, and kingship was plain to see, even if Nehemiah did not personally wish to become king (Neh 6:8). Sanballat leveraged this connection to corner Nehemiah. Furthermore, the dedication of Jerusalem's wall was celebrated as a cultic event in which the temple musicians used "the musical instruments of David" and processed past the old Davidic palace (Neh 12:36–37). Thereafter, the temple operated "according to the commands of David and his son, Solomon" (Neh 12:45). These details are neither incidental nor nostalgic, but programmatic. Nehemiah depicts Jerusalem as a royal Davidic city and the temple as a Davidic institution. Though the book of Nehemiah never mentions it overtly, the appeal to David as cultic initiator implies that Nehemiah repaired the temple and reinstated the cult. The later tradition of Nehemiah as a temple builder and cultic restorer (2 Macc 1:18–36) is, therefore, not wholly without historical basis.[41]

Nehemiah had a hard-edged personality, and he is understandably characterized as a separatist who sought to draw Judah away from Samaria. However, this is sometimes mistakenly attributed to a notion of Judah's superiority over the Samarians or that one had to have some connection to the experience of exile in Babylon to be a proper member of the people of God. Three factors, however, suggest otherwise.

First, Nehemiah enforced Torah as law, and this is something Judah had in common with Samaria. It did not mark Judah out as different or superior in any way. On the contrary, the Torah was pan-Israelite in its scope and not exclusively Judean. Its central tenet, "Hear, O Israel, Yahweh our God is one Yahweh" (Deut 6:4), implied a singular deity over all the tribes of Israel.

Second, the key difference between Judah and Samaria was the Davidic significance of Jerusalem. This is what lay behind Judah's promulgation of

---

41. This solves the dilemma of Nehemiah's role raised in Diana Vikander Edelman, *The Origins of the 'Second' Temple: Persian Imperial Policy and the Rebuilding of Jerusalem* (London: Equinox, 2005), 350–51.

the prophetic tradition alongside Torah. But even the Davidic tradition was pan-Israelite in scope. Although the Davidic dynasty came to rule the kingdom of Judah, Davidic theology cast David's kingship over all Israel (2 Sam 5:1–5). The Davidic undercurrents in Nehemiah's programs suggest that his separatism was pragmatic, not absolute. He was dealing with a context in which Sanballat's temple on Mount Gerizim had effectively detached most of Israel from its Davidic center. Nehemiah tried to preserve that center. Since Jerusalem was a small, beleaguered town that could not rival a large city like Samaria, Nehemiah could not force Samaria to adopt the prophetic traditions and their Davidic ideologies. Instead, he could only protect Judah from Samarian influence. He thus felt that he was working in the best interests of all Israelites, not just Judah (Neh 2:10). With this understanding of his mission, we can see Nehemiah as a pan-Israelite who felt the political climate demanded the pragmatic pursuit of isolationist policies to protect the conditions necessary for union at a later stage. In that sense, he was a protectionist, not a separatist, with a long-term goal in mind.[42]

This helps explain the third factor, which is that Nehemiah was not opposed to Samarians per se but to Sanballat and the temple on Mount Gerizim. In Nehemiah 2:20, Nehemiah responds to the first sign of opposition from Sanballat by stating, "The God of heaven will give us success. We are his servants. We will arise and build. But as for you, you have no share or claim or commemoration in Jerusalem." His language is reminiscent of the northern tribes' declaration of independence from the Davidic dynasty in the days of Rehoboam: "What share do we have in David? We have no possession in the son of Jesse. To your tents, O Israel! Look after your own house now, O David!" (1 Kgs 12:16). Nehemiah borrows this historic sentiment from the northern tribes to fend them away from meddling in Jerusalem. However, he aims this specifically at Sanballat and his allies rather than all non-Judean Israelites. In Nehemiah's estimation, Sanballat was leading the north astray, as Jeroboam I had done centuries earlier. This did not mean the northern tribes were beyond redemption. Nehemiah's execratory utterances were reserved specifically for Sanballat, Tobiah, and the prophetess, Noadiah (Neh 6:14), whom he believed compromised the welfare of all "Israelites" (Neh 2:10). Until they were removed from the scene and the "Israelites" outside Judah recognized Jerusalem, they could have no part in Jerusalem. To say that only Judah was the faithful remnant of Israel, therefore, was more descriptive than prescriptive.

---

42. I use the term "protectionist" not in its economic sense of imposing tariffs on imports but in the sense of putting up barriers to protect a religious community until threats to it subside.

Nehemiah aimed to protect Judah, but with a view to providing for the welfare of all Israelites (Neh 2:10) and thereby keeping Davidic hope alive.

In 432 BC, after twelve years governing in Jerusalem, Nehemiah returned to Artaxerxes in Susa (Neh 13:6–7). It was not unusual for high officials to return to the king from time to time.[43] Nonetheless, Nehemiah's return to Susa goes unexplained. This forces us to ask whether those who remained in Judah and Samaria thought that Nehemiah had departed permanently. Interestingly, Nehemiah had to ask for royal permission to return to Jerusalem (Neh 13:6–7), which might suggest that he had indeed been recalled permanently. This might also explain the seeming undoing of Nehemiah's policies after his initial departure.

During his absence (432–c. 429 BC), his opponents succeeded in permeating the upper echelons of the Judean community. For example, a recently appointed priest named Eliashib furnished Tobiah with a large office within the temple precinct (Neh 13:4–7). This was a different Eliashib to the elderly high priest of the same name, who died at about this time and was succeeded by his son, Joiada.[44] By the time Nehemiah returned to Jerusalem, Joiada's son had married Sanballat's daughter (Neh 13:28). This marriage was not illegal by the standards of Torah, for it was still endogamous. The integration of northerners into Judean society was to be encouraged. In this regard, the Chronicler's portrait of Hezekiah inviting the northern tribes to celebrate the Passover in Jerusalem (2 Chr 30) is telling. The Chronicler saw Israel as consisting notionally of all Yahwists "from Beersheba to Dan" (2 Chr 30:5), and the decision of some northerners to humble themselves and come to Jerusalem in Hezekiah's day was lauded (2 Chr 30:11–12, 18–20). The marriage of Joiada's son to Sanballat's daughter was not, therefore, like the marriages of other Judean men to foreign women from Ashdod, Ammon, and Moab (Neh 13:23; cf. Deut 23:3). What mattered was its political significance, since it tied the family of the high priest in Jerusalem to the family of the apostate, Sanballat, who built the temple on Mount Gerizim. More crucially, it is likely that Joiada's son was the heir apparent to the high priesthood (see 1.5.2 below). This meant that a grandson of Sanballat stood to become high priest in Jerusalem, giving the Samarian governor and his family pivotal sway over its temple. For many Yahwists, this would have been welcomed as strengthening a pan-Israelite

---

43. The Elephantine Papyri, for example, show that the satrap of Egypt, Arsames (Persian: "Arshama"), left his satrapy to attend to royal matters in 410 BC (*TAD* A4.7).

44. Knoppers, *Jews and Samaritans*, 161; *pace* Lester L. Grabbe, *Yehud: A History of the Persian Province of Judah*, vol. 1 of *A History of the Jews and Judaism in the Second Temple Period*, Library of Second Temple Studies 47 (London: T&T Clark, 2004), 231, 312.

identity. Yet, it also stood to unravel the prophetic traditions and the Davidic ideologies they supported. Social cohesion would come at the price of theological compromise. That made this particular marriage of great consequence for the future direction of "Israelite" identity, and neither would it be the last occasion a marriage held such gravity (see 1.7.3 below). Within the space of a few short years, it seemed that all of Nehemiah's efforts to protect Judah, the primacy of Jerusalem, and the Davidic traditions were coming to naught.

The events that took place while Nehemiah was gone imply that he was absent for a few years. Artaxerxes granted him leave to return in ca. 429 BC, whereupon he immediately evicted Tobiah from the temple precinct (Neh 13:8–9). Since the marriage of Joiada's son to Sanballat's daughter was not illegal, Nehemiah could not insist on a divorce. Instead, he drove Joiada's son away from Jerusalem (Neh 13:28)—an action reminiscent of ostracism, which was being practiced contemporaneously in Athens. However, Athens was a democracy, so an ostracized person's property was never confiscated, allowing them to return to the city after ten years of exile. Jerusalem was not a democracy, so Nehemiah's expulsion of Tobiah and Joiada's son were likely to have been permanent.

Nehemiah also punished the Judean men who had married foreign women during his absence (Neh 13:23–27). It is notable that, in doing so, he appealed to the precedent of King Solomon, whose numerous foreign wives had led him into apostasy (Neh 13:26). This shows Nehemiah reaching for a prophetic tradition outside the Torah and viewing it as just as legally binding as Torah. Solomon was also a Davidide and temple builder who had ruled over a united Israel—a significant figure in the Israelite ethos Nehemiah was seeking to preserve. Solomon's precedent not only demonstrated that he had broken the law but that he had endangered the integrity of all Israel as a Davidic kingdom. Israel had been torn asunder as divine punishment for his apostasy. The marriage of Judean men to foreign women, therefore, was a similar compromise that threatened to provoke divine wrath and sabotage the restoration program centered on Jerusalem as a Davidic capital. In all of this, there is no indication that Nehemiah outlawed marriages between Judeans and Samarians. It was only the marriage of Joiada's son to Sanballat's daughter and marriages to Ashdodite, Ammonite, and Moabite women (Neh 13:23) that provoked his ire.

Nehemiah also took measures to ensure tithes came to the Levites so that they did not need to draw a living from farming (Neh 13:10–13). By thus keeping the priests and Levites at the temple, he reinforced the centrality of Jerusalem. He also enforced the observance of the Sabbath (Neh 13:15–22), which promoted regular opportunities for communal convocations, the dissemination of authoritative traditions, and the consolidation of an Israelite identity rooted in both Torah and the Prophets. Though his policies had derailed in his absence, Nehemiah rectified the situation by stymying the influence of Sanballat and Tobiah. He thus kept alive Jerusalem's claim to be the one true place of worship for Israel, along with the prophetic traditions that undergirded it.

The precise date of Nehemiah's death is unknown, as his memoir cuts out at an ambiguous point. He may have persisted as governor of Judah into the reign of Darius II (423–404 BC), but if so, he probably died soon after Darius took power. Extrabiblical sources mention the next governor of Judah, Bagohi, being in office by 410 BC. By the time of Nehemiah's death (probably in the 420s BC), the issues he faced and the forces he fended off had not completely subsided. Nehemiah had insulated Judah to an adequate degree for the survival of the prophetic traditions and notions of Jerusalem's primacy, but he had not hermetically sealed Judah off from all external influences. This was practically impossible, since Judah was part of the larger Persian Empire. Sanballat lived a long life in Samaria, and his efforts to overshadow Judah and undermine Jerusalem did not abate. With Nehemiah's death and the rise of his successor, Bagohi, they received new impetus. Tobiah and his family also continued to be involved in Jerusalem's affairs for centuries to come. The isolationist policies that Nehemiah had pursued threatened to unravel. Even so, Nehemiah had set a precedent, whereby an isolationist agenda could preserve prophetic tradition, the Davidic legacy, and the primacy of Jerusalem. But many Judeans felt this agenda was inconvenient. Even if certain quarters of the Judean community still held out Davidic aspirations, the *Realpolitik* of the day tended to crowd them out. Nehemiah was a hardline idealist who shielded the prophetic traditions and the Davidic aspirations they engendered, but they were still in delicate condition when he died.

1.5 THE LATE FIFTH CENTURY BC

1.5.1 FROM ARTAXERXES I TO DARIUS II (424–404 BC)

During his reign, Artaxerxes I made ostensible peace with the Greeks, kept Egypt within the Persian domain, and curbed the rebellion that Megabyzus staged in Trans-Euphrates. He improved imperial infrastructure within the Levant and, through Ezra's implementation of Torah amongst Yahwists in the southern Levant, became the cultural benefactor of "Israel." He further strengthened his position as the benefactor of "Israel" by sponsoring the construction of the temple on Mount Gerizim and at the same time enabled the survival of Jerusalem and its attendant prophetic traditions under the leadership of a trusted advisor, Nehemiah.

Artaxerxes died in December 424 BC, leaving the empire to his son, Xerxes II. But Artaxerxes's seventeen other sons began to squabble with Xerses for the right to the throne. He was assassinated just forty-five days into his reign by a brother, Sogdianus. But it was another brother, Ochus, who managed to secure power by February 423 BC, taking the throne name Darius II (Ctesias, *Persica* 46–50).[1]

Darius II had to fend off further challenges from other brothers and relatives, demonstrating just how unstable the throne became after Artaxerxes's death. He then faced conflict on multiple fronts in his empire. There was unrest in Asia Minor, which destroyed the Peace of Callias and prompted him to send his teenage son, Cyrus the Younger, to deal with the satraps in the region (Thucydides, *P.W.* 8.5.5, 28.2–4; Andocides, *On the Peace* 29). Darius was also drawn into the long-running Peloponnesian War between Sparta and Athens. He backed the Spartans, enabling them to defeat the Athenians in 404 BC. Nevertheless, this collusion did not mask the general antipathy most Greeks still felt towards the empire.

A rebellion against Persian rule also broke out in Egypt in 410 BC when the satrap, Arsames, was absent (*TAD* A6.7; A6.10). Unrest spilled over to Upper Egypt, where the Yahwistic enclave at Elephantine suffered setbacks (see 1.5.3 below). While the insurrection was eventually contained, it fired a

---

1. Briant, *From Cyrus to Alexander*, 588.

sense of Egyptian nationalism right throughout the Nile Valley. According to Diodorus, the Egyptians and Arabs had designs on Phoenicia (Diodorus Siculus, *Bib. hist.* 13.46.6), presumably meaning the coastal plain of Palestine. It is possible that Qainu, son of Geshem the Arab, was involved in hostile activity, perhaps in concert with Egyptian nationalists, since the artefact bearing his name was discovered in Egypt. Exactly how such agitation affected the people of Judah and Samaria cannot be ascertained.

In 409 BC the Medes also rebelled against Darius (Xenophon, *Hell.* 1.2.19). The Medes were viewed as a sister nation of the Persians, so their dissatisfaction was a significant political barometer. Although the revolt was suppressed, another erupted in 404 BC among the Kadousians, neighbors of the Medes. Along with events in the Aegean, Egypt, and the Levant, Darius was clearly scrambling to keep his empire together. Though he was probably successful in quelling Kadousian unrest, he soon became gravely ill (Xenophon, *Hell.* 2.13–14) and died in Babylon soon after (Ctesias, *Persica* 58). Over the nineteen years of his reign, he did well to keep his empire intact, but the threads of Persian sovereignty were fraying at the fringes.

The Persians thus had to work hard to ensure the integrity of their empire. Darius I's restructuring of the empire in the late sixth century BC had proved remarkably steady and functional, but the machinery had to be oiled by both force and persuasion. Military movements and garrisons were as critical as infrastructure, wealth, and cultural benefaction, especially on the empire's fringes, where the Greek and Egyptian cultures were so different to that of the Persians. The antiquity of Egyptian culture, with its panoply of gods, mystical religion, visible monuments, and inherent potential for wealth derived from the Nile, lent the Egyptians a sense of ancient nobility that they felt was superior to the novel Persians. The agitation of local dynasts stoked this sentiment. The Greeks viewed Persian culture with both curiosity and disdain. This was especially the case in Athens, which had developed democracy a century earlier and had formed the backbone of Greek resistance to Persia. Though other parts of Greece, like Sparta, had not adopted democracy, they still viewed the Persians as barbarians. This meant that the occasional truce or alliance with Persia was purely pragmatic and usually involved considerable sums of money and resources. It was not because of any fundamental cultural or political alignment.

A century of interactions with the Greeks had revealed weaknesses in the Persian Empire. Although Persia was still a juggernaut, it could be resisted, and even attacked. This sparked a Panhellenic movement, which argued that Greeks should put aside their mutual differences and forge a more cohesive, singular Greek identity in the face of Persian opposition. The concept was, however, aspirational rather than politically plausible. Ethnic consolidation of this kind had occurred earlier in the Levant, as Ezra's implementation of Torah among all Yahwists in the region and the divorcing of foreign women had forged a specific "Israelite" identity. But, as in Greece, where the city-states still jostled with each other over fraternal differences, the divisions between Judah and Samaria continued. For Judeans who still clung to classic prophetic traditions, Greek and Egyptian resistance may have helped to keep alive their own hopes for an independent Davidic kingdom. Though it was still politically unrealistic in the final years of Darius II, it was not categorically impossible either, for the Persians were by no means invincible. As was soon to occur, the secession of Egypt from the empire added fuel to the flames of such aspirations.

1.5.2 JUDAH AFTER NEHEMIAH

The governor of Judah after Nehemiah was Bagohi (or Bigvai, Bagoas). We do not know the date of his appointment, but he was certainly governing by 410 BC, as a letter addressed to him by the leaders of the enclave at Elephantine indicates (*TAD* A4.7, line 18). In discussing his governorship, we must deal with the fact that Josephus conflates Bagohi, a contemporary of Artaxerxes II, with a Persian high official of the same name who was active during the reigns of Artaxerxes III and Artaxerxes IV (see 1.7.5 below).[2] The reason for Josephus's confusion is that he merges the reigns of Artaxerxes II (404–358 BC), Artaxerxes III (358–338 BC), and Artaxerxes IV (338–336 BC), who all ruled in succession.[3] Being aware of this helps us unravel most of the details related to this period.

Bagohi's name is the Aramaic form of the Persian name Bagavahya,[4] but this does not necessarily mean he was Persian. Adoption of names from a regnant culture is a well-documented phenomenon, and Judeans bearing this name appear in biblical texts (cf. "Bigvai" in Ezra 2:2, 14; Neh 7:7, 19; 10:16[10:17 MT]). In fact, it is tempting to identify Bagohi with the Bigvai of Nehemiah 10:16[10:17 MT], who was a civic leader and signatory to the accord that Nehemiah initiated in 444 BC (Neh 9:38[10:1 MT]). If this

---

2. To make the distinction clearer, I will refer to the Persian high official by the Hellenized name, "Bagoas."

3. Josephus's wording in *Ant.* 11.297 reveals this mistake. He associated the Persian general, "Bagoses," with "the other Artaxerxes," demonstrating that he knew of only one other Artaxerxes, namely Artaxerxes I, whom he discusses elsewhere.

4. Bob Becking, "Do the Earliest Samaritan Inscriptions Already Indicate a Parting of the Ways?," in Lipschits, Knoppers, and Albertz, *Judah and the Judeans in the Fourth Century B.C.E.*, 218.

identification works, we must reach two conclusions. First, he was quite young when he affixed his seal to Nehemiah's accord; and second, he would eventually stray from this accord as the known actions of Governor Bagohi went against Nehemiah's policies (see this section below). While both conclusions are plausible, we simply cannot be sure that they are probable. In all likelihood, Bagohi was a native Judean, as all other governors of Judah appear to have been.

Bagohi played a significant role in a controversy regarding the high priesthood in Jerusalem. Joiada had been high priest during Nehemiah's second term as governor and notched up approximately two decades in the sacerdotal office (ca. 432–412 BC). Nehemiah had expelled one of Joiada's sons from Jerusalem in ca. 429 for marrying Sanballat I's daughter (Neh 13:28; see 1.4.7 above). This was probably Joiada's eldest son, Jeshua, so that when Joiada died, it was a younger son, Johanan, who succeeded him as high priest.[5] As the Elephantine Papyri confirm, Bagohi was governor of Judah and Johanan was high priest in Jerusalem by 410 BC (*TAD* A4.7; cf. *Ant.* 11.297).

This helps to make sense of an incident related by Josephus (*Ant.* 11.298–299). He states that Bagohi was a personal friend of Johanan's brother, Jeshua (Gk. *Iēsous*), and worked to procure the high priesthood for him. If, as is likely, Jeshua was the eldest son of Joiada, whom Nehemiah had expelled from Jerusalem (Neh 13:28),[6] his attempt to wrest the high priesthood from his brother was motivated by the compelling conviction that he was the rightful heir to the high priesthood but he had been done out of his patrimony by the previous governor. Having the support of the new governor, Bagohi, added political clout to Jeshua's claim. This presented a significant challenge to Johanan, whose incumbency depended entirely on Nehemiah's policies and actions decades earlier. Questions over Johanan's legitimacy potentially threatened a major cultic crisis.

Bagohi's support for Jeshua indicates that, unlike Nehemiah before him, he was on good terms with the family of Sanballat I, governor of Samaria. This is supported by a memorandum sent to the Yahwistic enclave at Elephantine,

---

5. Frank Moore Cross (*From Epic to Canon: History and Literature in Ancient Israel* [Baltimore: Johns Hopkins University Press, 1998], 151–72, esp. 156) argues that the succession of high priests in Jerusalem during the Persian era involved considerable papponymy (naming a grandson after his grandfather), such that we need to differentiate two Eliashibs, three Jadduas, and four Johanans. Building on previous critiques, VanderKam (*From Joshua to Caiaphas*, 85–99) demonstrates convincingly that Cross's thesis is incorrect and that only six men held the high priesthood between Joshua in 522 BC and Jaddua in the time of Alexander (332 BC).

6. Josephus relates a similar incident just after the events of Bagohi, Johanan, and Jeshua that is sometimes seen as a different version of the same events because the governor of Samaria in both accounts is named "Sanballat." However, the later incident relates to Sanballat II and the brother of the high priest Jaddua, not the brother of Johanan. See 1.7 below.

composed jointly by Bagohi and Sanballat's son, Delaiah, in 407 BC (*TAD* A4.9).[7] Sanballat was still alive at that time but had delegated his duties to his two sons, Delaiah and Shelemiah (*TAD* A4.7.29). By resuming diplomatic relations with Sanballat's family, Bagohi undid some of Nehemiah's earlier actions and supported measures to bring the two provinces closer together.[8] This does not mean Bagohi was opposed to all of Nehemiah's policies. He was, after all, governor of Judah and not about to surrender Jerusalem's status altogether. The fact that he wanted Jeshua, whom he obviously felt was the legitimate high priest of Jerusalem, presiding at the altar also shows his regard for the temple in Jerusalem. He had a pro-Israelite posture, but he did not necessarily place the prophetic traditions on quite the same level. Unlike Nehemiah, he did not see the need to insulate Judah from Sanballat in Samaria or presumably from the Tobiads in Transjordan either. He felt that good relations were a higher priority. In other words, for Bagohi, the Jerusalem temple was an important cultic installation that needed the right priest presiding over it, but it did not need to be guarded as a Davidic monument.

Bagohi's support for Jeshua's claim to the high priesthood came to a head when Jeshua appeared in the temple precinct at Jerusalem. This had probably been engineered by Bagohi. We do not know whether Jeshua came merely as a supplicant in the hope of winning some support or to confront his brother. What is known for certain is that a row erupted between the brothers, and Johanan killed Jeshua in the temple precinct. Josephus vehemently condemns this violent act as "cruel and impious" (*Ant.* 11.299), but it was not the last time a high priest would act with such violence. The biblical character of Phinehas, who violently killed two people in the act of apostasy (Num 25:6–13), provided something of a precedent (cf. 3.4.1; 3.7.6). From Johanan's perspective, although he was the younger brother, historical circumstances had seen him anointed to what was a lifelong office. A high priest could not resign or be removed in favor of another candidate without committing sacrilege and damaging the cult. The only way, therefore, Johanan could be removed was to be killed. Knowing this threat, Johanan killed Jeshua instead. As extreme as this action was, it ensured that Johanan retained the high priesthood without any competing claim. Even if Jeshua had by this time fathered a son by Sanballat's daughter, that son was not in Jerusalem and would have been a teenager at best—well below the requisite thirty years of age for priestly service. Jeshua's death also deflected Sanballat's influence away from Jerusalem and limited

---

7. Fried, *The Priest and the Great King*, 228–29.
8. Knoppers, *Jews and Samaritans*, 167.

the ways Bagohi could interfere in temple affairs. As controversial as Johanan's actions were, they upheld Nehemiah's strategy of limiting Samarian influence in Jerusalem.

This was a critical result, for it gave those in Jerusalem who still clung to the prophetic and Davidic traditions some breathing space. Some generations later, the Chronicler's meticulous catalog of the Levitical and priestly castes connected the institutions of temple leadership to David and Solomon. In this way, he grounded the Levites and priests in an institution that was both cultic and Davidic. It was a combination of both Torah and prophetic tradition, which ideologically disqualified any attempts to weaken the links between the temple's leadership and its roots in Davidic monarchy. Thus, while the Chronicler reserved space for Samarians within Israel, he did so only under the aegis of Davidic monarchy, Davidic-sanctioned priestly leadership, and a single place of worship in Jerusalem (see 1.8).

1.5.3 THE YAHWISTS AT ELEPHANTINE

The Aramaic documents of the diaspora enclave at Elephantine reveal just how variegated Yahwism was at the end of the fifth century BC. Papyrus Amherst 63 (17.1–6) demonstrates that most of the Yahwists at Elephantine traced their origins back to the kingdom of Israel over three centuries earlier.[9] Their ancestors had been refugees from Samaria after the Assyrians captured the city in 723 BC. They initially headed south, where they became mercenaries for the Judean king. However, when Sennacherib decimated Judah in 701 BC they were on the move again and eventually found themselves in a "fortress of palms"—probably an allusion to the Syrian oasis of Palmyra—along with refugees from Babylon and Arameans from Hamath. Here they remained for several generations, adopting the local Aramaic dialect and forging a symbiotic relationship with their Babylonian and Aramean counterparts. Yet they still retained their distinctive Samarian heritage, which included the worship of Yahweh. They thus developed "a hyphenated identity" as Samarian Arameans.[10] At some point during the sixth century BC, this mercenary community of diaspora Samarians, Babylonians, and Arameans all migrated to Egypt, where they were known collectively as "Arameans."[11] The Samarians

---

9. This account of the enclave's origins follows the reconstruction offered by van der Toorn in his important study, *Becoming Diaspora Jews*.

10. van der Toorn, *Becoming Diaspora Jews*, 88.

11. The Elephantine Papyri frequently refer even to the Samarians with Yahwistic names as "Arameans," reflecting that period in their history spent in an Aramean context.

settled on the river island of Elephantine at Egypt's southern periphery, while their Babylonian and Aramean counterparts settled in Syene on the adjacent bank of the Nile. Here they worked as garrison soldiers and raised their families in their respective ethnic enclaves for the next two centuries.

Sometime before Cambyses's conquest of Egypt in 525 BC this enclave of Yahwists built a temple to Yahweh at Elephantine to facilitate their worship and express their cultural origins (*TAD* A4.7.13–15). The temple was, therefore, older than both the temples of Jerusalem and Mount Gerizim. Its campus measured approximately 27 × 9 meters and was enclosed by a wall punctuated by five stone gateways with bronze-hinged doors (*TAD* 4.7.9–10). The sanctuary was decked with lavish fittings and its roof was made of costly cedar (*TAD* A4.7.11). It was located among the houses of the community and was literally across the street (the "Royal Road") from a precinct devoted to the Egyptian god, Khnum. Some of the Elephantine documents refer to the temple as a *masged* (e.g., *TAD* B7.3.3), an Aramaic term for a place of prostration (cf. Arab. *masjid*, "mosque"). It appears to have been oriented towards the land of Israel, which, if deliberate, indicated a link to the enclave's ancestral origins.[12] Yet the Yahwists of Elephantine believed that Yahweh actually dwelt in the temple they had built for him (*TAD* B3.12.2). It is unclear whether this indicates that the temple housed a statue or a standing stone representing Yahweh, but the possibility cannot be discounted. In any case, they made animal, cereal, and incense offerings to Yahweh on the altar (*TAD* A4.7.22, 25–26).

After the classic Persian manner, they styled Yahweh as "the God of Heaven" (e.g., *TAD* A4.7.2). However, in addition to Yahweh, they recognized other deities. In some of their letters, they had no reservation in blessing people by "all the gods" (e.g., *TAD* A3.9.1)—a vestige of the enclave's henotheistic origins in syncretistic Samaria, as well as the century spent in an Aramean context. In fact, the community's syncretism shows clear lines of Aramean influences. A document dated to 419 BC (*TAD* C3.15) lists the names of all the Samarian Arameans in Elephantine who donated two silver shekels "to Yahweh the God" (line 1). When all the contributions were tallied, the money was split between Yahweh and two other deities, Ishum-Bethel and Anat-Bethel (lines 123–125). "Bethel" was either an Aramean deity worshipped throughout Syria or, more likely, a standard Aramean way of referring to any deity worshipped in the form of a sacred Bethel-stone (i.e., a standing stone [*matsebah*]).[13]

---

12. Porten, *Archives from Elephantine*, 112, 121. The orientation might have been purely pragmatic, dictated by the confines of the neighboring temple to Khnum and surrounding houses.

13. George Athas, *The Tel Dan Inscription: A Reappraisal and a New Interpretation*, JSOTSup 360 (Sheffield: Sheffield Academic Press, 2003), 310–11.

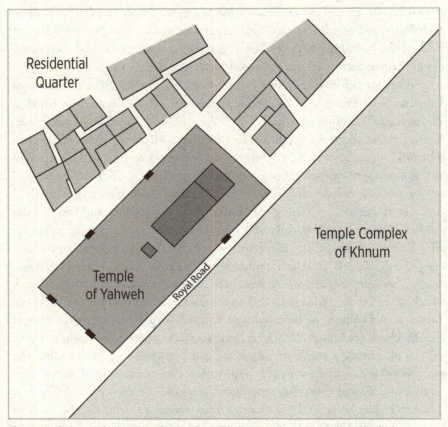

Theoretical plan of the temple of Yahweh at Elephantine, based on archaeological excavations and textual evidence from the Elephantine Papyri.

Ishum-Bethel (also known as Ashima) was a deity of Hamath (cf. 2 Kgs 17:30), whom the Samarian Arameans evidently came to revere during their sojourn in Syria. In all likelihood, Anat-Bethel, who received almost as many shekels in the distribution of funds as Yahweh, was worshipped as Yahweh's consort.[14] This compares with the Judean veneration of the "Queen of Heaven," which Jeremiah had tried to halt among the Judeans who migrated to Egypt after the fall of Jerusalem (Jer 44:1–30). In one affidavit, a member of the Elephantine enclave named Menahem swears his statement by "Anat of Yahweh" in addition to the *masged* (i.e., the temple) and what seems to be a deity named Herem (*TAD* B7.3.3; cf. B7.2.7–8). The close association between these deities and

---

14. Porten (*Archives from Elephantine*, 173–79) reserves judgment on possible religious syncretism within the enclave. However, such reservation rests on seeing a plethora of exceptions within the cache of documents. The evidence that Samarian Arameans were syncretistic is compelling.

Yahweh probably indicates that their shrines were part of Yahweh's temple precinct, perhaps as chapels in which sacred stones were placed. Moreover, the papyri show that intermarriage between the members of the enclave and their Egyptian and Aramean neighbors was unexceptional. Some even swore oaths by the Egyptians gods (e.g., *TAD* B2.8).

Evidence from the papyri is inconclusive as to whether the Yahwists of Elephantine observed the Sabbath. They did, however, observe Passover. One missive from 419 BC (*TAD* A4.1) was sent by a certain Hananiah to Jedaniah, the leader of the Yahwists at Elephantine, with instructions for observing Passover and the associated Festival of Unleavened Bread. Another letter refers to Hananiah's visit to Egypt (*TAD* A4.3.7), which demonstrates that he came from Judah or Samaria. It is tempting to identify this Hananiah with Nehemiah's brother, who brought him the news of Jerusalem's plight and who was later appointed mayor of Jerusalem (Neh 1:2–3; 7:2).[15] However, that was some twenty-five years earlier, and the name was one of the most common amongst Yahwists. Nonetheless, with his knowledge of Passover protocols, the Hananiah of the Elephantine Papyri must have been associated with the priesthood at either Jerusalem or Mount Gerizim. Even if the Passover had been celebrated at Elephantine prior to Hananiah's directions, his letter exemplifies the kind of work that Ezra had undertaken to disseminate and regulate Yahwistic religion in accordance with Torah, in this case across satrapal borders.

Interestingly, however, Hananiah blesses his "brothers" in Elephantine by "the gods" (*TAD* A4.1.1). This salutation is comparable to expressions that the Yahwists at Elephantine used themselves (e.g., *TAD* A3.7).[16] It shows that the kind of syncretism that prevailed at Elephantine had not yet been completely extinguished in Judah and Samaria either. Ezra's reforms and Nehemiah's governorship had given exclusive monotheism a fillip, but in an empire in which Yahwists rubbed shoulders with other cultures that entertained multiple gods, the embers of syncretistic Yahwism continued to glow. Furthermore, the high priest Joiada, who had crossed Nehemiah, survived him and was the incumbent high priest when Hananiah visited Egypt (419 BC). Joiada opposed Nehemiah's legacy by fraternizing with Samarians, as did Bagohi, governor of

---

15. Cf. Porten, *Archives from Elephantine*, 130.

16. Porten (*Archives from Elephantine*, 160) suggests that the use of the Aramaic plural "gods" (*'lhy'*) is congruent with the standard Hebrew practice of using the noun *'elohim*, which is plural in form but singular in usage. However, in such cases Hebrew uses singular verbs with the noun. The difficulty with Hananiah's Passover letter is that the text is fragmentary, so we cannot tell whether the verb associated with the plural noun *'lhy'* is plural or singular. In other letters from Elephantine, the associated verb is clearly plural (e.g., *TAD* A3.7). Porten suggests that this expression was a standardized greeting, which indicates that the documents were written by Aramean scribes. However, the argument rests on silence.

Judah. There was, therefore, a reflex against Nehemiah among those who survived him. It shows that key figures in Jerusalem were no longer as committed to Judah's isolation as he had been.

Hananiah directs his letter to Jedaniah and his colleagues as soldiers without mentioning the temple to Yahweh at Elephantine or any priests (*TAD* 4.1.1). This is significant, considering he discusses Passover protocols as a community endeavor affecting people's homes. He never suggests that the Passover lambs be sacrificed on the altar at Elephantine. Yet this does not mean that the Yahwists at Elephantine did not do so. The later friction between them and the priests of the Egyptian god, Khnum, may have been the result of this very practice (see this section below). Yet Hananiah's silence on any cultic dimension means we cannot determine whether he approved or disapproved of the temple at Elephantine.

By 410 BC, however, the relationship with Jerusalem changed. Joiada had died, and his son, Johanan, succeeded him as high priest. Johanan owed his position to the earlier policies of Nehemiah (see 1.5.2 above). To maintain his position, he would also have needed to keep any son of his brother, Jeshua, away from Jerusalem. Undoubtedly, therefore, he advocated Nehemiah's isolationist policies in opposition to Governor Bagohi, who maintained close relations with Samaria. This impacted the Yahwists at Elephantine when disaster struck them in 410 BC. The satrap of Egypt, Arsames, had left Egypt to attend to royal matters,[17] and unrest erupted throughout Egypt during his absence (*TAD* A6.7; A6.10). Exactly how it was quelled is unknown, but the Elephantine documents demonstrate that Persian rule in Egypt persisted for approximately another decade. Nonetheless, according to letters drafted by Jedaniah, the leader of the Yahwists at Elephantine, in 410 BC the priests of Khnum bribed the local Persian commander, Vidranga, into vandalizing the temple of Yahweh at Elephantine. The damage inflicted was so extensive that cultic functions could no longer be performed, sending the Yahwists into mourning. The incident was evocative of the damage inflicted on Jerusalem just before Nehemiah's appointment as governor (Ezra 4:21–23; Neh 1:3–4). Since Arsames was out of Egypt, Jedaniah asserts that the satrap could not have been complicit in the plot. Soon after the incident, Vidranga evidently met a grisly end, though whether this was by official punishment or mob justice cannot be determined. Either way, the Yahwists at Elephantine viewed his quick demise as divine retribution (*TAD* A4.8.14–16).

---

17. Whether Arsames attended the king personally or was called to help deal with Arabian incursions in the southern Levant (cf. Diodorus Siculus, *Bib. hist.* 13.46.6) cannot be confirmed.

The Egyptian priests were motivated by both religious friction and a resurgence of Egyptian nationalism. The daily slaughter of lambs in Yahweh's temple (cf. P. Amherst 63, 12.1–4)[18] would have been supremely offensive to the priests of Khnum, the ram-headed god of Elephantine. The annual celebration of Passover would have exacerbated this. Even if the Yahwists attempted to soften this by using goats rather than lambs (cf. Exod 12:5)[19] or butchering the animals in their homes, the festival itself would still have riled Khnum's priests as it celebrated Yahweh's triumph over Egypt, its pharaoh, and its gods. Hananiah's visit in 419 BC, which fostered an even livelier devotion to Passover, also stirred up trouble with the priests of Khnum, as another letter details (*TAD* A4.3.7). Most Egyptians could overlook this since they were not regularly confronted by it, but the priests of Khnum could not, for it was taking place across the street on a daily basis. Since the Yahwists were the garrison troops of the Persian authorities, there was little the priests could do to halt this. But by 410 BC the priests of Khnum were gripped with the rising fever of Egyptian nationalism. When the satrap, Arsames, left Egypt on official business in 410 BC, the priests were emboldened to strike, lighting the spark in what was already a potent mix of religious fervor, provocative symbolism, and ethnic pride. The damage inflicted on the Yahwistic temple was an act against the perceived offensive practices of the Yahwists and a stab at the imperial power that employed them.

Immediately after the incident, Jedaniah sent a letter to the high priest Johanan in Jerusalem and other leading Judeans, petitioning them for help to have the temple rebuilt (*TAD* A4 7.1.18–19). Even though the temple in Elephantine was older than the one standing in Jerusalem, Jedaniah's petition demonstrated the connection that Elephantine's enclave felt towards their cultural homeland and even the honor they accorded Jerusalem as a place of Yahwistic worship, perhaps as a result of Hananiah's visit a decade earlier. Nonetheless, Jedaniah received no reply from Johanan. This silence almost certainly stems from Johanan's pursuit of Nehemiah's isolationist policies, which sought to break Jerusalem off from external influence to preserve Jerusalem's exclusive eminence. Even if Jedaniah's petition was a diplomatic appeal to the primacy of Jerusalem, he was still asking for the restoration of a rival Yahwistic temple—something Johanan would never countenance.

Accordingly, three years later (407 BC) Jedaniah went over Johanan's head and petitioned Bagohi, the governor of Judah, along with the two

---

18. van der Toorn, *Becoming Diaspora Jews*, 168.
19. Porten, *Archives from Elephantine*, 280–81.

sons of Sanballat, Delaiah and Shelemiah, who were governing Samaria on behalf of their aged father. This shrewd move appealed to the dominant politics of the day, whereby most Yahwists could tolerate multiple Yahwistic shrines in a broad cultural solidarity, even as they accorded primary honor to Mount Gerizim. It also demonstrates how politically isolated Johanan was in Jerusalem, for Bagohi responded in concert with Delaiah, approving the essence of Jedaniah's request. The two officials sent a memorandum to solicit the permission of Arsames, satrap of Egypt, for the rebuilding of Yahweh's temple at Elephantine (*TAD* A4.9). Crucially, however, Bagohi and Delaiah did not approve the endeavor unconditionally. Their memorandum stated their support for the reinstitution of cereal and incense offerings at Elephantine, but they were conspicuously silent on the matter of animal sacrifice. Both officials could evidently tolerate a Yahwistic shrine in Egypt, but they either wished to preserve the distinction of their own cultic centers or else to promote the primacy of Mount Gerizim as the one place of animal sacrifice (cf. Deut 12). Their joint but qualified support, therefore, showed a pan-Israelite solidarity that stemmed back to their shared heritage but also a reinvigorated sense of the importance of Yahwism's homeland in the Levant. The land of Israel continued to be the only fully legitimate arena in which all aspects of covenant life could be conducted. People were thus encouraged to pursue covenant life in the diaspora, but they needed to demonstrate a conscious orientation towards the land of Israel.

Since Bagohi and Delaiah both replied to Jedaniah, the Yahwists at Elephantine had no recourse to further appeal. The highest "Israelite" authorities had exhibited a united front. Thus, if the temple to Yahweh at Elephantine was to be rebuilt, it would only be as an "altar house" (*TAD* A4.9.3) for cereal and incense offerings. Jedaniah and his colleagues had little choice but to acquiesce, which they did in a subsequent letter (*TAD* A4.10). The specific addressee of this letter has not been preserved, but it acknowledged that animal sacrifice had to cease and promised a considerable personal gratuity upon the recommencement of the now curbed cultic functions.

The Yahwists at Elephantine probably did rebuild their temple. A contract drawn up in December 402 BC for the sale of a house west of the temple (*TAD* B3.12) refers to Yahweh as "the God who dwells in Elephantine," suggesting the site was functional once again. Though the cessation of animal sacrifice was no doubt welcomed by the priests of Khnum, tension arising from the memory of the temple's destruction in 410 BC must have lingered, especially with the resurgence of Egyptian nationalism and the eventual overthrow of Persian power in Egypt by 400 BC. Soon after, the temple of Yahweh was destroyed again, though exactly when is a matter of speculation. A document dated to 400 BC (*TAD* B4.6) recognizes Egyptian rule at Elephantine by that time, which suggests that the garrison's employment had transferred from the Persians to the Egyptians. The latest document among the Elephantine Papyri dates to 399 BC and refers to the power struggles within Egypt at the time (*TAD* A3.9). The fate of the Yahwists is ultimately unknown. Their temple had certainly been demolished by the mid-fourth century BC when Nectanebo II expanded the temple of Khnum over its campus. This left Jerusalem and Mount Gerizim as the only Yahwistic temples still standing with authorized animal sacrifice.[20]

1.5.4 THE JUDEAN DIASPORA

The Elephantine Papyri attest to a thriving diaspora community of Yahwists in Egypt. They also give us insight into the fraternal dynamics between Judeans and Samarians in the Levant, demonstrating that Nehemiah's isolationist policy was atypical even as it was necessary for preserving the primacy of Jerusalem. The Elephantine enclave's cohesion came partially from their employment as garrison soldiers for the Persians, but their temple also gave them a focal point for expressing their culture and acknowledging their heritage. It is telling that they maintained their cultural distinction for over three centuries. However, unlike Judah and Samaria, where Yahwists formed the majority of the population, the Samarian Arameans of Elephantine were a tiny minority who did not receive the same level of cultural benefaction as their compatriots in the Levant. On the contrary, in Egypt it was the Egyptians whom the Persians needed to placate. This would, however, not be enough for the Egyptians, as they would break free of Persia's imperial control before the end of the fifth century BC.

The Judeans living in Mesopotamia were very well integrated into the society around them. As cuneiform documents from the sixth century BC indicate, this had begun with the Judeans whom the Babylonians had forcibly resettled, including in one town called Al Yahudu ("Judah Town").[21] This continued

---

20. The "house of Yahu" at Makkedah in Idumea, mentioned on an Aramaic ostracon (AL 283), might still have functioned while the Elephantine temple operated. Even so, it would have operated as an Idumean shrine to Qos, the Idumean guise of Yahweh, or even perhaps as a shrine where animal sacrifice was similarly not permitted. It was almost certainly no longer functional by the mid-fourth century BC. See Lemaire, "New Aramaic Ostraca from Idumea," 416–17.

21. Laurie E. Pearce and Cornelia Wunsch, *Documents of Judean Exiles and West Semites in Babylonia in the Collection of David Sofer*, Cornell University Studies in Assyriology and Sumerology 28 (Bethesda, MD: CDL Press, 2014).

well past the return of Zerubbabel to Jerusalem. Also instructive in this regard are the archives of the Murashu family from the fifth century BC. This was a Babylonian family based in Nippur (90 kilometers southeast of Babylon), whose members were involved in real estate management across Babylonia for several generations. Among their clients were numerous Judeans, identifiable by their Yahwistic names. These Judeans owned land and animals, worked the land as tenant farmers, were employed by Babylonians and Persians, and even worked on royal estates. For example, one Judean named Hanani ben-Menahem managed birds that supplied the kitchens of Darius II.[22]

The names of Judeans are a pertinent source of information for diaspora life in Mesopotamia during the fifth century BC. Like the names of Samarian Arameans at Elephantine, the use of Yahwistic theophoric elements shows continued adherence to Yahwism. However, some Judeans mentioned in the Murashu archives bear Babylonian or Persian names, many of which sported the names of foreign deities. Were it not for the Yahwistic names of their relatives, they could not have been readily identified as Judeans. These names do not necessarily imply that these Judeans were syncretists, though that is a possibility. As mentioned previously, the adoption of names across cultures was a common phenomenon, as even the book of Esther exemplifies. Mordechai's name is a Hebraicized version of Marduk, Babylon's patron deity. Esther exhibits two names, the first a Hebrew name, Hadassah ("myrtle"), and the second, Esther, a foreign name that has been variously derived from an Old Indian word for "young woman," the name of the goddess "Ishtar," or the Greek word "star" (*astēr*).[23] At the very least, it evinces a high level of cultural assimilation. But on analogy with the syncretism evident at Elephantine and that which persisted in Judah and Samaria, it is reasonable to assume that syncretism also continued to some extent amongst Judeans in Mesopotamia. Also parallel to the Samarian Arameans at Elephantine are names such as Haggai and Shabbetai, derived from the nouns for "festival" (Heb. *hag*) and "Sabbath" (Heb. *shabbat*) respectively. This suggests circumstantially that Judeans in Mesopotamia were observing religious festivals and keeping the Sabbath to some degree.

The question of whether the Judeans developed a cultic site in Mesopotamia is difficult to answer. An intriguing possibility comes from Ezra 8:15–20, where we are told that Ezra recruited personnel for the temple in Jerusalem from among the Levites and devotees at Casiphia. No consensus

---

22. Samuel Daiches, *Jews in Babylonia in the Time of Ezra and Nehemiah According to Babylonian Inscriptions*, Historical Monographs Collection 2 (London: Jews' College, 1910), 29.

23. Cf. *HALOT*. This is merely to draw attention to the adoption of names across cultures in the fifth century BC. The dating of the book of Esther and the time in which it is set are matters of dispute.

on the location of Casiphia has arisen,[24] but wherever it was, it hosted several people qualified for priestly work in Jerusalem. Of particular interest is the designation of Casiphia as the "place" (Heb. *maqom* [Ezra 8:17]), a term that often indicates a cultic site (cf. Deut 12:5; 1 Kgs 8:30; Jer 7:12), though not exclusively so. A certain Iddo is named "chief in Casiphia the place" (Ezra 8:17), which suggests some kind of guild or organized operation. It is not inconceivable, therefore, that a Judean cultic installation had been built in the early sixth century BC at Casiphia, perhaps even a fully-fledged temple like the one at Elephantine.[25] It has been suggested that Casiphia was not a cultic site but a Levitical school and that Ezra's recruitment of personnel from there was for both cultic functionaries and trained scribes.[26] The evidence is ultimately ambiguous and does not allow us to conclude definitively on the exact significance of Casiphia, but it was certainly home to a literate caste of Levites whose skills were transferrable to the temple in Jerusalem. Nothing further is known about any other possible Judean cultic site in Mesopotamia.

---

24. Leuchter suggests Casiphia was in northern Mesopotamia within old Assyrian territory, with its connection to Israelites going back to the deportations by the Assyrians in the eighth century BC. See Mark Leuchter, "Ezra's Mission and the Levites of Casiphia," in *Community Identity in Judean Historiography: Biblical and Comparative Perspectives*, ed. Gary N. Knoppers and Kenneth A. Ristau (Winona Lake, IN: Eisenbrauns, 2009), 179. While possible, there is no way to confirm this northern location. There is just as much, if not greater likelihood, that Casiphia was located within Babylonia.

25. H. G. M. Williamson, *Ezra, Nehemiah*, WBC 16 (Waco, TX: Thomas Nelson, 1985), 117; Joseph Blenkinsopp, *Ezra-Nehemiah: A Commentary*, Old Testament Library (London: SCM Press, 1989), 165–66.

26. Leuchter, "Ezra's Mission and the Levites of Casiphia," 182–83.

1.6 THE SHIFTING "COMPASS" OF THE FOURTH CENTURY BC

The rise of Alexander the Great was a momentous political, cultural, religious, and economic shift. However, Alexander did not initiate it. It had started long before him, when Darius I crossed the Hellespont into Thrace in 512 BC. This brought the Persians into the Aegean theater and put them at loggerheads with the Greek states, helping to create a new center of gravity. The Greco-Persian wars of the fifth century BC and the rise of the Greek states to international prominence were the first fluttering signs that the "compass" of the ancient world was shifting away from Mesopotamia towards a new magnetic center in the west. The entire fourth century BC was a pivotal transitional period that definitively reoriented the ancient Near East towards the west. Alexander was able to cap off the process with his astounding conquests. The people of Judah and Samaria were among those most affected by this transition. The fourth century BC was a period of great volatility for them, with enormous theological repercussions. Some of the critical events even occurred on their doorstep, beginning with the secession of Egypt from the Persian Empire.

1.6.1 ARTAXERXES II AND THE LOSS OF EGYPT

Before Darius II died in 404 BC, he appointed his eldest son, Arsaces, as his heir (Xenophon, *Anab.* 1.1.1). Arsaces was subsequently crowned as Artaxerxes II, but one of his brothers, known as Cyrus the Younger, challenged his rule. Cyrus, who was governing Lydia at the time, gathered an army of Greek mercenaries and in 401 BC marched them into Mesopotamia. He confronted his brother in battle at Cunaxa, but it was Artaxerxes who won the day, leaving Cyrus dead on the field of battle (Xenophon, *Anab.* 1.1.3–1.2.5; 1.4.11; 1.8.27). Cyrus's surviving mercenaries beat a long retreat back to Greece—an expedition recorded by their leader, Xenophon, in his famed account, the *Anabasis* ("Expedition"). Despite their defeat, the Greek mercenaries had demonstrated that they could penetrate the Persian Empire all the way to its heartland (cf. Xenophon, *Hell.* 3.4.2). It was a vulnerability that would percolate in the minds of Greek for decades to come. For now, though, they continued as a set of disunited city-states, with Athens reeling from its defeat to Sparta in the Peloponnesian War.

The Egyptian nationalism that had caused unrest in 410 BC surged again in 404 BC when Darius II died. The Egyptian cause was initially taken up by Amyrtaeus, possibly the grandson of the Amyrtaeus who had opposed the Persians after the defeat of Inarus in 454 BC. He declared himself pharaoh of Egypt, and by 400 BC his rule was recognized throughout Egypt, including at Elephantine, where the enclave of Yahwists switched their allegiance to him. Artaxerxes II thus lost the satrapy of Egypt—a massive territorial, military, and fiscal blow that once again put Judah on the Persian Empire's frontier.

1.6.2 A NEW MEDITERRANEAN "POLE" AND REORIENTATION IN THE LEVANT

In 398 BC Amyrtaeus was successfully challenged by Nepherites (398–393 BC). Though he is credited with founding the Twenty-Ninth Dynasty, Nepherites may have been a descendant of Inarus and the pharaohs of the Twenty-Sixth Dynasty. If so, it would demonstrate how long the claims of native dynasts in Egypt persisted during Persian rule and provide an analogy for the persistence of Davidic claims within Judah. During his short reign, Nepherites brought Egyptian rule to the southern coast of the Levant through the aid of Greek mercenaries. He displaced the Persians at some of the local garrisons,[1] secured the trade routes merging at Gaza, and created a territorial buffer all the way to Joppa.[2] His eventual successor, Hakoris (393–380 BC), then extended control north to Acco and Sidon.[3] With these territorial advances, Egypt and its Greek mercenaries gained indirect influence over Judah and Samaria. For the first time, we find Athenian-style coins in the region, including in Jerusalem and Samaria.[4] Judean coins still had "Yehud" (the Persian name of the province) stamped on them in Aramaic script, but one coin depicted a bearded deity, presumably Yahweh in similar guise to Zeus, seated on a winged and wheeled throne with a bird in his outstretched left hand.[5]

---

1. Cf. Fantalkin and Tal, "Judah and Its Neighbors," 163.
2. Stern, *The Assyrian, Babylonian, and Persian Periods*, 358.
3. Inscriptions of Hakoris have been found at Acco and Sidon. See Stern, *The Assyrian, Babylonian, and Persian Periods*, 358.
4. Yehoshua Zlotnik, "Minting of Coinage in Jerusalem during the Persian and Hellenistic Periods," 2012, https://www.academia.edu/5517837/Minting_of_coinage_in_Jerusalem_during_the_Persian; cf. Grabbe, *Yehud*, 67–68.
5. Michael Shenkar, "The Coin of the 'God on the Winged Wheel,'" *Boreas* 30/31 (2007): 13–23; pl. 7–8.

These Egyptian (and Greek) advances into the coastal plain were to prove crucial in the long-term weakening of Persian power in the region and a reorientation of the Judean and Samarian "compass." The political cooperation between Greeks and Egyptians against Persian power had been occurring for decades previously.[6] With Egypt's independence from Persia a new political axis developed, spanning the waves of the Mediterranean and strengthening the cultural and economic ties between Egypt and Greece. With Egyptian soldiers and Greek mercenaries now controlling the major ports and trade routes along the coastal plain, the economic artery of Judah and Samaria was diverted away from the heartland of the Persian Empire in Mesopotamia and towards the developing economy in the Mediterranean. For the first time in centuries, therefore, the political, economic, and cultural compass of Judah and Samaria began to swing away from the landward pole in Mesopotamia towards a new maritime pole situated in the Mediterranean. This magnetism was made stronger by the network of Greek and Phoenician colonies throughout the Mediterranean littoral, which reached as far west as Italy, Carthage, and Spain. Although Judah and Samaria were still ostensibly part of the Persian Empire, the shifting dynamics created a power vacuum in the region, which allowed provincial ties with Persia to slacken.

In Judah, these shifting dynamics are well demonstrated by a silver coin that bears the name of "Johanan the priest."[7] It is written in Hebrew with Paleo-Hebrew script rather than Aramaic, which indicates a heightened sense of local identity. However, the coin lacks the term "Judah," so there was not yet a sense of independence. The motif of an Athenian owl on the reverse evinces Greek influence via Egypt, but the weight of the coin accords with Persian standards.[8] It shows that the high priest in Jerusalem, Johanan ben-Joiada, had become de facto head of a province with a growing sense of autonomy in a politically ambiguous time. Judah could not attain independence, for it could not field its own army to withstand either Egypt or Persia. Any soldiers it could field were probably enlisted in the Persian army. But the political vacuum created by Egypt's incursions into the Levant allowed Judah some leeway to take care of its own affairs, perhaps with Egyptian and Greek encouragement. Johanan had the political nous to style himself as "the priest" on a silver coin, rather

---

6. The travels of the historian Herodotus, who was from the Ionian city of Halicarnassus (technically in Persian territory) in the late fifth century BC is testament to this.

7. D. Barag, "A Silver Coin of Yoḥanan the High Priest and the Coinage of Judea in the Fourth Century B.C.," *INJ* 9 (1986): 4–21; Lisbeth S. Fried, "A Silver Coin of Yoḥanan Hakkôhēn," *Transeuphratène* 26 (2003): 65–85.

8. Bradley W. Root, "Coinage, War, and Peace in Fourth-Century Yehud," *NEA* 68.3 (2005): 133.

than as "governor" or "king," thereby avoiding the charge of insubordination against the Persians. The Johanan coin is best dated to the late 380s BC, when Asia Minor and Cyprus dominated Persia's attention.[9] Thus, Johanan assumed leadership of Judah in his mature years, probably stepping into a breach created by the death of Governor Bagohi, his political rival. If so, his initiative shows Persia's inability to appoint a provincial governor in Judah during the 380s BC.

All of this confirms Johanan's continued commitment to Nehemiah's policy of insulating Judah against Samarian influence. By taking up provincial leadership, he ensured that Samaria could not exert political sway over Judah in the regional vacuum and thus undermine Jerusalem's primacy and the prophetic traditions that upheld it. This was critical since Bagohi died at this time (ca. 385 BC). Bagohi had been on friendly terms with Delaiah, who governed Samaria after his father's death (ca. 406 BC). Delaiah was succeeded in office either by his brother Shelemiah or by a son, Hananiah—the evidence is not altogether clear as to which it was. Hananiah certainly did become governor of Samaria in the first half of the fourth century BC, but whether his father was Delaiah or Shelemiah is uncertain.[10] In any case, since Hananiah had a son, Sanballat II, it seems clear that the local government of Samaria remained within the Sanballat dynasty. This suggests a measure of stability in Samaria, but no less a sense of growing autonomy. Indeed, the period witnessed an increase in locally minted coins and a proliferation of local names among the official class.

Under these politically ambiguous conditions, those in Judah who held to the prophetic traditions and the Davidic hopes they espoused probably longed for independence. But Judah was still politically and militarily a small player on the international stage. The only viable means for complete independence from

---

9. The coin is often dated to the mid to late fourth century BC on the basis of Cross's mistaken assumption of papponymy among Jerusalem's high priests, which led to the erroneous conclusion that there were four high priests named Johanan (*From Epic to Canon*, 156). For a refutation, see VanderKam, *From Joshua to Caiaphas*, 85–99. Fried ("A Silver Coin of Yoḥanan Hakkôhēn," 85) shows convincingly that the coin is that of Johanan ben-Joiada, dating it to 378–368 BC on the basis of comparison with firmly datable coins bearing similar motifs. However, even this bracket can be lifted to a slightly earlier period. *Pace* Edelman, *The Origins of the 'Second' Temple*, 65; Sylvie Honigman, "Searching for the Social Location of Literate Judean Elites in Early Hellenistic Times: A Non-Linear History of the Temple and Royal Administrations in Judea," in Honigman, Niham, and Lipschits, *Times of Transition*, 206.

10. Cross (*From Epic to Canon*, 152–57) argued that there were three Sanballats who governed Samaria, with the second being the son of Delaiah. However, Eshel exposes Cross's assumptions and argues persuasively for just two Sanballats, with the second governing later in the fourth century BC. Eshel proposes that Delaiah was succeeded by his brother, Shelemiah (cf. *TAD* A4.7.29; 4.8.28), who had authority to mint coins. In this case, Hananiah (known from coins and WDSP 7) was Shelemiah's son. But if Shelemiah never became governor, then Hananiah must be identified as Delaiah's son. See Hanan Eshel, "The Governors of Samaria in the Fifth and Fourth Centuries B.C.E.," in Lipschits, Knoppers, and Albertz, *Judah and the Judeans in Fourth Century B.C.E.*, 223–34.

foreign rule would have been to join with Samaria and neighboring provinces to create a large enough territorial bloc from which an army or militia could be drawn. This would create a new Israel of sorts—a united entity comprised of all Yahwists in the region, from the Jezreel Valley in the north to Idumea in the south. To succeed militarily and politically, though, the political vacuum between the Persian Empire and Egypt would need to deepen, allowing local soldiers to return from the Persian army. This was not an unrealistic expectation, but it had not sufficiently developed at the beginning of the fourth century BC. Furthermore, a united front would require the burial of differences between Judah and Samaria. Since Samaria was still by far the dominant province of the region, this would necessitate the surrender of Jerusalem's claim to primacy and the associated Davidic hopes that buttressed it. Since these hopes were the primary motivation for independence in Jerusalem, the entire notion was self-defeating. Johanan, whose leadership depended on political distance from Samaria, was not about to allow this. His pragmatic politics, therefore, continued the promotion of the prophetic traditions, but it also deferred any substantive political action to realize Davidic hopes and the establishment of an independent Judean kingdom. Instead, deference was still cautiously paid to Persia.

1.6.3 WEAKENING PERSIAN POWER IN TRANS-EUPHRATES

Artaxerxes II felt the loss of Egypt and the Levantine coast keenly. To retake them he had to free up his forces by pacifying the Aegean front. By 386 BC he had pushed the Spartans out of Asia Minor and successfully negotiated "The King's Peace" (also known as the Peace of Antalcidas) with the Greeks. Under its terms, all of Asia Minor and Cyprus were deemed possessions of Persia, and the Persians would guarantee the autonomy of all Greek city-states on the mainland, reserving the right to attack any Greek city that warred against another (Xenophon, *Hell.* 5.1.30–32). In this way, Artaxerxes cleverly fragmented the Greeks by pandering to their sense of individual city pride. However, the peace was not much of a blow to the Greek-Egyptian axis that now spanned the Mediterranean, for the city-states of Greece were still free to engage in indirect anti-Persian activity by supporting Egypt with mercenaries. Nevertheless, the King's Peace gave Artaxerxes the opportunity to disengage his forces from the Aegean front and redeploy them to Trans-Euphrates.

While negotiating in the Aegean, though, conflict broke out on other fronts. On Cyprus, one of the local kings, Evagoras, took advantage of Persia's weakness and asserted his sovereignty over the whole island. He received backing from Pharaoh Hakoris, and perhaps even from the Levant itself (Diodorus Siculus, *Bib. hist.* 15.2.3–4),[11] and convinced the city of Tyre to his cause. His success threatened to tear all of Trans-Euphrates away from Artaxerxes. But once the Aegean front was pacified, Artaxerxes domesticated Evagoras and retook the whole Levantine coast. By 380 BC all of Trans-Euphrates, including Judah and Samaria, was once again unambiguously Persian territory. Egypt thus lost its foothold in the Levant.

Artaxerxes bolstered Persian fortifications in the region[12] and began developing an army and fleet to attempt the reconquest of Egypt—a task that took some years to complete. In the meantime, dynastic squabbles rocked Egypt, resulting in the overthrow of the Twenty-Ninth Dynasty and the establishment of the Thirtieth Dynasty under a zealously pro-Greek pharaoh, Nectanebo I. Critically, though, the time that the Persians took to consolidate control of Trans-Euphrates gave Nectanebo time to fortify the Nile Delta (Diodorus Siculus, *Bib. hist.* 15.41.5). By the time the Persians were ready to invade (373 BC), they had lost any advantage and the Egyptians successfully fended them off.[13]

Jerusalem's high priest, Johanan, died soon after and was succeeded by his son, Jaddua. Since Johanan had functioned as de facto governor of Judah, his passing must have prompted the Persians to appoint a new secular governor to consolidate their power locally. Thus, as Jaddua took up the sacerdotal office in ca. 370 BC, another Judean was appointed provincial governor. Coins bearing the name "Hezekiah" and the title "governor" in Hebrew are basically identical to the Johanan coin, suggesting Hezekiah took over governing duties immediately after Johanan.[14] This Hezekiah was the last governor the Persians would appoint in Judah.[15] The use of Hebrew in Hezekiah's coinage attests to the sense of growing autonomy in Judah at the time, despite Persia's

---

11. Diodorus claims the king of Arabia sent troops to Evagoras (Diodorus Siculus, *Bib. hist.* 15.2.4), but it is difficult to ascertain the reliability of this statement, let alone who the Arab king was or what geopolitics might have been at work.

12. These fortifications in the Negev and Shephelah were built originally in response to Inarus's Revolt (see 1.4.1), *contra* Fantalkin and Tal ("Judah and Its Neighbors," 166–70). From ca. 400 BC, their garrisons constantly changed as control of the region swung several times between the Persians and Egyptians.

13. This was almost certainly the campaign mentioned by Isocrates (*Panegyric* 140), which lasted three years but ended in failure, *contra* Briant, *From Cyrus to Alexander*, 652.

14. Cf. Ya'akov Meshorer, *Persian Period through Hasmonaeans*, vol. 1 of *Ancient Jewish Coinage* (Dix Hills, NY: Amphora, 1982), 116.

15. On the possible chronologies arising from the numismatic evidence, see Fried, "A Silver Coin of Yoḥanan Hakkôhēn." Coins of "Hezekiah" dated to the Hellenistic era should be distinguished as relating to a different person from Governor Hezekiah in the early fourth century BC. Governor Hezekiah was almost certainly not in office at the end of the Persian era (see 1.7.5), as Jaddua was the ostensible leader of Judah when Alexander conquered the region.

ostensible sovereignty. Indeed, from about this time we also see overtly local motifs appear on Judean coins, such as the lily, which featured prominently in the temple's artistry (cf. 1 Kgs 7:19, 22, 26).[16]

After failing to retake Egypt, the aging Artaxerxes II found himself once again on the back foot. His forces had been decimated and his coffers were less full, which made it more difficult to keep a grip on the western portions of his empire. The Greeks and Egyptians continued to strengthen their axis, which included a flow of Greek mercenaries to Egypt and the marriage of Nectanebo to a female relative of the Athenian general, Chabrias.[17] So the magnetism in the west continued to grow. Nectanebo's son, Tachos, had high hopes of recovering Egyptian control over the Levant and raised taxes throughout Egypt to build an expeditionary force capable of achieving it. With Greek support, he stood a good chance.

In the meantime, Persian control in Asia Minor and northern Syria was challenged by the so-called Revolt of the Satraps. The historical sources provide conflicting and overly biased information, making it difficult to get a sense of the true course of events, but it prompted the Ionian Greek cities to seek independence from Persia.[18] Artaxerxes restored his sovereignty over the region by 360 BC, but it was with a weaker grip. The desire of the Ionian Greeks for complete independence never waned. Persian power in Asia Minor was fading.

Many throughout Trans-Euphrates, including Judeans and Samarians, probably questioned how long Artaxerxes could maintain his control. The region was experiencing constant political stress from being pulled between Persia and Egypt, resulting in imperial fatigue and the fragility of local Persian power. This grew yet more when Tachos invaded the Levant with Greek mercenaries shortly after the death of his father, Nectanebo I (361 BC). Tachos re-occupied the coastal plain and even tried to gain control of the highway through the Jezreel Valley. Egyptian control of this arterial road would have cut Judah and Samaria off from Persian control completely, but it is doubtful that Tachos succeeded.

An elderly Artaxerxes dispatched one of his sons, Ochus, to counter the Egyptian invasion and Tachos's progress was halted. Moreover, the high taxation Tachos had earlier imposed on Egypt prompted a *coup d'état* against him. In 359 BC he was ignominiously overthrown by his nephew, Nectanebo II, and left to find refuge with the Persians.[19] With the campaign in tatters,

---

16. Meshorer, *Persian Period through Hasmonaeans*, 29–30; cf. 62–63.
17. Joann Fletcher, *Cleopatra the Great: The Woman Behind the Legend* (London: Hodder and Stoughton, 2008), 19.
18. Briant, *From Cyrus to Alexander*, 656–59, 674.
19. Karol Myśliwiec, *The Twilight of Egypt: First Millennium B.C.E.*, trans. David Lorton (Ithaca: Cornell University Press, 2000), 169.

the Egyptian expeditionary force relinquished control of the coastal plain and skulked back to Egypt. Nonetheless, Tachos's campaign, coming so soon after the exploits of Nepherites and Hakoris, still managed to expose Persia's persistent weakness. Tachos's failure raises the question of how much someone with more fiscal sense, greater popularity, and better stability on the home front might have been able to achieve in a region experiencing perpetual imperial fatigue. That question would be answered within a generation with the rise of Alexander of Macedon. For now, the retreat of the Egyptians and Greeks left the Persians still officially in charge of Trans-Euphrates.

1.6.4 THE ACCESSION OF ARTAXERXES III

Artaxerxes II finally died in April 358 BC, and court intrigues clouded the succession. In the end, it was his third legitimate son, Ochus (the victor over Tachos), who succeeded him.[20] Ochus took the throne name Artaxerxes III (358–336 BC) and almost immediately faced problems on the Aegean front. The King's Peace (386 BC), which had kept a lid on the simmering rivalries between Greek cities, lapsed with the death of Artaxerxes II. This resulted in Greek cities not only jostling with each other but also taking openly hostile measures against Persia, such as encouraging rebellions within the satrapies of Asia Minor. One satrap, Artabazus, who defected from the empire, even sought refuge with the new young king of Macedon, Philip II (Diodorus Siculus, *Bib. hist.* 16.52.3).[21]

The maritime axis between Greeks and Egyptians was still strong, and Artaxerxes III intended to destroy it. To that end, he turned his attention to Egypt, now under the rule of Nectanebo I's successor, Nectanebo II. In 351 BC his imperial forces invaded. However, Nectanebo II held out successfully and dished out a humiliating defeat to the Persians.[22] Artaxerxes's depleted forces retreated. Not only did this allow Egypt to retain its independence, but it also loosened the bonds keeping Trans-Euphrates tethered to Persia. To attempt another invasion of Egypt, Artaxerxes would need to raise a new and bigger army as well as a navy—an expensive and time-consuming task. Then things went from bad to worse for Artaxerxes III.

---

20. Briant, *From Cyrus to Alexander*, 680–81.
21. Briant, *From Cyrus to Alexander*, 682; Robin J. Lane Fox, "Philip of Macedon: Accession, Ambitions, and Self-Presentation," in *Brill's Companion to Ancient Macedon: Studies in the Archaeology and History of Macedon, 650 BC–300 AD*, ed. Robin J. Lane Fox (Leiden: Brill, 2011), 354.
22. Unfortunately, the details of the campaign are unknown. All that can be ascertained from the ancient sources is the date of Artaxerxes III's defeat. See Briant, *From Cyrus to Alexander*, 682–85.

1.7   AN ISRAELITE COALITION

1.7.1   THE TENNES REVOLT (351–345 BC)

The Persian defeat in Egypt strengthened the Greek-Egyptian maritime axis. With Persian imperial magnetism over Trans-Euphrates at an all-time low, the new political pole in the Mediterranean exerted a strong pull on the Levant, Cyprus, and Asia Minor. In 351 BC the Phoenician cities made a bid for independence. Led by the Sidonian king, Tennes, they shored up support from Nectanebo II, which included the deployment of Greek mercenaries. They then moved against the personnel and paraphernalia of Persian colonial power in and around Sidon. They cut down the local Persian "paradise" (the palatial residence and botanical gardens of local Persian command), burned Persian cavalry provisions, and assassinated the colonial bureaucracy (Diodorus Siculus, *Bib. hist.* 16.41.1–6). In so doing, the Phoenician cities officially threw in their lot with the new maritime axis in the Mediterranean.

This "Tennes Revolt" and its calamitous conclusion (see 1.7.5 below) is remembered in the short but vivid oracle of Zechariah 11:1–3. The revolt was significant for numerous reasons. First, it demonstrated how fragile Persian hegemony over the lands bordering the Mediterranean had become. Although the regional Persian forces mobilized against the Phoenicians (ca. 349 BC), their strength had been seriously sapped by the recent defeat in Egypt and the current action of the Phoenician insurgents. Thus, with the help of the Greek mercenaries, the Phoenicians staved off the initial Persian counterattack (Diodorus Siculus, *Bib. hist.* 16.42.1–2). Persia's weakness in Asia Minor after the Revolt of the Satraps was also showing with local rulers acting with practical independence and adopting Greek culture almost wholesale. Perhaps the best example of this was Mausolus, the satrap of Caria, who ruled effectively as an independent king.[1]

Second, the Phoenicians' actions were diplomatically bold. Although the Persian defeat in Egypt was a clear spark for the revolt, the Phoenicians took the initiative to rebel on their own, thus preventing Nectanebo II from capitalizing and invading the Levant as his predecessors had done. The Phoenicians had Egyptian political backing and Greek mercenary reinforcement, but

---

1. At the death of Mausolus in 353 BC, his widow (and sister), Artemisia, commissioned the building of a fabulous tomb for him, the famed Mausoleum of Halicarnassus.

their initiative ensured that they did not simply trade one colonial power for another. Their independence from Persia added to the strength of the new maritime bloc developing in the Mediterranean, but it was also fragmented, lacking a unifying power to direct it. Like the Greeks, the Phoenician cities saw themselves as individual city-states rather than a singular political entity. Thus, while there was strength in the numbers being drawn to the new Mediterranean pole, there was still fragmentation.

Third, by removing all the Phoenician ports from Persian control, Tennes and his allies ensured Artaxerxes III could not build a new fleet to use against them. Persia's dilemma was compounded when the kings of Cyprus were emboldened to declare their independence also. They had been hankering for independence since the time of Evagoras three decades earlier (see 1.6.3 above). If the Persians wanted to recover these lands, they would have to raise infantry and cavalry from other quarters of their empire to recapture the Phoenician ports by land.

Fourth, the ferocity with which the Sidonians attacked the local Persian bureaucracy testifies to their resentment of colonial power. By cutting down the trees of the Persian "paradise," they symbolically depicted Persia's fall (cf. Zech 11:2). Sidon had benefitted economically as a base of Persian imperial power in the region,[2] but this benefit was insufficient to keep them tethered to Persian hegemony. It may be that the Sidonians themselves had lost considerable numbers of men fighting for the Persians in Egypt. Such discontent, combined with the emergence of a Mediterranean-centric perspective, cast the Persian regime as foreign and other. No longer were they the liberators who had turned back the tide of Babylonian oppression or benefactors who promoted local cultures. The Persians were relics of a colonial regime situated far in the east, suppressing the freedom of people whose identity was now located along the shores of a western sea brimming with new opportunities and ideas.

The scale of the threat to Persian imperial integrity was enormous, as the Athenian rhetorician, Isocrates, noted in an open letter to Philip II of Macedon, penned in 347 BC—the very time the Tennes Revolt was in full swing. Isocrates had been a proponent of Panhellenism, which sought to unite all Greeks into a single military and cultural force. He argued that the time was ripe for Philip to launch a military invasion of the Persian Empire, interpreting the empire's woes as the throes of death.

> Furthermore, Cyprus and Phoenicia and Cilicia, and that region from which the barbarians used to recruit their fleet, belonged at that time to the [Persian]

---

2. Briant, *From Cyrus to Alexander*, 684.

king, but now they have either rebelled against him or are so involved in war and its associated ills that none of these peoples is of any use to him; while to you [Philip], if you desire to make war upon him, they will be amenable ... and you will also induce many of the other satraps to throw off the king's sovereignty if you promise them freedom and broadcast over Asia that word which, when sown among the Greeks, has broken up both our [Athenian] empire and that of the Lacedaemonians [i.e., Spartans]. (Isocrates, *To Philip* 102–4)

Even reading past the rhetoric of Isocrates's words, it is apparent that there was widespread discontent with Persian colonial rule across the Mediterranean lands. Persia's strength was perceived to be at an all-time low.

1.7.2 THE POWER VACUUM IN THE SOUTHERN LEVANT

Naturally we must ask questions of how Judah and Samaria were affected by the Tennes Revolt and the growing anti-Persian movement across the Mediterranean seaboard. The half century of Egyptian independence, Greek-Egyptian incursions into the Levant, and the emerging Mediterranean bloc had impacted the two provinces in the first half of the fourth century BC. This is demonstrated archaeologically by the Attic (Greek) pottery in Judah and Samaria at this time, even though it is more sparsely attested than in the coastal regions.[3] The Judean and Samarian compass was in the process of reorientation.

Judah's political isolationism also allowed the prophetic traditions and the Davidic hopes of an independent kingdom to keep gaining traction. If Judean resentment at Persian colonial power was anything like that of the Sidonians, then an uprising was not inconceivable. Considering the entire Mediterranean coast from Cilicia to Egypt had declared independence and cut Samaria and Judah off from direct connection to Persian authority, there was little to keep the provinces in the Persian fold. Isocrates's letter to Philip implies as much (see 1.7.1 above). This is not to say that Judah and Samaria rose up in aggravated rebellion against Persia, but at the very least they found themselves in the middle of an imperial vacuum. Under such circumstances, Judah and Samaria began to operate on the assumption that Persian sovereignty over them was coming to an end.

Hundreds of Aramaic ostraca from Idumea on Judah's southern border provide a key piece of evidence on this front. They record the trading of various commodities across the mid to late fourth century BC.[4] Many of the ostraca

---

3. Fantalkin and Tal, "Judah and Its Neighbors," 142.
4. Lemaire, "New Aramaic Ostraca from Idumea," 414–15. Cf. Bezalel Porten and Ada Yardeni, "Makkedah and the Storehouse in the Idumean Ostraca," in *A Time of Change: Judah and Its Neighbours*

have incomplete or fragmentary dates, but many are dated by the specific year of the reigning monarch. Though the Persian kings are not named (the later Greek rulers often are), we are able to determine most of them by the length of their respective reigns, cross-checked by paleographical analysis of the handwriting. The ostraca positively dated by the reign of Artaxerxes III tell the story of how Idumeans on Judah's southern frontier acknowledged his sovereignty:

Year (Oct–Sept)	Positively Dated Ostraca	Possibly Dated Ostraca[5]
359/58	42	1
358/57	35	5
357/56	36	1
356/55	51	5
355/54	55	2
354/53	31	3
353/52	30	4
352/51	16	-
351/50	3	-
350/49	10	1
349/48	2	4
348/47	0	-
347/46	5	2
346/45	3	2
345/44	32	-
344/43	18	-
343/42	7	-
342/41	8	-
341/40	7	-
340/39	5	-
339/38	11	-

in the Persia and Early Hellenistic Periods, ed. Yigal Levin, Library of Second Temple Studies 65 (London: T&T Clark, 2007), 142–43.

5. This column tallies ostraca that the editors of *TAO* have assigned to a particular regnal year, but there is uncertainty over the dating due to such factors as faded ink, fragmentary evidence, or other ambiguities.

Many factors must have impacted these figures, such as agricultural productivity and supply and demand but also the local political situation. They demonstrate a robust acknowledgement of Persian sovereignty until the time of Artaxerxes III's disastrous campaign to Egypt in 351 BC when there is a sudden and sustained drop in the number of receipts dated by Artaxerxes's regnal year. A brief and low resurgence occurs in the summer of 349 BC, which can be correlated with the time of the Persians' unsuccessful attempt to quell the Tennes Revolt, after which the figures plummet again. It is not until the winter of 345/44 BC that acknowledgement of Persian sovereignty rebounds, corresponding to the successful quashing of the Tennes Revolt. The figures taper off again two years later, probably reflecting the altered economic condition resulting from the new taxes imposed by the vizier, Bagoas (see 1.7.5 below), and concomitant discontent at Persian sovereignty. The year that Artaxerxes IV came to the throne (338 BC) sees a brief resurgence, but the figures subsequently drop off again during the reign of Darius III.[6]

These ostraca show that there was a period when Persian sovereignty in Idumea was ambiguous and, at best, barely acknowledged. In 348/47 BC it was not acknowledged at all. The correspondence of this period with the years of the Tennes Revolt, when the entire Levantine coast broke away from Persian sovereignty, can hardly be accidental. Idumea does not appear to have acted in brazen rebellion as the Phoenician and Cyprian cities did, but the ostraca show a clear political vacuum due to Persian weakness. Since Judah and Samaria were in the same geopolitical situation as Idumea, it is reasonable to suggest that they too made little attempt to keep the Persian flag flying during these years.

The papyri brought to the Wadi Daliyeh by refugees from Samaria in 332 BC (see 2.2.4 below) tell a similar story. Most of these documents are contracts for the sale of slaves, and many are dated by reference to the regnal years of Persian and Greek monarchs, ranging from ca. 375 to 332 BC. Crucially, one document dated to January 351 BC (WDSP 2) refers to Artaxerxes III.[7] The next papyrus securely dated by the regnal year of Artaxerxes III dates no earlier than 345 BC (WDSP 37), and perhaps slightly later. No papyrus cites the regnal year of Artaxerxes III between 351 and 345 BC. Admittedly, this is an argument from silence, as the fragmentary nature of the papyri precludes us from knowing whether any of the contracts originated in this crucial period or

---

6. In the final three years of the Persian era (335–332 BC), there is no acknowledgement of Persian sovereignty among the ostraca whatsoever.

7. The date of WDSP 10 is fragmentary, but it can be reconstructed to 355 BC at the earliest and 350 BC at the latest.

if they cited the regnal year of Artaxerxes III. The silence is, therefore, by no means definitive. But when put beside the ostraca from Idumea, the Samarian papyri from Wadi Daliyeh appear to tell the same story of political vacuum.[8] Furthermore, the papyri refer to Idumeans operating freely within Samarian society (e.g., WDSP 2),[9] which shows a congruity in the political and economic situation between Samaria and Idumea, and presumably Judah, which was situated between them.

Additionally, from a cave overlooking Jericho, there is a document listing monetary contributions made by Yahwists. It is dated on paleographical grounds to this approximate period. The inaccessibility of the cave (Ketef Yeriho) makes it almost certain that the document was brought there by people seeking refuge, similar to the situation of the Samarian refugees in the Wadi Daliyeh.[10] The destruction of nearby Jericho by the Persians is dated to this time, making it likely that the bearers of the Ketef Yeriho document had fled from the Persians.[11] The timing and nature of the destruction are suggestive of punitive action taken by the Persians when they reasserted their power (ca. 345 BC).[12]

Finally, early church fathers refer to an old tradition that Artaxerxes III had banished some Judeans to Hyrcania on the southeastern shore of the Caspian Sea after his defeat in Egypt.[13] It is easy to dismiss these references as random or unreliably late, but four factors suggest there is an historical memory behind them. First, as mentioned above, the geopolitical situation makes it probable that Persia momentarily lost its grasp on the southern Levant at

---

8. Dušek argues that the papyri do not implicate Samaria in the Tennes Revolt. However, all they certify is that Samarians recognized Persian sovereignty outside the critical years of the revolt, without any specific evidence to contradict the notion that they believed Persian sovereignty over them had collapsed in 351–346 BC. See Jan Dušek, *Les Manuscrits Araméens Du Wadi Daliyeh et La Samarie Vers 450–332 Av. J.-C.*, Culture and History of the Ancient Near East 30 (Leiden: Brill, 2007), 601. Interestingly, the papyri before 351 BC refer to Samaria as the "citadel" (Aram. *birta*; e.g., WDSP 4), while those after 345 BC refer to Samaria merely as the "city" (Aram. *qerita*; e.g., WDSP 14). Again, the fragmentary state of the papyri means we cannot tell whether this was merely a synonymous variation or indicative of a change in official status.

9. Idumeans are identified by names bearing the theophoric element "Qos."

10. This destruction in Jericho must be distinguished from the aftermath of the Andromachus Affair, which made refugees of people from Samaria (see 2.2.4).

11. Hanan Eshel and Hagai Misgav, "A Fourth Century B.C.E. Document from Ketef Yeriho," *IEJ* 38.3 (1988): 174–76; D. Barag, "The Effects of the Tennes Rebellion on Palestine," *BASOR* 183.4 (1966): 11–12.

12. Buildings at En Gedi further south and Jebel Nimra also show evidence of damage in the mid-fourth century BC. Cf. Fantalkin and Tal, "Judah and Its Neighbors," 157; Igor Kreimerman and Débora Sandhaus, "Political Trends as Reflected in the Material Culture: A New Look at the Transition between the Persian and Early Hellenistic Periods," in Honigman, Nihan, and Lipschits, *Times of Transition*, 125.

13. D. Barag, "The Effects of the Tennes Revolt on Palestine," 8, n.10; Briant, *From Cyrus to Alexander*, 685.

this time. Second, Josephus cites Hecateus regarding a deportation of Judeans by the Persians to Babylon (*Ag. Ap.* 1.194). This is not a confused allusion to the Babylonian exile of 586 BC but to the fact that the Persians brought captives from the revolt to Babylon first, before transferring them to other regions (cf. *PE* 9.76; see 1.7.5 below).[14] Third, the name "Hyrcanus" enters the Jewish onomasticon in the Hellenistic era, shortly after this time. And fourth, Zechariah 11:4–17 and the book of Malachi allude to an attempt to unite Judah and Samaria that occurred in response to the weakness of Persia but had detrimental consequences (see 1.7.3 below). All these suggest that the Persians came down hard on at least some of the Judean population at about the time of the Tennes Revolt. It seems reasonable, therefore, to suggest that the Persians perceived a measure of disloyalty among some Judeans.

1.7.3 UNIFICATION AND THE MANASSEH AFFAIR

Josephus gives an anecdote that sheds light on Judah and Samaria in relation to the Tennes Revolt and that intersects with material in Zechariah 11 and the book of Malachi. Some of the details in Josephus's anecdote are confused, but they can be untangled. He relates how Sanballat, governor of Samaria, gave his daughter, Nicaso, in marriage to Manasseh, the brother of Jerusalem's high priest, Jaddua, as a means of securing the goodwill of the Judeans. However, Jaddua and his colleagues refused to let Manasseh continue as a priest in Jerusalem because of this marriage. Manasseh was unwilling to give up his priestly position for the sake of the marriage, whereupon Sanballat promised him the high priesthood at a new temple to be built on Mount Gerizim. Sanballat consequently built the temple and installed Manasseh as its high priest, causing numerous priests and Levites in Jerusalem to defect to the Samarians (*Ant.* 11.302–12).

It is clear that Josephus has blended two events into one: (1) the founding of the Samarian temple on Mount Gerizim, which occurred under Sanballat I in the mid-fifth century BC;[15] and (2) the Manasseh Affair, which occurred under Sanballat II a century later.[16] His confusion derives from the fact that

---

14. Josephus here cites a genuine and reliable statement from Hecateus, who lived not long after the events. See Bezalel Bar-Kochva, *Pseudo Hecataeus, "On the Jews": Legitimizing the Jewish Diaspora* (Berkeley: University of California Press, 2010), 87, 143–44.

15. The name "Nicaso" reflects a deference to Greek culture in Samaria, which could not have arisen before Greeks came into close contact with the Levant during the early fourth century BC. This confirms that Nicaso's father was not Sanballat I (from the mid-fifth century BC) but Sanballat II.

16. Grabbe (*Yehud*, 157) argues that Josephus blended Neh 13:28 into the mix, which relates how Nehemiah banished the son of the high priest Joiada from Jerusalem for marrying the daughter of

he thought there had been only one governor of Samaria called Sanballat, when in fact there were two.[17] Once we are aware of this, Josephus's testimony can be reliably untangled with the aid of archaeological evidence.[18] It can then be corroborated against biblical literature (Zechariah and Malachi) and the wider geopolitical situation, including Persian weakness and the rise of nationalist tides evident in the Tennes Revolt and the Panhellenic movement typified by Isocrates and Philip II of Macedon (see 1.7.1 above). We can, therefore, piece together a reliable reconstruction of the events of this volatile period.

After Persia's defeat in Egypt (351 BC), a Phoenician coalition led by Tennes of Sidon threw off Persian colonial rule and successfully repelled a Persian attempt to curtail them. Their newfound independence released Judah and Samaria from Persian control, as direct contact with the Persian regime was effectively cut off. Samaria, which had been exposed to elements of Greek culture for some decades, thus found itself with independent neighbors in its immediate vicinity. Emboldened by the independence of the Levantine coast all the way up to Cilicia and across to Cyprus, there was now a movement in Samaria that entertained notions of independence. It was not a rebellion against Persia per se but a realization that Persia's local authority structures had collapsed. Independence was a means of configuring the erstwhile province with a new authority structure that might allow it to operate in a new political environment. In other words, Sanballat II, who had become governor of Samaria in ca. 353 BC, had to determine what Samaria was going to be now rather than hold onto what it had once been under Persian hegemony.[19]

Sanballat. However, Josephus's account of Johanan murdering his own brother, Jeshua (*Ant.* 11.297–301), must be clearly distinguished from the affair of Manasseh, brother of Jaddua, for two reasons. First, Josephus names Jeshua (Greek: Jesus) as Johanan's brother, both being sons of the high priest Joiada. He also names Manasseh as the brother of Jaddua, both being sons of the high priest Johanan. We thus have two sets of completely incompatible names that speak to two distinct incidents. Second, the two incidents had very different outcomes: Jeshua was killed, while Manasseh defected. Manasseh and the events surrounding him must, therefore, be clearly distinguished from Jeshua and the earlier events that surrounded him, including Neh 13:28.

17. Frank Moore Cross suggested that there were three Sanballats. See "A Reconstruction of the Judean Restoration," *JBL* 94.1 (1975): 4–18. However, as Eshel ("The Governors of Samaria") has demonstrated, and as history bears out, there were only two.

18. Josephus also attributes the events to ca. 336 BC, when Philip II of Macedon was assassinated (*Ant.* 11.304–5). However, the Wadi Daliyeh documents correct this by showing that the Samarian governor in 336 BC was Jeshua, son of Sanballat II. This necessarily brings the Manasseh Affair to an earlier time, when Sanballat II was governor, coinciding perfectly with the Tennes Revolt.

19. Sanballat II's father, Hananiah, is mentioned as governor of Samaria in WDSP 7, dated to 354 BC, but by the time the Tennes Revolt broke out, Sanballat II had succeeded him.

Judah was in the same dilemma. This new situation was more pronounced than it had been when Nepherites I and Hakoris had held the coastal plain in the 390s and 380s BC. Back then, the high priest Johanan had acted as caretaker governor in an ambiguous situation because Persia had not lost its grip completely. But now with the Tennes Revolt, Persia had lost all practical sway over the satrapy of Trans-Euphrates. Thus, like Samaria, the leaders of Judah had to figure out how to negotiate the new political landscape.

In these new circumstances, Sanballat II attempted to form a regional coalition with the neighboring provinces of Judah and Idumea and with Yahwists in Transjordan, too. The aim was to form a new "Israelite" bloc throughout the traditional covenantal territory of Israel, with Yahweh as its patron deity. It was, in other words, an attempt to reunify the disparate parts of covenantal Israel as a national entity. As Josephus puts it, Sanballat was aiming to forge a "mutual society" (*Ant.* 11.307). Isocrates's letter to Philip II of Macedon demonstrates an analogous movement aimed at consolidating a political bloc on the basis of shared culture in the widely held perception of Persia's demise—something the Phoenicians on the coast had already pursued under Tennes. Each of the "Israelite" provinces on their own was relatively weak. A coalition would, however, allow the pooling of personnel and resources, and even create a centralized authority to organize a new territorial state united by a pan-Israelite culture. Being the governor of the most populous and economically developed of the provinces, Sanballat II would have emerged as the central potentate of this coalition (cf. Isocrates's perception of Philip II of Macedon as the potential champion of Panhellenism). The Tennes Revolt, therefore, created the opportunity for a new united Israel to develop under Samarian leadership. Indeed, the Israelite coalition seems to have taken a leaf out of Tennes's book, since the Persian administrative center at Ramat Raḥel, a few miles south of Jerusalem, was violently destroyed at this time.[20]

This proposed coalition was the event behind the "union" of Judah and Israel in the prophecy of Zechariah 11:4–17, which comes straight after the oracle recalling the Tennes Revolt (Zech 11:1–3). In that text, a prophetic sign is performed whereby two staffs, symbolically called "Goodwill" (Heb. *no'am*) and "Coalition" (Heb. *hobelim* [Zech 11:7]), are used to shepherd the "flock" of "all the people" (11:10) in a fraternal bond between Judah and Israel (11:14; cf. Ezek 37:15–28). The Zechariah text views this union from the Judean perspective and passes the judgment that it was doomed to failure (see this section below).

---

20. Kreimerman and Sandhaus, "Political Trends," 125, 128.

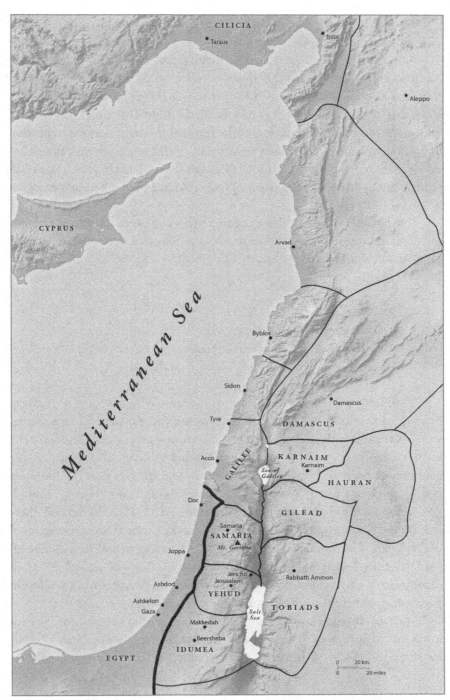

Trans-Euphrates during the Tennes Revolt and the Israelite Coalition (350–345 BC).

The entire prophecy of Malachi is best seen as a critique of the coalition. The prophecy is addressed not just to those in Jerusalem but "to Israel" (Mal 1:1)—that is, the whole nation. The inclusion of Idumea in the proposed coalition is implied by Malachi's denouncement of "Edom" and the appeal to Yahweh's election of Jacob (the forefather of Israel) over his brother, Esau (the forefather of the Idumeans).[21] For Malachi, the Idumeans could play no part within the people of Yahweh, despite the fact that they now occupied a portion of traditional Israelite land. They were, instead, "the people whom Yahweh has denounced in perpetuity" (Mal 1:4). Only the descendants of Jacob could participate in any national purposes—a policy that had been vigorously enforced by Ezra (cf. Ezra 10:1–8).

Israelite unity was desirable according to both the Pentateuch and the prophetic traditions, so the push towards a coalition was understandable. Malachi captures the sentiment of the historical moment in a quotation (a favorite technique in his diatribe):

> Do we not all have a single father?
> Did not a single deity create us?
> Why should we each betray our brother?
> To nullify the covenant of our ancestors? (Mal 2:10)

This verse quotes two justifications for reunifying the Israelite nation. First, the disparate parts of the nation all worshipped Yahweh, who was understood as the one who begat the nation as a whole—an evident allusion to the formation of Israel at the exodus. The fraternal language also reinforces the common ancestry of Israelites and Idumeans and the fact that the Idumean god, Qos, was a guise of Yahweh. Thus there was a concern to make Yahweh great again within the borders of the covenant land (cf. Mal 1:5). Second, there was a sense of obligation to unify on the basis of the national covenant espoused in the Torah. The covenant was seen as binding on all parts of the nation in all corners of the covenantal land. To maintain divisions was interpreted as an abrogation of the national covenant and, therefore, as unfaithful to Yahweh. This was a powerful argument against the detractors of the coalition.

Malachi, though, was one such detractor. For him, the basis of the coalition was ill-conceived. The appeal to a common deity as the "father" of all Israel masked the fact that there were two Yahwistic temples, one in Jerusalem

---

21. The involvement of Idumea is also inferred from the Aramaic ostraca, which have a gap in dating transactions by Persian regnal years at this precise time (see 1.7.2).

and another on Mount Gerizim, as well as a shrine to Qos (Idumean Yahweh) at Makkedah. If the Torah's demand for a single place of worship prevailed, then Mount Gerizim, as the temple with more adherents and greater sway, would naturally win out in the geopolitical climate. But a unification of Israel under Samarian leadership and a Samarian temple was anathema to those like Malachi who were committed to the notion that Yahweh had chosen Jerusalem. For Malachi this was not just about political power plays. It was about representing the true character of Yahweh, being faithful to his previous revelations, according him proper honor in the proper place, at the sanctuary he loved (cf. Mal 2:11), and ensuring the whole nation fell into line with this. Thus, Malachi critiqued the claim to a common deity as father:

> "'Son honors father,
> and a slave his master.'
> But if I am father, where is the honor due me?
> If I am master, where is the respect for me?"
> Yahweh of Ranks has said. (Mal 1:6a)

Of keen interest here is the fact that Malachi uses the divine title associated with Yahweh's cult in Jerusalem: "Yahweh of Ranks." He does not name Mount Gerizim (or Makkedah), but this is part of his rhetorical strategy of conscious forgetting, whereby he makes a clear allusion to people and places but deliberately avoids naming them. Thus, Malachi presents Yahweh of Jerusalem as the father of Israel—not the Yahweh worshipped at Mount Gerizim, and certainly not Qos. This, then, informs his critique of the unification movement in 2:10.

Like Malachi, the high priest Jaddua could not acquiesce to such a coalition under Sanballat's leadership. As desirable as unity was in accordance with the Torah, the prophetic traditions demanded that Israel be governed from Jerusalem as a Davidic estate. This necessarily meant the primacy of Jerusalem as the sole place of Yahwistic worship and government. The prophetic traditions were not held with the same esteem in Samaria. When it became clear that Sanballat had his own agenda, which would marginalize Jerusalem, Jaddua could not agree to the coalition. Not only would a Samarian agenda surrender Jerusalem's primacy to Mount Gerizim, but it would also effectively relinquish the authority of the prophetic traditions, which in Jerusalem were held on the same level of authority as the Torah.

Jaddua, therefore, seems to have had at least some affinity for the prophetic traditions. It is clear from biblical writings, such as the Book of the

Twelve Prophets (of which Zechariah and Malachi are a part), that apart from foreign rule, some of the elite in Jerusalem viewed the priests as one of the main impediments to the establishment of a Davidic kingdom.[22] Since much of Jerusalem's elite was comprised of priests, there must have been a division in priestly loyalties between those who actively perpetuated Davidic expectations, like the Chronicler (see 1.8 below), and those who held them loosely, being more interested in maintaining their own power. Over 170 years had passed since Zerubbabel's return to Jerusalem, and in that time, no Davidic kingdom had been established. Instead, leadership had been invested in non-Davidic governors and priests under foreign rule. All the while, pro-Davidic traditions were being preserved and perpetuated by at least some of the literati in Jerusalem. Even if Jaddua was motivated purely by self-preservation and the need to guard the viability of Jerusalem's temple as a cultic institution rather than a Davidic monument, his rejection of Sanballat's proposal aimed to preserve the prophetic and Davidic traditions.

Judah's governor, Hezekiah, however, was probably amendable to the notion of a coalition.[23] At the political level, Persia's effective collapse throughout the region made Hezekiah's position as governor tenuous, putting him in the same position as Sanballat. Under the proposed coalition, Sanballat would be the senior partner, and although this would relegate Hezekiah to a junior role, it still afforded him the opportunity to redefine his own role when he would otherwise have become politically obsolete. A coalition with Sanballat provided Hezekiah with the best means of political survival. He also shifted the weighting of Judean coinage from Persian weight standards to an Attic standard, showing that he was inclined to abandon Persian sovereignty in favor of a Mediterranean outlook.[24] He was, therefore, most likely sympathetic to Sanballat's proposal.

---

22. Athas, "The Failure of Davidic Hope?," 241–50.

23. Josephus never mentions Governor Hezekiah. The only evidence we have for him are the coins that bear his name and title ("governor"). See Lee I. Levine, *Jerusalem: Portrait of the City in the Second Temple Period (538 B.C.E.-70 C.E.)* (Philadelphia: Jewish Publication Society, 2002), 39, fig. 9. We may infer his attitude to the coalition by its eventual outcome and the shape of Judean leadership a decade later, when he is conspicuously absent and his governing role is taken instead by the high priest Jaddua (see this section below). Note, there are other Judean coins bearing the name "Hezekiah," but without the title "governor." These are often assumed to belong to Governor Hezekiah, but they exhibit very different iconography, showing they were minted during the Hellenistic era. They thus relate to the high priest Hezekiah at the end of the fourth century BC (see 2.6.2). A certain "Hezekiah son of Shemaiah," mentioned on a fourth-century BC Aramaic ostracon from Jerusalem (*TAHNDT*, A:360, B:120), is probably not be identified with the governor.

24. Appraisals of the various Hezekiah coins sometimes point to the change from the Persian to the Attic weight standard and conclude that the coins must all date to a time after Alexander; cf. Haim Gitler and Catharine ca. Lorber, "A New Chronology for the Yehizkiyah Coins of Judah," *Swiss Numismatic Revue* 87 (2008): 61–82. This, however, underestimates the extent of Greek influence in the Levant from

Since Sanballat II could not convince Jaddua to ally with him, he attempted to isolate him politically. To do this, he married his daughter, Nicaso, to Jaddua's brother, Manasseh. In this way, Sanballat made Manasseh a focal point within Judah and injected his own influence directly into Jerusalem's priestly circles, just as his namesake had done over eighty years earlier (see 1.4.7 above). That he could do this reveals the porous boundary between Judah and Samaria at this time. The elite in both provinces evidently continued to fraternize, despite the isolationist tendencies of some in Jerusalem. Indicative of this is the fact that many Jerusalem priests were already married to Samarian women (*Ant.* 11.312).

More than this, Nicaso's marriage to Manasseh ignited a halakhic scandal. It was not over the marriage of a Judean man to a Samarian woman, for this was evidently taking place *en masse*, and there was nothing in Torah to prohibit it. Rather, it had to do with monogamy and the restrictions on priestly marriage. The Torah permitted polygamy among laypeople, as the examples of the patriarchs Abraham and Jacob demonstrate, and there were laws to ensure the fair treatment of a man's multiple wives (Exod 21:10–11). Deuteronomy 21:15–17 even stipulated that a man was not permitted to privilege the children by his second wife over those by his first wife when it came to the inheritance; primogeniture was to be strictly followed. However, polygamy was not permitted for priests. According to Leviticus 21:7–15, priests were restricted in who they could and could not marry in order to preserve their holiness as those who presented food offerings to God (Lev 21:8). Part of the cultic logic of these laws was that priests had to be monogamous (cf. m. Yoma 1:1; b. Yebam. 59a).[25] The scandal surrounding Manasseh implies that he was already married, which made Nicaso his second wife, thereby compromising his own sacral status.

The evidence for this comes from Josephus, Malachi, and Zechariah 11. According to Josephus, the high priest Jaddua objected to his brother's marriage on the basis that it was "an illegal step concerning the cohabitations of wives" (*Ant.* 11.307).[26] The plural terms in the phrase "the cohabitations of

---

the early fourth century BC, as well as the inclination of locals in the Levant to be part of a Mediterranean world. As further evidence of this, we may point to the overt Greek pictorial imagery on several bullae from the Wadi Daliyeh, some of which were originally on Samarian documents dating decades before Alexander's conquest. See Mary J. W. Leith, *The Wadi Daliyeh Seal Impressions*, DJD 24 (Oxford: Clarendon, 1997).

25. Leviticus 21:7–15 does not overtly state that priests had to be monogamous, but in addressing the other restrictions on priestly marriage, it becomes evident that monogamy was assumed. Cf. the New Testament mandate that male church leaders should be "a husband of one wife" (1 Tim 3:2, 12; Titus 1:6).

26. Whiston's translation of Josephus adds an extra word to this clause by means of editorial brackets, but this significantly alters the original meaning: "transgressing about the marriage of [strange] wives." The Greek text of *Antiquities* does not contain the word "strange" at all. Whiston appears to have

wives" (Gk. *tas tōn gynaikōn synoikēseis*) are crucial here, for they do not simply refer to marriage in a generic way but more specifically to wives (pl.) who were dwelling together (pl.) within one household. In other words, the phrase refers to polygamy. If Manasseh had been a layman, there would have been no issue. But since he was a priest, his polygamy undermined the sacredness of his station. Yet more scandalous was the fact that he was the brother of the high priest—a member of the Zadokite line. Although Jaddua already had a son and heir by this stage, that son was still not of requisite age to participate in the temple cult.[27] This made Manasseh the direct successor to Jaddua at this point in time. It was necessary, therefore, that Manasseh observe all the restrictions on priestly marriage, including those predicated of the high priest himself. As Leviticus 21:7–15 implies, failure to do so would defile the sanctuary and compromise the holiness of the priestly Zadokite line.

The Manasseh Affair, therefore, engendered a damaging crisis within Jerusalem's priestly circles. Indeed, this was probably Sanballat's aim all along. The priests in Jerusalem who were already married to Samarian women were now, by virtue of those marriages, aligned with Manasseh and the reunification movement. It is this pro-Manasseh faction that Malachi has in his sights when he castigates the priests for failing to show proper honor to Yahweh and specifically for betraying the Levitical covenant (Mal 2:1–9). They had turned away from it by supporting Manasseh's marriage and in the process modelled a lackadaisical approach to holiness, which caused many to err along with them.[28] They had jeopardized the whole cult and put their descendants at risk.

Malachi addresses the scandal of Manasseh's marriage to Nicaso with caustic rhetoric:

> Judah has been disloyal.
> An abomination has been committed in Israel and in Jerusalem.
> For Judah has violated the sanctuary of Yahweh, which he loves,
> and married the daughter of a foreign deity.
> May Yahweh cut off the man who does this

---

been influenced by the second reason Josephus gives for the coalition, namely that Manasseh desired "also for this to be the beginning of a coalition with foreigners." Josephus offers this reason out of his first-century knowledge of the hostility between Jews and Samaritans, by which Jews characterized Samaritans as "foreigners" (cf. Sir 50:26; Luke 17:16–18).

27. Jaddua's son, Hezekiah (not to be confused with Governor Hezekiah), was born in 367 BC, meaning he was still a teenager when the Manasseh Affair broke in ca. 350 BC. See 2.6.2 below.

28. The issue is not that the priests had themselves entered illegal marriages but that they supported Manasseh's polygamous marriage, which compromised the holiness of the Jerusalem temple.

>   as a nemesis and a wretch[29]
>   from the tents of Jacob,
>   and from bringing an offering to Yahweh of Ranks.
>   (Mal 2:11–12; cf. 2:14–16)

Several points bear noticing here. First, Malachi points the finger of blame at Judah but sees the scope of the scandal as being "in Israel and in Jerusalem"—an allusion to the political and cultic dimensions of Manasseh's marriage to Nicaso. Intermarriage between prominent families in antiquity was common and had political value. Politically, the Manasseh Affair embroiled all the disparate parts of Israel in the attempt to form a regional coalition, but the eye of the storm was centered on the priesthood in Jerusalem. Indeed, the cultic dimension of the scandal meant that Manasseh's marriage had the potential to render the Jerusalem temple unclean and unfit for service—a situation that would play straight into Sanballat's hands and leave the temple on Mount Gerizim without any functional rival.

Second, "the sanctuary of Yahweh, which he loves" is a clear reference to the temple of Jerusalem, whose legitimacy and viability were now threatened by the impurity of Manasseh's situation. The use of Yahweh's Jerusalem title, "Yahweh of Ranks," backs this up further. Malachi's turn of phrase here is also part of his rhetorical strategy of conscious forgetting. He deliberately avoids mentioning Mount Gerizim as a subtle means of deconstructing its legitimacy. Yahweh loved Jerusalem; he did not love Mount Gerizim.

Third, Malachi equates the violation of Yahweh's sanctuary with Judah marrying the daughter of a foreign deity. Once again, he does not dignify the guilty parties by mentioning their names but rather consciously forgets them as a means of casting darkness rather than light on the culprits. Manasseh is "the man" (sg.) who is labelled "a nemesis and a wretch"; the "daughter" (sg.) whom he marries is Nicaso; and the foreign deity is an allusion to Sanballat, whose name included a theophoric element of the moon god, Sin. It is a dark theological satire on the notion that Sanballat could ever be the champion of Yahweh's people.

Fourth, the cultic ramifications of the marriage are clearly seen in the judgment Malachi passes on Manasseh. The prophet calls on Yahweh to cut Manasseh off to prevent him polluting the temple by making an offering in his

---

29. The Hebrew of this line is obscure, as comparison between the LXX and English versions shows. However, with the emendation of only a single vowel in the MT, which is not original anyway, the text can still be read contextually.

impure state (Mal 2:12). The terms in which he does this are reminiscent of the restrictions in the Torah on priestly marriage (Lev 21:7–15).

Jaddua could not risk his brother's new marriage polluting the Jerusalem temple, so he had Manasseh debarred from the altar. He also could not brook the marginalization of Jerusalem in favor of Mount Gerizim in a new era of Samarian-led unity—a prospect that would scupper the prophetic traditions on which the primacy of Jerusalem was based. Jaddua followed the precedent established by Nehemiah of preserving Jerusalem's primacy at all costs, even if that meant opposing national unity—a theological dilemma that must have been a public relations nightmare for him, in addition to the familial fracture it caused. Nonetheless, Jaddua and the priests allied to him put pressure on Manasseh to give up the marriage and thus pull the plug on the proposed coalition with Samaria. This would keep Jerusalem politically insignificant and defer hope for a reunification of Israel. Yet it would preserve the sanctity of the Jerusalem temple and keep alive the concept of "Israel" as defined by prophetic and Davidic traditions. For Judeans who did not cling to the prophetic traditions with any great principle, the benefits of a coalition far outweighed the potential relegation of Jerusalem. But this was an outcome that Jaddua, many of his priestly associates, and those with Davidic allegiances could not countenance. If Manasseh failed to divorce Nicaso, Jaddua would have no choice but to expel his brother from Jerusalem.

Manasseh was unwilling to divorce Nicaso, presumably because of the increased social standing it gave him. The situation reached breaking point when Jaddua (the implied writer in Zech 11:4–17) expelled his brother from Jerusalem, along with at least two of his prominent supporters (Zech 11:8). It was an action akin to Nehemiah's expulsion of Jeshua some eighty years earlier (Neh 13:28 [see 1.4.7 above]). The disqualification left Manasseh without standing as a priest and, as such, neutralized him in the political jostling.

Manasseh's desire for power now came to the fore. After the loss of his priestly status and his position as current heir to the high priesthood, he began to entertain the notion of divorcing Nicaso so that he could return to Jerusalem and resume his priestly station. This potential reversal shows us that Manasseh was only conditionally committed to Jerusalem's primacy and the concomitant prophetic traditions. He was willing to face whichever direction best promoted his own status.

Before Manasseh could divorce Nicaso and deal a serious blow to plans to create a regional bloc under Samarian leadership, Sanballat tried a different tactic. Sanballat did not need to work hard on winning over those in Jerusalem with little regard for Jerusalem's primacy, for they could be easily convinced of the viability of an Israelite coalition centered on Samaria and the temple at Mount Gerizim. In the strange political climate of the seeming collapse of imperial power, this was the most expedient political path Yahwists could take. The closure of the shrine to Qos (Idumean Yahweh) at Makkedah at around this time shows this kind of consolidating pragmatism amongst the Idumeans.[30] The isolationist approach of Jaddua was less pragmatic. But Sanballat recognized Manasseh's oscillation as a potential way of influencing those in the political and theological center at Jerusalem, who only held lightly to the prophetic traditions and Jerusalem's primacy. Their main motivation was the protection of their priesthood, which gave them social authority and a living drawn from tithes. Jerusalem was, however, still a small town, and Judah was far less densely populated than the Samarian hills. The tithes brought to Jerusalem, therefore, were modest. At this stage of history, when bartering was still the major mode of economic transaction, coins tended to be used for official purposes, such as taxation and tithes. Compared to Samaria, the number of Judean coins from this era is meager, demonstrating a lower population and a thinner base from which priests could draw tithes.

Sanballat II leveraged this reality by offering Manasseh the high priesthood at Mount Gerizim as an inducement not to divorce Nicaso or return to Jerusalem (*Ant.* 11.310–311). This would bring the Zadokite line to Mount Gerizim and effectively detach it from the primacy of Jerusalem and the prophetic traditions. Not only would this be a promotion from Manasseh's previous position as an associate priest in Jerusalem, but it also promised a wealthier future for Manasseh as his authority would be over more people and his tithes drawn from a wider base. In a regional coalition this base would include Samaria, Judah, Idumea, and Ammon. This motivation is aptly captured in Zechariah 11:5 by the sentiment expressed by those who abuse the flock: "Blessed be Yahweh that I am wealthy!"

Yet there was a catch. As long as Manasseh was married to two women, the Torah stipulated that his sacral status was still compromised. Furthermore, since Nicaso was not Manasseh's first wife, the rights of primary inheritance would not accrue to her children but to the children of Manasseh's first wife. This would mean that the high priesthood at Mount Gerizim would eventually pass from Manasseh to his eldest son by his first wife. To avoid this, Sanballat convinced Manasseh to divorce his first wife so that her children

---

30. An Aramaic ostracon (AL 283) refers to a "strip of land" associated with the "house of Yahu" at Makkedah at this time. This probably implies that the "house" was no longer functional and that Idumean Qos was now identified with Israelite Yahweh, presumably under the pressure of Samarian leadership. See Lemaire, "New Aramaic Ostraca from Idumea," 416–17.

would be disinherited. The result was that Manasseh became a monogamist once again and, therefore, fit to serve as priest at an altar. It also ensured that Sanballat's grandson by Nicaso would one day inherit the high priesthood at Mount Gerizim as a legitimate Zadokite—a figure of true national unity (cf. *Ant.* 11.324).

Although many must have viewed the divorce as unfortunate, the political gains it engendered were seen to outweigh it. The incident was, therefore, couched as a necessary evil for the greater good of Israel and was popularly hailed as having the approval of Yahweh (cf. Mal 2:17). Yet these developments drew the fierce ire of Malachi:

> This is the second thing you do: covering the altar of Yahweh with tears, weeping and sighing because he no longer turns towards the offering to receive it from your hands with pleasure.
>
> You ask, "Why?"
>
> Because Yahweh was witness between you and the wife of your youth, whom you have betrayed, though she was your partner and lawful wife. He [Sanballat II] has not made them [Samaria and Judah, or Manasseh and Nicaso] one—he has but flesh and breath! And what does that one person [Sanballat II] seek? Divine offspring? Guard your spirit and do not betray the wife of your youth. "For he [Manasseh] who divorced and expelled [his wife]," Yahweh, the God of Israel, has said, "has covered his own garment with violence," Yahweh of Ranks has said. "Guard your spirit and do not betray." (Mal 2:13–16)

Once again, Malachi employs conscious forgetting by going out of his way to avoid the names of Sanballat, Manasseh, or Nicaso—so much so that the syntax of his oracle becomes quite tortured. But once this device is understood in the context of the historical developments, it is clear that Malachi found the schemes of Sanballat and Manasseh worthy of divine wrath.

Sanballat's gambit proved a political masterstroke. Manasseh divorced his first wife and defected to Samaria, and along with him went most of the priests who had either married Samarian women or who were not partisan to Jaddua's conservative agenda (*Ant.* 11.311–312). Like Manasseh, they were drawn no doubt by the prospect of more lucrative circumstances in the north. The priesthood had become a profession for personal gain rather than of sacral service to the deity. If Judeans also began worshipping at Mount Gerizim, as would now seem likely, then the already modest operation of the Jerusalem temple would be threatened with irrelevance. Thus, in defecting, Manasseh and his associates were consigning Jerusalem to a future of impoverishment and potential dereliction. In light of these developments, Manasseh was dubbed the "useless shepherd who abandons the sheep" (Zech 11:15–17), while Sanballat II was characterized as one who buys the sheep only to exploit them (Zech 11:5).³¹

The wholesale defection brought priests and Levites to Mount Gerizim, which boosted its profile over Jerusalem, especially as a bastion for Torah. This, in turn, improved the prospects of the coalition under Sanballat's leadership. Malachi, however, interpreted the defection as a violation of the Levitical covenant:

> "But you have defected from the way.
> You have caused many to stumble in the Torah.
> You have ruined the Levitical covenant,"
> Yahweh of Ranks has said. (Mal 2:8)

According to Malachi, Manasseh and his cohort betrayed their Levitical commitments by abandoning the one true place of worship in Jerusalem. This necessarily meant that they formally gave up any commitment to the prophetic traditions preserved in Jerusalem and threw considerably more political and theological weight behind Sanballat's pan-Israelite agenda focused on Samaria and Mount Gerizim. And yet, despite seeming to uphold the unity demanded by Torah, Malachi argued it had compromised the observance of Torah. Corrupt priestly power had won out over the prophetic voice.

In the mind of Jaddua and his conservative allies, this made any cooperation with Samaria impossible. Jaddua's refusal to comply with the coalition was poignantly captured in Zechariah 11:

---

31. As Josephus's account implies, there was probably a delay in Manasseh's installation at Mount Gerizim. Josephus pins the delay on the need for Sanballat to gain the approval of the Persian monarch and then to build the temple on Mount Gerizim. But this claim is the result of Josephus's attempt to make sense of his own confused chronology. The temple on Mount Gerizim had been operating for a century by this time and must have had an officiating high priest with lifelong tenure. Manasseh would presumably have had to wait until the incumbent's death to succeed him. This also explains why Manasseh could be both an existing "shepherd" expelled by the implied writer of Zech 11:8 and the future "useless shepherd who abandons the sheep" (11:15–17). We do not know if, at this stage, the high priesthood at Mount Gerizim was hereditary. Current Samaritan tradition claims that all Samaritan high priests until 1624 were an unbroken chain of descent from Eleazar, son of Aaron (after 1624 they were descendants of Ithamar, son of Aaron). Manasseh is included in this chain. Documentation apparently existed in antiquity relating to the priestly succession, but it has not survived. The veracity of this hereditary tradition is, therefore, equivocal. See Alan D. Crown, "Samaritan Literature and Its Manuscripts," *BJRL* 76.1 (1994): 23–24.

So I said, "I will not herd you. Let the dying die. Let the lost be lost. And let the ones that are left eat each other's flesh." I then took my staff, "Goodwill," and snapped it in order to revoke the covenant I had forged with all the people. So that day it was revoked....I then snapped my second staff, "Coalition," to revoke the brotherhood between Judah and Israel. (Zech 11:9–11a, 14)

The breaking of the symbolic staffs was an act of execration—a cursing of the coalition and the proposed "brotherhood" between the two provinces. This was a reversal of the prophetic sign-act in Ezekiel 37:15–28 in which the aspirational reunification of Israel had been symbolized by joining two staffs and premised on Davidic kingship and the exclusivity of the Jerusalem temple. These premises had no place in Sanballat's coalition. The breaking of the "brotherhood" staff in Zechariah 11 also alluded to the irreconcilable rift between the brothers, Jaddua and Manasseh, and was undoubtedly behind the choice of words in Malachi 2:10 (see this section above) and the allusion to the brothers Jacob and Esau (Mal 1:2–4).

In addition to condemning Sanballat II and the priests who defected, Malachi criticized laypeople who only half-heartedly promoted the interests of Jerusalem. For Malachi, these people had devalued the standing of Jerusalem, vacillated towards Mount Gerizim, and created the conditions that allowed Sanballat to capitalize and the Jerusalem temple to face the prospect of closure:

"When you present a blind animal to sacrifice, is it not wrong?
When you present a lame or injured animal, is it not wrong?
Bring it to your governor [Sanballat II]!
Would he be pleased with you, or show you favor?"
Yahweh of Ranks has said.

"Well then, beseech the face of the deity,
so that he may show us favor."

"This is the work of your own hands!
Will he now show you favor?"
Yahweh of Ranks has said.
"If only one of you would shut the doors,
and not light up 'my altar' for nothing.
I have no pleasure in you,"
Yahweh of Ranks has said,
"and I will not accept an offering from your hands." (Mal 1:8–10)

Yet again, Malachi's rhetorical device of conscious forgetting and avoiding names is seen in the veiled allusion to Sanballat II as "your governor" and perhaps even to Mount Gerizim as a temple that Yahweh desires to see shut down.[32]

There is archaeological evidence that, around this time, a new building phase was begun on the top of Mount Gerizim, consisting of a new residential quarter to the south of the sacred precinct. The whole operation on Mount Gerizim thus received a materially appreciable boost, which gave the complex more pulling power across the region. Over subsequent decades, more monumental installations were built to facilitate Mount Gerizim's growing importance and the increase in the number of worshippers.[33] Sanballat succeeded in promoting Mount Gerizim as the one true center of Yahwistic worship for all "Israel" and laid the groundwork for a new Israelite political entity.

Quite telling are the Samarian coins from this era, which are stamped with the name "Jeroboam"—a significant name in northern Israelite heritage, recalling the first non-Davidic king of the Northern Kingdom of Israel. Considering the proliferation of names drawn from the Pentateuch in the Samarian onomasticon of this time—a testament to the authority that the Torah had attained in Samaria—the use of "Jeroboam," known only in the prophetic traditions, is particularly striking.[34] Nothing specific is known about this Jeroboam figure on the Samarian coins, but as a name of historic significance, it is possible that the most powerful man in the region, Sanballat II, adopted it as a prospective throne name.[35] After all, only the most powerful had the authorization to mint coins. Persian monarchs often took a new name on their accession as a nod to their Achaemenid heritage. It is not inconceivable that Sanballat, having interpreted the times as being of political transition and fresh promise, opted to take a new, overtly Israelite name laden with historic significance—known in Judah as well as Samaria—in place of his own foreign name ("Sanballat" comes from the Akkadian, *Sin-uballit*, meaning "May [the

---

32. A reference to Mount Gerizim here is not certain, since the text has Yahweh of Ranks (a Jerusalem title) refer to "my altar." There is emotive rhetoric here, but whether it expresses exasperation with Jerusalem or criticism of Mount Gerizim is debatable.

33. Some of the new installations at Mount Gerizim from subsequent decades may also have been built to accommodate a moving population after the decimation of Samaria in the wake of the Andromachus Affair (see 2.2.4).

34. Knoppers, *Jews and Samaritans*, 118–19, 127–29.

35. Eshel ("The Governors of Samaria in the Fifth and Fourth Centuries B.C.E.," 230) proposes that this Jeroboam was a high official or a high priest at Mount Gerizim. He does not specifically consider the possible connection to Sanballat because he does not consider the full implications of the Manasseh Affair.

moon god] Sin give life").³⁶ Malachi sharply insults Sanballat by alluding to the "foreign god" in his name (Mal 2:11), showing that there was a degree of odium associated with such a foreign appellation.

The obverse of one of the Jeroboam coins depicts the head of an elegant female figure. The reverse displays two male figures facing each other, the left figure holding a branch and the right holding an object that could be either flora (e.g., a lily) or a crown. The inscription "Jeroboam" (*yrbʿm*) divides the two figures. Do they pictorially represent the notion of a coalition? Do they represent Jacob and Esau, or Samaria and Judah? Is attention being drawn to the name "Jeroboam" not just as an historic name but also for its Hebrew meaning, "May he increase the people?" Is one of the figures Sanballat II being identified as a new Jeroboam? Is one of the figures Manasseh as the new high priest at Mount Gerizim? Is the elegant female head on the obverse perhaps Nicaso, who embodied the coalition?³⁷ There are so many ways to interpret the imagery, but if any of these possibilities holds, the minting of this coin would have signaled a new era with a new authority connected to Israel's heritage, not just Judah's. Ultimately, these possibilities tantalize us, so we can say only that the coin and the others like it are suggestive. Nonetheless, even if the Jeroboam of these coins was just a high official, the use of the name is still a barometer of emerging nationalism.

This pan-Israelite nationalism meant the idea of a new unifying covenant under a single leader had immense popularity in Judean and Samarian society. It had a groundswell of support, as it seemed to recover the greatness of Israel in centuries past. Malachi's rhetoric implies that the desire for such a covenant was commendable and congruent in principle with the divine will, but the conditions under which it was proceeding were misguided and would engender divine wrath. Yahweh's purposes for reunifying the nation would proceed very differently:

> "See, I am sending my messenger,
> and he will clear the way before me.
> Suddenly, the lord whom you are seeking will enter his palace,
> the messenger of the covenant you are proposing—look, he is coming,"
> Yahweh of Ranks has said.

---

36. Eshel, "The Governors of Samaria," 230.
37. Although many Samarian coins depict the head of the Greek goddess Athena, she is depicted with enough paraphernalia to identify her as the Greek goddess. The female head on the obverse of this Jeroboam coin, though, is elegant but unadorned. Since this would be most unusual for a representation of the goddess, it seems to be a deliberate replacement of the head of Athena.

> "But who will endure the day of his coming?
> Who will stand when he appears?
> For he will be like a refiner's fire,
> like a launderer's soap.
> He will sit and refine, purifying silver;
> he will purify the sons of Levi,
> he will filter them like gold and silver,
> so that they become righteous presenters of offerings.
> Then the offering of Judah and Jerusalem will satisfy Yahweh,
> as in days of old and yesteryear....
> "Since I, Yahweh, have not changed,
> you, sons of Jacob, have not come to an end.
> Since the days of your ancestors,
> you have strayed from my regulations, and have not kept them.
> Return to me, and I will return to you," says Yahweh of Ranks.
> (Mal 3:1–4, 6–7a)

The image of refining silver and gold might allude to the process of striking new coinage as an act of newfound sovereignty. At the very least it symbolizes the creation of new wealth, but Malachi appropriates it as an image of judgment. The implication was that Yahweh still intended to reunify Israel in accordance with his historic purposes. But this would not occur in line with Sanballat's plans, which simply replayed the mistakes of the past. Malachi was less despondent than the prophet of Zechariah 11 for the reunification of the nation, but both prophets interpreted Sanballat's coalition as putting the nation in grave danger. Zechariah 11 saw a coming punitive judgment, while Malachi saw judgment as both punitive and restorative. Both images would play pivotal roles in the ministries of John the Baptist and Jesus in the first century.

1.7.4 THEOLOGY AND SCRIBAL CULTURE

With the defection of so many priests and Levites to Mount Gerizim, Jerusalem was left as a small conservative bastion in the highlands of Judah. On the one hand, this isolated Jerusalem in the new political environment and threatened it with a dim future. On the other hand, it ensured at least the temporary survival of the prophetic and Davidic traditions alongside the Torah as markers of Judean identity. This was in clear distinction to the Samarians, for whom the Torah alone held authoritative status. The defection had flushed many (but not all) progressive elements out of Jerusalem's priestly circles, leaving those who promulgated the prophetic traditions in the clear majority. This does not mean that Judah was now devoid of people sympathetic to the Samarian cause, for there had been no forcible ejection of sympathizers—only inducements for priests whose loyalties could be bought (cf. Zech 11:5). Judeans who preferred political pragmatism over principled theological resistance undoubtedly remained. So although events left the Jerusalem temple in the hands of conservative elements committed to the prophetic traditions, the fault lines in Judean society more broadly did not disappear.

The sense of resignation wrought by these developments comes through strongly in Zechariah 11:4–17. The unity of all Israel was conceptually desirable, in accordance with both the Law and prophetic traditions. It was Samaria, however, that was steering Yahwists towards unity, and this was being pursued by consciously leaving prophetic traditions behind and marginalizing Jerusalem. The long-term prospect of destitution for Jerusalem's priests was now very real and must have made restoration of any Davidic descendants to power seem utterly implausible. On their own, conservative priests and their loyal followers were too weak to offer any substantive resistance, either armed or political. They had been left without a place at the table of this new political concord.

The only means conservatives in Jerusalem had for resisting their marginalization was theological persuasion. Through the renewed scribal activity of a class of literati, they could preserve and proliferate the prophetic traditions, which justified the primacy of Jerusalem and condemned the northern tribes of Israel for apostasy. They needed to show theologically and historically that the God of Abraham, Isaac, and Jacob, who revealed himself to Moses and constituted Israel as a single nation under the Law, was also the God who made an eternal covenant with David, who dwelt in the temple at Jerusalem, and who had spoken through the prophets to the northern tribes as well as to Judah. There was, therefore, a re-engagement of the prophetic tradition—scribal activity that transmitted past traditions but also brought them to bear on the present through redaction and recontextualization, thus creatively framing new hopes for the future. This centrist scriptural strategy, with both conservative and progressive elements, could itself be labelled prophetic, proceeding on the notion that God had not ceased his revelation with Moses, nor even with the previous prophets, but was continuing to guide Israel through new prophets and the prophetic activity of a scribal culture in Jerusalem—something reflected in the first-person voice and the depiction of Yahweh in Zechariah 11:4–17.

Since the primacy of Mount Gerizim was predicated on a commitment to Torah alone, it is unlikely that prophetic figures arose in the Samarian context. But this does not mean that Samarians were not also engaged in scribal activity. On the contrary, the primacy of Mount Gerizim was probably written into the Samaritan Pentateuch at around this time. But the scribal strategy needed by Samarians was necessarily minimalist, invested in a conservative program of preserving Torah alone to the deliberate exclusion of prophetic and wisdom traditions. By contrast, those in Jerusalem needed divine revelations beyond the Torah to sustain Jerusalem's primacy. Ironically, this meant that the onetime syncretistic Yahwists of Samaria had to become even more theologically conservative than the most principled conservatives in Jerusalem.

The conservatives in Jerusalem thus adopted a more centrist approach, looking both to past tradition and the notion of God's progressive and ongoing revelation through the prophets and other writings. A canonical consciousness emerged, which sought to develop and collate authoritative writings. Scribes were accordingly trained via a curriculum of these writings. This included the collation and redaction of classic prophetic traditions, applying their message from ages past to the current context with renewed prophetic authority. Though the Book of the Twelve Prophets would not be finalized for some decades yet, the stitching together of these old prophetic traditions and their recontextualization was begun in this late Persian era, with the "twelveness" of their witness being a testament to God sending prophets to all Israel. Wisdom collections associated with Davidic kings were brought together to guide the faithful in living wisely under the fear of Yahweh, the God of David, Solomon, and Hezekiah (Proverbs). Psalms were collected for communal use to put expressions of both Torah and Davidic traditions on the lips of the common person, encouraging pilgrimage to and worship in Jerusalem. These were collected into five books, just like the Torah, and prefaced with two psalms that promoted the authority of Torah (Ps 1) and Jerusalem as "Zion"—the "holy mountain" where Yahweh had once installed his anointed son, the Davidic king (Ps 2). In expressing this Zion theology, the kingdom of David was equated with the kingdom of Yahweh himself. We see, in other words, the first concerted framing of a messianic eschatology, which believed Yahweh would one day overcome all obstacles that prevented the reinstatement of a Davidic kingdom and establish this kingdom as an empire to rule the nations. And since God was now understood as transcendent to creation (see 1.2.3 above), his rule was necessarily cosmic. Over time, therefore, the vision of the future that would come from Jerusalem was bigger than just the Israelite nation. It was universal. Whereas Samaria would embed the anchor of its identity in the past through an outlook of Torah alone, Jerusalem would look both to the past and the future for God's revelation, but with an anchor resting in the future saving acts of God.[38] It was a centrist theological strategy with elements of both theological conservatism and progressiveness.

1.7.5 THE REASSERTION OF PERSIAN POWER

Losing Trans-Euphrates and Cyprus after the loss of Egypt came as a shock to Artaxerxes III. He was, however, determined to recover all these territories. Over the next few years, he built up a considerable army and marched on Trans-Euphrates in 345 BC. If the Phoenicians, now backed by Greek mercenaries, had stood their ground, the Persians might have been repelled again, allowing the Israelite coalition to solidify into a new territorial entity while Jerusalem slid into obscurity. As it turned out, the coalition was short-lived and never achieved its goal, for the Tennes Revolt fell apart.

It was all due to the perfidy of Tennes himself. The Sidonian king sold out his own city and allies by opening Sidon's gates to the approaching Persian king, perhaps intimidated by the size of Artaxerxes's army. Rather than surrender, the Sidonians put their own city and its fleet (made from local cedar) to the flame, preferring to "burn their bridges" rather than submit again to colonial rule (Diodorus Siculus, *Bib. hist.* 16.43.1–45.6). So great was the conflagration that, in Diodorus's account, Artaxerxes considered the city a "funeral pyre" (Diodorus Siculus, *Bib. hist.* 16.45.5). The calamitous events were summarily captured in the vivid words of Zechariah 11:1: "Open, O Lebanon, your doors, that fire may consume your cedars."[39] This grim end was juxtaposed in the very next verses (Zech 11:2–3) by allusions to the earlier destruction of the Persian "paradise" at the outset of the Tennes Revolt, which now became an image for the downfall of the revolt itself.

Determined to strike terror into the whole region, Artaxerxes was merciless. After killing Tennes, he went on a rampage through Sidon, killing civilians and deporting survivors to Mesopotamia. A small cuneiform tablet from

---

38. Fantalkin and Tal ("Judah and Its Neighbors," 171–82) argue that the canonization process of biblical literature began partially as a response to Egypt's independence from Persia in ca. 398 BC. This makes sense of some biblical literature but does not account for the full range of factors. It is also based on the low chronology for Ezra's mission (398 BC) rather than the earlier date (458 BC), which makes much better sense of the rise of Torah among all Yahwists in the Levant immediately prior to the building of the Mount Gerizim temple. The impetus in canonical consciousness that Fantalkin and Tal observe is better seen as having two stages: (1) the mission of Ezra in 458 BC, which established Torah in Judah and Samaria; and (2) the failure of the Israelite coalition in ca. 345 BC.

39. Theophrastus of Eresos, a contemporary of the events, states that the Phoenicians and Syrians made their triremes exclusively from the local cedar (*Enquiry into Plants* 5.7.1–2).

Babylon (*PE* 9.76) records the arrival of Sidonian captives in October 345 BC, followed shortly thereafter by Sidonian women forced into the king's service as slaves and concubines. The Phoenician efforts had come to naught, and this may be partially reflected in the sarcastic tone of Zechariah 9:2, which ridicules the wisdom of Tyre and Sidon in the context of an invading force.[40]

Upon the fall of Sidon, all resistance to Persia in Cilicia and Trans-Euphrates effectively ceased, and the region again came under Persian control (Diodorus Siculus, *Bib. hist.* 16.45.6). Artaxerxes did not wreak the same havoc in Tyre as he had in Sidon. Tyre's natural defenses as a small rocky island half a mile out to sea meant that conquering it would take far too long when Artaxerxes was more intent on retaking Egypt. Besides, Artaxerxes needed a functioning Phoenician port to resource a fleet after the Sidonians had destroyed their own fleet and port.

The Israelite coalition might not have been overtly seditious in purpose, but it nonetheless came to a swift end. Keen to avoid a similar fate to Sidon, the provinces did not put up resistance to Artaxerxes's forces. Still, the Persians secured the region with a show of strength, especially after finding the Persian "paradise" at Ramat Raḥel, south of Jerusalem, dismantled. The Persians destroyed Jericho, En Gedi, and Jabel Nimra (in Idumea) and reoccupied the palatial administrative center at Lachish and the nearby network of forts.[41] A portion of the Judean population, and probably also of the Samarian, was removed to Hyrcania at this time, either as a punitive deportation or as soldiers in the imperial army. Zechariah 11:6, which bemoans people "going out into the hands of their neighbors and their king," alludes to these measures and interprets them as divinely ordained consequences for the failure of Israel's "shepherds" (i.e., the priests and governors). The characterization of the people as a "flock for the slaughter" (Zech 11:4, 7) also probably alludes to the fate of many who lost their lives as Artaxerxes III took back control.

Even if some in Judah viewed these measures as divinely ordained, their harshness did not endear the Persians to them. The Tennes Revolt had broken out because the Persians had come to be seen as oppressive overlords, and this heavy hand did not dispel that notion. By removing people to Hyrcania, the

---

40. Zechariah 9:1–8 is a highly polished but much redacted text whose original kernel goes back to the march of Darius I on his way to Egypt in 519 BC. However, it was reworked after the Israelite Coalition, from which the sarcasm of 9:2 comes, and the invasion of Alexander, as the subtext of 9:3 alludes to his siege of Tyre in 332 BC (see 2.2.3).

41. Cf. Fantalkin and Tal, "Judah and Its Neighbors," 144, 161–65; Kreimerman and Sandhaus, "Political Trends," 125. The excavators of Jebel Nimra (near the Cave of the Patriarchs in Hebron) proposed its destruction as part of Alexander's conquest, but this would represent an anomaly. It should, rather, be connected with the reassertion of Persian sovereignty in ca. 345 BC.

Persians were employing the same colonial strategy of forced migration that the Assyrians and Babylonians had used. The legacy of Cyrus, which thrived on its juxtaposition to such policies and had earned him the title "messiah" among Judeans (Isa 45:1), had now been reversed, making the Persians indistinguishable from the brutal regimes that preceded them.

Re-subjugation devastated Sanballat II's plans for a unified Israelite state. He no longer appears as governor of Samaria after this time, meaning he was probably removed from office—either exiled or executed. We have no knowledge about whether the Persians fulfilled Malachi's execration against Manasseh (Mal 2:12). Sanballat's son, Jeshua, became the new governor, which reveals some level of Samarian cooperation with the resurgent Persians. Yet the Samarians had tasted freedom on their own terms, and they would savor its flavor during the tumultuous decade that followed.

If the Persians had removed Sanballat II, there is every reason to expect that they also removed Hezekiah from governing Judah. The high priest Jaddua's opposition to the coalition gained him the trust of Artaxerxes, and it seems he was appointed as de facto governor of Judah in place of Hezekiah. A decade later, when Alexander arrived in the Levant (332 BC), Jaddua was the civic leader of Judah, and his purported interactions with Alexander confirm his clear loyalty to the Persian regime (see 2.2.3 below). Under his leadership, Jerusalem seems to have replaced Ramat Raḥel as the administrative center for the collection of taxes.[42]

From Jaddua's perspective, the Persian reconquest must have seemed a godsend, for it ensured that Sanballat's coalition, which threatened to consign Jerusalem to oblivion, was itself consigned to oblivion. Samaria and Judah were now once again separate provinces within the satrapy of Trans-Euphrates. Jerusalem was still weak compared to Mount Gerizim, but the reassertion of Persian hegemony halted Jerusalem's slide into obscurity. This did not, however, obviate the need for Jerusalem to keep developing its scribal culture and prophetic outlook in opposition to the Samarian agenda.

To ensure quick regional stability, Artaxerxes III combined Trans-Euphrates with Cilicia under the oversight of the Cilician satrap, Mazaeus (or Mazday).[43] Mazaeus's coins, which blend Persian and Greek styles, feature his name and frequently portray a predatory lion, sometimes above the turreted

---

42. This is demonstrated by the sudden accumulation of "Yehud"-stamped jar handles in Jerusalem, rather than at Ramat Raḥel. See Honigman, "Searching for the Social Location of Literate Judean Elites," 207.

43. Briant, *From Cyrus to Alexander*, 709, 713.

wall of a city, probably Sidon.⁴⁴ Some of these coins also appear in Samaria and Judah and might explain some of the lion imagery in Zechariah 11:3. One of Mazaeus's coins issued in Samaria depicts the Persian king on his throne with the winged glory of Ahura Mazda and Mazaeus's name (abbreviated) on the reverse—seemingly a direct repudiation of a united Israel under Yahweh. Artaxerxes also coordinated the re-subjugation of Cyprus so that by 343 BC he had a solid base from which to launch an attempt to reconquer Egypt.

If Artaxerxes was to deal a mortal blow to the Mediterranean "pole," he needed to weaken both ends of the maritime axis. It was crucial that he recover Egypt and leave the Greeks in their perpetual state of rivalry and fragmentation. He had already struck a significant blow by bringing the Greek mercenaries used in the Tennes Revolt over to his side. These mercenaries brought with them considerable knowledge of Egypt itself, since they had been stationed there before the rebellion. Artaxerxes also convinced some of the Greek cities to send him yet more mercenaries (Diodorus Siculus, *Bib. hist.* 16.44.1–4), showing that nationalism was not the sole factor in determining allegiance—economics was just as powerful a reason. If, with numerical superiority, Artaxerxes could overpower Egypt, he would reattach it to his empire and regain Egypt's enormous revenue stream based on its perennial Nile economy. He would thus divert the wealth of Egypt and Phoenicia back towards Mesopotamia, breaking some of the magnetism that had grown in the Mediterranean.

In 343 BC Artaxerxes invaded Egypt. Despite some initial setbacks, his numerical superiority and the knowledge of his Greek mercenaries allowed him to overwhelm the country. Nectanebo II (360–342 BC) had poured considerable wealth into expanding temples throughout the country, including the expansion of the temple of Khnum over the grounds of the Yahwistic temple at Elephantine. But he seems not to have had the stomach for much resistance, and before long he fled south to Nubia. By 342 BC Artaxerxes had recaptured Egypt and installed a new satrap in Memphis. Artaxerxes's vizier, Bagoas, ensured the diversion of Egypt's revenue into Persian coffers, including his own. In fact, over the next decade Bagoas was to become so wealthy that just the apparel in his residence at Susa was said to have been worth 1,000 talents (Plutarch, *Alex.* 39.6).⁴⁵

---

44. Curtis and Tallis, *Forgotten Empire*, 205–6, figs. 358–62.
45. In modern terms, this would be the equivalent of approximately US$1.5 billion. While this is exaggerated out of all proportion, we should also remember that clothing in the ancient world was far more valuable than today, since it took far longer to produce without modern technologies. Only the wealthy tended to have many sets of clothes.

Although Artaxerxes reclaimed Egypt, he did not capture the hearts and minds of Egyptians or of the people of Trans-Euphrates. And his Greek mercenaries were not there out of loyalty to him but out of expediency and economic gain. Artaxerxes was still seen as a colonial oppressor, which meant a considerable portion of his empire was comprised of unwilling subjects who resented Persian authority. This was aggravated by both Artaxerxes's heavy military hand and the rapaciousness of his colonial staff, who used the reassertion of Persian hegemony to fleece the local population. The Demotic Chronicle from Egypt characterized the reconquest as the "ruination" of the Egyptians, whose "ponds and islands are filled with weeping" and whose houses were stolen from them (*PE* 9.79).

Artaxerxes's vizier, Bagoas, was particularly singled out in later sources for his supreme opportunism (Diodorus Siculus, *Bib. hist.* 16.50.8; 16.51.2). Diodorus calls him "exceptionally daring and impatient of propriety" (Diodorus Siculus, *Bib. hist.* 16.47.4) and "a eunuch in physical fact, but a militant rogue in disposition" (*Bib. hist.* 17.5.3). Josephus corroborates this portrait, though he confuses Bagoas the vizier with Governor Bagohi of Judah from seventy years earlier (*Ant.* 11.297–301).[46] It is still possible to untangle his testimony and deduce that Bagoas desecrated the Jerusalem temple by entering it. He also imposed a hefty levy on sacrifices made at the altar. This tax lasted seven years (*Ant.* 11.301), which coincides precisely with the period between the campaign in Egypt (343 BC) and Bagoas's own death (336 BC)—a time in which Bagoas was outranked only by the Great King himself. If Josephus's claim that the tax was fifty shekels per statutory sacrifice is correct, then the sum was exorbitant in the extreme—approximately five months wages. As a comparison, the annual temple tax that was levied on Jews for centuries was only half a shekel (cf. Exod 30:13; Matt 17:24).[47]

Bagoas's tax strained the already impoverished operations in Jerusalem and exploited the piety of Judeans for whom sacrifice was theologically and culturally vital. The tax was imposed on the two statutory daily sacrifices, so it was unlikely to have been imposed onto the sacrifices of common worshippers. Nonetheless, if Josephus's figure is to be believed, the cult was costing close to a year's wages per day to run, so the expense must have been defrayed to

---

46. "Bagoas" is derived from the Greek rendition of the Persian name Bagavahya, while "Bagohi" is the Aramaic equivalent of the same name. To distinguish the two men, I have adopted "Bagoas" for the Persian vizier, which is the Hellenized form of the name used by Josephus. This Persian eunuch Bagoas is not to be confused with another Persian eunuch named Bagoas, who became an intimate of Alexander the Great.

47. The half-shekel tax seems to have been an increase on the third of a shekel imposed during the time of Nehemiah (Neh 10:32–33[10:33–34 MT]).

commoners by increasing the cost of sacrificial animals. Worship at Jerusalem became an expensive enterprise. In response, the worshipper could take the financial hit by continuing to sacrifice. Alternatively, the worshipper could forego sacrifice and save the money but thereby underfund the cult, forfeit the means of attaining right standing with Yahweh, and risk divine disfavor. This was a serious predicament that made the pursuit of righteousness a means of suffering—a subversion of the entire theological system that the Torah (and the prophets) established.

For Jerusalem's priests and Levites, the tax meant effectively relinquishing most of the tithes from which they drew their living. Some temple personnel may have given up full-time service to pursue lay work for the sake of making ends meet, undoing Nehemiah's efforts to reverse this very circumstance a century earlier (Neh 13:10–13). Others may simply have given up service in Jerusalem altogether and sought employment at Mount Gerizim instead. We have no information about whether a similar tax had been imposed there, though it is likely. Even so, Samaria was in a fiscally more robust situation to cope with it. Its ability to defray costs across a wider population would have made Mount Gerizim a far more feasible center at which to worship than Jerusalem.

The oracle in Malachi 3:8–12 responds to this situation. Through a classic Deuteronomistic theology of retribution, Malachi encouraged full participation in Jerusalem's cultic system, despite the cost, to ensure the temple remained viable and to receive the blessing of economic security from God in return:

> "Should a human swindle God?
> Yet you are swindling me.
> You say, 'How are we swindling you?'
> In tithe and donation!
> You are suffering under a curse,
> yet it's me whom you, the whole nation, are swindling.
> Bring the tithe to the storehouse,
> so that there may be nourishment in my house.
> Test me in this."
> Yahweh of Ranks has said,
> "See if I do not open for you the floodgates of heaven
> and shower you with more than enough blessings,
> repelling your devourer,
> so that he does not ruin the fruit of your soil,

or lay waste the vine of your field,"
Yahweh of Ranks has said. (Mal 3:8–11)

Bagoas's predatory tax had made loyalty to the Jerusalem temple unsustainably costly. But Malachi insisted that full participation in the temple cult would bring divine blessing, which would overcome the economic burdens. How many heeded such calls is unknown.

The restoration of Persian control had stemmed the tide that had been rolling against Jerusalem, but Bagoas's tax brought it flooding back again. The Persians had forsaken their initial beneficence, becoming a foreign regime that wickedly exploited the innocent and turned their piety into a means of oppression. Artaxerxes III's martial ferocity and the avarice of his colonial staff sowed yet more seeds of discontent in soil that was already sprouting disaffection. He had delivered a blow to the maritime axis, but not a killer blow. Its resolve to work against him remained unbroken. Persian control, therefore, was a veneer, and it would not be long before insurgence would arise once again. In Judah, this began to take the form of eschatological thinking—a hope that looked for divine intervention to overthrow the oppressive weight of the foreign regime and allow a kingdom of God under a righteous Davidic ruler to blossom once again (cf. Zech 9:9–17). Artaxerxes had not reversed the magnetism of the new Mediterranean pole. He merely ensured that the desire for freedom from Persia had germinated in all the lands bordering the Mediterranean.

1.7.6 FROM ARTAXERXES III TO DARIUS III

After the reconquest of Egypt, Artaxerxes III returned to Mesopotamia. However, the expansionist activities of Philip II of Macedon drew his attention once again to the Aegean. Accordingly, he deployed the Greek mercenaries he now controlled to Asia Minor, appointing their leader, Mentor of Rhodes, as supreme commander of the western empire. But Mentor died soon after, leaving the Persian grip on Asia Minor weak.

Then, in 338 BC Bagoas had Artaxerxes poisoned (Diodorus Siculus, *Bib. hist.* 17.5.3), along with all but the youngest of the king's sons, Arses, whom he put on the throne.[48] Arses took the throne name Artaxerxes IV and in the third year of his rule grew tired of being Bagoas's puppet. He planned to

---

48. A Babylonian cuneiform tablet that implies Artaxerxes III died of natural causes (*PE* 10.1) should not be seen as authoritative. Its composer was primarily interested in chronicling solar eclipses and may not have been aware or even interested in the intrigues of the Persian court. The deaths of all but one of Artaxerxes's sons at the same time points to conspiracy. See Briant, *From Cyrus to Alexander*, 775.

have the powerful eunuch executed, but Bagoas pre-empted the maneuver and murdered him, along with all his children. In so doing, he created a dynastic crisis. When Cambyses and Bardiya both died in 522 BC, a similar dynastic crisis had occurred. Darius I had had both the initiative and adroitness to reconfigure the succession, command the respect of others, and mold the empire around himself as he molded himself around the legacy of Cyrus. By contrast, Bagoas was not even remotely related to the royal family and was incapable of fathering children to establish a dynasty. He needed to find another puppet among the relatives of the Achaemenid dynasty itself.

He gambled on Artashata, the satrap of Armenia, nicknamed Codomannus.[49] Artashata was a great grandson of Darius II via his father, Arsames. His mother, Sisygambis, might even have been the sister of Artaxerxes III, which would have made Artashata the closest living relative of both recently assassinated kings. Since he had so much to gain by the assassination of Artaxerxes IV, some have suggested that Artashata was the chief conspirator.[50] Alexander certainly accused him of such in a letter he later sent to him (Arrian, *Anab.* 2.14.5). However, Bagoas's ambition and unconventional power make it likely that he had already earmarked Artashata as Artaxerxes IV's successor before the murder. Artashata's succession was the logical course of action and appeared as though Bagoas was conceding to protocol rather than subverting it.

Thus, in 336 BC Artashata was crowned as Darius III. Like Artaxerxes IV before him, the new king planned to do away with Bagoas, but the eunuch again caught wind of the plan. Darius III's quick countermeasures show he was prepared for the eunuch's wiles. He had Bagoas poisoned, allegedly by drinking a toast to him and forcing him to drink from the goblet that the eunuch had intended for him (Diodorus Siculus, *Bib. hist.* 16.5.5). The measure of planning in this makes it likely that Darius III had indeed been part of the plot to kill Artaxerxes IV.

With the death of Bagoas, the tax on sacrifices in Jerusalem ceased. The "devourer" had been repelled (cf. Mal 3:11). His death instantly eased the financial strain on Judah, but not the rivalry with Mount Gerizim. Nor did it redeem the notoriety of the Persians as an oppressive regime. Moreover, since all the systems of government found their common focus in the person of the Great King, the dynastic crises of 338–336 BC and the switch to a collateral

---

49. The derivation of "Codomannus" is uncertain, but it is the way Greek writers often referred to Darius III. Cf. Briant, *From Cyrus to Alexander*, 771; Waldemar Heckel, *The Wars of Alexander the Great: 336–323 BC* (London: Bloomsbury, 2014), 24.

50. Briant, *From Cyrus to Alexander*, 776.

branch of the dynasty destabilized the empire as a whole. Darius III, though originally a satrap, had not been primed to become Great King. He came suddenly to the position at the age of 44.[51] Such volatility only increased the hunger of subject peoples for freedom, especially along the Mediterranean seaboard where the magnetic pull away from Persia was strongest.

At the accession of Darius III, then, the Persian Empire was militarily robust but politically turbulent, culturally divided, and colonially repressive. What was needed was wholesale reform to steady the administration and ingratiate the Persian regime once again with subject populations. Yet the entire western portions of the empire now faced the Mediterranean and desired to squirm free of Persia's reins. One could argue, therefore, that by the time Darius came to the throne, the proverbial horse had already bolted. The brutal force of the Persian military was the only thing holding the empire together. If, before any reforms could be implemented, the Persian military were to suffer momentous defeats, Persia would lose hold of its entire empire. It is significant, then, that Darius III's accession came just months before the assassination of Philip II of Macedon (336 BC) and the rise of Philip's son, Alexander III, who would inflict the fatal military defeats and unleash a cultural revolution that changed the course of history.

---

51. Arrian (*Anab.* 3.22.6) gives Darius III's age as approximately 50 at his death in 330 BC.

1.8 THE CHRONICLER

1.8.1 A MANIFESTO OF ISRAELITE IDENTITY

The work of the Chronicler (1 & 2 Chronicles) provides opportunity for an apt summary of the political, cultural, and theological attitudes present in Jerusalem on the eve of Persia's downfall. His access to genealogical information, biblical traditions, and knowledge of the temple's operations means he came from the upper echelons of society—either priestly, scribal, or Davidic circles. His initial work included eight generations of Davidic descendants after Zerubbabel, which was later updated to include another two generations (1 Chr 3:19–24 [see 2.6.1 below]). This puts his initial work in the 330s BC and a redaction in ca. 300 BC. He was writing initially, therefore, at a time when Persia's sovereignty had been challenged on multiple occasions. The leaders of Judah were negotiating questions about Judean polity and identity, especially in relation to Samaria but also with the various diaspora communities and the wider world that beckoned along the highways and shipping lanes—pressing concerns given the volatility of the fourth century BC and the emergence of the new Mediterranean pole. The Chronicler produced a new edition of Israelite history, which differed in focus from that of the Prophetic History (Joshua, Judges, Samuel, Kings). He essentially wrote a manifesto of Israelite identity to address the challenges facing Jerusalem in his day.

In producing this new edition of Israelite history, the Chronicler was not aiming to be comprehensive. He carefully selected and adapted material to achieve his specific aims. He was not a historian in the conventional sense of someone seeking to give an objective account of cause-and-effect across a period of time. Rather, he was presenting Israelite, or more specifically, Judean history, as a paradigm—a source from which to draw lessons and norms. His work is an ostensibly linear narrative that begins with Adam and ends with the decree of Cyrus to rebuild Yahweh's temple in Jerusalem. But this linear narrative is the framework for what is really a series of didactic vignettes. He focuses on precedents that model proper Israelite identity and practice, in the hope of shaping these into the future.

For the Chronicler, Israel's identity rested on five pillars:

1. Davidic dynasty
2. Jerusalem temple
3. Ancestry
4. Land
5. Torah

1.8.2 DAVIDIC DYNASTY

The Chronicler begins his work with extensive genealogies of all the tribes of Israel, tracing descent down to the time of the exile in the sixth century BC (1 Chr 1–8). In presenting these genealogies, he zeroes in on the line of David, for he views the Davidic dynasty as the only legitimate rulers of Israel. To that end, he does not recount the history of the Northern Kingdom of Israel and only mentions it when it directly intersects with the dealings of the Davidic kings of Judah (e.g., 2 Chr 18:3). Even Saul, the first king of Israel, is noted only for his death (1 Chr 10)—a mere curtain-raiser for David. Thereafter, the Chronicler focuses only on the Davidic kings, devoting the most space to David (1 Chr 10–29), the founder of the dynasty, and Solomon (2 Chr 1–9), the builder of the first temple. In this way, he paints Israel as an independent state with no foreign overlord in which an autonomous Davidic king presides over the priestly and Levitical functions in the temple.

The Chronicler was not a nostalgic admiring a glorious national past but a political formulator who viewed the Davidic dynasty as integral to Israel's future. This is why the Davidic dynasty is the only family line he traces beyond exile to his own time (1 Chr 3:17–24).[1] The Davidic patriarch in the Chronicler's own day was Shekaniah, who had six sons: Shemaiah, Hattush, Yigal, Bariah, Neariah, and Shaphat (1 Chr 3:22).[2] The Chronicler's purpose was also educative, seeking to instruct the prospective rulers, as well as the priests, Levites, and the laity, with positive examples to emulate and negative examples to avoid. In this way, the Chronicler's work was prophetic in scope: evaluating the past to elicit a specific response from a present audience and so shape the future.

---

1. In 1 Chr 9 the Chronicler does provide a list of people from the postexilic era. However, this list derives largely from Neh 11 and sits separately to the lines of descent traced in the first eight chapters.

2. Interestingly, the genealogy then follows the line of Shekaniah's fifth son, Neariah, despite clearly alluding to the sons of the eldest, Shemaiah, in aborted terms. This reflects a later redaction (ca. 300 BC), which updated the genealogy, reflecting the loss of Shekaniah's first four sons and their families (cf. Zech 12:12). See 2.6.3.

If we did not have the Prophetic History (Joshua, Judges, Samuel, and Kings) as a comparison, we perhaps would not fully appreciate the Chronicler's purpose. His selective portrait of David serves as the chief example of this. David's rape of Bathsheba and murder of Uriah, which appear in the Prophetic History, are left out of the Chronicler's account altogether. Absalom's rebellion, which the Prophetic History understands as punishment upon David for those earlier sins, is similarly cut. The Chronicler was uninterested in a "warts and all" portrait of David. Instead, he focused upon David as both the founder of Israel's only legitimate dynasty and the author of its temple structures. David's personal sins, therefore, were of no concern. He only discussed David's mistakes with regards to Israel's worship and corporate integrity. For example, the Uzzah incident in which David fails to follow the proper protocols for transferring the ark of the covenant, resulting in the humiliation of Yahweh himself, is treated at length and is corrected only by enforcing proper procedure and Levitical order (1 Chr 13–16). Likewise, the census that David takes of Israel's fighting men is interpreted as a gross overreach of royal power, a violation of the underlying tribal structures of Israel, and a dangerous infringement of the pacifistic vocation of the Levites (1 Chr 21). Thus, for the Chronicler, David was of immense significance but as a public figure—the king of Israel—rather than a private individual.

In depicting David this way, the Chronicler preserved the traditions of Israel's past and used them to project a model of how Israel should look in the prospective future. This was important in the uncertain political landscape after 351 BC. While the Chronicler viewed Cyrus in beneficent terms, and argued that Israel could cooperate with foreign powers, this could only ever be viewed as a temporary means to an end. Israel's fundamental identity included independence from foreign rule, for serving Yahweh as sovereign was ultimately at odds with serving foreign kings (2 Chr 12:8). If Judah now faced the Mediterranean and Persia's power was about to break, Judah's leaders would need to decide on a new polity. Sanballat II had cast a vision of a united Israel under Samarian leadership and the promotion of the temple on Mount Gerizim (1.7.3 above), but for the Chronicler, such a polity was unacceptable. His depiction of the reign of Jeroboam I, the founder of the breakaway kingdom of Israel, underscores this, made all the more poignant if Sanballat II had adopted the persona of a new "Jeroboam" (see 1.7.3 above). The Chronicler portrays faithful priests and Levites at the inception of the breakaway kingdom defecting back to Jerusalem, accompanied by loyal laity from every tribe of Israel who recognize the exclusive primacy of the Davidic dynasty and the Jerusalem temple (2 Chr 11:13–17). The Chronicler thus depicts the reverse of what had happened when Manasseh and other priests defected to Mount Gerizim, thereby passing judgment on them and theologically explaining the coalition's failure.

The Chronicler did not hold to the legitimacy of the Davidic dynasty merely for pragmatic reasons but on the principle of historic divine election. Yahweh had made a permanent covenant with David and entered the Davidic family itself as its eternal father figure. Thus, the Chronicler identified the Davidic throne with the throne of Yahweh himself (1 Chr 29:23). When Solomon inherits the kingdom from David, he sits on "the throne of the kingdom of Yahweh over Israel" (1 Chr 28:5). To put this aside in favor of another political configuration, be that serving foreign powers or being led by Samaria, was nothing short of apostasy. Only Davidic kingship could legitimately and permanently mediate Yahweh's rule and so provide equilibrium to the people of Yahweh. Israel was, therefore, both a Davidic estate and the kingdom of God.

Yet, in such a kingdom of God, there had to be a separation of powers whereby the Davidic dynasty ruled politically and the priests and Levites officiated cultically. The Chronicler does not mindlessly rubber stamp the Davidic dynasty, for he also evaluates its kings and condemns many for their excesses and failures in cultic matters. The Chronicler's argument was that the royal and priestly/Levitical institutions were complementary, with the one guaranteeing the other. Israel was not purely an autocracy with a king wielding absolute power, but nor was it a hierocracy led solely by priests. This was an important statement in the political vacuum of the fourth century BC when the priests were gaining civic power. Davidic kingship mediated the rule of Yahweh while the priestly and Levitical offices permitted Israel to worship Yahweh as his loyal subjects.

Recognizing the Chronicler's argument lets us see that he did not endorse the Persian regime. He could offer it only qualified support. He recognized that Cyrus had been a benevolent sponsor of the temple in the distant past (2 Chr 36:22–23), but his authority could only be approved insofar as Yahweh had granted it to him and used it to meet some of the conditions of Israel's full restoration, namely the return of people to the land of Israel and the reconstruction of the temple in Jerusalem. Read in isolation, the Chronicler's citation of Cyrus's decree sounds like an endorsement of Persian sovereignty over "all the kingdoms of the earth" (2 Chr 36:22–23). But when read against the Chronicler's argument about the inextricable link between Yahweh and the Davidic dynasty, the disparaging of foreign rule (cf. 2 Chr 12:8), and the Chronicler's own context in the fourth century BC, the reader is forced to ask,

"What happens when Yahweh takes all the kingdoms of the earth away from the Persians?" This was a distinct possibility from the mid-fourth century BC and might even have occurred by the time the Chronicler began to write. His answer was that the Davidic dynasty furnished all the tribes of Israel with the only faithful option for moving forward. This was not a call to arms to overthrow the Persians (or Greeks), for regime change was Yahweh's prerogative. The Chronicler saw the human usurpation of power as unnecessary and even objectionable. Instead, his message encouraged passive resistance through quiet hope and readiness. Therefore the Persians were at best caretakers until such time as Yahweh removed dominion from them. And since there were signs in the fourth century BC that Yahweh was intending to do just that, the leaders of Judah had to be prepared to reinstate Davidic kingship.

It is significant, then, that the Chronicler portrayed the Davidic kings as foils to the Persian regime, capable of filling any void left by Persia's demise. He cast the Davidic kings as independent potentates, commanders of armies campaigning abroad, fortifiers of cities, wealthy beyond measure, sponsors of Yahweh's temple, and promoters of the sacrificial cult. The Israelites contribute "darics" (Persian coins) for building the temple (1 Chr 29:7), and Solomon rules over all the kings from the Euphrates to the border of Egypt (2 Chr 9:26)—the same proportions as the Persian satrapy of Trans-Euphrates, which the Persians lost with the Tennes Revolt. In this way, the Chronicler cast the Davidic dynasty as a viable potential replacement of Persian imperial power.

Even though the Davidic dynasty provided the best paradigm of Israelite polity, the Chronicler also provided constitutional checks and balances to regulate and model the proper function of power. The dynamic of divine retribution provided the fundamental mechanism for this. One prominent example was King Uzziah, whose successful reign was marred when he usurped priestly authority by personally entering the temple to burn incense. He was subsequently punished by Yahweh (2 Chr 26:16–21). With this incident, not related in the Prophetic History (cf. 2 Kgs 15:1–7), one wonders whether there are subtle echoes of the Persian eunuch Bagoas and his intrusion into the temple.[3]

---

3. In the Prophetic History, Uzziah is named Azariah (2 Kgs 15:1), prompting us to ask why the Chronicler gives him a different name. It might be that the Chronicler wished to distinguish the king from the priest Azariah, who plays a prominent role in confronting Uzziah in the midst of his flagrant error (2 Chr 26:20). Yet why "Uzziah," as opposed to some other name? It could simply be a difference between the king's personal name and throne name. Interestingly, however, the name Uzziah is Hebrew for "Yahweh is my strength" and is comparable to the Persian name Bagavahya (Bagoas), which means "God is strong." The similarity may be purely coincidental, but the similarity between Uzziah's unauthorized entry into the temple and Bagoas's similar entry is suggestive.

Thus, unlike the Persian regime, the Davidic kings are not granted absolute power with a *carte blanche*. On the contrary, like all Israelites, they are compelled to right worship of Yahweh through the temple structures, which they guarantee, and are condemned when they violate them.

When operating properly, the Chronicler saw Davidic kingship as faithful to Israel's historic traditions and the most suitable alternative to anything offered by Samaria. The Davidic dynasty was the only prospective polity that could safeguard the viability of Jerusalem and its temple institutions, since the dynasty itself was so heavily invested in the Jerusalem temple as the essential "sacrament" of its own existence. At a time when Jerusalem's temple faced potential extinction, this was a notable point. Samaria had demonstrated indifference to Jerusalem's plight, and the Persians had recently proved callous. Since the Davidic dynasty was fundamental to the life of Israel, life without the Davidides impaired Israel's identity. But the survival of the Davidic line down to the Chronicler's day was a divine grace bestowed on Israel and offered the nation a chance to repair its identity fully.

The priesthood in Jerusalem would have been understandably spooked by events in the mid-fourth century BC, which had threatened their prospects and livelihood. Having gained a modicum of political power through Jaddua, they must have been reticent to relinquish it again and place their future in the hands of others. The Chronicler would have seen the benefit of Jaddua's leadership, since he had rightly resisted Sanballat II's coalition. But, like Cyrus, Jaddua also could only be a caretaker. As high priest at the temple that stood as a monument to the Davidic covenant, his rightful position was under a Davidic king. The Chronicler argued that the livelihood of the temple functionaries was best served by reinstating Davidic kingship, for it was reliant on a properly functioning cult in Jerusalem. His account of divine retribution for royal excesses and failures demonstrated the mechanism that would ensure the temple institutions would function properly under Davidic rule. By outlining royal transgressions, the Chronicler was providing a manual so that the nation's future leaders would not make the same mistakes again and jeopardize priestly viability and Israel's integrity.

The necessity of the Chronicler's work shows us that his views were not shared by all quarters of Judean society. For the average Judean seeking to make a simple living, it did not matter who steered the state so long as they enabled the average Judean to steer his own oxen in his own field. The Davidic dynasty provided little added value for such Judeans. For many, the ability of the priests to lead Judeans politically held a pragmatic attraction. The Chronicler, therefore, aimed to persuade people that the best possible future for all—priests,

Levites, and laity—was to have a fully operational Davidic dynasty in power, for only with it was Israelite identity given full expression and the blessing of Yahweh assured for all. The Chronicler attempted to shape expectation for Israel's future, assure those most nervous about their prospects, and create a patriotic enthusiasm among the otherwise indifferent.[4] If and when Yahweh was to grant Israel autonomy once again, the only course of action was to reinstate the Davidic dynasty.

1.8.3 THE JERUSALEM TEMPLE

In seeking to sell his vision of Israel, the Chronicler advocated the Jerusalem temple as another foundational pillar of Israelite life. This is why he spends so much time relating the organization of temple cult, as well as the genealogies of the Levites who ran it. He sees the roots of the temple going back to the institution of the tabernacle, established by Moses. But, for the Chronicler, the tabernacle was a preliminary institution reflecting a nascent stage of Israel's history. It is only with the establishment of the temple in Jerusalem that Israel's worship reaches maturity. Thus, in the Chronicler's estimation, Israel's life without the Jerusalem temple was underdeveloped.

The Chronicler sees an integral connection between the Davidic dynasty and the temple. This is expressed principally through the depiction of David as the author of its operating structures. While the Prophetic History, which is predicated on the Torah, gives Moses pride of place as the institutor of Israel's worship traditions and Solomon subsequently as the temple builder, the Chronicler gives pride of place to David, with the temple in all its facets being his brainchild. This is not to say that Moses and Solomon are disparaged. The Chronicler portrays Moses as the giver of formative law and tradition and Solomon as the executor of David's plans. Yet it is David who holds center stage in the Chronicler's estimation.

The location of the temple in Jerusalem was as important to the Chronicler as its functions and was tied to its Davidic significance. If the temple were just

---

4. In his book, *Chronicles and the Politics of Davidic Restoration: A Quiet Revolution*, LHBOTS 655 (London: Bloomsbury T&T Clark, 2017), David Janzen argues a similar understanding of the Chronicler's purpose. However, Janzen believes the Chronicler was arguing for the restoration of the Davidic dynasty as client kings within the Persian Empire. This, though, does not account for all points of the Chronicler's depiction of the dynasty whereby he casts them as independent monarchs ruling over swathes of territory, with foreign rule depicted as odious (2 Chr 12:8). In particular, the extent of Solomon's realm equates to the entire satrapy of Trans-Euphrates, which the Persians lost in 350 BC. When Chronicles is read in this context, the Davidides are not seen as the Persians' clients but as their replacements.

a cultic place, then Mount Gerizim could function legitimately as the one true place of worship for all Israel. But the Chronicler viewed David as the author of its institutions, and the permanence of its building reflected the permanence of Yahweh's election of the Davidic dynasty to rule Israel on his behalf. To move worship to another location was to deny Yahweh's election of David and his heirs. Thus even if the temple on Mount Gerizim performed the same cultic functions as the temple in Jerusalem and even had priests and Levites of the right ancestry serving there, it could never be the legitimate place of worship. The throne of David was the throne of Yahweh himself, and the temple in Jerusalem was both Yahweh's palace and a Davidic chapel. Any relocation was, therefore, treasonous.

Perhaps the best demonstration of this comes in the Chronicler's portrayal of the Passover celebrated under King Hezekiah (2 Chr 29–31). The king executes his role with aplomb, learning from the mistakes of his forebears, confirming the role of priests and Levites, and facilitating right worship in Jerusalem. Then, as an expression of Israel's full identity, Hezekiah invites all Israel "from Beersheba to Dan" to come to Jerusalem to celebrate the Passover (2 Chr 30:5). Many scorn Hezekiah's invitation, but the faithful gather in Jerusalem and celebrate the biggest and best festival in Judah's history. Hezekiah himself furnishes sacrifices and the means of cleansing for those who were ritually unclean. Consequently, the people rejoice, the priests and Levites receive tithes, and all rival altars and shrines are demolished.

Importantly, the Chronicler's vision for Israel's future left room for the participation of Samarians, despite the failure of Sanballat II's coalition and the pessimism expressed in Zechariah 11. But this future could stem only from a recognition of Jerusalem as the sole legitimate place of Yahwistic worship. In that regard, the Chronicler's vision of Israel was idealistic, but it was not unrealistic. He gives almost no coverage to the shrines established in the northern breakaway kingdom of Israel, yet he still included the genealogy of the northern tribes and punctuated his narrative with occasional references to the northern tribes and their kings. So while he viewed their place(s) of worship as illegitimate, the people themselves were still integral to the identity of Israel. Since it was they who had split from the true expression of Israel, they needed to return, just like the few northerners who celebrated the Passover in Jerusalem in Hezekiah's day. The recognition of Davidic monarchy and the Jerusalem temple were the only way that the estranged halves of the Israelite nation could be brought back together with integrity. The Chronicler's work can therefore be seen as a countermodel to the unity that Sanballat II had proposed.

1.8.4 ANCESTRY

The genealogies of the Israelite tribes are an important way in which the Chronicler delineated the extent of "Israel." They appear at the beginning of his work (1 Chr 1–9) before the narrative portions (1 Chr 10–2 Chr 36) to provide a sense of the nation's place in wider history and to assert the nation's composition. Ancestry is a passive marker in the sense that it is inherited rather than actively chosen. But for the Chronicler it reflected Yahweh's active choice of Israel. As the God of Israel, Yahweh had the right to determine Israel's composition, overriding any human choice over the issue. This choice can be traced back to Israel's inception. The inclusion of the northern tribes was, therefore, a vital expression of who the people of Yahweh were and, therefore, who should be expected to respond appropriately to divine instruction, especially if "Israel" was to establish its own polity. When combined with the previous two pillars of Israelite identity, ancestry stipulated who the citizens of a Davidic kingdom should be and who should worship at the temple in Jerusalem.

Ancestry was also important considering the impairment to Israel's identity in other areas. The nation's fracture in ages past and the destruction of Jerusalem by the Babylonians had compromised Israel's integrity. Davidic monarchy was still not a reality among any of the tribes of Israel in the Chronicler's day, and the primacy of Jerusalem's temple was upheld by only a small portion of the nation. Nevertheless, the people themselves continued to be carriers of Israelite identity, despite their waywardness or impaired status. This gave all the tribes of Israel the responsibility to work towards recovering the essentials of that identity. The Chronicler's genealogies, therefore, outlined who exactly was obligated to do this.

The "twelveness" of Israel's composition was important, as it reflected Israel's totality. But this led the Chronicler to an interesting configuration of the twelve tribes. In his initial catalogue, he lists the twelve sons of Jacob in their traditional order (1 Chr 2:1–2) but then departs from this order as he itemizes each tribal genealogy. Zebulun and Dan are left out of the detailed genealogies, probably because their territory in Galilee had become the hinterland of the Phoenician cities on the coast, with little of Israelite essence left. But this merely meant that Galilee had to be recovered and resettled rather than written off. To compensate for their absence, he includes the Levites like the other landed tribes (5:27–6:66) and treats the two halves of Manasseh on either side of the Jordan as distinct tribes (5:23–26; 7:14–19). Benjamin is also treated twice (7:6–12; 8:1–40). The Chronicler populated his genealogies with information he gleaned presumably from records and used it to show how

Israel had developed through the ages. Central to his purpose, however, was the sense of kinship between the tribes, even with those who had apparently been deported to distant lands (cf. 5:26).

1.8.5 THE LAND

One of the differences between the Chronicler's account and the Prophetic History has to do with the role of the land. In the Prophetic History, Yahweh's people could only observe the covenant within the land, which Yahweh had originally promised to the patriarchs. Exile was the ultimate punishment, representing the dissolution of Israel's identity as the people of Yahweh and the undoing of the covenant. This stemmed principally from a henotheistic worldview, which saw particular lands as belonging to particular peoples and their respective patron deities (see 1.2.1 above). This henotheistic worldview had, however, developed through the Babylonian exile and the subsequent Persian era. A far bigger and all-encompassing view of the divine had developed as Judeans came to realize that their patron deity, Yahweh, was not limited to the borders of their traditional homeland (cf. 1.2.3 above). Historical and prophetic reflection brought the conviction that his sovereignty extended over all nations. Yahweh had brought the Babylonians to his land as the instrument of his punishment. He had also visited his people in the land of their exile (cf. Ezekiel). He had raised Cyrus to overthrow Babylon and allow Judeans to return to their homeland (Isa 45:1–6). The prophet Zechariah had urged those pioneering Judeans who returned to cooperate with the Persians on the understanding that Yahweh was working through them (Zech 1:8–11; 6:1–8). This was why Ezra and Nehemiah could be both Persian functionaries and loyal Yahwists. Yahweh was understood to orchestrate events on the international stage, not merely those that impinged on the land of "his inheritance." Even so, Israel was "his people" (1 Chr 11:2) in a way that no other ethnos could be, and Yahweh was Israel's covenant deity.

With this sharpened awareness of divine sovereignty, the land took on a modified role for the Chronicler. It was not nullified as a pillar of Israelite identity, for it was still the homeland of all Israel and the rightful location of the Davidic kingdom, both past and prospective future. Yet, since the whole world was within the range of God's sovereignty, the people of God could now reside anywhere and still be considered constituent members of his covenant people, Israel. Distance from the land did not disqualify one from citizenship in Israel, for Yahweh had demonstrated his grace to Israel by continuing to relate to them, even in foreign countries. Nevertheless, the land was still the center of theological gravity and held pride of place in Israel's heritage and in hopes for a future Davidic kingdom.

As a means of holding the importance of the land together with a grander view of God's sovereignty and the hope of a Davidic kingdom, the Chronicler encouraged pilgrimage to Jerusalem. The Chronicler's picture of the ideal Israel was the gathering of all Israelites in the Jerusalem temple in celebration of the Passover as the quintessential national festival under the aegis of a Davidic king. This was an enactment of Israelite unity, a commemoration of God's past saving acts, and an expression of hope that God would once again grant his people freedom under their rightful Davidic king in the land.

This represented a development from the situation that had prevailed in the late fifth century BC as evidenced in the Elephantine papyri. There, the visit of Hananiah to the Yahwistic enclave in southern Egypt (419 BC) had encouraged local celebration of the Passover (*TAD* A4.1; see 1.5.3 above). The Chronicler might not have viewed such celebrations as illegitimate if they did not compromise the primacy of Jerusalem. Yet such celebrations outside of the land highlighted the impairments in Israelite identity. In his account of the great Passover under King Hezekiah, the Chronicler depicts "a very large assembly" gathered in the temple courts at Jerusalem (2 Chr 30:13). Obviously, this expectation was more easily realized if people resided in proximity to Jerusalem. Nevertheless, even Israelites living in other countries were expected to make pilgrimage. A similar expectation is reflected in Zechariah 14:16–19, which even creates the hope that, in the future, non-Israelites would make this pilgrimage too.[5]

1.8.6 TORAH

The significance of the land was closely aligned with the importance of Torah. Indeed, one could argue that the promise of the land was a central theme of the Torah. The Chronicler does not give any coverage to the giving of the Law to Israel, but not because he thought Torah unimportant. On the contrary, he affirms Moses as the conduit through whom God gave the Law and who built

---

5. Despite the initial statement that the nations would come to Jerusalem in pilgrimage (Zech 14:16), there continues to be a focus on Israelites in this passage. The "the clans of the land" (Zech 14:17) refers to all Israelites living within the land, rather than to all people throughout the whole earth. It would seem to be a reference to the Samarians and the expectation that, despite the rift within the nation (cf. Zech 11:14), they would return their allegiance to Jerusalem once again. Furthermore, "the clan of Egypt" (Zech 14:18–19) probably refers to Israelites living in Egypt. By the time this part of Zechariah had been composed (ca. 300 BC), many Judeans had either been deported or chosen to migrate to Alexandria (see 2.6.1). The author of this passage, however, still views pilgrimage as incumbent upon them.

the tabernacle (e.g., 1 Chr 15:15; 21:29). The Chronicler saw Torah shaping vital aspects of Israelite life through such things as the establishment of Yahweh as the nation's deity through a national covenant, the sacrificial cult, Sabbath observance, dietary laws, circumcision, and national commemorative festivals.

Torah was the major point of commonality between the Chronicler's Jerusalem-centered theology and the theology emerging in Samaria. But for the Chronicler, the Torah was just one of the pillars of Israelite identity, alongside others that emerged from the prophetic tradition. In Samaria, where the Torah was the only authoritative scriptural canon, the primacy of Mount Gerizim was being written into the text of the Torah. This was done primarily by combining the first two commandments (Yahweh as Israel's sole deity and the prohibition of idolatry) and then appending a new tenth commandment commissioning the erection of an altar that displayed the Law on Mount Gerizim. The Samaritan Pentateuch tenth commandment combined elements from various Pentateuchal texts (Exod 13:11a; Deut 11:29–30; 27:4–7) and asserted the primacy of Mount Gerizim, even adding directional data to ensure no ambiguity.[6] While this redactional activity is easily detected, the importance of Mount Gerizim was not invented by the Samarians at this time. Rather, it came from biblical precedent. Deuteronomy 27:4–7, one of the texts behind the Samaritan tenth commandment, has Moses command Joshua to build an altar on a mountain in the center of the land. The medieval Masoretic Text identifies this as "Mount Ebal," which lay directly across the valley from Mount Gerizim. Two biblical manuscripts from Qumran preserve portions of this passage, and unfortunately the fuller one (4QDeut^f) has a lacuna at this very point. The second, however, is a tiny fragment from the first century BC—centuries older than the medieval Masoretic Text—and clearly identifies the mountain as "Mount Gerizim."[7] Other ancient texts also reflect this reading, making it likely that the text did originally read "Mount Gerizim" and that later Jewish scribes changed this to "Mount Ebal" as an expression of anti-Samaritan sentiment.[8] Thus the importance of Mount Gerizim did have a basis in Torah.

---

6. Moses Gaster, *The Samaritans: Their History, Doctrines and Literature*, The 1923 Schweich Lectures (London: British Academy, 1925), 188; Jan Dušek, *Aramaic and Hebrew Inscriptions from Mt. Gerizim and Samaria between Antiochus III and Antiochus IV Epiphanes*, Culture and History of the Ancient Near East 54 (Leiden: Brill, 2012), 89.

7. James H. Charlesworth acquired this fragment separately to the Dead Sea Scrolls found in the Qumran caves but purchased it from Bedouin belonging to the family that first came across the Dead Sea Scrolls, who claimed it came from Cave 4 at Qumran. Yet, in light of its separate discovery, the manuscript has not received a standard reference tag as all other Dead Sea Scrolls have. See Charlesworth, "What Is a Variant?"

8. These are Papyrus Giessen 19, which is a revision of the LXX and the Old Latin text. See Dušek, *Aramaic and Hebrew Inscriptions from Mt. Gerizim*, 90.

By contrast, Jerusalem's claim to primacy did not stem from the Torah. Melchizedek is labelled "King of Salem" (Gen 14:18), which is usually equated with Jerusalem, and "Mount Moriah," the site of Abraham's near sacrifice of Isaac (Gen 22:2), is identified as Jerusalem's Temple Mount. Yet even the Chronicler, who makes the identification between Mount Moriah and the Temple Mount, draws the connection via David rather than Abraham (2 Chr 3:1). Thus the Jerusalem-centered theology of the Chronicler also looked beyond the Torah to the prophetic traditions for its theological underpinnings.

To this end, the Chronicler viewed the tabernacle that Moses built as a nascent stage of Israel's cultic life. The more mature stage of Israelite worship came with the Jerusalem temple, the planning of which was attributed to David. As the more mature expression of the relationship between Yahweh and Israel, there could be no turning back to the earlier generic worship associated with Moses's tabernacle or Joshua's altar on Mount Gerizim. Contrary to Samarian theology, Israel could not be Torah-only in outlook. For the Chronicler, Torah continued to shape Israelite life with its patriarchal promises, national covenant, customs, and regulations, but this did not represent the totality or completion of Israel's theological development. Torah was but one of the pillars on which Israelite identity rested.

1.9 CONCLUSION

For the people of Samaria, the rise of the Persians was not the watershed moment it was for Judeans. Since the Assyrian conquest of Israel in 723 BC, most Samarians were comfortably ensconced in villages and towns across the central highlands, with the city of Samaria as their thriving capital. For Judeans, the advent of the Persians signaled a major shift in fortunes after the Babylonians had destroyed the Davidic state in 586 BC. The Persians facilitated the return of those who were seriously committed to the recovery of a Davidic polity in the Judean highlands, and for the most part, the Persians were benevolent rulers. However, this perception changed through the course of the fourth century BC, as the political compass shifted towards the Greek and Egyptian world in the west. The persistent incursion of Greek and Egyptian forces into the Levant during this time brought significant turmoil and uncertainty to the region. To keep their empire intact, the Persians took measures that inevitably made them colonial oppressors, and they intermittently lost control over portions of their empire. The hope for independence gripped the entire Mediterranean seaboard, culminating in the Tennes Revolt (351–345 BC) and an attempted coalition between Samarians and Judeans. Both these initiatives failed. Persia reasserted its sovereignty over all the lands in Trans-Euphrates and over Egypt also (343 BC). Yet this sovereignty would not persist beyond the decade.

By the end of the Persian era, the henotheistic worldview in Judah and Samaria had developed into a fully orbed sense of the sovereignty of a transcendent God over all the world. The syncretism that had permitted the worship of other deities and the use of figurines and standing stones was receding, replaced by a blossoming aniconic monotheism. This development was enabled by the imperial oversight of the Persians, whose Zoroastrian beliefs viewed Yahwism as a religion compatible with their own. On the ground, it occurred largely under the tutelage of the Torah, which Ezra instituted as the cultural norm for all Yahwists with full Persian backing. Yet key differences in the perception of Israelite identity persisted. A sizeable diaspora of Judeans remained in southern Mesopotamia and perhaps also in Egypt. But the battleground for Israelite identity lay in the hills of Judah and Samaria, where the temples in Jerusalem and Mount Gerizim vied with each other for the patronage of all "Israelites" as the one true place of worship.[1]

On the eve of Persia's downfall, Judeans and Samarians alike were giving thought to their immediate future, longing for prospective freedom from colonial power and developing along rival theological lines with their rival temples. In this longing for freedom, most Yahwists were aligned with the Samarian view of Israelite identity. The hills of Samaria were still the popular heartland of "Israel," and the temple on Mount Gerizim was the most prominent center of worship. Jerusalem, although a provincial capital, was still a struggling temple town, consisting of the cultic precinct on the Temple Mount and a meager settlement of perhaps 3,000 people along the ridge to its south. But those committed to Jerusalem's primacy were fighting with prophetic fervor for its survival in the face of Samaria's bigger claim. This ideological struggle was predicated on the belief that Yahweh was continuing to reveal himself and his purposes beyond the Torah. It was being waged through the preservation, redaction, and composition of scriptural texts, the rise of prophetic figures, and, where possible, political maneuver. The Chronicler believed the way forward for Judah lay in the recovery of an independent Davidic state, to be enacted whenever Persia fell by the wayside. For others, the Davidic dynasty and the prophetic traditions were mere relics of the past, easily traded in the *Realpolitik* of the day. Despite its diminutive size, therefore, fault lines were still evident within Judean society.

The Judean-Samarian rivalry and the hopes for independence propelled Judeans and Samarians into the Hellenistic era. It would be an era of seismic political shifts, sharp cultural challenges, and profound theological and political disappointments, which would shape the character of both communities for the ensuing centuries.

---

1. The temple to Yahweh at Makkedah (Khirbet el-Qom) in neighboring Idumea was no longer functional by this time. It was probably decommissioned during the Israelite Coalition. See Lemaire, "New Aramaic Ostraca from Idumea," 416–17.

PART 2
THE HELLENISTIC ERA (331–167 BC)

2.1 UNITING GREECE

2.1.1 PHILIP II OF MACEDON (359–336 BC)

On a hot summer morning in 336 BC, Philip II of Macedon entered the theater at Aegae to celebrate the marriage of his daughter, Cleopatra. While he was unattended for a few moments, one of his bodyguards, Pausanias, stepped forward and thrust a blade between his ribs. The battle-scarred king dropped to the ground and died, his life taken not in the thick of battle but in a moment of peace and festivity. His assassination paved the way for the rise of his talented son, Alexander III, who was just twenty years old at the time.

Philip had come to the Macedonian throne unexpectedly in 359 BC at twenty-two years of age, after the deaths of his two older brothers, Alexander II and Perdiccas III. At the time, the Greeks were still a disunited ethnic group, divided into city-states and regional states. Although the Macedonians were ethnically and linguistically Greek and therefore allowed to compete at the Olympic Games, the rest of the Aegean viewed them as backward and uncultured, occupying the fringes of the Greek world.[1] Philip fought to change this perception, taking measures to bring Athenian culture to Macedon. For example, he adopted the *koinē* Greek of Attica to overcome the stigma attached to the Macedonian dialect, which other Greeks considered a blunt patois.[2] He promoted the study of classical Greek literature and patronized the visual and musical arts. He encouraged philosophy, even having his son, Alexander, educated by no less a figure than Aristotle.[3] Under his leadership, the Macedonian aristocracy became highly Atticized, though the rest of Greece viewed this as no more than a veneer of cultural polish on a raw and boorish people. Philip also showed great aptitude in military strategy, battle tactics, and political maneuver. He trained his infantry in phalanx units and wielded an effective cavalry with which he won numerous victories that expanded his power.

---

1. Robin J. Lane Fox, *The Classical World: An Epic History of Greece and Rome* (London: Penguin, 2006), 193–94.
2. Geoffrey Horrocks, *Greek: A History of the Language and Its Speakers*, 2nd ed (Chichester: Wiley Blackwell, 2014), 80.
3. Aristotle was himself a native of Macedonia, being born and buried in the town of Stagira. However, he spent much time in Athens, where he was a student of Plato at the Academy.

He was successful against Thracians, Scythians, and Illyrians to the north and sought to extend his sway over the Greek mainland. Over the course of his reign, he married seven women—an anathema to most Greeks, who viewed polygamy as brutish, but evidence of his political will to cement alliances. His most famous wife was the princess of Epirus, Myrtale Olympias, who became the mother of Alexander.[4] Over a decade after his father's death, Alexander would remind his Macedonian troops that Philip had transformed them from "helpless wanderers" into "city dwellers, and by means of laws and good customs gave [them] an orderly way of life" (Arrian, *Anab.* 7.9.2).

Yet Philip had many detractors throughout the Greek world, who viewed him as an uncouth barbarian. His most ardent opponent was the Athenian statesman Demosthenes, who perceived Philip as a threat to the freedom of the Greek cities. He had good reason for this perception. Philip's ambition had extended Macedon's sovereignty over northern Greece, Thrace, and Illyria. In this process, he had acquired numerous sources of revenue, including gold mines that he used to underwrite building projects and fund a potent army. This brought Philip into conflict with the city-states to the south, including Demosthenes's own city, Athens. Though Sparta had dominated Greece after winning the Peloponnesian War in 404 BC, its defeat by the Thebans at Leuctra (371 BC) allowed Athens to regain its status as Greece's leading city. Athens was also democratic—at odds with Philip's monarchic system of rule. For all his adoption of Athenian culture, Philip clearly wished to dominate Athens politically, and this contributed to the friction between him and the city. In 346 BC Philip concluded a peace with Athens, but this was purely expedient as neither side viewed the concord as permanent.

Nevertheless, there were others who saw in Philip a chance for Greek unity. The elderly Isocrates, also of Athens, was probably the best known of these. Having suffered hardship as a result of the Peloponnesian War, Isocrates advocated the Panhellenic ideal, which urged Greeks to put aside their differences and unite as a singular people. Only thus could they deal with one of the roots of their problems: the Persians. For Isocrates, the Great King of Persia was a source of division amongst Greeks, and he still held the Greeks of Asia Minor subject to his humiliating oriental rule. Isocrates's *Philippus*, an open letter to the Macedonian monarch, written in 347 BC (at the height of the Tennes Revolt), urged him to become a beacon of Greek unity and invade the Persian Empire. There is little doubt that Philip intended to do just that. He even had first-hand information about Persia's sway over Asia Minor from the

---

4. Myrtale was her original name. She received the name Olympias early in her marriage to Philip.

former Persian satrap, Artabazus, to whom he had given refuge. But Isocrates's Panhellenic ideal was just that: an ideal. In practice, the Greek states were never going to surrender their own agendas willingly, especially not to a king from a region considered the most backward in all of Greece. Greece was "a society obsessed with instability and poisoned with revolution."[5] If Greek unity was to become a reality, it would have to be imposed by force.

Philip did just that after he defeated a coalition of Athenians and Thebans at Chaeronea in central Greece in 338 BC. The following year he formed the League of Corinth (or "Hellenic League") in which all Greek states made peace with each other, and Philip became the guarantor of that peace.[6] Unity was imposed by a kind of *Anschluss*.[7] More importantly, the League created an expeditionary force to liberate the Greeks in Asia Minor from Persian rule (Diodorus Siculus, *Bib. hist.* 16.89.1–3). Philip thus brought most of Greece under his leadership and prepared for the invasion of the Persian Empire.

Of course, he never got the chance. Though he sent an advance force across the Hellespont in 336 BC, Philip met his end at the edge of Pausanias's blade. Some believed that Alexander's mother, Olympias, had put Pausanius up to the deed to ensure her own son, and not one of Philip's other sons, succeeded to the throne (Plutarch, *Alex*. 9.4; 10.4). Some even blamed Darius III (cf. Diodorus Siculus, *Bib. hist.* 17.7.1). Whatever the case, Philip was interred in a lavish tomb at Aegae (modern Vergina, Greece) amid great pomp and ceremony.[8] He was buried along with his seventh wife, eighteen-year-old Cleopatra Eurydice, and her newborn daughter, Europa—both murdered by Olympias a few days after Philip's assassination (Diodorus Siculus, *Bib. hist.* 17.2.3; Justin, *Epit.* 9.7).

2.1.2 THE ACCESSION OF ALEXANDER III

Alexander was born in the Macedonian capital, Pella, in 356 BC. Though ostensibly the son of Philip II and Olympias, questions about his paternity circulated at an early stage. When Alexander consulted the oracle of

---

5. Robin J. Lane Fox, *Alexander the Great* (London: Penguin, 2004), 69.
6. Sparta was the only Greek city not to join the League, but it had been thoroughly isolated by this time and rendered impotent.
7. Richard Stoneman, *Alexander the Great*, Lancaster Pamphlets (London, New York: Routledge, 1997), 12.
8. The tomb was lost to history until its rediscovery in 1977. After decades of debate, forensic analysis and corroboration with historical sources confirmed without doubt that Philip's remains were those contained in Tomb I. See Antonis Bartsiokas et al., "The Lameness of King Philip II and Royal Tomb I at Vergina, Macedonia," *PNAS* 112.32 (2015): 9844–48.

Zeus-Ammon at the Egyptian oasis of Siwa in 331 BC,[9] he was told that his father was Zeus. This appeal to divine parentage shows that Alexander became a figure of legend within his own lifetime, but this makes it difficult to know whether the attribution arose as part of the legend or whether it was used to cover up the embarrassment that Philip was not actually his father. There is probably an allusion to Alexander's questionable parentage in a biblical oracle associated with Alexander's conquests (Zech 9:1–8), which mentions a "bastard" (Heb. *mamzer*) coming to rule Ashdod (Zech 9:6).[10] Even so, we cannot determine whether there was any truth to the rumors. Philip certainly never marginalized Alexander. What we can say is that the motif of divine parentage was important for bolstering the image of Alexander as an exceptional individual bound for greatness—a veritable god among men.[11]

Alexander's rise to power was not straightforward. Alexander had a half-brother, Arrhidaeus, who was older, but he was disabled in some way.[12] Arrhidaeus was, therefore, never considered for the succession and so presented no threat to Alexander. But he did have to fend off a challenge from another half-brother, Caranus.[13] After this, Alexander had to re-subdue the Thracians and Illyrians and tame the League of Corinth, whose members now repudiated Macedonian leadership. Yet Alexander managed to assert his leadership with summary speed using a combination of force and persuasion, which included the destruction of Thebes and the intimidation of Athens.

As head of the League of Corinth, Alexander became the de facto leader of all Greece at the age of twenty-two. He also inherited the League's purpose, namely the liberation of the Greek cities of Asia Minor from Persian rule. To cement his leadership, he sought the approval of Apollo's oracle at Delphi. Legend has it that he arrived during an inauspicious season when the oracle was forbidden to issue prophecies. In the process of physically forcing her to prophesy, the oracle is said to have exclaimed to him, "You are invincible, my son!" (Plutarch, *Alex.* 14.4). Content with this, Alexander initiated the invasion that would launch him to legendary status.

---

9. The oracle at Siwa was devoted to the Egyptian god Amun, who was equated with the Greek god Zeus.

10. The core of Zech 9:1–8 dates to 519 BC, when Darius I marched to Egypt in his suppression of "revolts." However, the oracle was recontextualized and redacted in light of Alexander's campaign (see 2.2.3).

11. Peter Green, *Alexander of Macedon, 356–323 B.C.: A Historical Biography* (Berkeley: University of California Press, 1991), 35–36.

12. Arrhidaeus's exact condition is not known. He was not so incapacitated that he could not take a wife or travel, but he was easily dominated by others. This suggests something like, but not limited to, autism, Down Syndrome (Trisomy 21), or cerebral palsy.

13. Caranus was probably the son of Cleopatra Eurydice, though there is a possibility he was the son of another of Philip's wives.

2.2 ALEXANDER AND THE FALL OF THE PERSIAN EMPIRE

2.2.1 THE LIBERATION OF THE GREEK CITIES

In May 334 BC Alexander landed his expeditionary force on the Asian side of the Hellespont. The forces at his disposal were historically large for a Greek army—roughly 50,000 men accompanied by 160 ships. Yet, the Persians could muster over 120,000 men and 300 ships.[1] Persian forces relied on archers, slingers, and cavalry, which geared them towards swift engagement from a distance. Alexander's force, by contrast, was primed for close combat with soldiers arranged in phalanx units. Alexander's army, therefore, would need to rely on ingenuity to gain any advantage.

Alexander's first battle was at the nearby Granicus River. It was a battle he won, but he came very close to being killed (Diodorus Siculus, *Bib. hist.* 17.19.1–17.21.6; Arrian, *Anab.* 1.13.1–1.16.7; Plutarch, *Alex.* 16.1–5). Once he recovered, he headed south and liberated the Greek cities. The only substantive resistance he encountered was at Miletus and Halicarnassus (Arrian, *Anab.* 1.20.1–1.23.8). He permitted the Greek cities to govern themselves, usually through democratic processes. In reality he was making them dependent on himself by granting estates to his own men, ensuring that they would become prominent citizens in the local governments. This policy of injecting his own people into the local communities would become pivotal in the spread of Hellenism.[2]

At Miletus Alexander disbanded his fleet, figuring that he could not defeat the Persians on the sea, so he would save the exorbitant cost of trying to do so (Arrian, *Anab.* 1.20.1). He forged ahead and took the southern ports along the Mediterranean. With their submission, he successfully accomplished the mandate of the League of Corinth to liberate the Greeks in Asia Minor from Persian rule. But Alexander's ambitions were far grander than the League of Corinth's purpose. He intended to carve out an empire for himself that extended beyond the Greek arena. His intentions were captured in what was probably a deft piece

---

1. Fox, *Alexander the Great*, 100; Green, *Alexander of Macedon*, 157. Arrian puts Darius's numbers at an implausible 600,000 men (*Anab.* 2.8.8).
2. Fox, *Alexander the Great*, 140–41.

of propaganda from his time in the Phrygian capital of Gordium (May 333 BC). In Gordium's primary temple lay the wagon of legendary King Midas and his father, Gordius, which was tied to its yoke by an inextricable knot. A local prophecy stated that whoever could undo the knot would become master of all Asia. After inspecting it, Alexander reached for his sword and sliced through the "Gordian knot" (Arrian, *Anab.* 2.3.1–8). Whether staged or embellished, this propaganda, like the incident with the oracle at Delphi, attempted to portray Alexander as resourceful and his ambitions as inexorable and divinely ordained. The only question now was how far "Asia" extended.

2.2.2 THE BATTLE OF ISSUS (333 BC)

With Alexander's early successes, Darius III had little choice but to meet him head on in a land campaign. To this end, he gathered a colossal force at Babylon, giving him an overwhelming numerical advantage. Meanwhile, Alexander breached the imposing Taurus Mountains through the Cilician Gates and took control of the Cilician capital, Tarsus, on 3 September 333 BC.[3] He soon fell ill with fever after swimming in the Cydnus River, but with treatment from his physician, he recovered and established the first mint to strike imperial coins in his name.[4] He then prepared to cross the Amanus Range into Syria (Arrian, *Anab.* 2.4.1–2.5.9).

By this time, Darius had marched his enormous army into Syria and camped on a plain east of the Amanus Range, where his cavalry would have a tactical advantage. But his supreme confidence in his superior numbers induced him to cross the mountains and take the battle to Alexander (Arrian, *Anab.* 2.6.3–2.7.1). He surprised Alexander by emerging behind his army. Alexander had no choice but to double back and engage. The two armies met on a narrow strip of land between the sea and the mountains south of Issus on a late afternoon in November 333 BC.[5] But the location curtailed the effectiveness of Darius's superior cavalry, forcing the Persians to engage the center of Alexander's forces. Alexander's flanks swept around to press the Persian center where Darius himself was located, and a Persian retreat quickly ensued. The sources are clearly biased against Darius, so it is hard to tell whether he responded to the retreat or lost his nerve and caused it. What seems certain is that, at a crucial moment,

---

3. Stoneman, *Alexander the Great*, 31.
4. Pierre Briant, *Alexander the Great and His Empire: A Short Introduction*, trans. Amélie Kuhrt (Princeton: Princeton University Press, 2010), 9.
5. On dating the Battle of Issus, see James Romm, ed., *The Landmark Arrian: The Campaigns of Alexander*, trans. Pamela Mensch (New York: Anchor Books, 2010), n. 2.11.10b.

he personally took the reins of his chariot and fled the field. Alexander pursued him into the mountains, but Darius abandoned his chariot and escaped on horseback. The fall of night allowed him to get away. Alexander had won, but Darius lived to fight another day (Arrian, *Anab.* 2.7.2–2.11.10).

Alexander took possession of Darius's camp, including taking Darius's family into custody. The Levant and Egypt now lay open before Alexander. After just eighteen months of campaigning, the Macedonian had broken what remained of Persia's eastern-based magnetism and ensured that henceforth the western magnetism of the Mediterranean would hold sway over the Levant. It is understandable, then, that in biblical literature Alexander's agile success saw him depicted as a winged leopard (Dan 7:6) and a "shaggy goat" with "a prominent horn between its eyes coming from the west, crossing the whole earth without touching the ground" and ferociously attacking the "ram" of Persia (Dan 8:5–7, 21). Alexander had no traditional claim to the Levant, and he had already exceeded the objectives of his mission by conquering Asia Minor. The hot question now was what Alexander would do with the regions open before him. Autonomy was once again a very real possibility for Judah and Samaria.

2.2.3 CONQUEST OF TRANS-EUPHRATES AND EGYPT

The question was soon answered as Alexander took his armies south to assert his sovereignty over the Phoenician port cities. These cities, which had rebelled against Persia at the Tennes Revolt less than two decades earlier, were only too keen to overthrow Persia's colonial yoke. So they all surrendered willingly to Alexander. Only one city prevaricated: Tyre.

Tyre was a fortified island half a mile out to sea. Over the centuries it had created an extensive network of colonies throughout the Mediterranean, the most famous of which was Carthage. Tyre's maritime exploits had brought the city lavish wealth and made it a haven of merchants. Its natural defenses also made it practically invincible. In fact, though Tyre had previously submitted to foreign powers like Persia, it had never been militarily conquered. Nebuchadnezzar II had tried to conquer it for thirteen years (585–572 BC), and though he pressured them into terms, he never actually took the city.

Tyre's patron deity, Melqart, was equated by the Greeks with Heracles, from whom Alexander's family claimed descent. It so happened that Alexander arrived at Tyre in February 332 BC during a festival to Melqart, the climax of which was a sacrifice offered by the king of Tyre, Azemilcus. But Azemilcus was at sea with the Tyrian ships in the Persian fleet. When Alexander requested to make the climactic sacrifice himself—effectively a request for a *coup d'état*—the local nobles refused him and promptly crucified his envoys. The Macedonian saw red. For the next seven months, he set his men to building an earthen causeway from the coastal town of Ushu out to the island of Tyre. During this time, much of the Persian fleet defected to him, and Alexander used them against the Tyrians. Though they doggedly defended their city, Alexander prevailed, conquering the city in July 332 BC. He slaughtered many, sold 30,000 of its inhabitants into slavery, and surprisingly granted an amnesty to King Azemilcus (Arrian, *Anab.* 2.15.6–2.24.6).

Tyre's conquest is captured in highly sophisticated verse in the Poem of the Invader (Zech 9:1–8), which depicts the unstoppable march of an ominous invader heading south through the Levant. The poem was originally penned in response to Darius I's march to Egypt in the tumultuous early years of his reign (ca. 519 BC), but when Alexander followed essentially the same path, history seemed to be repeating itself. The poem was, therefore, reworked and recontextualized to reflect Alexander's arrival. Verse 3 particularly relates to Tyre. The Hebrew text was originally written without the vowels, forcing an original reader to choose between various possible vocalizations. The Masoretes supplied one set of vowels in the medieval era, which appears to praise Tyre's stellar reputation. But this is somewhat incongruous with the rest of the poem, which is clearly about invasion. The verse also exhibits distinctly narrative features that are highly unusual in a poetic text.[6] It appears to praise Tyre's economic mastery, but the military context conditions the reader to want to vocalize or interpret the text in line with military imagery. The reader must decide how exactly to vocalize the text, and the listener must listen attentively to choose what they intend to hear. The result of this dynamic is a double entendre that on the one hand appears to laud Tyre, but on the other gives a palpable sense of Tyre's cataclysmic downfall.

Surface Meaning		Subtext	
wattiben tsor...	Tyre built...	weteben tsor...	So Tyre is chaff!
matsor lah	...herself a bulwark.	matsor lah	A siege on her,
wattitsbor	She accumulated...	wettibtsor	and you must break [her].
kesep keʿapar	...silver like dust...	kesop keʿapar	Beat [her] like dust.
weharuts	and gold...	waharots	So mobilize.
ketit hutsot	...like mud of the streets.	katit hutsot	[She is] crushed in the open.

---

6. These narrative features are *wayyiqtol* verbs, which are characteristic of Hebrew narrative texts but extremely rare in Hebrew poetry.

Tyre is said to have built herself a bulwark. Yet, being an island, the Tyrians could not fortify their walls with a bulwark, for the sea, which was its natural defense, prevented the construction of one. The claim is, therefore, almost nonsensical, pressuring the reader and listener to reassess what is being said: is this about Tyre's defenses, or is it about a destructive siege on Tyre? Tyre is then praised for gathering silver and gold, but then these lines seem to use standard phrases alluding to victorious soldiers trampling through the streets of a conquered city (cf. 2 Sam 22:43; Ps 18:42; Isa 10:6; Zech 10:5). The implication is that, notwithstanding Tyre's wealth and natural defenses, its walls would be breached and enemy soldiers would run riot within her. This more sinister subtext creates a pressure upon both reader and listener, which poetically mimics the feeling of being forced to face the reality of Tyre's doom and her upended fortunes. The next verse is less subtle, as the double entendre is dropped for stark directness:

> See the Lord dispossessing her,
> beating her forces into the sea.
> She herself by fire will be consumed. (Zech 9:4)

The fall of Tyre struck the region like a thunderbolt. The untouchable city had been captured. Indeed, Alexander had literally changed the landscape by joining the erstwhile island to the mainland, as it remains to this day.[7] His industriousness provoked Darius into offering him sovereignty over Trans-Euphrates and Egypt, 10,000 talents of gold,[8] one of his daughters in marriage, and an alliance in exchange for his family members. Alexander refused, ensuring that Darius would face him once again in battle (Arrian, *Anab.* 2.25.1–3). It was now conspicuously clear that neutrality was not an option for the cities and provinces of the Levant. Alexander demanded both recognition and obeisance, though there was scope for his benevolence, as the amnesty extended to Azemilcus demonstrated.

Josephus's account of Alexander's arrival in the Levant (*Ant.* 11.306–345) is tainted by his confused chronology about the building of the temple on Mount Gerizim. It also includes a romantic story about Alexander deferring to the high priest Jaddua after seeing him in a dream before his

---

7. Over the centuries, each side of the causeway gathered silt, which filled the gap between Tyre and the mainland.
8. This would be the equivalent of approximately US$15 billion today.

campaign began and Jaddua then showing Alexander the book of Daniel in which his rise to world domination is foretold. Despite these fanciful details, there are elements of Josephus's account that can be aligned with information from other sources. Along with some of the biblical evidence, we can make some educated guesses as to how Samaria and Judah responded at this juncture.

Josephus states that, during the siege of Tyre, Alexander demanded troops from Jaddua to boost his war effort, but Jaddua refused out of loyalty to Darius. This accords well with Arrian's claim that, while the siege was being undertaken, Alexander sortied inland to bring more of the region to heel and gather more soldiers (Arrian, *Anab.* 2.20.4–5). That Jaddua features as Judah's civic leader in 332 BC shows that Artaxerxes III had confirmed the high priest as de facto governor of Judah a decade earlier, replacing the disloyal Hezekiah. It also explains Jaddua's reticence to defect from Persian sovereignty. He might also have been motivated by his opposition to Samaria, for Josephus relates how Samaria was keen to curry favor with Alexander in the hope of greater autonomy. While Jeshua, the governor of Samaria, quickly threw his lot in with Alexander, Jaddua took the opposite policy of isolation.

With the fall of Tyre, however, the political tide turned. Jaddua's refusal of Alexander's request put him in a precarious situation as Alexander arrived on the coastal plain and received the submission of the Philistine cities. There was no prospect of Jerusalem withstanding a siege, and Jaddua himself now risked his priesthood and the dissolution of the Jerusalem temple. This would leave Mount Gerizim as the sole temple to Yahweh, perhaps under the sacral leadership of his brother, Manasseh—a prospect that would prove fatal to the prophetic traditions and Davidic hope. Jaddua had little choice but to venture out and placate the Greek conqueror and try to secure concessions that might provide a measure of security to Jerusalem.

There is no archaeological or literary evidence to suggest that Alexander took Jerusalem by force.[9] Josephus has Jaddua meet him at a location called Saphein (*Ant.* 11.329), which he understood to be Mount Scopus near Jerusalem. But given Alexander's well-documented itinerary, it is more likely that Jaddua met him in the Shephelah or on the coastal plain.[10] It is also

---

9. Lester L. Grabbe, *The Coming of the Greeks: The Early Hellenistic Period (335–175 BCE)*, vol. 2 of *A History of the Jews and Judaism in the Second Temple Period*. Library of Second Temple Studies 68 (London: T&T Clark, 2008), 275–76.

10. Despite explaining the meaning of the name Saphein, it is possible that Josephus confused the

likely that he brought men for Alexander to draft into his army—something indirectly corroborated by Hecateus of Abdera (*Ag. Ap.* 1.200). The fact that Jaddua remained high priest for a few more years and was followed in office by his son confirms that this personal embassy to Alexander was a success. Jerusalem survived unscathed and retained its native institutions.

The entire region acknowledged Alexander's sovereignty (Arrian, *Anab.* 2.25.4), with the exception of Gaza. Its ruler, a eunuch named Batis,[11] defied Alexander, ultimately to no avail. Alexander breached the walls of Gaza in a matter of weeks, despite taking an arrow to the shoulder, and inflicted a fate on Batis reminiscent of the Trojan hero, Hector: he had straps threaded through Batis's ankles (unlike Hector, Batis was still alive) and dragged behind a chariot until he was dead (Arrian, *Anab.* 2.27.2; Curtius, *Hist.* 4.6.17–30). His gruesome fate is captured in the staid verse of Zechariah's Poem of the Invader (Zech 9:1–8), which also conveys the submission of the other Philistine cities of the plain:

> Ashkelon looks on in fear.
> And Gaza? She squirms about.
> And Ekron? Her expectations have wasted away.
> The king has perished from Gaza.
> Ashkelon no longer remains.
> A bastard rules in Ashdod. (Zech 9:5–6a)

As with the depiction of Tyre's downfall in the same poem (Zech 9:3), there is wordplay here too. The most common Hebrew word for "her expectations" is not used; a rare word (*mebbatah*) is employed instead. The choice is deliberate, producing a wordplay that means "Her expectations have wasted away" as well as "She has been failed by Batis" (or even, "Batis has wasted away"). The reference to the bastard ruling in Ashdod is probably a jibe at Alexander's questionable paternity.

Alexander installed one of his commanders, Andromachus, as governor of Syria. He also put garrisons in the major towns, including Samaria and Jerusalem, as reference to chariots in Ephraim and warhorses in Jerusalem

---

Hebrew name of Scopus (*tsopim*) with a similarly sounding locale on the coastal plain (e.g., Saphithah [Tell el-Safi=Gath], or Sappho).

11. Arrian (*Anab.* 2.25.4) and Curtius (*Hist.* 4.6.7) give the ruler's name as Batis (or Betis), while Josephus (*Ant.* 11.320) gives it as Babemeses. It is difficult to reconcile these two names and to know if Batis was physically a eunuch or simply bore the title as a high official.

prove (Zech 9:10). He then marched on Egypt, which was still nominally under Persian sovereignty. He found the country barely defended as the Persian satrap, Sabaces, had taken most of his troops with him to Issus, where he had fallen in battle. The new satrap, Mazaces, surrendered without a fight.[12] Alexander then ventured to the oracle of Zeus Ammon at the oasis of Siwa in the Libyan (Sahara) Desert, where the oracle confirmed him as the son of Zeus (Arrian, *Anab.* 3.4.5; Plutarch, *Alex.* 27.5–9). Even though Alexander had already been officially named pharaoh of Egypt, the oracle's pronouncement provided him with official religious backing and bestowed on him a sense of divinity. His likeness and cartouche were inscribed into the temple at Luxor.[13] Alexander had begun to take on the cultural airs of his conquered people—something that made some of his staunchly Greek colleagues uncomfortable (Arrian, *Anab.* 2.11.8; 3.3.1–3.4.5; Curtius, *Hist.* 3.11.10; 4.7.4).

On his return from Siwa, Alexander stopped at a fishing village named Rhacotis near the western tip of the Nile Delta with a small island, Pharos, just over a kilometer out to sea. He deemed the location ideal for a new city that might function as a Greek capital in Egypt. Alexander commissioned Cleomenes, the ruler of the nearby Greek colony of Naucratis, to develop the site, and the architect, Deinochares, drew up the plan.[14] The city would be laid out on a grid pattern and a causeway would join Pharos to the mainland (reminiscent of the siege of Tyre), creating two enormous harbors to either side. Alexander named the site after himself: Alexandria. It was officially founded on 7 April 331 BC.[15] In the following years, Cleomenes compelled locals to move to the developing city, and a new metropolis was born (Arrian, *Anab.* 3.2.1; Diodorus Siculus, *Bib. hist.* 17.52.1–7; Curtius, *Hist.* 4.8.5–6; cf. Pliny the Elder, *Nat.* 5.11). Alexandria's founding concretely represented the Greek-Egyptian axis and effectively became the New World of antiquity. In subsequent decades it would showcase Hellenism at its finest, developing into the definitive political, cultural, and economic pole of the Mediterranean—challenged only in later centuries by Rome.

---

12. Coinage issued by both Sabaces and Mazaces in Egypt still survives. See Curtis and Tallis, *Forgotten Empire*, 206, figs. 370–72.

13. Green, *Alexander of Macedon*, 276.

14. Deinochares would eventually draft plans for the new Artemision—the temple to Artemis (Diana) in Ephesus—after the previous structure had been burned in 356 BC, allegedly on the same day Alexander was born. It would become one of the seven wonders of the ancient world.

15. Green, *Alexander of Macedon*, 276; Stoneman, *Alexander the Great*, 41–42.

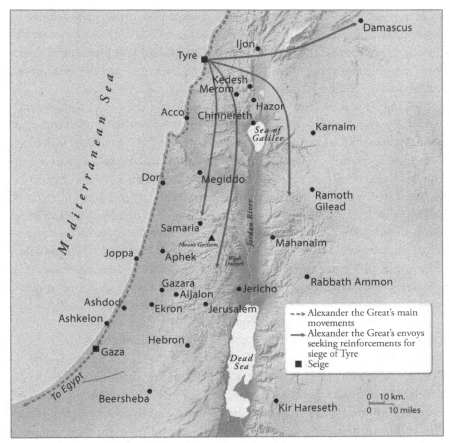

Alexander the Great's conquest of the Levant (332/1 BC).

2.2.4 SAMARIA AND THE ANDROMACHUS AFFAIR

The quick submission of Samaria's governor, Jeshua (son of Sanballat II), to Alexander definitively lifted the Persian yoke from the province. But while Alexander was in Egypt, the Samarians burned his governor, Andromachus, alive (Curtius, *Hist.* 4.8.10). Curtius gives no explanation for this horrific event, but evidence from the aftermath allows us to sketch some possibilities.

First, Andromachus seems not to have been killed accidentally. What the Samarians hoped to achieve by killing him is not clear, suggesting little forethought about the consequences of their actions. Second, Jeshua disappears from the historical record at about this time, and none of his sons ever succeed him. The Sanballat dynasty was snuffed out in response to the attack on Andromachus, though whether Jeshua died before or after Andromachus is unclear (see this section below). Third, since neither Arrian nor Diodorus mention the Andromachus Affair in their accounts of Alexander's campaign, it is safe to assume that the conflict did not engulf the whole province in rebellion. This entails a very sudden turn of events, limited to the city of Samaria and focused on Andromachus personally.

Alexander was swift in retribution. He captured the city of Samaria and turned it into a Greek *polis*. He executed or drove out its inhabitants and replaced them with Macedonian veterans.[16] Around 200 Samarians, including some from the family of Jeshua himself, fled the backlash, taking with them supplies and crucial documents. They made it to the honeycomb of caves in the Wadi Daliyeh, a steep ravine that spills into the Jordan River Valley. Two bullae (WD 22, 23) found among the documents discovered in the caves were stamped with Jeshua's personal seal.[17] They were affixed to documents written before the refugees came to the caves, so it is impossible to know if Jeshua himself was still alive at this point. In any case, Alexander's soldiers drove them all to starvation or surrender. The nobility of Samarian society thus met an ignoble end. Sanballat's petty dynasty was consigned to history, and the Samarian community lost its traditional leaders and the crème of its society.

The Samarians who survived the disaster dispersed across the region. Most made a new life for themselves at Shechem at the foot of Mount Gerizim. Shechem had for centuries been a mere village, but the influx of refugees turned it into the new bustling hub of Samarian life. The temple and residential area atop Mount Gerizim were also redeveloped to facilitate the influx. This included the enlargement of the temple campus, construction of a new perimeter wall, and a monumental staircase along the eastern slope of the mountain to give easier access between the valley and the summit.[18] Ironically, then, the disaster that struck the city of Samaria and its noble families resulted in a new concentration of people around Mount Gerizim, boosting the development of the temple and making its priests more important than ever before. As was the case in Judah (see 2.3 below), the priests became the unrivalled leaders of Samaritan society.

2.2.5 THE BATTLE OF GAUGAMELA (331 BC)

Alexander appointed a new governor in Syria named Memnon (Curtius, *Hist.* 4.8.11) and then marched north towards the Euphrates. Darius had replenished

---

16. See the Chronicle of Eusebius (updated by Jerome), entry for the 112th Olympiad.
17. Knoppers, *Jews and Samaritans*, 111–12.
18. Knoppers, *Jews and Samaritans*, 124–25.

his army while Alexander had been in Egypt, and although he probably did not field "a million infantry" (so Arrian, *Anab.* 3.8.6), his army still massively outnumbered Alexander's.[19] Darius marched his army into what was once the heartland of Assyria, northeast of Nineveh's ruins. The Great King had learned his lesson from Issus, so he camped his army where the terrain was favorable to him, and there he stayed. It was a dusty, open plain near a town called Gaugamela, with lots of room for his cavalry to maneuver.

On 1 October 331 BC, almost two years after the Battle of Issus, the two armies faced each other again. Darius put himself in the central ranks, with Mazaeus (former satrap of Cilicia and Trans-Euphrates) controlling the Persian right flank and Bessus (satrap of Bactria) controlling the left. With greater ranks of cavalry, Darius held a supreme tactical advantage in such open terrain. This forced Alexander to adopt a highly unconventional and risky formation, but it paid off. Alexander thrust his right flank wide, drawing the Persian left in response. As both armies tried to outflank each other, the Persian left became detached from the center. Alexander himself then charged into the gap, whence he headed straight for the chariot of Darius. Alexander got close enough to hurl a javelin at Darius, but it caught the driver of the Great King's chariot instead. Even though Darius was still very much alive, the troops around him believed he had been the one felled and so beat a hasty retreat. As his defenses rapidly depleted, Darius found himself exposed. He had no choice but to flee also, sparking a rout of the whole Persian center (Diodorus Siculus, *Bib. hist.* 17.60.1–4; cf. Arrian, *Anab.* 3.14.3).

Keen not to let Darius escape a second time, Alexander pursued the Great King. But when Alexander received word that his left flank was almost overrun by Mazaeus's cavalry, he called off the pursuit and came to the aid of his flagging troops. His arrival prompted Mazaeus to retreat. Darius escaped once again into the night, but, as at Issus, the day belonged to Alexander (Arrian, *Anab.* 3.14.4–15.7; Diodorus Siculus, *Bib. hist.* 17.60.5–61.3).

2.2.6 THE END OF PERSIA

Before Gaugamela, Babylonian documents were dated by the reign of Darius. Immediately after Gaugamela, a small cuneiform tablet marks the monumental change by being dated to the reign of Alexander, "King of the World."[20] He was twenty-five years old.

---

19. Stoneman, *Alexander the Great*, 45.
20. Romm, *The Landmark Arrian*, fig. 3.15, p. 125.

The Persian Empire was lost. As Darius hastened into the mountains of Media, Alexander headed to Babylon. As Cyrus had done two centuries before, he entered the metropolis unopposed. The biggest city of the Persian Empire, one of its four royal capitals,[21] fell into his hands. Alexander cast himself as the new Cyrus, a liberator and righter of colonial wrongs, by ordering the restoration of the Esagila—the temple of Marduk (or "Bel"), whose statue Xerxes I had destroyed in 482 BC.

A month later he was in Susa, where the local satrap welcomed him unopposed and turned over the vast treasury to him (Diodorus Siculus, *Bib. hist.* 17.65.5–66.7). He then took his army through the mountains into the Persian homeland where, in December 331 BC, he took possession of Persepolis. Diodorus flamboyantly described it as "the richest city under the sun," with over 120,000 talents of silver and gold in its treasury (Diodorus Siculus, *Bib. hist.* 17.70.2–71.1).[22] Alexander spent five months here, the most defining moment coming near the end of his stay when he ordered the Persian palaces to be torched. He targeted the quarters built by Xerxes I (so Diodorus Siculus, *Bib. hist.* 17.72.1–6), seemingly in calculated retribution for Xerxes's invasion of Greece in 480 BC and the fiery sacking of Athens (Arrian, *Anab.* 3.18.1–12). No other Persian capitals were so targeted by Alexander. He ensured that his new empire would be founded on the charred remains of Persian pride. With this catastrophic conflagration, the Persian homeland reverted once more to a mere mountain backwater.

In May 330 BC Alexander resumed his pursuit of Darius. In the summer heat of July, Darius's fate took its final turn. Bessus, the satrap of Bactria, broke ranks with the enfeebled king by clapping him in chains and imprisoning him in a wagon. Alexander soon learned of Darius's whereabouts in the mountains of Hyrcania and set off in hot pursuit. When Bessus and his men spotted Alexander through the dust behind them, they abandoned the wagon and fled, but not before plunging their spears into the hapless Darius. When Alexander reached the wagon, the Great King had bled out (Arrian, *Anab.* 3.20.1–21.10; Diodorus Siculus, *Bib. hist.* 17.73.1–4).[23] The Achaemenid Persian Empire died with him.

---

21. The four capitals of the Persian Empire hosted the royal court according to the seasons: Babylon in Autumn, Susa in winter, Persepolis in spring, and Ecbatana in Summer. This mobile tradition probably reflected something of the Persians' nomadic origins. See Jona Lendering, "Sacker of Cities: Why Did Alexander Burn Persepolis?," *Ancient History*, 2019, 20:34.

22. In modern terms, this would be the equivalent of approximately US$180 trillion, though it is doubtful whether Diodorus's accounting is accurate.

23. Both Arrian and Diodorus confirm that Darius was dead when Alexander reached him, though Diodorus knew of a fanciful version of Darius's death, preserved by Plutarch (*Alex.* 43) in which the Great King dies melodramatically in Alexander's arms.

Alexander's campaign now reached a watershed moment. He had liberated the Greek cities of Asia Minor, possessed Persia's entire Mediterranean seaboard, seized the Nile Valley, scooped up the fertile plain of Mesopotamia, and shot fire into the Persian homeland. With the Great King now dead, Greek vengeance against Persia was complete. Thus Alexander's troops fully expected to return home to Greece. Alexander discharged the soldiers given to him by the League of Corinth, even paying them far more than what he had initially promised. But Alexander's ambitions were still high, his sights set on lands further east. Accordingly, he offered to reenlist them for even higher pay if they would follow him there, and most took him up on the offer (Arrian, *Anab.* 3.19.5–8).[24]

They followed him through lands they had probably never even heard of before—regions that today form Iran, Turkmenistan, Afghanistan, Uzbekistan, Tajikistan, Kyrgyzstan, Pakistan, and India. During the expedition, Bessus, who had elevated himself as King Artaxerxes V, was captured by one of Alexander's bodyguards, Ptolemy, and painfully executed (Arrian, *Anab.* 3.29.7–30.5).[25] Alexander also fell in love with a Bactrian princess, Roxana, and, ignoring the protests of his companions, took her as his wife. Though romantically motivated, the marriage reflected Alexander's emerging policy of intermingling Greek culture with the local cultures of the conquered regions. Here were the early seeds of Hellenism.

In 326 BC Alexander crossed the towering Hindu Kush Mountains—Arrian's "Paropamisos" range (*Anab.* 5.5.3)—and forded the mighty Indus River. Such feats were astounding given the size of his army, the climatic conditions, and the unchartered territory. Then, not without some difficulty, he conquered the Indian principalities along the Indus and its tributaries. Allured by the wealth and exotic cultures before him, Alexander then desired to trek across the subcontinent via the great Ganges River. Like many in his age, he believed India to be the edge of the world. But by now, his troops were weary and affected by the stifling heat and humidity of India. Even Alexander's beloved warhorse, Bucephalus, succumbed to the conditions. The prospect of further perils made them yearn for the familiar climes of the Mediterranean. Unable to convince them to go any further and swayed by ill omens, Alexander agreed to turn back. He sent some of his men by ship along the coast and into the Persian Gulf.

---

24. Arrian places the decommission, reenlisting, and reconfiguration of the army before the death of Darius, while Diodorus places it afterwards. Arrian's version does not, however, account for Alexander's return to his troops after recovering the body of Darius, which Diodorus does (Diodorus Siculus, *Bib. hist.* 17.73.4).

25. The sources do not agree on the manner or location of Bessus's death.

166 THE HELLENISTIC ERA (331–167 BC)

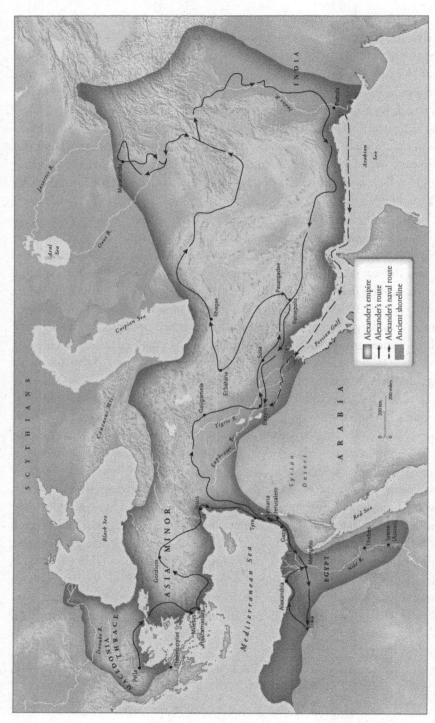

The Conquests of Alexander the Great (334–323 BC).

The rest made the perilous journey across the wastelands of Gedrosia (southern Pakistan and Iran). Thousands of Alexander's men fell during the sapping sixty-day march, but Alexander and his surviving men finally reached Cyrus's old capital at Pasargadae in Persia in the spring of 324 BC (Arrian, *Anab.* 6.29.1).

Cyrus's tomb at Pasargadae was in a dilapidated state, so Alexander ordered its restoration (Arrian, *Anab.* 6.29.3–11). He then continued to Susa where, as part of his policy of cultural intermingling, he married Stateira, the daughter of Darius III,[26] and Parysatis, the daughter of Artaxerxes III. In this way, he joined the Achaemenid dynasty to his own, boosting his legitimacy in the eyes of the locals. He also ordered his chief personnel to marry Persian women, which they did under duress. His aim was to amalgamate Macedonian and Persian nobility, thus creating a new ruling class that reflected the breadth of his new empire. His staff railed against this policy. They had sallied forth as Greeks on a crusade against barbarian enemies, but now Alexander was quite literally putting them into bed with the culture they had long despised. He had even taken to wearing Persian apparel (Arrian, *Anab.* 7.8.2). The weddings at Susa reveal that Alexander viewed his empire as an amalgam of east and west. Although his staff were still beholden to him personally, they felt his policy was a betrayal of fundamental Greek ideals, which drew an absolute distinction between Greeks and barbarians. An uncomfortable rift, therefore, opened up between Alexander and his men.

2.2.7 THE DEATH OF ALEXANDER

Over the next year, Alexander ventured between Babylon, Susa, and Ecbatana, reorganizing his administration. While many of his troops returned to Greece, others settled in colonies within conquered lands, spreading Greek culture in a tangible way. In autumn 324 BC his closest friend, Hephaestion, died, bringing Alexander disconsolate grief, which exacerbated his growing sense of isolation from those around him. Even so, he began planning an invasion of the Arabian Peninsula. But in early June 323 BC he was taken ill after a night of drinking. A week later, a fever took hold, rendering him unable to walk. Then, in the early hours of 11 June 323 BC, Alexander slipped into death (Arrian, *Anab.* 7.8.1–15.1; 7.19.3–28.1). He was thirty-two.

---

26. Arrian names Darius's daughter "Barsine" (*Anab.* 7.4.4), which is either a mistake or another name by which Stateira was known.

Alexander probably died from Guillain-Barré Syndrome, though typhoid and malaria have also been suggested.[27] His sudden death created a political crisis, for he died without an heir. Roxana was pregnant with their first child at the time, and though she gave birth to a son, Alexander IV, two months later, he could not rule immediately. Alexander's staff also objected to the fact that Roxana was a barbarian. They refused to be led one day by her son, who was not a full-blooded Macedonian as they were. Their objection thrust Alexander's disabled half-brother, Arrhidaeus, into the fray. Alexander's staff reached a provisional resolution: Arrhidaeus would rule symbolically as "Philip III" in a joint reign with Alexander's infant son, Alexander IV, while Alexander's senior general, Perdiccas, acted as regent on their behalf. The empire's satrapies were then divided among the remaining staff to govern.

The provisional solution was, however, unsustainable. In an empire forged by a single commander, no single person emerged to take control. By comparison, when Cambyses had died in 522 BC and left no heir, the Persian Empire had been rescued from oblivion by the strong leadership of Darius I. Alexander had spent most of his twelve years as king on campaign, but it took just two years for his empire to effectively implode. Its existence had been predicated on his personal rule and he had steered it in a multicultural direction that his staff, who held tenaciously to their Greek ideals, refused to countenance. The far-flung regions of Bactria and India broke away, though strong Greek influence would continue within them for centuries to come. In Greece the city-states, which had never been enthusiastic allies of Alexander and which now received back many of their veterans from his campaign, erupted into civil war (the Lamian War). Soon Alexander's generals were squabbling among themselves for supremacy. None of them had ever expected to succeed Alexander, and yet, having participated in his campaign, they had all become experienced warmongers with a taste for success.

Further exacerbating the fragmentation was the fact that the political pole of the ancient Near East was now in the Mediterranean. Alexander had adopted Persia's capital cities as his own, but he did not have the time or posterity to reorient the political magnetism back towards Mesopotamia. Now, with his empire in the hands of his parochially Greek staff, there was an inexorable pull back towards the Mediterranean. His successors relinquished the furthest territories in the east to duke it out among themselves for sovereignty over

---

27. See Katherine Hall, "Did Alexander the Great Die from Guillain-Barré Syndrome?," *AHB* 32 (2019): 106–28.

territories closer to the Mediterranean. Despite the attempt to mediate another resolution in 321 BC (the Partition of Triparadisus), hostilities between the generals soon broke out, bringing massive instability to the Levant. The constant warring, political turmoil, strain on resources, and the death of so many people—leaders, soldiers, and civilians alike—tyrannized society for the next two decades.

Despite the despair and tumult, the notion of Yahweh's sovereignty and the surety of his intentions was not overturned. Psalm 33 was probably composed during these decades to buoy the faithful amid the turbulent waters:

> Let all the earth be in fear of Yahweh,
> in dread of him all inhabitants of the world . . .
> Yahweh frustrates the plan of nations,
> foils the intention of peoples.
> The plan of Yahweh stands permanently,
> the intentions of his heart from generation to generation.
> Blessed is the nation whose god is Yahweh,
> the people he has chosen for his own estate.
> From the heavens Yahweh looks,
> he sees all the children of humanity.
> From the abode of his dwelling he gazes
> across all inhabitants of the earth . . .
> No king is saved by the greatness of his army.
> No soldier is saved by the greatness of his strength.
> Futile is the horse for victory,
> and by the greatness of his army, he does not escape.
> See, the eye of Yahweh is on all who fear him,
> on those who wait for his faithfulness,
> to save their lives from death,
> to preserve them through famine.
> Our being waits for Yahweh.
> Our help and our shield is he.
> For in him we will celebrate,
> for in his holy name we have trusted.
> May your faithfulness, O Yahweh, be upon us,
> even as we put our hope in you. (Pss 33:8, 10–14, 15–22)

For the people of Judah and Samaria, the entire fourth century BC was an experience of perpetual uncertainty and hardship.

2.2.8 ALEXANDER IN THE BOOK OF DANIEL

Alexander is never named in the Hebrew canon, but he is alluded to in the book of Daniel (see also 3.3.2 below). The first allusion comes in the interpretation of Nebuchadnezzar's dream (Dan 2). The statue in the dream has four segments representing the successive empires that ruled the ancient Near East. Nebuchadnezzar and the Babylonian Empire is identified as the "head of gold" (Dan 2:37–38). Various interpretations exist for the remaining three political entities, but some of these are based on misplaced eschatological speculation. The most appropriate configuration, which works with the context of the book and how the ancients viewed their world, is that the chest and arms of silver represent the Medes, the belly and thighs of bronze are the Persians (2:32–33a, 39), and Alexander's empire is the legs of iron, which fragment into feet of iron and clay (2:33b–34). The imagery is explained in Daniel 2:40–43:

> There will be a fourth kingdom, as strong as iron, for iron breaks and shatters everything. Like iron that destroys, it will break and destroy all these [previous kingdoms]. Just as you saw the feet and toes partly of potter's clay and partly of iron, it will become a kingdom divided, even though some of the hardness of iron will still be in it, for you saw the iron mixed with wet clay. As the toes of the feet were partly of iron and partly of clay, so some of the kingdom will be strong and some of it brittle. As you saw the iron mixed with wet clay, so will human progeny be mixed together. One part will not cling to another, the same way iron does not mix together with clay.

The explanation focuses on Alexander breaking down the structures of the Persian Empire as well as the swift disintegration of his own empire. His policy of cultural intermingling is depicted as doomed to failure. Nonetheless, some of Alexander's tenacity is imparted to the kingdoms of his successors. As we will see, Greek ideas were to have a profound effect on Jews, producing the hybrid culture of Hellenistic Judaism. Conflict would eventually arise over what proportion of Greek ideas could viably mix with traditional Jewish ideas. According to the author of Daniel, certain Greek notions were fundamentally incompatible with genuine Judaism, just as iron was incompatible with clay (see also 3.3.2 below).

Nebuchadnezzar's dream reaches its climax when a mere "pebble" of chipped stone topples the composite statue. The pebble then grows into a mighty mountain (Dan 2:34–35), depicting the downfall of foreign regimes and the establishment of the kingdom of God (2:44–45). Expressed here is not just a hope for Jewish independence but the inbreaking of a divine kingdom over the whole world. The Hellenistic era would witness the growth of such eschatological hope. There is no mention of a Davidic kingdom here, but neither is there mention of a priest or any other human agent. The focus is on divine action to overcome foreign obstacles that stand in the way of God's untrammeled rule upon the earth. Alexander's rise to power over most of the known world is a model of worldwide dominion. Yet it is dominion established by military muscle and political clout, building on preceding imperial structures in a vain attempt to establish something enduring and universal. The sudden fate of Alexander was testament to how fragile even the mightiest empire could be. The author of Daniel thus moves his readers from the model of Alexander's kingdom towards hope for a divine kingdom that would eclipse all others and promote genuine, universal faith in the one true God.

A similar progression appears in the first vision of Daniel (Dan 7). In contrast to Nebuchadnezzar's dream (Dan 2), this vision considers the kingdoms that arose within the ancient Near East as distinct from each other. Its emphasis lies on the sinister influence of the Hellenistic kingdoms (the fourth beast [Dan 7:7]) and the persecutions inflicted on Jews by the Seleucid king, Antiochus IV Epiphanes (the little horn [Dan 7:8]; see 3.2.5 below). The Babylonian Empire is depicted as a winged lion (Dan 7:4), the Medo-Persian Empire as a devouring bear (Dan 7:5), and Alexander's empire as a winged leopard (Dan 7:6). The four wings of the leopard symbolize the speed of Alexander's conquests while its four heads represent the four political blocs that sprang from his empire. The hybrid nature of these beasts gives a sense of monstrous abnormality and frightening viciousness, evoking the ancient imagery of the Rahab or Leviathan—the chaos monster, which Yahweh defeats to create the world (see 1.2.3 above). It is symbolic of the ruthlessness with which the conglomerations of empire were formed and the unnatural unity they imposed through violence and intimidation. There is no concern in this vision to consider any positive aspects of empire, such as the cultural benefaction of the early Persian Empire. Rather, the vision is concerned to depict the entirety of empires in one summary symbol and contrast them with the eschatological kingdom that will be the new creative work of God.

Daniel's second vision (Dan 8) depicts the Medo-Persian Empire as a ram with two horns—the smaller horn representing the Medes and the bigger horn representing the Persians (Dan 8:3–4, 20). It is then challenged by a shaggy goat, which charges it from the west without touching the ground (Dan 8:5–7). Alexander is not named, but he is undeniably "the first king," singled out as the prominent horn between the goat's eyes (8:21), which is snapped off at the height of its power (Dan 8:7–8, 22). The four horns that grow in its place symbolize the four political blocs of his successors and the continuity of Hellenistic influence (Dan 8:8, 22). The horn imagery in these visions might derive from associations with power throughout biblical literature (cf. Pss 75:10; 92:10; Lam 2:3) but might also come from the use of horns on the battle helmets of prominent commanders as depicted on Hellenistic coins from the third to the second century BC.[28]

Daniel's third and final vision (Dan 10–12) depicts the struggle between the Persians and the Greeks as a preface to the political machinations between the Ptolemies and Seleucids in the third and second centuries BC—all events that exerted influence over Judea. It couches these events in highly symbolic terms whereby the political figures of history are subsumed into spiritual "princes," "kings," and "kingdoms" that occupy an ethereal world—principalities and powers in the heavenly realms (cf. Eph 6:12). The text alludes to Xerxes I's invasion of Greece (Dan 11:2). Alexander is the "mighty king . . . who will rule with great power and do as he pleases" (Dan 11:3). Behind Alexander lies another figure, the "Prince of Greece" (Dan 10:20), who is a spiritual personification of Greek ideals. This enigmatic figure is akin to the Roman notion of the "genius"—a mythical character of spiritual protection who embodies the essence and ideals of that which it protects.[29] In this way, the reader begins to understand the rise and fall of empires not simply as historical events but as spiritual realities (see 2.4.3 below).

The turn of empires had a profound effect over the spiritual life of Jews and Samaritans. Alexander's sudden rise and demise was historically explosive and would have been a flash in the pan if not for two major factors: he destroyed the Persian Empire that had reigned over Judah and Samaria, and his empire gave way to the Hellenistic kingdoms that would suffuse subordinate cultures with a Greek flavor that was, in many ways, vastly different to Persia's influence.

---

28. For example, Seleucus I is portrayed wearing a horned helmet while the coins of Lysimachus show the deified Alexander (the Great) with a ram's horns (both early third century BC). The coins of Diodotus Tryphon (ca. 138 BC) portray a Boeotian helmet with a large horn protruding from the front. See Boris Chrubasik, *Kings and Usurpers in the Seleukid Empire: The Men Who Would Be King* (Oxford: Oxford University Press, 2016), 158–60.

29. In Dan 10:13, 21, Michael is depicted as the genius ("prince") of the Jews. Cf. Matthew L. Walsh, *Angels Associated with Israel in the Dead Sea Scrolls: Angelology and Sectarian Identity at Qumran*, Wissenschaftliche Untersuchungen Zum Neuen Testament, 2/509 (Tübingen: Mohr Siebeck, 2019), 66–83.

2.3 PRIESTLY POWER AND DAVIDIC HOPE UNDER GREEK RULE

2.3.1 JUDAH UNDER ALEXANDER

People like the Chronicler hoped that Persia's demise would lead to Judah's autonomy—perhaps even to the installation of a Davidic descendant, like Shekaniah or one of his sons, in a governing capacity (1 Chr 3:22–24). Judah's submission to Alexander, therefore, must have come as a demoralizing blow. Sovereignty over Judah simply passed from one colonial overlord to another, bypassing the Davidic dynasty completely. But this was probably viewed initially as a setback rather than a mortal blow. When Cambyses had died unexpectedly in 522 BC, the Persian Empire had begun to crumble. Alexander's sudden death thrust his empire into a similar dilemma, and this time there was no Darius I to prevent the collapse. Thus, hope for Judean independence was not lost, though it did underscore how small Judah was on the international stage.

Greek rule was also not without some benefits. The crippling economic burdens experienced under the Persians were lifted as Alexander permitted local institutions to continue. Jaddua's continued leadership over Judah exemplified this cultural leniency. The Greeks were also well disposed towards Yahweh, whom they equated with the head of their own pantheon, Zeus. Alexander's sovereignty was not, therefore, a threat to the cultural norm of Torah among Yahwists, nor even to the priesthoods in Jerusalem and Mount Gerizim. In this way, Alexander's rule was akin to that of Artaxerxes I, who had actively pursued a strategy of cultural benefaction in a multicultural empire.

Nonetheless, the possibility of Davidic leadership became much less likely. Despite gambling his leadership before Alexander, Jaddua was not set aside in favor of the scion of a dynasty that had last ruled Judah over 250 years before. Alexander found Jaddua as de facto governor and confirmed his ongoing tenure as ethnarch of the Jews. Under Persian rule, Jerusalem's priests did not by default hold political office—that had been the preserve of a civic governor appointed by the Persians (e.g., Nehemiah, Bagohi, Hezekiah). The high priests Johanan and Jaddua had only ever been caretaker governors in extraordinary circumstances (see 1.5.2 and 1.7.5 above), following the example of the high priest Joshua (cf. Zech 6:9–15; see 1.1.2 above). But from Jaddua onwards, the Greeks would recognize the high priest as the default holder of civic office, permanently combining cultic and political power.[1]

2.3.2 THE EXPROPRIATION OF DAVIDIC THEOLOGY

Jerusalem's primacy was predicated on the prophetic traditions from which Davidic ideology sprang. But with the high priest as the ethnarch of Judah, Davidic ideology was benched. On the one hand, the Jerusalem priesthood needed Davidic ideology to justify its existence and contradict Samaritan claims about Mount Gerizim. On the other hand, the emerging political reality could not allow a Davidic scion to take power of any kind. If the high priest was to retain power and still garner popular support, the priestly elite needed to stoke Davidic hope enough to justify Jerusalem's primacy while at the same time deferring indefinitely any actualization of Davidic hope. This was achieved in several ways across the next century.

First, the high priest in Jerusalem could not be ousted from civic office. When Jaddua died in ca. 325 BC, his son, Hezekiah, succeeded him, with local civic authority invested in him by the Greeks.[2] Even though Davidic descendants such as Shekaniah and his sons were in Jerusalem (1 Chr 3:22–24) and perhaps even lobbying for elevation, they were still barred from power and there was little they could do about it. The Davidic family was now a relic with little place in the *Realpolitik* of the late fourth century BC. Over time, this would allow some to turn Davidic hope into a pure ideal—a mythological model of power that could still captivate the hearts and minds of Jews while permitting non-Davidides to actualize leadership.

Second, the scribal tradition of preserving prophetic and pro-Davidic texts continued in Jerusalem unabated. This helped keep Davidic hope alive even as it was transformed by the ongoing marginalization of the Davidic family.

Third, despite this, Davidic hope was deemphasized by concentrating religious attention on the Torah. A greater concern for cultic purity and precision in following the commands of Torah emerged in the decades that followed. This would later be challenged by the influence of progressive Hellenism,

---

1. This situation is comparable to when the bishops of Rome took on de facto civic power, creating the papacy.
2. Onias I is often given as the son and successor of Jaddua, due to Josephus's account. However, as will be discussed below (see 2.6.2), Hezekiah was the son and successor of Jaddua, while Onias I was Jaddua's grandson.

but this legal trend would persist and lead centuries later to the development of such Jewish sects as the Essenes and Pharisees. It also enabled scribes to become officially sanctioned teachers of the Law—cultural guardians who could provide the population with a staple diet of Torah knowledge, with modest helpings of prophetic and associated traditions on the side.

Fourth, the priestly elite expropriated Zion theology for their own purposes, turning it into a promulgation of priestly power. The term "Zion" originally referred to the fortress in Jerusalem that David had captured and used as his residence, renaming it "city of David" (2 Sam 5:6–10; 1 Chr 11:5). It was not merely a synonym for Jerusalem but more narrowly a reference to the Davidic fortress and, by extension, to Jerusalem as the seat of Davidic power. Zion was also Jerusalem's first Yahwistic cultic site, for it was to the fortress that David brought the ark of the covenant (2 Sam 6:12–19; cf. 1 Kgs 8:1). In doing so, David performed a priestly function, wearing the priestly garb of a linen ephod, offering sacrifices, and mediating divine blessing to the people. The term "Zion," therefore, carried both royal and priestly overtones, both being grounded in Davidic ideology:

> I have authorized my king on Zion,
> my holy mountain. (Psalm 2:6)

> A Davidic Psalm.
> Declaration of Yahweh to my lord:
> "Sit at my right hand
> while I place your enemies as a footstool at your feet.
> The scepter of your sovereignty
> Yahweh will extend from Zion.
> Rule betwixt your enemies..."
> Yahweh has sworn and will not renege:
> "You are a perpetual priest
> by my word, O rightful king."[3] (Ps 110:1–2, 4)

Yahweh's passion for "Zion" in prophetic and psalmic literature, then, was about his commitment to the Davidic covenant and the restoration of a Davidic kingdom (cf. Zech 1:14). But during the Hellenistic era, a shift occurred and

---

3. This clause is often translated as "in the order of Melchizedek" (cf. NIV11, CSB, ESV, NRSV), following the LXX (cf. Heb 5:6, 10; 6:20; 7:11–17) The clause is most likely a deliberate play on words. Whichever way it is translated, the significance is unchanged: royal and priestly power are both conferred on the Davidic king.

"Zion" lost its royal core, leaving only its priestly shell behind. Soon it was little more than a generic appellation for Jerusalem as the city in which Yahweh's temple was located. That the temple had once been a monument and sacrament to the Davidic covenant was totally eclipsed by its role as a generic place of worship (cf. Sir 24:10; 36:19[MT]; Jdt 9:13). It was an ideological coup that promoted temple over palace, priest over king, cult over country. Davidic ideology was pressed into the service of the priesthood, reversing the preexilic norm. Priestly power could now be read straight off the scrolls of Scriptures, including the prophetic traditions, transforming the ideal Israel from Davidic kingdom into hierocratic community.

Fifth, while hope of reunion with the Samaritans was entertained in theory, in reality it was practically abandoned. Like prophetic texts espousing Davidic hope, Scriptures expressing the unity of all Israel were seen to reflect the distant past, creating a mythological ideal that was impossible to replicate in the present. By treating unity as a lost cause, the upper echelons of Jewish society created a separate Jewish national identity that defined Jews over against Samaritans. This identity was not entirely new, but a new line in the sand had been drawn. Many Jews (but not all), who still constituted the minority of Yahwists, came to see themselves not simply as the guardians of a larger Israelite identity but as the totality of Israel itself. From now on, to be an Israelite was to be Jewish and not Samaritan (or vice versa for the Samaritans).[4] Both Jewish and Samaritan communities claimed to be Israel to the exclusion of the other.

These developments were not immediate, yet they ensured that Judah came into the Hellenistic era as a hierocratic society centered around the supreme authority of the high priest. This did not eliminate Davidic loyalists like the Chronicler, who still held fervently to hope for a Davidic kingdom incorporating all the tribes of Israel. Their conviction that God still intended to restore the Davidic kingdom became the basis of messianic expectation. But this expectation was now largely confined to non-priestly classes, which widened the fault lines in Jewish society. In time, the privileged priestly classes who held political authority pursued a non-Davidic agenda, while some in the lower classes of society adopted the more prophetically charged desire for a

---

4. Many attribute this exclusive Jewish claim to Israelite identity to Ezra and Nehemiah in the fifth century BC. However, this misunderstands their pan-Israelite intentions and fails to account for both the consolidation of the Torah in Samaria and the ongoing interactions between Samarians and Judeans throughout the century that followed. It is only after the failure of the Israelite Coalition (see 1.7) and the dawn of the Hellenistic era that we see a definitive break between Judeans and Samarians. It was not unlike the schism between the Eastern Orthodox and Roman Catholic churches in the eleventh century or the break of Protestant churches from Roman Catholicism.

Davidic kingdom, though without the political power to do much about it. There was a growing divide being priestly and prophetic agendas, with both sides reading support for their claims off the same Scriptures.

Some members of the scribal middle class and urban plebs became the keepers of Davidic hope, in addition to the Davidic family itself. Though the priests and educated Davidic loyalists (like the Chronicler) might not have seen eye to eye on all matters in the past, there had nonetheless been a synergy between them over the matter of Jerusalem's primacy. Now, with the combination of the cultic and civic offices in the person of the high priest, Davidic loyalists were thrust to the margins. This is not to say there were no priests or Levites with Davidic loyalties—only that, over time, they became a distinct minority.

For members of the Davidic family, the slide into obscurity had begun the moment the Persians had clipped Zerubbabel's wings. Now the shadows encroached more fully, putting Shekaniah and his descendants on the road to becoming mere plebs. The more the shadows lengthened across them, the more light the priests received.

2.3.3 PROPHECY IN JUDAH

Zechariah 13:4–6, which dates to the early Hellenistic era, shows that prophetic figures existed within Jewish society at this time, in keeping with the notion that Yahweh had not fallen silent. Charismatic figures were still having visions and making public pronouncements, though the prophetic author of the oracle (Zech 12–14) critiques some practitioners as fraudulent. This facilitated an increased modesty in prophetic claims, leading to such things as anonymous prophecy (e.g., Zech 12–14) and a focus on the prophets of the past. The collation, editing, and reissuing of past prophecies alongside new prophecy is demonstrated by the Book of the Twelve Prophets. New literary genres were also created as quasi-prophetic outlets, such as apocalypses, novellas, psalms, wisdom reflections, histories, and *pesharim* ("interpretations" or commentaries on old prophetic texts). While many of these were never canonized, they attest to the continuing phenomenon of prophetic activity.

That a text like Zechariah 13:4–6 could take aim at perceived false prophets demonstrates that there was no unified theological outlook in Judah during the early Hellenistic era. The original core of Zechariah goes back to the prophet Zechariah in the early years of Darius I, when it was issued together with the prophecies of Haggai. Zechariah was himself a priest and advocated the elevation of the high priest Joshua to community leader during

Zerubbabel's absence from Jerusalem (Zech 6:9–15). Nonetheless, he was still a Davidic loyalist committed to the divine promises to "Zion" and all the Davidic freight that came with that term (Zech 1:14; cf. 2 Sam 5:7). This loyalist stance was adopted by the subsequent prophet(s) who supplemented his work with further prophecies in the Persian and Hellenistic eras.[5] These later prophecies were not correctives but worked with the ideological grain of the original prophet.

The Hellenistic era prophet who wrote Zechariah 12–14 does not describe the nature of the false prophecies in his own time. However, the nature of theological development at the time makes it likely that the ongoing place of the Davidic family in the life and prospects of Jewish society was at least part of it. He believed firmly in the primacy of Jerusalem and the need for pilgrimage to its temple (cf. Zech 14:16–21). Thus, he considered the priesthood integral to Jewish life. Yet, he also envisioned a time when "The house of David will be like God, like the Messenger of Yahweh" (Zech 12:8), in contrast to his own day. This view is wrapped within a hope for a universal kingdom of God (Zech 14:9), when false prophets would be ashamed of their own activities (Zech 13:4–6).

The prophet's concern for Davidic honor also explains his belligerent attitude towards Alexander. The Poem of the Invader (Zech 9:1–8), which he reworked to reflect the Greek advances, sees Alexander's conquests as unleashing irresistible terror throughout Trans-Euphrates. The survival of Jerusalem was due entirely to divine protection. Yet it also sparked longing for a time when invasions would cease—when the likes of Alexander (and Darius I and Artaxerxes II before him) would no longer treat the land as a thoroughfare or threaten its inhabitants:

> But I will garrison an outpost for my house
> against anyone traversing back and forth.
> No invader will again pass through,
> for now I have seen it with my own eyes. (Zech 9:8)

This prophecy is followed immediately by a recontextualization of what was originally a panegyric celebrating the return of Zerubbabel to Jerusalem after his unparalleled release by Darius I (ca. 518 BC). Zechariah's original prophecy provided the Hellenistic era prophet with just the right precedent for

---

5. The resulting book of Haggai–Zechariah was eventually incorporated into the Book of the Twelve Prophets (Hosea–Malachi) in the early third century BC.

shaping the hope that something similar might happen again in the future. In reworking the original prophecy, the later prophet contrasted the humility of an ideal Davidic king with the ostentation of Alexander astride his warhorse, Bucephalus. He also pined for a time when foreign occupation of Samaria ("Ephraim") and Jerusalem would end:

> Celebrate heartily, Daughter Zion!
> Shout out, Daughter Jerusalem!
> Look, your king comes to you.
> He is exonerated and liberated,
> humbled but riding on a donkey,
> on a colt, the offspring of asses.
> He wipes out chariotry from Ephraim,
> and cavalry from Jerusalem.
> The war-bow is wiped out.
> He promises peace to the nations,
> and his rule extends from sea to sea,
> from the River to the ends of the earth.
> "As for you,
> because of the blood of your covenant,
> I have released your prisoners from a waterless dungeon.
> Return to the stronghold, prisoners of hope.
> This very day, I tell you,
> I bring you back a second time.
>
> "Yes, I have loaded myself with Judah,
> fitted my bow with Ephraim;
> I am rousing your sons, O Zion,
> against your sons, O Greece,
> making you like a warrior's sword."
> Then Yahweh will appear above them
> and his arrow will shoot like lightning.
> Lord Yahweh will blow the trumpet
> and march in the siroccos of the south.
> Yahweh of Ranks will protect them,
> as they expend and conquer with sling-stones,
> drinking and rampaging as if with wine
> until they become as full as sacrificial bowls,
> as the edges of the altar.

> Yahweh their God will give them victory on that day.
> His people are like sheep,
> but they are crown jewels,
> shining across his territory. (Zech 9:9–16)

Crucially, the pairing of Ephraim (Samaritans) and Judah shows how the prophet retained a pan-Israelite hope, but the basis for this was still recognition of a Davidic king in Jerusalem. The demise of the Sanballat dynasty (see 2.2.4 above) had removed a significant obstacle to this, but the Samaritans were still beholden to Mount Gerizim. For Davidic loyalists, reunion under a Davidic king must have seemed a distant possibility with Greek authority stamped all over the region. For such loyalists, priestly leadership in Israel was permitted to fill a power vacuum, but it could never be a permanent arrangement. Over time, the priests ensured that it would be.

2.4 HELLENISM

2.4.1 GREEK RELIGION AND CULTURE

Hellenism was the combination of Greek ideals (religion, culture, ethics, philosophy, and science) with local cultures, and it exerted an enormous influence over Jews and Samaritans. Ancient Greek religion was decentralized, mostly because the Greeks were a politically fragmented ethnos. As such, it was comprised of several localized cults to various Greek gods and heroes, augmented by an ever-developing and often contradictory mythology. Although there were many temples, the priests never formed an official caste that controlled the religion in any authoritative way. There was, therefore, no such thing as "orthodoxy" and by corollary, no such thing as "heresy"—only "impiety" (Gk. *asebeia*), which was a failure to acknowledge the gods. Worship had few prescribed parameters, even though it often followed the same kinds of rites, such as animal sacrifice. This sometimes made it difficult to discern the will of the gods, which is why oracles were consulted (e.g., the oracle of Apollo at Delphi). Yet it provided considerable latitude in religious expression, which promoted personal ingenuity and free-thinking. This explains why the Greek poets (e.g., Homer, Hesiod), rather than priests, shaped Greek mythology and legend. It was also a logical consequence that, with such a decentralized religion, philosophical thinking and the pursuit of empirical knowledge would eventually grow. In all cases, there was room for considerable creativity and personal freedom.

This decentralized aspect of Greek religion made it quite different to Yahwism. When Israel and Judah had existed as independent kingdoms, henotheism enshrined Yahweh as the national deity of Israel, binding the entire land to his worship. The mandates of the kings were tied directly to the will of Yahweh, in whose land they ruled. The biblical prophets decried syncretism and religious laxity, seeing them as causes of the destruction of both kingdoms. Theirs was, however, a minority voice at the time. But during the Persian era, a more conservative and centralized form of religion emerged in both Judah and Samaria, leading to the decline of syncretism and the rising importance of the priesthood and of Torah to regulate orthodoxy. The temples at Jerusalem and Mount Gerizim vied for supremacy as the one legitimate place at which to worship Yahweh, who was increasingly recognized as the sole deity in existence. This competitiveness between the two centers gave yet more impetus to the attempts of the two respective communities to define orthodoxy and, by implication, define the other as heretical—a concept alien to Greek religion. Thus Yahwism was developing along a trajectory of centralization in direct contrast to the decentralized mode of Greek religion.

In contrast to the regnant monotheism in Judah and Samaria, the Greeks worshipped the Olympian pantheon. Chief among them was Zeus, god of the sky (or king of heaven), classically depicted with a thunderbolt in his hand, with jurisdiction over all gods and humans. His sister and consort was Hera, queen of heaven and patron of marriage and family life. Their brother, Poseidon, ruled the sea, while their other brother, Hades, governed the Underworld. Apollo, usually depicted as an athletic youth, was worshipped as a preserver of life, patron of the arts, and truth-teller. During the Hellenistic era, he also came to be viewed as the sun god, essentially replacing the Titan god, Helios, who had held that jurisdiction previously. Athena, who was said to have sprung fully formed from the head of Zeus, had her primary cult in Athens, which was named after her (or perhaps vice versa) and where her temple, the Parthenon, was magnificently rebuilt after Xerxes I sacked the city in 480 BC. The other Olympian gods were Demeter, Aphrodite, Ares, Artemis, Hermes, and Hephaistos. By the Hellenistic era, Dionysus had also earned himself a place in their company due to his intoxicating popularity as a god of wine.

In addition to the major deities were a host of lesser gods, often personifying concepts or serving etiological functions. For example, the Muses were the nine patron goddesses of the arts and sciences—all daughters of Zeus and Mnemosyne (the personification of "memory"). The goat-horned and goat-legged Pan was the god of rustic shepherds, while the nymph, Echo, was cursed by Hera to say nothing but the last words she heard from others. This array of major and minor gods presented an interesting mix of the predictable and unpredictable, giving rise to superstitions that often involved the interpretation of omens. There were also several "heroes"—mortals who could boast of at least one divine parent and who had earned veneration, much like the saints in medieval Roman Catholicism. The most famous hero was Heracles, the son of Zeus and the mortal Alcmene.

In addition to prayer and sacrifice, the Greeks developed a form of worship distinct to their ethnicity, namely the games (Gk. *agōnes*). These were festivals at which athletic and artistic competitions were held—organized pursuits of human excellence devoted to the gods. Any city could host games, but there were four Panhellenic Games held in a regular four-year rotation (an "Olympiad"), which attracted participants and spectators from all over the Greek world. These were (1) the Olympic Games, held in honor of Zeus at Olympia; (2) the Nemean Games, held in honor of Zeus and Heracles at Nemea; (3) the Isthmian Games, held in honor of Poseidon at Isthmia; and (4) the Pythian Games, held in honor of Apollo at Delphi. The competition was evocative of the perennial competitiveness between Greek cities. Athletes competed nude, partly to confirm their sex (only men could compete) and ensure that no assisting devices were used, but also to celebrate the human body. This was a logical outworking of the nature of the Greek gods, most of whom were human-like in both appearance and temperament. A similar focus on the human form can be seen in Greek sculpture in which representations of the nude abound, for to be nude was to be godlike.

The institution of the gymnasium developed in parallel to the Games. Gymnasia were arenas at which men trained physically, partly for fitness and battle-readiness, but also for competition and religious devotion. The term "gymnasium" comes from the Greek word *gymnos* ("naked"), indicating that physical training was pursued in the nude. Gymnasia were also places of education and socialization as men in the prime of life studied and fraternized together, preparing themselves for active military and civic life. The institution had wide appeal as a means of religious devotion, education, and social advancement. Indeed, the modern concept of the school stems from the ancient Greek gymnasium.[1]

The games, the gymnasium, and the public celebration of the nude in Greece were antithetical to the conformity and modesty inherent in Jewish and Samaritan worship (cf. Exod 28:42–43; cf. 20:26; Lev 6:10).[2] Furthermore, Greeks considered circumcision a barbaric practice and viewed the Torah's dietary restrictions as curious and unnecessary. Greek religion and culture tended towards latitude and freedom, whereas Judah and Samaria tended towards restrictions and regulations. These fundamental differences would contribute to the significant cultural clash between Greek-minded liberals and Hebraic-minded conservatives, which would develop in Judah and Samaria during the Hellenistic era.

The Greeks usually identified foreign gods with their own on the basis of similar functions. Such compatibilism saw the Greeks identify Yahweh with Zeus as the "God of the heavens" (cf. Let. Aris. 15), just as the Persians had

---

1. This connection is preserved in modern Greek today in which the word *gymnasio* denotes a middle school.

2. Paul's description of sinful human behavior in Rom 1:18–32 is, essentially, a denunciation of the gymnasium and the social culture it engendered among the elite of Greco-Roman society.

seen Yahweh as a local version of Ahura Mazda. The one critical difference, however, was that the Persians were essentially monotheistic, while the Greeks were not. This posed no problem to the liberal Greeks, who were content to allow foreigners to worship the gods in their own "barbarian" way. However, it posed a serious dilemma to conservative Jews and Samaritans, who understood Yahweh as the one and only God and who was exclusively in covenant with their own nation. Jews and Samaritans could not easily reverse the Greeks' compatibilism.

This dilemma was compounded by the nature and ethical character of Zeus (and the other gods). As a son of the Titan gods, Cronos and Rhea, Zeus was deemed to have had a beginning, whereas Yahweh was never depicted as having a source beyond himself (cf. Exod 3:14). Although designated as wise, just, merciful, and all-knowing, Zeus's impetuosity and escapades in mythology left much to be desired morally, whereas the biblical prophets portrayed Yahweh as without peer, steadfast, and abounding in his commitment to Israel, even at great cost to himself. Zeus was capricious and often more deeply flawed than humans, whereas Yahweh was wholly transcendent and infallible. Zeus often needed to be coaxed to dispense justice, whereas Yahweh was always perfect and just. Such incompatibility helps us appreciate the difference between biblical characterizations of Yahweh, like Psalm 113:5-6 ("Who is like Yahweh our God, the one who sits on high, who stoops to look at the heavens and the earth?"), and the nature of the Greek gods as caricatured by a critical Xenophanes (ca. 500 BC):

> Homer and Hesiod have attributed to the gods
> all sorts of things that are matters of reproach and censure among men:
> theft, adultery, and mutual deception. (Fragment B11)

> But mortals suppose that gods are born,
> wear their own clothes, and have a voice and body. (Fragment B14)

2.4.2 GREEK ETHICS AND PHILOSOPHY

In Judah and Samaria, the steadfastness of Yahweh's character and the centralizing trajectory of Yahwistic belief led to the development of ethical pursuit, characterized predominantly by wisdom motifs in various literary genres. Such pursuits were by no means foreign to Greek culture. Indeed, ethics was one of the most discussed matters in learned Greek society. However, the foundation of ethics was markedly different in the two cultures. In Judah and Samaria,

Yahweh himself provided the grounds of ethics—a tradition going back to Torah and the biblical prophets. Ethics was linked to revelation and the character of Yahweh and proceeded on the basis of observing the commandments (Deut 32:4; Lev 19:1–2; Prov 1:7; 3:5–6).

In Greece, however, the multiplicity of deities, with sometimes unreliable characters, meant that stable ethics required a basis other than the gods. The notion of "ethics" was the same as "custom" (Gk. *ethos*)—that which was done as a matter of course. But Greek philosophical reflection challenged such generic conventions so that the notion of moral "excellence" (Gk. *aretē*) developed. As philosophy grew, the goal of ethical inquiry became not the honor or emulation of the gods but the achievement of human happiness and political equilibrium. Greek philosophers began formulating various theories of moral excellence with the conviction that ethics was formulated through empirical observation, rational deduction, and human ingenuity rather than mythology or divine revelation. Because the Greek gods were so human in character and religion decentralized, ethics began with the human mind and worked towards human goals. In other words, while biblical ethics was primarily interested in relating properly to God, Greek ethics was primarily interested in applying human effort to being a good person. As Protagoras (fifth century BC) put it, "Man is the measure of all things, of the existence of the things that are, and the non-existence of the things that are not" (Plato, *Theaetetus* 152a).

Socrates's pupil Plato formulated a highly influential theory of all reality. Plato proposed that ultimate reality consisted of "the good"—that which was metaphysically perfect in every respect. Just as numbers are real and essential concepts in mathematics, so "the good" was the most real and essential concept of all, from which reality emanated in lessening degrees. The first such degree was the realm of "ideas" (or "forms") in which "the good" was disbursed into absolutes and attributes in their purest, archetypal form. For example, every circle participated in the a priori "idea" of a circle, which defined it. More accurate circles participated more fully in the "idea." The whole physical world was an imperfect embodiment of "ideas" radiating out from the ultimate metaphysical reality of "the good." Shadows and images, being themselves mere radiations of prior objects, were the lowest form of reality. In this schema, ethics was about humanity striving to know and participate in the ultimate good as the source of being. For Plato, then, ethics could never be subjective, for it necessarily had an objective source in ultimate metaphysical reality.[3]

---

3. Christopher Shields, *Ancient Philosophy: A Contemporary Introduction*, 2nd ed. (New York: Routledge, 2012), 68–72.

Plato's notion of "the good" approximated the Jewish understanding of God. Like "the good," Yahweh was transcendent beyond created reality and was the ultimate source of it. Where Judaism differed to Plato was in the ontological distinction it drew between Yahweh and created reality: creation was a coherent system that bore the fingerprint of Yahweh, but his being was not diffused through creation as Plato's "good" was. Nevertheless, Plato's metaphysics could accommodate Jewish notions of holiness, boundaries, ethical pursuit, and its repudiation of images in religious devotion. It would, therefore, come to have great appeal among Jewish thinkers (see 2.4.3 below).

Platonic philosophy was but one school of Greek thought. Plato's student, Aristotle, the tutor of Alexander, was more of a realist, arguing that ideas could not exist apart from or prior to their instantiations. He also advocated a notion of the divine as the unmoved mover—that which animates all reality by drawing it towards itself as the ultimate *telos* ("end"). This resonated with Jews who believed that history had an inexorable goal, such as the restoration of a Davidic kingdom and God's rule over the earth. The Epicureans objected to the Platonic striving for ultimate reality, preferring moderation in human activity and seeing the enjoyment of simple bodily pleasures as the goal of ethics—a notion that seems to have been an aspirational ideal of Qoheleth (see 2.6.16 below). The Stoics tried to eradicate desire from human endeavor through self-control, having satisfaction with whatever circumstances one was in as their ultimate goal. This focus on self-control also resonated with much Jewish thought.

Greek philosophy, especially the Aristotelian variety, also gave rise to scientific pursuits. Some of these endeavors were theologically innocuous, such as Aristotle's taxonomies of genus and species, which we still use today. Yet scientific thinking also attempted to explain the reality of the world through rational and natural processes rather than divine causation. This muddied the waters of theological formulation. In the Greek world, the development of the natural sciences tended to marginalize divine elements, relegating mythological explanations of reality to the quaint fantasies of past ignorance. For example, storms came to be understood as the observable product of water evaporation rather than the thunderbolts of a fickle Zeus or the mischief of water nymphs. For the first time, therefore, the word "myth" began to acquire a pejorative meaning—something it never had before this time (cf. 1 Tim 1:4; 4:7; 2 Tim 4:4; Titus 1:14). Some scientific explanations could still be accommodated within the parameters of classical Greek or biblical thought. Jesus, for instance, could point to the validity of meteorological predictions made through empirical observation (Matt 16:2–3) while still perceiving divine will behind the rising of the sun and the falling of rain (Matt 5:45). There were also things the sciences simply could not explain. No scientist could, for instance, explain why severe misfortune might befall one person and not another, whereas an oracle or a theologian might. Thus, throughout the Hellenistic era, Greek religion continued to thrive alongside Greek philosophy and science. But the strides in knowledge taken by Greek philosophers and scientists would, in time, mount a serious challenge to the older mythologically based modes of thinking. It sowed the seeds that would lead centuries later to the decline of the Olympian Greek religion and the widespread acceptance of Christianity.

2.4.3 THE DEVELOPMENT OF JEWISH APOCALYPTIC THOUGHT

Greek philosophy and science challenged Jewish and Samaritan understanding of the work of God by proposing causes to circumstances that were perhaps not the result of divine will. This spawned several theological questions. Was the current plight of God's people part of God's will or the result of political chance? Why would God allow the delay of the fulfilment of his purposes? Did God intend the nation of Israel to be perennially divided, or could this be attributed to human machinations? Was Yahweh sovereign but not omnipotent—simply wielding more power than anyone else but still having to struggle against challenges that might thwart him? To what degree could God's people trust him with their future and the fulfilment of his promises? Who or what, if anything, was guiding history? In what way could God's people talk about his perfection? Was life about striving for something within this world or beyond it? What impact did this have on political hopes for restoration? Where could one find true knowledge, wisdom, and certainty? These questions struck at the core of Jewish culture, politics, and identity.

In Judah, a major theological development arose in response to these tensions: apocalyptic thinking. The term "apocalyptic" comes from the Greek word *apokalypsis* ("revelation" [Rev 1:1]). In its broadest terms, apocalyptic is revelatory literature, which implies the uncovering of knowledge—not through deduction but through disclosure from another source. It traces its roots to both the prophetic and wisdom traditions of Judah. Like prophecy, apocalyptic sought to provide divine comment on human affairs. But whereas prophecy was about the word of Yahweh coming to a prophet, apocalyptic brought a human agent into the divine world to observe spiritual reality there. Just as a sage observed the world around him to perceive viable ways of engaging with it, the agent of apocalyptic observed the spiritual realm and then reported this knowledge to a human audience.

Apocalyptic was effectively the Jewish appropriation of Greek philosophy, especially Platonic metaphysics. Both Jewish apocalyptic and Greek philosophy were interested in metaphysical questions: ultimate reality, the purpose of history and being, the nature of the spiritual and physical realms, and the relationship between them.[4] Thus the topics that Jewish apocalyptic was interested in ranged from interpreting the spiritual realities behind historical events and perceiving God's will in them to the architecture of the cosmos (spiritual and physical) and the way the calendar worked. The book of 1 Enoch—a composite collection of works from the third to the first centuries BC—exhibits precisely these interests. Apocalyptic works are sometimes divided into prophetic apocalypses interested in history and theology, and sapiential apocalypses interested in cosmology. Yet both categories stem from the same concern to explain reality.

Apocalyptic also proved a fruitful mode for explaining foreign domination as the embodiment of metaphysical realities and for encouraging resistance to it.[5] There was also a mystical appeal in the way this unlocked knowledge. Greek philosophy and science thrived on new discoveries and theories, and apocalyptic served a similar function in Jewish society. But like Greek philosophy, there was no uniformity to Jewish apocalyptic thinking. Thus, one of the theological challenges within Jewish apocalyptic was an orthodox appropriation of it—not merely a flight of theological fancy but an understanding of reality that, while borrowing new notions from the Greek world, was still thoroughly anchored in the authoritative prophetic and wisdom traditions of Judah.

The challenge to do this is evident from the frequent use of pseudonymity in apocalyptic—attributing a book to an authoritative figure from the past. Pseudonymity is popularly viewed (and often denigrated) today as a device designed to fool the reader into thinking that a novel work was older and more authoritative than it actually was. In fact, the device was used to situate a book and its message in continuity with past revelation. A figure from the past was

---

4. This might partially explain early (fourth century BC) Greek depictions of the Jews as avid philosophers. See excerpts in Menahem Stern, *Greek and Latin Authors on Jews and Judaism*, 3 vols. (Jerusalem: Israel Academy of Sciences and Humanities, 1974), 1:10, 46, 49–50. Cf. Bezalel Bar-Kochva, *The Image of the Jews in Greek Literature: The Hellenistic Period* (Berkeley: University of California Press, 2010), 15–89, 136–163; Reinhard G. Kratz, "Greek Historians on Jews and Judaism in the 3rd Century BCE," in Honigman, Nihan, and Lipschits, *Times of Transition*, 264.

5. Anathea E. Portier-Young, *Apocalypse Against Empire: Theologies of Resistance in Early Judaism* (Grand Rapids: Eerdmans, 2014), 35.

nominated as a compere to the content, but the authority of the work came not from the figure chosen but from whether the work itself aligned with prior revelation. "Pseudonymity served not to hide the person or community who composed the apocalypse, but rather to assert that they were not the originators of this counterdiscourse. The guarantee of their revelation stood upon the givenness of tradition."[6] The sheer volume of disparate works in the category of Jewish apocalyptic shows how difficult this task was due to the divisions within Jewish society, as well as the perpetual political disappointment that Jews experienced in the Hellenistic era.

The nature of apocalyptic held considerable theological appeal for the way it dealt with such political disappointment. God's justice and faithfulness to his past promises were held in tension with the current suffering of the righteous before towering empires. This tension was resolved by the notion of eschatological intervention—a future moment when God would personally intervene with justice to fulfil his promises and vindicate his people. This was particularly important as, during the Hellenistic era, Jewish independence, especially in the form of a Davidic kingdom, seemed practically impossible to achieve through normal political process. Disappointments could be endured if history was still heading inexorably towards the fulfilment of God's promises through his direct intervention. In this way, the promised Davidic kingdom was identified as the future kingdom of God—the inbreaking of the spiritual realm into the physical, resulting in the untrammeled rule of God over all the earth.

This also brought more clarity to the notion of future judgment. The classic prophetic concept of the "day of Yahweh," which the prophets originally adapted to depict moments of Yahweh's decisive historical judgment through human agents, was developed into a day of definitive eschatological judgment. If God was just, then the wicked could not sleep in their graves unpunished, nor could the righteous waste away having never experienced vindication. God's perfect justice, aligned with his promises, entailed that God would raise and judge the dead and so bring about a new age in which the disorder and disappointment of the past would be replaced with order and fulfilment.

Apocalyptic became an intrinsic part of Judaism and the early church. The book of Daniel's supernatural realm of beasts, kings, and princes closely resembles Plato's realm of "ideas," especially in the direction of its hierarchy: the spiritual ranks above the physical. It is not the beasts, kings, and princes that represent human empires, but the other way around: human empires are

---

6. Portier-Young, *Apocalypse Against Empire*, 35.

historical instantiations of the beasts, kings, and princes that occupy a spiritual realm above the human world. The challenge for the Jew was to trust in God, who was ontologically distinct and transcendent over even the spiritual realm. This notion lies behind the early church's conceptuality of Jesus:

> He is the image of the invisible God, the firstborn of all creation. For in him all things were created—in the heavens and on the earth, the visible and the invisible, be they thrones, lordships, rulers, or authorities—they all were created through him and for him. And he is before them all, and in him they have been composed. And he is the head of the body of the church; he is the beginning, the firstborn from the dead, so that he himself might have primacy. For in him the entire fullness [of God] was pleased to dwell and through him to reconcile everything to himself, making peace through the blood of his cross—be they things on the earth or in the heavens. (Col 1:15–20; cf. Eph 1:3, 20–21)

We see similar principles in Hebrews, where the earthly tabernacle and its sacrifices are mere copies of the heavenly originals into which Christ entered and offered himself as a better sacrifice (Heb 8:1–2; 9:11–14, 23–28). The logic even informs Jesus's statement in the Lord's Prayer, "Your will be done on earth, as it is in heaven" (Matt 6:10).[7] Apocalyptic and its concomitant eschatological hope presented new theological developments, using Greek categories to build on the foundations of prophetic and wisdom traditions.

While Greek thinking promoted new modes of Jewish thought, it also sparked a liberal impetus in Judah and Samaria. As cleruchies (colonies of Greek veterans), gymnasia, stadiums, and agoras proliferated in the world around them, some Jews and Samaritans found their allure irresistible. Conservatives were soon jockeying alongside liberals within Judaism. These forces, pulling in opposite directions, facilitated the splintering of Judaism into various sects and contributed to the cultural, political, and theological explosion that occurred at the Maccabean Revolt (167–164 BC). Hellenism provoked a centuries-long battle for the heart of Jewish identity between multiple Jewish groups, ranging from hardline fundamentalists to liberal Philhellenic Jews.

---

7. Philo of Alexandria also used this metaphysical schema in his treatises.

2.5 THE WARS OF THE *DIADOCHI*

2.5.1 PTOLEMY I AND SELEUCUS I

The two decades following Alexander's death were characterized by the sprawling wars of his *diadochi* ("successors"), which traumatized populations far and wide. Several figures featured in these wars, but two are pivotal for our purposes: Ptolemy and Seleucus.

Ptolemy was born to a noble Macedonian family in ca. 367 BC. He was educated alongside Alexander and became one of his most trusted companions. He distinguished himself in battle, particularly in the capture of Bessus and the conquests along the Indus River, attaining the status of a general. He would later write a famous (but now lost) history of Alexander's campaign, which became the basis of the later works of Arrian, Diodorus, and Quintus Curtius.[1]

Seleucus was the son of a prominent Macedonian noble, Antiochus, and his wife, Laodice. He was commander of a phalanx unit (Arrian, *Anab.* 5.16.3) and was never part of Alexander's inner circle. At the mixed marriages that Alexander enjoined upon his men at Susa in 324 BC, Seleucus married a Sogdian princess, Apama. Unlike most of his peers, though, the match was not objectionable to Seleucus, and the couple had three children together: Antiochus, Achaeus, and a daughter, whom Seleucus named Apama after his wife—testament to the affection he had for her.

2.5.2 VYING FOR EMPIRE

In the provisional arrangement after Alexander's death, Ptolemy shrewdly bargained to become satrap of Egypt. Trans-Euphrates, which included Judah and Samaria, was granted to Laomedon, another of Alexander's boyhood companions, and renamed "Syria" in memory of the Assyrians who had once ruled the area. Seleucus was commissioned to head up the cavalry on behalf of the regent, Perdiccas.

---

1. Elizabeth Baynham, "Arrian's Sources and Reliability," in Romm, *The Landmark Arrian*, Appendix A: 325–32.

Before the end of 323 BC Ptolemy had taken up his post in Egypt, where the new *polis* of Alexandria was being developed. But when Alexander's embalmed body was transported from Babylon in a lavish hearse, Ptolemy was swift to act. There is conflicting information about where Alexander was to be buried (cf. Pausanias, *Descr.* 1.6.3; Diodorus Siculus, *Bib. hist.* 18.28.2–3). In any case, Ptolemy hijacked the hearse in Syria and diverted it to Memphis. Here he temporarily interred Alexander's body while he built a grandiose tomb for him in Alexandria (Diodorus Siculus, *Bib. hist.* 18.28.3–4). Through this act, he brazenly declared himself the practical heir of Alexander's legacy.

Using Ptolemy's impertinence as a pretext, Perdiccas invaded Egypt in 321 BC only to be assassinated by his own troops, with Seleucus as one of the chief conspirators. At the second agreement of the *diadochi*, reached at Triparadisus in Syria, Seleucus was promoted to satrap of Babylonia. However, he felt that Syria rightly belonged in his jurisdiction, raising the prospect of conflict with Laomedon. Among the other agreements, Alexander's old regent of Macedonia, Antipater, replaced Perdiccas as regent of the empire with the two rulers de jure, Philip III Arrhidaeus and Alexander IV, transferred to his custody. The whole agreement, however, was unsustainable.

When Antipater died in 319 BC, a battle for control of the two rulers de jure broke out. Alexander's own mother, Olympias, had the hapless Philip III Arrhidaeus murdered and became regent for her grandson, four-year-old Alexander IV. A few months later, she herself was murdered by Antipater's son, Cassander, who took custody of the boy and proclaimed himself regent.

Relations between the *diadochi* deteriorated quickly thereafter. The satrap of Phrygia, Antigonus, nicknamed "One-Eyed" (Gk. *Monophthalmos*) after the loss of an eye, annexed Syria, Babylonia, and Media to his own territories, bringing Judah and Samaria under his sovereignty. Seleucus had to abandon his satrapy and fled to Ptolemy in Egypt. Perceiving Antigonus now as a direct threat to Egypt, Ptolemy went on the offensive and invaded the Levant (Diodorus Siculus, *Bib. hist.* 18.43.1–2). Judah and Samaria thus suffered another military incursion. Josephus quotes the Greek historian Agatharchides in relating a story about how Ptolemy captured Jerusalem on a Sabbath, when the inhabitants refused to take up arms (*Ant.* 12.6). It is difficult to tell how much truth lies behind the story, but it is not inconceivable. In any case, Ptolemy added Judah, Samaria, and all of Syria to his jurisdiction.

Antigonus retaliated the following year (315 BC), and both Judah and Samaria reverted to him again. In 312 BC Ptolemy launched a counter-invasion and defeated Antigonus's son, Demetrius Besieger (Gk. *Poliorkētēs*), at Gaza. Ptolemy took control of the whole satrapy of Syria and then forced Antigonus to relinquish Babylonia to Seleucus. But because Ptolemy did not yield Syria to Seleucus, the two *diadochi* fell out with each other. The Levant thus became a bone of contention between them.

Once again, Ptolemy's control of the Levant lasted barely a year. In 311 BC Demetrius Besieger dealt him a defeat in northern Syria, and a subsequent accord returned the Levant, including Judah and Samaria, to Antigonus's control. Ptolemy's sovereignty was restricted to Egypt, Cyrene, and Cyprus, while Seleucus was confirmed as satrap of Babylonia. The situation was utterly dissatisfying to both Ptolemy and Seleucus, meaning the new accord was destined to be short-lived.

A critical tipping point came the following year (310 BC), just before Alexander IV turned fourteen and was able to take rule for himself. For most of the *diadochi*, having a boy of half-barbarian ancestry ruling in Greece itself was untenable. So Cassander had the boy and his mother poisoned. Thus, Alexander the Great's royal line came to a spluttering end, along with his vision for an empire that fused Greek and foreign elements in a new cultural unity.

The *diadochi* now dropped all pretense of maintaining Alexander's empire, and the realm clotted into distinct political blocs. Cassander emerged as the unopposed ruler in Macedon. Lysimachus held Thrace but harbored ambitions for Asia Minor. One-Eyed Antigonus ruled the greater part of Asia Minor and Syria (including Judah and Samaria), with ambitions for Babylonia and the regions to the east. Seleucus ruled in Babylonia, consolidated his rule all the way to the border of India, and continued to claim Syria as part of his domain. Ptolemy ruled Egypt, Cyrene, and Cyprus, and also had an ongoing claim to Syria. Thus, three of the *diadochi* competed for rule over Judah and Samaria. In 306 BC Antigonus took the official title of *basileus* ("king"), and the other four *diadochi* followed suit. In Alexandria, Ptolemy was formally recognized as *basileus* and pharaoh in 305 BC, thus inaugurating the Thirty-Second and final Dynasty of Egypt.[2]

The wars of the *diadochi* were not over yet, though. To curb the ambitions of One-Eyed Antigonus, the other four drew him into battle near the Phrygian town of Ipsus in 301 BC. But Ptolemy was himself absent from the battle, looking to make gains elsewhere. Antigonus fell during the battle, and his kingdom came crashing down with him. In the aftermath, most of Asia Minor was split between Lysimachus and Seleucus, with western Cilicia going to Ptolemy. Ptolemy had hoped to gain Syria also, but because he was not on

---

2. Ptolemy had been governing from Alexandria since 311 BC, as the Satrap Stele confirms. See Günther Hölbl, *A History of the Ptolemaic Empire*, trans. Tina Saavedra (Abingdon: Routledge, 2001), 26, 82.

the battlefield, it was awarded to Seleucus instead. Sovereignty over Judah and Samaria thus changed hands again.

After the Battle of Ipsus (301 BC), the world breathed a collective sigh of relief in the hope that the jumble of imperial pieces had finally settled into a sustainable order. Four kingdoms now dominated the map, echoed by the bestial imagery in the book of Daniel (Dan 7:26; 8:8, 22; 11:3–4). The third vision of Daniel also highlights the emerging rivalry between the Ptolemaic and Seleucid kingdoms:

> The King of the South [Ptolemy] will grow strong, but one of his officials [Seleucus] will grow strong against him, ruling a vast empire as his own empire. (Dan 11:5)

In the remainder of the vision, the Ptolemaic kings instantiate the metaphysical figure known as the "King of the South" while the Seleucid kings represent the metaphysical "King of the North."

2.6 PTOLEMAIC RULE

2.6.1 THE SIEGE OF JERUSALEM (301 BC)

In the half century leading up to the Battle of Ipsus (351–301 BC), sovereignty over Judah and Samaria changed nine times.

Before 351 BC	Persia
350–345 BC	Hiatus (Israelite Coalition under Sanballat II)
345 BC	Persia
332 BC	Alexander the Great
323 BC	Laomedon
316 BC	Ptolemy
315 BC	Antigonus
312 BC	Ptolemy
311 BC	Antigonus
301 BC	Seleucus

This list does not include the constant incursions of Egyptians, Greek mercenaries, and Persians during the first half of the fourth century BC. The persistent thoroughfare of armies wore deep grooves of trauma into the Jews and Samaritans, who were forced to provision these armies, billet them, man them, and often suffer the damage inflicted by them. The constant military shuffling, endemic political uncertainty, parlous pillaging, and high human toll made the fourth century BC turbulent, taxing, and profoundly traumatic. Yet as the world uttered its sigh of relief after Ipsus, there was no respite for Judah and Samaria. There was to be one more bloody, brutal chapter to the rapid-fire changes in sovereignty over them.

The reason Ptolemy was absent from the Battle of Ipsus was that he had launched his third invasion of the Levant. As part of this campaign he laid siege to Jerusalem, which contained one of Antigonus's garrisons (Appian,

S.W. 50).¹ Unlike his capture of the city in 316 BC, the ordeal in 301 BC was more protracted. The oracles in Isaiah 24–27, 62–66, and Zechariah 12–14 give some insight into the terrible struggles that eventuated. A veiled allusion to the downfall of One-Eyed Antigonus is contained in Isaiah 64:4[64:3 MT] with its oddly phrased declaration, "An eye [sg.] has seen no gods but you [Yahweh]." Other verses imply that Ptolemy used or threatened terror tactics, like the plundering and burning of crops, to force Jews in rural districts into his army to fight against Jerusalem (Isa 24:1, 4, 7, 9; 26:1–4; 27:2–4; 65:21–25; Zech 12:6). Ptolemy's aim was to displace Antigonus's garrison. He had little care if he was forcing Jew to fight Jew at their sacred city. Yet it caused enormous consternation among the Jews.

Members of the Davidic family were caught in the crossfire of the siege, as can be deduced from both the Chronicler's genealogy (1 Chr 3:17–24) and the oracle of Zechariah 12–14. The genealogy shows that the descendants of Shekaniah were the leading Davidic figures of the day. However, the genealogy through Shekaniah's eldest son, Shemaiah, has been apocopated. The genealogy breaks off mid-sentence (1 Chr 3:22), and the line of succession is traced instead through Shekaniah's fifth son, Neariah, passing over all four of Shekaniah's eldest sons.² Such an extreme diversion implies that Shekaniah's four eldest sons and their families all met a simultaneous and premature end at this time.³

When we remember that the Chronicler promoted the reinstatement of the Davidic family to civic authority, these details become significant. His genealogy initially included the sons of Shemaiah as the primary Davidic heirs, but after they and the families of Hattush, Yigal, and Bariah shared the same fate, they were removed from the genealogy and the dynasty traced through Neariah instead.

---

1. Cf. Odil Hannes Steck, "Tritojesaja in Jesajabuch," in *The Book of Isaiah–Le Livre d'Isaïe: Les Oracles et Leurs Relectures. Unité et Complexité de l'Ouvrage*, ed. Jacques Vermeylen, Bibliotheca Ephemeridum Theologicarum Lovaniensium (Leuven: Peeters, 1989), 397–400; *Der Abschluss Der Prophetie Im Alten Testament: Ein Versuch Zur Frage Der Vorgeschichte Des Kanons*, Biblisch-Theologische Studien 17 (Neukirchen-Vluyn: Neukirchener Verlag, 1991), 91–99.

2. The apocopation of Shemaiah's line is shown in the Hebrew text by the fact that the "sons of Shemaiah" are given an introductory formula but never listed. The five names that follow cannot be Shemaiah's sons, for a tally of "six" is specifically given after them, which must include Shemaiah as one of the six. The five names are, therefore, Shemaiah's brothers, not his sons.

3. Since the Chronicler does not give specific ages for anyone in his genealogy, we can only approximate them. The calculations here employ a schematic gap of approximately twenty years between father and eldest son, with three years separating the birth of each subsequent son.

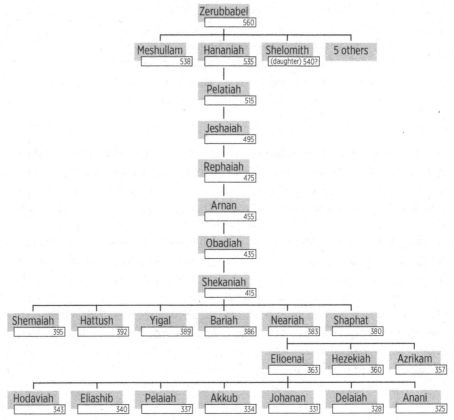

Davidic genealogy according to 1 Chronicles 3:17–24, with approximate years of birth indicated for each.

That the Davidic family was targeted in Jerusalem during or shortly after Ptolemy's siege is hinted at by Yahweh's words in Zechariah 12:

> "It will happen on that day that I will seek to annihilate all the nations that come against Jerusalem, pouring over the house of David and the resident of Jerusalem a spirit of grace and favor as they look to me, the one they have stabbed—
>
>> mourning over him as though mourning over an only child;
>> aching over him as though aching over a firstborn.
>> It will happen on that day,
>> the mourning in Jerusalem will be great,
>> like the mourning of Hadad-Rimmon in the Plain of Megiddo;

> the land mourning clan by clan, each in turn:
> the house of David's clan in turn, and their women in turn;
> the house of Nathan's clan in turn, and their women in turn;
> the house of Levi's clan in turn, and their women in turn;
> the Shimeite clan in turn, and their women in turn;
> all the clans that are left, clan by clan in turn, and their women in turn."
> (Zech 12:9–14)

The oracle unusually identifies Yahweh as the victim of a sinister stabbing but goes on to talk of the victim as also distinct from Yahweh. Along with the imagery of mourning a "son" (cf. 2 Sam 7:14), this strongly suggests that at least one Davidic figure was assassinated during the siege or executed after it, provoking the anguish of Davidic loyalists. The reference to the house of Levi shows that cultic personnel were either implicated in the attack on the Davidic family or also among the victims (see 2.6.2). Who the house of Nathan might be is not clear, but the "Shimeite clan" almost certainly refers to the family of Shemaiah (1 Chr 3:22). The fact that other clans "are left" (Zech 12:14) implies that the aforementioned clans had suffered significant loss. The reference to mourning at Megiddo evokes the fate of Josiah at the hands of Pharoah Neco (609 BC), suggesting that history had repeated itself as yet another Davidide fell during an attack launched from Egypt (2 Kgs 23:29–30; 2 Chr 35:20–25). Later in the oracle, Yahweh issues the following execration:

> "Awake, O sword, against my shepherd!
> Against the man of my community!"
> —Declaration of Yahweh of Ranks.
> "Strike the shepherd, so that the sheep scatter.
> I will swing my arm against the young." (Zech 13:7)

Was there a failed attempt to empower a Davidide in accordance with the Chronicler's agenda during the siege? Was there a bloody internecine struggle within the Davidic family? Did the high priest Hezekiah oppose the Davidides with murderous force? Did factions within Jerusalem war with each other over allegiance to competing *diadochi*? Did the common people turn on the Davidic family? Did Ptolemy execute the most prominent members of the dynasty to stamp out agitators? Such tantalizing questions cannot be answered without further evidence. What we can conclude plausibly is that the descendants of Shekaniah's four eldest sons seem to have been eradicated while the descendants of his fifth son, Neariah, survived. It was a new nadir for the

Davidic dynasty, which the Gospel writers would later see recapitulated in the execution of Jesus (Matt 26:31; Mark 14:27; John 19:37).

While the dust of battle at Ipsus was settling, Jerusalem succumbed to Ptolemy's forces. Sovereignty over the city thus changed for the tenth time in fifty years. This time Ptolemy did not relinquish it, defying the other *diadochi* who had apportioned Syria to Seleucus. Ptolemy won the whole southern half of the Levant and welded it fast to his own kingdom. Meanwhile, the Jews in Jerusalem suffered tremendous loss of life, and the temple compound sustained damage.

> For a short time, your people possessed your sacred site.
> Our enemies have now trampled your sanctuary. (Isa 63:18)
>
> The towns of your holiness have become a wasteland.
> Zion has become a wasteland, Jerusalem a desolation.
> Our holy and glorious house, where our fathers praised you,
> has become kindling for fire,
> and all our treasures have been ruined. (Isa 64:11–12[64:10–11 MT])

Ptolemy conscripted Jews into his army (Let. Aris. 12–14), joining those who had already fought for him against Jerusalem. He also deported swathes of the Jewish population to Alexandria.

> See Yahweh emptying the land,
> devastating it, marring its surface, scattering its residents.
> It will be
> > like people, like priest,
> > like slave, like master,
> > like slave-girl, like mistress,
> > like buyer, like seller,
> > like lender, like borrower,
> > like debtor, like creditor.
> He will empty the land,
> he will plunder it,
> for Yahweh has made this promise. . . .
> Therefore, a curse consumes the land,
> and its residents are guilty.
> Therefore, the residents of the land dwindle,
> and very few people are left. (Isa 24:1–3, 6)

200 THE HELLENISTIC ERA (331–167 BC)

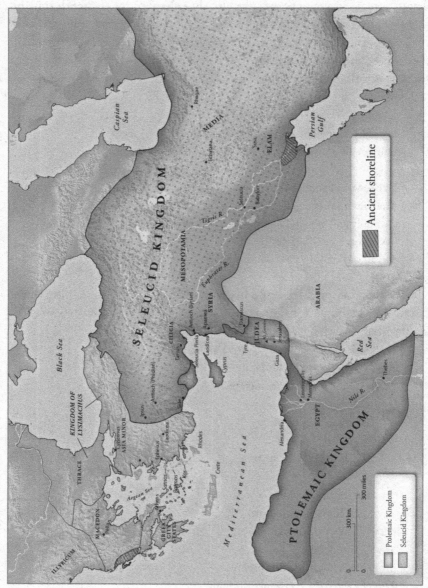

The Four Kingdoms of the *Diadochi* after the conquest of Jerusalem (301 BC)

The archaeological record demonstrates a sharp decline in settlement in the northern Shephelah and Jerusalem's districts at this time.[4] Ptolemy took similar actions against the Samaritans (cf. Josephus, *Ant.* 12.7). The pseudonymous Letter of Aristeas claims Ptolemy enslaved 100,000 Jewish commoners (Let. Aris. 12–14) while Josephus, quoting Hecateus of Abdera, claims a more modest "tens of thousands" (*Ag. Ap.* 1.194). These figures are inflated, and there are fictive elements in the Letter of Aristeas. Nonetheless, when read alongside the biblical texts and archaeological record, they reflect just how decimating Ptolemy's deportations were. It was nothing less than another exile. Jerusalem continued to exist as a small town, but almost overnight Alexandria became home to the largest urban Jewish population in the world—a position it would hold for centuries. As a result of Ptolemy's conquest, there were now more Jews in Egypt than in Judah.

The fall of Jerusalem in 301 BC and the subsequent deportations cut deeply into the Jewish psyche. There were profound feelings of grief and guilt, as well as an acute sense of divine abandonment. God seemed not merely transcendent but intransigent in his distance:

> If only you had torn open the skies and descended,
> and mountains quaked at your presence!
> As fire kindles brushwood,
> fire boils water,
> you could make your name known to your foes,
> nations would shudder at your presence. . . .
> But all of us became unclean,
> all our righteous acts like a menstrual cloth.
> We all withered like leaves,
> and our faults carry us away like the wind.
> No one calls on your name,
> or strives to keep hold of you,
> for you have hidden your face from us,
> and had us tossed about in the hands of our occupiers.[5]
>   (Isa 64:1–2, 6–7[63:19b–64:1, 5–6 MT])

---

4. Shalom et al., "Judah in the Early Hellenistic Period," 74–75.

5. The Hebrew word rendered "our occupiers" (*'onenu*) was understood by the Greek translator and the Masoretes as "our faults" (*'awonenu*), which uses the same consonants. However, the preceding phrase ("in the hands of") implies a human agent rather than a conceptual reference.

But prophetic impetus turned the disaster into a template for an apocalyptic-like hope for God's future intervention to right the wrongs and inaugurate a new age.[6] No longer would God sit impassively while foreign cavalry contested possession of Jerusalem and made Jew fight Jew. The dystopian present would be supplanted by a seismic utopian correction:

> See, I am making Jerusalem a bowl of staggering for all the surrounding peoples. The siege upon Jerusalem will be upon Judah as well.
> On that day, I will make Jerusalem an unliftable stone for all the people. All who lift her will be grievously injured, though all the nations of the earth gather against her.
> On that day, I will strike every horse with panic, and its riders with madness—but over the house of Judah I will open my eyes[7]—and strike every horse of the peoples with blindness. The squads of Judah will say in their heart, "The residents of Jerusalem have resolve through Yahweh of Ranks, their God."
> On that day, I will make the squads of Judah like a firepot among twigs, like a fire torch amid the sheaves, so that they consume to the right and the left all the surrounding peoples. But Jerusalem will remain intact, in its location, at Jerusalem. Yahweh will save the tents of Judah first, so that the majesty of the house of David and the majesty of the residents of Jerusalem does not exceed Judah's. (Zech 12:2–7)

> "It shall be throughout the whole land," declares Yahweh,
> "two-thirds will be cut down within it and perish,
> and a third will be left within it.
> But I will bring that third through the fire,
> refining it as one refines silver,
> testing it as one tests gold.
> It will call on my name,
> and I will answer it.
> I have said, 'It is my people,'
> and it will say, 'Yahweh is my God.'"
> See, a day is coming—Yahweh's day—
> when your spoil will be divided in your midst;
> when I gather all the nations to Jerusalem for war;

---

6. Cf. Gonzalez, "No Prophetic Texts from the Hellenistic Period?," 306–16.

7. This might be a taunt of One-Eyed Antigonus's failure to secure the countryside of Judah against Ptolemy's invasion in 301 BC.

when the city will be captured;
when the houses are looted
and the women will be raped;
when half the city goes into exile,
and the remainder of the people are not cut off from the city;
when Yahweh goes out and battles against those nations,
on his day of attack, on a day of engagement;
when his feet stand, on that day,
upon the Mount of Olives, to the east of Jerusalem;
when the Mount of Olives splits in half,
from east to west, a massive valley;
when half the mountain recedes northwards and half southwards . . .
Yahweh will become king over the whole earth.
On that day, Yahweh will be one and his name one. . . .
They will dwell in her [i.e., Jerusalem],
and there will no longer be such annihilation.
Jerusalem will dwell in safety. (Zech 13:8–14:4, 9, 11)

The Isaianic oracles convey similar sentiments:

On that day, the great trumpet will blast,
and those lost to the land of Syria,
and those banished to the land of Egypt,
will come and worship Yahweh
on the holy mountain in Jerusalem. (Isa 27:13)

"For I am about to create new skies and a new earth.
The former things will not be remembered,
nor even come to mind.
Rather, rejoice and cheer, on and on,
over what I am creating.
For I am about to transform Jerusalem into a joy,
and its people into cheerfulness.
I will rejoice over Jerusalem,
and cheer my people on.
Never again will the sound of weeping
or crying be heard in her. . . .
They will build houses and live in them.
They will plant vineyards and eat their fruit.

They will not build, and have others live there.
They will not plant, and have others eat of them....
The wolf and the lamb will pasture as one,
the lion like the ox will eat straw,
and the snake will have dust for its food.
They will no longer do harm, no longer destroy
anywhere on my holy mountain,"
says Yahweh. (Isa 65:17–19, 21–22a, 25)

The supernatural quality of the salvation envisioned in these oracle gives a sense of how hopeless the Jewish community felt in the face of Ptolemy's onslaught. Only the direct intervention of God could alter their plight. The focus on Jerusalem is also telling since, after the deportations, most Jews now lived in Egypt—the land that the Torah depicted as the "house of slavery" (Exod 13:3, 14; 20:2; Deut 5:6). If the Letter of Aristeas is anything to go by, many Jews (and Samaritans) entered Egypt under Ptolemy as actual slaves. The whole situation was antithetical to the essential identity of Israel as the people whom Yahweh brought out of slavery in Egypt (cf. Deut 5:15; 26:8; Jer 32:21).

2.6.2 THE HIGH PRIEST HEZEKIAH

Jaddua, the high priest of Jerusalem, must have died in ca. 325 BC at approximately eighty years of age.[8] Josephus states that he was followed in office by his son, Onias I (*Ant.* 11:347), who was in turn succeeded by his son, Simon I (*Ant.* 12.43). Yet, Josephus's account masks a major chronological problem.

Onias I was high priest when the Spartan king, Areus I (309–265 BC), sent him a letter initiating cordial relations between Spartans and Jews (1 Macc 12:19–23; cf. *Ant.* 12.225–227).[9] The circumstances of Areus's reign preclude this letter being written before 280 BC,[10] and it could have been written any time from then until his death in 265 BC. If Onias had succeeded Jaddua, he would have been high priest for a minimum of forty-five years before receiving Areus's letter—not inconceivable but potentially problematic if Onias had been much older than thirty when he became high priest and if Areus sent

---

8. Our knowledge of the precise timeframes for the high priests of this era is limited, but there are enough intersections with other people and events, about whom firmer dates exist, to allow reasonable approximations for their respective tenures.

9. Josephus erroneously credits Onias III rather than Onias I as the recipient of Areus's letter. Though the authenticity of the letter's contents is sometimes debated, there is no *a priori* reason to preclude correspondence between the Spartan king and the Jewish high priest.

10. VanderKam, *From Joshua to Caiaphas*, 133–35.

the letter any later than 280 BC. This would make Onias anywhere between seventy-five and one hundred years old when he received Areus's letter. This stretches probability but is still not categorically impossible.

What makes it practically impossible is the timeframe implied by what follows. Josephus states that Onias's successor, Simon, died prematurely and left a young son who was not old enough to become high priest (*Ant.* 12.44). Instead, two others occupied the position before Simon's son, Onias II, was old enough to assume the office at age thirty. The first was Simon's own brother, Eleazar, who presided for approximately fifteen years (ca. 275–260 BC). When Eleazar died, the high priesthood went to his uncle, Manasseh (*Ant* 12.156–157).[11] As Eleazar's uncle, Manasseh was the brother of Onias I. Assuming the youngest possible age for Onias I, we are forced to reckon Manasseh as being at least ninety to 105 years old when he attained the high priesthood in ca. 260 BC, which he then held for a few years more. If Onias I was any older than thirty when he became high priest in ca. 325 BC, we must then add several years more to both Onias I and Manasseh, making Manasseh potentially over 110 years old when he became high priest. The chronology simply is not credible (see diagram below).

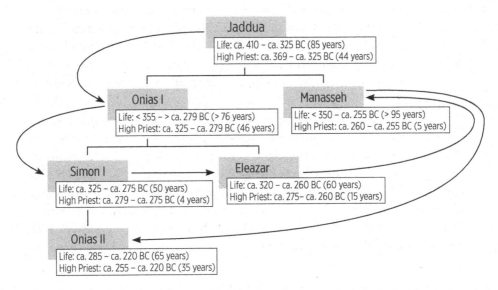

Problematic Chronological Schema of High Priests Implied by Josephus' *Antiquities*.

---

11. Josephus refers to Manasseh as "his uncle," raising the question of who the antecedent of "his" is. Since Josephus favors describing a new high priest by his relation to the preceding incumbent, Josephus was indicating that Manasseh was the uncle of Eleazar.

It seems that Josephus based his progression of high priests in *Antiquities* on the records available to him in which Onias I was listed as Jaddua's successor (cf. *Ant.* 20.227–234). However, in *Against Apion* Josephus leans on the testimony of Hecateus of Abdera, a leading Greek writer in the court of Ptolemy I,[12] who states that there was a Jewish high priest named Hezekiah who settled in Egypt after Ptolemy captured the Levant (*Ag. Ap.* 1.186–89). The lack of coverage for Hezekiah in *Antiquities* has led some to suggest that he was a priest of high rank or the civic governor of Judah and that he was erroneously called high priest.[13] However, four factors suggest otherwise.

First, even if Hezekiah was missing from the records Josephus consulted when writing his *Antiquities*, he still refers to Hezekiah in *Against Apion*. There is, therefore, positive evidence that a high priest named Hezekiah existed. Second, Hecateus's statements about Hezekiah have the hallmarks of eyewitness testimony (*Ag. Ap.* 1.187–89). Third, Hecateus gives Hezekiah's age as sixty-six years when he settled in Egypt, which occurred sometime after Ptolemy's success at the Battle of Gaza in 312 BC (*Ag. Ap.* 1.186–87). Since the deportations and migrations from Jerusalem to Alexandria began only after Ptolemy captured Jerusalem in 301 BC (technically "after" the Battle of Gaza), we should propose that date as the more likely time of Hezekiah's move. This would place Hezekiah's birth in 367 BC, which accords well with seeing Hezekiah as the son of Jaddua and pushes the birth of Onias I down to ca. 340 BC. This adjustment means that Manasseh was an older man (probably in his seventies) when he became high priest, but not too elderly to stretch credulity.

The fourth factor relates to the small number of Hezekiah coins, which date from this early Hellenistic period. Most analysts treat all the coins bearing the name "Hezekiah" as belonging to Governor Hezekiah and assume that he retained his position into the Hellenistic era.[14] However, it is impossible for Governor Hezekiah to have been sixty-six years old in 301 BC (or 312 BC). Besides, he was displaced as civic leader by Jaddua before Alexander's conquest. Furthermore, the coins of Governor Hezekiah show imagery consistent with the earlier coin of the high priest Johanan (see 1.6.2 above) and thus belong to

---

12. In his book *Pseudo Hecataeus, "On the Jews"*, Bezalel Bar-Kochva concludes that the work of "Hecateus," which Josephus used, was pseudonymous. Even if so, its information regarding the high priest Hezekiah can be corroborated with other sources, especially the coins of Hezekiah.

13. William F. Albright, "The Seal Impression from Jericho and the Treasurers of the Second Temple," *BASOR* 148 (1957): 29, https://doi.org/10.2307/1355656; Stern, *Greek and Latin Authors on Jews and Judaism*, 1:40–41; Bar-Kochva, *Pseudo Hecataeus, "On the Jews,"* 82–88.

14. Cf. Honigman, "Searching for the Social Location of Literate Judean Elites," 205–6.

ca. 370 BC.[15] By contrast, some of the Hezekiah coins show a figure sporting a Grecian hairstyle and realist features, comparable to the coins of Ptolemy I and his successors rather than coins minted during the Persian era. These Hellenistic coins must pertain to a different Hezekiah than the governor of Judah under the Persians. These later Hezekiah coins were minted in Judah down to ca. 301 BC when they were replaced by similar coins bearing the likeness of Ptolemy.[16] This accords perfectly with Ptolemy's capture of Jerusalem, as well as Hecateus's claim that Ptolemy brought Hezekiah to Alexandria. All the evidence, therefore, points strongly to identifying the Hezekiah who minted these later coins as the high priest, who was transferred to Egypt after Ptolemy captured Jerusalem in 301 BC.[17]

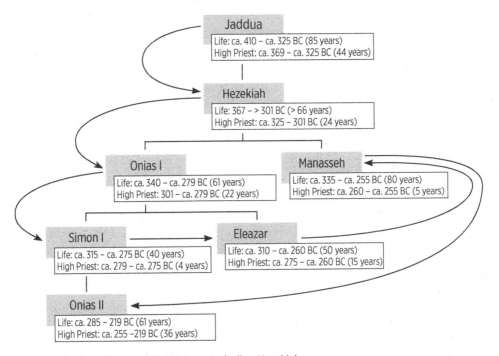

Chronological Schema of High Priests Including Hezekiah

---

15. Cf. Fried, "A Silver Coin of Yoḥanan Hakkôhēn." See also 1.6.3 above.

16. Bar-Kochva, *Pseudo Hecataeus, "On the Jews,"* 263.

17. Despite Honigman's assumption of a single Hezekiah identified as governor of Judah (dated to later in the fourth century BC), the identification of two Hezekiahs (the former as governor and the latter as high priest) bolsters her argument that the high priest took over the functions of civic governance. See Honigman, "Searching for the Social Location of Literate Judean Elites," 205–7.

Hezekiah (ca. 325–301 BC) was ethnarch of Judah during the turbulent decades of the wars between the *diodochi*. His coins show that, by the last quarter of the fourth century BC, a predilection for Greek culture had soaked into the highest echelons of Jewish society. From this time, certain Hebraic names sporting gutturals were softened with the more pastel sounds of Greek. Thus, the name of Hezekiah's son, Johanan, was softened to Onias. We cannot tell what Hezekiah's political allegiances were during the wars of the *diodochi*. In any case, he is unlikely to have countenanced the promotion of anyone from the Davidic clan, which must raise suspicions about his role in the apparent purge of Davidic ranks (see 2.6.1 above). We also cannot rule out the possibility that he adopted syncretistic practices. Isaiah 65:11 attests to Jews at this time performing rites to "Fortune" and "Fate"—clear references to the Greek divinities Tyche and the Fates.[18] It seems that the late fourth century BC witnessed a swell in foreign cultic practices, which occurred under the nose of Hezekiah.

The inclusion of Hezekiah in the register of high priests still leaves the quandary of why he was left out of the records that Josephus accessed. The likely answer comes from the cultic dilemma that must have ensued when Hezekiah left Jerusalem for Alexandria. According to Torah, the high priest retained his position for life by virtue of his anointing (cf. Exod 29:4–8, 29–30; Lev 16:32–33). His death had cultic and judicial ramifications, such as determining the end of the period during which a person charged with manslaughter had to live in seclusion (Num 35:25–32). Resigning the high priesthood created a legal ambiguity, for it meant there were two living high priests. The only precedent for the removal of a high priest had been an exception that proved the rule: Solomon's removal of Abiathar, which fulfilled the prophesied disqualification of the line of Eli (1 Kgs 2:26–27; cf. 1 Sam 2:27–36; 3:11–14). As long as Hezekiah was alive, his son, Onias, could not technically officiate as high priest, which compromised the operation of the temple cult in Jerusalem, not to mention the additional judicial ramifications it posed. The only way for Hezekiah's son, Onias, to operate legally as high priest would have been to expunge Hezekiah's entire tenure so that Onias was viewed as the successor to his grandfather, Jaddua.[19]

Hezekiah arrived in Alexandria as a result of Ptolemy's conquest of Jerusalem (301 BC). The oracle of Zechariah 12–14 refers to the house of Levi

---

18. Tyche was a goddess who governed the fate of cities, while the Fates (daughters of Zeus) ensured humans followed their divinely ordained destiny.

19. This situation no longer proved a dilemma after 175 BC when the legitimate high priest, Onias III, was ousted by his brother, Jason. After this, it was common for high priests to be removed from office and still be alive while the next incumbent officiated (cf. Luke 3:2; Acts 4:6).

mourning (Zech 12:13). Although not a direct reference to Hezekiah, he did belong to the tribe of Levi, so this might allude indirectly to his departure (cf. Isa 24:2; see also 2.6.4 below). But the oracle does not preclude the possibility that Hezekiah went voluntarily. Hecateus mentions his arrival in Alexandria while discussing people who came to Egypt voluntarily (*Ag. Ap.* 1.186–87).[20] The fact that Hecateus, a Greek litterateur, considered Hezekiah a person of high refinement suggests that Hezekiah might have been predisposed to migration anyway. Ptolemy was known to attract high profile figures to his new capital—Hecateus being one of them—and the transfer of Hezekiah fits with this perfectly (cf. Diodorus Siculus, *Bib. hist.* 19.86.2–3).

Hezekiah became a natural leader of the nascent Jewish community at Alexandria.[21] His presence struck balance between promoting Jewish life in the city and fostering its exposure to the undammed influence of a heaving Greek metropolis. According to Hecateus, Hezekiah "explained to them [i.e., Alexandrian Jews] every attribute of theirs, for he had all their dwellings and citizenship in writing" (*Ag. Ap.* 1.189). This might allude to the Jewish Scriptures,[22] but the wording suggests it might refer to records detailing where the Alexandrian Jews had all hailed from in Judah. Either way, possession of such documents attests to his high station.

Alexandrian Jews thus retained their Jewish identity even as, within two generations, they became native Greek speakers at home in the land that the Torah labelled "the house of slavery" (Exod 13:3). This dual dynamic became the hallmark of Alexandrian Jewry, which quickly became the largest Jewish community in the world. Although Jerusalem remained the cultic hub, it was now a provincial town in the Ptolemaic realm, whereas the Jews of Alexandria were at the cosmopolitan epicenter. Alexandria's meteoric rise as an international port also saw Jews spread across the Mediterranean. Within a few generations of Ptolemy's conquest of Jerusalem, the average Jew was a native Greek speaker who either lived in or whose ancestors had lived in Alexandria. Judaism had irreversibly become part of the Hellenistic world.

---

20. Ian Worthington, *Ptolemy I: King and Pharaoh of Egypt* (New York: Oxford University Press, 2016), 122.

21. It is not inconceivable that Hezekiah was an ancestor of Philo in the first century. Philo and his relatives were among the most prominent Alexandrian Jews of their era. Philo represented them in official matters and authored several Jewish philosophical works. He was evidently from a priestly family, though he never served at the temple in Jerusalem. This is quite curious, since priests who lived abroad would still ordinarily serve during an allotted time each year. Given the piety evident in his writings, Philo's failure to do priestly duty suggests he was ineligible for service. That his ineligibility stemmed from the disqualification of Hezekiah is not beyond reason. The Book of the Twelve Prophets might allude to this at Hosea 4:6–9 (see 2.6.4 below).

22. Cf. Kratz, "Greek Historians on Jews and Judaism in the 3rd Century BCE," 271.

2.6.3 THE HOUSE OF DAVID IN EGYPT

Ptolemy I seems also to have deported members of the Davidic family to Alexandria. The evidence for this comes from a Jewish tomb with the name "Akkabiah son of Elioenai" in large Aramaic letters painted onto the limestone over the entrance (*TAD*, D21.4; *TAHNDT*, A:384, B:129).[23]

Four factors point to this burial occurring not long after the deportation of Jews to the city in 301 BC. First, the inscription was written in Aramaic, and both Akkabiah's name and patronym (Elioenai) are of Hebraic Jewish origin. There is no element of Greek in the name. This suggests a milieu in the earliest decades of Jewish settlement in Alexandria. Second, the Aramaic script is formal in appearance and paleographically matches the early Ptolemaic era at the latest. Third, the ancient cemetery in which the tomb was discovered was situated outside Alexandria's eastern wall, adjacent to the Jewish quarter just inside the walls.[24] And fourth, two coins of Ptolemy I were found in a neighboring tomb, while coins from the time of Ptolemy I and Ptolemy II were found outside the tomb. All these factors strongly suggest that Akkabiah was buried during the reign of Ptolemy I (before 283 BC).

Who was Akkabiah son of Elioenai? The answer lies in the Chronicler's genealogy (1 Chr 3:17–24), which traces the Davidic line through Neariah, the fifth son of Shekaniah (see also 2.6.1 above). Neariah's eldest son was Elioenai, corresponding to the patronym on the tomb. Elioenai's fourth son was Akkub, a standard diminutive form of Akkabiah, the name of the deceased on the tomb. The birth of Akkub in the Chronicler's genealogy can be reasonably calculated to ca. 334 BC,[25] which would have put him in his thirties at the time of Ptolemy's conquest of Jerusalem in 301 BC. The collocation of the name Akkub/Akkabiah with the patronym Elioenai on both the tomb and in Chronicles, along with the prominence and date of the inscription, make the identification practically certain.

Akkabiah was probably deported to Alexandria by Ptolemy in 301 BC, perhaps with other surviving members of the Davidic dynasty. This might be the reason why the Chronicler's genealogy ends with Akkabiah's generation.[26]

---

23. William Horbury and David Noy, *Jewish Inscriptions of Graeco-Roman Egypt* (Cambridge: Cambridge University Press, 1992), §3 (3–6 [for a photograph of the tombstone, see pl. III]); Joseph Mélèze Modrzejewski, *The Jews of Egypt: From Rameses II to Emperor Hadrian* (Princeton: Princeton University Press, 1997), 77–78.

24. The find site was in the modern el-Ibrahimiya cemetery of Alexandria.

25. This uses a template of twenty years between father and son and three years between the birth of each son born to the same father.

26. By the second half of the third century BC there was at least one surviving member of the Davidic clan still in Jerusalem: Qoheleth, the author of the discourse in Ecclesiastes (see 2.6.16).

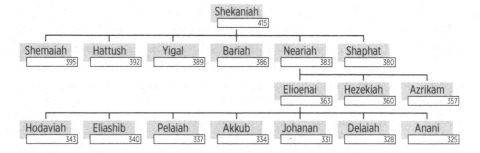

Akkabiah died in Alexandria sometime between 301 BC and 283 BC. But the prominence of the Davidic family in Alexandria did not quickly fade. When the Torah was translated into Greek (see 2.6.10 below), Jacob's blessing of Judah was rendered with modest but clearly messianic flavor, which perhaps hinted at the earlier deportation:[27]

> A ruler will not be missing from Judah,
> nor a leader from his loins,
> until the things stored up for him come about;
> he is the expectation of the nations. (Gen 49:10 LXX)

Nonetheless, Akkabiah's transference to Egypt demonstrates the waning importance of the Davidic family. For Davidic loyalists, this was a theological crisis of similar proportions to the Babylonian exile. Members of the dynasty elected by God to rule Israel (2 Sam 7:11–16; 1 Chr 17:10–14) were once again supplanted from the land of their inheritance.

2.6.4 THE BOOK OF THE TWELVE PROPHETS

A challenge for Davidic loyalists under the new conditions of Ptolemaic sovereignty was how to keep the flame of Davidic hope burning when the dynasty appeared to be descending into irrelevance. One strategy was the compilation of the Book of the Twelve Prophets. Before this time, the works of the twelve "Minor Prophets" had been collated into smaller separate collections.[28] But after 301 BC these works were brought together into a single scroll, perhaps by the anonymous prophet who produced its latest oracle (Zech 12–14).

---

27. Martin Rösel, "The Septuagint: Translating and Adapting the Torah to the 3rd Century BCE," in Honigman, Nihan, and Lipschits, *Times of Transition*, 258.

28. For a brief survey of models proposed for the growth of the various collections that contributed to the Book of the Twelve Prophets, see Jason T. LeCureux, *The Thematic Unity of the Book of the Twelve*, Hebrew Bible Monographs 41 (Sheffield: Sheffield Phoenix Press, 2012), 6–12.

This new collation preserved the prophetic word from the past, which had been fulfilled in the great catastrophes that had struck the Israelite nation, and implied that the authority of the past prophetic word had not expired. As it had spoken into those past catastrophes, so it was able to speak after the catastrophe of 301 BC. But the compilation of the book also required redaction and new prophetic insights for the new context. This implied that God was building on what he had said and done in the past and inspiring the redactors to issue new prophetic words with new revelations. The work also maintained a pan-Israelite agenda in which there was still room for Samaritans (minus the temple on Mount Gerizim) within Israel. This conviction sprang from Davidic theology, which identified Davidic rule over all Israelites as essential to the will of God. Thus the Book of the Twelve Prophets included the words of prophets, like Hosea and Amos, who had spoken to the northern tribes in past eras. The "twelveness" of the compilation, symbolic of the traditional twelve tribes of Israel, signified hope of the whole nation's reunification under a Davidic king based in Jerusalem.

The Book of the Twelve Prophets preserved the distinctive message of each past prophet while also providing additional prophecy that applied that past message to the Ptolemaic context. It is sometimes difficult to discern these later prophecies, especially as they were interspersed with earlier material. After all, the footnote had not yet been invented. However, prophecy was not mere prediction but divine comment on human affairs with an immediate relevance to the audience that first received it.[29] Understanding the course of history helps us become more sensitive to the contexts that prophecies addressed. In the case of the Book of the Twelve Prophets, this means appreciating the Ptolemaic context of the final compiler.

The last verses of Amos are a case in point. Amos prophesied during the eight century BC, when Israel and Judah were thriving and the Edomites still occupied their native territory southeast of the Dead Sea. But the verses that close the Amos section in the Book of the Twelve Prophets (Amos 9:11–15) address the situation shortly after Ptolemy's conquest of Jerusalem in 301 BC, when the Idumeans ("Edom") were entrenched in southern Judah and the Davidic dynasty no longer ruled. The author uses the phrase "On that day," familiar from Zechariah 12–14, to cast a vision of the longed-for future:

> "On that day, I will raise the fallen booth of David,
> repairing its gaps and its ruins.

---

29. A prophecy of little or no relevance to an audience is an indication that we have probably perceived the original audience and their context incorrectly.

> I will raise and rebuild it as in the days of old,
> that they might repossess the remnant of Edom
> and all the nations who invoke my name over themselves,"
> declares Yahweh, who does this.
> "See, days are coming," declares Yahweh,
> when the plowman will catch up to the harvester,
> and the one who treads grapes to the sower of the seed.
> The mountains will run with juice,
> and all the hills will flow.
> I will return the captives of my people, Israel;
> they will rebuild devastated towns and live in them;
> they will plant vineyards and drink of their wine;
> they will make gardens and eat of their fruit;
> I will plant them on their own land,
> and they will not be uprooted again
> from their own land, which I gave them,"
> says Yahweh your God. (Amos 9:11–15)

One hears the grief caused by Ptolemy's deportations, the "gaps" and "ruins" now evident in the Davidic royal family, angst at the Idumean occupation of southern Judah, and the estrangement with the Samaritans, who had essentially become another nation (though they still invoked the name of Yahweh). There are allusions to the damage inflicted by Ptolemy and the local resources lost to rapacious armies and deportation. The language of the Davidic covenant (2 Sam 7:10) provided the backbone of continued hope. The prophecy looked back to the days of Amos, when the Davidic dynasty had ruled strongly in Jerusalem, as the paradigm for what God intended to achieve in the future. It was a centrist theological strategy: the light of past prophecy was shone onto the early third century BC, bringing new revelation and proclaiming Yahweh's unfaltering commitment to his promises. It encouraged Jews to lift their eyes towards a future when God would intervene "on that day" to restore the fortunes of his people under a Davidic leader.

The Book of the Twelve Prophets also enjoined covenant faithfulness on its readers. The past prophets had warned of judgment for covenantal breaches, and they had been proved right with devastating effect. The God who had judged Israel and Judah in ages past could do so again. Indeed, the devastation inflicted by Ptolemy was interpreted as just such a judgment. The nation, especially its leaders who now gazed starry eyed at the Greek world, were cautioned to remain faithful to the right worship of God and his traditional customs so that history was not repeated. Judaism was undergoing unavoidable Hellenization, which was not in itself bad—much of it was beneficial to theological discourse (see 2.4.3 above). But it had to be tempered by devotion to Yahweh. To that end, the Book of the Twelve Prophets styled itself as a "book of remembrance":

> "Since I, Yahweh, have not changed,
> you, sons of Jacob, have not come to an end.
> Since the days of your ancestors,
> you have strayed from my regulations, and have not kept them.
> Return to me, and I will return to you," says Yahweh of Ranks.
>   (Mal 3:6–7)

> Those who feared Yahweh conferred with each other, and Yahweh was attentive and listened. A book of remembrance was written before him by those who feared Yahweh and who esteemed his name.
> "They will be," says Yahweh of Ranks, "my prize for the day I am
>   preparing.
> I will have mercy on them as a man has mercy on his son who serves him.
> You will once again see the difference between the righteous and
>   the wicked,
> between the one who serves God and the one who does not serve him."
>   (Mal 3:16–18)

> Remember the Torah of Moses, my servant, whom I issued with regulations and customs at Horeb for all Israel. See, I am sending to you Elijah the prophet before the coming of the great and fearful day of Yahweh, that he might turn the hearts of fathers towards children, and the heart of children towards fathers. Otherwise, I will come and strike the land with extinction.
> (Mal 4:4–6[3:22–24 MT])

The priests, as the new supremos of Judaism, received particular warning throughout the Book of the Twelve Prophets.[30] The partiality of the Jewish elite towards Greek culture, especially under the high priest Hezekiah, posed a substantive challenge to traditional devotion to Yahweh. Certain passages echo loudly in the context of Hezekiah's departure from Jerusalem:

---

30. Athas, "The Failure of Davidic Hope?," 241–50.

> Since you have rejected knowledge,
> I reject you from officiating as my priest.
> As you forgot the Torah of your God,
> so I too will forget your children.
> As they multiplied, so they have sinned against me.
> Their fame I will change to infamy.
> They will feed on the sin of my people,
> and in their own guilt their soul will revel.
> It is like people, like priest!
> I will deal their ways back upon them,
> and pay his deeds back to him. (Hos 4:6b–9)

In essence, therefore, the Book of the Twelve Prophets recontextualized the old prophetic word, calling all Israel to faithful devotion to God and his customs in the hope that God would fulfil his promises to restore Israel as a Davidic kingdom (cf. Zech 1:2–4).[31]

2.6.5 PTOLEMAIC ADMINISTRATION AND INFLUENCE

In the Persian Empire, provinces were bundled together into satrapies, and each satrapy was practically a kingdom of its own, sometimes with a ruling dynasty. The satrapies fitted neatly together to produce a complex but solid edifice, which was mutually supporting. The Persian monarch was the "Great King" or "King of Kings" who stood over the whole in a generally unobtrusive way. Persian administration was thus "present everywhere, and visible nowhere."[32]

Ptolemy's kingdom was quite different. Greek rulers tended to be much closer to their constituents. This was seen most clearly in democratic Athens but was also discernible in Ptolemy's native Macedon. The Macedonian king was like a chieftain—the first among equals. Ptolemy also witnessed how Alexander's force of personality bound people and regions to himself. Ptolemy brought these models to his own kingship, as well as the classic pharaonic model in which the ruler of Egypt was recognized as a god. In this Hellenistic fusion of Greek and Egyptian ideals, Ptolemy ruled his kingdom directly

---

31. LeCureux argues that Zech 1:3 epitomizes the controlling theme of the entire Book of the Twelve Prophets. See *The Thematic Unity of the Book of the Twelve*, 22–23, 180–92.

32. Flaubert, letter to Louise Colet (9 December 1852), cited in Josette Elayi and Jean Sapin, *Beyond the River: New Perspectives on Transeuphratène*, JSOTSupp 250 (Sheffield: Sheffield Academic Press, 1998), 146.

as a god with all territories belonging to him personally.[33] He abolished the Persians' provincial distinctions, bundling Samaria and Judah, or "Judea" (Gk. *Ioudaia*) as the Greeks called it, into a larger generic region known as "Syria and Phoenicia."[34] A bulky bureaucracy governed on Ptolemy's behalf, but the entire system was more fluid than it had been under the Persians, enabling it to adapt more easily to the king's will. "The whole structure was meant to buzz like a disciplined hive so that every conceivable form of enrichment could be extracted for the benefit of the king."[35]

This hive-like administration had numerous repercussions. First, the Ptolemaic kingdom was about the king himself. His will and that of his lackeys held more force than the administrative system. This promoted informal systems of control, like a veritable ancient mafia in which personal relationships could overcome systemic checks and balances.[36] Qoheleth, reflecting on Ptolemaic rule later in the third century BC, surmised that the safest policy was the path of least resistance to the king's will (Eccl 8:2, 4–6). Ptolemy and his successors governed more through personal appointees than rigid administrative machinery. Taxation, for example, was farmed out to contractors who negotiated directly with the king, making personal relationship with him crucial. In the Ptolemaic kingdom, who you knew mattered more than personal merit or systemic rules.

Second, the king's language and culture became hugely influential. Greek supplanted Aramaic as the lingua franca. Society's elite and literati had to be immersed in the Greek language to function. Along with the spread of Greek language went the dissemination of Greek literature, Greek ideas, and demand for Greek education. This, in turn, ensured the spread of Greek institutions like the gymnasium, stadium, and theater. Some aspects of this cultural influence were innocuous, such as the adoption of Greek personal names. But some presented a serious cultural clash, such as aspects of the gymnasium, which were so antithetical to conservative Jewish and Samaritan culture (see 2.4.1 above).

Third, Greek culture spread throughout the kingdom. Over the course of

---

33. Hölbl, *A History of the Ptolemaic Empire*, 28, 61; Worthington, *Ptolemy I*, 186–87, 193; Andrea M. Berlin and Sharon ca. Herbert, "The Achaemenid–Ptolemaic Transition: The View from Southern Phoenicia," in Hongiman, Nihan, and Lipschits, *Times of Transition*, 156.

34. Menahem Stern, "The Period of the Second Temple," in *A History of the Jewish People*, ed. H. H. Ben-Sasson (Cambridge: Harvard University Press, 1976), 186.

35. Michael Grant, *From Alexander to Cleopatra: The Hellenistic World* (London: Weidenfeld and Nicolson, 1982), 41.

36. Lester L. Grabbe, "Hyparchs, Oikonomoi and Mafiosi: The Governance of Judah in the Ptolemaic Period," in Grabbe and Lipschits, *Judah between East and West*, 88.

the third century BC each major city along the *Via Maris* became a Greek *polis* with all the requisite infrastructure: Gaza, Ashkelon, Joppa, Dor, and Acco,[37] the last being renamed Ptolemais by Ptolemy II. The Phoenician cities further north, such as Tyre and Sidon, had begun embracing Hellenism even before Alexander's arrival in the region. Some major inland cities also became *poleis* or cleruchies, such as Marisa (biblical Maresha) in Idumea,[38] Pella and Gadara in Transjordan, Philoteria on Lake Galilee,[39] and Beth-Shean in the Jezreel Valley, which was renamed Scythopolis. At Rabbath Ammon in Transjordan, the influential Tobiad family enthusiastically embraced Hellenism, and their city was renamed Philadelphia after it became a *polis*. Samaria had been a *polis* since the Andromachus Affair of 331 BC, but beyond this, no other *polis* emerged within either Judea or Samaria. This was due in part to both regions lying off the arterial highways but was also testament to the innate conservatism of Jews and Samaritans. Even with the appeal of Hellenism, the Jewish elite opted not to import the full freight of its infrastructure. Nonetheless, the presence of Ptolemaic garrisons in the major cities still exposed Jews and Samaritans to overt Hellenistic practices.

Fourth, since culture and religion were so intertwined, religious adaptations occurred. In Egypt a new Hellenistic god was promoted: Serapis, who fused the Egyptian deities Osiris and Apis with the Greek gods Hades and Zeus,[40] fostering the long-term blending of Greek and Egyptian culture. Since the Greeks identified Yahweh with Zeus, some Jews and Samaritans began to make this identification too. This was done to varying degrees. For some, it was the first step towards liberal Hellenization. For others, it provided a means of finding common ground with their overlords and neighbors. For example, the author of the Letter of Aristeas (an Alexandrian Jew writing under the guise of a Greek official) utilized this compatibilist attitude:

> For these people [i.e., the Jews] worship the god who oversees and created everything, as do all people, we included, O King, though we name him differently as "Zeus" and "Dio." (Let. Aris. 15–16)

---

37. Stern, "The Period of the Second Temple," 187.
38. Stern, "The Period of the Second Temple," 188; Oren Tal, "'Hellenistic Foundations' in Palestine," in Grabbe and Lipschits, *Judah Between East and West*, 254.
39. Hölbl, *A History of the Ptolemaic Empire*, 60.
40. The most plausible explanation for the derivation of the name "Serapis" is a combination of "Osiris" and "Apis" (Eg. *usir-hapi*). See Edwyn R. Bevan, *The House of Ptolemy* (Didactic Press, 2014), Kindle ed., locs. 694–725; Apostolos Polyzoides, *Alexandria: City of Gifts and Sorrows: From Hellenistic Civilization to Multiethnic Metropolis* (Eastbourne: Sussex Academic Press, 2014), 71.

218 THE HELLENISTIC ERA (331–167 BC)

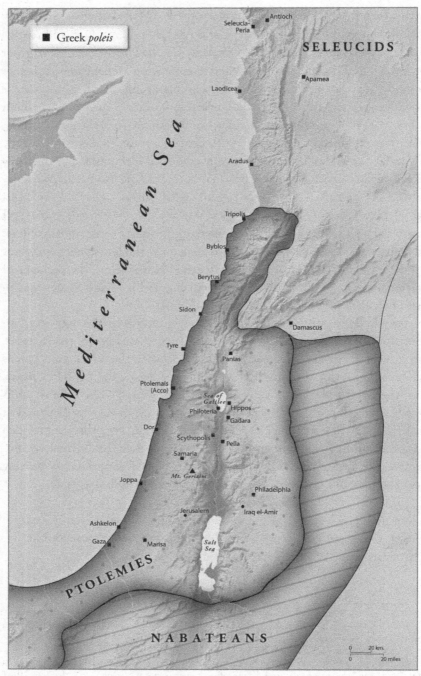

The Levant between the Ptolemies and Seleucids, showing the proliferation of Greek cities (*poleis*).

The pitfall associated with this strategy was potentially divesting Jewish theology of its particularities. For example, Yahweh's uniqueness, his faithfulness to covenant promises, and the election of Israel might be neglected in favor of viewing Yahweh as a generic deity over all people and Israel as one of many peoples united within a Hellenistic kingdom. For ultraconservatives, Greek influence was antithetical to Jewish identity, resulting in a hostility towards Greek culture and a deep introspection that tended towards sectarianism. Centrists and conservatives in Judea aimed to use Greek modes of thought while not compromising the substance of past revelation and Jewish particularity (see 2.4.3 above). Nevertheless, through the third century BC the impetus to embrace Hellenism more pervasively grew stronger.

2.6.6 GOVERNANCE OF THE JEWISH PEOPLE

The creation of "Syria and Phoenicia" as a regional unit created potential for strife. On the one hand, it allowed for more direct Greek influence upon Jews and Samaritans. On the other, it increased the possibility of friction between Jews and Samaritans. To the liberal Greek overlords, the theological rivalry between the two communities was mystifying and petty. But for the more conservatively minded locals, it became more imperative to differentiate the respective communities.

The bureaucratic changes also meant Jerusalem's high priest could no longer be the civic ruler of Judea. He was instead transformed into a *prostatēs*—a "custodian" of the Jewish people. The title indicates that the high priest became a vicar of the king, with ethnic leadership over all Jews within the kingdom. It made the high priest a refractor of royal power and Greek culture among the Jews, turning the supreme sacral office into a necessarily Hellenistic role, complicating the nature of Jewish identity. The high priest now owed his authority more to his personal relationship with the king in Alexandria than to the priestly tradition of the temple cult. The high priest at Mount Gerizim presumably received a similar custody (Gk. *prostasia*) over the Samaritans.[41]

As pharaoh of Egypt, Ptolemy took on the status of a living god, and worshipping him became a means of expressing loyalty. Since Jews (and Samaritans) were exclusive monotheists unable to engage in such worship, the Jewish high priest was instead required to pay for the privilege of being custodian and to take an oath of office. Josephus mentions the payment in relation

---

41. If Jaddua's brother, Manasseh, did become high priest at Mount Gerizim and was succeeded by his son (the grandson of Sanballat II through his daughter, Nicaso), then the high priests of Jerusalem and Mount Gerizim would have been cousins.

to the high priesthood of Onias II but states that it had been demanded of his forefathers (*Ant.* 12.158). Josephus puts the payment at 20 silver talents, which was steep for an annual payment.[42] The figure was certainly high enough to spark a crisis in the time of Onias II (see 2.6.16 below). The high priest was meant to pay this out of his own wealth, but since his estate was drawn from the tithes of the Jewish people, it was effectively a tax on worshippers. In this way, the high priest's annual fee was similar to the tax that the Persian eunuch Bagoas had imposed on the daily sacrifices (see 1.7.5 above).

The oath of office is an extrapolation from three pieces of evidence. First, Josephus mentions that Ptolemy I bound Jewish people to himself by oath because it was a reliable Jewish custom and that Jaddua had done this with Alexander (*Ant.* 12.8). Second, Ecclesiastes alludes to the taking and breaking of oaths, which aligns with the crisis that occurred under Onias II (Eccl 5:1–7; see 2.6.16 below). Third, it makes sense that Ptolemy would leverage the cherished monotheism of the Jews, which prevented them worshipping him as a god, as a means of expressing their loyalty to him.

The high priest was surrounded by a senate of elders (Gk. *gerousia*) that was based on the Greek model of oligarchic government in a city-state. It consisted of leading priests and heads of prominent families. Qoheleth, who authored the discourse of Ecclesiastes, was probably one of its members as he was well-known (Eccl 12:1), a member of the house of David (Eccl 1:1), and had intimate knowledge of domestic and international affairs (Eccl 4:1, 13–16; 5:8–9; 6:2; 8:2–4; 9:12; see 2.6.16 below). The Jewish Senate was the precursor of what would evolve into the Sanhedrin of later centuries (see 3.7.13 below).

2.6.7 THE ALLURE OF ALEXANDRIA

Since the Ptolemaic kingdom revolved around the person of the king, radical centralization occurred around the royal court in Alexandria. The city also attracted migration from the Aegean so that, before long, it became the chief Greek city of the world. It was ideally situated to take advantage of fresh water from the Nile, the supply of grain from Upper Egypt, a favorable climate, and trade networks throughout the Mediterranean. Its two vast harbors fostered an enormous naval base and commercial shipping industry so that it quickly eclipsed Memphis as Egypt's commercial center. Ptolemy also set up his realm as a closed currency system that required merchants to exchange foreign money for Ptolemaic currency, turning Alexandria into a major financial

---

42. In modern terms, this is the equivalent of approximately US$30 million.

center.⁴³ Imports and exports abounded, creating an affluent lifestyle that attracted yet more upwardly mobile people. Alexandria became a riviera metropolis.

With the influx of people, it was also a cosmopolitan city. Its Jewish community lived in the northeastern sector and made up a quarter of the city's population. All the requisite infrastructure of a Greek *polis* was present, exposing all residents, including Jews, to Ptolemy's Hellenistic ideals. Civic life was conducted in Greek, according to Greek cultural norms. Jews continued to observe their distinctive practices such as Sabbath observance, dietary restrictions, and circumcision (practiced also by native Egyptians), but it was inevitable that Jews living in the largest Greek *polis* in the world would also adopt the Greek language and facets of the Greek worldview.

Ptolemy also built the *Sōma*—a mausoleum for Alexander's body, which he transferred from its temporary tomb in Memphis.⁴⁴ He augmented it with a full temple cult in Alexander's honor. He also began building the famous lighthouse on the island of Pharos, which gave its name to the monumental structure.⁴⁵ The three-tiered tower was over thirty stories tall, and the constantly burning furnace of its beacon was visible to ships dozens of miles out to sea.

Alexandria also became the principal seat of learning in the Greek world. Ptolemy created a new research school modeled on Aristotle's Lyceum at Athens but on a far grander scale. It included lecture halls, meeting rooms, work studios, a library, a colonnade, and accommodation for a community of scholars, set amid extensive gardens. Ptolemy dedicated it as a temple to the Muses, the nine patron goddesses of the arts and sciences. From them, it received its name: the Museum of Alexandria.⁴⁶ It was essentially the forerunner of the modern university.⁴⁷ The vast sums Ptolemy poured into it allowed its library (technically his personal collection) to become the most extensive repository of knowledge in the world. This was in an age when written works had to be copied manually—a fastidious, time-consuming, and expensive process. Yet with Ptolemy's patronage, which his son, Ptolemy II, continued even

---

43. M. Lianou, "Ptolemy I and the Economics of Consolidation," in *The Age of the Successors and the Creation of the Hellenistic Kingdoms (323–276 B.C.)*, ed. Hans Hauben and Alexander Meeus, Studia Hellenistica 53 (Leuven: Peeters, 2014), 399–409; Hölbl, *A History of the Ptolemaic Empire*, 28–29; cf. Polyzoides, *Alexandria: City of Gifts and Sorrows*, 71–72.

44. Worthington, *Ptolemy I*, 129–33. In Greek, *sōma* means "body."

45. It took over a decade to build and was completed in the reign of his son, Ptolemy II.

46. Timothy H. Lim, "The Idealization of Ptolemaic Kingship in the Legend of the Origins of the Septuagint," in Honigman, Nihan, and Lipschits, *Times of Transition*, 232–33.

47. George Athas, *Ecclesiastes, Song of Songs*, Story of God Bible Commentary (Grand Rapids: Zondervan Academic, 2020), 224–25.

more indulgently, the book trade flourished. An anecdote preserved by Galen (second century AD) details the lengths Ptolemy II went to in order to procure old works for the Royal Library:

> He gave [to the Athenians] a deposit of fifteen silver talents,[48] and received the books of Aeschylus, Sophocles and Euripides, but only to copy and return them intact in next to no time. When he had prepared a magnificent copy on the best of paper, he kept the books which he received from the Athenians, and sent the copies back to them, asking them to keep the fifteen talents and accept the new books instead of the old originals they had given him. Even had he not sent the new books back to the people of Athens and kept the old ones, they could have done nothing, since they had accepted the silver on condition that they might keep it if he would keep the books. Therefore, they accepted the books, and kept the money. (Galen, *Commentary on Hippocrates' Epidemics* 3.239–240)[49]

The growth of the Royal Library was prolific. It is alleged that in Ptolemy II's day it held 200,000 volumes and aimed eventually to reach half a million (Let. Aris. 9–10a). How accurate these figures are is beyond investigation.

Ptolemy I understood that knowledge was power. His generous sponsorship enticed the most agile minds to Alexandria to trade ideas, conduct research, and compose new works. The result was an explosion of knowledge so incandescent that much of our current knowledge of mathematics, astronomy, geography, music, and history still bears the glow of research conducted at the Museum. It was an age of intellectual discovery, with an exciting sense of collaboration, freedom, and progress.

For the scribal culture in Jerusalem, the Museum of Alexandria presented an interesting dilemma. On the one hand, it was an attractive beacon of knowledge. Learning, particularly through the empirical observation of patterns inherent in nature and society, was critical to the wisdom tradition. So much could be gained by the kind of research and collaboration going on in the Museum. Jerusalem was also a scribal center where ancient books were kept, copied, and used in teaching. At the Museum, books were being collected and produced on an unprecedented scale. On the other hand, the legal and

---

48. In modern terms, this would be the equivalent of approximately US$22.5 million.
49. Adapted from Michael W. Handis, "Myth and History: Galen and the Alexandrian Library," in *Ancient Libraries*, ed. Jason König, Katerina Oikonomopoulou, and Greg Woolf (Cambridge: Cambridge University Press, 2013), 364.

prophetic traditions were a vital means by which Jews held to their identity, particularly to the notion of past revelation. They were not averse to new discovery and progress. After all, the dynamic prophetic tradition was premised on the notion of progressive revelation and believed that God was moving history forward towards the fulfilment of his ancient promises. But this sense of progress was still inextricably linked to past revelations. The notion that God had inspired the archaic traditions promulgated in Jerusalem was a controlling factor in the quest for knowledge. It is why even the biblical wisdom tradition, for all its links to international wisdom, still had its foundational tenet summed up in the statement, "Fear of Yahweh is the beginning of knowledge" (Prov 1:6a).

As attractive as the pursuits of the Museum were, there was no bypassing the fact that it was a temple dedicated to the Muses. Zeus was said to have sired the nine goddesses when, in the guise of a shepherd, he seduced their mother, Mnemosyne, on nine successive nights. In his famed *Theogony*, which tells of the birth of the gods, the Greek poet Hesiod claimed their inspiration:

> Once they taught Hesiod beautiful singing
> as he shepherded his sheep 'neath holy Helicon.
> This is what the goddesses spoke first of all to me,
> the Olympian Muses, daughters of shield-bearing Zeus:
> "Wild shepherds, evil louts, mere bellies,
> we know how to state many falsehoods as if they were right,
> and, when we want, we know how to present truth."
> Thus spoke the articulate daughters of great Zeus.
> They gave me a staff, plucked an admirable branch of thriving laurel,
> and breathed into me a voice inspired,
> to celebrate what will be and what has been. (Hesiod, *Theogony* 22–32)

Hesiod's poetry highlights the connection between the Muses and Zeus, the interweaving of truth and lies, the Muses' sense of whim, the notion of divine inspiration, the guiding symbol of a shepherd's staff, and the idea that the Muses bring both understanding and betterment. In the Greek world, Hesiod's *Theogony* was de facto scripture along with Homer's *Iliad* and *Odyssey*, which also referenced the Muses in their opening lines. Yet such undercurrents ran contrary to Jewish theology, which claimed Yahweh was the only deity in existence, that he was steadfast and true in character, and that divinely inspired knowledge came from him alone. In this vein, we read the epilogue to Ecclesiastes:

> The words of the wise are like goads,
> the expert collectors like firmly planted spikes,
> given by one shepherd.
> Beyond them, my son, beware!
> Of making many books there is no end,
> and much fervor wearies the flesh.
> The end of the matter—it has all been heard.
> It is God you should fear and his commands you should keep,
> for this is everything for a person.
> For God will bring every deed into judgment—
> every hidden thing, whether good or bad. (Eccl 12:11–14)

These words, written in the late third century BC, resonate with protest against the religious aspects of the Museum and the bibliomania found there. The Jewish writer does not advise reactionary separation from the scholarship of the wider world but rather cautious and critical engagement with it. For him, the foundational element of wisdom and knowledge was Yahweh himself, the one true shepherd. This in turn engendered the need for utmost loyalty to God and obedience to his past revelation. These were the non-negotiables of Jewish identity.

2.6.8 THE LAST OF THE *DIADOCHI*

In 283 BC Ptolemy I died in Alexandria, aged eighty-four. He passed over his eldest son, Ptolemy Thunderbolt (Gk. *Keraunos*), and handed his realm to a younger son, Ptolemy II. Over in Macedon, Cassander had died in 297 BC and his dynasty was subsequently expelled by Demetrius Besieger. But Demetrius was in turn squeezed out, and Macedon was incorporated into the realm of seventy-eight-year-old Lysimachus. He and seventy-five-year-old Seleucus were the last of the *diadochi* left alive.

Seleucus established several new cities in his enormous kingdom. One such city was Seleucia-on-the-Tigris, near Babylon, which initiated the ancient city's decline. He also founded four key cities in Syria: the Mediterranean ports of Seleucia-Pieria and Laodicea, and Apamea and Antioch further inland.[50] But since Asia Minor was split between him and Lysimachus after Ipsus (301 BC), a showdown between the two *diadochi* loomed. It came in 281 BC

---

50. John D. Grainger, *The Rise of the Seleukid Empire (323–223 BC): Seleukos I to Seleukos III* (Barnsley: Pen and Sword, 2014), 92–94.

in the "Field of Cyrus" (Corupedium) outside Sardis. Lysimachus lost his life in the battle, leaving Seleucus as the last remaining *diadochus*. Seleucus set off across the Hellespont to take possession of Lysimachus's territories in Thrace and Macedon. But scarcely had he landed on European soil than Ptolemy Thunderbolt made an opportunist move. Thunderbolt had allied himself with Seleucus in the hope of gaining Macedon for himself. But with Seleucus moving to occupy the country, Thunderbolt had him assassinated and proclaimed himself king of Macedon.[51]

Thunderbolt's rule in Macedon, though, was fated to be brief. Just two year later (279 BC), bands of Celtic Gauls swept into Macedon, captured him, and beheaded him. For the next few years, the Gauls wreaked havoc in Greece until they were defeated by Antigonus II Knock-Knees (Gk. *Gonatas*), the son of Demetrius Besieger and grandson of One-Eyed Antigonus. With this victory, Antigonus II re-established the Antigonid dynasty in Macedon, and it would endure until the Roman conquest of Macedon in 148 BC (3.6.6 below).

2.6.9 FIRST SYRIAN WAR

After Seleucus I's death, his son, Antiochus I, spent the first part of his reign quelling unrest in the Seleucid heartland of Syria and Mesopotamia. This left Asia Minor exposed, and the Gauls who had invaded Greece started pouring in. Antiochus managed to contain them in central Asia Minor, where they settled down to sedentary life. The region even took on a new name to reflect their arrival: Galatia.

Despite the passing of the older generation, the rivalry between the Seleucids and Ptolemies did not dissipate. Antiochus had designs on the southern Levant and tried to distract Ptolemy II's attention from it by creating strife for him in Cyrene. It ultimately failed, and Ptolemy launched a pre-emptive strike in what would come to be known as the First Syrian War (275–271 BC)—the first of six Syrian Wars the Ptolemies and Seleucids would fight over the next century. Ptolemy first overran the Mediterranean coast of Asia Minor[52] before taking the war to Syria. But a stalemate ensued, and a peace settlement was eventually hammered out. Ptolemy had clearly won in Asia Minor, so he agreed to maintain the status quo in the Levant. The line

---

51. Bob Bennett and Mike Roberts, *The Wars of Alexander's Successors 323—281 BC. Volume 1: Commanders & Campaigns* (Barnsley: Pen & Sword Military, 2008), 216–17.

52. This acquisition of territory in Asia Minor is sometimes attributed to an earlier campaign immediately after the death of Seleucus I (cf. Hölbl, *A History of the Ptolemaic Empire*, 37). However, the circumstances better reflect those that prevailed in the First Syrian War.

demarcating their realms ran along the Eleutheros River (the modern Kabir River separating Syria and Lebanon). Judea and Samaria thus remained within the Ptolemaic kingdom.

Ptolemy's victory put him in a politically and economically dominant position, a fact celebrated by a lavish parade in Alexandria during the Ptolemaia Games. The parade was remembered as one of the most flamboyant exhibitions of opulence the ancient world had ever seen (Atheneus, *Learned Banqueters* 5.196a–203b). The legendary event earned Ptolemy II a reputation as a fabulously wealthy monarch, epitomizing the ideal of *tryphē* ("luxury").[53] It was almost certainly part of the inspiration behind Qoheleth's characterization of the rich oriental despot in Ecclesiastes 2:1–26 (see 2.6.16 below).[54]

Ptolemy II also divorced his first wife, Arsinoe, who had borne him his future heir, Ptolemy III Benefactor (Gk. *Euergetēs*), and married his own sister, Arsinoe II. Together they ruled as "sibling gods,"[55] a situation that earned Ptolemy the epithet "Sibling Lover" (Gk. *Philadelphos*). The incestuous union combined the ideals of Egyptian and Greek gods, who married their siblings (e.g., Osiris and Isis; Zeus and Hera). It thus distinguished the dynasty from mere mortals and raised them to the level of the gods—something that had been common in pharaonic custom. It also promoted the Ptolemaic royal cult and made the dynasty self-sufficient. It was a practice that would characterize the Ptolemies right down to its last monarch, Cleopatra VII.

2.6.10 THE SEPTUAGINT

Onias I replaced Hezekiah as high priest in 301 BC. Onias was succeeded in ca. 279 BC by his son, Simon I. But Simon died prematurely (ca. 275 BC), leaving a son, Onias II, who was too young (under thirty) to take up the high priesthood. Thus the office passed to Simon's brother, Eleazar (see also 2.6.2).

During the incumbency of Eleazar, the Torah was translated into Greek at Alexandria. Our chief evidence for this is the pseudepigraphal Letter of Aristeas, a Greek work by an Alexandrian Jew in the mid-second century BC. The account contains several fictive elements. It has Ptolemy II send a delegation to Eleazar with a request for six Jewish translators from each of the twelve tribes of Israel. Under the sponsorship of Ptolemy and the auspices of the Museum's Royal Library, the seventy-two men work for seventy-two days on the translation. Their translation is

---

53. Catharine ca. Lorber, "The Coinage of the Ptolemies," in *The Oxford Handbook of Greek and Roman Coinage*, ed. William E. Metcalf (Oxford: Oxford University Press, 2012), 215.

54. Athas, *Ecclesiastes, Song of Songs*, 71–73.

55. Hölbl, *A History of the Ptolemaic Empire*, 46.

judged to be flawless and accepted by the Jewish community as divinely inspired. The story led to the translation being labelled as "The Translation of the Seventy" (the seventy-two translators being rounded to seventy; cf. Josephus, *Ant.* 12.57). From this came the Latin term *Septuaginta* ("Seventy").[56] Despite the fanciful elements, some of the details in the Aristeas narrative intersect with verifiable historical contexts and Philo's less embellished account (Philo, *Mos.* 2.27–29).[57] The translation dates to the co-reign of Ptolemy II and Arsinoe II (Let. Aris. 41)—that is, the 260s BC.[58] This aligns perfectly with the tenure of Eleazar (ca. 275–260 BC; Let. Aris. 1, 33, 35, 41),[59] whose involvement in the endeavor as custodian of the Jews in the Ptolemaic realm is logical.

The Greek of the Septuagint is not of the polished literary quality associated with Classical Greek works. It is, rather, a *koinē* ("common") Greek associated with everyday language, but that is aware of technical terms in a Greek Egyptian context.[60] It also shows signs of preserving underlying Hebrew linguistic structures.[61] Textual analysis shows that it was based on a Hebrew text that came from Palestine.[62] These characteristics have led some to suggest that the translation was not made under the auspices of Ptolemy II and the Royal Library.[63] However, two factors undermine this. First, the Septuagint was a translation of a Hebrew text, which was foreign to the Greek scholars of the Royal Library. The well-known bibliomania of the Ptolemies makes it plausible that Ptolemy II could have sponsored the translation as a project of the Royal Library, even though the translation itself must have been carried out by Jews. Second, the needs of the Jewish community in Alexandria were probably the dominant motivation for its production. By the 260s BC at least one generation of Jews had grown up in Greek-speaking Alexandria, and the prestige of Greek probably amplified the need for a translation of the Torah. By sponsoring the translation of Jewish laws, Ptolemy would have given expression to his

---

56. The term "Septuagint" technically refers only to the Greek translation of the Torah, but it is often used in a more generic sense to mean the Greek translation of all the Hebrew Scriptures.

57. Lim, "The Idealization of Ptolemaic Kingship," 131–39.

58. Arsinoe II died in ca. 260 BC.

59. *Pace* Rösel, "The Septuagint," 253.

60. Benjamin G. Wright, "The Production of Greek Books in Alexandrian Judaism," in Honigman, Nihan, and Lipschits, *Times of Transition*, 244–45.

61. James K. Aitken, ed., *The T&T Clark Companion to the Septuagint* (London: Bloomsbury, 2015), 3–4.

62. Emanuel Tov, "The Palestinian Source of the Greek Translation of the Torah," in *Die Septuaginta—Themen, Manuskripte, Wirkungen*, ed. Eberhard Bons et al., Wissenschaftliche Untersuchungen Zum Neuen Testament 444 (Tübingen: Mohr Siebeck, 2020), 18–39.

63. Erich S. Gruen, *Heritage and Hellenism: The Reinvention of Jewish Tradition* (Berkeley: University of California Press, 1998), 208–10; Benjamin G. Wright, "The Letter of Aristeas and the Question of Septuagint Origins Redux," *JAJ* 2.3 (2011): 304–26.

bibliomania and made himself a beneficent patron of the burgeoning Jewish community in his capital, to whom he granted limited autonomy.[64]

Contrary to the portrait in Aristeas, the translation was not a unified effort. Different translation styles are evident across the five books of the Torah, and sometimes within a book too.[65] That the Torah was, at least initially, the only portion of the Jewish Scriptures to be translated might suggest the input of the high priest Eleazar. Priestly prestige was predicated on the Torah rather than the prophetic traditions, which contained some vitriolic critiques of the priesthood (e.g., Jeremiah, Ezekiel, the Twelve). Yet by the late second century BC the Prophets had been translated into Greek, and other books were also being translated, as the preface to Ben Sira indicates (Sira 0:21–26). Some of the books that would ultimately make it into the canon of the Writings (Lamentations, Ecclesiastes, Song of Songs) would not be translated until the first century AD.[66] Nevertheless, the translation of key texts into Greek was pivotal to developing the Hellenistic complexion of Judaism, and the texts themselves were then exported via the shipping lanes from Alexandria to other Mediterranean cities where Jews settled.

2.6.11 PRAYER HOUSES: THE BEGINNINGS OF THE SYNAGOGUE

Concomitant with the translation of the Septuagint was the rise of prayer houses—the earliest form of synagogues. Various theories exist about how prayer houses and synagogues developed, the most cogent being that Jews initially met for communal piety at city gates.[67] In Judea, such meetings became critical for the regular dissemination of scriptural traditions, which were so vital to the survival of the Jerusalem temple (see 1.7.4 above). City gates across Palestine were multi-chambered, often with adjoining public squares—adequate infrastructure for public assembly. But from the Hellenistic era, architecture changed. City gates became simple points of ingress and egress, and activities previously conducted there were transferred inside or outside the city.[68] In Palestine, where Jews were the majority and older style gates persisted much longer, dedicated synagogues did not develop until the first cen-

---

64. Cf. Lim, "The Idealization of Ptolemaic Kingship," 235–37.
65. Rösel, "The Septuagint," 253–54.
66. Aitken, *Companion to the Septuagint*, 4.
67. Lee I. Levine, *The Ancient Synagogue: The First Thousand Years*, 2nd ed. (New Haven: Yale University Press, 2000), 28–44.
68. Donald D. Binder, *Into the Temple Courts: The Place of the Synagogues in the Second Temple Period*, SBL Dissertation Series 169 (Atlanta: Society of Biblical Literature, 1999), 217; cf. Tal, "'Hellenistic Foundations' in Palestine," 251.

tury BC (see 4.2.1 below). In Egypt, Jews were in a minority, and the agora did not provide them with appropriate space for their endeavors. It was, therefore, in the early third century BC, around the time that the Torah was translated into Greek, that dedicated buildings for communal prayer, the reading of Scripture, and the safe storage of scrolls began to appear throughout Egypt.

These buildings were called *proseuchai* (sg. *proseuchē*), meaning "prayer" houses. Due to the concentration of the Jewish population in Alexandria, it is reasonable to assume that the first prayer houses were erected there. Artefactual evidence from Alexandria, however, is meager because of the paucity of modern archaeological excavation. The first (fragmentary) epigraphic evidence from the city comes from the second century BC (*JIE* 9=*CIJ* 2.1433; cf. *JIE* 13-*CIJ* 2.1432),[69] but literary evidence exists in relative abundance. Although much of this dates to the first century BC and later (e.g., 3 Maccabees, Philo),[70] it demonstrates an institution that had become a staple of Jewish life in Egypt.

The earliest known prayer house in all of Egypt dates to the reign of Ptolemy III Benefactor (246–222 BC) and was located in Schedia, east of Alexandria.[71] It carried a dedicatory inscription (*JIE* 22=*CIJ* 2.1440):

> On behalf of King Ptolemy and Queen Berenice, his sister and wife, and their children, the Jews [dedicated] the prayer house.

The dedication shows that the Ptolemaic monarchs approved of Jewish prayer houses, though it is unlikely that they sponsored them financially. An almost identical dedicatory inscription comes from a prayer house at Crocodilopolis-Arsinoe in the Fayum Oasis (*JIE* 117=*CPJ* 3.1532a).[72] That particular prayer house is mentioned in a land survey (*CPJ* 1.134), from which we know that it stood on two-and-a-half acres of land outside the city. It lay beside a canal, which provided access to water and perhaps facilitated ritual bathing. The congregation was represented by a man named Pertollos, and about an acre of the land was leased to a tenant as a "consecrated garden" growing flowers and vegetables.[73] Prayer houses were considered sacred, as confirmed by a legal petition from 218 BC, which states that an accused thief found asylum in a Jewish prayer house (*CPJ* 1.129; cf. 3 Macc 2:28; 3:29; 4:18; 7:20).[74]

---

69. Binder, *Into the Temple Courts*, 131, 248.
70. Binder, *Into the Temple Courts*, 43–54.
71. Binder, *Into the Temple Courts*, 240.
72. Binder, *Into the Temple Courts*, 112.
73. Binder, *Into the Temple Courts*, 236–38. It is hard to know whether "consecrated" indicates a sacred function or simply connotes a "dedicated" garden.
74. Binder, *Into the Temple Courts*, 238–39.

Gentiles referred to them as "shrines" (Gk. *hiera*; cf. 3 Macc 2:28), and Jews themselves eventually adopted this terminology, too.[75]

This helps explain a bizarre anecdote told by Josephus. He relates how, during the reign of Ptolemy VI (180–145 BC), a heated dispute arose between the Jewish and Samaritan communities in Egypt over whose temple in Palestine was legitimate. They brought the dispute to Ptolemy VI on the agreement that those who lost the case would be put to death (*Ant.* 13.74–79). The anecdote contains embellishment, but since Josephus names the specific proponents of the debate, there probably was some historical substance behind it. It was most likely a dispute over "shrines" (*hiera*)—that is, prayer houses (synagogues), especially if Jews and Samaritans sometimes had to share them. Which temple in Palestine they prayed for or towards would have caused considerable friction, and an appeal to the Ptolemaic crown, in whose name prayer houses were constructed, was logical.

Prayer houses also became something of a cultural lodge, fostering Jewish cultural life in Egypt. For example, they provided hospitality to Jewish travelers and became de facto schools for Jewish boys. This occurred particularly in Alexandria, where well-to-do Jewish families were impelled to educate their children in a city dominated by the Museum and the gymnasium (cf. 4.2.1 below). The skill of literacy also enabled social betterment in a world that began to develop rapidly with the monetization of the economy (see 2.6.12 below).

2.6.12 THE PTOLEMAIC ECONOMY

Up until the mid-third century BC, bartering was the dominant mode of trade.[76] In this system, goods were exchanged for other goods, which meant that goods always travelled in two directions. Taxation was also usually paid in kind, mainly in the form of agricultural produce. Coinage tended to be used sparingly, being reserved to pay soldiers, purchase offerings for sacrifices, or to use in lending. Ptolemy II changed this by monetizing his realm. During his reign, the minting of coins increased fivefold.[77] The cash economy grew as a result, so that trading goods for coins became the dominant means of exchange. This meant that goods increasingly travelled in just one direction, with coins

---

75. Binder, *Into the Temple Courts*, 122–30.

76. Primitive money in the form of *hacksilber* (piece of silver offcuts) had been around for centuries beforehand.

77. Mark R. Sneed, *The Politics of Pessimism in Ecclesiastes: A Social-Science Perspective*, Ancient Israel and Its Literature 12 (Atlanta: Society of Biblical Literature, 2012), 97–98; Martin Hengel, *Judaism and Hellenism: Studies in Their Encounter in Palestine during the Early Hellenistic Period*, 2 vols. (London: SCM Press, 1974), 1:43–44.

substituting for goods in the opposite direction. Theoretically, a seller who received cash for a transaction now had greater choice as a consumer, for cash could be used to purchase from a greater range of goods than in a bartering system. However, with the radical centralization that occurred around the Ptolemaic king, an overwhelming amount of goods streamed into Alexandria while fewer goods went out to other centers. This effectively reduced the supply of goods in those other centers, which in turn drove up prices in those centers, reducing consumers' purchasing power. The result was a massive redistribution of goods towards Alexandria and an increase in prices outside it.

Ptolemy also imposed a barrage of cash taxes in addition to the taxes paid in produce. The average person in the Ptolemaic kingdom was taxed multiple times, and many were taxed out of independent production. As a decree of Ptolemy II from 261 BC demonstrates, tax evasion attracted crippling fines, and people were encouraged with financial incentives to inform on their tax evading neighbors.[78]

What made things worse for the average person was the method of tax collection. The Ptolemies sold the right to raise tax revenues to private contractors. These tax farmers (Gk. *telōnai*) were obliged to deposit an agreed amount of tax revenue into the royal coffers by a particular date. The profession was so profitable because tax farmers exacted more revenue than they were obliged to raise, keeping the difference as their own profit margin. Intimidation was a standard *modus operandi*, which made tax farmers veritable mafia bosses. The system bred a sense of Sisyphean frustration among the general populace, who often forfeited much of their own wealth. This explains the general hostility towards tax farmers that persisted into the first century (cf. Matt 9:10–11; Luke 15:1; 19:7), as well as the profoundly countercultural attitude of Jesus, who not only reached out to them (Matt 11:19; 21:31; Luke 7:29; 19:1–10) but even counted one repentant tax farmer among his inner circle (Matt 9:9; 10:3; Mark 2:14). In the Ptolemaic kingdom, taxation ensured that, while goods tended to flow into Alexandria, most of the cash that went out to pay for those goods also came back in the form of taxes. Under such circumstances, many people were drawn to urban life, especially in Alexandria.

As if this were not enough, Ptolemy II and his inner circle monopolized numerous industries. This allowed them to control the supply and price of goods even further. Among the state-controlled industries were olive oil, fine textiles, brewing, papyrus production, salt, and timber, to name but a few.[79]

---

78. The decree is preserved in the Vienna Papyrus. See Lawrence H. Schiffman, *Texts and Traditions: A Source Reader for the Study of Second Temple and Rabbinic Judaism* (Brooklyn: KTAV, 1998), §4.2.6.

79. Bevan, *The House of Ptolemy*, 148–49.

Palestine, with its renowned olive oil and wine industries, experienced an economic boom. But on the personal level, few of the producers involved in these industries benefitted from their work. They were poorly paid and often unable to meet tax demands or loan repayments. Defaulters were compelled to sell their land to the state or to the wealthy elite and become tenant farmers instead, creating a class of peasants connected to the landowning elite. Some simply abandoned land and trades to become hired laborers instead. Others were forced into taking loans they could never repay, binding them to their creditors in perpetual debt slavery. Others offered themselves for military service, which explains the vast armies the Ptolemies could muster. What was particularly attractive in military service was the system of cleruchies in which soldiers were granted small parcels of land in exchange for permanent service as reservists. Some escaped the realm for opportunities in other lands, while those who were able resorted to bribery and illicit favors. The utterly desperate were driven to sell children into slavery or enter the sex trade (the two were often indistinguishable). Some faced perpetual threat, physical harm, detention, kidnapping, and even death. Under the burdens of monetization, taxation, monopolization, intimidation, fines, and redistribution, many slid into economic and social servility while the elite grew exceptionally wealthy.[80]

Under such pressures, many Jews and Samaritans were probably attracted to mortgaging ("consecrating") their property to their respective temples. Leviticus 27:14–21 made provision for this, valuing land by its agricultural potential and stipulating a 20 percent flat interest rate on paying off the mortgage. These stipulations were in existence well before the Ptolemaic era, such that temples also functioned as banks. With the monetization of the Ptolemaic economy and the economic hardship this entailed for so many, temple-based mortgages made the banking function of temples more prominent. Consequently, the wealth of the priests grew steadily through the receipt of interest payments or the foreclosure of property. In time, the Jewish and Samaritan priests became real estate moguls, ranking among the biggest landowners in the region and thus taking their place among the elite of Hellenistic society in the Ptolemaic realm. The once struggling priesthood of Jerusalem was socioeconomically elevated.

Some of the most telling evidence for the polarizing effects of Ptolemy's economic policies comes from an archive of some 1,800 papyri belonging to Zenon, the senior executive officer (Gk. *oikonomos*) of Apollonius, the chief

---

80. Ptolemy II's tax decree for the Levant in 261 BC demonstrates the extent of the exploitation. See Schiffman, *Texts and Traditions*, §4.2.6.

minister (Gk. *dioikētēs*) of Ptolemy II. Apollonius engaged in large-scale business ventures across the Ptolemaic realm. He owned a fleet of ships that plied the ports of the eastern Mediterranean, with agents conducting business for him in the major centers. Among his vast holdings was a large wine estate in Galilee.[81] Zenon assisted Apollonius in managing both his governmental and personal business pursuits. To that end, Apollonius sent Zenon on a tour of Syria and Phoenicia in 258 BC as part of a royal census and audit of his own business interests. It was a journey that included a stop at Jerusalem,[82] which was probably the occasion for introducing the annual fee for the high priest's custodianship (cf. *Ant.* 12.158).

Zenon's archive indicates that Apollonius had ties with Tobias, the head of the Jewish Tobiad family, who administered Ammanitis (Ammon) in Transjordan.[83] Tobias was married to the daughter of the Jewish high priest, Simon I, making him an important figure in Jewish society. Zenon's papyri reveal Tobias's openly Hellenistic attitudes, which also reflects on Simon. They show that Tobias supplied Apollonius and Ptolemy II with gifts, undertook business deals with them,[84] and facilitated the economic exploitation of locals. One papyrus details the sale of a seven-year-old Sidonian girl named Sphragis to Zenon as a slave for fifty drachmas.[85] Another details the gifting of a eunuch and four boys aged between seven and ten as slaves to Apollonius.[86]

From Zenon's archive we also learn of debt collection and the hostility it engendered towards the wealthy. One letter relates how Zenon sent two henchmen to extract money from a Jewish man named Jeddous (a Hellenized form of "Jaddua" or "Iddo") and how Jeddous defended himself by physically attacking them.[87] How Zenon responded to Jeddous's recalcitrance is undocumented, but it is unlikely that there were no repercussions.

2.6.13 EXCURSUS: ECONOMICS AND THE GOSPEL

Monetization and the hardships it induced persisted for centuries. The Romans also employed tax farmers, who were notorious for fleecing subject

---

81. Bevan, *The House of Ptolemy*, 134.
82. Campbell Cowan Edgar, *Zenon Papyri in the University of Michigan Collection* (Ann Arbor: University of Michigan Press, 1931), 31.
83. Tobias was the descendant of "Tobiah the Ammonite," the ally of Sanballat I (Neh 2:10, 19; 4:3, 7; 6:1, 12, 14, 17, 19). It is also likely that the Tobiah mentioned in Zech 6:9–15, who lived in the late sixth century BC, was an ancestor.
84. Schiffman, *Texts and Traditions*, §4.2.5, Papyrus 5.
85. Schiffman, *Texts and Traditions*, §4.2.5, Papyrus 1.
86. Schiffman, *Texts and Traditions*, §4.2.5, Papyrus 4.
87. Schiffman, *Texts and Traditions*, §4.2.5, Papyrus 6.

peoples. Several of Jesus's parables referred to such economic and social realities. For example, the parable of the tenants (Matt 21:33–46) described a landowner who installed tenant farmers to work his vineyard. The hostility of these tenants towards the landowner and their desire to acquire the property for themselves (Matt 21:35–39) manifested their economic helplessness. Jesus used this socioeconomic dynamic to critique some of the wealthiest landowners in the Levant—"the chief priests" (Matt 21:45). He appealed to the outrage that they as landowners would have felt at the belligerence of such tenants before stunningly casting them as the wicked tenants, using this to explain God's outrage and rejection of their leadership.

Jesus's critique of the priests continued the sentiments of John the Baptist's preaching. John repudiated the trappings of his own priestly heritage and made his home in the Judean Desert, from where he decried (among others) the Sadducees—the faction that included the wealthiest priestly families in the Jewish world. We also see the real estate ventures of the priests in the acquisition of the field associated with Judas Iscariot and his death (Matt 27:5–8; cf. Acts 1:18–19). Such real estate dealings made the precedent of Joseph Barnabas in the early church so surprising. Barnabas was a landowning Levite from Cyprus, yet he sold a farm he owned and contributed the proceeds to the apostolic community (Acts 4:36–37).

Cancelling debt also featured highly in Jesus's teaching. In his parable of the unmerciful servant (Matt 18:23–35), Jesus played on the hierarchy of credit, the inability of people to pay their debts, the violence and intimidation used in debt collection, and the concept of debt slavery to highlight the depths of God's forgiveness. But appealing to such realities was not just illustrative. The forgiveness of debts was Jesus's leading analogy for the forgiveness of sins, which also exposed the spiritual condition lying behind the harsh economic injustices of the day (cf. Luke 7:40–50). It is what made Jesus's announcement of forgiveness so revolutionary. This explains why he configured blessing and salvation in similar terms with such statements as, "Blessed are the poor in spirit, for theirs is the kingdom of heaven" (Matt 5:3) and "Forgive us our debts, as we also have forgiven our debtors" (Matt 6:12).

2.6.14 SECOND SYRIAN WAR (261–253 BC)

Antiochus I was unable to prevent the fracturing of Asia Minor. In the 260s BC Pergamum seceded and became a state in its own right, ruled by the Attalid dynasty. Pontus, along the northern coast, followed suit. There were additional blows after Antiochus had lost the southern coast to Ptolemy II. Antiochus's dynasty was also suffering. He had elevated his son, Seleucus, to joint rule with him, but the father-son relationship festered so badly that Antiochus had his son executed in 267 BC. He then replaced him with a younger son, Antiochus II.

The peace that Antiochus I and Ptolemy II had struck at the end of the First Syrian War in 271 BC was in force until Antiochus died in 261 BC. The peace treaty thus lapsed, and Ptolemy immediately went on the offensive in the Aegean and Asia Minor. Details of the campaign are scant, but two years later he invaded Syria and seems to have threatened Antioch and Seleucia-Pieria. The invasion forced Antiochus II to focus his defensive efforts there, with the result that more regions across Asia Minor seceded from Seleucid rule. Antiochus was compelled to make diplomatic and territorial concessions to these emerging states to prevent them from siding with Ptolemy against him. It was just enough to ensure that Antiochus maintained a semblance of authority as the senior among a number of junior kings, but it set a precedent that would haunt the Seleucid kingdom for centuries.

Antiochus II's diplomatic scrambling worked. Ptolemy was repelled from Syria and Asia Minor and defeated on the sea.[88] The census, which Zenon undertook in Palestine in 258 BC (see 2.6.12 above), was conducted in response to Ptolemy's defeats, with the aim of securing new revenue streams to bolster the Ptolemaic military. The demand that the high priest in Jerusalem pay for his custodianship of the Jews probably derives from the pinch of this moment and was probably policed by Zenon.

Ptolemy was unable to bounce back quickly, and soon Antiochus was dealing with strife in Babylon. Hostilities between the two kings turned into shadowboxing until they both assented to a formal end of the conflict. In the rapprochement, Ptolemy agreed to marry his daughter, Berenice, to Antiochus. But there was one major sticking point to the match: Antiochus II was already married to his cousin, Laodice, and she had borne him two sons, Seleucus and Antiochus Hierax, who had been listed alongside their father in official documents since their infancy.[89] The boys were now seventeen and fifteen respectively—both in the midst of military training. While it was not unusual for a king to take two wives, the whole point of Antiochus's marriage to Berenice was to produce a new heir to the Seleucid throne, who would also be Ptolemy's grandson. Antiochus reluctantly agreed to divorce his first wife,

---

88. Hölbl, *A History of the Ptolemaic Empire*, 62.

89. Boris Chrubasik, "The Epigraphic Dossier Concerning Ptolemaios, Son of Thraseas, and the Fifth Syrian War," *Zeitschrift Für Papyrologie Und Epigraphik* 209 (2019): 123.

Laodice, and sent her into exile at Ephesus along with her two sons, removing them from the succession.

Ptolemy sent Berenice to Syria in the custody of his chief minister, Apollonius (the employer of Zenon), and the wedding took place in 252 BC. Five years later, Berenice gave birth to a baby boy, named Antiochus after his father. The baby became the new heir to the Seleucid kingdom, thus ensuring the permanent marginalization of Antiochus II's two older sons by Laodice.

2.6.15 THIRD SYRIAN WAR (246-241 BC)

A year after the birth of Berenice's son, everything changed again. In January 246 BC the treaty between the Ptolemies and Seleucids came to end when Ptolemy II died at the age of sixty-two. The status quo might have prevailed, except that Antiochus II hastened to Ephesus to reconcile with his first wife, Laodice. In so doing, he alienated Berenice and offended her brother, the newly regnant Ptolemy III. Laodice's eldest son, the former crown prince Seleucus, was now twenty-four—old enough to be cemented back into the channels of power at the expense of Berenice's infant son. The only chance Berenice stood of surviving was if her brother, Ptolemy III, put enough pressure on Antiochus to make him repudiate Laodice and her sons again. But Laodice was not about to let that happen again. In a bold and sinister twist, she poisoned Antiochus in July 246 BC and proclaimed her eldest son, Seleucus II, king. Berenice appealed to her brother and he leapt to her defense, launching the Third Syrian War.

Ptolemy made with haste for the Seleucid capital at Seleucia-Pieria and took the city. He then marched inland to Antioch, only to find that his sister and her infant son had been murdered by Laodice's henchmen. Ptolemy's forces sailed to Ephesus to deal with Laodice, but she and her sons had fled across Asia Minor shoring up support for Seleucus. In an attempt to dispossess Seleucus of his kingdom, Ptolemy cut through northern Syria and Mesopotamia. He plundered far and wide, acquiring lavish amounts of booty, which included repossessing antiquities originally removed from Egypt in the time of Cambyses. It was to little avail, though, for in 245 BC Ptolemy was forced to return to Egypt to deal with a major crisis caused by extremely low flooding of the Nile. Famine took hold in Egypt for the next seven years (245–238 BC).[90] To quell the unrest, Ptolemy remitted taxes and imported

---

90. Modern scientific studies suggest that the Nile's flow was affected by volcanic eruptions that impeded the normal cycle of monsoon rains in central east Africa. See Joseph G. Manning et al., "Volcanic

grain from Cyprus and the Levant (Canopus Decree, 9–10). These initiatives were enough to bring Egypt through the crisis, and a grateful people gave their king the sobriquet "Benefactor" (Gk. *Euergetēs*).[91]

The Egyptian crisis allowed Seleucus II to establish his own rule in Syria. He appointed his younger brother, Antiochus Hierax, as commander over volatile Asia Minor, while he himself headed east to deal with the damage wrought by Ptolemy. He then attempted an invasion of Ptolemy's lands in the Levant but was held at bay in southern Syria. In 241 BC the two kings agreed to another peace treaty, with Ptolemy coming out stronger. Among his gains was the retention of Seleucia-Pieria as a Ptolemaic enclave in Syria, which forced Seleucus to remove his court to Antioch.

These events between the end of the Second Syrian War and the end of the Third Syrian War would have repercussions in Judea (see 2.6.16 below). They are also related in Daniel 11, with the Ptolemaic kings embodying the quintessential "King of the South" and the Seleucid kings embodying the "King of the North."

> At the end of some years, they will reach an accord. The daughter [Berenice] of the King of the South [Ptolemy II] will come to the King of the North [Antiochus II] to make an agreement. But she [Berenice] will not retain her power, so his [Ptolemy II's] influence will not endure. She, her retainers, her son, and her supporter [Ptolemy II] will be taken in time. But a branch of her own stock [Ptolemy III] will arise in his place and come with the army and enter the stronghold [Seleucia-Pieria] of the King of the North [Seleucus II], prevailing successfully. Even their gods, with their libations and prized vessels of silver and gold, he will bring to Egypt. Then he [Ptolemy III] will stay away from the King of the North. He [Seleucus II] will come against the kingdom of the King of the South, but then return to his own territory. (Dan 11:6–9)

2.6.16 ONIAS II, JOSEPH TOBIAS, AND THE PESSIMISM OF QOHELETH

The waxing and waning fortunes of the Ptolemies and Seleucids lie behind two seemingly innocuous comments of Qoheleth, the author of the discourse in Ecclesiastes:

Suppression of Nile Summer Flooding Triggers Revolt and Constrains Interstate Conflict in Ancient Egypt," *Nature Communications* 8.1 (2017): 1–9.

91. Hölbl, *A History of the Ptolemaic Empire*, 49.

Off to the south, and around to the north, round and round goes the wind, and then back on its circuit goes the wind again. (Eccl 1:6)

Whether a tree falls to the south or to the north, the place in which the tree falls is where it will be. (Eccl 11:3b)

Both these statements are philosophical in tenor, but they derive from Qoheleth's setting in Jerusalem during the late third century BC, where the terms "north" and "south" were loaded with political freight (cf. the vision of Dan 11). Indeed, most of Qoheleth's reflections are not purely philosophical but prompted by the political upheaval he lived through. Judea, caught between the Seleucid north and the Ptolemaic south, was continually buffeted by their effervescent rivalry. Furthermore, Judea had witnessed such rivalries between north and south ever since the secession of Egypt from the Persian Empire in 400 BC. This made the life of average Jews a lottery of miserable outcomes. To Qoheleth, the teetering fortunes of the Seleucids and Ptolemies were like the swirling of the wind (an allusion to the inscrutability of God's will in political affairs) or the random fall of a tree (often used as an image of imperial downfall). They could not be predicted, much less controlled by insignificant Jews in Judea. To even try was like "chasing the wind" (Eccl 1:14)—an attempt to herd God's spirit and bend divine initiative to human will.[92]

According to Qoheleth, though, this is exactly what the high priest in Jerusalem, Onias II, tried to do. Qoheleth never names Onias outright since anonymity is one of his rhetorical strategies, but the contours of his discourse trace the clear shape of Onias and the events in which he was involved.[93] We know of his incumbency from Josephus's *Antiquities*, which relies partially on the *Tobiad Romance*. This source traced the career of Joseph Tobias (son of the Tobias known from the Zenon archive [see 2.6.12 above]) and the youngest of his eight sons, Hyrcanus. Though some question the reliability of the *Tobiad Romance*, many details can be corroborated with other sources, including Ecclesiastes, to gain an accurate picture of events.

Onias was initially too young to succeed his father, Simon I, as high priest in ca. 279 BC, so it was not until ca. 255 BC that he came into the position (see 2.6.2 above). Unlike Ptolemaic subjects in other lands, monotheism prevented Onias from demonstrating his loyalty to the Ptolemaic king by participating in the Ptolemaic royal cult. Instead, his continuance in office depended on

---

92. Athas, *Ecclesiastes, Song of Songs*, 58, 207–9.
93. George Athas, "Qoheleth in His Context: Ecclesiastes 4,13–16 and the Dating of the Book," *Biblica* 100.3 (2019): 358–60, 371.

paying an annual fee (see 2.6.6 above)[94] and swearing allegiance to the king via an oath taken in Yahweh's name.[95] Such an oath placed Onias and the whole Jewish nation under divine obligation to obey the king, such that disloyalty was tantamount to treason against God himself.

When Ptolemy III scaled back taxation for seven years to ease the effects of the Egyptian famine in 245 BC (see 2.6.15 above), he seems also to have paused the payment demanded of Onias. But when the famine was over, Ptolemy III sought to recoup his losses and fund a new campaign against Macedon (the Demetrian War of 238–234 BC). The annual fee for Onias's position was thus reinstated.[96] Onias, however, refused to pay the 20 silver talents demanded of him. According to Josephus, this was because he was "a great lover of money" (*Ant.* 12.158). But there was a political dimension to Onias's decision also. Ptolemy had paid for grain from the Levant to help ease the Egyptian famine (Canopus Decree, 9–10), which placed Ptolemy morally in Onias's debt. The high priest's political stock within the Ptolemaic kingdom soared as a result, only to fall again with the reintroduction of the annual fee after 238 BC.

Ptolemy's involvement in the Demetrian War gave Onias room to maneuver. The high priest began courting young Seleucus II in Antioch for support, leveraging the latent rivalry between the two kingdoms in an attempt to force Ptolemy into concession. Seleucus would have welcomed Onias's overtures as a means of swinging the regional balance of power his way. With the threat of Judea declaring for the Seleucids, Seleucus's chances of undoing Ptolemy's gains in Syria increased exponentially, especially the retaking of Seleucia-Pieria. Ptolemy was keen not to open a new front in Syria whilst prosecuting a war in Greece and dealing with ongoing challenges in Upper Egypt.[97] It was strategically wiser for Ptolemy to play a long game and avoid pushing Onias to more brazen disloyalty. Ptolemy therefore allowed the high priest to get away with defaulting on the annual payment in the short term, which kept Judea docile.[98]

But before long Onias found himself on the back foot. Seleucus's younger

---

94. Cf. Honigman, "Searching for the Social Location of Literate Judean Elites," 210.

95. This is logically inferred from the fundamental Jewish aversion towards participation in foreign cults, the similar concessions given to Jews at other times, and Josephus's statement about the Jews of Jerusalem taking oaths as a means of demonstrating fidelity (*Ant.* 12.8). It also makes sense of the placement of Qoheleth's discussion about the taking and breaking of oaths (Eccl 5:1–7), which pertains to the actions of Onias II (see discussion immediately below).

96. The easing of Onias's obligatory fee is never specifically referred to in ancient sources but is logically deduced from the known course of events, including Onias's documented refusal to pay the fee after the Egyptian famine ended.

97. Hölbl, *A History of the Ptolemaic Empire*, 52.

98. Ptolemy's delay in addressing Onias's recalcitrance lies behind Qoheleth's statement in Eccl 8:11. See Athas, *Ecclesiastes, Song of Songs*, 180.

brother, Antiochus Hierax, undermined the integrity of Seleucid power by declaring himself king of a new state in Asia Minor. He began making alliances with the petty rulers around him (e.g., Mithridates II of Pontus, the Galatians) and soon had enough of an army to challenge his brother. The two fought a battle in 236 BC near Ancyra, which Hierax won. Seleucus survived the confrontation, but his political, military, and economic clout had been sapped. Soon other parts of Seleucus's realm began to break off, such as Parthia, where a new kingdom was established by the enigmatic figure of Arsaces.[99] Seleucus was clambering to keep his kingdom intact and therefore had little scope for challenging Ptolemaic power in Syria. This pulled the rug from under Onias. The storm of strength that the high priest had hoped to whip up through Seleucus turned out to be a sputtering puff. He had chased the wind and failed to grab it.

These foibles lie behind Qoheleth's vignette in Ecclesiastes 4:13–16:

> Better a poor but wise youth [Seleucus II] than an old but foolish king [Antiochus II], who no longer knows how to take advice. For he [Seleucus II] came out of the house of exile to reign, even though within his kingdom he had been born first. I saw all the living who walk about under the sun following the second youth [Antiochus Hierax] who would stand in his place. There was no end to all the people—to all who were before them. But even those who come later will not celebrate him. For this too is meaningless, and chasing the wind. (Eccl 4:13–16)[100]

Qoheleth alludes here to Seleucus II's initial exile as crown prince, his unexpected resurgence, and then the curbing of his sovereignty at the hands of his own brother. He also alludes to Antiochus Hierax's demise. Despite his victory at Ancyra, Hierax was unable to retain the loyalty of his regional allies and ended up warring with them. After several defeats, he lost his state and found himself on the run. He eventually crossed over to Thrace, where he was captured by the Gauls who had settled there and was unceremoniously executed in ca. 227 BC.[101]

From this sketch of the fluid fortunes of the Seleucids (Eccl 4:13–16), Qoheleth launches immediately into a discussion of oaths made in the temple

---

99. This Parthian kingdom and its Arsacid dynasty would endure for almost five centuries, eventually becoming the eastern nemesis of the Roman Empire (see 4.4).
100. On the ambiguities and text-critical issues of these verses, see Athas, "Qoheleth in His Context," 358.
101. Grainger, *The Rise of the Seleukid Empire*, 200–7.

(Eccl 5:1–7[4:17–5:6 MT])—an allusion to the oath of loyalty to Ptolemy III, which Onias had sworn in Yahweh's name and on which he reneged by refusing to pay the annual fee for his position. Qoheleth advises circumspection and avoiding vows that one has no intention of keeping, as this would provoke the wrath of God. Qoheleth thus brings the religious dimension of Onias's actions into focus, in addition to the political. Onias had not just broken faith with Ptolemy but with God—a fateful action for the high priest and custodian of the Jewish nation. Qoheleth characterizes Onias here and throughout his discourse as "a fool" for incurring the ire of both God and man (Eccl 5:3[5:2]). And since Qoheleth viewed God as utterly unpredictable and frightening in his sovereignty (Eccl 3:14),[102] he perceived Onias's folly as driving the Jewish nation into divine judgment and the prospect of destructive reprisal.

The enormity of the situation became apparent in ca. 229 BC when Ptolemy finally demanded that Onias pay up. Once again, the high priest refused. Disinclined now to let such obstinacy go unchecked, Ptolemy dispatched an ambassador named Athenion (the "messenger" of Eccl 5:6[5:5]) to Judea in 228 BC to collect the payment. Yet again Onias refused to pay (*Ant.* 12.159, 171). This led to a significant escalation in tension as Ptolemy III threatened military intervention, the confiscation of land, and the establishment of cleruchies in Judea. Not only would this make some of the population destitute, but it had the potential to turn Jerusalem into a Greek *polis*. Panic broke out in Jerusalem. Onias had brought his people and their distinctive culture to the brink of potential ruin. His leadership was denounced by many, including Davidic loyalists like Qoheleth. One of the key themes of the Book of the Twelve Prophets was playing itself out, namely that the priesthood was imperiling rather than preserving the nation.[103]

What made things worse in Qoheleth's eyes was that he himself was a Davidic descendant.[104] The prophetic promises and the illustrious heritage of his family gave Qoheleth a keen sense that he, not Onias (or even Ptolemy), should have been ruling Judea and that he would have brought sagacity and intellect to the role. Instead, Qoheleth, a "son of David" (Eccl 1:1), was not in

---

102. Athas, *Ecclesiastes, Song of Songs*, 99–102.
103. Athas, "The Failure of Davidic Hope?," 241–50.
104. Many commentators view the royal persona adopted by Qoheleth as a pure fiction that he discards after two chapters, for at later points in his discourse another figure of unpredictable temperament (Ptolemy III) is clearly reigning (cf. Eccl 8:2; 10:16, 20). However, the appellation "son of David, king in Jerusalem" in the title (Eccl 1:1) is relevant to Qoheleth's entire discourse, not just part of it, and indicates that he was a Davidic descendant. "Qoheleth" is undoubtedly a *nom de plume*. The Epilogist who published Qoheleth's discourse called him "a sage" (Eccl 12:9), and this is probably part of the tragedy of Qoheleth, the man of royal heritage who was not actually king. See Athas, *Ecclesiastes, Song of Songs*, 20–25.

charge of the nation that was his rightful inheritance (cf. Eccl 7:11). He was just "a sage" (Eccl 12:9), powerless to prevent the implosion of his nation at the hands of a high priest he deemed an utter fool and a foreign king of frightening power and faint regard for commoners. What's more, it seemed to Qoheleth that God was doing nothing to rectify the situation, and Onias was simply compelling God to act in judgment.

With the threat of reprisal, other leaders in Jerusalem launched efforts to find a diplomatic solution to the crisis. One of those who weighed in was Joseph Tobias. We may presume that, like his father, Joseph had become cleruch in Ammanitis and was an unabashed Hellenizer.[105] After all, his seat at Rabbath-Ammon had already become a Greek *polis* named Philadelphia in honor of the sibling-loving Ptolemy II. But since Joseph's mother was the sister of Onias II (*Ant.* 12.160), he still had standing in Jerusalem. Joseph travelled to Jerusalem, where he urged his uncle to perform a volte face and head to Egypt to placate the king personally and so avoid a Jewish catastrophe. Qoheleth captures this advice and the wider predicament in his discourse:

---

105. Some date Joseph Tobias to the early second century BC (e.g., Hengel, *Judaism and Hellenism*, 272–76; Daniel R. Schwartz, "Josephus' Tobiads: Back to the Second Century?," in *Jews in a Graeco-Roman World*, ed. Martin Goodman (Oxford: Clarendon, 1998), 47–61; Catharine ca. Lorber, "The Circulation of Ptolemaic Silver in Seleucid Coele Syria and Phoenicia from Antiochus III to the Maccabean Revolt: Monetery Policies and Political Consequences," *Electrum* 26 (2019): 9–23, https://doi.org/10.4467/20800909EL.19.001.11204.). There are two reasons for this. First, Josephus has Joseph Tobias interact with a Ptolemy whose queen was Cleopatra (Josephus, *Ant.* 12.167), and the first known Cleopatra was married to Ptolemy V in 194/3 BC (Livy, *Ab urbe cond.* 35.13). However, Josephus's enumeration and dating of the various Cleopatras in Ptolemaic history is fraught with difficulty, since he did not know how many there were, nor when exactly they lived, nor to whom they were married—a problem compounded by the proliferation of the name "Ptolemy." Second, Joseph Tobias's chronology is pinned to details about his notorious son, Hyrcanus, who is said to have had a fortune deposited in the Jerusalem temple in the time of the Onias III (2 Macc 3:1–11). Hyrcanus eventually took his own life during an attack by a Seleucid king named Antiochus. Josephus inferred this to be Antiochus IV Epiphanes and thus claimed that Hyrcanus governed Ammanitis during the reign of Seleucus IV (187–175 BC [*Ant.* 12.234–36]). However, it is politically impossible that Hyrcanus ruled Transjordan as a taxpaying province of the Ptolemaic kingdom after the Levant had been conquered by the Seleucids in 198 BC. Hyrcanus could only have governed in Transjordan before the Seleucid conquest. As will be seen below (2.6.19 and 2.8.1), the imbroglio between Hyrcanus and his Jerusalem-based brothers makes it highly unlikely that he kept his own wealth in the Jerusalem temple, especially when he himself was based in Transjordan (supposedly in another kingdom!). Furthermore, Hyrcanus does not appear to have had control over the funds associated with his name—that control belonged to Onias III (cf. 2 Macc 3:1). It is more plausible that Hyrcanus's wealth was brought to the temple by his brothers after his death during the Fifth Syrian War. Hyrcanus's incomplete building activities at Iraq el-Amir are dated to the period ca. 200 BC, before Seleucus IV and Antiochus IV. Finally, Hyrcanus's father, Joseph Tobias, was the son of the cleruch Tobias mentioned in the Zenon Papyri (258 BC). It becomes chronologically problematic to date the rise of Joseph Tobias to the period after 193 BC (sixty-five years after the Zenon Papyri), during the high priesthood of Onias III. All such problems are resolved when we realize that Joseph Tobias was a contemporary of Onias II (not Onias III) and that Hyrcanus committed suicide during the reign of Antiochus III (not Antiochus IV).

> Obey the king's command. Because of the oath to God, do not hurry away from him [the king]. You should budge. Do not persist in a bad cause because he will do whatever he wants. For the word of the king is supreme. Who will say to him, "What are you doing?" He who obeys a command will not experience any harm. A wise mind knows timing and judgment. For every purpose there is timing and judgment, for the people's predicament is great. They do not know what will happen, for who can tell someone what will happen? No man has authority over the wind, to control it. And there is no authority over the day of death, and no discharge during war. A wicked man does not escape his master. (Eccl 8:2–8)[106]

When Joseph's admonition fell on deaf ears, he called a meeting of the Jewish Senate in the temple. He canvassed support to represent the elders before Ptolemy's ambassador, Athenion, and then head to Egypt himself to defuse the situation. The plan earned Joseph considerable praise (*Ant.* 12.161–165). He charmed Athenion and, with his support, proceeded to Egypt in 227 BC. Reading between the lines of the *Tobiad Romance*, which Josephus uses, it seems Joseph brought an ample bribe for Ptolemy, which he procured from backers in Samaria (*Ant.* 12.168–173). Ptolemy was placated by the payment and backed down from his threat of drastic action. Joseph Tobias had saved the day.

However, what happened next engendered feelings of betrayal in Qoheleth and the general populace, which drove them to complete despair. Ptolemy had backed down, but he could not simply leave Onias and Judea untouched. Yet as high priest, Onias could not be deposed. Ptolemy could not hand Onias a moral victory, and so had to find some other punitive measure to demonstrate his authority. Joseph Tobias leveraged this dilemma in his own favor. He lingered in Egypt and was present for the auction of tax farming rights. He pledged to double the tax revenue for Ptolemy and accordingly won the right to oversee the farming of taxes throughout the Levant (*Ant.* 12.174–179). The arrangement enabled Ptolemy to save face by humiliating Onias through the promotion of his nephew and filling the royal coffers with the money Onias had never paid. The already hefty tax burden on Judea and its neighbors doubled overnight, turning the lives of thousands into abject misery (cf. Eccl 5:13–17).

Joseph embarked on an extremely lucrative tax farming career, which earned him a fortune for the next twenty-two years. Josephus details how he

---

106. Athas, *Ecclesiastes, Song of Songs*, 175–76.

used intimidation, violence, and murder to force compliance to the new tax regime (*Ant.* 12.180–185; cf. 2.6.12 above). The exploitation of local landowners and workers and the wholesale redistribution of wealth to the powerful few, endemic as it was in the monetized Ptolemaic system, reached stupendous levels as wealth fell into the hands of Joseph Tobias. He quickly became a powerful mafioso.

So dismal and desperate did Qoheleth find the lot of the average person that it led him to question all the conventional wisdom of his inherited Jewish orthodoxy. Immediately after his "advice" to Onias (Eccl 8:2–8), he ruminated on the effects of Joseph Tobias's intervention:

> I have seen all this, applying my mind to every deed done under the sun: a time when a man [Joseph Tobias] wielded authority over his fellow man for harm. Yes, I have seen wicked people brought to burial. Though they might go about in a holy place [the temple] and extol themselves in the city [Jerusalem] where they have done so, this too is meaningless. When a sentence is not carried out, evil deeds hasten. Because of this, the heart within humans is filled with evil intent. When a sinner does evil a hundred times, he lengthens his life. Yes, I too know that it should go well for those who fear God, who are afraid of him, and that it should not go well for the wicked. They who are not afraid of God should not lengthen their days like a shadow. But this is the absurdity in what occurs on the earth: there are righteous people who get what the wicked deserve, and there are wicked people who get what the righteous deserve. I say that this too is an absurdity. I applaud happiness, in that there is nothing better for a person under the sun than to eat, drink, and be happy. That should be added to his toil during the days of his life, which God gives him under the sun. But as I set my mind to comprehend wisdom, seeing the drudgery that takes place on the earth—how both day and night a person's eyes have no sleep—I considered all the work of God, but no person can figure out what will occur under the sun. As much as a person might toil to discover it, he cannot figure it out. Even if the sage claims to know, he cannot really figure it out. (Eccl 8:9–17)

Pessimism and hopelessness pervade Qoheleth's entire discourse.[107] He wanted to affirm the received orthodoxy of his tradition—that the righteous were rewarded and the wicked punished, enabling people to live fruitful lives and enjoy the deserved labors of their hands under the eye of a just God.

---

107. Athas, *Ecclesiastes, Song of Songs*, 176–82.

But he failed to observe this. He believed the ability to eat, drink, and be happy was fundamental to life but that this has been put out of reach of the average person by the folly and evil of his nation's leaders.

Elsewhere in his monologue, Qoheleth reflected on these realities. In one salient passage, he plays on the Hebrew word for "high official" (*gaboah*), which sounds very similar to the word for "tax farmer" (*gobeh*).[108] With this device, he highlights the inherent villainy of the Ptolemaic system and the avarice of Joseph Tobias:

> If you see the oppression of a poor person or the perversion of justice and righteousness in the district, do not be surprised over the matter. For "high official" is above "high official," keeping watch, with "high officials" above them. Though the profit of the land should be for all, yet it is a king who is served by the field. . . .
>
> There is a sickening evil I have seen under the sun: wealth kept for its owner to his own harm. That wealth was lost in an evil incident, so when he had a son, there was not a single thing left in his hand. Just as he came naked from his mother's womb, so he will return as he came. And he will not carry a thing in his hand for all his labor when he goes.
>
> This too is a sickening evil: just as everyone comes, so they go. What profit does a person have when he toils for the wind? All his days he eats in darkness with much frustration, suffering, and anger. (Eccl 5:8–10, 13–17[5:7–9, 13–16 MT])

All this led Qoheleth to question the purposes of God. He never repudiated divine sovereignty, for he saw God governing history and the various seasons of human life (Eccl 3:1–14). Yet he found it difficult to reconcile this with the misery and inversion of justice that confronted him after Joseph Tobias's opportunism. As a pious Jew of Davidic descent, Qoheleth could not bring himself to charge God with evil intent. This moral bind led him instead to craft his famous motto, "Meaningless! Meaningless! Utterly meaningless! Everything is meaningless!" (cf. Eccl 1:2).[109] This mantra of pessimism expressed the profound disconnection Qoheleth felt between his orthodox theology and his empirical observations.

Qoheleth did not engage in abstract philosophy or systematic theology.

---

108. In a consonantal text, the two words can be indistinguishable. See Athas, *Ecclesiastes, Song of Songs*, 127–28.

109. While I have translated the key Hebrew term *hebel* here as "meaningless," Qoheleth cycles through the whole semantic range of the word in his discourse. See Athas, *Ecclesiastes, Song of Songs*, 36.

His gloomy reflections were contextually based, inextricably rooted in the reality of Jewish politics and Ptolemaic economics. Even his frequent use of the phrase "under the sun" had Ptolemaic allusions. The Ptolemies bought into pharaonic ideology, by which they were understood as the earthly avatars of the sun god who ruled all the earth. The Ptolemaic king was "a king like the Sun"[110] and all decrees inscribed in stone displayed the traditional image of the sun disk, whose outstretched wings curved like a vault over all that lay below.[111] To be "under the sun," therefore, was not just to be a human on earth but more particularly to be "under the Ptolemies" as their subject. Qoheleth was thus a sage with a prophetic voice, commenting on the harsh realities of his own day. He despaired of the future of the Jewish nation. In his estimation, the prophetic hopes for restoration under a Davidic king seemed to have failed. Instead, the nation seemed headed for shipwreck on the reefs of economic exploitation, political gambling, and liberal Hellenization. The final movement of Qoheleth's discourse captured this pessimism with a haunting poem on death metaphorically depicted as the cessation of urban and rural life. It was not just individual death he was picturing but the death of the Jewish nation through cultural and economic asphyxiation.

Interestingly, Qoheleth was himself influenced by Hellenistic thought. His adoption of a royal persona at the beginning of his discourse appealed to his actual royal heritage but also used a sense of theatrics common in Greek drama. He donned an actor's mask, as it were, which was part of the tragedy of his situation. He was himself the descendant of kings, but his crown was purely imaginary and without substance. His reflections also bore affinity to the philosophy of Epicurus, who flourished earlier in the third century BC, demonstrating his learning within a Hellenistic milieu. The pursuit of happiness that characterized Epicureanism characterized Qoheleth's assessments too. His royal experiment in which he tested pleasure and wealth (Eccl 1:12–2:26) functioned as an assessment of both his own royal heritage and the rampant hedonism of the Ptolemaic court and its hangers-on, like Joseph Tobias. Like Epicurus, Qoheleth saw the good life consisting in the moderate goals of eating, drinking, and finding satisfaction in work—something he viewed as completely congruent with the covenantal dynamic of blessing for

---

110. From the Raphia Decree of Ptolemy IV (217 BC); See Edwyn R. Bevan, "Raphia Decree," *Translations of Hellenistic Inscriptions 17*, 3 October 2018, http://www.attalus.org/docs/other/inscr_17.html.

111. Examples include the Satrap Stele of Ptolemy I (311 BC), the Pithom Stele and Mendes Stele of Ptolemy II, the Tanis Chapel Steles of Ptolemy II and Ptolemy IV, and the Canopus Decree of Ptolemy III. The Rosetta Stone of Ptolemy V almost definitely included the motif of the winged sun-disk, but the surviving fragment does not include the uppermost edge where the motif was always placed.

obedience (Eccl 2:24–26). And yet, he observed that the average person had been robbed of such simple pleasures and possibilities by the rapacious greed of the elite. Alongside the complete sovereignty of God over all affairs "under heaven" (Eccl 1:13; 2:3; 3:1), this left Qoheleth in an ethical and theological depression, fearing for the future of the Jewish nation.

The anonymous Epilogist who published Qoheleth's discourse also felt the weight of Qoheleth's pessimistic appraisal. In the epilogue he appended to Qoheleth's words (Eccl 12:9–14), he advised a twofold strategy for his readers to deal with such sinking feelings as well as the magnetic appeal of a better life in Hellenistic Egypt: (1) to take a critical approach to Greek learning (Eccl 12:12); and (2) to remain faithful to the demands of God in the biblical tradition (Eccl 12:13–14). This was not a call to disengagement with the Hellenistic world but rather to moderate, critical interaction that did not rush to embrace the novel but set it within an educational framework that prioritized relationship with God.

This strategy had two repercussions. First, by prioritizing relationship with God over engagement with the wider world, it buttressed classic Jewish identity. The Epilogist felt that Jewish identity had to be preserved, and this was done by observing Torah and maintaining allegiance to the classic prophetic hopes of the past. By anchoring current culture and practice in past revelation, Jewish identity would not be diluted in the cultural melting pot of Hellenism. Second, this would produce eschatological hope, which would help negotiate the future. This did not shy away from theological quandaries or the harsh historical realities facing the Jewish nation but attempted to grapple with them within a framework of faith. And like Qoheleth, it was acceptable to be brutally honest and not to have all the answers. If God's sovereignty was to be upheld alongside his justice and truth, then the grand promises of the past meant that the current reality could not be the final word. There must be more to come. Orthodoxy and orthopraxy, even if they resulted in temporal suffering and confusion, were integral to hope and therefore the basis of a quiet resistance strategy. The faithful Jew was not to abandon his identity or his God but was, rather, to leave space for God to act and make good on his promises. In the meantime, obedience had to be the norm.

Just two years after the crescendo of the crisis, Seleucus II fell from his horse and succumbed to his injuries (225 BC). This deprived Onias II of any external backer amongst the Seleucids and isolated him even further. Though he could not be ousted from his position, he was now politically overshadowed by Joseph Tobias and lived out the remainder of his high priesthood in his nephew's shadow and despised by his people.

2.6.17 FOURTH SYRIAN WAR (219–217 BC) AND THE SIEGE OF JERUSALEM

With the death of Seleucus II, war between the Ptolemies and Seleucids became a live prospect again. Seleucus was succeeded by his teenaged son, Alexander, who took the name Seleucus III on his accession. He was nicknamed "Thunderbolt" (Gk. *Keraunos*) for his fiery temperament, and it showed almost immediately. He sallied forth into Asia Minor, bent on reconquering the territories that had broken away. But he was defeated and, while still on campaign, was assassinated by two of his commanders in April 222 BC.

Seleucus III had no son to succeed him, so the throne passed to the sole surviving member of the dynasty, his younger brother, Antiochus III. His reign began in chaos. He tried to launch an invasion of the Ptolemaic kingdom, but his army became trapped by a Ptolemaic blockade of the Orontes Valley, forcing him to abandon the effort.[112] His uncle, Achaeus, whom he had commissioned to bring Asia Minor to heel, was accused of conspiring against him. Rebellion broke out in Media and Persia. One of his generals, Molon, declared himself king at Seleucia-on-the-Tigris, staunching the flow of taxation and trade that was so vital to Seleucid finances. And then, when Antiochus realized he needed to intervene in Mesopotamia, his soldiers who had retreated from the Orontes Valley were on the verge of mutiny. The Seleucid kingdom was on the brink of complete rupture.

Ptolemy III stood to gain significantly from the apparent devolution of the Seleucid kingdom, but he never got the chance. He died in December 222 BC, just eight months into Antiochus III's reign, and was succeeded by his eldest son, Ptolemy IV Philopator, aged twenty-three. Ptolemy IV began his reign by murdering his mother and younger brothers. He then surrounded himself with courtiers who pandered to his rampant hedonistic tendencies. Rather than take an active interest in governance, he was "absorbed in unworthy intrigues, and senseless and continuous drunkenness" (Polybius, *Hist.* 15.34–36). One of Qoheleth's statements resonated with the situation under the new king:

> Blessed are you, O land, whose king is a son of nobles, and whose princes eat at the right time for strength, rather than for drunkenness. (Eccl 10:17)

By referring to a king as "a son of nobles" rather than a "son of kings," Qoheleth probably had his own pedigree in mind. The Davidic family was

---

112. Hölbl, *A History of the Ptolemaic Empire*, 128.

nobility in Jewish society but had not actually held royal power for centuries. The statement subtly critiqued Ptolemy IV (and all Hellenistic rulers) while expressing the opinion that things would be better for the Jewish nation under a temperate Davidic descendant, like himself.[113] In the rivalry between the Ptolemies and Seleucids, it was hard for Jews not to feel like they were mere commodities to be owned. And now they had become the plaything of a spoiled, privileged, pleasure-seeking prince.

Back in Syria, Antiochus III successfully dealt with all his prevailing issues by 220 BC, except for his uncle in Asia Minor, Achaeus (Polybius, *Hist.* 5.56). Antiochus intended to deal with him, but an opportunity fell into his lap that changed his plans. A Ptolemaic general named Theodotus who was based in Palestine fell out of favor with his playboy master, Ptolemy IV. He defected to Antiochus, pledging his assistance to turn over to him all the regions of "Coele Syria," as the Seleucids called Palestine (Polybius, *Hist.* 5.40). It was a bolder version of the strategy Onias had tried to employ against Ptolemy III, but unlike Onias, Theodotus had the advantage of commanding military units. Antiochus could not ignore the stroke of luck that Ptolemy's own reckless character had engineered. So he launched the Fourth Syrian War in 219 BC.

It is ironic that Onias II died at around this time (ca. 219 BC), just as the Seleucid challenge to Ptolemaic rule in Coele Syria gained momentum. He was succeeded in the high priesthood by his son, Simon II, who would later play a pivotal role in the Ptolemaic-Seleucid conflict. For now, Antiochus retook Seleucia-Pieria, and Theodotus ensured that the Ptolemaic navy at Tyre and Ptolemais-Acco never left port. This allowed Antiochus to contemplate invading Egypt via the overland route without risking a naval invasion behind him. But he was dissuaded from this after Ptolemy's military staff stationed more troops at the Egyptian border-post of Pelusium. Instead, Antiochus tried to consolidate his grip on Coele Syria by occupying all the ports along the Levantine coast. He was, however, unable to capture Sidon or Dor, which still left potential for a Ptolemaic counterstrike. What gave him breathing space was Ptolemy's singular commitment to a hedonistic lifestyle rather than war (Polybius, *Hist.* 5.61–62).

Ptolemy's ministers took matters into their own hands by petitioning Antiochus for a four-month ceasefire to negotiate the future of Coele Syria. Antiochus agreed and spent the next four months arguing that he was simply taking back what had been lawfully awarded to his ancestor, Seleucus I, after the Battle of Ipsus in 301 BC (see 2.5.2 above). But during the ceasefire,

---

113. Athas, *Ecclesiastes, Song of Songs*, 204–5.

Ptolemy's advisors furtively recruited a massive army from the Aegean and, for the first time, from the native Egyptian population also (Polybius, *Hist.* 5.63–67). The ceasefire ended in early 218 BC with no agreement, and Antiochus resumed his campaign. He captured territory around Lake Galilee and the Jordan Valley. Buoyed by these successes, he pushed south and took possession of Philadelphia, the hometown of Joseph Tobias (Polybius, *Hist.* 5.70–71).

At this point, Antiochus sent some of his forces into Samaria, while he returned to Ptolemais-Acco on the coast (Polybius, *Hist.* 5.71). Polybius's account only mentions the *polis* of Samaria and its "district" as the objective of this sortie,[114] but Antiochus could not bypass the Jewish center in Jerusalem. Consequently, Jerusalem came under siege also. Confirmation of this comes from words penned by Jesus ben-Eleazar ben-Sira—better known simply as "Ben Sira"—a contemporary of Simon II and witness to the events. Ben Sira refers to damage sustained by the city and its temple during a siege that had to be subsequently repaired (Sir 50:1, 4). Daniel 11:10, which follows the course of the Fourth Syrian War, probably alludes to the siege also:

> His sons [Seleucus III and Antiochus III, sons of Seleucus II] will wage war, gathering a multitude of great forces. He [Antiochus III] will keep coming, pouring back and forth, and waging war on the stronghold. (Dan 11:10)

It is possible that this "stronghold" is Seleucia-Pieria, as in Daniel 11:7. However, the war on the stronghold here is said to occur in the context of constant movements, which better fits Antiochus's campaign in Palestine. What's more, it is said to provoke the King of the South to battle (Dan 11:11), which happened shortly after the siege of Jerusalem (see this section below). From these fragments of evidence, it appears that Jerusalem was besieged in the winter of 218/7 BC by Antiochus III's troops. We may further surmise from Ben Sira's statements that the city put up some resistance, presumably under the compulsion of the Ptolemaic garrison within it (cf. Polybius, *Hist.* 5.86). Serious damage was inflicted, including upon the sanctuary itself, so much so that Ben Sira described its later repair as the temple receiving new foundations (Gk. *ethemeliōthē* [Sir 50:2]). What we cannot tell is whether Jerusalem (or Samaria) succumbed to Antiochus's siege. Ben Sira mentions that Simon "protected his people from collapse and strengthened the city during siege" (Sir 50:4), but it is hard to know if this means that the city resisted successfully.

---

114. Cf. Andrea M. Berlin, "Between Large Forces: Palestine in the Hellenistic Period," *BA* 60.1 (1997): 13.

Polybius states that Antiochus ordered his attacking troops to protect those who submitted to him (Polybius, *Hist.* 5.71), so it is possible that Simon successfully negotiated the safety of the people. Either way, he was remembered for his protective role in the crisis.

The war reached its decisive battle in the summer of 217 BC. Ptolemy's advisers convinced him to march with the massive force they had recruited. With his sister-wife, Arsinoe III, by his side, he crossed the desert and met Antiochus's army at Raphia, near Gaza. On 22 June 217 BC battle was joined.[115] While initially it seemed that Antiochus had won the day, Ptolemy showed himself on the battlefield and his native Egyptian recruits rallied to defeat Antiochus's army. Against the odds, the playboy prince, Ptolemy IV, was victorious, and Antiochus was forced to retreat (Polybius, *Hist.* 5.79–86).[116] The outcome was recalled in Daniel 11:11:

> The King of the South [Ptolemy IV] will be incited to go out and fight with him—with the King of the North [Antiochus III], who will employ a vast horde. But that horde will fall into his [Ptolemy IV's] hand. (Dan 11:11)

Seleucid power in Coele Syria collapsed at once. When peace was finally agreed upon in late 217 BC, Ptolemy appeared lenient by retaining Coele Syria and Phoenicia while conceding Seleucia-Pieria back to Antiochus. Ptolemy demonstrated largesse by handsomely rewarding his army and returned home to Egypt, where he was feted widely. The playboy prince with little interest in politics or war had ironically won a decisive battle and now settled down to resume his sybaritic lifestyle.

2.6.18 ANTIOCHUS III AND THE JEWS IN ASIA MINOR

After his defeat at Raphia, Antiochus III turned his attention to Asia Minor. He defeated his separatist uncle, Achaeus, and brought the strategic city of Sardis under his control by 213 BC (Polybius, *Hist.* 5.107; 7.15–18; 8.22–23). He then employed a series of astute measures to mitigate the ill-feeling towards Seleucid dominance. First, he made an alliance with Attalus of Pergamum, demonstrating that he was willing to recognize local dynasts in return for their support (Polybius, *Hist.* 5.107). Second, he appointed a new commander,

---

115. Hölbl, *A History of the Ptolemaic Empire*, 131.
116. Stefan Pfeiffer, "The Representation of the Victorious King: Comments on the Dedication of a Statue of Ptolemy IV in Jaffa (SEG 20.467 = *CIIP* 3.2172)," in Honigman, Nihan, and Lipshits, *Times of Transition*, 45–47.

Zeuxis, to govern Asia Minor as a self-contained unit. Third, he instituted a royal cult like that employed by the Ptolemies. It worshipped him as a god and provided inducements to important locals to become ministrants of it, thereby making loyalty to the Seleucids attractive and profitable. It also made Seleucid rule more visible and entrenched Hellenistic culture among the disparate people groups across the region. It was a policy that would affect Judea crucially a generation later.

Antiochus's fourth measure was to transplant some 2,000 Jewish soldiers and their families from Babylonia to Lydia and Phrygia. There he granted them land and generous tax concessions. Josephus cites a letter of Antiochus to Zeuxis that sanctioned this arrangement (*Ant.* 12.147–153).[117] Antiochus effectively created a cluster of Jewish cleruchies in Asia Minor in which the people had no native connection to the land and, therefore, no impulse for its independence. Their connection to the land and the economic standing this gave them was entirely dependent on their lord's munificence. Antiochus anticipated that their presence would help dilute separatist tendencies in the regions.[118]

According to Josephus, Antiochus permitted these Jews to observe their own customs (*Ant.* 12.150)—a Jewish parallel to the cleruchies of Greek soldiers. Lack of hard evidence makes it difficult to know if these soldier-colonists immediately created synagogues to facilitate the observance of their Jewish customs, but it is possible.[119] Yet, even if they did not, their descendants certainly did, for the apostle Paul visited these synagogues on his missionary journeys in the mid-first century (Acts 13:14; 16:6; 18:23; cf. 2:10). Interestingly, the letter of 1 Peter is addressed to the Jewish diaspora in Asia Minor, some of whom were probably descendants of these early reservists, and described them in terms reminiscent of the Jewish cleruchies: *paroikous*, denoting those who live beside others, and *parepidēmous*, denoting those who live in a foreign land, especially civil servants who distinguish themselves during international duty (1 Pet 1:1; 2:11).[120]

Having thus dealt with affairs in Asia Minor, Antiochus headed east again in 212 BC to recover the territories that had become disconnected from his

---

117. The letter's authenticity has been called into question, but evidence for Jewish communities throughout Asia Minor begins at approximately this time. See Abraham Schalit, "The Letter of Antiochus III to Zeuxis Regarding the Establishment of Jewish Military Colonies in Phrygia and Lydia," *JQR* 50.4 (1960): 289–318, https://doi.org/10.2307/1453606.

118. John D. Grainger, *The Seleukid Empire of Antiochus III (223–187 BC)* (Barnsley: Pen and Sword, 2015), 52–53.

119. Cf. Schalit, "The Letter of Antiochus III to Zeuxis," 315–16.

120. BDAG, s.v. "παρεπίδημος."

rule (Polybius, *Hist.* 10.27–31). He did not dislodge some of the new dynasts who had arisen in places like Armenia, Parthia, and Bactria, but he succeeded in making them his client kings. His expedition took him as far as the Hindu Kush Mountains and down the Persian Gulf, with constellations of Greek cities founded as far back as Alexander's day facilitating the renewal of his authority. Thus Antiochus's sovereignty was recognized across a territorial expanse as wide as Seleucus I's realm—a feat that earned him the moniker "Antiochus the Great."

2.6.19 DISCONTENT IN JUDEA UNDER PTOLEMY IV (217–204 BC)

Just months after Raphia, the native priests of Egypt gathered in synod at Memphis, from where they issued the "Raphia Decree" (October 217 BC). This recounted Ptolemy IV's victory and its aftermath and instituted new cultic rites to honor the king and his sister-wife. The decree included an account of how Ptolemy donated generously to restore temples in Coele Syria and Phoenicia:

> He [Ptolemy IV] conducted a tour through the other places which were in his kingdom. He went into the temples that were there. He offered burnt offerings and libations, and all the inhabitants of the cities received him with gladness of heart, keeping holiday, and standing in expectation of his arrival with the shrines of the gods (in whose heart lies power), crowned with wreaths, bringing burnt offerings and grain offerings. Many caused a wreath of gold to be made for him, undertaking to set up a royal statue in his honor and to build temples. It came to pass that the king went on his way as a man divine. As for the images of the gods which were in the temples, which Antiochus had defaced, the king commanded that others be made in their stead and set up in their place. He gave much gold, silver, and precious stones for this and to replace the vessels in the temples which those men had carried away. He took thought to replace them. The treasure which had previously been given to the temples, and which had been diminished, he ordered to be restored to its former quantity.[121]

The account is given in generalized terms and through a decidedly Egyptian religious lens. Nevertheless, we can determine that Ptolemy IV went

---

121. Translation adapted from Bevan, "Raphia Decree."

on a victory march through the major centers of Palestine, making promises to local cults as part of a wider policy aimed at ingratiating himself with the local population and their gods. Tangible evidence of this comes from Joppa in the form of a plaque (originally on a statue) dedicated to Ptolemy by a local ministrant of the royal cult.[122] This victory march included Jerusalem, where he promised to repair and renovate the temple, which had sustained damage during the siege of 218/7 BC.[123] The renovation of the temple on Mount Gerizim might also be seen in line with this policy.[124]

Interestingly, the book of 3 Maccabees, written in the mid-first century BC, is set in this precise period.[125] It is a mixture of historical memory and dramatic Jewish legend. The story begins with Ptolemy's victory at Raphia and his subsequent tour of sacred sites in Coele Syria. When he comes to Jerusalem, Ptolemy adamantly desires to enter the sanctuary, despite the people's protest that his entry would desecrate it. When the high priest Simon II petitions God before the sanctuary, God convulses Ptolemy so violently that the king is rendered harmless. However, on his return to Alexandria, he takes his frustration out on the Jewish community there, eventually rounding them up in the hippodrome to be trampled by drunk elephants. Once again, however, the Jews are saved by the prayer of a righteous priest. The elephants turn on their handlers, and Ptolemy's attitude is changed. Thereupon, he sponsors a weeklong festival for the Jewish community. Although most of the story is fictional, Ptolemy's visit to the Jerusalem temple echoes real history, as the Raphia Decree and Polybius's account (*Hist.* 5.80–86) corroborate.[126]

Ptolemy IV's pledge to renovate the temple in Jerusalem promised to increase its prestige and finally put it on a par with the well-developed temple campus on Mount Gerizim. For the high priest Simon II, it would also have come as a reward for his loyalty during the war. Ptolemy's magnanimous promises, however, turned out to be mere bluster. Even if he had initially intended on being true to his word, there was a significant catch that virtually guaranteed he would not follow through: his promises needed financing. He had already used some of his own wealth to bestow rewards on his native Egyptian soldiers and enhance temples in Egypt (see Raphia Decree). He was not,

---

122. Pfeiffer, "The Representations of the Victorious King," 43–52.
123. Zeitlin, "'The Tobias Family and the Hasmoneans': A Historical Study in the Political and Economic Life of the Jews of the Hellenistic Period," *Proceedings of the American Academy for Jewish Research* 4 (1932/3): 184.
124. Cf. Kreimerman and Sandhaus, "Political Trends," 126.
125. 3 Maccabees was probably written in response to Pompey's conquest of Jerusalem and desecration of the temple in 63 BC (see 4.1.2 below). Ptolemy IV was seen as providing an interesting precedent.
126. Cf. VanderKam, *From Joshua to Caiaphas*, 183–85.

therefore, willing to compromise his playboy lifestyle by dipping further into his personal finances to pay for building projects in Coele Syria. If he had any intention of making good on these projects, he would do so with the tax revenues of Coele Syria itself. In other words, the Jews themselves would foot the bill for the repairs to their own temple while Ptolemy received the credit as benefactor.

But Ptolemy failed even to do this. Some twenty years later, a decree of Antiochus III implied that work on the temple had begun but never been completed (*Ant.* 12.137–144). Ben Sira, who lived through these years, gave Ptolemy no credit whatsoever for the eventual renovation, laying all the glory instead at the feet of Simon II (Sir 50:1–4; see this section below). This means that Ptolemy continued to harvest high taxes from his subjects in Judea but did not direct anywhere near enough funds back into the country to pay for the promised repairs. Instead, Ptolemy continued to fund his own lavish lifestyle and maintain little interest in government, causing perilous instability for his realm. Polybius states that after Raphia, Ptolemy "abandoned entirely the path of virtue and took to a life of dissipation" (*Hist.* 14.12.3). He was keenly interested in literature and the arts, so he continued to sponsor the activities of the Museum in Alexandria.[127] But these activities did not govern a realm. The main decisions of policy and governance lay with his staff who, as time would tell, turned out to be every bit as self-seeking as he was. The Ptolemaic ship of state was drifting aimlessly.

The prodigious scale of Ptolemy's administrative and fiscal negligence coupled with his uncompromising commitment to personal indulgence did nothing to endear him to his subjects after Raphia. Taxation reached dizzying heights, with the brunt borne by the working classes. In Coele Syria, Joseph Tobias continued to hold the tax farming rights, fleecing the commoner in the name of funding a temple renovation that failed to materialize. The money kept pouring into Ptolemy's coffers, but with little benefit to anyone else. Discontent bubbled throughout the realm.

Ptolemy's empty promises even perturbed the Jewish elite who had historically benefitted from Ptolemaic rule. Simon II, whose fidelity to the Ptolemies is notable before Raphia, seems to have adjusted his loyalties in the decade after it. He enhanced support for his own leadership by harnessing the widespread resentment against Ptolemy. Ben Sira's testimony implies that Simon oversaw the beginning of repairs to the temple and the city (Sir 50:1–4),

---

127. Hölbl, *A History of the Ptolemaic Empire*, 133; Sebastiana Nervegna, "Performing Classics: The Tragic Canon in the Fourth Century and Beyond," in *Greek Theatre in the Fourth Century BC*, ed. Eric Csapo et al. (Berlin: de Gruyter, 2014), 162.

but from political developments over the next two decades, it is clear that he was unable to complete them while Ptolemy ruled. Even Joseph Tobias wavered in his loyalty as association with the prodigal prince became a political liability through the 210s BC. He had grown wealthy through his association with the Ptolemaic crown. But with Ptolemy indifferent to government, Egypt on the verge of explosive strife, and Antiochus III gaining in strength, Joseph could see that Ptolemy was not a safe bet for the future. Along with most of the Jewish elite in Judea, he distanced himself from the prodigal prince. For the remainder of Ptolemy's reign, a significant political shift occurred throughout Coele Syria. Ptolemy's relationships with the key figures who upheld his power locally rusted over, making his control brittle. The region was rapidly turning against him.

Joseph himself was now an older man. He had so ensconced himself as a powerbroker in Judea that he had become a kind of *capo dei capi*—a *mafioso* godfather, with his eight sons standing in the wings to take over the family's dirty business after him.[128] His seven eldest were born to his first wife, but his youngest son, Hyrcanus, was born to his niece. Josephus, relying on the *Tobiad Romance*, tells the sordid tale of how Joseph had once wanted to bed a Greek actress in Alexandria when his brother, Solymius, substituted the actress with his own daughter instead, thus preventing Joseph from having a tryst with a gentile (*Ant.* 12.187–189). Whether the bawdy details are historically true is difficult to know, but it is clear that Joseph fathered Hyrcanus by another woman, setting Hyrcanus oddly apart from his other seven sons.

In ca. 208 BC Ptolemy IV held grand birthday celebrations at Alexandria for his son and heir, Ptolemy V, who had been born in 210 BC. Joseph Tobias pleaded that the infirmity of his old age prevented him from attending. While he may have been incapacitated, his seven eldest sons (whose names are unfortunately lost to us) also declined to attend. The *Tobiad Romance* states that their excuse was that they were not able conversationalists (*Ant.* 12.197). Such an excuse hardly flies. It is more likely that Joseph and his sons perceived the political tide turning against Ptolemy IV and did not wish to be seen supporting his regime. They had begun to move their political capital towards the Seleucid regime instead. Yet they still needed to keep up appearances with Ptolemy, who was still officially their overlord. Thus Joseph's youngest son, Hyrcanus, who stood on the family's fringe, was sent to represent them at the celebrations in Alexandria.

---

128. Cf. Lester L. Grabbe, "The Ptolemaic Period: A Dark Age in Jewish History?," in Honigman, Nihan, and Lipschits, *Times of Transition*, 24.

It is perhaps because Hyrcanus was a fringe figure that he was also an opportunist. In this regard, he resembled his father. Whilst at Alexandria, he gained considerable favor with Ptolemy IV and came away from Alexandria with an official commission as a new tax farmer (*Ant.* 12.196–222). Ptolemy seems to have figured that if Joseph was too old to attend festivities for the royal successor in Alexandria, he might also be too old to fulfil his tax-collecting duties. Whether Hyrcanus was appointed as his father's replacement or simply as a rival to him is difficult to know. Either way, Ptolemy ensured that he had an energetic whelp keen to do his bidding in Coele Syria rather than depend solely on a doddering old man with dithering loyalties.

The favor bestowed on Hyrcanus politically isolated his father and brothers, who now resorted to violence. When Hyrcanus returned to Judea, they met him with an armed ambush. In the ensuing melee, two of Hyrcanus's brothers died (*Ant.* 12.222) while the remaining five escaped to Jerusalem. Undeterred, Hyrcanus continued to Jerusalem, armed with his bodyguard and his official commission. But once there, no one fraternized with him, as most were afraid of falling afoul of his brothers, who were clearly calling the shots in the city. In this way, Joseph's five surviving sons clawed back some sway and galvanized Jerusalem in an anti-Ptolemaic stance.

Hyrcanus might have taken up residence at the palatial administrative center at Ramat Raḥel, south of Jerusalem. In any event, he became a marked man and soon abandoned Judea altogether for Transjordan (ca. 205 BC) and managed his tax farming operations from there. The ascendancy of his brothers in Jerusalem must have put a dent in the revenues he could garner. But, ever the opportunist, he made up the shortfall by making constituents of the "barbarians" (*Ant.* 12.222), that is, the Nabatean Arabs on the fringes of Ammanitis. Taxing them was by no means easy, as Josephus asserts that Hyrcanus was constantly skirmishing with them (*Ant.* 12.229). His efforts, though, were successful enough to offset any decline in revenue from Judea and keep Ptolemy happy with brimming coffers. Hyrcanus also took a chapter out of Ptolemy's book by constructing for himself a lavish country mansion (or mausoleum—the exact purpose of the building is disputed) between Philadelphia and the Jordan River (*Ant.* 12.230–233).[129]

The animus between Hyrcanus and his brothers raises certain questions. If taxes were not going from Judea to Alexandria via Hyrcanus, were taxes going from Judea to Alexandria at all? Did the remaining Tobiad brothers

---

129. The ruins of Hyrcanus's estate are still visible today, known locally as the "Castle of the Slave" (*Qasr al-Abed* at Iraq el-Amir, Jordan).

continue collecting taxes on behalf of their aged father, Joseph, and ship them to Ptolemy? Or did they do something else with the monies? They did not stop collecting taxes, as Joseph is noted for being a tax farmer right up to the time of his death (*Ant.* 12.224). And though anti-Ptolemaic feeling was running high in Judea, all of Coele Syria was still under Ptolemaic military command. Withholding taxes would have been an act of blatant treason that would incur military intervention. Indeed, Simon's father, Onias II, had thrown Jerusalem into fear of such a deadly reprisal a generation earlier (ca. 230 BC) merely by withholding the fee for his *prostasia* (see 2.6.16 above).

If we trace the wider political, social, and economic trajectories, we can reconstruct what occurred in the period 208–204 BC in a way that makes sense of all the disparate pieces of evidence. Simon II and his cousins, the Tobiad brothers, approached the situation vis-à-vis Hyrcanus and Ptolemy IV pragmatically. They must have kept up some appearance of loyalty to Alexandria while actively seeking to distance themselves. A good way to do this was to continue collecting taxes in Judea and sending a portion to the king, while directing most of the money to the temple in Jerusalem to fund its renovation. This would have instantly put the Judean public on side with the Tobiad brothers, consolidating their political position, especially if they reduced the amount of taxes they collected. It meant that at least some of the money people forfeited in tax now benefitted them locally. Furthermore, Hyrcanus's appointment as tax farmer put the onus on him to deliver tax revenues to Ptolemy, relieving the Tobiad brothers of this obligation to some extent. The taxes Hyrcanus extracted from the Nabateans made up for any shortfall of revenue from Judea. This effectively turned any payment the Tobiad brothers offered the king into a personal gratuity rather than dues owed by obligation, putting them back in favor with the king. Then, by directing money to the temple treasury, they could inform Ptolemy that they were acting on his behalf to fulfil his own promise to repair the temple and the city, magnifying his prestige and bringing him the favor of the Jewish god. By so appealing to the king's greed and vainglory, they could appear to be doing his bidding while actually loosening their political and fiscal ties to him and consolidating their own power locally. And they could do all this by getting behind their relative, the high priest Simon II, as the legally recognized figurehead of the Jewish community and head of temple operations. Indeed, the whole scheme might have been engineered by Simon himself, whose prestige increased so greatly at this time that he was popularly remembered as "Simon the Just." Ben Sira's gushing praise of Simon (Sir 50:1–21) at the conclusion of his extensive "Praise of the Fathers" (Sir 44–49) testifies to the acclaim that Simon earned at this time.

This reconstruction of events aligns plausibly with five key pieces of evidence.

First, as implied by Antiochus III's decree of 196 BC, repairs to the temple in Jerusalem had begun before the Fifth Syrian War broke out in 202 BC (see 2.8.2 below)—that is, while the Ptolemies still ostensibly controlled Judea. The funding for these repairs must have come from somewhere, but it does not seem to have come from Ptolemy IV himself.

Second, the wording of Antiochus's decree (*Ant.* 12.137–144) implies that the Jews themselves were responsible for financing the temple works through the taxation system, and Antiochus capitalized on this with further concessions (again, see 2.8.2 below). The modest donations of Jewish worshippers alone would have been insufficient to pay for such public works. The redirection of their taxes, though, would certainly have provided the necessary means, and the Tobiads were still handling taxes at this time. It also explains why the repairs seem to have begun but not been completed by 196 BC.

Third, Ben Sira, who lived through these events in Jerusalem, credits Simon II, not Ptolemy IV, with the eventual renovation of the temple:

> Simon, son of Onias, was the high priest,
> who, during his lifetime, repaired the house,
> and in his day reinforced the temple,
> and under whom it was refounded with double the height,
> a tall fortification around the sanctuary.
> In his day was hewn a water cistern,
> a reservoir like the sea in perimeter.
> He protected his people from collapse,
> and strengthened the city during siege. (Sir 50:1–4)[130]

Ben Sira clearly describes the renovation of the temple not simply as a cultic site but also as a fortification with a secure water supply. Although these constructions had still not been completed by 196 BC (cf. *Ant.* 12.137–144), their design must have already been in place before the Seleucids came to control the city. Simon II and his Tobiad relatives could easily have convinced Ptolemy that Jerusalem's temple needed renovation in keeping with his own

---

130. This is a translation of the Greek version of Ben Sira. The Hebrew version has slight differences, including the characterization of the temple compound as a "royal palace." Otto Mulder, *Simon the High Priest in Sirach 50: An Exegetical Study of the Significance of Simon the High Priest as Climax to the Praise of the Fathers in Ben Sira's Concept of the History of Israel*, Supplements to the Journal for the Study of Judaism 78 (Leiden: Brill, 2003), 115–17, 259.

promise after Raphia and that the city needed fortification against the growing threat of Antiochus III, who had recovered from his defeat at Raphia and was once again in a formidable position. Moreover, Ptolemy himself would not need to cough up a cent to pay for it because it would all be paid for internally within Judea, and Ptolemy would himself receive fringe benefits for sanctioning it. The Tobiads could thus demonstrate their loyalty in securing the realm against foreign invasion, even though practically they were consolidating their own power in Coele Syria. In so doing, they were also enhancing the life of the Jews in Judea—a popular measure, for not only was the institutional center of Jewish life being revitalized, but the construction itself would have provided employment for thousands.

Fourth, events in Egypt provided the perfect opportunity for Simon and the Tobiads to enact their venture. After Raphia (217 BC) the native Egyptian units who had won the battle returned to their homeland filled with confidence in their own abilities. Over the next decade, this turned into ambition and nationalism as they sought to free themselves of the yoke that bound them to a wanton and dissolute monarch (Polybius, *Hist.* 5.107). To make matters worse, Ptolemy increased taxes to recoup his expenses after the Fourth Syrian War. Before long, inflation had become so severe that bronze currency was devalued to the point of near worthlessness, driving many to penury.[131] Then, in 208 BC the Nile experienced another abnormally low annual inundation. While Ptolemy and his court lived in the lap of luxury and celebrated the crown prince's birthday, most of Egypt fell into the grip of famine, in addition to the economic woes already rampant throughout the country. The following year, a full-scale revolt erupted in Upper Egypt, which saw the nationalist Egyptian soldiers proclaim one of their own, Hyrgonaphor (Eg. *Horwennefer*), pharaoh in Upper Egypt.[132] This so-called Great Revolt jolted Ptolemy from the stupor of negligence. As his loyal troops mobilized in Upper Egypt, the population at large was enveloped in civil war.[133] These developments are alluded to in the final vision of Daniel:

---

131. Lorber, "The Coinage of the Ptolemies," 220.
132. The Ptolemaic temple to Horus at Edfu, begun in 237 BC, was nearing its completion when the revolt halted its construction. Reference to the revolt was engraved onto the temple walls when it was eventually completed in 176 BC. Willy Clarysse, "The Great Revolt of the Egyptians (205–186 BCE)" (Center for the Tebtunis Papyri, University of California at Berkeley, 2004), 2–3, http://www.lib.berkeley.edu/sites/default/files/files/TheGreatRevoltoftheEgyptians.pdf.
133. One papyrus (Trinity College Dublin, Pap. Gr 274) reports how several farmers near one town on the Middle Nile were massacred during the war and their surviving neighbors desperately took over the vacant land. The papyrus dates to 186 BC but recalls events of the Great Revolt. See Clarysse, "The Great Revolt of the Egyptians," 4–5 (Text 4).

The masses will rise up. His [Ptolemy IV's] heart will be haughty, and bring multitudes down. But he will not prevail. (Dan 11:12)

With his armies bogged down in the conflict, Ptolemy must have been nervous of the frontier with Syria, particularly as Antiochus III's stature grew after his own domestic successes (see 2.6.18 above). The fortification of Jerusalem that the Tobiad brothers sponsored with Jewish taxes must have allayed some of his fears of an imminent Seleucid invasion or of Judea's potential disloyalty. The irony, however, was that in fortifying Jerusalem, Simon II, Joseph Tobias, and his sons were cleverly prizing Ptolemy's fingers off Judea, making themselves far more influential over the political fate of the region and tipping the balance of power towards Antiochus.

Finally, this reconstruction helps explain a seemingly incongruous statement from Josephus. Despite the calumny in how Joseph Tobias came to be chief tax farmer in Coele Syria and the misery he and his sons foisted on the Jewish people through extortion and thuggery, Josephus ends his account of Joseph's life with a positively glowing statement:

> Now Joseph, the father of Hyrcanus, died, having become a good and magnanimous man, who brought the Jewish people out of poverty and weak circumstances into a brighter standard of living. (*Ant.* 12.224)

This evaluation could be a bald-faced lie. Alternatively, Josephus could have relied on a questionable source or misunderstood his source. However, it is better explained by this reconstruction of events. Josephus later states that when Joseph Tobias died, Judea became seditious "because of his sons" (*Ant.* 12.228). By this phrase, he indicates that most Jews threw in their lot with the Tobiads in opposing Hyrcanus (cf. *Ant.* 12.229). This does not mean that the Senate and the people became affectionate supporters of the Tobiads overnight, for the villainy of the *mafioso* family could not be erased from popular memory so quickly. Rather, it indicates that many began to support them in the name of political expediency. If the Tobiad brothers were still collecting and sending taxes to Ptolemy in the same way as before, there would have been no reason for most people to get behind them in opposing Hyrcanus, for their money would have ended up in Alexandria either way. But if the Tobiads reduced taxes and redirected some to the temple in Jerusalem, then the Jewish taxpayer was no longer enriching a spoilt, distant monarch but investing in Judaism's most vital institution and creating jobs in the process. All this helps make sense of Josephus's assessment of Joseph Tobias. It is likely, therefore, that the Tobiads siphoned Jewish tax money into the temple treasury, where at least a portion was used for the beginning of temple repairs.

This also had the advantage of turning the temple treasury into a profitable Tobiad bank. Prior to this moment, the temple treasury would have held meager funds from what little money Jewish worshippers could donate or deposit after the payment of their taxes. On that meager basis, the temple could only offer few, modest loans to the Jewish public. But with the redirection of tax monies, the temple treasury expanded massively, which made enormous amounts available for potential loans. Investment within Judea thus received an enormous boost, promoting economic growth to enhance the employment opportunities that came with the rebuilding of the temple. At the same time, the repayment of those loans would have increased the temple's treasury even further and presumably grown the accounts of the Tobiads, who effectively bankrolled the whole system.

Although the outbreak of the Fifth Syrian War in 202 BC halted much economic activity, the rudiments for developing Jewish society in Judea under its own steam had been put in place. Though Simon II was probably the brains behind the whole scheme, it was Joseph Tobias and his sons who were able to implement it soon after the outbreak of the Great Revolt in Egypt in 207 BC and before Joseph's death in ca. 205 BC. This explains Josephus's assertion that the old tax farmer "became" (Gk. *genomenos*) a good and magnanimous man who helped enrich the Jewish nation. Ptolemy's gargantuan greed and astonishing irresponsibility induced Joseph and his older sons to convert their predatory tax farming activities that had once beggared the general populace into a public banking system based in the temple, which benefitted Jewish society at large. The *mafiosi* Tobiads reinvented themselves as investment bankers to rapturous public applause.

2.6.20 DEATH OF PTOLEMY IV (204 BC)

Although Ptolemy IV made some initial efforts to deal with the civil war in Egypt, he was not a tactician, let alone a politician. The affairs of government were handled by his two chiefs of staff, Agathocles and Sosibius, who also governed with a large measure of self-interest (Polybius, *Hist.* 14.11; 15.25). As the rebels gained the upper hand in the country's south and Alexandria itself felt the pinch, questions were raised about how much longer Ptolemy's Egypt could survive. Then, in the summer of 204 BC Ptolemy IV suddenly died. He was not even forty years of age. What caused his early demise is unknown, but Daniel 11:12 describes his fate with the laconic statement, "He will not prevail."

The dead king's son, Ptolemy V Epiphanes, was six years old when his father died. It was expected that his mother, Arsinoe III, would reign as regent on his behalf. However, she fell victim to Agathocles and Sosibius, who then took custody of her son before word of Ptolemy IV's death was even made public. When they finally did announce the deaths of both Ptolemy and Arsinoe and how they themselves would act as regents for the new boy king (September 204 BC), they were met with immense suspicion by the cosmopolitan residents of Alexandria (Polybius, *Hist.* 15.25). Public opinion towards the Ptolemaic regime now festered in the capital itself. Meanwhile, Ptolemaic garrisons throughout Egypt were capitulating to the native pharaoh, Hyrgonaphor.[134] The new boy king, Ptolemy V, thus inherited a kingdom that his father had put into a tailspin and that his chiefs of staff now struggled to bring under control. The heyday of the Ptolemaic kingdom was over.

Furthermore, with Ptolemy IV's death, the peace treaty hammered out with Antiochus III after Raphia came to an end. In the thirteen years since that momentous battle, Antiochus had consolidated his own realm and now had significantly more resources to pour into an invasion of Coele Syria. The specter of war rose once again over the Levant. Thanks to the efforts of Simon II and the Tobiads, Judea was poised to play a crucial role in it.

---

134. Hölbl, *A History of the Ptolemaic Empire*, 155.

2.7 THE RISING IMPORTANCE OF ROME

At this juncture, it becomes important to consider the rise of Rome. Its ascent would draw the Jews more deeply into the Mediterranean's political, economic, cultural, and religious waters. After Alexander the Great, Rome is most responsible for making the ancient world's horizons bigger, such that the ripples that began on one Mediterranean shore could send waves crashing against another. The Jews in the eastern Mediterranean would become inextricably affected by persons and events from distant shores, so we cannot rightly do justice to Jewish history and theology without tracing the ebb and flow of Rome's influence.

2.7.1 THE DAWN OF ROME

According to its most popular foundation myth, Rome was established in 753 BC by Romulus, after whom the city was named. Archaeological evidence suggests sporadic settlement at the site before this, but the development of an organized town does begin in the eighth century BC.[1] Initially, the city was governed by non-hereditary monarchs, though this period is shrouded in mystery and legend. In 509 BC, just a handful of years after the temple in Jerusalem was rebuilt and at precisely the same time that the Athenians were establishing democracy, the Romans overthrew their kings and established a republic that would prevent any one man from holding inordinate power. An elaborate governmental system was developed over subsequent centuries, at the center of which was the Roman Senate, supported by a hefty weight of laws and customs. This produced a highly stratified society with the patrician class (representing the oldest families of Rome) at the peak, plebeians in the middle, and slaves at the base.

A military and merchant ethos also developed, especially as distinction on the battlefield or financial success provided opportunity for gentrification. Rome thrived on military discipline and trade. Like Ptolemaic society, however, there were also informal systems of social interaction and preferment.

---

1. Marcel Le Glay et al., *A History of Rome*, trans. Antonia Nevill, 4th ed. (Chichester: Wiley-Blackwell, 2009), 21–23.

But whereas the extent of such systems in Egypt was entirely dependent on the personal will of the king, Rome's penchant for law meant that its informal systems were essentially legal loopholes—gaps (often deliberately left) that preserved unwritten traditions privileging the upper classes. The most notable such system was the tradition of patronage, whereby those without means or of low social standing looked for a patron in the upper classes to assist them in a particular matter. In return for such support, a client promised his patron full loyalty with a view to enhancing the patron's honor, influence, and wealth. Since patrons often acted out of self-interest and class distinction, this *quid pro quo* system inevitably worked in the patron's favor.

Patronage and military discipline led Rome to pursue a foreign policy of intervention and defensive expansion. It aimed initially to arbitrate disputes between other political entities and create buffers that protected Roman interests. Beginning with its immediate neighbors, Rome pushed its influence southwards. At the beginning of the third century BC Rome's state consisted of territory on the western side of the Apennine Mountains between Rome and Neapolis (modern Naples). Neapolis and the nearby city of Cumae were originally part of a disparate network of Greek colonies in southern Italy and Sicily known as *Magna Graecia* ("Greater Greece"). But by the beginning of the third century BC they had mixed with Italic peoples, recognized Roman sovereignty, and had begun receiving Roman colonists.[2] The population under Rome's control, therefore, burgeoned, giving it a healthy supply of men to man its armies.

The Etruscans to Rome's north influenced the Romans culturally for several centuries.[3] But as Rome's territory expanded in the third century BC, the Greek language and culture of Italy's southern cities had a profound effect on Roman culture, especially in the arts and religion—so much so that the Romans eventually saw themselves as the heirs and perfecters of Greece's classical legacy.[4] Thus while Hellenism was an infiltration of Greek culture into the societies of the Near East, the infiltration of Greek culture into Roman society produced what has come to be known as Greco-Roman culture. This (in part) even led the Romans to produce a new foundation myth at the end of the first century BC: Virgil's *Aeneid*, which traced Rome's roots back to the Trojan War, thereby giving Rome a stake in the classical legends. Rome's gods were easily identified with the Greek gods: Jupiter was equated with Zeus; Minerva

---

2. Gianfranco Adornato, "Southern Italy," in *A Companion to Greeks Across the Ancient World*, ed. Franco De Angelis (Hoboken, NJ: Wiley Blackwell, 2020), 285–86.
3. Le Glay et al., *A History of Rome*, 8–12.
4. Le Glay et al., *A History of Rome*, 16–18, 68–72.

with Athena; Mars with Ares; and Bacchus with Dionysus. The Greco-Roman ideal was also reflected in the apostle Paul's letter to the Romans (AD 55) in which he identified the gentile Christians of Rome as "Greeks" (Rom 1:13–16)—a term they evidently used to distinguish themselves from "barbarians."

In 280–275 BC, just prior to the First Syrian War between the Ptolemies and Seleucids, Rome fought the Pyrrhic War. This conflict was sparked when the Greek city of Tarentum at the "heel" of Italy invited Pyrrhus, king of Epirus, to champion their cause in resisting Rome's growing influence. Pyrrhus was eventually defeated in 275 BC, and over the next decade, Rome inserted itself into the "boot" of southern Italy. It established new colonies throughout the region and soon controlled almost the entire Italian Peninsula. Before the Pyrrhic War, Rome was a small regional state with less clout than the nearby Carthaginian Empire and a minnow in comparison to the Seleucids and Ptolemies. But victory over Pyrrhus put Rome on the map, making it an international power comparable to Epirus and Macedon. It induced Ptolemy II to send an embassy to Rome in 273, establishing a mutual concord (Dio Cassius, *Hist. rom.* 10.41).[5]

2.7.2 ROME AND CARTHAGE

Rome's expansion southwards put it on a collision course with the larger Carthaginian Empire. Carthage, originally a colony of Tyre, had developed a vast trading empire that included colonies in Sicily, Sardinia, Corsica, the Balearic Islands, Spain, and North Africa. In 264 BC Rome was invited to act as protector of the city of Messana (modern Messina) in Sicily against the aggression of the Greek city of Syracuse to its south. But the Carthaginians, who controlled most of the island, also intervened in the crisis, and this sparked the first of the so-called Punic Wars.[6] This first war (264–241 BC) was a protracted affair, fought on land and sea. It took a heavy financial toll on both sides, prompting Carthage to seek a loan from Ptolemy II, with whom it was on good terms. However, Ptolemy was keen to maintain his concord with both Carthage and Rome and so refused the loan. He even tried before his death to negotiate peace between the warring states, but to no avail (Appian, *Sicily* 1). Both Rome and Carthage were drained by the long conflict, but when they finally negotiated a peace treaty, Carthage was forced to cede its Sicilian colonies to Rome. This gave Rome a significant source of grain to feed its

---

5. Hölbl, *A History of the Ptolemaic Empire*, 54, 73, n. 105.
6. The term "Punic" is a Latin form of the word "Phoenician," reflecting the ethnic background of the Carthaginians.

growing population and ensured the flourishing of both Roman trade and its military machine. However, the war and its outcome only ensured the continued enmity between the two states.

Over the next decades, Roman foreign policy became imperialistic.[7] It led Rome to challenge Carthaginian dominance in the western Mediterranean. The spark for the Second Punic War (218–201 BC) occurred when the Carthaginian general Hannibal tried to create a buffer zone to prevent Rome gaining access to the mineral-rich territories of southern Spain.[8] At the same time that Antiochus III's forces were laying siege to Jerusalem (218/7 BC), Hannibal famously marched his infantry, cavalry, and war elephants from Spain through southern Gaul and across the Alps into the Italian Peninsula. He took the Romans so utterly by surprise that he forever became their archetypal bogeyman and forced them to adopt an entirely new war strategy. Hannibal was successful at every turn in Italy, inflicting a heavy defeat on the Roman legions at the Battle of Cannae in 216 BC—a loss that became imprinted on the Roman psyche.

Victory at Cannae gave Hannibal a clear shot at Rome itself. However, traversing the Alps had deprived him of siege engines, and he found it difficult to feed his army, let alone replenish its numbers and resources so far from its bases. Unable to take the shot, he was forced instead to attempt the slow asphyxiation of the Roman state. Hannibal spent several years bogged down in southern Italy and Sicily but succeeded in sapping Rome of its fighting men and grain supply. Roman and Carthaginian forces also continued to skirmish in Spain. Hannibal's brother, Hasdrubal, decided the best strategy was not to continue battling on the periphery but to strike at Rome's head in Italy. Hasdrubal abandoned Spain and replicated his brother's feat by crossing the Alps with an army. Had he linked up with Hannibal, their combined forces would undoubtedly have delivered the *coup de grace* that would have finished Rome off. Yet the Romans intercepted communications between the brothers and were able to obliterate Hasdrubal's army at the Metaurus River in 207 BC.

At this, Hannibal lost his grip on Rome's jugular and Rome breathed anew. Under the direction of the Roman general Publius Cornelius Scipio, Rome invaded the Carthaginian heartland. Carthage recalled Hannibal home, but Scipio defeated him at Zama in 202 BC. The victory earned Scipio the epithet "Africanus," making him a household name in Rome. Carthage

---

7. This development towards imperialism was neither steady nor linear. See Le Glay et al., *A History of Rome*, 91–93.

8. William G. Sinnigen and Arthur E. R. Boak, *A History of Rome to A.D. 565*, 6th Ed. (New York: Macmillan, 1977), 106–14.

was demilitarized, fined a humiliating 10,000 talents of silver,[9] and all its colonial holdings were ceded to Rome. Carthage was thus reduced to a minor regional state.

The Second Punic War won for Rome an extensive empire in the western Mediterranean. Its economic stability and military prowess were bolstered by Italy's agricultural capacities, Sicily's vast wheat fields, Spain's prodigious metal mines, a booming population, and an extensive trade network throughout the Mediterranean. The construction of Roman roads facilitated the movement of its armies and lubricated the flow of trade, encouraging mercantile activity and migration. Like Alexandria, Rome boomed. By the end of the third century BC Rome had become a colonial powerhouse in the west whose clout rivaled the Ptolemaic and Seleucid realms in the east. Its soldiers, senators, and suppliers had made their mark and could not be ignored by any polity in the Mediterranean world. Thus the cultural, economic, and political pole that had moved from Mesopotamia to the eastern Mediterranean by the end of the fourth century BC was now steadily being drawn further west by the gravitational pull of Rome.

---

9. In modern terms, this would be the equivalent of approximately US$15 billion.

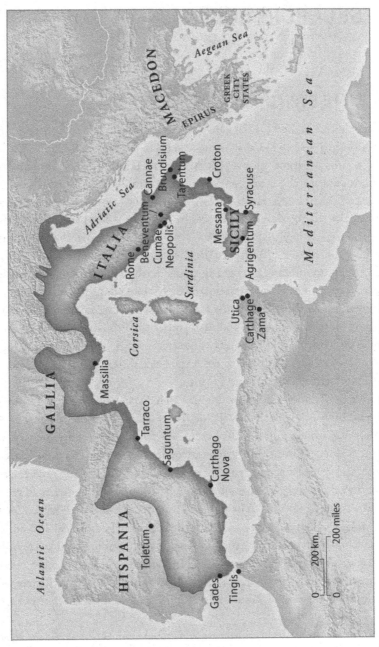

The Growing Influence of Rome in the Western Mediterranean (to 202 BC).

2.8 SELEUCID RULE

2.8.1 FIFTH SYRIAN WAR (202-195 BC)

After Joseph Tobias died (ca. 205 BC), his sons and the Jewish Senate got fully behind Simon II and the secessionist cause (*Ant.* 12.138, 228–229). While no specific records of negotiations with Antiochus III exist, they were undoubtedly conducted, as the later course of events imply. In Egypt, the regents, Sosibius and Agathocles, realized they needed new troops who were loyal to them to deal with the domestic threats in Egypt as well as the inevitable war with Antiochus. They dispatched a Greek general, Scopas the Aetolian, to recruit new mercenaries in Greece. But while he was away, both regents fell victim to intrigue and public lynching, particularly as the Ptolemaic army itself attempted a coup. The administration of Egypt looked directionless.

Antiochus saw this as his prime moment. In 202 BC he struck a deal with Philip V of Macedon to attack and dismember the Ptolemaic kingdom and its allies in Asia Minor. The Ptolemaic ambassador to Antioch protested loudly, but there was little he could do to repel the Seleucid king (Polybius, *Hist.* 3.2; 15.20). The Fifth Syrian War had begun.

In charge of Ptolemaic garrisons in Coele Syria was Ptolemy Thraseas, a general and high priest of the royal cult. The instability of the regency back in Egypt deprived him of allies, such that he now faced the likelihood of trying to withstand a Seleucid invasion without adequate support amid a populace eager to rid themselves of Ptolemaic rule. Sensing an opportunity, the Jewish leadership convinced Ptolemy Thraseas to throw in his lot with the Seleucid regime. After corresponding with Antiochus, Ptolemy Thraseas defected in late 202 BC and swung the entire balance of the region away from the Ptolemies.[1]

Antiochus launched his invasion of Coele Syria, establishing a strategic base at Damascus (Polyaenus, *Strategems* 4.15). In Judea, the Tobiad brothers went to war against Hyrcanus (*Ant.* 12.228–229). It is unlikely they had the means for an assault on his position in Transjordan, for he himself survived this internecine

---

1. This correspondence is preserved in the inscribed dossier found at Hephzibah in the Jezreel Valley, where Ptolemy Thraseas had a personal estate. See Chrubasik, "The Epigraphic Dossier Concerning Ptolemaios," 115–30. Cf. Dov Gera, "Ptolemy Son of Thraseas and the Fifth Syrian War," *Ancient Society* 18 (1987): 63–73.

conflict. It is more likely that they raided his allies and assets in Judea itself. To that end, the lavish complex at Ramat Raḥel that had served as an administrative center for the Ptolemies ceased to function at this time. That the site was also dismantled suggests that it probably had been connected to Hyrcanus.[2]

With the Jewish leadership on his side, Antiochus did not need to go to Jerusalem.[3] Instead, he marched on Gaza to secure the coast against a possible landing by Scopas and his Greek mercenaries. But Antiochus found himself delayed by Gaza's dogged resistance (Polybius, *Hist.* 16.22a). Although he eventually defeated its garrison, the delay meant he was unable to secure the rest of the coast. Thus, when he quartered his army for the winter of 201/200 BC, his hold over Coele Syria was loose.

Scopas seized this chance and launched a lightning counterattack with his mercenaries over the winter and spring. Because of the pivotal role that the Tobiads had played in tearing the region away from Ptolemaic control, Jerusalem was one of Scopas's prime targets. A Ptolemaic garrison was still stationed there, so he got into the city without much of a struggle. Once there, he wreaked harsh vengeance on the population, to which Daniel 11 alludes:

> The King of the North [Antiochus III] will return and employ a horde larger than the first. After an interval of some years [after the Battle of Raphia], he will come with a large force and many provisions. In those times, many will stand against the King of the South [Ptolemy IV/V], and the sons of violent men among your people [the Tobiads] will raise themselves up to fulfil a vision,[4] but they will stumble. (Dan 11:13–14)

What the vision is in this context is a matter of debate. If it does not refer to the vision of Daniel 10–12 itself, it might refer to a vision announced by a prophetic figure in Jerusalem in support of the secessionist cause. Either way, the "sons of violent men" is a clear allusion to the erstwhile *mafiosi* Tobiads

---

2. Lipschits et al. (*What Are the Stones Whispering?*, 113–18) connect the decommissioning of Ramat Raḥel with the general change from Ptolemaic to Seleucid sovereignty. However, the dismantling of the site seems redundant to the eventual shift in sovereignty, especially since its infrastructure could have been adapted to Antiochus's administration. Its demolition speaks to a more personal purpose, such as the animosity between the Tobiad brothers and Hyrcanus.

3. Zeitlin erroneously asserts that Simon II welcomed Antiochus into Jerusalem at this juncture ("The Tobias Family and the Hasmoneans," 184). In following Josephus's chronology, however, he does not account for its non-linear presentation at this point or some of Josephus's more egregious chronological errors, which can be disentangled with more thorough corroboration.

4. The vowels of the Masoretic Text read the phrase this way, employing a *hithpael* verb. However, a purely consonantal text could read the relevant verb as a *niphal*. In that case, the text could read, "the sons of violent men will be carried off," referring to Scopas's deportation of Jewish aristocracy to Egypt.

and their allies in the Jewish Senate. Scopas deported secessionists among the Jewish aristocracy to Egypt. Whether the Tobiads were among them is difficult to know. The family was still influential in Jewish politics a handful of years later, so they may have escaped before Scopas took the city (Jerome, *Daniel* 11.13–14).[5] Either way, as the vision of Daniel puts it, the effort to break with the Ptolemies stumbled.

By the end of spring 200 BC Scopas had reasserted Ptolemaic control over Coele Syria (Polybius, *Hist.* 16.39) and induced Antiochus to abort his campaign. The following year, Antiochus was aiding Philip V of Macedon in his efforts against Pergamum. But Philip had also invaded the rest of Greece, provoking the Second Macedonian War with the Romans. Unwilling to be drawn into direct conflict with Rome, Antiochus quickly backtracked.

He soon got a second run at Coele Syria after Ptolemy V took the reins of kingship at age eleven (199 BC). While the boy king used Scopas to try to quell ongoing unrest in Egypt, Antiochus invaded again. Scopas scrambled to meet him, and the two forces met near Panias at the foot of Mount Hermon in late 198 BC. Antiochus overwhelmed Scopas with vastly superior numbers, forcing him to flee to Sidon.[6] Ptolemaic control over Coele Syria was decisively broken (Polybius, *Hist.* 16.18–19; Livy, *Ab urbe cond.* 31.43).[7]

Antiochus's forces swept south through Transjordan, and pro-Ptolemaic Hyrcanus soon came to the bleak realization of his impending doom.[8] According to Josephus, he took his own life, having governed Transjordan for the Ptolemies for seven years (*Ant.* 12.234–36). His palatial estate west of Philadelphia was left unfinished—a monument to both the height of his aspirations and the depth of his downfall. His monetary wealth was confiscated, and at least part of it was deposited as a fund in the temple treasury at Jerusalem (2 Macc 3:11), demonstrating the role that the Tobiads and Simon II played in his undoing.

---

5. Jerome's exact source is unknown, but an interpretive error he makes tells us his source was credible. He describes those Jews whom Scopas deported as belonging to the faction of Ptolemy, which he took to mean that they were loyal to Ptolemy V Epiphanes. However, as Gera rightly points out, with the loyalty of Coele Syria hanging in the balance, it is unlikely that Scopas removed pro-Ptolemaic elements from the country when they were most needed there. It is most likely that the faction was loyal not to Ptolemy V but to General Ptolemy Thraseas, who had defected to Antiochus III (cf. *Ant.* 12.139). See Gera, "Ptolemy Son of Thraseas and the Fifth Syrian War," 63–66.

6. The date of the Battle of Panias is usually given as 200 BC, but this is based on a faulty reconstruction of Polybius's fragmentary evidence. Epigraphic and numismatic evidence allows for greater accuracy, which puts the battle in late 198 BC. See Chrubasik, "The Epigraphic Dossier Concerning Ptolemaios," 120–29; Catharine ca. Lorber, "Numismatic Evidence and the Chronology of the Fifth Syrian War," in Honigman, Nihan, and Lipschits, *Times of Transition*, 31–41.

7. Grainger, *The Seleukid Empire of Antiochus III*, 112–13; Lorber, "Numismatic Evidence," 34–38.

8. Lorber, "Numismatic Evidence," 32.

According to Antiochus's own account, the people of Jerusalem welcomed him to the city, provisioned his army, and assisted him in ejecting the Ptolemaic garrison (*Ant.* 12.133–46; cf. Polybius, *Hist.* 16.39; see 2.8.2 below). Antiochus then brought the coast under his control before returning to Sidon where his forces had been blockading Scopas. Sidon capitulated (197 BC), and Antiochus gave an emaciated Scopas safe conduct back to Egypt. The vision of Daniel describes the incident:

> The King of the North [Antiochus III] will come and put up a blockade, capturing a well-fortified city [Sidon]. The mercenaries of the South [Scopas's forces] will not stand and its elite troops will have no power to resist. (Dan 11:15)[9]

This was not the end of the Fifth Syrian War, though, for the conflict now merged with the Second Macedonian War playing out in Greece. Antiochus had already put himself in Rome's bad books through his alliance with Philip V of Macedon. Rome considered the Macedonian king a general menace, especially for his harassment of Attalus I of Pergamum, a solid Roman ally, and for his earlier alliance with Hannibal, which sparked the First Macedonian War (214–205 BC [Polybius, *Hist.* 3.2]). After securing Coele Syria, Antiochus was faced with a choice. He could continue forward to Egypt and attempt to end the reign of the Ptolemies completely—a daunting prospect, since any invasion of Egypt was never straightforward. Alternatively, he could return to Asia Minor, eject the Ptolemaic enclaves there, and aid Philip against Pergamum. He chose the latter and, in so doing, returned to the fringes of the conflict between Rome and Philip.

Antiochus picked off what remained of Ptolemaic holdings in Asia Minor and wound up on the threshold of Pergamum in 197 BC. Shrewdly, he never breached Pergamum's borders, so the Roman Senate opted not to take direct action against him (cf. Livy, *Ab urbe cond.* 32.8, 27). Roman efforts instead concentrated on hounding Philip V until he capitulated. The subsequent treaty (196 BC) forced Philip to renounce all his territories outside Macedon, surrender his navy, and pay war reparations—similar terms to those Rome had imposed on Carthage just five years earlier (201 BC). He was thus turned into

---

9. Jerome understood the blockade as a siege against the Ptolemaic garrison in Jerusalem (*Daniel* 11.15–16). This is possible, though it entails an anonymous reference to Jerusalem. We also have to reckon with Antiochus's own account, which states that he was welcomed into Jerusalem. The verse more likely refers to the defeat of Scopas and his mercenaries at Sidon, which signaled the collapse of Ptolemaic sovereignty in Coele Syria.

a minor regional dynast and client of Rome. But Antiochus took advantage of Philip's chastening and occupied much of the territory he was forced to abandon. This brought Antiochus into Europe, where he laid claim to Thrace, which had been theoretically absorbed into the traditional Seleucid realm after the Battle of Corupedium (281 BC), though it had never been officially occupied by the Seleucids (see 2.6.8 above). With this move, Antiochus effectively encircled Pergamum and came hard up against the Romans. While the Romans were eager to see the dust of war settle, they also understood that they needed to halt Antiochus's advances and still the rivalry between the Seleucids and the Ptolemies (Livy, *Ab urbe cond.* 32.27; 33.38–40).

The situation in Egypt changed demonstrably in 197 BC after an abundant annual inundation of the Nile. Ptolemy V sponsored the building of dams to store water and prevent widespread famine from reoccurring. This pivotal administrative change from prodigality to planning saw the tide of opposition to Ptolemaic rule begin to ebb. A synod of grateful priests, meeting at Memphis in 196 BC, issued a decree celebrating the king's beneficence.[10] It would be another decade before Ptolemy regained full control of Egypt. For now, he realized that he needed to write off the loss of Coele Syria and enter negotiations with Antiochus. Under the terms of their treaty, Ptolemy recognized Seleucid control of Coele Syria and agreed to marry Antiochus's daughter, Cleopatra. This was a major win for Antiochus as it ensured that the heir to Ptolemy's throne in Alexandria would be his own grandson with Seleucid blood—a similar ploy to the one Ptolemy II had used at the end of the Second Syrian War (see 2.6.14 above). The marriage occurred in the winter of 194/3 BC at Raphia (Livy, *Ab urbe cond.* 35.13), the site of the battle between the two kingdoms in 217 BC. Thus the Fifth Syrian War finally came to an end, as described in Daniel:

> The one who comes [Antiochus III] against him [Ptolemy V] will do as he pleases, with none to stand against him. He will stand in the glorious land [Judea] with conquest in his hand. He will set his face to come with the authority of his entire kingdom and make agreements with him [Ptolemy V]. He [Antiochus III] will give him [Ptolemy V] a girl-child [Cleopatra] to ruin him, but she will not remain or be there for him [Antiochus III]. (Dan 11:16–17)

---

10. A fragmentary stone copy of this Memphis Decree would be discovered in 1799 at the Egyptian town of Rosetta by troops of Napoleon—the famed Rosetta Stone, whose trilingual inscription enabled the modern decipherment of the ancient Egyptian language.

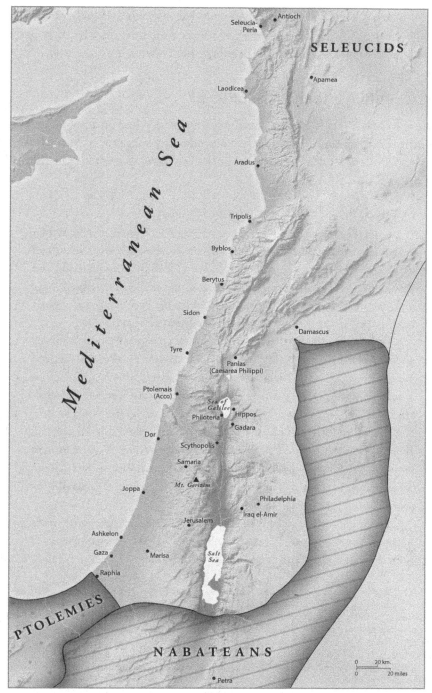

The Levant after the Seleucid Conquest of Coele Syria (198 BC).

The last part of this testimony is somewhat difficult to decipher but most likely refers to the fact that, over the course of the next decades, Cleopatra would prove of no lasting political benefit to her father.[11]

2.8.2 JUDEA UNDER ANTIOCHUS III

The transfer of Coele Syria to Seleucid sovereignty had an immediate and significant effect on Judea. Josephus reproduces a letter from Antiochus to General Ptolemy Thraseas, whom Antiochus now appointed governor of Coele Syria (*Ant.* 12.137–144):

> King Antiochus to Ptolemy [Thraseas]: Greetings.
>
> From the moment we entered the country of the Jews, they showed their devotion toward us. They warmly received us into their city, their senate met us, they provided our troops and elephants with abundant provisions, and they helped us eject the Egyptian garrison in the citadel. Therefore, we see fit to reward them by restoring their city, which has been ravaged by various wars, and repatriating those who have been deported from it.
>
> First of all, we judge that, by virtue of their piety, a subsidy be bestowed upon them for the sacrifice of sacrificially suitable animals, wine, oil, and incense, to the value of 20,000 pieces of silver; sacred artabae of fine flour in accordance with their native law; 1,460 medimni of wheat; and 375 medimni of salt.[12] I would have these payments completed as I have stipulated.
>
> Regarding their temple, the work on the stoas should be completed, along with anything else still in need of reconstruction. Wood materials should be procured from Judea itself, or from other nations, or the Lebanon without any toll charged. The same applies for other apparent materials that are needed for the repair of the temple.
>
> Everyone who is part of their nation may live according to their ancestral laws. The senate, priests, temple scribes, and sacred cantors are exempted from the poll tax, the crown tax, and any other tax. So that the city might

---

11. This was not because Cleopatra was insignificant. Rather, she only became significant after her father's death. Josephus also states that Antiochus gave Coele Syria to Ptolemy V as Cleopatra's dowry and divided its tax revenue with him (*Ant.* 12.154). The claim is, however, preposterous after Antiochus had gone to such lengths to win Coele Syria for himself. The claim probably comes from later Ptolemaic propaganda. See Hölbl, *A History of the Ptolemaic Empire*, 145; Grainger, *The Seleukid Empire of Antiochus III*, 143–44.

12. An artaba was a dry measure of approximately 27 liters. A medimnus was approximately 52 liters (1.5 bushels). The letter does not specify the precise quantity of fine flour to be supplied, perhaps because the number was overlooked in the copying. Of the other quantities, Antiochus pledges 60 tons of wheat (75,920 liters, or 2,190 bushels) and 22 tons of salt (19,500 liters).

be speedily resettled, I grant the current residents and those who migrate to it before the month of Hyperberetaios [i.e., September] an exemption from taxes for three years. We also hereafter relieve them of a third of their taxes, so that they might recover their damages. Also, all from the city who were seized for slavery, along with those born to them, we set free, and command the return of their property.

The letter dates to ca. 196 BC, shortly after the peace treaty between Antiochus III and Ptolemy V. A Jewish priest named John, the father of Eupolemus (who wrote a Jewish history in Greek, now almost completely lost), was pivotal in negotiating the concessions (2 Macc 4:11). Antiochus evidently secured the return of those whom Scopas deported from Jerusalem in the winter of 201/200 BC—prominent citizens who had been instrumental in turning Judea over to him, perhaps even some of the Tobiads. In any case, the Tobiads now emerged with even more influence as the champions who had fostered the regime change and helped fund a veritable Jewish renaissance. The book of Tobit, which extols them in veiled terms for such virtues, was written at this time (see 2.8.3 below), as was the *Tobiad Romance*, which Josephus drew upon.

The generous tax exemptions for the Jewish Senate and temple personnel demonstrates the leading role they had played in the Fifth Syrian War. The declaration of Jerusalem as a tax haven extended tax relief to commoners also, showing that Antiochus was committed to undoing the crippling burdens of the Ptolemies and repopulating the city. His concessions provided the major stimulus for the growth of Jerusalem as both a sacred city and a commercial center. Despite the difficulties in determining the population of Jerusalem,[13] a marked upturn is evident in the archaeological record from the beginning of the second century BC. All pockets of the ridge south of the Temple Mount (the Ophel and so-called city of David) were filled,[14] increasing the population to approximately 5,000. Within a few decades of Antiochus's decree, settlement was spilling over to the larger Western Hill, which had not been occupied since the fall of Jerusalem in 586 BC. The population mushroomed, transforming Jerusalem into a bustling city of tens of thousands. Jerusalem became an officially recognized "holy city" (Gk. *hiera polis*). In fact, the Greek name of Jerusalem (*Ierousalēm*) underwent a popular modification at this time

---

13. Lipschits, "Jerusalem Between Two Periods of Greatness," 164–65.
14. Lipschits, "Jerusalem Between Two Periods of Greatness," 174; cf. Oded Lipschits, "Demographic Changes in Judah between the Seventh and the Fifth Centuries B.C.E.," in *Judah and the Judeans in the Neo-Babylonian Period*, ed. Oded Lipschits and Joseph Blenkinsopp (Winona Lake, IN: Eisenbrauns, 2003), 366.

and hereafter was often called *Hierosolyma*, reflecting a play on the Greek word *hieron* ("temple").[15]

Antiochus did not offer to pay for the temple renovation himself. Rather, he provided tax breaks that enabled the Jews to pay for the construction themselves. Essentially, this capitalized on the momentum generated by the scheme of Simon II and the Tobiads to renovate the temple and fortify the city (see 2.6.19 above). The monies that now landed in the temple treasury were no longer taxes to the crown but the freewill offerings of the Jewish people to their God, donated from the abundance of their untaxed income. Antiochus was officially facilitating Jewish worship and promoting the financial function of the temple.[16] His decree also recognized the Jews as a distinct ethnos within his realm, with the right to observe their own ethnic customs. They were thus exempted from participation in the Seleucid royal cult, which worshipped the Seleucid king as a god.

Antiochus's policy achieved several goals. It promoted the temple institution at the heart of Jewish life; it bound the Jewish people to him as a benefactor; it helped integrate Judea within the Seleucid realm; it provided security for the population by fortifying their growing city; it kickstarted the local economy by injecting money into it and encouraging a growing workforce; and it laid out a viable stream of revenue for the crown into the future (after the three years of tax-free status expired). The situation was a win for both Antiochus and the Jewish people. At the same time, it underscored that the prophetic promises of Davidic restoration were evaporating into the air of prospective prosperity. Were the Davidic promises even relevant anymore?

2.8.3 THE BOOK OF TOBIT

The book of Tobit was originally composed in Aramaic and later translated into Greek. It tells the story of a pious Jewish man, Tobit, who lives in Nineveh during the days of Sennacherib. This setting is not historical but a legendary projection of Jews living within a Syrian state—that is, the Seleucid kingdom.[17] The names of the hero (Tobit), his father (Tobiel), and his son (Tobias) all play on the phrase "God is good" and indicate that the book is a theodicy couched

---

15. Eupolemus, Fragment 2 (in Eusebius, *Praeparatio Evangelica* 9.34.13), gives the etymology of *Hierosolyma* as a corruption of the term *hieros Solomon* ("temple of Solomon"). Cf. Hecataeus as cited in Diodorus Siculus, *Bib. hist.* 40.3.3; Josephus, *Ant.* 7.67; *J.W.* 6.438.

16. Vasile Babota, *The Institution of the Hasmonean High Priesthood*, Supplements to the Journal for the Study of Judaism 165 (Leiden: Brill, 2014), 42–43.

17. Assyria and Syria were often used interchangeably, especially in Hellenistic contexts.

as an entertaining tale. More than this, though, it provides multiple intersections with the Tobiad family. This, along with several themes in the story, show that the book reflects conditions prevalent in the early years of Seleucid sovereignty over Judea.

For example, Tobit's property is confiscated by the evil king Sennacherib, reflecting a common Jewish experience under the grueling tax regime of the Ptolemies. Yet Tobit's property is eventually returned to him when there is a change of king, echoing the beneficent policies of Antiochus III. Tobit sends his son, Tobias, to recover some money deposited with a compatriot named Gabael in Media (Tob 1:14). Though many take "Gabael" simply to mean "God is high," it can also be rendered "tax collector of God," thus alluding to the Tobiads as tax agents who reinvented themselves as bankers financing loans to fellow Jews and bankrolling the repairs to the Jerusalem temple (see 2.6.19 above). This allusion is reinforced by the fact that the Tobiad brothers took possession of their half-brother Hyrcanus's estate and brought his money into the temple treasury. The conversion of the Tobiads from local *mafiosi* to pious temple bankers is also seen in the book's claim that charitable giving (including lending), rather than storing up gold for oneself (tax farming), is better than prayer and fasting, delivers one from death, and cleanses all sins (Tob 12:8–9). In other words, the Tobiads' latter deeds exculpated their former crimes, and their tax farming could be seen in the grander scheme of God's sovereignty as paving the way for a Jewish renaissance. Their collusion with Antiochus III against the Ptolemaic regime is also echoed in the statement, "It is good to keep the secret of a king" (Tob 12:7). Finally, the book ends with the hope that Israel's captives would be gathered from the nations where they had been deported, that God would cheer the captives within Jerusalem, that the nations would come to them with gifts (Tob 13:11), and that Jerusalem and its temple would be rebuilt (Tob 13:5, 10–11, 16–17; 14:5). All these hopes reflect the policies of Antiochus III (see 2.8.2 above). They are not eschatological hopes, for the author shows no belief in a future resurrection. On the contrary, the author sees physical death as the ultimate end of human life and presents its hero, Tobit, as one who piously buries the dead. Hope is very much centered on the mundane world, and since charity is seen to stave off death, the Tobiads are extolled as righteous.

When seen against the context of its composition, the book of Tobit gives a sense that the past hardship under the Ptolemies was giving way to a new era of prosperity and even fulfilment of prophetic promises, thanks in large measure to the efforts of the Tobiads. The family that had once brought such misery to the common person is turned into the common person's champion. Righteousness, particularly in the form of charity, is held up as the ultimate good, which leads to blessing. In this way, the Tobiads are celebrated as paragons of piety, with nary a Davidic promise in sight. The house of David was little more than a curious throwback (Tob 1:4).

2.8.4 SIMON II AND THE JERUSALEM TEMPLE

As ethnarch and high priest, Simon II oversaw the renovation of the temple, which received a Hellenistic makeover. Antiochus's letter to Ptolemy Thraseas makes mention of stoas (*Ant.* 12.141)—architectural features typical of Greek temples. Simon built a retaining wall around the complex, and the height of its enclosing walls was doubled (Sir 50:2). The inspiration for this might have come partly from the impressive complex on Mount Gerizim, which by this time exhibited distinct Hellenistic features. The Jerusalem temple thus became an imposing acropolis at the northern edge of the city, putting it on a more equal footing with its Samaritan rival.

The temple design also facilitated Jerusalem's transformation from small Near Eastern town to more classic Hellenistic city of the Mediterranean world. For example, the precinct's configuration and security structures enabled the transfer of certain civic functions from the city gates to the sacred precinct.[18] Thereafter, the temple grounds began to function as a de facto agora—a trend that continued with the Herodian temple (see 4.5.6 below).[19]

In superintending the renovation, Simon emulated the accomplishments of the Davidic kings, especially Solomon, the legendary builder of Yahweh's temple in Jerusalem. That role, which had previously been the preserve of Davidic heirs, was now firmly in the hands of the priesthood. In Ben Sira's mind, it made Simon a fitting heir of the royal legacy. For Davidic loyalists, who must surely have applauded the promotion of the temple, it raised ongoing doubts regarding God's past promises. For most Jews, the temple in Jerusalem was a cultic installation doubling as an agora. It was no longer the symbol of Yahweh's covenant with David—the Zion tradition had lost all its royal trappings, and its transformation into solely a priestly tradition was now complete. If any members of the Davidic family still sat in the Jewish Senate by this stage, the temple's renewal under Simon II deepened their growing irrelevance. Certainly, a generation later, the only Davidic voice heard in Jewish society was the archaic

---

18. This kind of relocation is exemplified in 1 Esd 9:38, which retells the story of Ezra's public reading of the Torah and changes the setting for the scene from the square by the Water Gate (Neh 8:1) to the square by the temple's east gate. Binder, *Into the Temple Courts*, 219.

19. Sylvie Honigman, *Tales of High Priests and Taxes: The Books of the Maccabees and the Judean Rebellion against Antiochus IV* (Berkeley: University of California Press, 2014), 340–42.

prophetic traditions. This period, then, spelled the end of substantive Davidic involvement in Jewish politics, as the trajectory between the Chronicler (340s BC), Qoheleth (220s BC), and Ben Sira (180 BC) highlights. Davidic expectation was fading into an ethereal apocalyptic eschatological hope.

Simon completed the temple construction shortly after the expiry of Jerusalem's three-year tax haven status (ca. 192 BC). He was by now around seventy years of age, but he officiated at its dedication, which Ben Sira (see also 2.8.7 below) recalled a few years later with vivid lyrical nostalgia (ca. 180 BC):

> How glorious he [Simon] was when he processed around the laypeople,
> when he came forth from behind the temple's curtain—
> like the morning star amidst the clouds,
> like the moon with fulsome days,
> like the sun beaming upon the sanctuary of the Most High,
> and like the rainbow shining amidst glorious clouds . . .
> when he donned the glorious attire,
> and clothed himself with a consummate achievement;
> when he ascended the holy altar,
> and consecrated the sacred precinct;
> when he received the portions from the hands of the priests,
> as he himself stood at the hearth on the platform. . . .
> Then all the laypeople hastened
> and fell to their faces on the ground
> to worship their Lord,
> the Almighty God, the Most High. . . .
> When he came down, he raised his hands
> over the whole assembly of the sons of Israel
> to give the blessing of the Lord from his lips,
> and to exult in his name.
> And they fell to the ground once again,
> to receive the blessing from the Most High. (Sir 50:5–7, 11–12a, 17 20–21)

2.8.5 JEWISH MODERATES, PROGRESSIVES, AND CONSERVATIVES

Antiochus III's measures gave the Jewish people considerable autonomy. Spirits rose across the board, and the new latitude invigorated national life and the pursuit of piety. With such latitude came diversity. The blending of politics, culture, religion, and economics under a beneficent Hellenistic regime generated a wide spectrum of worldviews among the Jews of Judea. We may discuss each of these as discrete categories in theory, but in reality they were initially an organic spectrum that gave rise to concrete factions and movements in subsequent decades.

Moderates

Occupying the center of the spectrum were moderates like the high priest Simon II. For Simon and many of his serving priests, national life and piety were about the preservation of Jewish identity in the here and now. A later rabbinic tradition, which termed him "Simon the Just," attributed to him a statement that comported with the cultural and political reality of his day. For that reason, it probably distils his genuine thought and was telling both for what it did and did not say:

> On three things the world stands: on the Torah; on the [temple] cult; and on demonstration of piety. (m. 'Avot 1:2)

The "world" implied by Simon's slogan was the world as he knew it—one in which Torah and temple were pivotal, alongside personal "piety." This was a manifesto for a moral culture. There was no mention of the importance of the land, political independence, or Davidic hopes. On the contrary, the emphasis on the temple cult implied that pilgrimage was sufficient to fulfil all righteousness. Prophetic traditions were, therefore, only important insofar as they bolstered a temple-based religion in Jerusalem. The priestly content of Zion theology was, therefore, sufficient to sustain this—royal Davidic hope was irrelevant to it. While we cannot discount the possibility that Simon and his priests hoped for something better in the future, such as Jewish independence, the phrasing of Simon's slogan grounded Jewish hope in *Realpolitik*—what was achievable now rather than in some age to come. It was non-eschatological and non-apocalyptic in ethos, much like the hopes expressed in the book of Tobit (see 2.8.3 above). Thus all three elements of the slogan could be fulfilled under foreign rulers, provided those rulers were beneficent.

Simon was politically progressive in that he was content with foreign rule but religiously conservative in his promotion of native Jewish institutions and preservation of the status quo. Culturally, Simon was a moderate, having given his sons a Greek education and permitted Greek architecture in the renovated temple while still promoting the distinctiveness of Jewish identity. There must have been an element of expediency in such eclecticism. Hellenistic sympathies were practical for someone in regular contact with Hellenistic officials, and giving the upcoming generation an education among the upper echelons of the colonial power was useful and not necessarily a betrayal of Jewish values. The tradition of Daniel and his three companions receiving an elite Babylonian education (Dan 1) also serves as a primary lesson for this. However, it did walk a fine cultural line. After all, even the protagonist in Daniel 1 takes precautions to ensure his Jewish piety is not undermined by his engagement with a foreign culture.

This mix of progressive politics, conservative religion, and eclectic culture probably explains why Simon had such wide appeal. Those more progressive and those more conservative than him could still find common ground with him. He was, therefore, a unifying figure at a critical juncture in Jewish life. However, he died in ca. 185 BC and attention turned to his Greek-educated sons, Onias III and Jesus.

Progressives

Cultural progressives in Jewish society embraced Greek education and all it brought, including Greek literature, art, philosophy, and ethics. Some progressives were religiously moderate, still holding to traditional Jewish religion while viewing it as essentially compatible with Greek religion. They were, therefore, at ease with a generic identification between Yahweh and Zeus. Within Judea they were probably a minority but still influential, especially as Jerusalem grew into a truly international hub.

Other progressives, however, retained little link to Jewish tradition at all, becoming Greek in practically every way. This trend was evident at least a century beforehand, when Ptolemy I conquered Jerusalem (cf. Isa 65:1–5, 11). At the beginning of Seleucid rule, they were a tiny minority, mainly because no Greek *polis* had been established inside Judea. It was, therefore, mainly the elite with ties outside Judea, such as the Tobiads, who were in thrall of Hellenism. Yet as Jerusalem grew in the early decades of the second century BC, its population could not help but be increasingly exposed to the Hellenism that had gripped the surrounding world. Gaza, Ashkelon, Joppa, Marisa, Samaria, Dor, Ptolemais-Acco, Scythopolis, Philoteria, Gadara, Pella, and Philadelphia were all Greek *poleis* by this time, exerting a cultural pull around the borders of Judea. For liberal Hellenizers, circumcision was not necessarily abandoned, but it was considered an embarrassment. By the late 170s BC some Jews were even taking measures to reverse their own circumcision, especially for the scorn it drew from Greeks at gymnasia (1 Macc 1:14–15). Judea was already an island in a Hellenistic sea. The question was whether it could withstand the rising cultural tide around it.

Conservatives

The majority of Jews in Judea were culturally conservative. They held an allegiance to Jewish tradition and observed the essential dictates of Torah, such as circumcision, food laws, the Sabbath, and worship in the Jerusalem temple. For many, the motivation for Torah observance was purely cultural. Righteousness was about orthopraxy—the preservation of a certain lifestyle and morality. They were generally opposed to Greek cultural influence, even though they could not escape it completely—Hellenism was simply the contextual reality. They harbored hopes for independence as the ideal means for preserving Jewish culture. Yet there were many who tended to a more moderate position as political pragmatists, willing to live as a cultural island in the Hellenistic sea. An excellent example was Ben Sira, who could call on God to maintain this cultural independence by acting against foreign aggression while hoping for international recognition of the Jewish God in a way that put Jews in the cultural ascendancy (Sir 36:1–22; see also 2.8.7 below). "For God and country" would have been an apt description of this position. Such pragmatism meant that they had little interest in a Davidic agenda. While there was little impetus for political activism in the early years of beneficent Seleucid rule, it was not long before cultural conservatives would be forced to take on politically active roles, which would turn some into extremists.

Other Jews were conservative out of religious conviction. The distinction between culture and religion is familiar to the modern mind, but in antiquity the two were practically indistinguishable. Nonetheless, it is a useful heuristic for appreciating the dynamics and conflicts that arose between certain Jewish groups at this time, as well as tracing the trajectory that would eventually see Jews and gentiles, with all their cultural differences, congregate together in the early church on the basis of belief.

Conservative Jews whose observance of Torah was a product of religious convictions were most concerned with orthodoxy—belief about who the deity was and what he required above all else. They were, of course, still concerned about culture (orthopraxy), but this stemmed from a religious persuasion. The new lease on life granted to Judea by Antiochus III propelled their theological pursuits. In the early years, some such conservatives were quite moderate, calling themselves "Intellectuals" (Heb. *maskilim*; Dan 11:33, 35; 12:10). They were steeped in Jewish tradition, blending Torah-based piety with sophisticated theological discourse and literary activity while adapting eclectically to the Hellenistic culture around them. Among their ranks were priests, scribes, sages, and laity from the educated middle class. They adopted those Greek modes of thought that permitted the expression of Jewish theology and ethics with greater clarity, such as quasi-Platonic metaphysics, the distinction between body and soul, and an academic curiosity that sought structure in history and creation. Their ideological forebears had already pressed these into the service of conservative theology and produced a highly developed apocalyptic eschatology. This is exemplified chiefly by the development of the book of 1 Enoch, which began life as various literary traditions in the early third century BC and achieved its final form in the late first century BC. It included discussion on the architecture of the spiritual realm (cf. Plato's realm of the forms), the nature of time and its correct observance, and spiritual criticism of political currents through apocalyptic metaphor and the retelling of Torah traditions. Thus the conservative authors of the five books of 1 Enoch (reminiscent of the five books of Torah) expanded biblical traditions as a vehicle for theological formulation and political critique.[20]

As time wore on, divisions among these moderate Intellectuals became more pronounced, especially as many were pulled towards the vortex of political power and more deeply conservative views. Some coalesced initially into a movement known as the *Hasidim* ("pious ones" or "devotees") in ca. 182 BC. But in the volatility and high stakes of the 160s BC, the political whirlpool would fling them apart and far from power (see 3.5.4 below). They would fragment into disparate groups with their own theological agendas and a growing intolerance of others, which the book of Daniel decries (Dan 11:35). These groups eventually tended to more fundamentalist attitudes, which critiqued other worldviews sharply. This was not a fundamentalism exhibited in a tendency to violence but to separatism—a flight mechanism rather than a fight mechanism. Arguably, this was prompted by quasi-Platonic metaphysics, which sought reality in the spiritual over the physical—something that distinguished religious conservatives from cultural conservatives. As such they became more interested in the word than the world or the sword. Some would leave Jewish politics behind to form an exclusive group of "Torah practitioners" (Heb. *'osey hatorah*)—a label that would give rise to the term "Essenes" (Gk. *essaioi* or *essēnoi*).[21] They prized the Scriptures and concentrated their efforts on preserving and interpreting them while practicing Torah-based piety. The Essenes would eventually look back to the early days of Seleucid rule—196 BC

---

20. The book of 1 Enoch was written originally in Aramaic, as fragments from Qumran prove. It was subsequently translated into Greek and thence into Ethiopic, the language in which it was predominantly preserved for centuries.

21. The etymology of the term "Essenes" is still contested. The derivation offered here is the one with the most scholarly support and appeals to the way the Qumran community referred to themselves (e.g., 1QpHab 7.10–12). See James C. VanderKam, *The Dead Sea Scrolls Today*, 2nd ed. (Grand Rapids: Eerdmans, 2010), 118–19.

to be precise—as "the end of wrath," which had begun with Nebuchadnezzar's destruction of the temple in 586 BC. It was a time when God "visited them, and caused an embedded root to flourish from Israel and from Aaron to possess his land, and to make his territory fat with goods" (CD 1.5–8). But they would also see these initial decades when they were undifferentiated from other Intellectuals and *Hasidim* as a time when they groped about "like blind men" (CD 1:9–10), for it was the time before the rise of their feted leader, the "Teacher of Righteousness," in 162 BC (see 3.5.4 below).[22]

Then there were the ultra conservatives, mainly scribes and educated laity, who did not wish to abscond from society but rather to leaven it with meticulous piety. Despite using Greek modes of thought, they advocated a strict cultural separation from the Hellenistic world to preserve a distinct Jewish identity that sought the deity's favor above all else. They would come to be known as "Separatists"—*parishin* in Aramaic (Heb. *perushim*), from which the term "Pharisees" would come. The educated in their ranks would lead them to discuss what was required to keep the Torah with granular precision. From this, they would develop new regulations and customs, which would eventually form their Oral Torah—a supplement to the written Torah, which they would hold as fundamental to correct observance and obedience to the deity.

Finally, there were Davidic loyalists. Their conservatism came from their belief that Yahweh's historic commitment to the Davidic dynasty had not expired (2 Sam 7:15–16; Ps 89:19–37[89:20–38 MT]) and that Yahweh was permanently faithful to his promises (cf. Ps 33:4; Isa 55:3). The restoration of a Davidic kingdom over a united Israel was, therefore, not negotiable. But the disappointments of history and their belief in ongoing prophetic activity led them to a more moderate outlook. There were Davidic loyalists among the ranks of the early Intellectuals and *Hasidim*, but those who were eventually pulled into the political whirlpool tended to have their Davidic convictions either diminished or stripped away in the ideological centrifuge. This explains why Davidic hope survived mainly away from the corridors of power rather than as an organized movement—an orthodoxy of mild-mannered moderates. Though the hope of Davidic loyalists was ultimately political, their faith was not invested in political process so much as the direct intervention of God in history—an apocalyptic eschatology grounded in messianic expectation. They thus shared much in common with religious and political conservatives, but they were culturally more moderate—uninterested in

---

22. Ḥanan Eshel, *The Dead Sea Scrolls and the Hasmonean State*, Studies in the Dead Sea Scrolls and Related Literature (Grand Rapids/Jerusalem: Eerdmans/Yad Ben-Zvi Press, 2008), 30–31.

legal minutiae for observing Torah and content to adapt within society as long as their religious and political convictions could be upheld.[23] We might describe their outlook as being "For God, king, and country," in that very order. Indeed, without a Davidic "king" in this formulation, "country" made no sense to them.

Thus there was considerable growth among Jewish conservatives in the early years of Seleucid rule, as well as division over the subsequent decades. With increasing internationalism and the concomitant rise in the Hellenistic tide, the challenge to religious conservatives grew, even as it provided the opportunity for them to flourish.

Summary

At the beginning of Seleucid rule over Judea, Jewish life found new invigoration but with little unity to guide it into the future. The country had been briefly united in its desire to heave the Ptolemaic yoke off its neck, but once removed, Judaism grew in various directions. This would eventually weaken its controlling center, where the priesthood lay. As long as Simon II occupied that center, the nation was somewhat stable, for no particular group was more privileged than another. Simon's tenure thus provided some cohesion. But with Simon's passing in ca. 185 BC Judaism became unfastened from this center and grew susceptible to the forces of the various groups pulling it in different directions. In time, this threatened to fray and even tear Judaism asunder.

	Politics	Culture	Religion	*Priority*
Simon II, Priests	Progressive	Moderate	Conservative	*All*
Hellenizers	Progressive	Progressive	Progressive	*Culture*
Ben Sira	Moderate	Conservative	Conservative	*Culture*
Intellectuals	Conservative	Moderate	Conservative	*Religion*
Hasidim	Conservative	Conservative	Conservative	*Religion*
Davidic Loyalists	Conservative	Moderate	Conservative	*Politics*

Added to this was the rising influence of Hellenism in Judea. Greek patterns of thought had already renovated the essential structures of Judaism,

---

23. Such cultural adaptability would prove pivotal when the early church opted to incorporate gentiles into its ranks without the need for circumcision.

with even the most conservative Jews making use of them in their theological formulations. Hellenism had transformed how to think about God, what it meant to be Jewish, and even how Judaism looked.[24] Thus all of Judaism had become porous at this time, but this was not necessarily detrimental. The question was just how porous it would be in the longer term—culturally, politically, and theologically. How would Judea manage its identity as Jerusalem took its place as a major urban center in a thoroughly Hellenized world? Would people resist ongoing change and tend towards an insular identity, becoming an unshakeable enclave distinct from all others—even their compatriots in the diaspora? Would they absorb change by engaging with it while keeping clear links to their heritage, like a Daniel among the Babylonians who retained certain boundaries of conscience and culture? Or would they trade the old for the new, seeking integration into the wider world that was moving apace with Greek ideals, thus becoming truly international citizens? The new latitude of Antiochus III's concessions gave the various schools of thought in Judea the opportunity to jockey not just for their own ideological turf within Judaism but for the right to define Jewish identity on an international stage. A tug-of-war for the heart of Judaism was developing, which would ultimately result in open conflict a generation later.

2.8.6 ANTIOCHUS III AND ROME

In addition to marrying his daughter, Cleopatra, to Ptolemy V, Antiochus III married two of his children to each other—the first time sibling marriage occurred among the Seleucids (194 BC). The match was between the crown prince, Antiochus, and his full sister, Laodice IV (Appian, *S.W.* 1.4).[25] Antiochus had made the crown prince co-ruler and co-signatory to his treaties in a bid to ensure their validity beyond his own death. But this plan came unstuck when the crown prince died just a year later (Livy, *Ab urbe cond.* 35.15). Antiochus took the death of his son hard, compounded by the death of his own wife, Laodice III, at about the same time.[26] He then married his daughter to his next eldest son, Seleucus, whom he promoted as his new heir.

---

24. Hengel, *Judaism and Hellenism*, 103–6; John J. Collins, *Jewish Cult and Hellenistic Culture: Essays on the Jewish Encounter with Hellenism and Roman Rule*, Supplements to the Journal for the Study of Judaism 100 (Leiden: Brill, 2005), 21–26.
25. Grainger, *The Seleukid Empire of Antiochus III*, 152.
26. Livy concocts the notion that Antiochus III feared his son would surpass his own achievements and so had him poisoned. It is more likely that an epidemic claimed both the crown prince and his mother. See Grainger, *The Seleukid Empire of Antiochus III*, 155–56.

The royal cult thus continued throughout the Seleucid realm[27] though the Jews, as a distinct ethnos within it, were not obliged to participate in it.

Antiochus went on to conquer Thrace and convince many Greek states to ally themselves to him. His creeping influence made the Romans nervous. They felt that their international interests were best served by a passive, compliant Greece serving as a buffer zone against Antiochus. But despite diplomatic concessions, the Greeks were increasingly seeing Rome as a meddling western bully, which made Greek-descended Antiochus seem like the protective big brother to many of them. The Roman Senate tried to convince Antiochus to stay out of Europe, but he argued that the Seleucid claim to Thrace was older than Rome's arrival in Greece. When Antiochus granted asylum to Rome's Carthaginian nemesis, Hannibal, the Roman Senate saw this as a step too far (Livy, *Ab urbe cond*. 34.40). Conflict became virtually inevitable.

The key moment came in 191 BC. Greece was in political pandemonium. The Romans had pulled their troops out of Greece in the hope that diplomacy might be the more effective weapon in influencing the Greek states. But when Antiochus arrived in Greece with a small force to intervene in the mayhem, the Romans sent several armies against him. Eventually, the two forces met at the famous Pass of Thermopylae where, three centuries earlier, Leonidas had led the Greeks' famous last stand against the army of Xerxes I. Now in 191 BC, both sides knew the tactical lessons of that battle and tried to outmaneuver each other. The Romans won the day. Unwilling to go down like Leonidas, Antiochus evacuated (Livy, *Ab urbe cond*. 36.16–19).

Though defeat was humiliating for Antiochus, it was not fatal. The question was how the Roman bear would respond now that it had been poked. He probably banked on the Romans simply re-stamping their authority over Greece, but they did much more than that. The Senate recruited a massive force that they put under the command of both Publius Cornelius Scipio Africanus, who had defeated Hannibal at Zama (202 BC), and his brother, Lucius Cornelius Scipio, who had been elected consul for 190 BC (Livy, *Ab urbe cond*. 36.45; 37.2). The brothers marched their army towards the Hellespont with a view to confronting Antiochus in Asia.

While they did, a major threat to Antiochus's control of Coele Syria emerged. Ptolemy V, now twenty years of age, commissioned a naval raid of the Phoenician coast, which saw the city of Aradus looted in violation of the

---

27. Angelos Chaniotis, "The Divinity of Hellenistic Rulers," in *A Companion to the Hellenistic World*, ed. Andrew Erskine (Malden, MA: Blackwell, 2005), 437, https://doi.org/10.1002/9780470996584.ch25.

treaty between the Seleucids and Ptolemies.[28] It is possible that the Romans put Ptolemy up to it. In any case, Antiochus was forced to dispatch troops to defend Coele Syria, leaving him weaker in the main theater of war in Asia Minor.[29]

Antiochus went into damage control by trying to reach a diplomatic solution to his unfolding crisis. The Scipio brothers demanded Antiochus pay war reparations and relinquish all of Asia Minor (Livy, *Ab urbe cond.* 37.34–36), but Antiochus did not agree to such terms. A showdown finally came in December 190 BC when Lucius Cornelius Scipio fought Antiochus near Magnesia in Lydia and inflicted a heavy defeat upon him (Livy, *Ab urbe cond.* 37.40–44).[30] The victory earned the younger Scipio the epithet "Asiaticus."[31]

Just as Scipio Africanus's defeat of Hannibal at Zama in 202 BC changed the political complexion of the western Mediterranean, so now Scipio Asiaticus's defeat of Antiochus at Magnesia in 190 BC changed the balance of power in the east. The event is described in the final vision of Daniel:

> He [Antiochus III] will turn his face towards the coastlands [the lands of the Aegean], and will capture many of them. But a commander [Scipio Asiaticus] will put a stop to his audacity, and turn him back without his audacity. He will turn his face to the fortresses of his own country, but will stumble, fall, and be found no more. (Dan 11:18–19)

With the subsequent Treaty of Apamea (188 BC), Rome imposed a humiliating surrender on Antiochus, akin to the modern Treaty of Versailles. He was compelled to abandon Thrace and all of Asia Minor up to the Taurus Mountains. Much of this territory was awarded to Eumenes II of Pergamum, whose kingdom now became a regional "kingdom of Asia" (Polybius, *Hist.* 21.46). Eumenes also received 477 silver talents from Antiochus as a fine.[32] Antiochus was also forced to pay Rome 15,000 silver talents over twelve years as war reparations.[33] He was practically stripped of his whole navy and prevented from acquiring elephant units or recruiting mercenaries outside his

---

28. John D. Grainger, *The Roman War of Antiochos the Great* (Leiden: Brill, 2002), 315, 362–63.
29. Grainger, *Roman War*, 315–16.
30. Magnesia in Lydia is to be distinguished from Magnesia on the Meander, located near Ephesus.
31. His brother, Scipio Africanus, had fallen ill before the battle and took no part in it.
32. In modern terms, this would be the equivalent of approximately US$715 million. Edwyn R. Bevan, *The House of Seleucus* (Cambridge: Cambridge University Press, 1902), 2:116.
33. In modern terms, this would be the equivalent of approximately US$22.5 billion.

own realm. He was to surrender Hannibal as a prisoner,[34] along with other notables to whom he had given asylum, and provide twenty hostages of Rome's choosing to be retained in Rome as guarantee of his compliance (Livy, *Ab urbe cond.* 37.45; 38.37–38).[35] The most notable of the hostages was Antiochus's youngest son, Mithridates.

The utter humiliation of both Carthage and the Seleucid kingdom within little more than a decade of each other gave Rome monumental clout throughout the Mediterranean and rich streams of revenue from multiple sources. After Apamea, the political pole in the Mediterranean shifted further west and settled upon the city of seven hills.

The punitive measures foisted on Antiochus were potentially crippling. He was not consigned to obscurity, but he was confined to a sphere in which his economic center of gravity was no longer in the Mediterranean but in Mesopotamia.[36] He quickly set about consolidating his sovereignty there and securing his far eastern frontiers where strife was brewing. He also had to find a means of funding the war reparations without stressing his internal economy. The following year (187 BC), he raided a temple in Elymais (i.e., Elam) said to contain an enormous deposit of gold and silver (Diodorus Siculus, *Bib. hist.* 29.11.15). This drew the extreme ire of the locals, who viewed his actions as both sacrilege and grand larceny. Antiochus was lynched and killed (Diodorus Siculus, *Bib. hist.* 28.3; 29.15).[37] The man who had turned around the fortunes of Judea had his own fortunes turned by the growing juggernaut of Rome and a mob of angry Elamites.

2.8.7 THE WISDOM OF BEN SIRA

Jesus ben-Eleazar ben-Sira is better known to us via his book simply as "Ben Sira."[38] Like Qoheleth before him, Ben Sira was a sage among Jerusalem's literati and probably a member of the Jewish Senate. Approximately a decade after Simon II dedicated the refurbished temple, Ben Sira penned his book in Jerusalem. He wrote originally in Hebrew (a nationalistic choice), and his grandson translated the work into Greek at Alexandria in 132 BC, adding an

---

34. Hannibal managed to flee Antiochus's service before he could be apprehended and given over to Rome. He escaped to Crete but soon after went to Bithynia, where he remained actively involved in agitations against Rome. He died there a few years later, though exactly when and how is disputed.
35. The treaty allowed for the hostages to be swapped with Rome's approval every three years.
36. Michael I. Rostovtzeff, *The Social and Economic History of the Hellenistic World* (Oxford: Oxford University Press, 1941), 2:696.
37. Grainger, *The Seleukid Empire of Antiochus III*, 190–91.
38. The book of Ben Sira is also known as "Sirach" or "Ecclesiasticus" (via its Greek title).

introductory preface to it.[39] The book is a discourse on wisdom, which gives us insight into Judaism when sovereignty over Judea passed from the Ptolemies to the Seleucids. Ben Sira even alludes to this seismic political change:

> Sovereignty is transferred from nation to nation,
> because of injustice and hubris and money. (Sir 10:8)

Although the early years of Seleucid rule were a positive boom for Judea, Ben Sira also experienced the significant downturn in fortunes after the Treaty of Apamea in 188 BC (see 2.8.6 above). These political and economic undulations led him, as a Jewish nationalist, to decry the rule of foreigners and call on God to overawe them:

> Have mercy on us, O Despot, God of all, and take heed.
> Lay the fear of you upon all the nations.
> Lift your hand against foreign nations,
> and let them see your sovereignty.
> As in their presence you have been sanctified by us,
> so in our presence may you be magnified by them.
> Let them acknowledge you, just as we acknowledge
> that there is no God but you, Lord.
> Give new signs and various wonders.
> Glorify your right arm and shoulder.
> Raise your anger and pour out your wrath.
> Carry away the opponent and crush the enemy.
> Hasten the day and remember your oath.
> Let them recount your great deeds.
> In fiery wrath let the survivor be consumed,
> and may those who harm your people find destruction.
> Crush the heads of enemy rulers,
> who say, "There is none but ourselves." (Sir 36:1–12 [36:1–9, LXX])

This was not a call to arms but to resistance through devotion to the God who could act on behalf of his chosen nation. These words exhibit a desire for Yahweh himself to conquer the nations and enforce their recognition of him as the one true God. This was not about conversion but cultural subjugation.

---

39. For centuries, only the Greek version of Ben Sira was known. It was not until the twentieth century that manuscript fragments of the Hebrew version were discovered.

Ben Sira's language imbibed both the prophetic spirit that pined for national restoration and the apocalyptic imagination that called on God to act personally to establish a divine empire protecting Jewish culture—a kingdom of God.

Jaded as he was by the ebb and tide of international politics, Ben Sira also disapproved of Joseph Tobias and his sons. Ben Sira makes indirect reference to them at various points throughout his work. For example, he describes the poor as "the feeding ground of the rich" (Sir 13:19), discusses the exploitation of the poor and the choice of some to wander about in search of employment, and offers cautions regarding lending and borrowing (Sir 13:1–26; 29:1–28). He also has pragmatic wisdom on avoiding precarious situations with "sinners," who are described in terms reminiscent of Joseph Tobias:

> Do not fight with a dominant man,
> or you might fall into his hands.
> Do not challenge a rich man,
> or he might oppose you with his influence. (Sir 8:1–2)

> Do not envy the prestige of a sinner,
> for you do not know what catastrophe will be his.
> Do not seek the good graces of the impious;
> remember that even in Hades they will never be justified.
> Keep far from the man who has the authority to murder,
> and you will never be anxious with the fear of death.
> And if you approach him, do not offend him,
> so that your life is not forfeited. (Sir 9:11–13a)

As an unabashed Jewish nationalist, Ben Sira openly criticized the peoples on Judea's periphery:

> By two nations is my soul outraged,
> and the third is not even a nation:
> the residents of Seir, and the Philistines,
> and the deplorable nation that lives at Shechem. (Sir 50:25–26)[40]

In referring to the Idumeans as "residents of Seir," Ben Sira rhetorically put them back in their native homeland, southeast of the Dead Sea, rather than

---

40. This reading follows the manuscripts of Ben Sira's original Hebrew version. Ben Sira's grandson, who translated the book into Greek, replaced the reference to "the residents of Seir" with "the residents on the mountain of Samaria."

the southern hills of Judea, which they occupied in his day. The Philistines on the coastal plain had now become thoroughly Hellenized.[41] By describing the Samaritans with reference to Shechem rather than Mount Gerizim, he denied any legitimacy to the Samaritan temple.

Ben Sira hoped for Jewish independence so that the Jews might be free to practice their culture in their own land unhindered. Critically, even though he had historical sympathy for the Davidic covenant, he did not see the need for restoring a Davidic king. On the contrary, he consigned the importance of the Davidic dynasty entirely to the past:

> Except for David and Hezekiah and Josiah,
> they all went absolutely wrong.
> Since they abandoned the Law of the Most High,
> the kings of Judah ceased.
> For they gave their horn [i.e., power] to others,
> and their glory to a foreign nation.
> They [i.e., a foreign nation] burned the chosen holy city,
> and desolated its streets,
> as per the hand of Jeremiah, whom they mistreated,
> though from the womb he was consecrated a prophet,
> to uproot and harm and destroy,
> similarly, to rebuild and to replant. (Sir 49:4–7)

Ben Sira deduced that Davidic rule came to an absolute end because of the dynasty's failure to obey the Torah and its mistreatment of the prophets. In his estimation, of chief importance for the Jewish nation was the temple cult, the priesthood, and the culture that emanated from these:

> With all your soul, respect the Lord,
> and revere his priests.
> With all your strength, love your maker,
> and do not abandon his ministers.
> Fear the Lord and honor the priest,
> and give him his share, as you are commanded. (Sir 7:19–31a)

---

41. Philistine roots went partially back to peoples in the Aegean, albeit from the twelfth century BC. Their seafaring culture meant they had maintained links with the Aegean world for centuries, and they were, therefore, open to Hellenism.

In his "Praise of the Fathers," the three figures Ben Sira deemed worthy of the greatest commendation were Moses, Aaron, and Phinehas (Sir 45:1–23)—all priestly figures. He even used the Davidic covenant as a mere analogy for the greatness of the perpetual covenant of Aaronic priesthood (Sir 45:24–25). He equated Zion wholly with the temple as a cultic institution, without any vestige of its royal Davidic significance (Sir 36:18–19). The prophecies concerning Zion were, in his mind, entirely wrapped up with the temple and the priesthood rather than the Davidic dynasty. The Davidic kings were integral to Jewish heritage but as a phenomenon of the past. David's temple-building dynasty had been eclipsed by Simon II, the builder of a new temple, for whom Ben Sira gushed with praise (Sir 50:1–21). When Ben Sira called upon God to deal with Israel's enemies and restore the nation, he couched it as the restoration of the people around the temple and its city (Sir 36:13–22 [36:10–16, LXX]), without a royal messiah anywhere in sight.[42]

As a sage living in a Hellenistic world, Ben Sira eclectically adapted Hellenistic notions that were compatible with Jewish ideals. For example, he reiterates the ideas of the Greek poet Theognis of Megara on the subject of friendship (Sir 6:5–17).[43] He contemplated what made a good life and found this anchored in observing Torah and earning a favorable legacy. He approved of the pursuit of learning and of travel to foreign lands for knowledge (Sir 39:4), but he could not approve of training in the gymnasium, with its shameless focus on the body. He was open to Greek thought, as long it could be "Judaized," and opposed those elements that could potentially dismantle Judaism.[44] He deemed those who absorbed Greek culture without an appropriate Jewish filter as "sinners" who would "ruin their inheritance" and derided those Jews who were embarrassed by circumcision and the dietary laws (Sir 41:5–15). To his mind, Hellenism was no idle threat. Certain aspects of Greek culture could be adapted to Jewish ideals, but some could be profoundly damaging. And it was the elite he saw as the most susceptible to liberal Greek culture, which put the entire nation at risk of losing its essential identity.

In political terms, Ben Sira's wisdom trod a delicate line. The Tobiads, who wielded considerable power and influence, had bankrolled the temple reconstruction, but they were open to Hellenism and its excesses. For Ben Sira,

---

42. In the LXX, the final line reads, "according to the blessing of Aaron concerning your people." The text of Ben Sira is notoriously difficult to establish at certain points due to the variety of manuscripts.

43. Jack T. Sanders, *Ben Sira and Demotic Wisdom*, Society of Biblical Literature Monograph Series 28 (Chico, CA: Scholars Press, 1983), 29–38.

44. Sanders, *Ben Sira and Demotic Wisdom*, 58.

such syncretism risked diluting Jewish identity and needed to be opposed. In Simon II, who was related to the Tobiads, Ben Sira identified a trustworthy stalwart who could anchor the nation to its conservative ideals through fastidious devotion to Torah and the promotion of the temple cult. But Simon died in ca. 185 BC, shortly before Ben Sira penned his wisdom, and Simon's sons, Onias III and Jesus, had evidently received a Greek education.[45] By this time, Jerusalem had become an important city in a progressive Hellenistic world. Ben Sira's book provides a moderate prelude to the machinations that would shortly unfold.

2.8.8 SELEUCUS IV AND THE HELIODORUS AFFAIR

With the death of Antiochus III in 187 BC, Seleucus IV inherited both the Seleucid throne and the Treaty of Apamea with Rome. As a republic ruled by the "Senate and people of Rome," the Roman state had legal status in and of itself rather than being synonymous with the person of a king. Thus its treaties survived the death of any foreign signatories. It was for this reason also that Rome could embody the essence of its own state in the image of a goddess—the genius Roma—while the Hellenistic kings only ever embodied the state in the image of themselves and their royal cult.

Nevertheless, Seleucus soon began flouting the restrictions of Apamea by rebuilding his military machine to defend Coele Syria against Ptolemy V.[46] This became more urgent after 186 BC when Ptolemy finally extinguished the Great Revolt in Egypt. Seleucus skimped out on some of the war reparations to Rome, but he could not afford to neglect them altogether and risk Roman reprisal.[47] What's more, his brother, Mithridates, was still being held hostage in Rome, along with other Seleucid notables, as security against his failure to pay. Any royal death would be a blow to the royal and divine honor of the Seleucid dynasty.

Seleucus adopted two policies to pay for all his expenses.[48] First, he tightened the taxation screws. This hit Judea hard and dredged up memories of the burdensome years under the Ptolemies. His second policy, implemented

---

45. Simon's sons were probably in their teenage years when the battle of Raphia confirmed Ptolemaic political ascendancy over Judea in 217 BC. They would have been in the midst of their education at the time, making it distinctly possible that the sons of the Jewish ethnarch were given privileges in the very hub of Greek learning: the Museum of Alexandria.
46. Benjamin Scolnic, "Heliodorus and the Assassination of Seleucus IV According to Dan 11:20 and 2 Macc 3," *JAJ* 7.3 (2016): 361, https://doi.org/10.13109/jaju.2016.7.3.354.
47. *Pace* Scolnic, "Heliodorus and the Assassination of Seleucus IV," 360.
48. Ernst Haag, *Das hellenistische Zeitalter: Israel und die Bible im 4. bis 1. Jahrhundert v. Chr.*, vol. 9 of *Biblische Enzyklopädie* (Stuttgart: Kohlhammer, 2003), 102.

in 178 BC, was to take state control of temple treasuries throughout Coele Syria.[49] This was probably prompted by the sudden death of Ptolemy V in 180 BC. According to Diodorus (Diodorus Siculus, *Bib. hist.* 29.29), Ptolemy was poisoned by his courtiers for suggesting that they were the "moneybags" who would fund his war to recover Coele Syria.[50] His heir, Ptolemy VI Philometor, was still a child, so his mother, Cleopatra I, assumed leadership of the Ptolemaic state on his behalf. Cleopatra was Seleucus's full sister, and the Egyptians nicknamed her "The Syrian." Though she had been of little direct value to her father, Antiochus III (Dan 11:17), she now became immensely valuable to her brother, for she immediately curtailed all Ptolemaic plans to recover Coele Syria. Though no ancient sources tell us that Seleucus saw in this an opportunity to make a grab at Egypt for himself, it is the most likely explanation of the geopolitical chess match he played over the next few years. With his sister, Cleopatra, as his queen piece, Seleucus had a member of his own family able to keep in check any anti-Seleucid moves in Egypt. But though she was onside with her brother's intentions, she was also unwilling to sacrifice the future of her own son. Realizing that his queen piece was only of use to him while she was regent, Seleucus had to act quickly and nab Egypt before his nephew came of age. Once accomplished, Seleucus would gain himself an illustrious kingdom to rival that of Alexander the Great, and he could then challenge the supremacy of Rome in the Mediterranean. Such a prospect would undoubtedly have alarmed Rome. Therefore, if Seleucus was to have any success, he needed to play a decoy game, which diverted Rome's attention to another place on the Mediterranean chessboard.

In 178 BC Seleucus played his gambit: he sacrificed one of his own pieces by marrying one of his daughters to Perseus, the new king of Macedon.[51] He thereby forged an alliance with a state that Rome deemed an endemic troublemaker (Diodorus Siculus, *Bib. hist.* 29.30). This hoodwinked the Roman Senate into thinking that the Seleucids were itching once again for a leading role in the Aegean. Rome, therefore, focused its attentions on Greece. To put Seleucus back in his place, the Roman Senate hankered for the payment of

---

49. Hannah M. Cotton and Michael Wörrle, "Seleukos IV to Heliodoros: A New Dossier of Royal Correspondence from Israel," *Zeitschrift für Papyrologie und Epigraphik* 159 (2007): 203; Scolnic, "Heliodorus and the Assassination of Seleucus IV," 364.

50. We cannot tell whether there is any historicity to the anecdote, for we cannot rule out other potential causes of Ptolemy V's death. Since his parents were full siblings, Ptolemy's health may have been compromised by congenital issues. We should not preclude foul play on the part of Cleopatra, his wife, either. Cf. John D. Grainger, *The Fall of the Seleukid Empire (187–75 BC)* (Barnsley: Pen and Sword, 2015), 7.

51. Perseus succeeded his father, Philip V, who died the year before. See Grainger, *The Fall of the Seleukid Empire*, 8.

its war reparations, which were due in full in 177/6 BC. To lull the Romans into a false sense of security, Seleucus was prepared to surrender the money for these reparations. But to do this and fund an expeditionary force to invade Egypt, Seleucus needed plenty of money. The source of this money was to be the temple treasuries of Coele Syria.

The Heliodorus Stele, a fragmentary Greek inscription from Marisa in the Idumean lowlands, contains a communiqué of Seleucus IV to his chief minister and most trusted friend, Heliodorus, dated to August 178 BC. It notes the appointment of an official named Olympiodorus as minister for temple affairs throughout Coele Syria. His appointment brought Coele Syria into administrative line with the rest of the Seleucid kingdom.[52] Before this time, the temples of Coele Syria had enjoyed considerable autarchy and Jerusalem, with the many concessions granted to it, had gained the most. But this came to an end with the appointment of Olympiodorus, to whom the high priest in Jerusalem now became an underling. A stone copy of the edict, like the one found at Marisa, was almost certainly erected in Jerusalem also.

Most citizens in Judea were probably outraged by the appointment and viewed it as administrative overreach. Seleucus's claim that he was "taking the greatest care for [their] security" and "inclined to [increase] the honor of the gods" (lines 14–15, 36) must have seemed culturally insensitive to the Jews.[53] In accordance with the classic theology of retribution, the blessing of God flowed to the Jewish people when proper honor was accorded to the deity, which included the unfettered operation of all temple institutions under the rightful high priest. The banking function of the temple, which had helped renew the civic life of Jerusalem, was a product of this and demonstrated the veracity of the theological principles. But the appointment of Olympiodorus threatened all this. Onias III had by now succeeded his father as high priest and steered an ideologically and politically centrist course, like his father had. He had, after all, received a Greek education. But having Olympiodorus as his direct superior put him at odds with the Seleucid bureaucracy, forcing him to adopt an ideologically and politically more conservative stance. Even if Olympiodorus did nothing to the temple or Onias, he was a gentile idolater given supreme authority over the institution that defined Jewish identity.[54] The halcyon days of Seleucid rule over Judea had come to a thudding halt.

---

52. Cotton and Wörrle, "Seleukos IV to Heliodoros," 195–98.
53. Dov Gera, "Olympiodorus, Heliodorus and the Temples of Koilē Syria and Phoinikē," *Zeitschrift für Papyrologie und Epigraphik* 169 (2009): 130–31.
54. Gera, "Olympiodorus," 136, 149. In modern terms, Olympiodorus's appointment was akin to a non-Muslim being appointed administrator of the Kaaba in Mecca or a non-Catholic becoming overseer of the Vatican.

Only liberal Jews, who were less scrupulous about the temple's administration, took less exception to Olympiodorus's appointment. Now, some twenty years into Seleucid rule, their ranks had grown to include principal members of the temple personnel. The instillation of a Greek temple minister, then, was not a matter of great concern to them as it facilitated the integration of Jerusalem into the wider Hellenistic world. They were ready and willing to be citizens of the kingdom, not just of Judea. But with Onias moving towards a conservative stance, the ideological divide between liberal and conservative Jews widened appreciably.

Ironically, the liberal Tobiad family sided with Onias. This might not have been out of theological principle so much as economic necessity. Their monies were still the fiscal backbone of the treasury, with the money from the estate of Hyrcanus still a notable deposit (2 Macc 3:11). Whether they continued to hold tax farming rights under the Seleucids is unknown. Regardless, the appointment of Olympiodorus made their monies vulnerable to confiscation by the crown.

As Onias III stepped towards conservativism, he vacated the political center where he might have held all Jewish parties together in solidarity. Thus, Seleucus's policy polarized Jewish society more starkly between its conservatives and progressive Hellenizers, all in the context of integrating Judea within a Hellenistic milieu. Moreover, there was no single conservative bloc within Judaism. There were, rather, many emerging and competing conservative factions, each with their own distinct ideology and vision for the future (see 2.8.5 above). While Onias could still unite them in opposing the royal decree, he could not dissolve their theological differences.

For the events that transpired after the appointment of Olympiodorus, we are dependent on the author of 2 Maccabees, who relied on the five-volume work of Jewish historian Jason of Cyrene (late second century BC). Along with other key sources, we may discern a timeline of events.[55]

One of the key figures was a certain Simon, who was custodian (*prostatēs*) of the temple (not to be confused with the high priest as custodian of the Jewish nation). Simon was part of a liberal family of priests in favor of

---

55. Extrapolating the developments is no easy matter, since Jason's work is no longer extant. Thus, we do not know how faithfully the author of 2 Maccabees summarized his work, nor how accurate Jason's history was. There is also the issue of trying to see past the presentation of the miraculous. Contra Gera, I discern differentiated roles for Heliodorus, who is mentioned in 2 Maccabees, and Olympiodorus, who is not. I also disagree with Gera's estimation that Apollonius Thraseas (brother of Ptolemy Thraseas [2 Macc 3:5]) was actually Apollonius, son of Menestheus (2 Macc 4:4). In discerning a timeline of these events, I see General Ptolemy Thraseas being succeeded as governor of Coele Syria by his brother, Apollonius Thraseas. He, in turn, was succeeded by Dorymenes (mentioned on the Heliodorus Stele) who was then succeeded by Apollonius, son of Menestheus. Cf. Gera, "Olympiodorus," 140–47.

integrating Judea into the wider Seleucid kingdom.⁵⁶ Simon and Onias III had a falling out over the administration of the agora in Jerusalem, which suggests that the agora had become part of the temple's function. The nature of the disagreement is never spelled out, but it is likely that it pertained to whether commercial revenues landed in the temple treasury or in Seleucid coffers.⁵⁷ As a liberal Hellenizing Jew, Simon was inclined to collaborate with the Seleucids.

Simon appealed over Onias's head to Apollonius Thraseas, governor of Coele Syria and Phoenicia. This suggests that the disagreement occurred in ca. 181 BC, shortly before the death of Ptolemy V and before the appointment of Olympiodorus. It brought the wealth of the Jerusalem temple to the attention of Seleucus IV, who was then able to incorporate it into his plans to invade Egypt. Seleucus used one of his most trusted friends, his chief minister Heliodorus, to investigate matters in 179 BC. The wealth stored in Jerusalem's temple was confirmed, along with that of neighboring sanctuaries like Mount Gerizim. All this allowed Seleucus to pursue his grand strategy by making an alliance with Perseus of Macedon and appointing Olympiodorus as minister of temple affairs to gain direct access to the temple treasuries.

Not long after his appointment, Olympiodorus was tasked with commandeering funds from the temples, ostensibly to pay for the war reparations owed to Rome but surreptitiously to fit out a Seleucid expeditionary force. Seleucus still owed the Romans at least 2,000 silver talents, the amount due for at least two years (178–177 BC), if not more. The temple custodian, Simon, had intimated that something close to this amount was stored in the Jerusalem temple. But when questioned for a direct accounting, Onias claimed there were only 400 talents of silver and 200 talents of gold, comprising the deposits of "widows and orphans" and the estate of Hyrcanus (2 Macc 3:10–11).⁵⁸ It is possible that Onias deliberately underplayed the amount held in the treasury. In this case, his position was now under serious threat for misleading his superiors,

---

56. According to the Greek text of 2 Macc 3:4, Simon was a Benjamite and therefore a layman. However, two factors suggest that he was a priest. First, his position as temple custodian (*prostatēs*) was almost certainly given to a priest, as a layman would be unqualified to enter certain parts of the temple. Second, the Old Latin and Armenian versions of 2 Maccabees associate Simon with the priestly order of Bilgah (cf. 1 Chr 24:14; Neh 12:5, 18). The author of 2 Maccabees has a transparent bias against Simon and his brothers, Menelaus and Lysimachus, so we should understand the claim of Benjamite ancestry as a deliberate fabrication. See Gabriele Boccaccini, *Beyond the Essene Hypothesis: The Parting of the Ways Between Qumran and Enochic Judaism* (Grand Rapids: Eerdmans, 1998), 90, n. 19.

57. Cf. Honigman, *Tales of High Priests and Taxes*, 340–42; idem. "Searching for the Social Location of Literate Judean Elites," 211–12.

58. In modern terms, this amounts to approximately US$900 million. In antiquity, the value of silver was close to that of gold because it was rarer than it is today.

playing right into the hands of his rival, Simon. It is even possible that Simon caught wind of a secret account (Hyrcanus's money) in the temple. The specific mention of the funds from Hyrcanus's estate in 2 Maccabees 3:11 makes it entirely likely that the high priest Simon II had become trustee of the estate as part of his agreement with the Tobiad brothers and that Onias III inherited this trusteeship when he succeeded him. Furthermore, sensing a potential threat to their wealth, the Tobiads (and perhaps others) probably made a run on their own deposits in the treasury, drastically reducing its available capital. Thus, when Olympiodorus took stock of the treasury in Jerusalem, a secret account might well have been uncovered, but the treasury still contained far less than what Simon had originally reported.[59]

Even so, Seleucus needed to secure monies to make his political strategy work. This placed Onias in a precarious position. If he turned the money over to Seleucus, he would be pulling the plug out of a booming economy and betraying the Jewish people, whose liquid assets were held in the temple and who depended on its good function for their financial welfare and the blessing of God. Onias was risking a financial and theological depression. But to take a stand against Seleucus's wishes meant potentially causing a rebellion. According to 2 Maccabees 3:16–17, Onias grew pale and physically trembled under the pressure.

Perhaps Olympiodorus tried to extricate the money from the temple and failed. Perhaps he realized the amount of fierce opposition the move was igniting in Judea and appealed to his superiors for backup. Whatever the case, it was Heliodorus who stepped into frame, as Seleucus delegated to him the task of extracting the money from Jerusalem. Since Heliodorus was the king's most trusted friend and advisor, this immediately raised the stakes and put Judea into panic. But the fate of Antiochus III, who died trying to extricate money from a temple in Elymais a decade earlier, probably played on Heliodorus's mind. It is probably for this reason that Seleucus himself did not head to Jerusalem but sent the next most powerful person in his kingdom.

According to 2 Maccabees 3:14–35, Onias and the population of Jerusalem went into immediate mourning and made perpetual supplication to God. Here the account takes a miraculous turn. Upon his arrival at the temple treasury, Heliodorus and his bodyguard are said to have been confronted by a divine cavalryman in golden armor. The horse's hooves kicked Heliodorus to the ground, whence two other divine figures of muscular proportions began flogging him.

---

59. We do not know whether the money from Hyrcanus's estate was held secretly in the temple or with public knowledge, but its mention (2 Macc 3:11) is conspicuous and feels rhetorically like an exposé.

Heliodorus's bodyguard managed to spirit him away, but he was now fighting for his life. Onias interceded with the deity on behalf of Heliodorus, who was then miraculously restored. After another visitation by the divine messengers, Heliodorus offered a sacrifice to the deity in gratitude and departed Jerusalem in humility, without a penny taken from the temple treasury.

It is tempting to dismiss the account out of hand and propose that Seleucus never got the chance to raid the temple's coffers. However, this seems unlikely in the larger political machinations of the period and subsequent events. It is more probable that what transpired had such a surprising outcome that it was immediately interpreted as divine intervention, and memory of it was quickly embellished. The image of Heliodorus that emerges from various sources is of a deeply religious and even superstitious man. Perhaps he felt he was being asked to commit sacrilege and did not wish to anger the deity whose temple he was robbing. Perhaps he did not wish to suffer the fate of Antiochus III and got cold feet or had a dream that dissuaded him from carrying out the king's command. Alternatively, he may very well have been ambushed by armed men who prevented him accomplishing his mission. The Tobiads were certainly known for using violent tactics, and the divine figures in the story do appear rather human and thuggish. If Heliodorus was physically attacked, he might also have been nursed back to health on Onias's orders, as a gracious gesture towards a religious man. Whatever the case, Heliodorus returned to Antioch without securing any money from the Jerusalem temple, and Onias was feted as the hero of his people.

The Heliodorus Affair left Seleucus without the funds he needed to pay the Romans and with his plans for Egypt fading away. When the war reparations failed to materialize in Rome by 176 BC, the Senate turned the screws on Seleucus. Under the Treaty of Apamea, the Seleucid hostages in Rome could be swapped every three years for other hostages of Rome's choosing (Polybius, *Hist.* 21.43). Invoking this clause, they demanded a swap, trading Seleucus's brother, Mithridates (now about forty years of age), for Seleucus's nine-year old son, the crown prince Demetrius. The maneuver told Seleucus that the Senate still recognized his rule but that they expected him to behave circumspectly, which included paying what he owed them. Thus the young Demetrius was shipped off to Rome in late 176 BC and his uncle, Mithridates, who had lived the previous twelve years in Rome and acquired a penchant for Roman ways, was released (Appian, *S.W.* 45). Jerusalem had played an unexpected role in the foiling of Seleucus's plans.

These plans took a further hit when, in the spring of 176 BC, Seleucus's sister, Cleopatra I, died unexpectedly in Alexandria. Seleucus thus lost his "queen" piece in Egypt.[60] More damaging to Seleucus, though, was the rift that developed between himself and Heliodorus. It seems the king's once trusted friend never forgave him for sending him to Jerusalem and putting his life at risk (2 Macc 3:38). He lost faith in Seleucus as a king and, on 3 September 175 BC, assassinated him in Antioch and took the reins of government for himself. The final vision of Daniel refers to the Heliodorus Affair and its murderous consequences in the most economical terms:

> In his [Antiochus III's] place, will arise one [Seleucus IV] who makes an inspector [Heliodorus] intrude for the majesty of his kingship. But in a few years, he [Seleucus IV] will be broken, though not in the heat of battle. (Dan 11:20)[61]

It is possible, though not certain, that Heliodorus was put up to the assassination by the Roman Senate.[62] If so, Heliodorus may have informed the Romans of Seleucus's plans for Egypt, and rather than starting an expensive international war to stop Seleucus, the Senate employed a disgruntled Heliodorus to work some cutthroat diplomacy. Whatever the case, Heliodorus had aimed to rule as regent for Seleucus's infant son, Antiochus, since the actual crown prince, Demetrius, was now a hostage in Rome. But Heliodorus had barely settled himself as regent when he was ousted by Rome's ally, Eumenes II of Pergamum, who handed power to Seleucus's recently released brother, Mithridates (Appian, *S.W.* 45). If Heliodorus was on Rome's payroll, he quickly became their dispensible patsy.

When news reached Mithridates of his brother's assassination, he was in Athens on his leisurely way back to Antioch. When he finally arrived and became regent for his infant nephew, he signaled his intention to take the throne itself by taking a throne name: Antiochus IV Epiphanes ("Antiochus, the divine manifestation"). The vision of Daniel marks his rise to power with an ominous announcement:

> And in his [Seleucus IV's] place will arise a despicable one. (Dan 11:21a)

---

60. Hölbl, *A History of the Ptolemaic Empire*, 143.
61. The phrase "not in the heat of battle" signifies that Seleucus died an ignoble death rather than a valiant death in pursuit of his own policies. See Scolnic, "Heliodorus and the Assassination of Seleucus IV," 360–61.
62. Grainger argues that the real assassin was Mithridates (Antiochus IV), since he eventually controlled the information about Seleucus's death (*The Fall of the Seleukid Empire*, 11). It seems more credible that Heliodorus was indeed the assassin and that, if Mithridates had any hand in his brother's death, it was via his handlers in Rome.

2.9 CONCLUSION

Hellenistic rule changed the complexion of Judaism. Greek influence was already apparent in the Levant before the fall of the Persian Empire, but it was modulated by the imperialism of the Persians. With Persia's downfall, the magnetism of Greek culture and language over the Levant became far stronger. The political, cultural, and economic pole shifted from Mesopotamia to the Mediterranean, and Judea and Samaria accordingly turned west.

The change in sovereignty spelled the end of the Sanballat dynasty in Samaria, and Greek settlement came into the heart of the Levant with the conversion of Samaria into a *polis*. Shechem became the new center of the Samaritan community, and the Samaritan temple on nearby Mount Gerizim continued to flourish. Alexander's conquests alleviated the stress on the temple in Jerusalem, bringing it back from the brink of oblivion, but it did not compare with Mount Gerizim for size and constituents until the onset of Seleucid rule.

The political volatility in the Levant after Alexander's death was stemmed by Ptolemy I's conquest of Jerusalem in 301 BC. This brutal event was a harsh blow to the Jews, many of whom now found themselves as residents of the new Greek *polis* at Alexandria. This city now effectively became the hub of Judaism, such that by the reign of Ptolemy II, the average Jew was a native Greek speaker in Egypt. Jewish synagogues or "prayer houses" (Gk. *proseuchai*) appeared throughout Egypt, and the translation of the Jewish Scriptures into Greek began with the Torah. The Jerusalem temple held pride of place even in the heart of Jews in Egypt. But Jerusalem remained a small provincial town in the hills of Judea, far from the corridors of powers and the shipping lanes of trade.

The relative political unimportance of Jerusalem is, at least initially, what spurred conservatives to preserve and develop the prophetic traditions and the Psalms. These traditions undergirded the ideological centrality of Jerusalem in the Jewish psyche. The roots of Jerusalem's importance lay in Davidic or Zion theology—the notion that God had elected the dynasty of David to rule Israel on his behalf and that the temple of Jerusalem was the physical symbol of this divine election. "Zion" was the nexus of Davidic kingship and temple worship. Yet the priestly leadership of the Jewish nation continued unchallenged throughout the Hellenistic era, excluding members of the Davidic family from the exercise of actual power. Zion theology was accordingly expropriated by the priestly circles in Jerusalem for their purposes so that, by the end of the Hellenistic era, "Zion" was synonymous solely with the temple cult, without any vestige of its original Davidic significance. The Davidic family also disappeared from the circles of Jerusalem's elite, experiencing a decimating event at the time of Ptolemy's siege of Jerusalem in 301 BC. The clan was reduced but survived, with at least some of its members deported to Alexandria. It was similar to what had happened to the dynasty at the hands of the Babylonians in the early sixth century BC. Despite its descent into practical irrelevance, the Davidic family and its ideological allies firmly believed that the character of God was unchanging. They thus clung to the eternal covenant that God had made originally with David, believing that Davidic leadership was still central to his purposes and that without it, Israel's identity was impaired. The political realities of the Hellenistic era, though, meant that hopes of Davidic rule developed into apocalyptic eschatological hopes.

For the entire third century BC Judea and Samaria were caught in the middle of the rivalry between the Ptolemies and the Seleucids while Rome grew in stature over in the west. Under the Ptolemies, most Jews experienced backbreaking taxation. This made some, like the Tobiads, extremely wealthy but drove many others to poverty and misery. The Seleucid conquest of Coele Syria in 198 BC alleviated this. Antiochus III granted special privileges to Jerusalem, which transformed it from a lowly highland town into a burgeoning holy city of international significance. The temple was refurbished as a veritable acropolis, which the high priest Simon II rededicated in ca. 192 BC, and the Tobiads helped turn it into a fully functioning bank, which funded an economic recovery.

Under Antiochus III, the Jews of Judea thrived. But the latitude he granted them also enabled the disparate groups within Judaism to grow in disparate ways, each with their own vision of Jewish identity. With the passing of Simon II (ca. 185 BC) the political center within Judaism quickly disappeared, and the gulf between conservative Jews and liberal Hellenizing Jews widened even further, pulling Judea in opposite directions. This tension had already been exacerbated after the Romans defeated Antiochus at Magnesia (190 BC) and then imposed the damaging Treaty of Apamea (188 BC) on his realm. During the subsequent reign of Seleucus IV, Judea began once again to feel the stringencies of taxation, and Seleucus's political ambitions brought Judea to the brink of rebellion. By this stage, the cracks of division within Judaism were opening up. With Jerusalem now a major international city in the Hellenistic world, the stakes were much higher for all involved.

When Antiochus IV ascended the Seleucid throne, the Jews still retained their cultural distinctiveness as an official ethnos within the Seleucid kingdom. This gave them the right to practice their ancestral laws unhindered, without the need to participate in the royal cult. But liberal Hellenizing Jews had also become a major faction, and the culture war with Judaism was one of the factors behind the conflict that would erupt during the reign of Antiochus IV. Hellenism had renovated the thought structures of Judaism, even in the most conservative Jewish circles. Greek philosophical ideas had irreversibly entered Jewish theological discourse and become mainstream. These ideas did not enter Jewish thought *de novo*; they found purchase in prior theological and cultural notions within Judaism. Thus they did not hijack Jewish thought but developed it along prior trajectories. These ideas would persist into the first century, such as the quasi-Platonic metaphysic of a spiritual reality lying behind the structure of the mundane, physical world and its institutions; that the body and the soul could, in theory, be distinguished; that life might be possible beyond death; that thought was as important as practice; and that the individual was as important as the corporate.

This last notion was particularly consequential as it brought the tenet of decentralization, which lay at the heart of Greek religion, to bear on the highly centralized religion of Judaism. The resultant tension was lived out in the growing competition between the various groups within Judaism towards the end of the period, as each group vied for the supremacy of its own vision of corporate Jewish identity. According to Jewish conservatives, Yahweh, the God of Israel, was one, so Israel too was necessarily one. But which conservatives deserved to define and lead Israel in worship of its one God? The attitude of "live and let live," which characterized most Greek culture, could not prevail in the tension of a highly centralized Judaism during this era. This tension would become a key factor in the political and theological developments of the subsequent Hasmonean era.

Finally, the political, cultural, and economic pole shifted westward over the course of the Hellenistic era. It started in the eastern Mediterranean, but as the Ptolemies, Seleucids, and the Greek states of the Aegean vied with each other for supremacy, it ended beyond them all in Rome. By 175 BC the Romans dominated the Mediterranean world. In the subsequent Hasmonean era, the Romans would continue to exert a huge influence. It meant that Jews (and Samaritans) continued facing west across the sea, which the Romans would eventually come to call *mare nostrum*—"Our Sea."

PART 3
THE HASMONEAN ERA (167–63 BC)

3.1 INTRODUCTION

3.1.1 SOURCES FOR THE HASMONEAN ERA

On 6 December 167 BC (the fifteenth day of Kislev) a small altar was built along the side of the large altar of burnt offering before Yahweh's sanctuary in the Jerusalem temple.[1] Ten days later, sacrifices were offered upon it in the name of Olympian Zeus (1 Macc 1:54–59; 2 Macc 6:1). In the visions of Daniel, this event was described as an "abomination of desolation" (Dan 9:27; 11:31; 12:11). It desecrated the temple precinct and plunged Judea into a civil war that involved fighting betwixt Jewish factions, harsh persecution of conservative Jews, and guerrilla warfare against the Seleucids. It was a battle for the identity of the Jewish nation.

Our information for the conflict and the subsequent period comes from several sources. The books of 1 and 2 Maccabees are perhaps the most important. Contrary to the suggestion of the nomenclature, they are not successive volumes, but separate works. The author of 2 Maccabees summarized the (now lost) five-volume work of Jewish historian Jason of Cyrene, written in Greek in the mid-second century BC. The author traced the conflict back to the Heliodorus Affair (see 2.8.8 above), focusing on the struggle for control of the temple from 178 to 161 BC. He exhibited a pro-Hasmonean bias, though his belief in an eschatological resurrection of the righteous (cf. 2 Macc 7:14, 23) set him slightly apart from the Hasmonean inner circles. His beliefs were similar to those of the Pharisees, but he himself was probably a priest or scribe (see 3.7.6 below).[2]

The author of 1 Maccabees was probably a Sadducee who did not believe in resurrection. By starting his account with the conquests of Alexander the Great (1 Macc 1:1–4), he placed the Hasmonean conflicts in the context of Judaism's ongoing struggles with Hellenistic kings, seeing the reign of Antiochus IV Epiphanes as the crucial spark that lit the conflagration. The author's aim was

---

1. Joseph Sievers, *The Hasmoneans and Their Supporters: From Mattathias to the Death of John Hyrcanus I*, South Florida Studies in the History of Judaism 6 (Atlanta, GA: Scholars Press, 1990), 20, n. 75.

2. *Pace* Babota, *Hasmonean High Priesthood*, 15–20; Honigman, *Tales of High Priests and Taxes*, 2–4, 7.

to foster loyalty to the Hasmonean dynasty by extolling the virtues of the earliest Hasmoneans and their fighters, the Maccabees. He had access to primary documents, though he sometimes doctored these to suit his characterizations. He probably wrote in Hebrew in the late second century BC, but the work was translated into Greek, and the original Hebrew version was subsequently lost.[3]

Though veiled in symbolism, the Hebrew visions in the book of Daniel (Dan 7–12) are also an excellent source. The book sees the years from 171 to 163 BC as the culmination of the long historical wait for Jewish restoration, extending all the way back to the Babylonian exile (sixth century BC).[4] It redefines the notion of exile as not simply absence from the land but as the state of being under foreign rule even after repatriation to the land.[5] The reign of Antiochus IV is placed in the context of the struggle between the Ptolemies and Seleucids for control of Judea, and like the author of 1 Maccabees, Antiochus's policies are seen as the immediate cause of the conflict. But unlike the author of 1 Maccabees, the book of Daniel is not patently pro-Hasmonean. The book focuses instead on the Intellectuals (Heb. *maskilim*; Dan 11:33, 35; 12:3, 10) as the ultimate champions of faithful Judaism. By the time of the Maccabean Revolt, a politically active faction known as the *Hasidim* ("pious ones" or "devotees") had emerged from the ranks of the Intellectuals and gone rogue by allying with the Hasmoneans. The remainder of the Intellectuals could not fully endorse the Hasmoneans' methods, viewing them as providing only "a little help" to the Jewish cause (Dan 11:34). The Intellectuals did not wish to take up the sword, but the scroll.[6] The figure of Daniel himself embodies the Intellectuals' centrist ideal of quiet resistance: he engages foreign culture but remains faithful to Jewish convictions, even when that threatens his life. There is an eschatological thrust to the book, as it looks beyond the Maccabean conflict and the disappointments of history to ultimate salvation in the establishment of an eternal kingdom of God.

The book of 1 Enoch also contains information about the Hasmonean conflict (mainly in 1 En. 90), though its symbolism is more opaque than

---

3. Babota, *Hasmonean High Priesthood*, 9–15; Lawrence H. Schiffman, "1 Maccabees," in *Outside the Bible: Ancient Jewish Writings Related to Scripture*, ed. Louis H. Feldman, James L. Kugel, and Lawrence H. Schiffman (Philadelphia: Jewish Publication Society, 2013), 2769–70.

4. Most scholars date the visions of Daniel to 164 BC, but there is a vocal minority who date the whole book to the sixth century BC.

5. George Athas, "In Search of the Seventy 'Weeks' of Daniel 9," *Journal of Hebrew Scriptures* 9 (2009): Article 2.

6. This scribal impetus made the Intellectuals allies of those conservative priests and Enochic Radicals who also clung to the scriptural traditions. Some of them would eventually combine to form the Essene sect. See further Philip R. Davies, "The Scribal School of Daniel," in *The Book of Daniel: Composition and Reception*, ed. John J. Collins and Peter W. Flint (Leiden: Brill, 2002), 247–65.

Daniel. It relates the extraterrestrial journey of Enoch into the heavenly realms, where the secrets of history and the universe are revealed to him. The book comes from multiple sources across a wide period and reflects the perspective of a group we may call the Enochic Radicals. Originally part of the Intellectuals, they eventually took over leadership of the politically active *Hasidim*, which took them into the eye of the political storm in the 160s BC. First Enoch reflects their initial support of the Hasmoneans' efforts against foreign influence, though the group eventually split from the Hasmoneans under the guidance of the "Teacher of Righteousness" (see 3.5.4 below). Thereafter, their concerns became more broadly philosophical, making them analogous to the Greek Pythagorean communities—a factor that also shaped the content of 1 Enoch.[7] After they abandoned political activism, they became the backbone of the Essene sect and continued to produce other literature.[8]

A surprisingly earthy and romantic source comes from the biblical book, Song of Songs. Though dressed in the metaphors of erotic poetry, this highly sophisticated piece of literature expresses the mindset of a persecuted people desperately clinging to their God under the most dystopian circumstances (see 3.3.1 below).

Josephus is another key source for the period. He made use of 1 Maccabees, as well as the 144-volume *Universal History* of Nicolaus of Damascus, a courtier of Herod the Great. Considering Nicolaus's prolific output and access to documentation, Josephus's account has much to commend it.[9] Though his chronology is at times tangled by unwitting mistakes, comparison with other sources usually allows us to unravel these satisfactorily.

For the later portion of this period, an indispensable source is the Dead Sea Scrolls—the large cache of biblical and sectarian documents produced over the course of two centuries by the Essenes, who eventually established a monastic settlement at Qumran by the Dead Sea. The scrolls are particularly useful for filling in gaps that are simply passed over in silence by 1 and 2 Maccabees. The evidence for these developments must be harvested from the sectarian writings, but their interpretation is still hotly contested for two basic reasons. First, the sectarian scrolls employ opaque expressions and symbolism as well as esoteric exegesis of biblical texts, often exacerbated by the fragmentary nature of the scrolls. Second, the scrolls use labels to discuss important figures, such as the "Teacher of Righteousness," the "Wicked Priest," the "Man of Mockery,"

---

7. First Enoch has an interest in the structures of the cosmos and the mechanism of time. In this way, it delves into the same spheres of interest as Greek scholarship, but from an overtly Jewish perspective.
8. Fragments of 1 Enoch were discovered among the Dead Sea Scrolls at Qumran.
9. Babota, *Hasmonean High Priesthood*, 20–34.

THE HASMONEAN ERA (167–63 BC)

and the "Liar," without ever naming who these figures were. This leaves the historian with the task of decoding the labels to identify the historical personas behind them—a task compounded by the difficulty of not knowing whether the labels have a one-for-one match with historical personas. For instance, some argue that the "Wicked Priest" is identical to the "Man of Mockery" and the "Liar," while others make a distinction between them. The so-called Groningen Hypothesis argues that the "Wicked Priest" is to be identified with five different historical personas. The variety in interpretation is symptomatic of the difficulties. A consensus has descended on scholarship, which identifies Jonathan Apphus as the "Wicked Priest" (and the "Man of Mockery" and the "Liar"), but this is an uneasy consensus, for several aspects of this identification still do not fully match. It is as though Jonathan Apphus is the square peg that slides the furthest into the round hole, but the peg still does not slide in completely.[10] It is a consensus of convenience for lack of a hypothesis that better fits the data. This propels us to reconsider the respective identifications of these figures. In our accounting of this period, we will take an alternative view to the uneasy consensus, but one that arguably has more explanatory power of the data. It is based on evidence from the Dead Sea Scrolls themselves and their convergence with persons, events, and currents corroborated in other sources.

Of course, we continue to draw on sources from the wider Mediterranean world, such as Polybius and Diodorus. All the sources mentioned above come from a variety of vantage points and help us piece together the course of the Maccabean Revolt and the developments it set in train. They also testify to the pivotal importance of this period for the shape and flavor of Jewish society in the Second Temple period.

---

10. For example, the "Wicked Priest" is said to have suffered from a painful disease (1QpHab 9.9–11), but Jonathan Apphus never did. Elsewhere the "Wicked Priest" is said to be killed at the hands of gentiles (4QpPs^a [4Q171] IV.8–10), which did happen to Jonathan Apphus, but it is unclear whether this is seen as a past event or an eschatological prediction that need not be historical. Many have settled on the reference as historical and used this as the basis for identifying Jonathan Apphus as the "Wicked Priest." But this means that an uncertain element about the "Wicked Priest" (dying at the hands of gentiles) has outweighed a certain historical element (suffering from a painful disease). Then one must also consider how the exegetical strategy used to depict the "Wicked Priest" affects these considerations. These factors make the identification of Jonathan Apphus as the "Wicked Priest" counterintuitive, propelling us to search for a better candidate. Cf. Rick van de Water, "The Punishment of the Wicked Priest and the Death of Judas," *DSD* 10.3 (2003): 395–419.

3.2 THE ROAD TO REVOLT

3.2.1 THE HIGH PRIEST JASON AND THE CULTURAL DIVIDE (175–171 BC)

Antiochus IV arrived at Antioch in November 175 BC and assumed the regency of his eight-year-old nephew, also named Antiochus. He married his sister, Laodice IV, who for the third time became the wife of one of her brothers. The marriage made Antiochus the focus of the royal cult throughout the Seleucid kingdom and signaled his intention to rule as the divine king of the realm. As part of this, he took on the epithet "Epiphanes," signifying his status as a god "made manifest." His nephew, the younger son of Seleucus IV, was a mere puppet.

While the tension between Rome and Seleucus IV was now gone, the Roman Senate still needed to ensure Antiochus was compliant with their aims. The twelve years Antiochus had spent as a hostage in Rome had conditioned him to Roman ideals, but he was an extroverted character, supremely ambitious, and probably narcissistic (he eventually named his son "Antiochus Goodfather" [Gk. *Eupatōr*]). As he took the reins of government in Antioch, he pursued his own agenda with little regard for Roman policy. He undoubtedly realized the opportunities that lay before him for taking Egypt, especially as the regency for the young Ptolemy VI began to flounder. But he faced the same dilemma as his now dead brother: he needed money to pay war reparations to Rome and to fund an expeditionary force to invade Egypt.

An opportunity presented itself within a few months. Onias III had moved towards a conservative political outlook, which opposed the interference of the Seleucids in Jewish affairs. But Onias's brother, Jesus, leaned far more towards Greek culture. Early on, he dropped his original Hebrew name in favor of the similar sounding but classical Greek name, Jason (*Ant.* 12.239). He had fewer scruples about Seleucid oversight and was keen to give Jews a more prominent place at the Hellenistic table.[1] And if Egypt could be added to the Seleucid kingdom, its large Jewish community could be brought into the fold, further stimulating the status of Jerusalem and its high priest.

---

1. As a modern analogy, this dynamic was akin to that which drove eastern states in the former Soviet bloc to join the European Union, which had developed in Western Europe.

In early 175 BC Jason had an interview with Antiochus in Antioch (2 Macc 4:7–10). Jason promised to give Antiochus 440 silver talents from various sources if the king granted him the high priesthood in Jerusalem. He also offered an annual payment for his appointment. The confidence of his offer makes it likely that Jason had the estate of Hyrcanus, held in the temple treasury, in mind as one of the sources of his payment. If Jason were appointed high priest, he would become the trustee of the estate and could then easily make it over to the Seleucid king. If he financed his exploits by dipping into the deposits of commoners in the temple treasury, he was likely to spook its patrons and even instigate a popular uprising, such as that which nearly occurred during the Heliodorus Affair (see 2.8.8 above). It is more likely, then, that he anticipated gouging the price of sacrificial animals, raising levies on commerce in the temple, and perhaps even intimidating people with *mafiosi* tactics.

In Antiochus's estimation, Jason was a stellar candidate for high priest. In addition to the funds he promised, Jason was of the requisite Zadokite line. He was also the primary heir to the office, as Onias's own son was still too young to inherit it. His appointment might create a level of discontent, but this was not a pain Antiochus would have to bear personally. He would gain a financial windfall through a diplomatic coup, and it would be Jason's job to ensure the Jewish people were compliant.

Jason went a step further, though. He also promised a further 150 silver talents if the king granted him the rights to establish a gymnasium in Jerusalem and to register people as citizens of Antioch (2 Macc 4:9). This is where we see Jason's true Hellenizing colors. He was proposing to turn Jerusalem into a fully-fledged Greek *polis*. This was not a secularization of Jerusalem's holy status, a demotion of Jewish culture, or the imposition of Greek culture upon the Jewish people. The Jews were still a recognized ethnos in the Seleucid kingdom. It was, rather, a graduation of Jerusalem's political status and an opening of the city to multiculturalism. This was probably born of the tolerance and compatibilism of Jason's cultural views. He identified Yahweh as the Jewish version of Zeus, as most Hellenizing Jews did. In his mind, he was not compromising Yahwism or Jerusalem's sacred status but rather enhancing them by embracing multiculturalism. Indeed, he was giving the Jewish God more international appeal. By registering Jerusalem's residents as citizens of Antioch, he was winning them greater rank and putting Jerusalem in the same league as the Seleucid capital itself. He was, therefore, integrating Jerusalem and the Jewish nation more firmly into the Hellenistic world of the eastern Mediterranean.

For religious and cultural conservatives such multiculturalism was a threat, for behind it lay the specter of pluralism, which compromised the exclusivity of monotheistic Yahwism at the heart of Jewish identity. For most Jews, Yahweh could never be identified with Zeus. Jewish culture, particularly as it was prescribed by the Torah, was incompatible with other cultures and their religions. For cultural conservatives, this might have been spawned of xenophobia, but for others it was borne of religious conviction about what the deity desired. Ritual purity and holiness were at stake. The problem was that a sizeable quarter of the Jewish elite, especially those exposed in their earlier years to Greek principles, had few such qualms.

Jason and Antiochus struck their bargain. Onias III was officially deposed as high priest in 175 BC, and Jason was appointed in his stead. Antiochus had his financial windfall, and Jerusalem officially became a *polis*. The city's oldest quarter (the so-called city of David) was transformed into the requisite Greek colony. Yet another fraternal fracture over the high priesthood rocked Jewish society (cf. 1.5.2; 1.7.3), and it would not be the last (see 3.7.17 below).

Onias refused to acknowledge his deposition. As high priest, he was committed to the office for life and could not resign it without instigating a judicial crisis in Judaism. Either he had to continue in office or have his entire tenure expunged (cf. the high priest Hezekiah [see 2.6.2 above]). This he was not prepared to do, for it would amount to an admission of his personal unfitness to be high priest. He firmly believed that Jason's maneuver was illegal by the statutes of Torah and that Jason's liberal multiculturalism was a potent threat to Jewish society. Many priests, Intellectuals, and conservatives agreed. With their backing, Onias refused to step aside—a brave move, as he was effectively exerting pressure on Antiochus to execute him, since that would technically solve the legal issue. But Antiochus was unwilling to implement such a hamfisted measure, which would cause more instability than he was prepared to live with.

If Jason raided the estate of Hyrcanus to pay for his position, then the deposits of commoners in the temple treasury remained untouched, which quelled potential unrest. But Jason still had to raise the rest of his pledge, meaning volatility was never too far away. With the money from Jason (and perhaps other temples also), Antiochus paid off a significant tranche of the reparations owing to Rome. In return, Antiochus received *amicitia*—a formal alliance of friendship with the Senate and people of Rome (Livy, *Ab urbe cond.* 42.6).[2]

---

2. The full amount was evidently not paid off, for Demetrius continued as a hostage in Rome for almost another decade.

Meanwhile in Jerusalem, new infrastructure was built. The biggest project was a military compound constructed over buildings on the Ophel ridge between the temple precinct to the north and the *polis* in the city of David to the south. Its size and strategic position allowed the Seleucid garrison to guard the approaches to the temple. In this way, the compound also functioned as a *propylaea*—a monumental entrance to a sacred complex.[3] Known as the "Acra" (Greek for "elevated citadel"), the fortress would, in time, include at least one tower tall enough to rival the height of the temple itself (*Ant.* 12.252, 362).[4] Along with the temple, therefore, it created an imposing acropolis that dominated Jerusalem. The Greek-speaking families of the garrison soldiers became colonists in the adjoining *polis*, and shrines to the Greek gods were erected throughout it.

Jason built the gymnasium on the edge of the Western Hill, directly opposite the Acra (1 Macc 1:14; 2 Macc 4:12).[5] As a dynamo of Greek culture, its establishment attracted more foreigners to Jerusalem, increasing the profile of Hellenism in the very heart of Judaism's sacred city. Liberal Hellenizers among the Jewish elite began to frequent the gymnasium. The author of 2 Maccabees opined that even priests were sucked into its more despicable activities (2 Macc 4:11–15):

> There was such a burgeoning of Hellenization and uptake of foreign custom because of the ungodliness and surpassing impurity of the fake high priest, Jason, that the priests were no longer eager for their service at the altar. Instead, despising the sanctuary and neglecting the sacrifices, they hurried to take part in the unlawful program of the wrestling arena, just as soon as they were inclined to throw a discus. (2 Macc 4:13–14)

By participating in nude athletic training, Jewish men were exposing the characteristic mark of their circumcision to the foreigners also training at the

---

[3]. Ayala Zilbersetin, "Hellenistic Military Architecture from the Giv'ati Parking Lot Excavations, Jerusalem," in *The Middle Maccabees: Archaeology, History, and the Rise of the Hasmonean Kingdom*, ed. Andrea M. Berlin and Paul J. Kosmin, Archaeology and Biblical Studies 28 (Atlanta: SBL Press, 2021), 37–52.

[4]. Josephus claims that the Acra overlooked the temple complex. However, its location at the Ophel ridge, on ground that was lower than the temple, makes it difficult to comprehend this. Either Josephus exaggerated the height of the Acra, or it was built to a dizzying height to match the elevation of the temple courts. A subsequent collapse of ashlar blocks, unearthed in excavations, might be testament to its precarious height. Cf. Zilbersetin, "Hellenistic Military Architecture," 44. See also 3.7.2 below.

[5]. The location of the gymnasium is known by the fact that its *xystus* (open garden with peristyle) lent its name to the plaza that occupied it at a later date. Josephus describes the location of this later plaza quite precisely (*J.W.* 2.344).

gymnasium. Since Greeks viewed circumcision as culturally barbaric, some Jewish men attempted to reverse their circumcision (1 Macc 1:15). This challenged one of Judaism's most essential cultural features, which literally embodied membership in the covenant community of Israel under the tutelage of the Torah. Some might have done this in repudiation of their Jewish identity, but most did not feel they were abandoning their heritage or disobeying God. Most likely, they believed they were redefining Jewishness rather than repudiating it. Most of the population, who were still conservative in outlook, were panicked and outraged. If some put such skin in the game that they were prepared to reverse their circumcision, then laxity towards other cultural markers, such as the Torah's dietary restrictions or Sabbath laws, was bound to creep in.

This spawned critical questions about the role of Torah in the life of the Jew. Was it an historical epic explaining the origins of Jewish identity, prized above all other documents but without imposing ongoing restrictions on the Jewish nation? If so, the Torah was like the Greek Homeric epics of the *Iliad* and the *Odyssey*. Hellenizing Jews adopted this perspective, seeing the Torah as defining the nation's historical psyche but by no means mandating the shape of its future. It was a cultural classic of sentimental worth. One can see this attitude emanating from the gymnasium, where liberal Jews were now regularly reading the Homeric epics.

But non-liberal Jews headed the opposite way. Ultra-conservatives began reading the Torah in a hyper-literal fashion, understanding it as a manifesto stipulating the precise shape, hue, and texture of every aspect of Jewish life. It was an all-or-nothing proposition, and to treat it as anything less was to cut the Jewish nation loose from its moorings and jeopardize its future. More moderate conservatives and centrists preserved a milder approach. For them, the Torah did not straightjacket the nation's future, but it certainly provided precedents and guidelines, which the nation ignored to its peril. The Torah was not necessarily a detailed map, but it certainly was a compass. Jews in this camp tended to view the prophetic traditions as equally authoritative, with ongoing prophetic activity integral to how Torah should be applied. But as more Jews careened towards the liberal end of the spectrum, some centrists and conservatives recoiled in the opposite direction. This galvanized support for Onias III as the jilted darling of the conservatives but left the theological center almost empty. The centrist Intellectuals, amorphous as they were, had their ranks sapped as some found common cause with hardline conservatives who could not sit idly by while Jason and Antiochus rode roughshod over the legitimate high priest. It left the moderately minded Intellectuals alone at the center, beseeching God for redress and waiting patiently for prophetic guidance to point the way forward. The previous decades of Seleucid rule had seen a discernible increase in Hellenizing tendencies within Jewish society, and the introduction of the gymnasium to Jerusalem accelerated this rapidly. Now, within the space of just a couple of years, a swift and weighty shift occurred in Judea as the ranks of the liberal Hellenizers swelled. Conservatives began spoiling for a fight.

What added further momentum to this was the authority Jason received to register inhabitants of Jerusalem as citizens of Antioch, with special rights and privileges.[6] This was a powerful means of inducing people to his side and promoting the station of his own supporters. It also blurred cultural lines, undermining the actuality of the Jews as a discrete ethnos in the Seleucid kingdom.

Jason's appointment polarized Jewish society. But with Jerusalem now officially a *polis*, a gymnasium within its walls, and the Acra rising on its skyline, the critical momentum lay with the liberal Hellenizers. As the balance swung, conservatives in Jerusalem bunkered down, seeing themselves as the defenders of the rest of the country, which was generally conservative. The Hellenizing Jewish elite thus grew detached from the rest of the country, but with momentum on their side, it was likely that the country would, in time, join them.

3.2.2 THE HIGH PRIESTHOOD OF MENELAUS

With questions over the legality of Jason's appointment, those who were not prepared to depend on his cultic leadership and mediation might have been induced to withdraw their offerings and finances from the temple. This would have curbed Jason's revenue streams, putting more pressure on the Judean economy, the cost of worship, and on Jason's ability to fulfil his pledges to Antiochus IV. The movements of Onias III during these years are unclear, but cultic ambiguity certainly smoldered.

In 172 BC Jason took a significant step towards pluralism when he sent 300 drachmas to the Tyrian Games to pay for a sacrifice to Heracles. While the envoys bearing the money were content to be at the games, even they chafed against offering a sacrifice. Rather than using the money as stipulated, the envoys gave the money directly to Antiochus IV to construct war galleys (2 Macc 4:18–20). Antiochus welcomed the payment as he was clearly planning to invade Egypt (cf. 1 Macc 1:16). There was an urgency to his plans, for in 172 BC fourteen-year-old Ptolemy VI came of age and started making

---

6. Victor Tcherikover, *Hellenistic Civilization and the Jews* (Grand Rapids: Baker, 1999), 160–61.

noises about returning Coele Syria to the Ptolemaic fold. Antiochus went on a recruitment drive that included a visit to Jerusalem, where Jason welcomed him with much fanfare (2 Macc 4:21–22).

The following year (171 BC), Jason sent Antiochus the next annual payment for his position as high priest. In charge of delivering it was Menelaus, brother of Simon, the custodian of the temple who had clashed with Onias III some years earlier. Menelaus was a priest and unabashed Hellenizer.[7] Taking his lead from the Greek world, where priesthoods could be bought by anyone, Menelaus made a brazen counterbid for the high priesthood, offering the king 300 silver talents more than Jason (2 Macc 4:23–25). The offer was timely for Antiochus, who was keen to finance his invasion of Egypt. The sticking point was that Menelaus was not from the Zadokite line. Antiochus probably figured that the long-term momentum of Hellenization in Judea would soon right any short-term destabilization caused by Menelaus's appointment, so he accepted the offer and removed Jason from office. For the first time in eight centuries, a non-Zadokite was high priest of Yahweh in Jerusalem.[8] It was a watershed moment.

The appointment set the proverbial cat amongst the pigeons in Judea. Menelaus returned to Jerusalem with an armed escort and violently drove Jason from the city. The author of 2 Maccabees caricatures Menelaus as "having the temper of a cruel tyrant and the rage of a savage beast" (2 Macc 4:25). Jason fled across the Jordan to Ammanitis, where he planned his next move (2 Macc 4:26). For centuries now the sacerdotal office had had political elements attached to it, but the militarism of Menelaus's arrival in Jerusalem added a martial dimension to it. Menelaus came as both cleric and commander of the ruling regime, making him much like Ptolemy Thraseas under the Ptolemies (see 2.8.1 above).

Menelaus still had to make good on his pledge to Antiochus. In this he had the support of the Tobiad family (cf. *Ant.* 12.239–240), who now distanced themselves from both Onias and Jason. Onias's retreat into conservativism might have been enough to dissuade them from his cause. In opposing Jason, they had probably been excluded from Antiochene citizenship. With Menelaus, they could receive the relevant rights and privileges and lend him

---

7. Josephus's testimony about Menelaus is mudded by his assertion that Menelaus was a brother of both Onias III and Jason (*Ant.* 12.238–239), all three being sons of Simon II. Menelaus's original Hebrew name was Onias, which probably led Josephus to confuse him with Onias III at certain points. Nonetheless, Menelaus was the brother of Simon, the custodian of the temple (2 Macc 4:23), who was unrelated to Onias and Jason.

8. Some scholars doubt the Zadokite line was so ancient, interpreting the appointment of Zadok under Solomon (1 Kgs 2:35) as a mythic interpolation from a much later time.

the muscle required to raise money within Judea. It is not inconceivable that they put Menelaus up to the bid in the first place. The population seethed with discontent.

3.2.3 CRISIS IN THE HIGH PRIESTHOOD (171-170 BC)

The price for Menelaus's appointment as high priest proved beyond his ability to raise. This must have caused misery for the population beneath him, not just for the economic consequences, but for the obstructions to their worship and the rising specter of violence. If Menelaus raided the temple treasury to pay for his pledge, he risked instigating an armed uprising. Half of Jewish society refused to acknowledge his tenure since two Zadokite priests were still alive.

When Antiochus IV pressed him for the funds, Menelaus resorted to secretly melting down golden vessels and fixtures within the temple—items probably out of public view (2 Macc 4:27–28, 32). It was the high priest's job to maintain and promote the temple, and Menelaus was doing just the opposite. Onias III somehow caught wind of this and hastened to Antioch to expose Menelaus before the king (2 Macc 4:33). It was a daring maneuver, for he was risking his own life by going. Antiochus could cauterize at least some of his problems in Judea by doing away with Onias. It is unlikely that Onias wished to put in a counterbid to regain his priesthood. Rather, he probably planned to show that he had the support of most Jews in Judea and that reinstalling him would pacify Judea enough to ensure that the province was not up in arms on the eve of Antiochus's planned campaign to Egypt. Aware of the extreme risk to his life, Onias did not enter Antioch itself. Instead, he went to Daphne, a sacred settlement devoted to Apollo and Artemis, a few miles south of the capital. Ironically, here in this sacred Greek temenos, he found asylum.

In the meantime, Antiochus ordered Menelaus to report to him in the capital and explain his failure to pay up. But leaving Jerusalem was risky for Menelaus, for Jason stood ready to pounce and reoccupy the city. So before he left for Antioch, Menelaus appointed his brother, Lysimachus, to hold the fort on his behalf (2 Macc 4:29).

Although the Jewish high priesthood had now become a thorn in Antiochus's side, a bigger thorn was now starting to torment him: his young nephew, Antiochus, for whom he was technically still regent. Now aged thirteen, the boy was fast approaching the age when he could assume rule for himself and dispense with his uncle as regent. If the elder Antiochus was to launch his own invasion of Egypt, he needed to secure the throne for himself.

The events that subsequently transpired in August 170 BC were so coincidentally convenient to Antiochus IV that it is unreasonable to suggest he did not orchestrate them. He left Antioch ostensibly to quell a rebellion in nearby Cilicia, but this was probably an alibi for being absent from the capital. In his wake, he appointed a certain Andronicus as his plenipotentiary in Antioch and ordered him to confirm Menelaus as Jewish high priest and offer him a gesture of goodwill. When Menelaus had his audience with Andronicus, he proceeded to bribe the plenipotentiary with some of the gold he had melted from the temple. The bribe secured Menelaus a tangible favor: the murder of Onias III. Of course, as long as Onias stayed within the temenos at Daphne, his person was inviolate. But Andronicus persuaded Onias that he would come to no harm in Antioch and that his accusations against Menelaus would be heard favorably, since Menelaus had essentially proved the case against himself with his bribery. With great reticence, Onias left Daphne to meet with Andronicus but was callously murdered the moment he stepped beyond the limits of the temenos (2 Macc 4:30–35).

While he was allegedly quelling rebellion in Cilicia, Antiochus also arranged for his henchmen to murder his nephew, the young Antiochus.[9] Since the lad's demise occurred while he himself was elsewhere, Antiochus could not be implicated. Thus, when he returned to the capital, he assumed sole rule of the kingdom and sought the alleged perpetrators of the boy's murder. But he did not betray his own henchmen. Instead, he pinned the blame on Andronicus. The murder of Onias had given Antiochus the perfect precedent for this: if Andronicus could murder the former high priest of Jerusalem in cold blood, then he could also go as far as murdering the young prince out of political ambition. The author of 2 Maccabees states that Antiochus had Andronicus executed for Onias's assassination (2 Macc 4:35–38), while Diodorus attributes his downfall to his assassination of the young prince Antiochus (Diodorus Siculus, *Bib. hist.* 30.7.2–3). The best explanation of all the evidence is that Antiochus IV engineered the whole situation, and Andronicus became the fall guy for both murders.[10]

Onias's assassination came as a huge blow to his supporters. The Intellectuals of the book of Daniel viewed it as a critical moment, which saw

---

9. Antiochus IV's sister-wife, Laodice IV, could not have taken well to the murder of her own son. She disappears from the historical record at about this time, though whether she withdrew from active court life or was herself assassinated also is unknown. She had, however, borne Antiochus a son in ca. 172 BC—the future Antiochus V. Antiochus was already consorting with another woman, Antiochis, by whom he had two other children. See Grainger, *The Fall of the Seleukid Empire*, 28–29.

10. Athas, "In Search of the Seventy 'Weeks,'" 9–12; Erich S. Gruen, "The Origins and Objectives of Onias' Temple," in *The Construct of Identity in Hellenistic Judaism: Essays on Early Jewish Literature and History*, Essays on Early Jewish Literature and History (Berlin: de Gruyter, 2016), 361–62.

"a leader of the covenant" swept aside by "a despicable one," initiating a new era of wickedness (Dan 11:21–22).[11] In Daniel 9, the historical schema of "seventy weeks" configured the Jewish experience of exilic and postexilic history into seventy periods of seven years, amounting to 490 years. These were not 490 linear years, for two of the periods seem to overlap.[12] But Onias's death was understood as the key turning point that initiated a final catastrophic "week":

> Seventy "weeks" are decreed over your people and over your holy city, to complete rebellion and consolidate sin; to atone for iniquity and re-institute permanent righteousness; to authorize vision and prophet, and anoint the holy of holies. Know and understand from the issuing of the word to return and rebuild Jerusalem: until an anointed leader [Zerubbabel or the high priest Joshua] there will be seven "weeks" [587–538 BC]. In sixty-two "weeks," [605–171 BC][13] you will have returned, and street and reservoir will be built, but with the anguish of the times. But after the sixty-two weeks [in 171/70 BC], an anointed one [Onias III] will be cut off and have nothing. Then the people of the coming leader [Antiochus IV] will ruin the holy city, its end overwhelming, with the ravages of war decreed to the very end. (Dan 9:24–26)

Onias's murder was seen to mark the outbreak of a great evil, characterized by the ruin of Jerusalem, the ravages of war, the completion of rebellion, and the consolidation of sin—a reference to Jews turning from the dictates of Torah towards liberal Greek customs. This description of cultural betrayal was placed in the context of Daniel's penitential prayer (Dan 9:4–19), which supplicated God for the forgiveness of the whole Jewish nation. Thus, despite the course of events, hope for redemption was also held out in the form of re-establishing the temple cult.

Onias's supporters naturally turned to his son, Onias IV, as his logical successor. However, he was still too young to take the office of high priest, being only around twenty years of age at this time. By rights, therefore, the high priesthood now legitimately fell to Jason. This presented conservatives with a dilemma: could they bring themselves to endorse Jason, considering his

---

11. Porphyry mistakenly believed the leader of the covenant was Judas Maccabeus (see Jerome's commentary on Daniel 11:24).
12. Athas, "In Search of the Seventy 'Weeks,'" 7–19.
13. The use of 605 BC comes from the date given for the opening events in the book of Daniel (Dan 1:1). For a fuller explanation of this, the translation of these verses, and the overlapping configuration of 490 years, see Athas, "In Search of the Seventy 'Weeks,'" 13–19.

Greek predilections and evident pluralism? For pro-Zadokites, the pedigree of the high priest was not negotiable, so despite Jason's questionable cultural affiliations, they felt obliged to back him. Yet this put them in league with the Hellenizers and pluralists who had subverted the office in the first place. For others, like many Intellectuals and *Hasidim*, Jason had disqualified himself by his actions and could never be endorsed. For them, culture and morality held more weight than pedigree. But this itself presented an institutional quandary: who at all could they back without undermining the very institution they prized so dearly? Onias's death fractured the ranks of Jewish conservatives and produced a crisis of seemingly insurmountable proportions. Their divisions ensured that they had no direction, which simply played into the hands of the Hellenizers in Judea.

The social, ideological, and political temperature in Jerusalem now rose to fever pitch. Menelaus's brother, Lysimachus, resorted to violence to maintain order. But when Menelaus's pilfering of the temple's gold became public knowledge, an enormous riot broke out in the temple. Lysimachus deployed men to contain it, but they were met with dogged resistance by the angry crowd.[14] Probably by sheer weight of numbers, the crowd overpowered Lysimachus's detachment, hunted Lysimachus down, and lynched him to death next to the chambers of the temple treasury (2 Macc 4:39–42).

Menelaus rushed back to Jerusalem to put a lid on the unrest. He no longer feared a challenge from Jason, and he had good support from the Hellenizers in Jerusalem. But he was now more unpopular than ever, seen by the majority as a despoiler of the temple and a tyrannical leader. There were still enough conservative members of the Jewish Senate to produce a groundswell of opposition to him. Three senators were picked to make a case impeaching Menelaus before Antiochus.

But Antiochus was now in the full swing of preparations for an invasion of Egypt. The Romans were bogged down by conflict in Macedon and not in a position to prevent him. Since Ptolemy VI was planning his own invasion of Coele Syria, the Romans were prepared to let the two kingdoms duke it out as long as the conflict did not spill over into other states.

The three Jewish senators put their case to Antiochus in Tyre. The fact that they were arguing for the removal of a Jewish high priest before a foreign king reveals the dire circumstances they felt they were in. Antiochus must

---

14. Second Maccabees states that Lysimachus deployed 3,000 men, which seems an exaggerated figure. They were commanded by an older man named Auranus (2 Macc 4:40). No further information about him is given, but we may wonder whether he belonged to the Tobiad family, who were now backing Menelaus as high priest (cf. Josephus, *Ant.* 12.239).

have been tempted to remove Menelaus and reinstall Jason who, despite the opposition to him, had the benefit of being a Zadokite. But Menelaus, true to character, manipulated the decision by sending a considerable bribe. Antiochus dismissed the case for impeachment and had the three senators summarily executed for daring to challenge a royal appointment (2 Macc 4:43–50).

The summary callousness with which Antiochus handled the situation soured most of the Jewish nation against him. Even Hellenizers in the Jewish Senate must have seen in these cold executions both the whim of a tyrant and an unscrupulous attack on a venerable institution. It confirmed in no uncertain terms that, with the Seleucids, the king was both god and state. Any other institutions within the realm existed purely at his pleasure. Even Hellenizers had to face the reality of what subscribing to Greek ideals in a Seleucid context meant. For some, it was reason enough to jump ship from Judaism altogether and assimilate completely with the liberal Hellenistic culture around them. The rest had to figure out how to negotiate the challenges that Antiochus's acid personality presented in such a polarized society as Judea. The crisis in the high priesthood, therefore, deepened into a profound existential crisis for the whole Jewish nation.

3.2.4 SIXTH SYRIAN WAR (170–167 BC)

It is difficult to determine the precise order of events that occurred over the next few years due to confusions in our available sources. The following analysis is offered as the most likely sequence of events.

Young Ptolemy VI busied himself with preparations for an invasion of Coele Syria, but Antiochus pre-empted him by marching on Egypt. The two armies met outside Pelusium and the Seleucid forces won the day. In the truce that followed, Antiochus occupied Pelusium, securing a bridgehead from which he could coordinate the rest of his campaign (1 Macc 1:16–19; Polybius, *Hist.* 28.18; Diodorus Siculus, *Bib. hist.* 30.16–18). Building on this momentum, he proceeded to Memphis, where he declared himself king of Egypt[15] and began to sell off land in the Nile Delta to raise more money (cf. Dan 11:24, 39; 4Q248).[16]

But one of the challenges facing him at this point was not presenting himself as an aggressor to the international community. The fact that Ptolemy had an army ready to invade Coele Syria gave him reason enough to launch a

---

15. This information comes from Porphyry, cited in Jerome's commentary on Dan 11:24.
16. Eshel, *The Dead Sea Scrolls and the Hasmonean State*, 16.

pre-emptive strike. In the watchful eyes of Rome, his victory at Pelusium had settled the issue. His continued presence in Egypt was, therefore, a contentious international affair. Rome would not stand for a Seleucid Empire that added Egypt to its realm, as this would challenge the authority Rome itself wielded throughout the Mediterranean. So Antiochus needed to keep Rome at bay, or even get them onside, while he gained mastery of Egypt—a diplomatic balancing act, which Antiochus had the audacity to try.

At this point, young Ptolemy sent envoys to negotiate directly with Antiochus who was, after all, his maternal uncle. Ptolemy's advisors took this as a sign of the lad's eagerness to capitulate, so they conspired to remove him from power (Polybius, *Hist*. 29.19–21) and raised Ptolemy's younger siblings to the throne: his own sister-wife, Cleopatra II, and younger brother, Euergetes II ("Benefactor"). Euergetes has come to be known as Ptolemy VIII, but for his obesity was popularly known by the unflattering nickname, "Fatso" (Gk. *Physkōn*).[17] With these new heads of state acting essentially as their puppets, the courtiers aimed to put up resistance to Antiochus's aggression.

In Memphis, Antiochus came to an agreement with his nephew. He realized that conquering Alexandria required a herculean effort, including a massive naval blockade and an enormous, protracted land siege. With his current army and fleet, he could not hope to accomplish this. He had to find a way of unlocking Alexandria covertly and decided to use Ptolemy VI as his key. Antiochus would magnanimously relinquish his claim over Egypt, much to the relief of the international community, but he would back his nephew's claim to return to the Ptolemaic throne. If the courtiers in Alexandria refused him, as Antiochus expected they would, it would give him an honorable reason to raise more troops and ships to besiege Alexandria on his nephew's behalf—a *casus belli*, which the international community could hardly dispute. He would then be able to stamp his own authority over the country. Even if the courtiers in Alexandria willingly accepted Ptolemy VI back, Antiochus would still install him as his own client king. Either way, Antiochus would be seen as

---

17. Ptolemy VIII's actual given name was Euergetes—the second Ptolemy (after Ptolemy III) to bear that name, hence his enumeration as Euergetes II. Confusingly, Ptolemy VIII is occasionally enumerated as Ptolemy VII when his coregency with his older siblings is taken into account, even though he was but a child at the time. The putative Ptolemy VII was a son of Ptolemy VI, though which precise son is debated. He was most likely the boy who nominally reigned under the regency of his mother, Cleopatra II, in 145 BC before Fatso Ptolemy VIII murdered him but who is sometimes left off the roster of Ptolemaic rulers altogether. Some equate the boy Ptolemy VII with Ptolemy Memphites, another son of Ptolemy VI and Cleopatra II whom Ptolemy VIII also murdered, though this identification is almost certainly incorrect. Yet others suggest that Ptolemy VII be equated with Ptolemy Eupator, the son of Ptolemy VI who died at age thirteen on Cyprus in 152 BC. To complicate matters even further, when Fatso Ptolemy VIII is counted as Ptolemy VII, the boy Ptolemy VII (whoever he was) is then counted as Ptolemy VIII.

upholding the honor of Egypt while simultaneously gaining the foothold he desired in Alexandria. When Ptolemy VI agreed to his uncle's offer, Antiochus knew he had outwitted his young and impressionable nephew (Livy, *Ab urbe cond.* 45.11).

While Ptolemy VI remained in Memphis, Antiochus advanced on Alexandria to determine what he needed for a concerted chokehold of the city (Livy, *Ab urbe cond.* 45.11). He then returned to his own realm in 168 BC to raise the extra troops and ships he needed to bring his plans to fruition.

Daniel's last vision portrays this whole first phase of the Sixth Syrian War as follows:

> With confidence and with the best resources of the province, he [Antiochus IV] will come and achieve what his fathers and their fathers could not achieve. The plunder, spoil, and wealth they had taken he will spend in devising plans against fortresses, but for a time. He will rouse his strength and his heart against the King of the South [Ptolemy VI] with a large force, and the King of the South will provoke him to war with a very large and substantial force, but will be unable to withstand him, for they [Ptolemy VI's advisors] will plot against him; those who eat from his royal provision will break him, and his force will be overwhelmed, with many falling slain [at the Battle of Pelusium]. The two kings [Antiochus IV and Ptolemy VI], their hearts bent on evil, will speak lies to each other at a common table. This will not succeed, for the end will yet come in time. So he [Antiochus IV] will return to his country with great wealth. With his heart set against the holy covenant, he will act and return to his country. (Dan 11:24–28)

This final detail in Daniel 11:28 alludes to Antiochus's arrival in Jerusalem on his return from the first phase of his Egyptian campaign. Menelaus welcomed him to the city and, in sycophantic style, gave him free access to the temple and its treasury, which Antiochus, with an eye on funding the second phase of his campaign, plundered freely.[18] He also stripped the temple of most of its golden paraphernalia, such as the golden altar of incense, the menorah, and most of the remaining ceremonial vessels that Menelaus had not already melted down (1 Macc 1:21–23). Poignantly among the valuables Antiochus IV

---

18. First Maccabees 1:20 implies that Antiochus raided the temple in 168 BC, after the first phase of his Egyptian campaign, while 2 Macc 5:1 implies it came in 167 BC, after the second phase. In light of Antiochus's strategic aims and the outcome of the second phase, it is most probable that he raided the temple after the first phase with the purpose of funding the second.

helped himself to were "the crowns" (1 Macc 1:22)—most likely the two crowns fashioned by the prophet Zechariah in 519 BC, one for the high priest Joshua in his capacity as surrogate "Sprig" during Zerubbabel's arrest, and the second as a symbol of hope for the return of the "Sprig" (Zerubbabel) and the survival of Davidic hopes (Zech 6:9–15; see 1.1.2 above). The value of the loot Antiochus carried off was estimated at a staggering 1,800 talents of gold (2 Macc 5:15–21).

This cavalier act crushed the psyche of conservative Jews. Jewish heritage and symbols used in the worship of God had been stolen by a rapacious man who thought himself a god, to fund his own megalomania through a war in a foreign land. What's more, it had all been facilitated by the man who claimed to be their high priest. The Intellectuals prayed for God to intervene by overthrowing the rulers of the age and instituting a new kingdom of God (cf. Dan 7:11–27). Davidic loyalists pined for the Davidic "Sprig," whose crown was now pilfered. Zadokite loyalists and Enochic Radicals hoped for a priestly messiah to redeem the priestly institutions. The apocalyptic nature of such hopes demonstrates the utter despair that many Jews felt at this moment in history. For, paralyzed into inaction by the forces Antiochus had with him, they could do nothing but watch the Seleucids carry off the temple's goods.

A similar thing probably occurred at the Samaritan temple on Mount Gerizim, for Antiochus appointed two new superintendents over both temple complexes. In Jerusalem, he appointed a Phrygian man named Philip, and at Mount Gerizim he appointed a man named Andronicus (2 Macc 5:22–23).[19] They enabled Antiochus to suppress any active resistance more directly. It is likely that Samaritan hopes for their own messiah who would defend them and their temple began to develop at this time, if they had not begun already (see also 3.7.7 below). Hellenism and Seleucid power struck the roots of both communities.

It is difficult to know how long Antiochus anticipated it would take to muster additional forces for his war effort, but he was prompted to return to Egypt much sooner than expected. Ptolemy VI reneged on their Memphis agreement and returned to Alexandria, where he promptly reconciled with his two siblings and came to an agreement for them all to rule jointly. By this maneuver, eighteen-year-old Ptolemy VI diplomatically outwitted Antiochus, thirty years his senior. If, as Antiochus asserted, he was merely defending the claim of Ptolemy VI to rule Egypt, then Ptolemy's return to Alexandria

---

19. This Andronicus is not to be confused with the plenipotentiary executed for the murders of Onias III and the boy Antiochus two years earlier (see 3.2.3).

and confirmation as ruler had duly accomplished this, even if it was alongside his siblings. By virtue of their Memphis agreement, Antiochus should therefore honorably withdraw his forces from Egypt. But if Antiochus refused and advanced on Egypt again, he would demonstrate that the Memphis agreement had been a sham, revealing to the international community that he had encroached on foreign territory out of pure aggression—an attitude the Romans could not overlook. Not one to brook such a clear diplomatic outflanking, Antiochus threw caution to the wind and launched the second phase of his war before he was ready, bent on making his nephews and niece in Alexandria pay for ingeniously thwarting his plans (Livy, *Ab urbe cond.* 45.11).

Antiochus realized that he could not enforce a naval blockade on Alexandria, for the Ptolemies could send for supplies from their territories in Cyprus and Cyrenaica. To mitigate this, Antiochus deployed his fleet to Cyprus, where he occupied the island's ports and possessed its ships. He himself then began the march back to Egypt. But Ptolemy VI pre-empted him and decided to play a diplomatic game. He sent envoys to Antiochus to dissuade him from attacking and so preserve his honor. Antiochus issued an ultimatum in return, demanding that the Ptolemies cede Cyprus to him and acknowledge Seleucid sovereignty over Pelusium and the adjacent area of the eastern Nile Delta (Livy, *Ab urbe cond.* 45.11). When his demands were refused, Antiochus pressed forward towards Alexandria.

Ptolemy VI's diplomacy exposed Antiochus before the Romans. The previous year (168 BC), they had won the Third Macedonian War, defeating Perseus of Macedon and dismantling his troublesome Macedonian state. The spoils of victory filled Roman coffers to such an extent that the war tax on Roman citizens, which used to pay soldiers' wages, was abolished.[20] Victory over Macedon came just in time for the Romans to turn their attention to Antiochus in Egypt. Keen to avoid the destabilization of the whole eastern Mediterranean, the Romans dispatched a former consul, Gaius Popilius Laenas, to Alexandria. He arrived in Egypt carrying an ultimatum from the Roman Senate. Antiochus was at the time camped at Eleusis, one of the suburbs of Alexandria, preparing to lay siege to the city. Popilius, armed only with a walking stick and accompanied by a handful of Roman commissioners, marched out to meet him. As he approached, Antiochus put his hand out to greet the senator in friendship, since they knew each other from Antiochus's years as a hostage in Rome. But Popilius placed the ultimatum in Antiochus's open hand instead, stating that he was unsure whether Antiochus was indeed

---

20. Sinnigen and Boak, *A History of Rome*, 125–26.

a friend. Antiochus read the ultimatum. The Senate gave him a deadline for a complete withdrawal from all Ptolemaic realms, including Cyprus. When Antiochus demurred that he needed to confer with his advisors, Popilius took his walking stick, traced a circle in the ground around Antiochus, and advised him not to step outside it until he had reached a decision. Antiochus stewed, but after some minutes agreed to comply with the Senate's demands. At this point, Popilius and the other commissioners jovially grasped his arm in friendship, and Antiochus was allowed out of his circle (Polybius, *Hist.* 29.27; Livy, *Ab urbe cond.* 45.12).

This juicy little incident demonstrates how, despite Antiochus's mastery of manipulation and aggressive ambition, Rome was the dominant power of the Mediterranean. To entice Rome into hostilities, especially now that its armies were no longer engaged in Macedon, was to tempt a fate worse than the one imposed by the Treaty of Apamea. A single senator and a few commissioners were all it took to turn Antiochus and his whole army around and send them back to Syria. Antiochus evacuated all his forces from Egypt and Cyprus in April 167 BC (*Ant.* 12.242; Polybius, *Hist.* 29.27; Livy, *Ab urbe cond.* 45.12). The Sixth Syrian War thus came to an abrupt end with a very public humiliation of Antiochus on an international stage. The final vision of Daniel describes these very developments:

> At the appointed time, he [Antiochus IV] will return and enter the South [Egypt], but this latter time will not be like the first. Ships of Kittim [the Romans] will come, and he will be intimidated into turning back. (Dan 11:29–30a)[21]

3.2.5 THE ABOMINATION OF DESOLATION (167 BC)

While Antiochus IV was still in Egypt, a rumor of his death spread through Judea, presumably prompted by the sudden halt to hostilities through the intervention of Gaius Popilius Laenas. Thinking that Menelaus had now lost his patron, Jason seized the opportunity to take the high priesthood back for himself. He gathered a small army of about a thousand pro-Zadokites

---

21. The term "Kittim" derives originally from the town of Kition on the southern coast of Cyprus. In Gen 10:4, the *kittim* are closely associated with the Rhodians (Heb. *rodanim*), showing that "Kittim" became a general term for the islands of the Aegean or the Mediterranean generally. In Dan 11:30, it refers either to Roman territory or the fact that Popilius sailed from the Aegean to confront Antiochus and thence to Cyprus to ensure the Seleucid withdrawal from the island. The Essenes used the term as a cipher for the Romans—a common Jewish feature, since the Old Greek version of Daniel renders the term explicitly as "Romans" (*rhōmaioi*).

and Hellenizing Jews and took possession of Jerusalem in a lightning raid. Thereafter, he went on a violent rampage to rat out his opposition. In fear for his life, Menelaus sought refuge in the Acra (2 Macc 5:5).

For Jewish conservatives, this new development presented a dilemma. Should they support Jason because of his Zadokite heritage, or should they distance themselves from him because he had sold out to Greek culture? Would withholding support play into the hands of Menelaus? Was it more expedient to get behind Jason and ensure Menelaus was dispensed with? Would neutrality cost them their lives, as Jason went on his murderous spree? And what would happen with the Seleucid kingship? Who was king now?

That final question was answered in a matter of days, as Antiochus arrived back in Coele Syria very much alive. Still smarting from his humiliating withdrawal from Egypt, he was in no mood for diplomacy. He considered Jason's occupation of Jerusalem a revolt against his own authority, and he was not about to suffer another blow to his royal dignity. As Antiochus sent his armies to Jerusalem, Jason scampered back to Transjordan, his cause utterly lost. He never appeared in Judea again and lived out his days running from country to country as a political refugee, eventually dying in Sparta (2 Macc 5:5–10).

Antiochus's army arrived in Jerusalem under the leadership of a captain named Apollonius. He halted his troops outside the city while he himself approached with overtures of peace. But then, on the following Sabbath, he savagely set his men upon the city, knowing that most locals would be observing the weekly rest. The frustration that Antiochus had pent up for Alexandria was thus vented on Jerusalem instead. A violent three-day slaughter ensued. A bloody massacre occurred on the temple grounds. Houses were pillaged and burned. As swords swung and parts of the city went up in flames, thousands of Jews perished or were enslaved. Those who could fled into the neighboring villages or the desert. Some departed Judea altogether, bound for new lives in Egypt or Mesopotamia. Conservative priests and scribes who had avoided the sword until now ran for their lives, some clinging to as many scrolls of Scripture and associated writings as they could carry (cf. 2 Macc 2:14). There was a wholesale abandonment of the city and its temple by Jewish conservatives (1 Macc 1:29–40; 2 Macc 5:11–14, 24–27; *Ant.* 12.251–252).[22]

The brutality inflicted on the city resulted in a new social profile for Jerusalem. The conservative Jewish population was decimated, leaving the

---

22. Second Maccabees splits Antiochus's taking of the city into two events at the end of the two respective phases of the Sixth Syrian War. However, this is the result of confusion over the timing of Antiochus's pilfering of the temple. Apollonius's attack in 2 Macc 5:24–26 should be equated with the deceitful attack of Antiochus's anonymous tax collector in 1 Macc 1:29–40.

city in the hands of liberal Hellenizing Jews and gentile colonists. Menelaus emerged from the Acra and was once again confirmed as high priest, now surrounded by an urban population that was largely on his side. Apollonius ordered that the walls surrounding the temple, which had been doubled in height during the time of Simon II, be torn down. He also ordered the demolition of those parts of the city that had been burnt and that the Acra be enlarged, with a glacis built around it (1 Macc 1:33–35).[23] This turned the Acra into a massive rectangular fortification approximately 200 meters long and 100 meters wide—a footprint that extended across half the city of David, turning this original part of Jerusalem into a veritable Greek citadel.[24] Its height was accentuated by the demolition of the temple walls, so that it visibly dominated the skyline from within the city—a monument to Seleucid sovereignty and Greek culture. Thus, just twenty-five years after Simon II celebrated the dedication of the refurbished temple (Sir 50:1–21), Jerusalem found itself a Greek *polis* with a population of liberal Hellenizing Jews and gentiles.[25]

Hellenization now took off with even more pace. With practically no conservative priests left in the city, the temple cult was left in the hands of Menelaus and his backers. For conservative Jews, Jerusalem and the very temple itself now felt like foreign territory.

Antiochus decided to set the new social profile of Jerusalem in more institutional concrete. According to the author of 1 Maccabees, he issued a kingdom-wide decree to make all the disparate peoples of the Seleucid realm into a single people (1 Macc 1:41–53). There is no external evidence for such a universal decree, but taking account of the author's rhetoric and the trajectory of events, we can determine that Antiochus revoked the status of the Jews as an ethnos ("nation") within the Seleucid kingdom.[26] In other words, Jews lost the right to have their ancestral customs recognized as legally normative for themselves. We do not know if this was applied to Jews elsewhere in the Seleucid kingdom, such as in Mesopotamia, but Judea itself lost its status as an ethnic

---

23. See Zilbersetin, "Hellenistic Military Architecture," 44; Dafna Langgut, "Palynological Analysis of the Glacis of the Seleucid Acra in Jerusalem: Duration of Construction and Environmental Reconstruction," in *Rethinking Israel: Studies in the History and Archaeology of Ancient Israel in Honor of Israel Finkelstein*, ed. Oded Lipschits, Yuval Gadot, and Matthew J. Adams (Winona Lake, IN: Eisenbrauns, 2017), 207–20.

24. By comparison, this made the Acra about a third of the size of the whole Acropolis of Athens.

25. It is possible that Jerusalem was renamed Antioch at this time, in honor of Antiochus. This is based on 2 Macc 4:9, which states that Menelaus enrolled the citizens of Jerusalem as citizens of Antioch, which mirrors the authority given to Jason in 175 BC (see 3.2.1). However, this could simply refer to the change in the legal status of its citizens, who were now directly responsible to the Seleucid capital, Antioch in Syria.

26. Babota, *Hasmonean High Priesthood*, 59.

enclave of the Jews and became a generic administrative unit, like all other administrative units in the kingdom.

This change in status had colossal ramifications. First, since Judea was now a generic administrative unit, the Seleucid royal cult was instituted as mandatory, as it was everywhere else in the Seleucid realm. The previous exemption for Jews had existed only insofar as they were a recognized ethnos. Jews now had to express loyalty to the crown through sacrifice to Antiochus as a god. Antiochus sent an Athenian elder (his name is not known) to Jerusalem "to compel the Jews to convert from the ancestral laws and not to live politically by the laws of God" (2 Macc 6:1). This almost certainly means the Athenian elder was appointed as priest of the royal cult in Jerusalem. This was followed up by the appointment of superintendents to enforce the royal cult throughout the rest of Judea (1 Macc 1:51–53).

Second, the worship of other gods was now openly sanctioned in Judea. The Greek gods were already worshipped in the Acra and in private by foreign colonists, but this now became public. Jerusalem was no longer the holy city of the Jewish deity alone. It was now a place where any deity was tolerated, as long as the king himself was worshipped among them. Shrines and idols, therefore, appeared throughout the city.

Third, the loss of ethnic status meant the loss of recognition that Yahweh was the distinct God of Israel. This did not entail the eradication of worship in the temple but rather its homologation to Greek standards. The Jews had long worshipped Yahweh as the Most High God who, in Greek minds, naturally corresponded to Zeus. And now that the Most High God worshipped in Jerusalem was no longer tethered strictly to the ethnos of Israel, the normal ethnic strictures that governed his worship disappeared. This meant no one could be excluded from worshipping in the temple, and no one was legally required to follow the prescriptions of the Torah in how they worshipped there. In accordance with the deregulated nature of Greek religion, anyone could come and offer any sacrifice they pleased, whether that was in the Jewish fashion or otherwise. Yahweh was thus officially baptized into the Greek religion and his temple in Jerusalem was rebranded as the temple of Olympian Zeus (2 Macc 6:2).

In the eyes of liberal Hellenizing Jews and most foreigners, these were welcome developments. It brought the Jews more firmly into the family of nations and opened doors of tolerance, mutual respect, and even religious cooperation. It was a milestone of integration and social progress, which did not eradicate Judaism but rather desegregated it. Hellenizing Jews must have viewed it as a theological triumph, whereby Yahweh was now worshipped by all nations (albeit in the guise of Zeus), fulfilling what had been spoken through the prophets. The nations could now stream to Jerusalem and worship the Most High God (cf. Jer 3:17; Zech 8:20–22). Indeed, liberal Hellenizing Jews could go so far as to proclaim that the whole world now recognized and worshipped the Most High God, in fulfilment of God's promise to bless all peoples through Abraham (Gen 12:3). Scripture could now be read in a new light:

> All peoples, clap your hands!
> Shout to God with a joyful voice!
> For Yahweh Most High is awesome,
> a great king over all the earth. . . .
> Since God is king of all the earth,
> sing a creative song.
> God reigns over the nations,
> God sits on the throne of his sanctuary.
> Nobles of the peoples are gathered,
> the people of the God of Abraham,
> For the shields of the earth belong to God,
> who is highly exalted. (Psalm 47:1–2, 7–9[8–10])

> Sing to Yahweh a new song!
> Sing to Yahweh, all the earth!
> Sing to Yahweh! Bless his name!
> Announce from day to day his salvation.
> Declare his glory among the nations,
> his miracles among all the peoples. . . .
> Give to Yahweh, O clans of the peoples,
> give to Yahweh glory and strength.
> Give to Yahweh the glory of his name.
> Carry an offering and enter his courts.
> Worship Yahweh in the majestic sanctuary.
> Pay homage before him all the earth.
> Say among the nations, "Yahweh reigns."
> Indeed, the world is set firm, nevermore to totter.
> He defends the peoples with fairness. (Psalm 96:1–3, 7–10).

But in the estimation of conservative Jews, Antiochus's decree was not a theological triumph but a theological catastrophe that lethally poisoned the Jewish nation. It repudiated the prophetic promises and denied the God who made them. Rather than bringing the nations to the God of Israel, it dissolved Israel into the nations and disfigured Yahweh beyond recognition. It was a wholesale compromise of the national covenant that had conferred the status of "holy" upon Israel and that necessitated its distinction from other nations—a conviction that stemmed from understanding that Yahweh himself was intrinsically different to other deities. Jews would be unable to pursue the moral and cultural mandate laid out in the Torah (Deut 4:5–8). Rather than allowing Jews to be a moral and cultural beacon to attract the nations to their God through the observance of Torah, Jewish distinctiveness officially evaporated into Greek cultural air. Judaism became indistinguishable from idolatrous polytheism. Antiochus's decree undid the notion that Yahweh was the God of Israel and that they were his people, dissolving the very core of Jewish identity.

Psalm 79 was most likely penned in response to these developments, including the massacre in Jerusalem that preceded them:

> O God, gentiles have invaded your inheritance.
> They have desecrated your sacred temple.
> They have turned Jerusalem into piles of rubble.
> They have given the corpse of your servants as food to the birds
>   of the air,
> the flesh of your devotees [Heb. *hasidim*] to the beasts of the earth.
> They have shed their blood like water all around Jerusalem,
> and there is none to bury them.
> We have become the scorn of our occupiers,
> a mockery and derision to those who surround us.
> Until when, O Yahweh? Will you be angry forever?
> Does your passion burn like fire?
> Pour your fury on the gentiles who do not know you,
> and the kingdoms that do not call on your name.
> For they have consumed Jacob,
> and devastated his precinct.
> Do not recall our former guilt.
> Hurry! Let your mercies meet us,
> for we have sunk very low.
> Help us, O God of our salvation, for the sanctity of your name.
> Rescue us, and atone for all our sins, for your name's sake.
> Why should the gentiles say, "Where is their God?"
> Let the avenging of the blood your servants have shed

be known among the gentiles, before our very eyes.
Let the groans of the prisoner come before you.
With the greatness of your arm safeguard those bound for death.
Pay back sevenfold into the arms of our occupiers,
for the scorn with which they scorn you, O Lord.
Then we, your people, the sheep of your pasture, will acclaim
    you always.
From generation to generation, we will recite your praise.[27]

When the Athenian senator appointed as priest of the royal cult arrived in Jerusalem, Antiochus's decree took force. In accordance with classical Greek religious standards, sacrifice in the temple was deregulated. The morning and evening sacrifices to Yahweh were abolished as unnecessary (Dan 9:27; 11:31; 12:11). Since the Torah stipulated the necessity of these sacrifices (Num 28:1–10), their abolition amounted to the removal of the Torah from statutory authority (cf. 2 Macc 6:1). The large altar of burnt offering before the sanctuary was still in use, so technically a Jew could continue offering sacrifice to Yahweh upon it. But since the entire temple had been rebadged as the temple of Olympian Zeus, this was now interpreted as worship of Zeus. Furthermore, Menelaus and the Hellenizing priests now operated the cult in complicity with its new Greek norms.

On the fifteenth day of Kislev (6 December 167 BC), a new altar was erected to facilitate the worship of Antiochus IV Epiphanes in conformity with the royal cult.[28] It was a small platform, built either on top of the altar of burnt offering or directly adjacent to it (1 Macc 1:54–59). A statue of Antiochus was also erected nearby (*Ant.* 12.253). Ten days later, on the twenty-fifth of Kislev, the royal cult was inaugurated with a sacrifice offered to Antiochus upon the new altar (1 Macc 1:59). The stark manner in which this was recalled by the author of 1 Maccabees suggests it was a solemn ceremony that finalized the legal transformation of Judea from an ethnic administrative unit into a generic unit. The claim that "the altar was covered with unlawful things that deviated from the laws" (2 Macc 6:5) indicates that pigs were offered, as was

---

27. This psalm is often understood to describe the fall of Jerusalem to the Babylonians in 586 BC. However, it depicts the temple being desecrated, not destroyed, and the nations are understood as occupiers in the immediate vicinity rather than invaders. There is no notion of exile but of being present in Jerusalem during an ongoing crisis in which the name of Yahweh is disrespected and his temple defiled. It makes overt reference to the death of *Hasidim* (Ps 79:2), and this verse is quoted in 1 Macc 7:17 in specific reference to the later slaughter of *Hasidim* (see 3.5.4). The psalm also makes use of more generic terms for Yahweh ("God" and "Lord"), which became common from the Hellenistic era.

28. Sievers, *The Hasmoneans and Their Supporters*, 20, n. 75.

standard practice in Greek and Roman worship (*Ant.* 12.253).²⁹ In Roman custom, a formal treaty of alliance between Rome and another state was conducted by the slaughter of a pig on an altar before a temple, accompanied by the swearing of an oath in Jupiter's name.³⁰ Being a Romanophile, Antiochus IV appears to have adapted this ceremony as the means by which the subjects of his kingdom legally bound themselves to him. The Athenian commissioned as priest by Antiochus (2 Macc 6:1) presumably presided over proceedings at the new altar, while Menelaus undoubtedly officiated at the traditional altar of burnt offering.

For conservative Jews, this event drew a line in the sand. The altar had been ritually polluted, rendering it unfit for use in the worship of Yahweh and the atonement of sin. The situation was not unlike that described in Ezekiel 8–11 in which Yahweh demonstrates to the prophet Ezekiel how the foreign worship within the first temple and the perfidy of the priesthood had forced Yahweh to abandon his own house, leaving it fit for destruction. The crisis in Judaism now reached tipping point.

The effects of Antiochus's policies are described in the visions of the book of Daniel:

> He [Antiochus IV] will overpower the public covenant for one "week." Halfway through the "week," he will stop sacrifice and offering, and along an edge [of the altar] will be abominations—a desolation, right until the end, when what is decreed will be poured out on the desolator. (Dan 9:27)

> He [Antiochus IV] will sabotage the holy covenant, by reaching an understanding with those who abandon the holy covenant. Forces from him will oppose and desecrate the sacred stronghold, abolish the daily sacrifices, and set up the abomination of desolation. Those who contravene the covenant he will corrupt with ease, but the people who know their God will stand firm. (Dan 11:30b–32)

The murder of Onias III in 170 BC was interpreted as the beginning of a cataclysmic period ("week") of seven years. The middle of this period was marked by Antiochus's decree to revoke the ethnic status of the Jews establish the Seleucid royal cult. This was seen as an "abomination of desolation"—an

---

29. Gunnel Ekroth, "Animal Sacrifice in Antiquity," in *The Oxford Handbook of Animals in Classical Thought and Life*, ed. Gordon Lindsay Campbell (Oxford: Oxford University Press, 2014), 326.

30. Linda Zollschan, *Rome and Judaea: International Law Relations, 162–100 BCE* (Abingdon: Routledge, 2017), 109.

event of such repulsive enormity that it subverted the national covenant and wrecked the Jewish nation.

The Samaritans suffered a similar loss of status as a recognized ethnos. The Athenian senator whom Antiochus commissioned as priest of the royal cult rebadged the Samaritan temple in honor of Zeus Xenios—Zeus, the hospitable friend of foreigners (2 Macc 6:1–2). This appellation suggests that opening up the Jewish and Samaritan cults to the participation of gentiles was a motivating principle of the reforms—an antidote to perceived xenophobia. What we do not know is what kind of resistance Samaritans put up to the reforms.

3.2.6 EXCURSUS: THE OLIVET DISCOURSE

These events give us greater perspective on Jesus's Olivet Discourse (Matt 24; Mark 13), in which he issues a prophetic pronouncement on the fate of the temple and the Jewish nation in the first century AD. Pivotal to Jesus's prophecy is what he refers to as the "abomination of desolation" (Matt 24:15; Mark 13:14), with Matthew even linking this explicitly to the use of the term in Daniel. This does not mean that Matthew understood Daniel to be prophesying about something that had yet to occur in Jesus's day. Rather, Matthew has Jesus recycle the concept from Daniel, where it clearly refers to the desecration of the temple in 167 BC, and apply it to a new situation. This theological link is, however, crucial for deciphering what Jesus meant by it.

In the Olivet Discourse, Jesus foresees a foreign imposition on the temple, which would prompt the end of the national covenant for Israel. There is a twofold theological rationale for this, laid out within the discourse itself but also throughout the rest of the respective Gospels. First is the nation's rejection of Jesus as their messiah. The nation and its leaders fail to heed Jesus's call to repent, and this leads to an unpreventable national disaster, which will overthrow the temple and ruin the nation. Second is the establishment of a new covenant and a new people of God under Jesus himself. Jesus sees the old order as characterized by the temple (including its bad leadership) and a national culture that had lost its way, whereas the new order would be characterized by righteousness and an international mission that required no physical temple building (see 3.5.6 below).

The abomination of desolation in the Olivet Discourse can be identified with one (or both) of two events that occurred in the first century. The first is the intention of Caligula to erect a golden statue of himself within the Jerusalem temple in AD 40—almost an exact repeat of the events of 167 BC. Caligula's decision caused Jewish protests across the Roman Empire and a national crisis in Judea itself (Philo, *Gaius* 202–203, 207, 265). It was only the assassination of Caligula in January AD 41 that aborted the whole endeavor. The second event is the Roman siege of Jerusalem during the Jewish Revolt (AD 70), the pillaging of the temple that ensued, and the temple's subsequent destruction. This catastrophic event was reminiscent of Apollonius's massacre and changed the Jewish nation, as they lost the vital institution at the heart of their culture. For the Gospels, this event signaled the end of the old covenant and the arrival of the new, which would culminate in the establishment of the eternal kingdom of God.

3.2.7 THE PERIOD OF PERSECUTION (167–164 BC)

For most Jews in Judea, the enforcement of Antiochus's decree felt like a national persecution. The Seleucid administration diligently pressed the application of the decree, backed by the ardent efforts of local civic authorities. Jews were compelled to eat of the sacrifices offered in the royal cult on the occasion of Antiochus's birthday (2 Macc 6:1a). Participation was used as a test of loyalty to the crown, with failure to participate inferred as treason, carrying a sentence of death. At Ptolemais-Acco, civic authorities forced the royal cult on local Jewish residents—a measure subsequently adopted by other cities also (2 Macc 6:8–9). A festival to Dionysus, the god of wine and fertility, was held (probably in Jerusalem), with all the associated pageantry. The author of 2 Maccabees states that the people were "forced to wear ivy in procession to Dionysus" (2 Macc 6:1b), which was probably a modest understatement as a traditional Dionysia festival included the parading of enormous phallic images. Not only did this breach conservative Jewish standards of decorum, but it was an insult to the Jewish practice of circumcision. From a conservative perspective, a dystopia had descended on Judea.

The persecution forced centrist and conservative Jews at critical moments either to seek refuge in hideouts or to face martyrdom. Social pressure had damaging psychological effects and produced distrust among neighbors. The author of 2 Maccabees provides several anecdotes of persecution. For example, he described the case of two women who had circumcised their infants being publicly shamed and hurled to their deaths from the city wall, their babes still at their breasts (2 Macc 6:10; cf. 1 Macc 1:60–61). He recounts the martyrdom of a ninety-year-old scribe named Eleazar, who refused to eat pork sacrificed on the altar or even to eat kosher meat while pretending it was pork. He preferred not to give any impression of giving up his religion and culture and so willingly submitted to torture and death. The author also describes at length how a woman and her seven sons were brutally tortured before the king himself, even refusing attractive inducements to eat sacrificial pork. Instead, they willingly endured gruesome fates in the hope of a future resurrection on the last day (2 Macc 7:1–42). These accounts were all crafted as stories of heroic martyrdoms, and they bear many affinities to the narratives of persecution in Daniel 3 and 6. Yet, despite the veneer of legend, they testify to the psyche of centrist and conservative Jews at this time. They felt their world was caving in and that they were experiencing a crisis of apocalyptic proportions. The very existence of the Jewish nation was at stake (cf. Qoheleth [see 2.6.16 above]). Such a crisis could only be met by faithful endurance under the most extreme pressure to compromise, and even then, the prospect of death was real. Yet death was preferable to compromise.

3.3 RESISTANCE LITERATURE

3.3.1 SONG OF SONGS

The notion that death was preferable to compromise is one of the key ideas in the Song of Songs. Though many modern interpreters treat the book as a collection of disparate love poems, the book shows evidence of a narrative integrity. That is, there is a consistency to the characters who speak within the poem, which helps us discern a storyline unfolding throughout it. Once the Song's plot is understood, we may see how it relates metaphorically to the crisis of the Antiochene persecution.

On the surface, the Song is about a young woman who has fallen in love with a shepherd boy.[1] The two characters love each other and desire to express their love in the intimate sexual union of marriage. They rightly belong to each other and therefore their union is both logical and natural. However, a complication has arisen: the young woman's brothers, who have guardianship over her, have promised her in marriage to the king, and they will gain much wealth and standing from this. The king is none other than Solomon. The woman is confined and kept under guard so that she can be prepared as a bride for Solomon. In a dream sequence, she dreams of finding her shepherd boy and bringing him into her mother's house to experience intimacy. But her anxieties also come through in the dream, as she sees Solomon and his warriors, armed for conquest, arrive to claim her. When the dream sequence ends, harsh reality sets in: the shepherd boy is not there, and the woman is instead beaten for trying to find him. The shepherd boy is at a distance watching her being prepared as a bride. But the ornaments that decorate her are symbols of her conquest. English translations have the shepherd describe her as "my bride," but the Hebrew text never actually uses the pronoun "my." Rather, he observes his beloved being prepared as "a bride" for the king. The brothers' pledging her to Solomon, a distant figure with no care for her at all, is a catastrophic injustice that has subverted the bond between the two lovers.

The extreme nature of their predicament leads the woman to flee her

---

1. For a fuller exposition of the interpretation given here, see Athas, *Ecclesiastes, Song of Songs*, 249–369.

confinement and sleep with her beloved shepherd boy. This action exposes the illegitimate claim of the king over her but also forces the issue towards a resolution. Either the woman will now be acknowledged as rightly belonging to the shepherd, or both she and the shepherd will be condemned and face death for contravening the king's claim. The woman takes this extreme measure because she does not belong to the king but to her shepherd boy, who truly loves her. She determines that it is better to give up everything and die in honor of her love for the shepherd than to capitulate to the distant king (Song 8:6–7). At the climactic end of the Song, Solomon arrives to claim the woman as the shepherd begs her to choose him. The Song ends with the woman's words, giving us the impression of her capture or ensuing death. However, the reader never witnesses these, as the Song ends abruptly. This permits the reader to imagine a scenario in which the woman and her shepherd triumph against the severe injustice perpetrated against them.

On the metaphorical level, the Song draws on the prophetic marriage metaphor used to describe the covenant relationship between Yahweh and Israel. In this way, the Song's protagonist, the young woman, is representative of Israel, and the shepherd represents Yahweh, the divine shepherd. The argument of the Song is that Israel rightly belongs to Yahweh and to no one else. To take Israel away from Yahweh is criminal and should be resisted at all costs. Solomon, therefore, is a cipher for Antiochus IV and the woman's brothers stand for the Jewish elite, like Menelaus, who should protect the nation's interests but instead sell the nation out to Antiochus for personal gain. The extreme measures the woman takes in sleeping with the shepherd are an encouragement for Jews to remain steadfast in their devotion to their divine shepherd, Yahweh, even though such devotion has become illegal and might attract capital punishment. The woman of the Song does not attack the king himself but rather enacts her commitment to her shepherd boy, which in the Antiochene persecution encourages a non-aggressive pietism prepared for martyrdom rather than armed uprising.

The key verses of the entire Song appeal to Yahweh to remember his people and act on their behalf as they face death for the love and devotion they maintain towards him under the most traumatic of circumstances:

> Set me as a seal on your heart,
> like a seal on your arm,
> for love is just as strong as death,
> devotion just as harsh as Sheol.
> Its flames are fiery flames—an inferno!

> Many waters cannot extinguish love,
> and rivers cannot overwhelm it.
> If a man gives up the entire wealth of his house for love,
> he would be utterly despised. (Song 8:6–7)

The arm of Yahweh is an image of divine intervention, familiar from traditional formulations of the exodus (cf. Deut 4:34). Both the heart and arm also evoke the classic call to faithfulness in the exposition of the *Shema* (Deut 6:4–9). Just as the Torah calls on Israel to remain radically faithful to Yahweh, so the Song calls on Yahweh to remember his people and act for them in their plight.

Furthermore, the word "inferno" (Heb. *shalhebetyah*) in Song of Songs 8:6, which occurs only here in biblical literature, carries double significance. The word derives from the Hebrew word for "flame" (Heb. *lahab*) and has been compounded with intensifying elements to yield the sense of "inferno." The compound element *-yah* at the end of the word is also the shortened form of Yahweh's name. Hidden within the word, then, is a reference to Yahweh. Indeed, when the Hebrew word *shalhebetyah* is pronounced, one hears within it the Hebrew phrase *bet yah*, meaning "house of Yahweh," a surreptitious allusion to the temple in Jerusalem, which the faithful with ears to hear could indeed hear. Using such a sophisticated auditory device to hide the divine in plain literary sight is itself a form of passive resistance and coded encouragement for the faithful. It captures in lexical form the illicit nature of worshipping Yahweh after 167 BC and demonstrates both devotion to Yahweh and the intensity of fervor that such devotion inspires, despite the "many waters" of persecution (Song 8:7). The high cost of such devotion is captured in the scenario of a person giving up the wealth of his entire house for love—a reference to the potential of forfeiting one's personal property in persecution. Although an outsider might consider such willingness to lose life, limb, and property to be weak and nonsensical, the Song views it as an expression of fervent loyalty to Yahweh. It also passes satirical judgment on Menelaus, who had despicably surrendered the wealth of Yahweh's house to Antiochus in 167 BC.[2]

Throughout the Song, one finds other devices and allusions reflecting the Antiochene persecution. For example, the anonymity of the woman reflects the loss of identity through the removal of the Jews' ethnic status. The anonymity of the shepherd evinces the dedication of Yahweh's temple to another deity (Olympian Zeus), despite the "fragrance" (an allusion to sacrifice and incense)

---

2. Athas, *Ecclesiastes, Song of Songs*, 349–50.

of his name (Song 1:3). The only active figure named in the Song is the king (Solomon), reflecting the imposition of the royal cult to demonstrate that the Jews now belonged to Antiochus. The fact that he is named as Solomon rather than Antiochus is a subversion of Antiochus's policies—a *damnatio memoriae* that refuses to dignify the despicable Seleucid king with his own name when Yahweh's name has been despoiled. He is, instead, substituted for a temple-builder from native Jewish culture who nonetheless bore a questionable legacy (cf. Neh 13:26). The imagery of Solomon coming from the desert with his warriors to claim the woman (Song 3:6) evokes Antiochus's journey through the desert after his aborted second invasion of Egypt in 167 BC and his subsequent decrees regarding the Jews. This combines with the shepherd's description of the woman's charms, which includes the following lines:

> Like the tower of David is your neck,
> built in rows,
> a thousand shields hung on it,
> all the quivers of the soldiers. (Song 4:4)

The allusion is to the tower of the Acra, its location in the city of David, and the stationing of the Seleucid garrison within it. By describing it with reference to David, the Song passively resists the transformation of Jerusalem into a Greek *polis* and instead reaches back beyond the immediate king and his new temple to the original conqueror of Jerusalem, Israel's beloved King David. These lines, therefore, have tones of both admiration and melancholy, portraying the woman as stunningly attired (the Acra must have been an impressive citadel) but nonetheless militarily conquered. This links thematically with the watchmen guarding the city who beat the woman while she seeks her beloved shepherd (Song 5:6–7), reflecting the massacre in Jerusalem perpetrated by Apollonius and the subsequent persecution of conservative Jews. The woman's desire to bring her beloved shepherd into her "house" (Song 3:4; 8:1–2) also represents the desire of conservative Jews to see normative Yahwistic worship reinstated in their temple, overturning the need to observe classic customs in secret (cf. Song 1:7) or to do so with public disapproval (Song 8:1).

The ubiquity of these allusions demonstrates that this quaint, erotic, tragic love story testifies to the deep feelings of devotion, despair, and desperation that many Jews felt during the Antiochene persecution. The Song encouraged Jews to pursue their devotion to their covenantal God even though it had become an illicit activity that could cost them their lives, for death was preferable to compromise.

3.3.2 THE BOOK OF DANIEL

Some interpreters view the book of Daniel as the writing of a Judean visionary during the period of exile in the sixth century BC. Most scholars, though, place its composition in the period of the Antiochene persecution in the second century BC. Regardless of the view taken on dating, the interpretive focal point of the book is the persecution of conservative Jews under Antiochus IV, which it interprets as a time of pre-eminent consequence for the Jewish nation. This is seen in both the narrative and visionary sections of the book.

For example, in the interpretation of Nebuchadnezzar's dream (Dan 2), the sequence of historical empires embodied by the statue's segments leads down to the Hellenistic kingdoms (the feet of clay mixed with iron). Seleucid power is thus the base of the entire stature, with elements that expose it as brittle and weak. The expectation, therefore, is that the structure will fall, like all the empires before it. Though interpreters usually see the segments of the statue as each being made of distinct elements (gold, silver, bronze, iron, and clay), it is more likely that the dream depicts the stripping away of the statue's layers as one moves from its head to its feet. In this way, all foreign empires are depicted as having impressive veneers, but in essence they have a flimsy, earthly basis. This is supremely demonstrated when a mere pebble smashes its clay feet and topples the statue (Dan 2:31–25). The Seleucid kingdom could, therefore, be successfully resisted by covenant faithfulness, and this resistance propels hope in the establishment of an invincible kingdom of God.

This puts into perspective the next chapter in which Nebuchadnezzar erects a golden statue and commands all peoples to worship it (Dan 3). The multi-ethnic scene recalls the dilution of the Jews' ethnic status within the Seleucid kingdom, while the statue itself evokes the institution of the Seleucid royal cult with its altar and idol in the Jerusalem temple. But in light of the previous chapter, the statue of solid gold is understood to be insubstantial and worthless. Thus it should be resisted by a faithful refusal to worship before it. The decree of Darius the Mede, that all should pray only to him for thirty days (Dan 6), evokes the royal cult, the month-long celebration of Antiochus at Daphne (see 3.4.2 below), and perhaps even the celebration of Antiochus's birthday (cf. 2 Macc 6:7). The opening chapter (Dan 1) raises the question of what Jews may eat so that they do not compromise the dietary laws, especially in a context in which the temple has been raided and rendered unfit for worship.

The visionary section of the book (Dan 7–12) also focuses on the Antiochene persecution. In like manner to Nebuchadnezzar's dream (Dan 2), the visions portray the sequence of historical empires through the ages, culminating in the Seleucid kingdom. All these empires are viewed as earthly instantiations of monstrous beasts that occupy a spiritual realm standing behind the earthly reality, as per the quasi-Platonic metaphysic of Jewish apocalyptic thought. Antiochus IV is the earthly personification of a horn "with eyes and a mouth speaking grandiose things" and that "engaged in battle with the saints, and prevailed against them" (Dan 7:20–21). Yet, the beast on which this horn sits "was slain, its body destroyed, and thrown into the blazing fire" (Dan 7:11), a fate reminiscent of the three companions in Daniel 3 and just deserts for the execution of Jews (cf. 2 Macc 7:3–5, 17). Antiochus and the Seleucid kingdom are thus represented as savage persecutors of God's people (the "saints"), but the book maintains hope even amid such opposition.

This hope is achieved in four ways. First, the book urges quiet resistance through adherence to covenantal tenets—the main strategy of the centrist Intellectuals (Heb. *maskilim*; see 2.8.5 above). Daniel and his companions exemplify this strategy in the narrative chapters (Dan 1–6). They engage foreign culture but without compromising their Jewish identity or religion. Theirs is not a separatist mentality that withdraws from the world but one that deals eclectically with culture by using the national covenant as their essential compass. Daniel and his companions embody the covenantal wisdom that Moses urges of the Israelites in Deuteronomy 4:5–8. At times, this earns them the praise of the gentiles, even advancing their careers among them. But at other times, it earns them fierce opposition. In all cases, they adamantly obey God and keep his Law, even when that costs them dearly. Death is seen as preferable to disobedience. One of the clearest expressions of this comes from the lips of the three companions in their resistance of Nebuchadnezzar's demand that they worship his statue:

> Shadrach, Meshach, and Abednego replied and said to the king, "O Nebuchadnezzar, we have no need to give you a response to this. If our God whom we serve exists, he is able to save us from the blazing fiery furnace. From your hand he just might save us, O king. But if he does not, let it be known to you, O king, that we are not going to serve your god, or honor the statue of gold you have set up." (Dan 3:16–18)

Secondly, the book deconstructs the power of the Seleucids (and all foreign empires). It does this in two ways. First, in the narrative chapters, foreign kings are defanged through caricature. They are depicted as foolish, shallow, short-sighted, impetuous, brimming with hubris, and sometimes comically stupid.

They stand in stark contrast to Daniel and his companions—Intellectuals who are measured, wise, sensible, responsible, and heroic in their devotion to God. This type of literary political cartooning exposes the wickedness of kings like Antiochus and undermines the raw power they wield. It thereby reconfigures how the faithful should view them and empowers the faithful to resist and endure. Second, both the narrative and visionary sections employ the quasi-Platonic metaphysic of Jewish apocalyptic to expose the spiritual reality behind kings like Antiochus. The statue in Nebuchadnezzar's dream (Dan 2) exposes the feeble substance behind the impressive veneer of Seleucid royal power. In the visions, the hideous hybrid beasts are avatars embodying the spiritual realities behind the foreign empires of history. They are abominations of nature, figurative of disorder and the misuse of power on a colossal scale. The power of Antiochus and other earthly kings to inflict harm is thus never denied, but the beasts are themselves subordinated to the sovereign power of God, who is over and above them and who acts on behalf of his covenant people. The power of the God of Israel thus confines and controls human power. This knowledge empowers the faithful to trust this God and endure persecution.

The third way the book of Daniel inspires hope is through its depiction of the character of God. He is distinguished as the particular God of Daniel and his companions whom they, as ethnic Jews, serve (cf. Dan 2:47; 3:17–18, 28; 6:5, 10, 16, 20, 26). In this way, it affirms Yahweh as the God of Israel and denies the possibility of his identification with any other god. In contrast to statues, he is a living God, and while the kings have the lives of humans in their hands, God has the lives of the kings in his hand (Dan 5:23). Even more critically, God is depicted as just. Daniel's first vision (Dan 7) culminates in a judgment scene that takes place in the spiritual realm occupied by beastly avatars. The "Ancient of Days," the avatar of God himself, takes his seat as a ruling judge on a fiery throne as documents are opened before him. This consulting of documents depicts God as judging by attested facts and consistent, righteous standards. Unlike Zeus, he does not operate according to whim and fancy, and he cannot be hoodwinked, distracted, or swayed from achieving what is good and right. Thus, when he passes judgment, he rules in favor of the saints (Dan 7:22). In this way, Daniel inspires the faithful to trust that God will vindicate them.

Finally, the book of Daniel generates hope through its eschatology. By placing the sequence of historical empires into a grand divine plan, the book imparts the sense that history is moving towards a culmination in the establishment of an unfettered kingdom of God. This means that, for the saints, the current moment of history is not the totality of one's reality. One needs to lift their gaze beyond the current moment. On the one hand, this means looking back to what God has done and revealed in ages past—we see this demonstrated in Daniel's penitential prayer, recounting God's historic dealings with his people (Dan 9:4–19). On the other hand, it means looking ahead to what God is yet to do. The faithful are to anchor their hope in the future rather than the present. In Daniel's first vision, this is epitomized by the "son of man" figure:

> I was looking in the night visions and there, amidst the clouds of the sky, was coming one like a son of man. He approached the Ancient of Days and they brought him before him. To him was given sovereignty, honor, and kingship. All the peoples, communities, and languages were to serve him. His sovereignty was to be a permanent sovereignty that would not vanish, and his kingdom, one that would not perish. (Dan 7:13–14)

Like the other figures in the vision, the "son of man" (or "human") is an avatar embodying the spiritual reality behind earthly figures and institutions. This helps us understand the explanation of the imagery given in Daniel 7:27, where he is identified as "the highest saints" (pl.), and "his" (sg.) kingdom is permanently established. The son of man figure is, therefore, singular insofar as he is one avatar in the spiritual realm but corporate in that he embodies all the saints of God. This produces a solidarity and unity amongst the people of God. To borrow Platonic categories, the son of man is the perfect "idea" of the faithful human, from which all the faithful in God's people derive their being. To put it another way, just as Antiochus and his Seleucid kingdom partake in the spiritual reality of a hideous hybrid beast, so the faithful partake in the glorious son of man. The saints, therefore, can anchor their hope in a future kingdom in which they will be supreme.

In the Gospels, when Jesus adopts the title "son of man" for himself (e.g., Matt 9:6; Mark 10:45) and appeals to it during his trial (Matt 26:64), he appropriates the theological facets of the figure in Daniel 7. He identifies himself as the incarnation of this spiritual avatar (John 3:13), which explains some of the logic behind the grand statements associated with Jesus. He is portrayed as both a faithful Jew devoted to God at all costs and the physical embodiment of the organizing principle behind the faithful. He therefore provides the faithful with their being, their faithfulness, their unity, and their eschatological salvation. He receives an everlasting kingdom from God, which gathers within it all the faithful who derive from him, and he is to reign over all the nations in a kingdom of divine quality and proportions. To reject him, therefore, is to repudiate life, being, and salvation.

In Daniel's final vision (Dan 10–12), an eschatological resurrection is promised. This doctrine of resurrection develops out of two factors. First is the classic Deuteronomistic theology of retribution, which is the backbone of justice in the national covenant. It stipulates that one gets what one deserves. Obedience to God results in blessing and life, while disobedience results in punishment and condemnation. The Torah views this as operative within the lifetime of Israelites and understands God to be the enforcer of this justice. Yet under Antiochus, the faithful were undergoing extreme persecution precisely because of their obedience to God. Many were suffering and perishing, and God was not coming to their immediate rescue in their lifetime. The only way the faithful could maintain the justice of God in the face of their harsh historical experience was to posit a time of eschatological judgment, when God would finally put all things right and true justice would be served beyond their own lifetime:

> Many will wake from sleeping in the dust of the ground—some to permanent life, and some to scorn and permanent shame. (Dan 12:2)

It is unclear whether this verse envisions a universal resurrection for all humanity or a narrower resurrection for the covenant nation only. The author of 2 Maccabees certainly thought Antiochus was disqualified from any resurrection because of his wickedness (2 Macc 7:14), but it is unclear whether he thought it was ever possible for him as a gentile. In any case, the author of 2 Maccabees demonstrates how the hope of resurrection steeled many Jews to quiet resistance, choosing martyrdom over armed conflict or compromise (cf. Dan 3:16–18).

When the doctrine of eschatological resurrection is seen in the light of its development, we see how the New Testament writers interpreted Jesus's resurrection as the harbinger of the eschaton. They viewed it not as something limited to Jesus himself but as the first event in the victory of God over the enemies of his people, the enactment of final judgment, the resurrection of all the righteous, and the establishment of the everlasting kingdom of God. Those Jews, like the Sadducees, who did not believe in resurrection probably did not hold Daniel as authoritative.[3] This makes it all the more poignant when, in answer to the questions of the Sadducee high priest, Caiaphas, Jesus appealed to the apocalyptic imagery of Daniel in response (Matt 26:63–64).

---

3. Daniel 12:2 and Isa 26:19 are the only two unambiguous references to resurrection in the Hebrew Scriptures.

3.4 THE MACCABEAN REVOLT

3.4.1 THE OUTBREAK OF REVOLT

After fleeing Jerusalem, centrist and conservative Jews began crystallizing into new groups and forming various alliances. These groups were characterized by such things as social class, their level of attachment to the Zadokite priesthood, convictions about prophetic activity, beliefs around resurrection, and attitudes towards political activism and armed resistance. In the early stages, many of these groups were nebulous and had competing ideologies within their own ranks. Some divided and re-formed in new configurations. Over the years, they solidified into more discrete groups, which dominated Judaism for the next two centuries. One thing they all shared was a commitment to Torah and classic Jewish identity, even if they differed over how to achieve its reinstatement or how it should be applied to the Jewish nation. Tracing the complex development and associations of these groups is fraught with difficulty. The following diagram is, therefore, purely schematic, as it attempts to plot linear links in what was an intricate sociopolitical web that was being constantly re-spun.

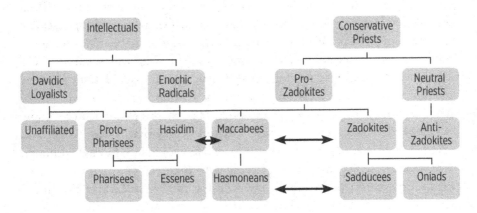

For some, like the Intellectuals and those who emerged from their ranks, the doctrine of resurrection provided the impetus for quiet resistance and martyrdom, in the belief that God would ultimately vindicate them in justice (cf. Dan 12:2–3). But others, like the pro-Zadokites and even some of the *Hasidim*, held no prospect of resurrection (cf. Sir 17:27; 41:4). For them, current earthly existence was the totality of human experience and, therefore, human society was the only locus of hope. To surrender to martyrdom was to give up everything. This generated an urgency within their ranks to undo the Antiochene persecution and achieve tangible change. They, therefore, sought active resistance, and since change could not be achieved through legal process, they were prepared to take up the sword.

Among those who escaped Jerusalem in 167 BC (2 Macc 5:24–26) was an old pro-Zadokite priest named Mattathias (1 Macc 2:1), a descendant of a certain Hasmoneus, from whom the name of the "Hasmonean" family derived (*Ant.* 12.265; *Life* 2). Mattathias had five sons: John, Simon, Judas, Eleazar, and Jonathan. With four of them, he fled the slaughter in Jerusalem and escaped to the family estate at Modiin, a small town in the lowlands along the road between Jerusalem and the port of Joppa (1 Macc 2:1). Mattathias's middle son, Judas, initially fled into the desert, where he survived with a small group away from the reach of the Seleucid authorities (2 Macc 5:27). Whether Judas returned to the family estates in Modiin at this early stage is unknown.

In 166 BC the enforcers of the royal cult arrived in Modiin. According to 1 Maccabees 2:15–28, Mattathias was singled out as a leading citizen and invited to be the first to offer a sacrifice, whereupon he and his family would be granted special rank as "friends of the king." Mattathias refused. When another leading citizen stepped forward to offer the sacrifice instead, an enraged Mattathias struck the man down before turning on the royal official presiding over the event. The account has been deliberately crafted to resemble the incident of Numbers 25 in which Phinehas, grandson of Aaron, acted out of zeal for Yahweh by slaughtering an Israelite who was sleeping with a Moabite woman after sacrificing to the Baal of Peor. It casts Mattathias in the mold of Phinehas as a means of showing the Hasmoneans to be the rightful heirs of Phinehas's perpetual priesthood.[1] It is, therefore, difficult to know what exactly transpired at Modiin; suffice it to say that it was violent and resulted in Mattathias's sons fleeing Modiin and going into hiding. Although 1 Maccabees depicts Mattathias fleeing with them, it is more likely that he died shortly before or during the incident, for he was evidently buried in the family's tomb at Modiin (1 Macc 2:70).[2]

We do not know whether Judas was involved in the incident at Modiin.

---

1. Sievers, *The Hasmoneans and Their Supporters*, 30–31.
2. Part of the purpose of 1 Maccabees is to justify the rise of all Mattathias's sons by portraying Mattathias as the instigator of the revolt—the grand patriarch who blesses all his sons and whose death is mourned by "all Israel" (1 Macc 2:70). It is unlikely that Mattathias was able to kill both a Jewish man and

Nevertheless, soon after it, all five Hasmonean brothers were together. At first, they were simply a family of vigilante priests on the run from the Seleucid state. But the incident at Modiin gained them enough notoriety to attract others who, like them, felt that active resistance to Antiochus's decree was necessary. In the early stages, this did not amount to many people. Most Jews, though conservative, were probably bullied into participation in the royal cult and were willing to comply in order to save their own skins. For the Hasmonean brothers this was unacceptable, as it imperiled the long-term future of Jewish identity.

Judas quickly emerged as the leader of the rebel band. They would secretly enter Jewish villages to foster resistance against the Seleucids and encourage villagers to take an active stand (2 Macc 8:1–4). Exactly what form this encouragement took is unknown, but judging by some of the brothers' later methods, it is not inconceivable that they used tactics every bit as threatening as the Seleucids. According to 2 Maccabees 8:1, Judas gathered some 6,000 people to his cause, but this number probably reflects more the level of general support he managed to drum up among the rural population. The number of men who flocked to his side was probably much smaller.

Before long, the Hasmonean brothers were commanding a small but dedicated underground resistance movement in the Judean hills. Each brother earned a nickname, which was either a codename used during covert operations or earned through their reputation in subsequent years. They were John Gaddi ("Lucky" John), Simon Thassi ("Clever" Simon), Judas Maccabeus (Judas the "Hammer"), Eleazar Avaran ("Pale" Eleazar),[3] and Jonathan Apphus (Jonathan the "Trickster").[4] Simon became the movement's strategist while Judas led armed operations.

Initially, the band's fighters were poorly armed, wielding makeshift weapons. Their earliest operations were of a vigilante nature, such as vandalizing the altars used for the royal cult and worship of the Greek gods. But the movement soon grew bolder and began acquiring human targets, particularly as it met resistance from fellow Jews. The band started to terrorize Hellenizing Jews and even those of a more neutral disposition. The author of 1 Maccabees called such people "sinners" and "lawless ones," in contrast to "those who took up the cause of the Law" and supported the rebels (1 Macc 2:42, 44). Their tactics became

---

the royal official at Modiin. It is more probable that he was either killed during the incident or had died shortly before it and that his sons were involved in the violence.

3. The meaning of "Avaran" is contested. Despite some linguistic difficulties, some connect it to the Hebrew word 'eran, meaning "alert." See Bezalel Bar-Kochva, *Judas Maccabaeus: The Jewish Struggle against the Seleucids* (Cambridge: Cambridge University Press, 1989), 334.

4. The precise meaning of "Apphus" is disputed because the original Hebrew or Aramaic name has been obscured considerably by its Greek form.

brazenly violent and included intimidation, driving people from their property, assassination, and burning (1 Macc 2:44, 47; 3:3–9).[5] They also forcibly circumcised boys as a means of guaranteeing Jewish covenantal identity (1 Macc 2:46).

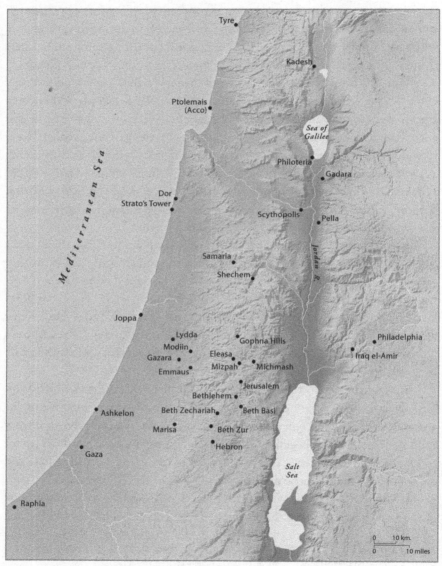

Sites relating to the Maccabean Revolt.

---

5. Second Maccabees 8:6 states that the Maccabees burned villages, but the wording of 1 Macc 3:5 makes it difficult to ascertain whether the Maccabees burned only the property of their enemies or the people themselves.

The rebels were soon called Maccabees ("Hammers") after the nickname of its primary leader, Judas. The rhetoric of 1 Maccabees places emphasis on the zeal of the Maccabees for the Torah (cf. 1 Macc 2:50, 67–68; 3:5–6). They viewed themselves as defenders of Jewish culture rather than defenders of the God of Israel per se. This does not mean God was unimportant to them, for the Hasmonean brothers were qualified priests who believed they were averting the wrath of God by eradicating apostasy (cf. 1 Macc 3:8). However, their primary motivation was cultural rather than religious. This distinction is somewhat artificial since Jewish culture was intrinsically religious, but it is a conceptually helpful distinction, as the variegated nature of Judaism at this time demonstrates (see 2.8.5 above). The Maccabees saw their task as a national effort to counteract Antiochus's revocation of the Jews' ethnic status and the adverse effect this was having on conservative Jewish identity (cf. 1 Macc 3:20–21). Theirs was a cultural crusade that sought to "snatch the Law from the hand of the gentiles and the kings, and not give the sinner any power" (1 Macc 2:48).[6] In this way, they were the heirs of the same cultural brand of Judaism expressed by Ben Sira.[7]

3.4.2 EARLY MACCABEAN SUCCESSES

In the summer of 166 BC Antiochus IV held a month-long festival at Daphne, south of Antioch, to celebrate the so-called success of his Egyptian campaign—a veritable propaganda jamboree. Being a connoisseur of Roman culture, he modelled the opening procession on a Roman triumphal march. The historian Polybius, who was in attendance, stated that the festival's extravagance was paid for by Antiochus's looting of Egypt and local temples (Polybius, *Hist.* 30.25–26), including the temple in Jerusalem. In Daniel 6, the thirty-day embargo on praying to anyone other than king might be a veiled allusion to this month-long celebration. If so, then the book of Daniel countered the festival and its propaganda by encouraging Jews to continue praying towards Jerusalem, even though worship in the temple was impossible. The faithful were enjoined to turn their backs on Antioch and look forward to the temple's restoration.

---

6. The word translated here as "power" is literally "a horn," a classic symbol of power, and indeed the dominant image of Antiochus IV in the book of Daniel.

7. Second Maccabees gives a more religiously motivated account, which preserves the apocalypticism prevalent among many *Hasidim*. Whether this reflects the underlying perspective of Jason of Cyrene (which it summarizes) or is a veneer added to Jason's work cannot be known. Either way, the concentration on martyrs who had nothing to do with the Maccabean movement (2 Macc 6–7) shows that the author of 2 Maccabees, though praising the Maccabean movement, was an allied outsider, able to maintain his own perspective.

The Daphne festival showed that Antiochus no longer saw Judea as a serious flashpoint. The Hellenization of Judea was continuing according to royal policy, with Maccabean resistance still a small endeavor. But as the months wore on, Maccabean operations grew more violent and conspicuous. By garnering support among conservative sympathizers and provoking terror among neutrals, the Maccabees began to make their mark on Jewish society so that they could no longer be safely ignored. Their persistent agitation against Seleucid policy and its erosion of classic Jewish culture made them an odious nuisance to the Seleucid authorities and the Hellenizing Jewish elite.

In late 166 BC the Seleucid administration decided to take action. Apollonius, who had been appointed governor of Samaria, put together a police force, which he personally marched into the hills bordering Judea.[8] His intent was to rat out the Maccabean fighters, who were operating near a town called Gophna. But Judas Maccabeus demonstrated his military acumen. He knew that his Maccabean fighters could never prevail against Apollonius's troops in open combat. So he opted to employ guerilla tactics, which played to the strengths of the small rebel band.[9] They ambushed Apollonius, and several Seleucid troops fell in the skirmish. More importantly, Judas killed Apollonius. The sacker of Jerusalem received his comeuppance, and his police force was put to flight. The rebels stripped the dead, which provided them with useful weapons and armor. Judas himself is said to have taken the sword of Apollonius, which he brandished for the rest of his life (1 Macc 3:10–12)—a patent David and Goliath moment (cf. 1 Sam 17:51; 21:9). The victory catapulted the Maccabean cause to prominence and escalated the level of their threat to the Seleucid authorities. As far as we know, it was the first successful military resistance to Seleucid power since the implementation of Antiochus's decree in 167 BC. The rebel band continued to operate in the Gophna Hills and attracted new followers, encouraged by the recent victory.[10]

There was little reprieve for the Hasmonean brothers, though. A more serious assault soon came from the coastal plain, led by a Seleucid commander named Seron.[11] He set out to smash the rebels in their highland hideouts

---

8. First Maccabees 3:10 describes it as a "large force," but this almost certainly refers to its size in comparison to the smaller band of Maccabean fighters. For discussion on Apollonius as governor of Samaria, see Bar-Kochva, *Judas Maccabaeus*, 202–3.

9. See Bar-Kochva, *Judas Maccabaeus*, 205.

10. We can infer this from the later size of the movement. It compares with the growing forces of slaves attracted to Spartacus's side after the initial successes of his rebel movement in Italy (73–71 BC).

11. Josephus calls Seron the "general" (Gk. *stratēgos*) of all Coele Syria (*Ant.* 12.288), while 1 Maccabees dubs him "leader of the force of Syria" (1 Macc 3:13). Both are either mistaken or exaggerations. He was probably the garrison commander at Gazara (Gezer). See Bar-Kochva, *Judas Maccabaeus*, 132–33, 209.

before their menace grew worse. But the Hasmonean brothers expected such a reprisal and sprang a surprise attack. Judas brought a small contingent from the Gophna Hills and attacked Seron's men as they began the steep climb between Lower and Upper Beth Horon, inflicting many casualties and routing the rest (1 Macc 3:13–26),[12] The success against Seron again demonstrated Judas Maccabeus's prowess in using guerilla tactics to maximum effect against a superior foe. It boosted his prestige and the appeal of the Maccabean cause. They were no longer viewed as a band of disparate vigilantes but as an organized resistance force to be reckoned with.

Despite the quiet resistance promoted by the book of Daniel, the appeal of armed resistance now gained considerable traction. It was at this time that some of the Intellectuals joined with several Zadokite priests to form the group that came to be known as the *Hasidim* ("pious ones" or devotees" of the covenant). They were convinced to make common cause with the Maccabees, viewing Judas as the most promising means of regaining the ethnic status of the Jews.[13] The War Scroll (1QM), despite its veneer of later apocalyptic eschatology, contains an echo of this alliance in its opening chapter.[14] It effectively created a new conservative political bloc in Jewish society. The Maccabees gave the *Hasidim* a military wing with some sting, while the *Hasidim* gave the Maccabees political clout and broader social appeal. The priestly pedigree of the Hasmonean brothers must also have been appealing to the *Hasidim* as it gave them prominent qualified figures with whom to rally in opposition to the Hellenizing high priest Menelaus. The alliance with the *Hasidim* swelled the numbers of Maccabean fighters and escalated their goals. They were now fighting realistically for the overthrow of Menelaus, the reinstatement of the Jews' ethnic status, and the reclamation of the temple for Torah-observant Judaism.

With such aims, the "elephant in the room" was who would replace Menelaus if he could be ousted. The most direct and legitimate candidate was

---

12. First Maccabees 3:24 places the number of the slain at 800. The wording of 3:23 makes it difficult to ascertain whether Seron was killed in the battle. See John D. Grainger, *The Wars of the Maccabees: The Jewish Struggle for Freedom (167–37 BC)* (Barnsley: Pen & Sword, 2012), 14–16; Bar-Kochva, *Judas Maccabaeus*, 207–18.

13. The chronology of 1 Maccabees puts the alliance of the *Hasidim* with the Maccabees much earlier (2:42), but realistically, the alliance only makes political sense after Judas's victories against Apollonius and Seron.

14. The War Scroll alludes to warfare against the "Kittim of Assyria" (1QM 1:2), originally a reference to the Seleucids, which was reworked and redefined in the final recension of the War Scroll. Cf. Jean Duhaime, "War Scroll," in Feldman, Kugel, and Schiffman, *Outside the Bible*, 3117; David Flusser, *Qumran and Apocalypticism*, vol. 1 of *Judaism of the Second Temple Period*, trans. Azzan Yadin (Grand Rapids: Eerdmans, 2007), 149, 154.

Onias IV, the young son of the murdered high priest Onias III. But Onias IV was still too young to take up the office. If the Hasmonean brothers themselves had any pretensions to the highest sacerdotal office at this stage, they were certainly muted. In any case, the Seleucid king still had the authority to appoint any high priest, so the most the Hasmoneans and *Hasidim* could hope for was to exert enough pressure to gain some leverage over any future appointment. That goal, however, was still a long way off.

3.4.3 THE BATTLE OF EMMAUS (165 BC)

With the expansion of the Maccabean movement, the Hasmonean brothers realized that they could no longer continue as an underground resistance. They needed to prepare themselves for more conventional troop warfare. The brothers chose a new base for their operations: Mizpah. The town was symbolic, for in Israelite history it had been a place of pan-Israelite convocation, especially before battle (Judg 10:17; 20:1; 1 Sam 7:5; 10:17). It was also strategic, for the town was situated at one of the highest points north of Jerusalem, affording views of all the major roads into the highlands. Here, Judas set to training a fledgling Jewish army (1 Macc 3:46–56).

The notoriety of the Maccabees reached Antiochus IV. His first response was not direct military intervention but rather measures for controlling the roads and fostering the progress of Hellenization. He granted royal status to key coastal cities such as Gaza and Ptolemais-Acco, as well towns east of Lake Galilee and the Jordan Valley.[15] This surrounded Judea and Samaria with strongly Hellenized centers buttressed by strong garrisons, with Jerusalem already a royal colony since the time of Jason. Antiochus was effectively placing colonial pillars around Judea and Samaria to support a greater weight of Greek culture across the region. He eventually acknowledged the need for military intervention but did not consider the Maccabean menace big enough to warrant his own involvement. Instead, he turned his attention to Armenia and the eastern reaches of his kingdom, which lay outside Rome's purview. Before he embarked on his expedition, he made his seven-year-old son, Antiochus V Goodfather (Gk. *Eupatōr*), co-ruler and made a trusted relative, General Lysias, regent for the boy.[16] In Antiochus's absence, Lysias would deal with the Maccabees.

---

15. Grainger, *The Fall of the Seleukid Empire*, 30–31.
16. Antiochus V was the son whom Laodice IV bore to Antiochus IV. Her fate by this time is entirely unknown.

Lysias appointed a new governor of Coele Syria (Ptolemy, son of Dorymenes) and put two military legates, Nicanor and Gorgias, at his disposal.[17] Plans for a strike on the Maccabees were drawn up in consultation with Menelaus in Jerusalem. In September 165 BC Nicanor and Gorgias brought a sizeable force into the Judean foothills and pitched a conspicuous camp near Emmaus, not far from the Hasmonean hometown of Modiin.[18] From there, Gorgias was to take a division into the hills under the cover of night to surprise the Maccabees at dawn (1 Macc 3:38–41; 2 Macc 8:8–11).

At this point, Judas acted with great alacrity. He chose not to dig in or flee into the desert. Instead, he took his modest militia and, putting a line of hills between them and Gorgias's forces, headed quickly and quietly through the night via a different route to Emmaus. As morning broke, "Pale" Eleazar was charged with reading aloud from a scroll of Scripture and sounding the signal for attack with the words "Help of God" (the meaning of the Hebrew name "Eleazar"). While Nicanor's forces still slept, Judas's men struck. Panic ensued among the Seleucid soldiers, and they fled towards the coastal plain, Nicanor included (1 Macc 4:1–18; 2 Macc 8:12–25).

In the highlands, Gorgias found an empty Maccabean base at Mizpah. Only when he spotted the fire emanating from Nicanor's camp down at Emmaus did he realize what had happened. He turned his men around and marched back to Emmaus, but by the time they arrived, they were exhausted from over 50 kilometers of marching. The Maccabean fighters had plundered the weapons left behind in the camp. Seeing them thus armed, Gorgias chose not to engage and also retreated to the coastal plain (1 Macc 4:19–25).

The following day was a Sabbath, which the Maccabean militia observed solemnly—a potent demonstration of Jewish cultural piety. In addition to the arms they had plundered, they also came across a trove of money brought to the Seleucid camp by slave traders seeking to buy prisoners of war. Over the coming weeks, the Maccabees distributed some of this money and other spoils to Jewish people throughout the countryside who had lost loved ones to the Antiochene persecution. In this way, the Maccabees made themselves champions of the people, and their victory at Emmaus began to unite more Jews behind their cause (2 Macc 8:25–29).[19]

---

17. This Ptolemy was probably son of the Dorymenes mentioned on the Heliodorus Stele of Seleucus IV (178 BC).
18. Inflated figures for the force are given in both 1 Macc 3:39 (40,000 infantry, 7,000 cavalry) and 2 Macc 8:9 (20,000 men). In light of the size of the entire Seleucid army, the contingent is likely to have been less than 10,000.
19. Bar-Kochva, *Judas Maccabaeus*, 219–74.

3.4.4 NEGOTIATIONS WITH THE SELEUCIDS

After Emmaus, the Hasmonean brothers effectively controlled the roads leading from the foothills to the highlands north of Jerusalem. From the Seleucid perspective, a rebel army was now in possession of crucial territory. Lysias pressured Governor Ptolemy to resolve the problems in Judea, so he urged Gorgias to raid the Jewish rebels. But over the early months of 164 BC Judas's militia repelled these raids, delivering brutal deaths to any Seleucid soldiers who fell into their hands (2 Macc 10:14–17). Lysias fired Ptolemy Dorymenes and replaced him with Ptolemy Macron (2 Macc 10:13).[20] Macron encouraged Lysias to take a conciliatory approach to the Jewish rebels, so negotiations were opened. What role Menelaus had in the process is unknown. In the late summer of 164 BC the rebels sent a delegation of two men, John and Absalom,[21] to Antioch, where they put forward their demands. We can only infer what these were from the official response given afterwards by Lysias (2 Macc 11:16–21). They seem to have demanded the removal of Menelaus as high priest, the right of appointment for all subsequent high priests, the abolition of the royal cult in Judea, and the reversion of the temple in Jerusalem to pure Yahwistic worship—in short, nothing less than the reinstatement of the ethnic status of the Jews.

From the Seleucid perspective, the regime could not afford to grant all the rebels' demands, for it would have wider regional repercussions. Reversing the status of the temple in Jerusalem would raise expectations that the same be done for Mount Gerizim. And yet, the rivalry between the Jewish and Samaritan communities made this a delicate matter. Furthermore, Antiochus would have been keen to ensure that any concession to the Jewish rebels did not come across as weakness on his part. A compromise was required.

Lysias delayed a ruling because he desired to know the imperial mind before repealing imperial decrees. After receiving communications from Antiochus out on campaign, Lysias sent an official response in early October 164 BC. He addressed it to "the multitude of the Jews" (2 Macc 11:16), conspicuously avoiding the term "nation" (Gk. *ethnos*),[22] demonstrating that Antiochus

---

20. Ptolemy Macron had been governor of Cyprus for the Ptolemies but defected to the Seleucids when Antiochus invaded Cyprus in 167 BC.

21. It is impossible to know whether this John was the eldest of the Hasmonean brothers or someone else.

22. Lysias's letter (2 Macc 11:16–21) appears with several other communiques from the Seleucid regime to the Jews, giving the impression that they all relate to the reign of Antiochus V after November 164 BC. Despite their arrangement, though, the date of Lysias's letter demonstrates that it relates to October 164 BC, during the reign of Antiochus IV.

was not inclined to reinstate the Jews' ethnic status. But he was prepared to "concede what was acceptable" (2 Macc 11:18). Lysias encouraged the rebels to maintain goodwill towards the authorities, and he would endeavor to secure their welfare.

This response fell well short of what the Hasmonean brothers and their *Hasidim* allies desired. Consequently, the Maccabean militia intensified their operations to demonstrate their rejection of it. The Hasmoneans had effectively thrown down the gauntlet and turned their cause into a struggle for complete secession from the Seleucids. Lysias had little choice but to respond directly, quickly, and with overwhelming force. He gathered his troops and marched swiftly south to quash the rebels.

3.4.5 THE DEATH OF ANTIOCHUS IV (164 BC)

Lysias studied the previous defeats of Apollonius, Nicanor, and Gorgias and opted for a new tactic. In late October he attempted to outflank the Maccabees by approaching Judea from the south through the highlands of Idumea. Thus, in November 164 BC he reached the southern border of Judea at Beth Zur along the watershed road. From here, he had a dominant view of the region and could thrust into the heart of Judea from higher ground (1 Macc 4:26–29).

The Hasmonean brothers tracked Lysias's movements and deployed their modest but keen militia into southern Judea to surprise him. The literary and archaeological sources give conflicting information, making it difficult to determine exactly what happened. The most plausible interpretation is that Lysias was in the process of improving the fortifications at Beth Zur when the Hasmonean brothers and their Maccabean fighters arrived. Lysias was in the dominant position with the advantage of fortifications, higher ground, and open terrain. For the Maccabean fighters to engage his troops head on would have been to invite catastrophic defeat. Thus, despite the valorous claim of 1 Maccabees 4:34 that a pitched battle occurred, it is far more likely that the Maccabees employed sabotage to avoid a direct confrontation.[23] The longer Lysias continued to dig in, the bleaker the Maccabean prospects became. The odds were stacked completely against them, and it was only a matter of time before Lysias would deliver the *coup de grâce*.

Then, there suddenly came a *coup de théâtre*—a completely unexpected twist that changed everything. It was late November 164 BC and by this time, Antiochus IV had been on campaign for over a year. He had tamed Armenia

---

23. Cf. Bar-Kochva, *Judas Maccabaeus*, 284–89; Grainger, *The Wars of the Maccabees*, 24–25.

and ensured the loyalty of Mesopotamia. He even attempted to pilfer a temple in Elymais, though a different one to that in which his father, Antiochus III, lost his life (1 Macc 6:1–4).[24] It seems he was in Persia gathering resources to meet a challenge from the Parthians in the east when he was suddenly struck by disease and died just days later (Polybius, *Hist.* 31.9; Appian, *S.W.* 66; cf. 1 Macc 6:5–16; 2 Macc 9:1–28).[25] Word of his death was conveyed quickly along the royal roads to Antioch and relayed instantly to Lysias at Beth Zur. Upon receiving the news, Lysias immediately abandoned his operations against the Maccabees and hastened back to Antioch to oversee the royal succession (cf. 1 Macc 4:34–35).

The Maccabean fighters probably did not understand the reason for Lysias's abrupt departure, for news of Antiochus's death had not yet become public knowledge. Therefore, they interpreted it as a retreat sparked by divine intervention on their behalf. When news of Antiochus's demise filtered into the public domain over the following days, the notion of divine intervention gained yet more traction. Lysias's departure confirmed that Antiochus's death was no mere rumor, such as the one that had circulated some years earlier when Antiochus had reinvaded Egypt. The Seleucid tyrant was indeed dead. The lethal pressure that Lysias had been exerting against the Maccabees suddenly dissipated. To everyone's surprise, the Antiochene persecution was over.

3.4.6 THE REDEDICATION OF THE TEMPLE

The death of Antiochus IV Epiphanes in late November 164 BC caused an immediate political change. Antiochus's body was in the custody of Philip, one of his generals who had been campaigning with him. This gave Philip considerable political clout as he conveyed the body back to Antioch.[26] Lysias's peremptory departure from Beth Zur was to ensure that Philip did not capitalize on this by gaining control over the new boy king, Antiochus V Goodfather.

In Judea, the Maccabees took possession of Beth Zur and then made a beeline for Jerusalem. By the time they arrived, their numbers had swelled. With them was a small army of fighters, priests, and civilians intent on enforcing

---

24. Second Maccabees 1:13–16 contains a similar account but is linked with the death of Antiochus IV, which contradicts the account in 2 Macc 9:1–28.

25. Antiochus is said to have died at "Tabae" in Persia. This is probably a corruption of "Gabae" (modern Isfahan, Iran). The accounts of his demise in 1 Maccabees and 2 Maccabees, though differing in various details, drip with melodramatic schadenfreude. His sudden and rapid demise may be likened to that of Alexander the Great.

26. To understand the political value of taking possession of the body of a deceased king, we have only to turn to the efforts of Ptolemy I to gain control over the body of Alexander the Great.

the demands that Antiochus had effectively turned down. No conservative had been in Jerusalem since Apollonius's massacre in May 167 BC. With his appointing patron now dead, Menelaus was in an extremely vulnerable position, so he bunkered down with the Seleucid garrison in the Acra. Aware of the violent tactics the Maccabees had used in the past, some of the civilian population retreated there also, whilst others fled the city entirely.

The Maccabees occupied Jerusalem's Western Hill, the Baris fortress north of the Temple Mount, and then took the temple itself. But the Acra and the *polis* in the city of David still defied them, and its inhabitants survived easily. Jerusalem effectively became a partitioned city.

The Hasmonean brothers had the statues, altars, and shrines throughout their zone of control demolished. In the temple precinct, the altar for the royal cult and its accompanying statue were removed and destroyed. Similarly, the large altar of burnt offering was dismantled and a completely new altar constructed. New equipment was also fashioned, such as a menorah for the sanctuary, the incense stand, sacrificial bowls, and the like. Once the temple had been cleansed, an official period was organized to rededicate it to Yahweh. This would draw a line in the sand, putting the dystopia of the Antiochene persecution in the past. It marked the de facto reinstatement of the ethnic status of the Jews, even if that status had not been reinstated de jure by the Seleucids. The period of rededication commenced on the 25th day of Kislev (14 January 163 BC)—three years to the day (according to Jewish reckoning) since the old altar had been desecrated by the first sacrifice offered in the royal cult.[27] The rededication period began with a ceremony to light new fire on the new altar by the striking of flint. Incense was burned, the menorah inside the sanctuary was lit, and freshly baked bread of the presence was placed on the sanctuary table. The Hasmoneans then offered a sacrifice to consecrate the new altar and led the people in worship, seeking Yahweh's favor in repentance for the nation's sin.

The rededication lasted eight days, the length of time stipulated in the Torah for ritual cleansing (cf. Lev 14:10–11, 23; 15:13–15, 29) and for the consecration of Aaron and his sons for priestly office (Lev 8:31–9:24). The period thus re-consecrated all conservative priests for service. They and the

---

27. The date of the rededication is commonly identified as 25 December 164 BC. However, as Bar-Kochva notes, there was a discrepancy between the calendrical system used in Judea and that used in official Seleucid chronicles. Along with the use of intercalary months, an adjustment is required that means the beginning of the rededication must have taken place on 14 January 163 BC. See *Judas Maccabaeus*, 280–82, though note the typographical error in Bar-Kochva's table on 282, which mistakenly gives "14 January 164 B.C." instead of 14 January 163 BC.

laity remained in and around the temple campus for the duration of the rededication, living in makeshift booths like during the Festival of Sukkot. At the end of the rededication ceremony, the full gamut of sacrifices recommenced. A decree was then issued that this event should be commemorated annually for eight days, beginning on 25 Kislev (1 Macc 4:36–59; 2 Macc 10:1–7). The festival, known as Hanukkah ("Dedication"), thus became a standard feature in the Jewish ritual calendar.[28]

There is no evidence that a high priest officiated at the rededication. Although the Hasmonean brothers were themselves priests, they did not make any claim to the supreme sacral office at this moment. They were not of the requisite Zadokite line, so any attempt to grab the office would have put them in the same category as Menelaus. Rather, they and the *Hasidim* supported the claim of Onias IV, son of the murdered Onias III. His undoubted presence at proceedings would have given the conservative cause a shot in the arm. The young man was now in his twenties, so not too many years from being able to take office at age thirty. Until then, the intervening years would give the Hasmoneans and the *Hasidim* valuable influence over him.

3.4.7 DANIEL AND THE END OF THE ANTIOCHENE PERSECUTION

The book of Daniel describes the end of the Antiochene persecution in the following terms:

> At the time of the end, the King of the South [Ptolemy VI] will backstab him, but the King of the North [Antiochus IV] will storm against him with chariots, cavalry, and many ships. He will invade lands, overwhelm them, and continue campaigning. He will invade the glorious land, and many will stumble. But these will escape his hand: Edom, Moab, and the leading sons of Ammon [the Tobiads]. He will stretch his hand out against lands, and the land of Egypt will have no escape. He will command hidden stores of gold and silver, and the treasures of Egypt, with Libyans and Nubians in his wake. But reports from the east [Parthia] and the north [Armenia] will trouble him, so that he departs with great fury to annihilate and confiscate many.

---

28. The celebration of Hanukkah also came to include a legend about the lighting of the temple menorah. It was said that there was insufficient olive oil to ensure the menorah would burn for the duration of the rededication. However, what little oil there was kept the menorah miraculously burning for the full eight days. Thus, Hanukkah also came to be known as the Festival of Lights. The legend was perhaps a timely appropriation of Zech 4.

Though he pitches his palatial tents between the seas [the Mediterranean] and the mountain of glorious holiness [Jerusalem], he will yet come to his end with none to help him. But at that time, Michael, the great chief who stands over the sons of your people, will take his stand. Though it be a time of trouble that has not occurred since the time the nation came into being until that time, yet at that time your people will escape. (Dan 11:40–12:1b)

Most scholars who date Daniel to the Antiochene persecution see these verses as an imaginative but failed prediction, arguing that they were written shortly before Antiochus's death without knowledge of what eventually transpired.[29] Even those who argue for composition in the sixth century BC struggle to interpret these verses. However, such confusion is largely the result of getting the direction of interpretation back-to-front. Scholars tend to see the "King of the North" as a cipher for Antiochus IV when actually the reverse is true: Antiochus is a cipher for the "King of the North." This final vision of Daniel (chs. 10–12) represents a single "King of the North" who is instantiated by multiple Seleucid figures, Antiochus being but one of them. The quasi-Platonic metaphysic of apocalyptic reality in Daniel means the various avatars occupying the visionary spiritual realm represent ultimate reality, and the earthly figures merely embody them as representative subordinates. The "King of the North" is the spiritual genius behind all Seleucid power, just as the "King of the South" is the spiritual genius of Ptolemaic power and "Michael" is the spiritual genius of the Jewish people.[30]

Furthermore, scholars tend to assume that the entirety of Daniel's last vision is chronologically linear. This is true in broad outline but does not prevail at every point. Daniel 11:29–12:1 is a dossier of information, and there is no compelling necessity for it to be strictly chronological. Thus, Daniel 11:40 is best understood not as a failed prediction of a third invasion of Egypt but as a reference back to Antiochus's capture of Cyprus and his second invasion of Egypt in 167 BC. The escape of "Edom, Moab, and the leading sons of Ammon" (Dan 11:41) is not a failed prediction of these regions breaking away from Seleucid rule, but a testament to the fact that the citizens of these regions, including their Jewish inhabitants, were highly Hellenized and so escaped the heavy-handed oppression that the faithful in Judea and the Phoenician cities suffered. The "leading sons of Ammon" (Dan 11:41) is probably a reference

---

29. Louis Francis Hartman and Alexander A. Di Lella, *The Book of Daniel*, Anchor Bible 23 (Garden City, NY: Doubleday, 1978), 303.

30. Cf. Walsh, *Angels Associated with Israel*, 66–83.

to the Tobiad family, whose ancestral estates lay in Ammonite territory.[31] The situation of Antiochus's two invasions of Egypt (168 and 167 BC) are then mentioned again (Dan 11:42–43) to contrast with his final expedition to deal with Armenia and Parthia in 165–164 BC (Dan 11:44). The pitching of "his palatial tents between the seas and the mountain of glorious holiness" (Dan 11:45) is not a wild guess that Antiochus would return to Judea and finally meet his end there. Rather, it is a reference to the camp of Nicanor at Emmaus in the foothills between Joppa and Jerusalem and the subsequent Seleucid loss to the Maccabean militia in September 165 BC. After all, the subject who pitches his tents here is not, strictly speaking, Antiochus but the spiritual genius of Seleucid power known as the "King of the North." The final demise of the "King of the North" is then noted, actualized in the earthly sphere by the death of Antiochus in November 164 BC. This is then contrasted with the prevailing rise of "Michael," the spiritual genius behind the Jewish people (Dan 12:1), who is instantiated by all who took their stand against Antiochus's decree by clinging faithfully to Jewish ideals.[32]

The visions of Daniel also give insight into the timing of events during the Antiochene persecution. In general terms, the persecution is said to last for "a set time, set times, and a half" (Dan 12:7)—that is, for three and a half years.[33] This corresponds to the time between the return of Antiochus from his aborted second expedition to Egypt in mid-167 BC and the rededication of the temple in January 163 BC. The first vision of Daniel sets down 2,300 evenings and mornings before the "rectification [i.e., rededication] of the sanctuary" (Dan 8:14), referring to the number of evening and morning sacrifices foregone after their abolition. This is clearly a rounded number, so we must be prepared for some give-or-take in a more precise calculation. It corresponds to 1,150 days (3 years and 55 days). It was 1,143 days between the erection of the altar for the royal cult (6 December 167 BC) and the end of the rededication ceremony when regular sacrifice recommenced (22 January 163 BC). Furthermore, the abolition of the daily sacrifices had occurred just prior to the erection of the altar for the royal cult. Thus, the calculation of 1,150 days, even if a rounded figure, is still remarkably accurate.

---

31. This is further boosted by Nehemiah's characterization of the family's fifth century BC ancestor as "Tobiah the Ammonite" (Neh 2:10, 19; 4:3), the reference to Tobias (father of Joseph) as the cleruch of Ammanitis in the Zenon Papyri (258 BC), and the location of Hyrcanus's estates at Iraq el-Amir in Ammanitis at the end of the third century BC.

32. This means that the opening chapter of the War Scroll is not an alternative vision based on the non-fulfilment of Dan 11:40–44 but a reminiscence of what did indeed happen. *Pace* Flusser, *Qumran and Apocalypticism*, 144–45.

33. The Hebrew word for "set time" is *mo'ed*.

Another timeframe for this period is given in the final vision of Daniel:

> From the time of the abolition of the daily sacrifices and the institution of the abomination of desolation there will be 1,290 days. Blessed is the one who waits and reaches 1,335 days. (Dan 12:11–12)

This calculation has been characterized as an educated guess at the duration of the lapse in daily sacrifices (1,290 days) followed by a later revision (1,335 days) to correct it.[34] If this were the case, why the revision did not simply amend an initial faulty guess is inexplicable. Either way, this understanding fails to appreciate the dynamics in both the text and history. There are two key factors to consider.

First, the word used for "time" here (Heb. 'et) refers to a period rather than a specific day. This period is noted by both the lapse of the daily sacrifices and the abomination of desolation. These two events were clearly related but not identical. Indeed, they occurred at least ten days apart. They cannot, therefore, function together as a single starting point for calculating either the 1,290 days or the 1,335 days. Instead, the period is characterized generally by these two salient events, which is rather different to stating that the period began with them.

Second, the final vision of Daniel is interested in details concerning the "King of the North" (the genius of Seleucid power) and the "King of the South" (the genius of Ptolemaic power) and how they affected the Jewish people. The forces of the "King of the North" abolish the daily sacrifice and institute the abomination of desolation (Dan 11:39). Thus, the period of 1,290 days is described as a time in which the forces of the "King of the North" prevail in Jerusalem. To this is added a further forty-five days, the end of which is characterized by blessing.

Putting these factors together, the end of the 1,335 days must refer to the rededication of the temple on 14 January 163 BC. Working backwards from this date, forty-five days earlier (the end of the 1,290 days) brings us to 30 November 164 BC. This is seen as the time in which the power of the forces of the "King of the North" was broken. It must, therefore, refer to the death of Antiochus IV in Persia, which is known to have occurred between 20 November and 19 December 164 BC.[35] The beginning of the 1,290 days can then be pinned to 21 May 167 BC, which corresponds to the time that

---

34. Cf. Hartman and Di Lella, *The Book of Daniel*, 313–14.
35. André Lacocque, *The Book of Daniel*, trans. David Pellauer (London: SPCK, 1979), 233; Hartman and Di Lella, *The Book of Daniel*, 305.

Antiochus IV returned from his aborted second expedition to Egypt and authorized the massacre in Jerusalem perpetrated by Apollonius. We also know that the Seleucids expanded the Acra and built a glacis around it immediately after the massacre. Archaeological evidence confirms that the glacis was built in late spring, according perfectly with the timeframes in Daniel.[36]

The visions of Daniel peek behind the veil of earthly experience to ultimate spiritual reality. The need to do this is testament to the severity of the situation that centrist and conservative Jews at the time faced. There was a desire to find explanations for the grave injustices they experienced and what felt like a world caving in on them. The apocalyptic mindset, which combined Greek philosophical categories with traditional biblical thought, provided the conceptual architecture for doing this. It enabled a seemingly unhinged historical experience to be pinned to the immovable mast of the ultimate justice of God. It thereby enabled the faithful to cling to their beliefs about God and endure the assaults upon their cult and culture. It cast the imperial forces that assaulted them as manifestations of evil realities. But however beastly they might be, they were still subject to the overarching sovereignty of the God of Israel, who circumscribed their power. Gaius Popilius Laenas may have intimidated Antiochus IV into a monumental backdown by drawing a circle around him, but the book of Daniel enabled Jews to resist Antiochus (and liberal Hellenization) by drawing a theological circle around his power.

3.4.8 THE LONG-TERM THEOLOGICAL RAMIFICATIONS OF REDEDICATION

For centrist and conservative Jews who lived to see the rededication of the temple in January 163 BC, a new era had dawned. The temple had been recovered from gentiles and ungodly Jewish leaders. For those with an apocalyptic mindset, it entrenched a theological principle, namely, that the symbols of an old order needed to be dismantled to legitimize a new order. This precedent of discontinuity went back to the Deuteronomic commands to dismantle Canaanite society before building Israelite society (Deut 7–11), continued with the destruction of the temple in 586 BC and its reconstruction by Zerubbabel, was echoed in the dedication of the renovated temple under the Simon II (ca. 191 BC), and now received further confirmation under the Hasmoneans. It was a principle that would shape the theological attitude of various groups in the coming centuries, including those who would found the community at

---

36. Langgut, "Palynological Analysis of the Glacis of the Seleucid Acra in Jerusalem," 213–18.

Qumran and also of Jesus, who announced that the coming of the kingdom of God required the fall of the old temple and the rise of a new one.

For the Hasmonean brothers and their allies, cultural restoration of the Jewish nation was the primary goal of the rededication. This necessarily led to the ongoing pursuit of political leverage to guarantee these cultural outcomes. For others, like the remaining Intellectuals and Davidic loyalists, the primary outcome of the rededication was the vindication of the justice of God and a new impetus to look forward to what God might yet achieve in the future. For them, the cultural and political outcomes, as welcome as they were, did not obviate the excesses of human power. A hearty doctrine of universal human sinfulness caused them to look beyond human institutions for ultimate salvation. They recognized that even conservative Jews were prone to falter (cf. Dan 11:35) and perpetrate acts of injustice and greed. After all, the Maccabean extremists were known for the cruelty they inflicted upon their victims, including fellow Jews. For the Maccabees, whose hope was invested in the vindication and restoration of Jewish culture in the present age, such cruelties were a necessary evil and could therefore be justified. But for the Intellectuals and Davidic loyalists, whose hope lay in vindication by God himself, all human sin, whether perpetrated by foreign regimes or native Jewish priests, was necessarily problematic and could not simply be tolerated as a means to an end. What the Maccabees had achieved could be celebrated, but the extremist means behind their victory underscored the deeper problems of human sinfulness. Thus, the Intellectuals and Davidic loyalists did not just long for mundane power to express their culture but for a completely renovated world—a new age in which God's ultimate transcendent reality subsumed the sinful mundane reality, dealing once and for all with the ills of human society. It looked for a divine conquest of all earthly power and an atoning and sanctifying work to transform all humanity and establish justice.

This apocalyptic outlook had the critical result of delineating faith and ethics from culture, such that justice was not merely that which was done culturally but that which was morally right. This would prime the soil for the early church in later centuries to propose that the person and work of Jesus had been effective for all people, not just for Jews, so that belonging to an ethnic culture could never be a prerequisite for salvation. It was the theological impetus behind the theology of Paul and his insistence that gentiles could be saved as gentiles, without the need for circumcision (see this section below).

For apocalyptically minded Jews, God himself could not be vindicated if his prior promises were not fulfilled. Davidic loyalists understood that this required a Davidic messiah. Only with the appearance of such a messiah could the new transcendent reality be established. As such, the Davidic messiah, though a fundamentally political figure, would also have to be an apocalyptic and eschatological figure who ushered in an entirely new age. It is precisely this dynamic that framed Jesus's self-understanding and the beliefs of the early church. The book of Daniel does not really express Davidic hope, but the book's theology certainly leaves room for it. For example, the son of man figure is a royal figure, for he receives untrammeled dominion that directly contrasts with the circumscribed power of the four imperial beasts (Dan 7:13–14, 18). The son of man, therefore, projects easily onto a Davidic canvas, allowing for the inbreaking of God's kingdom to come through a Davidic messiah. It is this apocalyptic mindset of divine inbreaking that would eventually give birth to such Christian ideas as the Word made flesh (John 1:14), the regeneration of the human person (2 Cor 5:17; Gal 6:15), an eschatological resurrection of the dead, a new creation, and a new Jerusalem descending from heaven as the final home of the saved (Rev 21:1–4).

It also paved the way for the inclusion of gentiles within the people of God in Christian thought. At the end of the Antiochene persecution in 163 BC, this must have seemed not just impossible but even repulsive. For the Maccabees, whose hope was primarily cultural, the presence of gentiles within the people of God was the very thing they were struggling against. Yet the divergent emphases among various Jewish groups at this time set in motion theological trajectories that would each produce different theological results in centuries to come. They would not have seen it in the second century BC, but the hope of the Intellectuals and Davidic loyalists for a supernatural inbreaking of a transcendent God would eventually become the theological basis upon which to include gentiles in the people of God. The early church struggled with the question of the gentiles for decades because of the strong cultural legacy of conservative Judaism from this period in the second century BC. This is why the early church did not actively seek gentile converts for some time, and once it did, why there was initially a conservative Judaizing tendency that demanded gentiles become Jews through circumcision in order to be saved. Both Acts and Paul's letter to the Galatians testify to this program. However, as gentiles came to faith in Jesus without circumcision, especially through the apostolic ministry of Paul, the early church realized that culture and faith could, and indeed should, be distinguished from each other. If the inbreaking work of God had indeed dealt with human sinfulness and not just Jewish politics, then no person was beyond salvation—not even gentiles.

The experiential catalyst for this was gentiles coming to believe in Jesus as the Messiah in the first century. The theological catalyst was the notion of a new covenant, which traced its roots back to prophetic literature (cf. Jer 31:31) and could, in turn, be connected back to the patriarchal promise that all nations would be blessed through the descendants of Abraham (Gen 18:18; 22:18; 26:4). This enabled the early church to propose that Torah-based culture was fulfilled in a new covenant appropriated by faith in the atoning work of Jesus the Messiah. This obviated the need for any person to become a Jew culturally as a prerequisite for salvation. Faith unlocked righteousness, and this stemmed not from observance of cultural norms that made one a member of Israel but from the comprehensive atoning work of Christ, which enabled any human to become a member of the new covenant people, the church. It was a new type of righteousness that did not come from the Law (culture), though the Law and the Prophets testified to it (Rom 3:21–26). It came solely from faith.

We can appreciate the theological challenge that gentiles posed for the early Jewish Christians when we see the political, cultural, and religious challenges of the Antiochene persecution. Gentiles within the people of God were the antithesis of covenantal faithfulness according to the Torah, for they diluted the holiness of the chosen nation, rendering them indistinguishable from any other nation. This was the very dilemma facing Jews when Antiochus IV revoked their ethnic status. We can also understand just how inextricably linked culture and faith were in Judaism. The breaking of this nexus between culture and faith was one of the main theological achievements of the early Jewish Christians, which ultimately saw Christianity spread throughout the gentile world and become an international faith. It also distinguished the earliest Christians from their Jewish compatriots who continued to hold the nexus together and who viewed the breaking of this nexus as a betrayal and an abomination of similar proportions to what Antiochus IV had done in 167 BC.

3.5 AFTERMATH OF REVOLT

3.5.1 THE NEW STATUS QUO

The rededication of the temple did not result in independence for Judea. On the contrary, not a single concession was granted to the Jews. As far as Lysias was concerned, the Maccabean extremists had infiltrated a Seleucid *polis* that was attempting to maintain loyalty to the Seleucid crown. The Seleucids would not take this lying down.

For their part, the Hasmoneans understood that their mission was far from accomplished and that they had not seen the last of Seleucid power. Thus, they set about rebuilding the walls around the temple, which Apollonius had torn down in 167 BC. Their immediate aim was to restore the temple's previous design and create a fortified position against the Acra. Their more ambitious aim was complete independence from the Seleucids.

Menelaus tried to secure his own position as high priest in the new status quo by brokering an agreement between the new king, young Antiochus V Goodfather, and the conservative Jews now running the temple. Operating out of the Acra, he sought to win concessions for the conservatives, his erstwhile opponents, by convincing the new king to reinstate the ethnic status of the Jews and to remove any threat of military reprisal. He evidently hoped to ingratiate himself with the Hasmoneans and their allies, the *Hasidim*, by becoming their advocate. However, the entire basis of Menelaus's high priesthood was anathema to conservatives, who did not acquiesce to anything that included the continuation of his tenure as high priest. What's more, the conservatives could now get behind young Onias IV as the legitimate successor to the Zadokite high priesthood.

In April 163 BC, documents from Antiochus V arrived in Jerusalem, drafted under the guidance of his regent, Lysias. The first letter (2 Macc 11:22–26) had the ring of an official communique for public display. In it the new king recognized the restoration of Jewish worship in the temple and the will of the Jews to live by their traditional customs. This pandered to Jewish conservatives but did not mean Hellenizing Jews were forbidden from living by Greek-oriented ways; it merely entailed that they could no longer offer Greek-styled sacrifices in the temple. The second document (2 Macc 11:27–33) was addressed to "the Senate of the Jews" and "the other Jews"—an allusion to the Hasmoneans and their allies in a manner that deliberately avoided recognizing their leadership. The letter was a thinly veiled ultimatum urging them to abandon their military stations in Jerusalem and return home within two weeks. Compliance would ensure no military backlash and guarantee recognition of the Jews' ethnic status. The letter also referred to Menelaus's attempts to secure concessions and assumed his authority as high priest.

The Hasmoneans and the *Hasidim* now faced a quandary. They could accept the king's terms and return to a relatively peaceful life, which resembled the one before Antiochus IV's decree in 167 BC. In that case, they would also be recognizing Seleucid sovereignty over the Jews, including the king's right to appoint the high priest. This meant settling for a non-Zadokite high priesthood and, therefore, the continued power of gentiles and liberal Hellenizers at the epicenter of Jewish life in the temple. If they rejected the king's terms, they would be committing themselves to a long-term armed struggle against the Seleucid imperial juggernaut.

As they brooded over the dilemma, cracks began to form in the unity of the conservative ranks. The Hasmoneans and their Maccabean fighters were keen to continue the struggle, despite the odds against them. They had, after all, come a long way in four years as hardened fundamentalist fighters, and their recent achievements must have filled them with confidence. However, this was an overinflated confidence since they had not actually broken Seleucid sovereignty but rather benefitted from the political distraction that Antiochus IV's death caused. The *Hasidim* took a more pragmatic approach that was willing to settle for a short-term compromise. If they could cement concessions today, they might be in a better position to negotiate further gains tomorrow. Unlike the Hasmoneans and their adherents, the *Hasidim* were more genteel and politically minded. Their moderate stance gave them significant sway over the general populace, and the Hasmoneans could ill afford to lose their alliance with them.

Consequently, the Hasmoneans went along grudgingly with the compromise, choosing to live and fight another day. The Maccabean militia dispersed from Jerusalem and a relative calm descended upon Judea. Menelaus emerged from the Acra and once more took up his role as high priest in the temple. It was as if the clock had been turned back and the last four years had not happened.

3.5.2 REGIONAL CONFLICT (163/2 BC)

The new calm was a momentary lull before the next inevitable storm. The Hasmonean brothers took advantage of the lull to conduct operations outside

Jerusalem. The disparate accounts in 1 and 2 Maccabees make it difficult to determine the precise nature and order of these operations, but a general impression is possible.[1]

First, the alliance between the Maccabees and *Hasidim* was put under strain by the Maccabees' continued operations in defiance of the Seleucid terms, which the *Hasidim* had accepted. Second, with the legal reinstatement of traditional Jewish customs, there was a patriotic resurgence of public Torah observance throughout Judea and the neighboring regions. Third, the Jewish year beginning in September 163 BC was declared a Sabbatical rest for the land (cf. 1 Macc 6:49).[2] Conservatives would not sew or harvest crops during the whole upcoming year. Liberal Jews and their gentile neighbors had no scruples in working the land, especially to guarantee a stable food supply. This became a point of contention in areas where conservative Jews lived alongside of, and perhaps worked for, liberal Jews and gentiles. The lack of sowing, therefore, sowed the seeds of cultural discord and potential famine, which explains the sudden spike in pogroms in the regions around Judea.[3] Fourth, the fact that a Sabbatical rest for the land was declared shows that conservative Jews were thinking again in terms of the entire promised land as described in the Torah. This traditionally extended from Dan in northern Galilee to Beersheba in the far south. The cultural friction, therefore, was felt throughout these regions. Thus, the concessions granted to Jews and the dispersal of the Maccabean fighters did not take the heat out of Judea. On the contrary, it dispersed it more widely and ensured the cultural temperature of the whole region continued to rise.

The Maccabees conducted expeditions of both terror and rescue in various districts. Their first target was the Hellenizing Jews who had fled Jerusalem when the Maccabees had advanced on the city. They had ended up in the pro-Hellenizing areas of Idumea and the coastal plain. These revenge attacks resulted in the death and displacement of many Hellenizers and the sabotage of various installations (1 Macc 5:1–5; 2 Macc 12:2–9), but no territory was captured. After this, Judas and Jonathan evacuated conservative Jews out of

---

1. Sievers, *The Hasmoneans and Their Supporters*, 49–57.

2. The first month of the seasonal Jewish year (Nisan) fell in March-April. However, the cultic festival of "New Year" (*Rosh haShanah*) fell in the seventh month (Tishri), which corresponded to September-October. Year-long cycles, such as the Sabbatical rest of the land and the Jubilee, were calculated by the cultic year, beginning with Tishri. It is hard to know whether the seven-year cycle was already in operation or reinitiated at this point.

3. The law of a Sabbatical rest for the land appears in Lev 25:1–7 and states that Israelites could not harvest cultivated land but only pick what grew wild and uncultivated. Normally, the previous six years could be used to store supplies for the seventh Sabbatical Year, but this had become practically impossible over the previous four years while Antiochus IV's anti-Torah policies prevailed.

Transjordan, where they were being harassed. In the process, they sabotaged local Seleucid garrisons and destroyed a temple dedicated to Atargatis at Karnaim in Gilead (1 Macc 5:6–13, 24–54; 2 Macc 12:17–28).[4] Simon managed a similar evacuation of conservative Jews in western Galilee who were being targeted by their Phoenician neighbors (1 Macc 5:21–23, 55).

By April 162 BC, the Hasmoneans and their Maccabean fighters were back in Judea for the celebration of Passover and Pentecost. The resettlements they had facilitated grew their fundamentalist support base just when it seemed inevitable that the *Hasidim* would break ranks with them. Menelaus was also still high priest, and the Acra in Jerusalem continued to stand defiantly as a bastion of Hellenization. The Hasmonean brothers and their fundamentalist supporters were intensely dissatisfied with this status quo and hankered for complete independence. Thus, immediately after the festivals, the Maccabees undertook fresh skirmishes in Idumea and the coastal plain (1 Macc 5:65–68; 2 Macc 12:32–45).

At this point, Lysias could no longer ignore them, for they had turned their cause into a region-wide conflict. In May 162 BC he took the boy king, Antiochus V Goodfather, and marched with a force to confront the Maccabean partisans.[5] For the second time, he approached Judea from Idumea in the south. He easily punched through the Maccabean border fortress at Beth Zur (1 Macc 6:48–50; 2 Macc 13:18–22) and came upon the main Maccabean band, commanded by all five Hasmonean brothers, at a village called Beth-Zechariah, southwest of Jerusalem. Here a pitched battle occurred in which Lysias employed all his forces, including his war elephants. The Maccabees were hopelessly outnumbered and yet stood to fight. In the melee, "Pale" Eleazar, one of the Hasmonean brothers, targeted the tallest elephant, which was festooned more than the others, on the surmise that the young king was inside the cab on the animal's back. Eleazar fought through and stabbed the elephant from underneath, bringing it down. The king was not, however, in the cab, and the flailing pachyderm crushed Eleazar to death as it slammed down on top of him. The remaining four Hasmonean brothers fled the field, and the Maccabean stand dissolved. The Seleucid army won the day (1 Macc 6:32–47).

Lysias marched on Jerusalem, where the Maccabean garrison was weakened by food shortages (1 Macc 6:48–54). Lysias easily took back control of the city, bringing its partition to an end. He also proceeded to break down the

---

4. Atargatis was probably identified with Artemis and worshipped by the semi-nomadic peoples of the Hauran. See H. J. W. Drijvers, "Atargatis," in *Dictionary of Deities and Demons in the Bible*, ed. Karel van der Toorn, Bob Becking, and Pieter W. van der Horst (Leiden: Brill, 1995).

5. See Bar-Kochva, *Judas Maccabaeus*, 544–49.

fortifications that the Maccabees were building around the temple. Powerless to stop him, the Hasmoneans and their remaining squads fled Judea altogether, their cause now looking completely lost.

3.5.3 THE DILEMMA OF THE HIGH PRIESTHOOD

While Lysias was in Jerusalem with Antiochus V Goodfather, word reached him that his rival, Philip, was taking control of Antioch. Lysias, therefore, sought a quick resolution to the power struggles among the Jews so he could return to Syria and confront Philip. Under the pressure of time, Lysias could not afford a wholesale reorganization of Judea. He, therefore, committed to maintaining as much of the status quo as possible, which permitted the Jews to continue observing their ancestral customs. But by this time, he realized that Menelaus's high priesthood was an ongoing liability.

The *Hasidim* took advantage of this. They now disassociated themselves completely from the Maccabean cause, ensuring that the Hasmoneans and their partisans were thoroughly marginalized politically. This conscious move away from an extremist stance gained the *Hasidim* favor and the necessary leverage to encourage Lysias and the boy king to remove Menelaus from the high priesthood. Menelaus was deposed, arrested, and summarily executed (2 Macc 13:3–8).

A major dilemma now ensued: who to appoint as the new high priest? To appreciate the scale of this dilemma, we must take stock of the political spectrum in Judea at this moment in time (162 BC). On the political left were the liberal Hellenizers, consisting of Jewish elite (e.g., the Tobiads), those priests and Levites who had been allies of Menelaus, progressively minded Jewish laity, and the local gentile population. The center was the least populated part of the spectrum, occupied by the remaining Intellectuals, a few priests, Levites, and scribes, and some Davidic loyalists. On the right were the disparate ranks of the conservatives, including the majority of the priests, Levites, and scribes, the supporters of the Zadokites (including Onias IV), the *Hasidim*, some Davidic loyalists, and most laity. The break with the *Hasidim* had left the Hasmonean brothers and their Maccabean fighters isolated as extremists on the far right, along with those ultra-conservatives who would eventually become the Pharisees. Davidic loyalists were not an organized faction but were part of the laity occupying the center and center-right.

This complexity helps us evaluate the choices facing Lysias over the high priesthood. Most of Jewish society was conservative, and the candidate they favored was Onias IV, the legitimate successor to the Zadokite high priesthood. Onias was very close now to the sacral office's requisite age of thirty—a factor that lent more weight to the *Hasidim*'s request for Menelaus's removal. However, for Lysias and the boy king, the appointment of Onias IV was completely unacceptable, for Onias was also the candidate favored by the extremist Maccabees. Appointing him would effectively invite them back into mainstream Jewish society, rendering the current campaign to eradicate them futile and prolonging the instability of the region. And yet, if the Jews were legitimately being allowed to live by their ancestral laws, returning the priesthood to the Zadokite line was practically a necessity. If Lysias did not permit Onias to take office, he would be effectively repressing the Jewish nation and putting most of it offside. For the Seleucid authorities, the key lay in eliminating the Maccabees, so that Onias IV was disconnected from their influence altogether.

Lysias had two options. His first was to leave the high priesthood vacant for the few years until Onias attained the requisite age for the office. But this simply delayed the inevitable decision about what to do with him. It also raised questions about how the temple cult would operate in the interim, which could ignite a chaotic power struggle among the conservative factions. The other option was to fill the vacancy with someone moderate enough to appeal to the *Hasidim*, now the leading faction of the conservatives. Turning their back on the Maccabean extremists had given them political credibility with Lysias, and they were now prepared to enter negotiations with centrists. Since the high priest was an appointment for life, the man would ideally be older, so as not to hold office for too long. But he would need to be in office long enough to allow Lysias to stamp out the Maccabean movement once and for all, but not so long as to inordinately delay the appointment of Onias IV.

Lysias and the boy king opted to fill the vacancy with an older man as a stop-gap measure. Although this delayed the appointment of Onias IV, it was a soft commitment from the Seleucids to install him as high priest after the new incumbent. It was enough of a commitment to receive the approval of the *Hasidim*.[6]

We do not know the range of candidates Lysias had to choose from for high priest, but we do know the man he appointed: an old priest named Alcimus. His Hebrew name was Jakim (*Ant.* 12.385), a shortened form of Eliakim. That he took the similar sounding Greek name, Alcimus, tells us that he was at the very least a centrist conversant with Greek language and ideals. Though not

---

6. No historical source mentions the Seleucids' commitment to install Onias IV later on. However, the *Hasidim*'s dealings with Alcimus and the subsequent movements of Onias IV make it clear that he was in the picture for the sacral office in 162 BC.

a Zadokite, he was an Aaronide priest (cf. 1 Macc 7:14) and therefore a bona fide minister of the altar. As an older man, perhaps with pre-existing ailments (cf. 3.6.3 below), he was expected to occupy the high priesthood for only a short time. He was, therefore, a paper tiger with appeal to both the Seleucids and pro-Zadokite conservatives. Lysias departed Judea to deal with matters in Antioch and left the installation of Alcimus to a trusted general, Bacchides.

3.5.4 THE "TEACHER OF RIGHTEOUSNESS" AND THE CALENDAR CONTROVERSY

Though Alcimus was not a member of the *Hasidim*, he was someone the *Hasidim* felt they could work with (cf. 1 Macc 7:14). The promise of fruitful cooperation was conveyed in the Pesher of Habakkuk among the Dead Sea Scrolls, which states that Alcimus was "called by the name of truth at the start of his tenure" (1QpHab 8:9).[7]

The *Hasidim* themselves were now led by a priest whose name has unfortunately been lost to history. In the sectarian writings of the Dead Sea Scrolls, he is known simply as the "Teacher of Righteousness." His elevation to the leadership of the *Hasidim* occurred shortly before this time, and he was almost certainly responsible for the *Hasidim* breaking ranks with the Hasmoneans. His leadership came twenty years after the inception of the movement, and the Essenes who later emerged out of the *Hasidim* would describe those twenty years as a time when they were "like blind men groping for the way" (CD 1:13).[8] The priest's title, "Teacher of Righteousness," carried dual connotations, for the term "righteousness" in Hebrew (*tsedeq*) comes from the same root as the name "Zadok," the implication being that he promulgated righteousness and held firmly to the exclusive right of the Zadokite line to the high priesthood. It is possible that he himself was a member of the wider Zadokite clan, but even if so, he was not the direct heir of the Zadokite priesthood. He was also probably

---

7. Alcimus is not specifically named in 1QpHab. Rather, the quoted description describes the beginning of the "Wicked Priest's" tenure. The identity of the "Wicked Priest" is one of the most contested issues in Dead Sea Scrolls scholarship, with an uneasy consensus identifying him with Jonathan Apphus. However, identifying him with Alcimus makes much better sense of all the data from the Dead Sea Scrolls and other sources (1 and 2 Maccabees, Josephus). See also 3.1.1.

8. According to the Damascus Document, the movement's inception occurred 390 years after Nebuchadnezzar destroyed Jerusalem (CD 1:5–11). Strictly speaking, this would place the sect's inception in 196 BC, but the figure of 390 years is a clear allusion to the sign act in Ezek 4:5 in which the prophet bears Israel's guilt for 390 days. There is also some doubt as to whether the sect was able to date historical events with absolute accuracy. Therefore, we should see "390 years" as both symbolic and approximate rather than precise. If the "Teacher of Righteousness" came to the movement's leadership in 162 BC, then the inception of the *Hasidim* as a recognizable group occurred in ca. 182 BC.

a younger priest than Alcimus, which counted against his appointment as interim high priest. Under his leadership, the *Hasidim* offered to cooperate with Alcimus, with a view to shaping how temple operations would look after him.

The *Hasidim* underestimated Alcimus's antipathy towards them. Alcimus was an outspoken critic of the Hasmoneans and their Maccabean militia, which probably endeared him to Lysias, and he may well have been targeted by the Maccabees during their raids in 163/2 BC. The *Hasidim* were still allies of the Maccabees at that time. Despite the cancellation of that alliance, Alcimus was still highly suspicious of the *Hasidim* (cf. 2 Macc 14:6). Thus, cooperation between Alcimus and the *Hasidim* would take considerable diplomatic effort.

The *Hasidim* came, perhaps with other groups also, to negotiate with Alcimus in the late summer of 162 BC. He guaranteed them safety and cooperation despite the bad blood between them (1 Macc 7:12–15). It is unknown whether Onias IV was present, but he was surely a significant factor in their discussions. But the agenda of the Teacher of Righteousness contained a raft of other demands pertaining to cultic procedures and legal customs in accordance with a solar calendar. He submitted these to Alcimus in a document that has come to be known as *Miqṣat Ma'aseh haTorah* ("Some of the works of the Law"), or Halakhic Letter.[9] Six fragmentary copies of this document were preserved among the Dead Sea Scrolls (4Q394–399, or 4QMMT collectively). In it, the Teacher of Righteousness aimed to ensure that holy days fell on prescribed dates, calculated according to a 364-day solar calendar, that proper protocols for sacrifice were observed, that priests maintained ritual purity, and that tithes from the public were handled appropriately. The document also probably argued against the acceptance of sacrifice from gentiles—an important condition considering the temple had recently been a place of gentile worship.[10] That these matters were tabled reveals that they were in dispute among the negotiating parties. If Alcimus was willing to accept sacrifices from gentiles, the *Hasidim* may have believed that he was not taking adequate measures to protect the nation's holiness after its previous loss of ethnic status.

---

9. While most scholars agree on the contents and purpose of 4QMMT, debate continues about the precise historical moment into which it originally spoke. The proposal I offer here (that it was a submission to Alcimus in 162 BC) is based primarily on my identification of the key figures in the scrolls, namely the "Teacher of Righteousness," the "Wicked Priest" (Alcimus), and the "Man of Mockery" (Judas Maccabeus), as well as the convergence of the document's concerns with the theological and political developments known from 1 Macc 7:12–18 and 2 Macc 14:3–14.

10. The manuscripts of 4QMMT are poorly preserved at this point. They mention (1) the "wheat of the gentiles" in the same context as becoming "defiled"; (2) the "sacrifice of gentiles" in close proximity to statements of who these sacrifices were offered to (unfortunately the object of worship is not preserved); and (3) "whoring" activity (4QMMT B3–5, B8–9). All these statements are in an indisputable context of sacrifice in the temple.

Alcimus evidently also observed the traditional lunar calendar, which had prevailed in Judaism and the wider Near East since time immemorial. He would, therefore, have observed Sabbaths and festivals on different dates to those espoused by the *Hasidim* and perhaps with varying nuance of ritual.

These issues were not easily ignored, nor could a compromise be reached by proposing that different groups observe the rituals on different days. There was only one Israel with one God, so there could only be one high priest who was pivotal to the efficacy of all rituals. From Alcimus's perspective, these issues meant the potential insubordination of his priestly staff. If a large proportion of his ancillary priests were not prepared to comply with how he, as high priest, operated the temple, it could generate a major crisis at the center of Judaism. From the perspective of the Teacher of Righteousness, the lunar calendar needed reform. Its inherent inexactitude required constant correction to compensate for large discrepancies with the seasons and wider astronomical movements. His proposed solar calendar removed most of the inexactitude and need for compensatory methods. This was a shift from previous practice but one that the Teacher of Righteousness and his supporters believed was divinely authorized, since God was in control of the seasons and astronomical movements.

The rationale for the proposed calendar reforms came from two documents. The first was the Aramaic Levi Document, composed in the late third century BC, of which only incomplete fragments have survived. Its importance to the *Hasidim* and the Essenes who emerged from them is demonstrated by the fact that it is one of the sources for the book of Jubilees, the Damascus Document, the Testament of Levi, the Testament of Kohath (4Q542), and the Visions of Amram (4Q543–48). The work contains a revelatory journey to the heavens by the patriarch Levi, gives stipulations for sacrifices, argues for establishing a royal priesthood in Israel, presumes a solar calendar, and assigns the priests a didactic role within Israel.[11]

The second significant document was the Book of the Heavenly Luminaries, written in Aramaic in the third century BC, partly as a conservative Jewish response to Greek astronomical theories. The document was eventually incorporated into the 1 Enoch corpus (1 En. 72–82). In this book, the antediluvian hero Enoch journeys into the heavens where an angel, Uriel, discloses to him the nature and measurement of the times in accordance with a 364-day solar calendar.[12] It argued that the solar calendar was woven into the

---

11. Michael E. Stone and Esther Eshel, "Aramaic Levi Document," in Feldman, Kugel, and Schiffman, *Outside the Bible*, 1490–1506.
12. The Book of the Heavenly Luminaries was originally composed in Aramaic. Four Aramaic fragments of the book were found at Qumran (4Q208–211). See George W. E. Nickelsburg, *Jewish Literature between the Bible and the Mishnah*, 2nd ed. (Minneapolis: Fortress, 2005), 44.

fabric of spiritual reality, as per the quasi-Platonic metaphysic of an apocalyptic worldview. Failure to observe a solar calendar, therefore, was a failure to work in concert with the spiritual essence of reality as God created it, putting the nation out of touch with its God and rendering the temple cult null and void.

The *Hasidim* distilled pivotal tenets from the Book of the Heavenly Luminaries into the book of Jubilees, which was composed in response to the aftermath of negotiations with Alcimus.[13] This book, which the *Hasidim* knew as "the book of the division of the times by their Jubilees and Weeks" (CD 16:2–3), purports to be part of the divine revelation to Moses on Mount Sinai. It was so important to the group that fragments from sixteen copies were discovered at Qumran. In Jubilees, the revelatory Angel of the Presence explains the rationale for a solar calendar to Moses in polemical terms:

> And you, command the children of Israel to guard the years I thus number —364 days—and it will be a complete year. Let none corrupt its appointed time from its days or from its festivals because all the appointed times will arrive during them according to their testimony. Let them not pass over a day or corrupt a festival. But if they are transgressed, and they do not observe them according to their respective commandments, then they will corrupt all their fixed times. The years will be moved from within this order, and they will transgress their regulation. Then all the sons of Israel will forget, and they will not find the course of the years. They will forget the new moons, appointed times, and sabbaths. They will misalign all the regulations of the years. For I know, and henceforth I shall make you know—but not from my own heart because the book [of the Heavenly Luminaries] is written before me and is ordained in the heavenly tablets of the division of days—lest they forget the festival of the covenant and walk in the festivals of the gentiles, after their error and after their ignorance.
>
> But there will be those who examine the moon diligently because it corrupts the appointed times and advances ten days from year to year. Therefore, the years will come to them as they corruptly make a day of testimony a reproach, and a profane day a festival. They will mix up everything—a holy day as profaned, and a profane day as a holy day—because they will misalign the months, sabbaths, feasts, and jubilees. Therefore, I command you and

---

13. As Wintermute rightly argues, "the content of Jubilees' revelation is directed toward all of Israel and not to just a small group of embattled faithful. The author of the book may have been a member of a relatively small band of Hasidim, but there is no reason to believe that his group had yet broken sharply away from the larger Jewish community." See O. S. Wintermute, "Jubilees (Second Century B.C.): A New Translation and Introduction," in *The Old Testament Pseudepigrapha*, ed. James H. Charlesworth, 2 vols. (New York: Doubleday, 1985), 2:37–38.

bear witness to you, so that you may bear witness to them. For, after you have died, your sons will be corrupted, so that they will not make a year only 364 days. And so they will misalign the months, the appointed times, the sabbaths, and the festivals, and they will eat all of the blood with all flesh. (Jub. 6:32–38)[14]

By this rationale, the calendar was not just about measuring time but about observing the quality of time.[15] Both the protocols and their timing gave the rituals their efficacy. Thus, even if the high priest had good intentions, if he did not enact sacred rituals on their appropriate days, he would compromise their efficacy. Indeed, if atonement could not be achieved, the altar would be rendered ineffective and the deity would be incited to wrath against the nation. At a time when conservatives felt they had just emerged from a period of great wrath, tribulation, and compromised holiness, this was utterly unacceptable.

In the fragmentary *Miqṣat Maʿaseh haTorah* (4QMMT), we see the Teacher of Righteousness use forthright yet conciliatory rhetoric to persuade Alcimus towards the perspective of the *Hasidim*:

We have written what you must understand in the Book of Moses, in the books of the Prophets, in David, and in the actions of each generation. . . . It is written that if you stray from the way, evil will befall you. It is written also that when all these things will happen to you in the end of days—the blessing and the curse—you should set your heart to it, turn to him with all your heart and all your soul at the end of time. . . . We recognize that some of the blessings and curses written in the Book of Moses have happened. But this is the end of days when they will turn within Israel to the Torah and not turn back. Yet, those who are wrong will do wrongly. . . . Remember David, who was a man of piety. As he was saved from great distress and received forgiveness, so we have written to you some of the works of the Torah that we consider good for you and your people. For we have seen that you have intelligence and knowledge of the Torah. Reflect on all these and seek from him that he may correct your counsel, and distance poor thinking from yourself and worthless counsel. Then you will celebrate at the end of time when you find that some of our words are right, and it will be reckoned to you as righteousness when you do what is correct and good before him, to your own good and the good of Israel. (4QMMT C9–32)

---

14. Adapted from the translation by Wintermute, "Jubilees," 68.
15. Wintermute, "Jubilees," 38–39.

The Teacher of Righteousness encouraged Alcimus with evangelistic zeal to activate divine blessing for the nation by bringing them back to covenantal faithfulness, as outlined in the document. The Teacher of Righteousness believed he spoke as an authoritative interpreter of the Scriptures, which he enumerated as the Torah, the Prophets, and David (probably a reference to the Psalter). While there is some flattery in his comparison of Alcimus to David, he also subtly claimed biblical backing for his agenda by referring to David as a "man of piety," or more literally, "a man of the *Hasidim*."[16] Alcimus, however, rejected the demands, alienating the *Hasidim*.

The timing could not have been worse for a string of major festivals was fast approaching in September-October, namely, the Day of Remembrance (the New Year festival), the Day of Atonement, and the Festival of Sukkot. There can be little doubt that Alcimus exerted pressure on his ancillary priests who belonged to the *Hasidim* in the lead up to the festivals. This might have created divisions within *Hasidim* ranks between those prepared to stand with the Teacher of Righteousness in defiance of Alcimus and those with a more conciliatory posture. Nonetheless, Alcimus was facing a major revolt from his subordinate priests, led by the Teacher of Righteousness.

What then transpired can be pieced together from the corroborating testimony of 1 Maccabees 7:12–20 and the Pesher of Habakkuk (1QpHab). Alcimus prepared to celebrate the New Year Festival in accordance with the lunar calendar, which was earlier than the Teacher of Righteousness was prepared to do. When the day arrived, the priests who sided with the Teacher of Righteousness treated the day as an ordinary day and thus failed to perform the duties expected of them. Ten days later when Alcimus celebrated the Day of Atonement, the dissenting priests again refused to participate. From their perspective, Alcimus offered unauthorized sacrifice upon the altar, polluting the sanctuary rather than consecrating it. It was an error of similar magnitude to that committed by Aaron's sons, Nadab and Abihu, who provoked the lethal wrath of the deity (Lev 10:1–5; cf. 1QM, 17.2). The Teacher of Righteousness publicly denounced Alcimus as the "Wicked Priest" (Heb. *hakohen haresha'*)—a powerful pun on the title "high priest" (Heb. *hakohen harosh*). Alcimus was thus publicly insulted.

Lysias's paper tiger now grew fangs and pounced. With the backing of Bacchides (cf. *Ant.* 12.396), Alcimus instigated a bloody purge of the *Hasidim* on the day they had calculated by a solar calendar as the Day of Atonement. As justification, he may have appealed to precedents and laws in the Torah related

---

16. Cf. Honigman, *Tales of High Priests and Taxes*, 61.

to apostasy and failure to consume sacrificial meat (Exod 32:25-29; Lev 17:3-4, 8-9; 19:5-8).[17] The murderous rampage resulted in the deaths of sixty members of the *Hasidim* (1 Macc 7:16).[18] The Teacher of Righteousness was Alcimus's main target, but he evidently escaped the massacre and went into hiding. His followers interpreted this as the fulfilment of Habakkuk 2:15:[19]

> This is about the "Wicked Priest" [Alcimus], who chased the Teacher of Righteousness into his place of exile, in order to swallow him up in the frustration of his rage. At the appointed time of rest on the Day of Atonement, he turned up to swallow them up and bring them down on the fast day, the Sabbath of their rest. (1QpHab 11:4-8)

The bloody purge gave Alcimus personal revenge upon the *Hasidim* for the role they had played alongside the Maccabees in the previous years. It also revealed that he would tar those who disagreed with him with the same political brush as the Maccabees. The Teacher of Righteousness and his closest followers who survived the massacre departed Jerusalem. The Damascus Document refers to their escape when it says the repentant of Israel "went out from the land of Judah and migrated to the land of Damascus" (CD 6:5). The War Scroll (1QM 1:2-3) implies the group was exiled to "the desert of the peoples," which probably refers to desert regions on the fringes of the covenantal land, such as those near Damascus.[20]

The purge had massive ramifications for Jewish society. It broke the back of the *Hasidim* as a unified political movement at a critical juncture when the *Hasidim*, the leading conservative group in Judea (cf. 1 Macc 2:42; 7:13), had separated from the Hasmoneans and taken a more moderate stance. The promise of constructive cooperation that this generated towards the center

---

17. In both 1 Maccabees and *Antiquities*, the massacre is dated to the reign of Demetrius rather than Antiochus V. This, however, fails to account for Judas Maccabeus's activities in 161-160 BC. Their mistaken chronology is the result of the assumption that Alcimus's entire tenure as high priest had been continuous. However, see 2 Macc 14:3 and 3.6.3 below.

18. First Maccabees does not present the issue(s) behind the breach between Alcimus and the "group of scribes" (1 Macc 7:12). It simply pins the massacre on the character of "Alcimus the ungodly" (1 Macc 7:9)—a term similar to "the Wicked Priest." The calendrical issues are derived from the sectarian writings of Qumran.

19. The MT reads the final word of Hab 2:15 as *me'oreyhem* ("their naked bodies"). The Qumran sect read the *resh* in this word as a *daleth*, yielding the word *mo'adeyhem* ("their appointed times"). Although this produced a contextually implausible reading, it allowed them to interpret the calendar controversy with Alcimus as the fulfilment of this Scripture (1QpHab 11:2-8).

20. This place is differentiated from the group's later arrival in the "desert of Jerusalem" (1QM 1:3), which refers to the establishment of their community at Qumran (ca. 90 BC). While some take "land of Damascus" in a figurative sense, it is most likely literal.

of Judaism had stalled over the calendrical controversy, but now all hopes for fruitful synergy were dashed. The massacre decimated the leadership of the *Hasidim*. Those who fled Judea with the Teacher of Righteousness eventually stiffened into the sect that would come to be known as the Essenes. The massacre left an indelible mark on their psyche, as the War Scroll (1QM) demonstrates. This document sees eschatological justice being achieved through a future apocalyptic battle in which the "sons of light" defeat the "sons of darkness," whose ranks include "the troops of the Kittim of Asshur" (i.e., the Seleucid Greeks of Syria) and "the violators of the covenant" who help them (1QM 1:2). The vision seeks redress for the massacre and vengeance upon the corrupt power structures that enabled it to happen (cf. 1QM 3:7–11).

But not all survivors of the purge followed the Teacher of Righteousness into exile. Some dissociated themselves from him as a polarizing figure. Being left leaderless, they were flung in various directions. Most began associating with other pro-Zadokite factions in Jerusalem and developed into the Zadokite sect—the Sadducees. Some lay members dropped out of political life altogether or joined with ultra-conservative separatists to become the Pharisees. Yet others reverted to active association with the extremist Maccabean movement of the Hasmonean brothers (cf. 2 Macc 14:6). In this way, Alcimus strengthened the Hasmoneans' cause. But this was a calculated risk, as he was still banking on the Seleucids to hunt them down until their movement was no more.

The purge also violently ended the hopes of Onias IV to one day claim the high priesthood as the rightful Zadokite heir. Alcimus had slaughtered some of Onias's most powerful supporters, demonstrating in no uncertain terms that he was no longer prepared to be a mere placeholder for him. The Hasmoneans still supported Onias's claims, but they were marked men. We do not know whether Alcimus intended to have Onias slaughtered during the purge, but either way, the city was no longer safe for the Zadokite heir. And so, like the Teacher of Righteousness, Onias escaped. Anxious to avoid a similar fate to his murdered father, he fled the Seleucid kingdom altogether and found refuge in Ptolemaic Egypt (*Ant.* 13.62; cf. *J.W.* 1.33; cf. 7.423).[21] The ancient Zadokite line of high priests was thus uprooted from Judea.

---

21. Josephus's testimony about Onias IV is consistently muddled with that of his father, Onias III. The reason for Josephus's confusion is that Onias IV never officially held the high priesthood in Jerusalem and so never appeared in the list of high priests among Josephus's sources. Yet, many viewed him as the rightful high priest. Josephus, therefore, attributed all Onias IV's exploits as a supposed "high priest" to his father, Onias III, who was on the roster of the sacral office. Once this mistake is accounted for, Josephus's chronologically impossible account can be unraveled. See also VanderKam, *From Joshua to Caiaphas*, 214–22.

3.5.5 ONIAS IV AND THE TEMPLE OF LEONTOPOLIS

In the years before Onias IV's arrival in Egypt (late 162 BC), uprisings of native Egyptians had broken out again across the Ptolemaic realm. Ptolemy VI had been ruling jointly with his siblings, Cleopatra II and Fatso Ptolemy VIII, before he fell out with them in 164 BC. He fled Alexandria for Rome but returned the following year with backing from the Roman Senate for his claim to rule. A compromise was imposed on the realm, whereby Ptolemy VI ruled Egypt and Fatso Ptolemy VIII ruled Cyrenaica. When Onias IV arrived in Egypt, therefore, he came to a divided and destabilized kingdom.

Ptolemy VI received him in Alexandria and both men realized how much they had in common. Both were vehemently opposed to the Seleucids and had been recently forced to flee their home city. Onias gave up hopes of recovering the high priesthood in Jerusalem. The dystopia of the Antiochene persecution had led many conservative Jews to migrate and find welcome relief in Egypt. With Judea now descending once more into chaos, Egypt, despite its own upheavals, must have felt like the promised land. And so, Onias found a warm welcome with the thriving Jewish community there.

Onias capitalized on the situation by asking Ptolemy VI to grant him land in Egypt to build a Jewish temple in which he could function as high priest. His request exposed some major theological currents of the day. For starters, it showed that Onias now rejected the legitimacy of the temple in Jerusalem (cf. *Ant.* 13.62–73; *J.W.* 1.33; 7.420–432). Others too rejected the temple because of the perceived illegitimacy of its leadership, but they did not call for a new temple elsewhere. What this shows, then, is that Onias believed the institution of the high priesthood, rather than the temple itself, was the vital center of Jewish life and of greater theological significance than the covenantal land. For him, the one true place of Yahwistic worship was wherever the high priest was, and this did not have to be in Jerusalem or even in the promised land. Both the temple and the land were simply the working domain of the high priest—mere satellites orbiting his person. This was the logical endpoint of the theology of Ben Sira, influenced also by the political ideology of the Hellenistic kings who viewed themselves as the state. The temple was no longer a monument to the Davidic covenant. The once grand dynasty of David was but a trophy from the distant past, now adorning the cultural mantlepiece of the high priest who had inherited all the dynasty's prerogatives, including the right to build the temple. David was little more than a prominent practitioner of Torah (cf. 4QMMT, C25–26). The high priest was now everything.

Onias evidently subscribed to a concept of ongoing theological development. Though the Torah placed great emphasis on the consecration of the high priest and the need for one place of worship within the land of the covenant, Onias did not feel so constrained by this that he could not propose something new. This was not a rejection of the authority of the Torah, for the sacral office he was aiming to preserve was dependent on that authority. Instead, this was a theological evolution, which Onias, as the self-accredited vital center of all Jewish life, felt he was entitled to make. He clearly saw the office of high priest as above the Law.

Onias was almost certainly motivated by personal ambition, but his actions cannot be reduced to this. He had precedent and a reasonable theological basis for what he was doing. He was, after all, the legitimate Zadokite high priest who by rightful pedigree was an anointed one of Yahweh. Whether directly or indirectly, Alcimus had lifted his hand against Yahweh's anointed. So, like David under the persecution of Saul, Onias had been driven from his homeland into the service of a foreign king. Moreover, Judaism had moved along from the henotheism that had prevailed during the early Persian era and was now on a more definitive monotheistic footing. Jews viewed Yahweh as not just their national covenantal deity but as the one true God over all nations. There was nowhere Onias could go, then, where he could not worship God. As the legitimate high priest in an age when most Jews cared very little about Davidic monarchy, Onias saw himself as the magnetic center of Judaism who had the right to gather the nation around himself, wherever he might be.

One additional factor gave impetus to Onias's desire to build a new temple. He found a scriptural mandate for it in Isaiah 19:18–22:

> On that day, there will be five cities in the land of Egypt speaking the language of Canaan and swearing oaths to Yahweh of Ranks. One of them will be called, "City of the Sun." On that day, there will be an altar to Yahweh within the land of Egypt with a pillar to Yahweh beside its territory. It will be a symbol and a testimony to Yahweh of Ranks in the land of Egypt. When they cry to Yahweh for help from their oppressors, he will send them a savior. He will advocate for them and rescue them. Yahweh will be acknowledged by Egypt, and Egypt will know Yahweh on that day, making sacrifice and offering, making vows to Yahweh and fulfilling them. Yahweh will inflict injury on Egypt and healing, and they will return to Yahweh. He will be propitiated by them, and he will heal them.

It is likely that this prophecy was updated to reflect Onias's temple in Egypt, but the original prophecy gave Onias enough impetus to see it as directly relevant to himself and his context.[22] Egypt had recently been afflicted by the invasions of Antiochus IV, the uprisings of native Egyptians, and discord within the Ptolemaic dynasty itself. Under Rome's influence, these "injuries" had been largely "healed." By building an altar to Yahweh in Egypt, Onias was casting himself as the divinely appointed savior of the Jews, perhaps even attracting Egyptians to the worship of Yahweh. Indeed, it was during this precise period (the reign of Ptolemy VI) that a series of Jewish oracles were composed in Egypt, which were critical of gentile religion and culture but favorable towards gentile people, urging them to repent and find blessing in the one true God. These oracles would eventually be compiled into Book Three of the so-called Sibylline Oracles.[23]

Ptolemy VI granted Onias's request. Onias found a disused temple once dedicated to the feline deity, Bastet, in a town the Greeks called Leontopolis ("Lion City").[24] It was within the nome of Heliopolis, the "City of the Sun" (Isa 19:18) in the southern Delta. Onias renovated the ruins and built an altar resembling the one in Jerusalem. Unlike Jerusalem, though, the sanctuary at Leontopolis was a tower close to 30 meters tall, with a golden chandelier suspended from the ceiling by a golden chain. Some disaffected Levites joined Onias, and the temple began attracting Jewish worshippers (*J.W.* 7.426–430).

This was different to the Yahwistic temple at Elephantine from centuries earlier. Onias's temple was not established as a satellite shrine for a satellite community but as a rival cult to Jerusalem, much like the Samaritan temple on Mount Gerizim (cf. *J.W.* 7.431).[25] The territory surrounding the temple came to be known as "the Onios" district after Onias (*War* 7.421)—a veritable New Judea for disenchanted pilgrims. Onias was propelled by ambition, but he was also partaking in an eschatological vision for a new Jerusalem. The book of Isaiah was evidently his guiding light. In addition to the mandate of Isaiah

---

22. The clause "One of them will be called, 'City of the Sun'" is almost certainly a late addition to the text. The LXX names the location as "City of Asedek," which is a transliteration of Hebrew's "City of Righteousness" (*'ir hatsedeq*). Whether this conveys connotations of Onias's Zadokite ancestry is unknown. In any case, it is quite different to the Hebrew manuscripts (e.g., 1QIsa^a) which read "City of the Sun" (Heb. *'ir haheres*), which itself reflects an updating of the Hebrew text after Onias's temple was built. The Masoretes subtly changed their inherited reading to "City of Demolition" (Heb. *'ir haheres*), reflecting a later negative assessment of Onias's temple.
23. See Nickelsburg, *Jewish Literature*, 193–96.
24. The settlement, located some 20 kms north of modern Cairo, was quite ancient and included remains from the time of Ramesses II (thirteenth century BC). The site later came to be known as the "Mound of the Jews" (Tell el-Yehudiyeh).
25. *Pace* E. Mary Smallwood, *The Jews Under Roman Rule: From Pompey to Diocletian* (Leiden: Brill, 1976), 367–68; Livia Capponi, *Il tempio di Leontopoli in Egitto: identita politica e religiosa dei giudei di Onia, ca. 150 a. C.–73* (Pisa: ETS, 2007), 61–90.

19:18–22, the manifesto of Isaiah 61:1–9 spoke loudly to Onias and how he perceived his role:

> The Spirit of Lord Yahweh is upon me,
> because Yahweh has anointed me to be a herald to the poor . . .
> to set up the mourners of Zion,
> to give them a turban instead of ashes,
> the oil of happiness instead of mourning,
> a mantle of praise instead of a spirit of despair,
> naming them "oaks of Righteousness,"
> a planting of Yahweh, regaining stateliness,
> as they rebuild ancient ruins,
> raise former desolations,
> renovate cities of ruin, desolate for generation upon generation.
> Strangers will stand and shepherd your sheep,
> the sons of foreigners becoming your farmers and vintners,
> as you are called, "priests of Yahweh,"
> addressed as "ministers of our God."
> . . . Their offspring will be recognized by the gentiles,
> their issue amid the peoples.
> All who see them will acknowledge that
> they are the offspring Yahweh has blessed. (Isa 61:1a, 3–6a, 9)

The book of Isaiah culminates in a vision of a Jerusalem recreated for the faithful who endured the opposition and exclusion of their brethren (Isa 66:5). Onias used this to frame his new program in the hope that, under his leadership, the Jewish nation might be born again.

However, Onias's vision never gained the traction he hoped for. Most Jews could not transfer their loyalty from Jerusalem to Leontopolis. Jewish worship still faced Jerusalem. Jewish prayer houses in Egypt continued to function as satellites of the Jerusalem temple, and the annual temple tax was still paid to Jerusalem. Onias's theology was still tied to a sacrificial cult on a specific cultic campus, and therefore most only ever saw it as a cheap imitation of the real thing. Furthermore, the Jewish community of Alexandria, which had long since attained the status of a *politeuma* (a semi-autonomous ethnic enclave), was the indisputable hub of Jewish life in Egypt.[26] Leontopolis had neither the

---

26. Smallwood, *The Jews Under Roman Rule*, 225–26.

political nor cultural capital to sway Alexandria, nor the theological clout to displace Jerusalem.

Despite this, Onias's temple did have a modest stream of adherents. It continued to operate with a Zadokite line of priests for over two centuries, until Vespasian ordered it closed in AD 74 in the wake of the Jewish Revolt (*J.W.* 7.407–432).

3.5.6 EXCURSUS: THE EARLY CHURCH AND THE TEMPLE

The theology of the early church had much in common with Onias IV's vision for a new temple and a new Jerusalem. The strict monotheism of the early Christians fed the conviction that God could be worshipped anywhere. They also believed that the old order had come to an end in judgment, giving rise to a new order. Crucially, however, the early church moved away from the notion of a sacrificial cult at a specific sacrificial campus, and this distinguished it from Onias IV's program of a transplanted cult. This was achieved in three ways.

First, the conviction that the Holy Spirit was granted to all who believed in Jesus transcended the notion of place. The Spirit was received by faith in Jesus, which was not culture-bound and thus not fettered by the ethnic strictures of a temple precinct. Onias's vision was for a nation born again, but this amounted to replicating the nation's structures in a new location. The early church, however, saw Jesus's vision being for a transformed people of God, transcending nation, land, and temple. In the Gospel of John, the miracle of Cana has Jesus turn water into wine, which is indicative of the transformation from the old order to the new (John 2:1–11). Jesus's conversation with Nicodemus then shows that the new people of God are to be "born from above"—that is, born of the wind, which blows over and above the earth, rather than "born of water," which is tied to the lower earthly regions and represents the old covenantal order of Law and land (John 3:3–8). Crucially, between the miracle at Cana and the conversation with Nicodemus, Jesus demands the destruction of the old temple and the erection of a new one (John 2:19). This was not a call for the replication of the old system but for a wholesale transformation, which John interprets as a reference to Jesus's resurrection (John 2:21–22). The granting of the Spirit meant there was no need for people to worship at one cultic location, for now anyone could worship the transcendent God who was Spirit at any place "in spirit and in truth" (John 4:23–24). The pneumatology of the early church, connected as it was to the notion of Jesus's resurrection with his body as the new temple, thus gave its theology much greater impact than Onias IV's vision of a transplanted cult.

Second, Jesus's death was interpreted as a definitive sacrifice once and for all time, obviating the need for ongoing sacrifice. The writer to the Hebrews, who wrote to Jewish Christians after the destruction of the temple in AD 70,[27] argued against the need for a physical temple because of Jesus's superior priesthood in accordance with the quasi-Platonic metaphysic of Jewish apocalyptic thinking. Jesus was, according to this thinking, a priest in the royal order of Melchizedek, which far surpassed the Levitical priestly order (Heb 5:6–7:22). For, while the Levitical priests had ministered in a physical location, Jesus entered the sanctuary's heavenly template—the spiritual temple in the heavenlies, where ultimate reality resided. There he offered up his own blood as the ultimate and perfect sacrifice. As both high priest and perfect victim in the heavenly realm, Jesus fulfilled the purpose of the old cult and rendered all subsequent earthly sacrifice defunct (Heb 9:1–15).

Third, the early church was convinced that the death and resurrection of Jesus brought about the end of the old covenant. The writer to the Hebrews argued that, since Jesus's priesthood in the royal order of Melchizedek was a change from the old Levitical order, a new covenant naturally ensued to facilitate it (Heb 7:11–21; 12:24). Furthermore, Jesus's atoning work was so all-encompassing that an entirely new order was required (Heb 7:22–25). Jesus was the builder of a new "house," which consisted not of a physical building but of a new people who clung to him in hope (Heb 3:2–6; cf. 2 Cor 6:16; Eph 2:11–12; 1 Pet 2:5). This moved Jewish Christians away from the need for temple-based worship altogether by showing that Israel's historic destiny had all along been a heavenly city without physical foundations (Heb 11:10)—a heavenly Jerusalem (Heb 12:22) reached by faith in Jesus. To turn back from this was tantamount to apostasy, akin to the rebellion of the Israelites who failed ultimately to reach the promised land (Heb 3:16–4:11; 10:26–31).

The early church's theology of the Spirit and atonement, built on the foundations of Jewish apocalyptic thought, thus did what Onias's theology could not: it provided a theological mandate for graduating from Jerusalem-based temple worship. This was not sacrifice-less worship, such as that which

---

27. There is no scholarly consensus about the date of Hebrews beyond a broad bracket of AD 60–100 (cf. Harold W. Attridge, *The Epistle to the Hebrews*, Hermeneia [Minneapolis: Fortress, 1989], 6–9). However, the rhetoric of Hebrews implies that the Jewish Revolt had already occurred and reached its incendiary end with the destruction of Jerusalem and its temple (cf. Heb 3:6–19; 4:12; 6:8; 9:8–10; 10:26–27, 30–31, 39; 11:8–10, 14–16; 11:29–34; 12:28–29; 13:3). The reflex response of Jews would have been to desire the reconstruction of the temple. But the writer to the Hebrews urges his readers to resist this seemingly natural instinct by arguing that Jesus's sacrificial death brought the old order to an end and obviated the need for a physical tabernacle/temple (Heb 7:18–19; 8:1–2, 7–13; 9:11–15, 24–26; 12:22–24; 13:11–14). Cf. Athas, "Reflections on Scripture," 127–28.

eventually developed in rabbinic Judaism. The death of Jesus was the singular sacrifice that stood perpetually at the heart of Christian worship, appropriated by faith and celebrated in the Lord's Supper.

3.5.7 THE ACCESSION OF DEMETRIUS I

Upon his return to Antioch in the late summer of 162 BC, Lysias successfully put down Philip's challenge to his regency. But Seleucid power structures soon began to fray, with unrest in Media, Babylonia, and Commagene in the mountains of far northern Syria.[28]

At the same time, Demetrius, the son of Seleucus IV and cousin of Antiochus V Goodfather, was making loud counterclaims to the Seleucid throne in Rome. Demetrius had been just nine years old when the Romans took him as a hostage in place of Antiochus IV (see 2.8.8 above). Since Antiochus's death in 164 BC, the now adult Demetrius began petitioning the Roman Senate to support his claim to the Seleucid throne. But the Romans preferred to keep the Seleucids weak and so denied his claim in favor of the more impressionable boy king, Antiochus V Goodfather. It led Demetrius to escape Rome in November 162 BC. He landed at the Phoenician city of Tripolis, where he was hailed as the savior of the unraveling Seleucid realm. On his orders, both Lysias and Antiochus V Goodfather were executed. He then took power in Antioch (1 Macc 7:1–4; 2 Macc 14:1–2) and launched immediately into a campaign to retrieve Commagene, Babylonia, and Media. All these actions would generate political waves, whose effects would be felt for the next century.

3.5.8 THE ZADOKITE CRISIS

The regime change in Antioch led Bacchides, whom Lysias had left in Jerusalem to assist with Alcimus's installation, to head back to Syria. This left Alcimus vulnerable, with only a small force for his protection (cf. 1 Macc 7:19–20). Jewish sentiment had also shifted manifestly against Alcimus after his murderous purge of the *Hasidim* and the consequent flight of the Teacher of Righteousness and Onias IV. Many now sympathized once again with the Maccabean cause. The Hasmonean brothers and their Maccabean fighters took advantage of this and returned to Judea. The longer the Seleucids delayed in dealing with them, the more chance they stood of clawing power back.

---

28. Bar-Kochva, *Judas Maccabaeus*, 347–48.

With the fibers of Seleucid rule unraveling, Alcimus did not know whether the Seleucids would even deploy forces to hunt them down. Alcimus was perilously isolated, which emboldened conservatives in Jerusalem in their opposition to him (cf. 2 Macc 14:3). The specter of violence rose again over Jerusalem, and Alcimus realized he was no longer safe. In an ironic twist, he who had put both the Teacher of Righteousness and Onias IV to flight fled the city himself (cf. 2 Macc 14:4, 7).

Alcimus's departure left the door open for the Hasmonean brothers to return to Jerusalem. The Seleucid garrison in the Acra bunkered down, and once again Jerusalem became a partitioned city. The Hasmoneans acted quickly to sew up their own control over the rest of Judea and press for complete independence while the country was largely devoid of Seleucid armies. This was no easy task, for in addition to fortifying the country, they also needed to secure the leadership of all the conservatives on the home front. Although many had welcomed them back to Jerusalem, Jewish conservatives were still far from united. Then there was the matter of dislodging the Seleucid garrison from the resolute Acra and its adjacent *polis*.

But a more immediate crisis now confronted them: Who would replace Alcimus as high priest? The conservative factions could have rallied behind Onias IV as the legitimate Zadokite heir, which would have produced some far-reaching solidarity. However, Onias IV may have still been under the requisite age for the office. In any case, he had probably already disqualified himself by inaugurating his rival temple at Leontopolis in Egypt. Furthermore, his association with Ptolemy VI meant that, even if he did return to Jerusalem, he might bring Ptolemaic sovereignty with him. Onias, a Zadokite, was no longer a practicable option. Someone else had to be found.[29]

The Teacher of Righteousness might have been a logical choice to solve the Zadokite crisis, especially if he was a member of the wider Zadokite clan and had taken some Zadokite priests into exile with him.[30] As such, he probably expected to return to the city to take up the high priesthood.[31] But he was a

---

29. Cf. VanderKam, *From Joshua to Caiaphas*, 245–46.

30. This likelihood arises from the Essene writings, which give a position of leadership in the sect to the "sons of Zadok," who are distinguished from the "sons of Aaron" and the Levites (CD 4:3–4; 1QS 5:2; 1Q28a 1:2, 24; 2:3; 1Q28b 3:22–23). This suggests that, as leader of the sect, the Teacher of Righteousness was one of the "sons of Zadok."

31. The Damascus Document castigates those who did not listen to the Teacher of Righteousness, including while he was in exile in the "land of Damascus" (CD 19:33–35; 20:28). In particular, it denounces those who followed the "Man of Mockery" (CD 1:14–21). This figure, who should be identified with Judas Maccabeus, is seen as a leader of the "men of mockery" (CD 20:11), a reference to the Maccabees who fought under Judas's codename. Behind the references is a memory that the nation chose to follow the "Man of Mockery" rather than the Teacher of Righteousness.

polarizing personality with an unsparing hardline stance on the solar calendar. Pro-Zadokites existed throughout Jewish conservative ranks, but many opposed the imposition of the solar calendar on the temple cult, while others viewed it as adiaphora at best. Thus, many pro-Zadokites were reticent to accept the leadership of the Teacher of Righteousness, even if they wanted a Zadokite as high priest. The Hasmonean brothers certainly could not countenance him as high priest after he had withdrawn the *Hasidim* from their alliance with them. Furthermore, Judea had by this time experienced eleven years of non-Zadokite high priests (Menelaus and Alcimus) and become somewhat acclimatized to living without them. If the nation could not get Onias, and it did not wish the leadership of the pontifical Teacher of Righteousness, it might be willing to live without the Zadokite line altogether.

The last eleven years had also seen the sacral office take on military characteristics. The high priest was no longer simply the ethnarch of the Jewish people but the representative of the Seleucid authority who appointed him.[32] Along with this power came military dispensations, as Jason and Menelaus had demonstrated. The high priesthood was now a role that required martial clout behind it. The disavowal of armed resistance by the Teacher of Righteousness ruled him out as a viable candidate.

The Hasmonean brothers had the military muscle to install the next high priest. They wanted someone who was not a stooge for the Seleucid government but a man who could stand valiantly for Jewish independence, able to wield a sword as much as a censer. The Hasmoneans' position as powerbrokers was aided by the fact that they themselves were Aaronide priests, albeit not from the Zadokite line. And so, without a viable Zadokite candidate to choose from, Judas "The Hammer" assumed the high priesthood for himself in the winter of 162/1 BC (*Ant.* 12.419).[33]

---

32. Cf. Babota, *Hasmonean High Priesthood*, 53–57, 88, 94.

33. First Maccabees does not overtly claim that Judas Maccabeus assumed the high priesthood, which has led some to doubt that it occurred (e.g., Babota, *Hasmonean High Priesthood*, 99–101, 105–109). However, 2 Macc 14:26 does state that Judas was appointed as Alcimus's successor—a clear reference to the high priesthood. Furthermore, Josephus states that Judas became high priest (*Ant.* 12.419), which explains why Alcimus was prevented from serving at the altar, how Judas could have had authority over priests before the altar (2 Macc 15:31), why Alcimus needed to be installed a second time at a later point (2 Macc 14:13), and how he was characterized as one who had "previously been high priest" (2 Macc 14:3). See VanderKam, *From Joshua to Caiaphas*, 242–43; Daniel R. Schwartz, *2 Maccabees*, Commentaries on Early Jewish Literature (Berlin: de Gruyter, 2008), 474–75, 551–52. Judas's high priesthood was, however, quickly eclipsed by Alcimus's counterclaim. The omission of Judas's tenure in 1 Maccabees and the mere allusion to it in 2 Maccabees can be explained by the theology of retribution in both books. Since Judas was killed shortly after assuming the office, the authors risked presenting his death as a divine judgment in the same league as Menelaus and Alcimus. It was theologically safer to scrub Judas's short tenure altogether and focus on the divine judgment enacted upon Alcimus instead (cf. 1 Macc 9:54–57).

The Teacher of Righteousness had probably returned from exile in the "land of Damascus" in the expectation of taking up the high priesthood and imposing a solar calendar on the temple. But Judas denied him and threatened him with violence. The Teacher of Righteousness was either forced to retreat from Jerusalem again or was killed (see quote below).[34] Ultimately, we do not know his precise fate or the whereabouts of the Essenes at this time.[35] They were now thoroughly marginalized in Jewish society, and this fostered their isolationist apocalypticism (see 3.6.1 below). In the sect's later writings, Judas's subversion of the priesthood and the alienation of Essene customs was recalled as a tragic fulfilment of prophecy that led the whole nation astray:

> [God] raised up for them [i.e., the faithful of Israel] a Teacher of Righteousness to set them on the path of his heart . . . and he made known in later generations what he did with later generations—with the company of traitors [i.e., the Maccabees]. They were the ones who strayed from the way. It was the time of which it was written, "Like a stubborn cow, so has Israel been stubborn" [Hos 4:16a]; when a Man of Mockery [i.e., Judas Maccabeus] arose, who spread the waters of fraud upon Israel, and made them roam in a pathless wasteland, throwing down the ancient heights, straying from the pathways of righteousness, and removing the demarcation that the ancients marked out as their inheritance. . . . They looked for easy answers [lit: "smooth things"],[36] and so chose the ridiculous. They searched for loopholes and chose a fine neck.[37] They justified what was wrong and condemned what was right. They contravened the covenant and broke the standard. They conspired against the life of the righteous one and found abominable all who would walk with integrity. They pursued them with the sword and celebrated conflict among the people. (CD 1:11–16, 18–21)

---

34. The Damascus Document was written after the death of the Teacher of Righteousness (cf. CD 19:35–20:1, 13–15), but since it is difficult to pinpoint the date of its composition, we cannot pinpoint the date of his death either.

35. The Essenes did not yet settle at Qumran. Roland de Vaux suggested they established the Qumran community between ca. 130 and 100 BC, but the archaeological evidence points to their arrival in the early first century BC. See Jodi Magness, *The Archaeology of Qumran and the Dead Sea Scrolls* (Grand Rapids: Eerdmans, 2002), 68.

36. The "seekers of smooth things" usually refers to the Pharisees in the Essenes' sectarian writings. The phrase here in the Damascus Document, however, is early and does not use the ordinary nominal form of this sobriquet; it is, rather, a verbal clause. In this instance, it refers not to the Pharisees but to one of the many actions taken by Judas Maccabeus and his brothers. The label might simply be a way the Essenes denigrated those they saw as extremists.

37. To choose a "fine neck" denotes saving one's life to live a life of ease, as opposed to being prepared to live with difficulty (cf. Mic 2:3).

The pro-Zadokites who were not aligned with the Teacher of Righteousness now faced the fact that the Zadokite line was, for all intents and purposes, dead. All they could do was to claim it as their spiritual heritage and get behind Judas Maccabeus as high priest. Those who did so coalesced into a new denomination that came to be known as the Sadducees—the heirs of the Zadokite legacy.

3.5.9 JUDAS MACCABEUS AS HIGH PRIEST

Judas Maccabeus seems to have declared Judea's independence—a bold move considering Judea consisted of little more than a partitioned city and the district surrounding it. Judas was lighting a political bonfire to add to those already burning in Commagene, Babylon, and Media. But when it became clear that Demetrius was quenching those other bonfires, Judas realized he needed more robust backing. So he dispatched an embassy to Rome to seek *amicitia*, a formal treaty of friendship (1 Macc 8:1–20). He was astutely aiming to leverage the Roman Senate's role as Mediterranean powerbroker, its opposition to Demetrius, and its desire to keep the Seleucid kingdom torpid. The two ambassadors he commissioned were Eupolemus ben-John and Jason ben-Eleazar.[38]

While the ambassadors were on their mission, Alcimus swung into action and sought an audience with Demetrius the moment the king returned to Antioch in 161 BC. He made the very simple and evident case that Judas and his allies had compromised Seleucid sovereignty in Judea (2 Macc 14:3–10): "As long as Judas is around," he told the king, "it is impossible to achieve peace in any matters" (2 Macc 14:10). Demetrius needed little convincing. He appointed Nicanor, one of his closest friends, who had helped him escape Rome (*Ant.* 12.402), as governor of Judea (2 Macc 14:11–13). Nicanor headed south to confront Judas with an army, plunging Judea into panic once again (2 Macc 14:14–15). That panic escalated when Nicanor repelled an attempted ambush by Simon Thassi near a village called Dessau (2 Macc 14:16).[39]

The return of Eupolemus and Jason from Rome gave Judas only minimal extra hope. According to the overcooked claims of 1 Maccabees 8:21–32,

---

38. Eupolemus is almost certainly the same Eupolemus who wrote a history of the Jewish nation in Greek in ca. 157 BC (see Clement of Alexandria, *Stromata* 1.141). Only fragments of it survive in the writings of later authors (e.g., Alexander Polyhistor).

39. The location of Dessau is unknown, though it might be the same as Adasa, between Jerusalem and Beth Horon, and which featured in the unfolding conflict. See Bar-Kochva, *Judas Maccabaeus*, 349–50.

Rome entered a military alliance that bound Rome and Judea to mutual assistance if the other was invaded. But the mighty behemoth of Rome did not need Judas's tadpole state to come to its potential aid. This rendition of the embassy's result probably reflects what Judas had hoped to gain rather than what he actually did gain.[40] Rome did not wish to manufacture a conflict with Demetrius, but it did want to curtail his power. Giving some backing to Judas served Rome's foreign policy, but the Senate needed to do this without violating its treaty with the Seleucids. Thus, Rome recognized Judea as a "free and autonomous" hierocracy, which was "under the leadership, not of a king, but of a high priest" (Diodorus Siculus, *Bib. hist.* 40.2.1).[41] This diplomatic-speak was vague enough to imply that Rome did not recognize Judea as an independent state with its own king, but it did recognize the Jews as a discrete *ethnos* with the right to live according to their own customs under their high priest. These conditions could be met with Judea still within the Seleucid realm, so long as Judea was led by the high priest rather than a Seleucid civic governor. Now that the royal cult had been repealed in Judea, the Jewish people were no longer swearing direct fealty to the Seleucid king but rather being represented before him by their high priest. It was, in other words, only a slightly modified form of the status Judea held before 167 BC.[42]

The pact was enough to give Nicanor pause from attacking Judas.[43] Instead, he entered into negotiations with him (2 Macc 14:18–29)—something Judas probably felt he had little choice but to entertain. By involving Rome in Judea's affairs, Judas had unwittingly let the Romans reframe the nature of the conflict. Jewish independence was now firmly off the table. What was on the table was the high priesthood and Jewish autonomy within the Seleucid realm. Nicanor cleverly offered Judas recognition of his position as high priest in return for his recognition of Seleucid sovereignty. This essentially put flesh

---

40. See Linda Zollschan's detailed work, *Rome and Judaea*, 65, 160, 187.

41. The Roman concept of "freedom" (*libertas*) did not imply absolute autonomy but rather freedom from arbitrary rule through the rule of law. Since Jewish custom was all about law (Torah), the Romans interpreted "freedom" for the Jews as adherence to their Torah, regardless of who else might have been imposed over them. See Zollschan, *Rome and Judaea*, 210–12.

42. The historicity of the embassy to Rome and the consequent pact has been called into question, but there is enough evidence to support it in broad outline; see Babota, *Hasmonean High Priesthood*, 106–9; Zollschan, *Rome and Judaea*, 187. Furthermore, the chapter does contain one reliable historical anomaly, namely the statement that the Romans "entrust one man to lead them annually and rule their entire territory" (1 Macc 8:16). Rome elected *two* consuls annually, but in 162 BC an electoral irregularity led to the removal of both consuls and the appointment of an *interrex*—something that occurred shortly before Judas's embassy arrived in Rome (see Zollschan, *Rome and Judaea*, 30–31, though note that she dates Judas's embassy to 162 BC rather than 161 BC).

43. Contra 2 Macc 14:18, it was almost certainly Rome's response to Judas's embassy, rather than the reputation of Judas himself, that halted Nicanor's military endeavors.

on the bones of Rome's level of recognition. It was an offer that pinned Judas on the horns of an agonizing dilemma. Should he accept the offer and continue as high priest in Jerusalem, with a guarantee of Jewish autonomy, but betray the cause of Jewish independence? Or should he reject the offer and stay loyal to the cause for independence but face a clearly superior foe with the risk of losing everything he had fought so hard for?

Judas's theology, which advocated the use of the sword in the defense of Jewish culture, had no room for accepting Seleucid sovereignty. He did not believe in resurrection and nor did his Maccabean fighters or Sadducean supporters.[44] His ideology was primarily invested in the here-and-now, which made the social, political, and cultural struggle more vital to him than the spiritual. To that end, for example, he had long been willing to fight on the Sabbath if attacked (1 Macc 2:41). This priority of politics over piety was viewed by the emerging Essenes (their former allies) as a sell-out—the route of compromise and easy answers ("smooth things" [CD 1:11–21]).

But since Nicanor had the numbers, Judas reluctantly acquiesced to his demands. It was a colossal backdown. The author of 2 Maccabees spun this as Nicanor developing a camaraderie with Judas, which convinced Judas "to marry and have children" (2 Macc 14:23–25). The historical reality behind this fatuous presentation is that Nicanor compelled Judas to give up Judea's independence in return for a hereditary high priesthood that he could pass down to a son.[45] Judas was given a Hasmonean priesthood to replace the Zadokite priesthood in exchange for an end to the Maccabean cause for independence. Although it was a serious ideological retreat for Judas, it was an offer too good to refuse. Not only did it affix him and his descendants as the hereditary high priests, it returned the Jewish nation to the status it had enjoyed shortly after Antiochus III had wrested Coele Syria off the Ptolemies: a recognized Jewish *ethnos* under the authority of a hereditary ethnarch, only this time it was without a Seleucid governor above him. From Nicanor's perspective, it was a compromise Rome would approve of, and it pacified a turbulent province in the Seleucid realm. In one masterstroke, Nicanor had taken Judea off the political flame and restored peace to the region.

Judas's backdown represented a step away from belligerent extremism

---

44. The author of 2 Maccabees, who clearly believed in resurrection, includes an anecdote (12:39–45) that he claims proves that Judas also believed in resurrection. This is, however, purely the author's own interpolation. Judas's actions should instead be framed within a standard Deuteronomistic theology of retribution rather than a doctrine of resurrection.

45. This is the only historically viable interpretation of what is otherwise a "mysterious staccato" (Schwartz, *2 Maccabees*, 482) in 2 Maccabees.

towards a more peaceable conservative posture, which appealed to just about everybody. Alcimus, however, was incensed at being completely sidelined. He appealed again to Demetrius, accusing Nicanor of treason for reaching an understanding with a flagrant rebel like Judas. He argued that only he (Alcimus) could bring enduring stability to Judea because he was both the legitimate high priest and a compliant centrist, whereas Judas had assumed the high priesthood for himself and was at heart a militant fundamentalist. Alcimus rattled Demetrius's confidence, so the king overruled Nicanor and commanded him to arrest Judas and transport him to Antioch (2 Macc 14:27).[46]

Forced to comply with the king's demands, Nicanor adopted a different disposition towards Judas. The moment he did, Judas grew skittish. It is easy to see how Judas might have surmised that the regime he distrusted so much wanted to backstab him (cf. 2 Macc 15:10). Eventually, Nicanor demanded that the priests in the Jerusalem temple hand Judas over to him (1 Macc 7:29–38; 2 Macc 14:31–36).[47] Judas, however, had done as Alcimus, the Teacher of Righteousness, Onias IV, and Jason had all done before him: he fled the city.

Of course, Judas was used to operating out of such conditions. His brothers and the Maccabean fighters rallied around him and once again went to ground in the Gophna Hills north of Jerusalem. Nicanor dispatched a search party, but Judas and his posse ambushed them near a village called Kefar Salama, leaving the survivors to crawl back to Nicanor in Jerusalem (1 Macc 7:31).

The success at Kefar Salama was a Rubicon moment for Judas, for it represented a definitive reversal of his earlier backdown and committed him and the Maccabees to the cause for complete independence from the Seleucids. The stakes were now all or nothing. It was also a political victory for Alcimus, as it confirmed what he had been telling Demetrius all along: Judas could not be trusted to recognize Seleucid sovereignty and observe the peace.

In February 160 BC, Nicanor ventured out with a small force and encamped along the main road near Beth-Horon. Judas based his freedom fighters in a village called Adasa, cutting Nicanor off from Jerusalem. Despite the testimony of 1 Maccabees 7:39–50 and 2 Maccabees 15:20–25, it is doubtful that the two forces faced each other in open battle, since Judas's men were not adequately armed for that (2 Macc 15:11). It is more probable that Judas employed guerrilla warfare. On the 13th day of Adar (23 February

---

46. Demetrius may have wanted to bring Judas to Antioch, rather than have him executed in the field, to deliberately demonstrate to the Romans that he was treading with cautious legality and not wanton abandon.

47. First Maccabees places Nicanor's appearance in the temple even before the embassy to Rome, which disagrees with the more preferable order in 2 Maccabees.

160 BC),[48] Judas used his superior knowledge of the terrain to ambush Nicanor's camp and successfully routed the Seleucid soldiers.

When the dust settled, the Maccabees found that Nicanor had fallen in the melee. Judas now determined to make an example of the fallen governor to rally support for the cause for independence. He ordered that Nicanor's head and arm be hacked from his corpse and conveyed to Jerusalem. There, in front of the altar, before an assemblage of priests, Judas appeared as a warrior high priest. He produced the grisly trophies and gruesomely cut the tongue from Nicanor's lifeless mouth. It was a graphic show of strength, reminiscent of David cutting off Goliath's head (1 Sam 17:51) and the Levite dismembering the corpse of his concubine to unite Israel in outrage against a common foe (Judg 19:29–30). After commissioning the annual public celebration of his victory, Judas had Nicanor's rotting head displayed before the Acra (1 Macc 7:44–50; 2 Macc 15:28–36). It was a brazen act of violent defiance that sent a clear message: Judas would stop at nothing to ensure the death of his enemies and the independence of Judea. And yet this horrific act was thoroughly devoid of apocalyptic significance, for Judas was not trusting in the eschatological intervention of God but in his own agency as God's chosen instrument to bring about a political solution for the Jewish nation in the here-and-now.

When word of his friend's morbid fate reached Demetrius in Mesopotamia, he was jolted into action. He commissioned Bacchides, who had local knowledge of Judea, to avenge Nicanor's death, bring Judas Maccabeus to justice, and install Alcimus a second time as high priest in Jerusalem (1 Macc 9:1). Demetrius was at no risk of offending Rome with this course of action, for Judas had proved himself the aggressor. What's more, by reinstalling Alcimus as high priest, he was not contravening Rome's declaration that Judea should be under the authority of a high priest.

Thus, in April/May 160 BC, barely two months after his victory over Nicanor, Judas Maccabeus faced a fresh onslaught.[49] Bacchides brought

---

48. This was the day before Purim (2 Macc 15:36), which falls in February-March. It is common to place the skirmishes between Nicanor and Judas in 161 BC, but this is too compressed a timeframe. Demetrius escaped from Rome in November 162 BC, and the Battle of Adasa occurred in the Jewish month of Adar (February-March). Judas's embassy to Rome occurred during the consulship of Gaius Fannius Strabo (*Ant.* 14.233), which was the Roman year between March 161 BC and March 160 BC (Sievers, *The Hasmoneans and Their Supporters*, 68–70). Judas's embassy to Rome must have arrived in March 161 BC, putting the negotiations between Nicanor and Judas later that year. Only after this did Alcimus parley with Demetrius, putting the skirmishes between Judas and Nicanor in late 161 BC or early 160 BC. The Battle of Adasa must, therefore, be dated to February 160 BC.

49. It is practically certain that an intercalary month (Adar II) was inserted into the lunar calendar this year, meaning that at least two months elapsed between the death of Nicanor on 13 Adar (23 February 160 BC) and the arrival of Bacchides in the month of Nisan (late April or early May 160 BC). See Bar-Kochva, *Judas Maccabaeus*, 385; Sievers, *The Hasmoneans and Their Supporters*, 67.

a force of 20,000 troops and 2,000 cavalry to Judea, trekking through the Jordan Valley and ascending into the mountains north of Jerusalem (1 Macc 9:2–4).[50] This cut Judas off from his Maccabean fighters in the Gophna Hills further north. Without Judas's leadership, they were helpless to repel Bacchides's superior forces. Bacchides easily eliminated them and confined Judas to Jerusalem.

With his forces drastically reduced and the defenses of Jerusalem in no condition to withstand an assault, Judas found himself in a situation of impending doom. If he surrendered, he risked certain execution. If he fled, he would have to abandon Judea altogether, spelling the end of the whole Maccabean cause. But if he chose to fight, he faced almost certain defeat.

Judas chose to fight. He mustered approximately 3,000 men (1 Macc 9:5) and ventured north to confront Bacchides's army. They encountered them north of the village of Elasa along the main road (at modern Ramallah). When Judas's militia saw the strength of Bacchides's army, many attempted to dissuade him from fighting, arguing that it was wiser to live and fight another day than to go down in battle now (1 Macc 9:6, 9). But Judas refused to be swayed and vowed an honorable fight to the death. Most of his men, though, abandoned him, leaving him with barely 800 diehard fighters (1 Macc 9:6). In a moment of uncharacteristic frankness, the author of 1 Maccabees admits that at this point, Judas was "heartbroken" (1 Macc 9:7). He had faced many battles against the odds before, but in this moment he faced certain doom. Despite this, Judas persuaded his remaining warriors to stand and fight. The author of 1 Maccabees has him tell them, "If our time has come, then let us die with manliness on behalf of our brothers and not leave behind a question about our honor" (1 Macc 9:10). This was not a statement of hope in a future resurrection but of making the current moment count as much as possible in the face of certain loss.

Judas fell in battle against Bacchides at Elasa in May 160 BC (1 Macc 9:11–18). His brothers survived the fight and, according to the sources, retrieved his body after a truce with Bacchides and buried him in the family tomb at Modiin (1 Macc 9:19; *Ant.* 12.432). But this is hardly plausible, since immediately after the battle, Bacchides was hunting them down in the Judean Desert (1 Macc 9:32–34). Thus, despite the reports of his burial and national lamentation (1 Macc 9:19–21), it is likely that Judas's body fell into

---

50. First Maccabees 9:2 states that Bacchides came via Maisaloth in Arbela. Maisaloth may be a misrepresentation of the Hebrew word *mesilloth* ("highways"). Arbela overlooks Lake Galilee, so its mention is either a curious detail regarding Bacchides's route or perhaps a mistake for *har bethel* ("Mount Bethel"). See Bar-Kochva, *Judas Maccabaeus*, 382–84.

the hands of Bacchides's army while the survivors fled (cf. 1 Macc 9:18).[51] The Maccabean resistance and the cause for independence was over.

When the Essenes reflected upon the death of Judas Maccabeus, whom they dubbed the "Man of Mockery," and the failure of his freedom fighters, they concluded that it was divine judgment for his usurpation of the priesthood and failure to adopt the piety that the Teacher of Righteousness had espoused:

> The curses of his [God's] covenant clung to them, consigning them to the sword, which enacts the vengeance of the covenant. . . . The wrath of God was kindled against their party, annihilating their entire horde. Their deeds had become unclean before him. (CD 1:17; 1:21–2:1)

---

51. Judas's brother, Simon, later built seven tombs at Modiin, one for each Hasmonean brother and two for their parents (1 Macc 13:28–29). This gives the impression that Judas was buried in Modiin, but these were probably monumental cenotaphs, not actual tombs.

3.6 THE REASSERTION OF SELEUCID SOVEREIGNTY

3.6.1 JEWISH SECTS UNDER THE SELEUCIDS

After the death of Judas, Bacchides reinstated Seleucid sovereignty over Jerusalem and reinstalled Alcimus as high priest. It was a time of mixed emotion in Jerusalem but also of continued theological evolution. Most would have been glad that hostilities had finally come to an end, but many conservatives had harbored great sympathy for Judas's cause, even if some did not condone his methods. Now the notion of Jewish independence seemed dead in the water, with no one to take up the cause.

All Jewish parties needed to adjust to this new reality. With the end of the Zadokite priesthood and the failure of the Maccabean cause, Judas's priestly allies, the Sadducees, found themselves largely alone. They had little choice but to accept the leadership of Alcimus, even if they disliked him personally. Their existence was, after all, predicated on priestly power. They thus moved from a conservative stance towards a more centrist posture.

The conservative Essenes kept their distance now that their arch-nemesis, Alcimus, was back in power. They developed their own movement as one of conscientious objection to the status quo. Like the Sadducees, they viewed themselves as the true heirs of the Zadokite legacy, especially as there probably were Zadokite priests in their midst. But unlike the Sadducees, they rejected the legitimacy of the temple's leadership and so turned away from it towards prayer and ascetic monasticism within their own community (cf. CD 11:18–23; 1QS 9:3–5; Josephus, *Ant.* 18.18–19). This helped fuel their growing apocalyptic eschatology and the expectation of God's imminent intervention to set right what was wrong in Jewish society.

Their isolation would see conservative ranks thinned and turn instead towards the ultra-conservative Pharisees. Judas's death brought the Pharisees out of the Maccabees' shadow into a more prominent role as the main fundamentalist party in Jewish society. This gave them significant lay influence and the momentum to continue developing pietistic practices. The Intellectuals were a more nebulous group to begin with, and many of them joined the other factions that became organized sects. Those who did not simply continued as unaffiliated members of society—an educated class of Scripture-devoted scribes, officials, and entrepreneurs with moderate views. Most continued to hold Davidic hopes, an apocalyptic worldview, and belief in ongoing prophecy and eschatological resurrection. We cannot tell whether Hellenizing Jews formed an organized sect, but they were still present in Jewish society. The volatility of the previous years might have induced many to leave or perhaps form even closer association with local gentiles. But the reinstatement of Seleucid authority and Alcimus's high priesthood let them breathe a sigh of relief. Alcimus himself was, of course, the biggest winner of all. Originally a centrist, he had become an avowed anti-fundamentalist, and this moved him towards a more progressive stance.

Theological formulation within the various groups took place in response to major events and to each other. For example, a famine took hold soon after Alcimus's reinstatement (1 Macc 9:24). The Essenes believed this had been foretold in Psalm 37:19–20 and interpreted it as divine judgment on the Jewish nation for rejecting the Teacher of Righteousness while they themselves were spared its rigors in exile (4Q171 3:2–5). The harsh conditions only intensified the conservative distaste for Alcimus and the Seleucids, with a continued rise of prophetic figures claiming to interpret the signs of the times. On the other hand, it encouraged progressive Jews to take a further step away from traditional beliefs and find solace in Greek learning as it sought empirical explanations for such phenomena rather than divine causation. For the educated Sadducees, who were conversant with Greek ideas and on the move away from conservatism, it induced a kind of agnosticism about divine intervention. In the long term, it bred the deistic notion that became characteristic of Sadducee theology, namely that Yahweh was a distant deity who rarely got his hands dirty in human affairs. This was a way of affirming the value of Greek philosophy, especially Aristotelianism with its emphasis on empirical observation and natural causation, while still holding resolutely to the Jewish idea of God's holy transcendence. This deism, in turn, promoted the Sadducee belief in complete human free will, for if God was rarely involved in human affairs, then it was impossible to say that God actively predestined things to occur. To the Sadducee mind, the entire notion of prophets was thereby rendered obsolete (cf. 1 Macc 9:27), for God was not in the business of regularly intervening in the world—at least not anymore. Similarly, there was no scope for eschatological judgment, resurrection, or an afterlife (*War* 2.164–165; *Ant.* 18.16). It was a theology grounded in the world of the now, driven by the concerns of politics and power rather than piety.

This contrasted with the apocalyptic outlook of the Pharisees and Essenes who developed beliefs in God's direct intervention in human affairs. The Pharisees came to believe in predestination, which included both God's determining election and a circumscribed human free will—an apocalyptic perspective that depended chiefly on the apocalypticism and eschatology of the book of Daniel, which became evident also in the early church.

The Essenes, on the other hand, believed that humans had less say in their own destiny, not because humans were mere puppets of God's will but because humans were influenced in an essential way by a multitude of evil spiritual forces that had rebelled against God—an idea that owed much to the metaphysics of Platonic philosophy with its realm of forms. However, they also viewed history as imbued with the impetus to head inexorably towards the goal ordained for it by God—a theology that owed much to the Aristotelian notion of the unmoved mover and an ultimate *telos* (see 2.4.3 above). Their ideological forebears, the Enochic Radicals, had adapted these ideas into narrative form in the Book of the Watchers (1 En. 1–36), which portrays the descent of angelic beings ("Watchers") to earth, where they couple with human women and lead the human race astray. The Essenes developed this idea through their cosmology and angelology. The "Prince of Light" and the "most sacred spirits" governed the faithful, while the "Angel of Darkness" or "Belial" governed the wicked and enticed the faithful to corruption (1QS 3:13–4:19; 4Q403; 1QM 1:1). History was, therefore, not just the unfolding of God's pre-determined plan but also a departure from it. It was an apostasy constrained by the gravity of God's foreordained times, but an apostasy nonetheless, which required repentance and realignment with God's sanctioned equilibrium. The sacrificial cult played a pivotal role in this, which is why the Essenes saw the ultimatum of the Teacher of Righteousness to Alcimus (4QMMT) as so vital (see 3.5.4 above). But it would ultimately require God's eschatological intervention to destroy the rebellious spiritual forces and the "sons of darkness" whom they controlled in an imminent cosmic battle (1QM 1:1–15). Thus, while the Essenes believed that God's sovereignty and knowledge were supreme and his eschatological intervention inevitable, their view of history was one of charismatic open theism. History was about God bringing a rebellious world back under his control even as it headed towards a pre-ordained goal (cf. 1 En. 91:1–19; 108:1–15). Personal piety and right cultic practice were able to shake off the control of evil spiritual forces and align with God's cosmic purposes.

The view that history was an aberration, even as it was under the gravity of a divine plan, also explains how the Essenes developed a hermetic monasticism that sought escape from the world and protection from its evil influence.

Both experience and theology told the Essenes that the world was a dangerous place. In this regard, Essene theology owed more to the book of 1 Enoch than to Daniel, and it would find expression in the books of Jubilees and the Genesis Apocryphon.[1] But although the Pharisees and Essenes differed slightly on the mechanisms of predestination, both groups believed in the continued agency of prophets in mediating divine revelation and the need for personal spirituality (*J.W.* 2.160–163; *Ant.* 18.12–15, 18–22).

3.6.2 THE WANING MACCABEAN CAUSE

The survival of Judas's brothers—Lucky John (Gaddi), Clever Simon (Thassi), and Jonathan the Trickster (Apphus)—meant that Bacchides's task was not fully completed, and he continued to hunt them down. The brothers retreated into the Judean Desert with the few men who still remained to them (1 Macc 9:33). Leadership of their battered band fell to the youngest brother, Jonathan Apphus (1 Macc 9:28–31), and plans were made to retreat east into Transjordan. In the process of transferring supplies across the Jordan, the eldest brother, Lucky John, ran out of luck when he was ambushed and killed by a Nabatean chieftain, Jambri of Medeba (1 Macc 9:35–36). Whether Jambri acted out of desperation to secure provisions during famine or whether his loyalty had been bought by Bacchides is not known. But the death of John, so soon after Judas's, was another severe blow to the Maccabean cause. It left only two of the original five brothers: Simon and Jonathan.

It was about to get worse, though. John's death tipped Bacchides off to the group's whereabouts, and he brought a force down to rat them out. The account in 1 Maccabees 9:43–49 gives the impression that a close-run pitched battle occurred, but the final outcome gives away the true nature of the incident: Simon, Jonathan, and their small band escaped Bacchides's clutches by swimming desperately across the Jordan. Being thus chased from their homeland was a new nadir for the Hasmoneans and their cause. They vented their frustration by taking murderous revenge on Jambri and his whole family (1 Macc 9:37–42).[2]

Bacchides could now claim to have accomplished his mission of quashing the revolt in Judea, for there were no more rebels left in the region. To reinforce Seleucid sovereignty and prevent the rise of new insurgents, he initiated a

---

1. For an insightful summary of the theology of 1 Enoch, see Seth Schwartz, *Imperialism and Jewish Society, 200 B.C.E to 640 C.E.* (Princeton: Princeton University Press, 2001), 30.

2. The account in 1 Maccabees puts this incident before the escape from Bacchides, but this is only to keep the story of the revenge for John's death together with the account of his actual death.

fortification program throughout Judea, which included enhancing the Acra in Jerusalem (1 Macc 9:50–52). He also took the sons of leading Jewish citizens as hostages to guarantee their compliance with Seleucid authority and Alcimus's leadership. He held them within the confines of the Greek *polis* in the city of David (1 Macc 9:53) in the hope that they would soak up Greek culture and become good Philhellenes who would one day lead the province. Thus, while the Jewish people continued to have cultural autonomy, Hellenization had not been stemmed.

3.6.3 THE SECOND TENURE OF ALCIMUS

Opposition to Alcimus's high priesthood grew among conservative Jews, naturally driving him towards the progressives. This probably explains his decision to demolish the inner wall around the sanctuary (1 Macc 9:54), which Judas appears to have hastily erected again shortly before his death. In the eyes of Alcimus and his Seleucid overlords, it was a relic of a rebel past. But with the Acra and the Greek *polis* just yards from the temple, the removal of the sanctuary's inner boundary would effectively dilute the temple's own sacred space, mixing the holy with the profane and even potentially being defiled by the unclean. And it would all be the doing of the high priest himself.[3] Whether he had plans to permit gentiles to worship in the temple again is unknown, but conservative Jews were outraged nonetheless.

The demolition had barely gotten underway, though, when Alcimus was struck by a debilitating illness. He was rendered immobile, unable to speak, and racked with pain—symptoms suggesting a degenerative disease, like Guillain-Barré Syndrome, rather than a stroke.[4] The inauspicious coincidence with the demolition of the sanctuary wall led to the demolition being abandoned (1 Macc 9:55). The Essenes saw Alcimus's plight as part of the fulfilment of the book of Habakkuk—a divine punishment both for his treatment of the Teacher of Righteousness and his followers, and for his actions against the temple (N.B., the following excerpts are fragmentary):

> The interpretation of the passage [Hab 2:7–8a] refers to the priest [Alcimus] who rebelled and violated the standards of [God] . . . his affliction with the condemnations due for wrongdoing. The horrors of terrible illness acted upon him, with retaliations against his fleshly body. (1QpHab 8:16–9:2)

---

3. Sievers, *The Hasmoneans and Their Supporters*, 75.
4. *Pace* Sievers, *The Hasmoneans and Their Supporters*, 75.

Its interpretation [of Hab 2:8b] refers to the Wicked Priest [Alcimus]. Because of his guilt towards the Teacher of Righteousness and the men of his party, God put him in the hands of his enemies,[5] to bring him low with an affliction that consumed him with personal agony on account of his wrongdoing against his [God's] chosen one. (1QpHab 9:9–12)

The interpretation of the passage [Hab 2:17] refers to the Wicked Priest [i.e., Alcimus], to have retribution enacted against him for what he enacted against the vulnerable [i.e., the Hasidim]. . . . God will condemn him with annihilation, just as he [Alcimus] planned to annihilate the vulnerable. And where it says, "because of the bloodshed in the citadel and the violence of the land" [Hab 2:17], the interpretation of the citadel is Jerusalem, where the Wicked Priest committed acts of abomination and polluted the sanctuary of God.[6] (1QpHab 12:2–3, 5)

Alcimus's incapacitation led eventually to his death, but calculating when he died is not straightforward. First Maccabees states that he died "at that time in great agony" (1 Macc 9:56), but this links his fate with his plan to demolish the temple wall and need not have been immediate. The Essenes' Pesher of Habakkuk (see quotes above) does not give the impression of a swift death at all. The focus on Alcimus's suffering in both sources implies a prolonged period, which might have lasted some years.

This possibility becomes more likely when we examine the subsequent period. First Maccabees 9:54 puts Alcimus's illness in 159 BC, and most infer that his death occurred that same year.[7] But none of the extant sources mention any subsequent high priest in Jerusalem for the next seven years (159–152 BC). This has led to two competing theories about what occurred during these years. The first is that the Teacher of Righteousness became high priest for these seven years.[8] Yet, while the Essene writings state that the Teacher of

---

5. Van de Water ("Punishment of the Wicked Priest," 410–12) argues the "enemies" here are supernatural, spiritual enemies rather than human agents. See also 3.6.5.

6. The "acts of abomination" could refer to Alcimus's plan to demolish the temple's inner wall or to his carrying out the Day of Atonement on an unauthorized day (according to Essene calculation [see 3.5.4]), or both.

7. E.g., Sievers, *The Hasmoneans and Their Supporters*, 75.

8. This theory was first espoused by Hartmut Stegemann in his PhD dissertation, "Die Entstehung der Qumrangemeinde" (Rheinische Friedrich-Wilhems-Universität, 1971), 210–25. It is, however, predicated on the uneasy consensus that the "Wicked Priest" who pursued the Teacher of Righteousness into exile was not Alcimus but Jonathan Apphus, who did become high priest in 152 BC. As seen previously, though, this uneasy consensus fails to explain all the evidence, whereas the identification of the "Wicked Priest" with Alcimus congruently matches all the data.

Righteousness was a priest (4Q171 3:15–16), nowhere do they ever claim that he became the high priest—a glaring omission if he had.[9] The sectarian writings never bemoan the loss of what the Teacher of Righteousness once had but rather express disappointment that his views were never adopted—an unlikely situation if he had been high priest. Furthermore, if he had been high priest, we would expect the solar calendar to have been instituted and to know his name from the roster of high priests, which Josephus consulted. But no sources ever mention such reforms or another incumbent during 159–152 BC. It is historically implausible, therefore, that the Teacher of Righteousness or anyone else functioned as high priest in Jerusalem during these years.[10]

The second theory is that there was a seven-year *intersacerdotium* in which Jerusalem had no high priest at all. Josephus makes this very claim (*Ant.* 20.237), but his chronology is contradictory. These contradictions can be traced back to the assumption that Alcimus died the same year he fell ill—something he infers from 1 Maccabees 9:56, despite the author never stating it overtly.[11] Furthermore, the suggestion that there was no high priest in Jerusalem during this period is highly problematic, for the cult of Yahweh in Jerusalem required a high priest to function—a cultic crisis mentioned in no extant source. What is mentioned is the illness of Alcimus (1 Macc 9:55). His suffering, rather than his eventual death, is the chief feature of his demise recalled by the sources, implying that he survived in his incapacitated state for some time. Although a deputy must have performed his priestly duties for him, the lifelong tenure of the office precluded anyone else from taking the office while Alcimus was still alive.

Alcimus, therefore, probably survived beyond 159 BC. The abandonment of his plans to demolish the temple's wall and his eventual immobility undoubtedly mollified the conservatives in Jerusalem, and the tension in the city receded accordingly. As long as the high priest was a harmless invalid, Judea was in a holding pattern. By 157 BC, Bacchides completed his network of forts, which galvanized the region against possible rebellion. The following year (156/5 BC)

---

9. VanderKam, *From Joshua to Caiaphas*, 246–47.

10. *Pace* Hartmut Stegemann, *The Library of Qumran: On the Essenes, Qumran, John the Baptist, and Jesus* (Grand Rapids: Eerdmans, 1998), 147–48.

11. Despite claiming that there was no high priest for seven years (*Ant.* 20.237), Josephus elsewhere states that it was only for four years (*Ant.* 13.46). He also has contradictory information about the length of Alcimus's incumbency (cf. *Ant.* 12.413; 20.237). His confusion arises from the assumption that Alcimus died the same year he fell ill (159 BC), which opens a gap to 152 BC, when Jonathan Apphus became high priest (see 3.6.5). A hiatus in the sacral office is merely his attempt to make sense of his own mistaken assumption. His chronology is further compromised by the need to account for the high priesthood of Judas Maccabeus. The list of high priests, which Josephus drew upon, treated Alcimus's two discrete periods in office as a single tenure, which completely scrubbed Judas's tenure. This leads Josephus to mistakenly put Judas as high priest after Alcimus, even though this contradicts his narrative.

was a Sabbatical rest for the land, during which the Jews were prohibited from warfare. Bacchides used the opportunity to return to Demetrius in Antioch.[12]

3.6.4 RETURN OF THE HASMONEANS

Bacchides's departure and the Sabbatical Year (156/5 BC) allowed Jonathan Apphus and Simon Thassi to return to Judea. Fearing another outbreak of violence, Hellenizing Jews petitioned Bacchides to return. Their fears were well-founded, for Jonathan initiated a time of terror, resulting in the assassination of some fifty leading figures throughout Judea (1 Macc 9:58–61). Alcimus himself was not a target, because as long as he was alive, he prevented anyone else occupying the high priesthood, keeping the office in a torpor and the Seleucid authorities at bay. The incapacitated high priest thus unwittingly provided Jonathan and Simon with scope for their clandestine operations.

With each assassination, the Hasmoneans clawed back another inch of political power. Of course, with each assassination, the noise of their methods grew louder, until eventually it reached a crescendo that could be heard in Antioch. But Demetrius's ears were filled with the din of opposition to Seleucid dominance among the client kings in Asia Minor. He was able to mute these intermittently over the years but doing so occupied many of his staffers and resources. Bacchides was probably one of these, which is why he was not sent immediately back to Judea. His delay gave the Hasmoneans leeway to continue their assassinations throughout Judea.

But the loudest problem for Demetrius came from a challenger to his throne. Alexander Balas was a teenager who claimed to be a son of Antiochus IV Epiphanes. Whether he actually was is impossible to say, but some of the most powerful people in Asia Minor, like Attalus II of Pergamum, supported his claim, at least out of political expediency.[13] In 154 BC, the Roman Senate voted to acknowledge Alexander Balas and his sister, Laodice, as royal offspring with the right "to return to the kingdom of their forefathers" (Polybius, *Hist.* 33.18).[14] It was a guarantee that Rome would not interfere with

---

12. First Maccabees 9:57 states that Bacchides returned to the king after Alcimus died. But if Alcimus had died at this juncture, Bacchides would have needed to oversee the succession. Furthermore, the fortification network that guaranteed the security of Judea had not been completed by 159 BC. It is more likely that Alcimus was incapacitated, perhaps "as good as dead," when Bacchides eventually left Judea.

13. Both Polybius (*Hist.* 33.18) and Justin (Justin, *Epit.* 34.1.6) state that Alexander Balas's claim was fraudulent.

14. Polybius states that there was division in Rome over the veracity of Alexander Balas's claims (*Hist.* 33.18). Despite this, the Senate threw its support behind Alexander, showing its determination to destabilize the Seleucid realm.

Alexander's attempt to wrest the throne off Demetrius, effectively providing him with a legal imprimatur to raise an army and initiate a Seleucid civil war.

Demetrius was by this stage an alcoholic (Polybius, *Hist.* 33.19), so his judgment probably became increasingly impaired. Soon after Rome back-slapped Alexander with tacit approval, Demetrius bungled an attempt to take control of Cyprus, which was still part of the Ptolemaic kingdom.[15] In so doing, he incited the enmity of Ptolemy VI, who subsequently acknowledged Alexander Balas as his cousin, throwing Ptolemaic weight behind his claim to the Seleucid throne.[16]

It was a crucial turning point. Demetrius had dispatched an under-resourced Bacchides to Judea in 154 BC. His mission was undoubtedly to ensure the readiness of the garrisons throughout the fortifications he had built a few years earlier, in the event of an invasion by Alexander Balas. But Demetrius did not send extra troops with Bacchides. Had he done so, Bacchides might have avoided an embarrassing defeat at the hands of the Hasmonean brothers. The account of their confrontation at Bethbasi, east of Bethlehem, is grossly exaggerated to amplify the victory of Jonathan and Simon (1 Macc 9:63–69),[17] but Bacchides was unable to counter their covert operations. It was at this point that news of the failure in Cyprus broke. In all probability, Bacchides saw the writing on the wall for the alcoholic Demetrius. Keen not to fight a war he had little hope of winning, Bacchides seems to have engineered a coordinated defection to Alexander Balas of all the garrisons for which he was responsible.

This explains the sudden volte face in Bacchides's attitude towards the Hasmonean brothers. He, the slayer of Judas Maccabeus, abandoned the hunt for Jonathan and Simon and reached an agreement with them to facilitate the defection (see 3.6.5 below). While no source overtly states that Bacchides planned the defection (though see 3.6.5 below), the suddenness and sheer irony of the situation hints that there was more going on than meets the eye. This novel hands-off policy put the Hasmoneans squarely back into the mainstream of Jewish politics, and they were suddenly able to relocate to a more prominent position at Michmash, north of Jerusalem. From there Jonathan "began to judge the people," like one of the Israelite judges of old (1 Macc 9:73)—a hint

---

15. Grainger, *The Fall of the Seleukid Empire*, 56–57.
16. Ptolemy VI's mother was Cleopatra I Syra, the sister of Antiochus IV Epiphanes.
17. Excavations at Bethbasi (Khirbet Beit Bassa, on the outskirts of modern Bethlehem) show that it was probably not settled until the first century AD. See Ibrahim Abu Aemar and José C. Carvajal Lopez, "The Pottery of Khirbet Beit Bassa," *Medieval Ceramics* 36 (2011): 1–12. It therefore did not require a protracted military siege by a huge army, as 1 Macc 9:63 claims. Furthermore, the brothers were evidently still able to venture out from Bethbasi for operations, suggesting they were not consistently harangued by Bacchides.

that he was abandoning terror tactics and not causing trouble for Bacchides. The agreement with the Seleucid commander also explains why Bacchides suddenly turned against the Jewish Hellenizers ("men of lawlessness") in Jerusalem, who had called for the brothers' elimination (1 Macc 10:69). Once again, Jews were playing a key role in a regional defection.

3.6.5 SELEUCID CIVIL WAR AND THE RISE OF JONATHAN APPHUS

While Jonathan Apphus waited for the arrival of Alexander Balas and the planned defection, he grew his political power in Judea. The sources do not mention what exactly Jonathan was up to, but we can create a sketch from the general information we have and the trajectory of events that followed. First Maccabees 9:73 says that Jonathan "did away with the ungodly from Israel," which suggests he was able to diminish the influence of Jewish Hellenizers. But he did not achieve this through continued assassinations, for 1 Maccabees also states that during Jonathan's time at Michmash the "sword ceased from Israel" (9:73). This pertains as much to the intra-Jewish situation as it does to the cessation of hostilities with the Seleucid authorities. Jonathan ceased employing terror tactics and began to use more diplomatic means to extend his influence. If, as seems likely, he was privy to an upcoming defection by Bacchides, he could afford to use less violent techniques and bide his time. His priestly pedigree gave him influence, enticing the centrist Sadducees to abandon Alcimus and support him. His active patriotism also appealed to many at the conservative end of the Jewish spectrum. Thus, even while at Michmash (154–153 BC), he became a rallying point for a broad swathe of factions.

There is little doubt that many wanted him to vie for the high priesthood when Alcimus eventually died. Jewish Hellenizers probably wanted the ailing high priest to die sooner than later so that Demetrius could appoint a progressive high priest before Alexander Balas challenged Demetrius.[18] But Alcimus clung to life, putting the high priesthood into a holding pattern. Since Jonathan was privy to Bacchides's planned defection to Alexander Balas, it is almost certain that one of the deal-sweeteners for Jonathan was the promise of the high priesthood (see this section below).

With Alexander Balas raising forces to invade the Seleucid kingdom, Demetrius's actions became desperate. He whisked two of his sons, Demetrius

---

18. The royal right of Demetrius to appoint the Jewish high priest is yet another reason why it is patently implausible to suggest that there was an *intersacerdotium*—a period of four or seven years without a high priest in Jerusalem (see 3.6.3 above). Cf. VanderKam, *From Joshua to Caiaphas*, 244–50.

and Antiochus, off to safety at Cnidus (Justin, *Epit.* 35.2.1)[19] and made a frantic attempt to persuade the Hasmonean brothers to his side. We are told, "Demetrius sent letters to Jonathan with promises of peace, in order to promote him, for he said, 'Let us get to them [Jonathan and Simon] first and make peace with them before they make peace with Alexander against us'" (1 Macc 10:3–4).[20] It may be that Demetrius caught wind of Bacchides's planned defection, but either way his overtures towards the brothers shows how probable it is that Bacchides had done the same. In another supremely ironic moment, Demetrius made Jonathan a general of the empire with the right to raise and equip Jewish troops. As a gesture of goodwill, he also offered to release the young Jewish hostages being kept in the *polis* at Jerusalem's city of David (1 Macc 10:6–7). Critically, though, Demetrius did not offer Jonathan the high priesthood, probably because Alcimus was still clinging to life. In any event, this did not matter to Jonathan, for Demetrius's offer still put him in an unassailable position. He had been granted the right to arm the Jewish nation and enter Jerusalem armed, all with immunity against harassment by the garrison at the Acra, which was still loyal to Demetrius. Then, all he had to do was wait until the regional defection to Alexander Balas, at which point he would be proclaimed high priest by the new regime. And he would come to the office with all the military trappings that the high priesthood had acquired over the decades, all thanks to his unwitting promotion by Demetrius himself.

Jonathan hastened to Jerusalem, where he publicized his new credentials to the consternation of the Jewish Hellenizers. In compliance with the imperial edict, the garrison at the Acra released the young Jewish hostages (1 Macc 10:7–9)—a clear victory for conservative Judaism, as it removed the leadership of the coming generation from under the thumb of direct Greek influence.

Jonathan did not lift a hand against Alcimus. The paralyzed high priest was now thoroughly isolated and completely at his mercy. All the ancient sources recall that Alcimus merely succumbed to his debilitating illness rather than met his end through sinister means.[21] Jonathan had no desire to execute

---

19. Grainger, *The Fall of the Seleukid Empire*, 66. Another son, Antigonus, was kept home in the kingdom (cf. Livy, *Per.* 50.4).

20. The order in which 1 Maccabees presents events suggests that Demetrius contacted Jonathan after Alexander Balas arrived in the Seleucid kingdom but before Alexander Balas contacted him (1 Macc 10:1–4). However, no specific chronological marker is given for when Demetrius reached out to Jonathan, and it is unlikely that he waited until after the arrival of Alexander Balas to do so. It also makes more sense that Alexander Balas would publicly promote Jonathan immediately after landing at Ptolemais-Acco rather than wait passively for Demetrius to try enlisting the Hasmonean brothers first.

21. When the Essenes looked back at the fate of the "Wicked Priest," they recalled that, in addition to his illness, "God put him in the hands of his enemies" (1QpHab 9:10). This might refer to supernatural "enemies" that caused his illness rather than human agents, as argued by van de Water ("Punishment of

the high priest, particularly since he had arrived in Jerusalem putatively as Demetrius's man, as Alcimus also was. He was not about to set the precedent of slaying the Jewish high priest when he himself was about to inherit the office. However, to consolidate his own position, he began rebuilding the walls around the temple with "squared stones for fortification" (1 Macc 10:10–11). While he could claim that this was done in his role as military commander, it deliberately reversed the program of demolition that Alcimus had tried to implement seven years earlier. Jonathan was clearly pressing his authority over the temple ahead of his inevitable installation as high priest.

He did not have long to wait either. In the spring of 152 BC Alexander Balas landed at Ptolemais-Acco, the seat of government in Coele Syria (1 Macc 10:1). Upon landing, the local garrison defected to him, allowing him to make the port his own headquarters (*Ant.* 13.35–36). The ease with which Alexander took the city testifies to the fact that he had suborned the region's top brass before his arrival. Bacchides was almost certainly one of them, for at the same time the garrisons of his fortification network in Judea defected as part of a coordinated mutiny against Demetrius across the region (1 Macc 10:12–14; *Ant.* 12.58).[22] The only exceptions were the garrisons at Beth Zur on Judea's southern frontier and the Acra in Jerusalem, both of which were not under Bacchides's direct control. Thus, most of Coele Syria was in Alexander Balas's pocket as soon as he landed.

Alexander Balas then dispatched a letter to Jonathan. In it he styled himself "King Alexander" and bestowed upon Jonathan the high priesthood (1 Macc 10:17–20). Jonathan's role in the regional defection now became apparent and gave Alexander Balas a foothold in Jerusalem, where the garrison was still loyal to Demetrius. Jonathan's appointment was still provisional at this stage, as Alcimus was still alive, but the old priest died during the summer of 152 BC.[23]

---

the Wicked Priest," 410–12). But it is also possible that the Essenes were recalling that Alcimus ended his days as a paralytic at the mercy of Jonathan Apphus. This possibility is usually overlooked because most erroneously assume that Alcimus died almost seven years earlier in 159 BC at the onset of his disease.

22. First Maccabees 10:12–14 does not state that the troops defected to Alexander Balas. It merely implies that their departure from the fortifications was permanent. The fact that the text does not say that they mobilized on behalf of Demetrius is a blaring silence. The author seems not to have known that the garrison at Ptolemais-Acco defected to Alexander Balas, and therefore it is no surprise that he did not specifically know of other defections, including Jonathan's. But Josephus draws upon a source that was aware of the defection at Ptolemais-Acco (*Ant.* 13.35) and of troops throughout "Syria" (*Ant.* 13.58). All this helps us understand the abandonment of the garrisons in Judea as part of a wider regional defection to Alexander Balas and Bacchides's instrumental role in orchestrating it.

23. This surmise comes from the fact that Alexander Balas landed at Ptolemais-Acco in the spring of 152 BC (see Sievers, *The Hasmoneans and Their Supporters*, 93, n. 75), but it was not until Sukkot in the fall that Jonathan began his tenure as high priest. The delay must have been due to the fact that Alcimus was still alive.

This final note in his demise was deemed confirmation to fundamentalists and conservatives that God had judged him for his crimes (cf. 1QpHab 9:9–12). The centrist Sadducees, who had begrudgingly accepted Alcimus's leadership, now gladly acclaimed Jonathan as high priest. The progressive Hellenists no doubt felt outflanked. Those among them with less allegiance to Demetrius, however, may have resigned themselves to Jonathan's leadership. For Davidic loyalists, Jonathan's rise highlighted yet again how far the restoration of a Davidic kingdom must have seemed, fueling apocalyptic hope for the rise of a Davidic messiah. While they might not necessarily have endorsed Jonathan's priesthood, they probably accepted it. Thus, Jonathan brought a reasonable amount of unity to the Jewish nation at this moment. He was no longer an outlawed fundamentalist extremist; he was a conservative cleric, commander, and politician.

The only ones whom we know did not acclaim him were the Essenes. In their writings, they label Jonathan "the Spreader of Fraud" (Heb. *mattif hakazab*)—a sardonic interpolation of his moniker, Apphus ("Trickster"). It might also allude to Jonathan's unapologetic two-faced pragmatism in accepting Demetrius's offer of making him a general at the same time as planning a defection to Alexander Balas, whose own claim to the Seleucid throne many deemed fraudulent. Jonathan's assassinations and building program in Jerusalem also come in for targeted criticism:

> The interpretation of the passage [Hab 2:12–13] refers to the Spreader of Fraud [Jonathan Apphus], who led many astray to rebuild a town of nothingness with blood, and raise a society with falsehood for his own glory; to make many toil in service of nothingness, and to instruct them in deeds of falsehood; to have their toil come to nothing, so that they come to fiery judgments because they blasphemed and mistreated the elect of God [the Essenes]. (1QpHab 10:5–13)

3.6.6 JONATHAN APPHUS AND INTERNATIONAL AFFAIRS (152–142 BC)

Jonathan's rise to the high priesthood was largely the result of being in the right place at the right time and testament to how much Judea had become woven into the fabric of the Mediterranean world. The significance of Jonathan's high priesthood was then magnified by how turbulent the Mediterranean world was during his tenure, as some major political shifts occurred in the 140s BC. Indeed, the account of his high priesthood in 1 Maccabees 10:21–13:24 is taken up largely with international affairs.

Despite the commencement of the Seleucid civil war, there was no immediate showdown between Demetrius and Alexander Balas. Demetrius tried desperately to win the Jews back to his side with a raft of economic and political inducements, including tax exemptions, the remission of debts, the release of prisoners, and the annexation of three districts from Samaria. Demetrius even offered to relinquish control of the Acra and the *polis* "to the high priest," to fund the renovation of Jerusalem's temple and city walls, and to grant Ptolemais-Acco (Alexander Balas's capital) as a permanent endowment to the temple establishment. Demetrius put these inducements into a letter addressed to the wider Jewish nation rather than to Jonathan specifically (1 Macc 10:25–45).[24] But, of course, the price of these concessions was loyalty to Demetrius, with the demand that the Jews levy up to 30,000 men for Demetrius's army (1 Macc 10:36).[25] Jonathan rejected the offer, for the momentum now clearly lay with Alexander Balas, who had granted him the high priesthood (1 Macc 10:46–47).

Two years later (June 150 BC), Alexander Balas and Demetrius finally faced each other in battle near Antioch. Jonathan presumably lined up alongside Alexander Balas. To everyone's surprise, Demetrius won the day by using his war elephants. It was not, however, a comprehensive victory, and a few weeks later Alexander Balas decisively defeated Demetrius, this time with his own elephants. Demetrius fled on horseback but was soon picked off by his pursuers (1 Macc 10:48–50; *Ant.* 13.58–61; Appian, *S.W.* 67).[26] Alexander Balas, a teen of suspicious parentage, became the undisputed ruler of the Seleucid kingdom.

The outcome showed just how much the political climate had shifted in two decades. Jonathan Apphus, one of the five Hasmonean brothers who battled for years as outlaws against the regime of Antiochus IV Epiphanes, had now become the incumbent high priest, the head of a legally sanctioned Jewish army, and a friend of Antiochus's alleged young son, Alexander Balas. His rise had also entailed his step away from fundamentalist extremism towards milder

---

24. Some doubt the authenticity of the letter (see Sievers, *The Hasmoneans and Their Supporters*, 93), but the letter follows standard epistolary form and makes sense of the geopolitics in 152–150 BC. Of critical importance is Demetrius's reference to the high priest by the generic office title rather than by the name of its incumbent. This accords with the fact that Demetrius never appointed Jonathan to the office. While some details might have been touched up, the essence of the letter is historically sound.

25. It is questionable whether Jonathan could realistically recruit 30,000 men from Judea (cf. 1 Macc 1:74). It probably represents an upper threshold rather than a minimum levy, *pace* Israel Shatzman, *The Armies of the Hasmonaeans and Herod: From Hellenistic to Roman Frameworks*, Texte und Studien zum antiken Judentum 25 (Tübingen: Mohr Siebeck, 1991), 28–30, 34; Babota, *Hasmonean High Priesthood*, 148.

26. The time of the two battles is known from the Babylonian Astronomical Diaries (*AD* 3.149). The author of 1 Maccabees knew of only the second battle and its outcome.

conservatism, fostered in part by his dealings with the Hellenistic monarchs. He had reinvented the Maccabean cause. The extremist tide from the days of the Maccabean resistance was ebbing.[27]

Jonathan attended the marriage of Alexander Balas to Cleopatra Thea, the young daughter of Ptolemy VI, at Ptolemais-Acco (1 Macc 10:51–60; *Ant.* 13.80–82).[28] For a once-fundamentalist Jewish priest, this must have been an occasion of conflicting interest, as he had to tolerate the ostentatiously Greek religious and cultural elements. But he was now an international dignitary recognized by two imperial powers, whom he also had to acknowledge by his own presence and gifts.

Whilst there, a fresh challenge to his leadership was brought by Hellenizing Jews from Jerusalem.[29] But with Jonathan's relationship with Alexander Balas rock solid, the challenge was dismissed. Instead, Alexander Balas enlisted Jonathan among the chief "friends of the king," promoted him to general (Gk. *stratēgos*) and provincial governor (Gk. *meridarchēs* [1 Macc 10:61–66]), and granted him the right to wear purple. This latter distinction marked him out as a Hellenistic high priest,[30] an office similar to that held by Olympiodorus (see 2.8.8 above) and the Athenian elder who had enforced the royal cult (see 3.2.5 above). Ironically, then, the Hellenizers' challenge saw Jonathan transformed into a high priest in the classic Hellenistic order of the Seleucid kingdom.[31] It also aided the eventual political slide of the Hasmoneans towards a more progressive outlook.

Jonathan's promotion converted Judea into an autonomous province of the Seleucid kingdom. Religious, civic, and military powers in Judea were concentrated in his hands, bolstering the institutional infrastructures that would enable Judea to rule itself. The only things Alexander Balas did not put under Jonathan's control were the Acra and its adjoining *polis*. These Hellenistic bastions kept the heart of Judea fastened directly to the Seleucid kingdom[32] and ensured the Hellenistic Jews in Jerusalem were not completely marginalized.

---

27. If one may be permitted a modern analogy to Jonathan Apphus we may consider Yasser Arafat (1929–2004), whose political career took him from guerrilla extremist to recognized political head of the Palestinian people.

28. Ptolemy VI was only thirty-six years of age. Josephus refers to his daughter as a "child" (Gk. *paida* [*Ant.* 13.82]), no more than fourteen. Four years earlier, she had been promised in marriage to her uncle, Fatso Ptolemy VIII ("Physcon"), who governed Cyrenaica (Polybius, *Hist.* 39.7.6). That marriage never eventuated because her father found a more politically significant match for her in Alexander Balas.

29. See Babota, *Hasmonean High Priesthood*, 175.

30. See the comparable anecdote regarding Diogenes the Epicurean in Athenaeus, *Learned Banqueters* 5.211a–b.

31. Babota, *Hasmonean High Priesthood*, 154–59.

32. Since the death of Demetrius, the garrison in the Acra had no choice but to acknowledge Alexander Balas, but many of its soldiers probably nursed animosity towards Jonathan.

It was not long before Ptolemy VI adopted a patriarchal posture over Alexander Balas, his cousin-cum-son-in-law. He imposed Ptolemaic advisers on the Seleucid government (Livy, *Per.* 50.4) and had Seleucid coins minted, which copied Ptolemaic currency almost exactly.[33] The teenaged Alexander Balas was given little room to move within his own kingdom. This inevitably caused friction, heating up the age-old rivalry between the Seleucids and Ptolemies, especially over Coele Syria, where Jonathan was now ascendant.

Pressure also came from dead Demetrius's two surviving sons, Demetrius and Antiochus.[34] In 149 BC the elder of the two, Demetrius II, who was no more than eleven years of age, began to buy the support of Cretan mercenaries with a view to invading the Seleucid realm, just as Alexander Balas had done a few years before. Most Seleucid forces were kept in the Levant against a possible invasion, but this exposed the empire's eastern territories. In 148 BC, the Parthians, under the leadership of Mithridates I, attacked Media, which induced several other eastern provinces to secede from the Seleucids.[35] By 147 BC, Alexander Balas had lost all provinces east of Mesopotamia, along with the revenue they brought.

When Demetrius II's invasion came the following year, Jonathan proved his worth to Alexander Balas. The governor of Coele Syria, Apollonius Taus, defected to the young invader, but Jonathan and his brother Simon deployed their forces and defeated him. In the process, they captured the coastal towns of Joppa, Azotus (Ashdod), and Ashkelon, even burning down the temple to Dagon (and those sheltering inside it) at Azotus (1 Macc 10:74–86). As a reward, Alexander gifted the town of Ekron to Jonathan as a personal holding (1 Macc 10:87–89). In capturing these cities, Jonathan ostensibly acted in Alexander Balas's interests, but he also acted as a de facto sovereign. He was now in possession of the southern coastal plain as well as Judea. The mortar holding the region within the rapidly dwindling Seleucid edifice was starting to crumble.

Ptolemy VI saw this and swung into action. Alexander Balas was struggling to contain Demetrius II in Cilicia, so Ptolemy brought his army from Egypt, ostensibly to come to his aid. But as he worked his way along the

---

33. Hölbl, *A History of the Ptolemaic Empire*, 193; Grainger, *The Fall of the Seleukid Empire*, 66.

34. A third son, Antigonus, who had not been sent into safekeeping with the other two, was murdered along with his mother, Laodice V, by Ammonius, the chief advisor whom Ptolemy VI had imposed upon Alexander Balas's government (Livy, *Per.* 50.4).

35. Daniel T. Potts, *The Archaeology of Elam: Formation and Transformation of an Ancient Iranian State* (Cambridge: Cambridge University Press, 1999), 384–91; Grainger, *The Fall of the Seleukid Empire*, 68–70; Peter Thonemann, *The Hellenistic World: Using Coins as Sources* (Cambridge: Cambridge University Press, 2016), 93–95.

coastal plain, he installed Ptolemaic garrisons in the cities, including those secured by Jonathan (1 Macc 11:1–3). Although Ptolemy was always the power behind Alexander Balas, this unapologetic landgrab was a transparent vote of no-confidence in the young Seleucid king and a way of checking Jonathan's growing importance. It also revealed Ptolemy's motivation for initially backing Alexander Balas in the first place: the reassertion of Ptolemaic sovereignty over Coele Syria. It was effectively a seventh Syrian War.[36]

Rather than challenge Ptolemy, Jonathan showed his diplomatic side by meeting him at Joppa. First Maccabees implies that the two came to an agreement, which must have been Jonathan's recognition of Ptolemy's sovereignty over Coele Syria. It was a shrewd move since Jonathan could never overcome the might of the Ptolemaic empire on his own. He was not about to squander all his recent gains on one bad political decision. So, Jonathan threw in his lot with Ptolemy (1 Macc 11:4–7).

Ptolemy VI then continued north, alleging that, while he had been at Ptolemais-Acco, an attempt had been made on his life at the orders of Alexander Balas. Whether the allegation was true cannot be said, but it gave Ptolemy a pretext to openly oppose Alexander Balas. This he did by taking control of the entire coast up to Seleucia-Pieria. With Alexander Balas still in Cilicia, Antioch was open to Ptolemy, so he marched up the road and occupied the Seleucid capital.

At this point, Ptolemy took the Seleucid throne for himself (1 Macc 11:13; *Ant.* 13.113). There was substance to his claim, too, since he was a grandson of Antiochus III (via his mother), and there was no question over his parentage, unlike Alexander Balas. By taking the double diadem of Egypt and Asia, Ptolemy became potentate of the largest empire in the Mediterranean, achieving what his Ptolemaic and Seleucid forebears had failed to do: the recovery of the most prodigious portion of Alexander the Great's colossal empire.

It was to last but a moment. The merging of the two kingdoms attracted the immediate attention of Rome. Two decades earlier, the Roman Senate had prevented Antiochus IV from trying to merge the two kingdoms (see 3.2.4 above). Now that Ptolemy VI had succeeded in doing it, Rome was not about to sit idly by as a grand new empire rose in the eastern Mediterranean.

That particular year, 146 BC, was a watershed moment in the Mediterranean world, which definitively placed the political and economic pole in Rome itself. During the previous years, Rome had engaged in regional conflicts that

---

36. John D. Grainger, *The Syrian Wars*, Mnemosyne Supplements: History and Archaeology of Classical Antiquity 320 (Leiden: Brill, 2010), 350.

convinced its Senate to switch to a more aggressive foreign policy (cf. Diodorus Siculus, *Bib. hist.* 32.4). Thus, when Rome intervened yet again in Macedon (150–148 BC), it opted for a more definitive solution: it dissolved the Macedonian state and two years later (146 BC) converted it into a Roman province (Pausanias, *Descr.* 7.13.1). While this was going on, the city-states of the Greek mainland stubbornly refused to comply with Rome's demands for order, so the Romans skewered the rest of Greece, too. Corinth was savagely sacked and its people enslaved, and the Greek city-states of southern Greece were reorganized as the new Roman province of Achaea (Polybius, *Hist.* 39.12; Livy, *Per.* 51.7–52.6; Pausanias, *Descr.* 7.16–17).

At the same time, Rome was busy intervening in North Africa. Many Romans had feared the resurgence of Carthaginian nationalism. Senator Marcus Porcius Cato (the Censor) even famously took to ending every speech with the words, "Moreover, I consider that Carthage must be destroyed." Roman fears were stoked when Carthage took up arms to defend itself against harassment by the neighboring kingdom of Numidia (Diodorus Siculus, *Bib. hist.* 32.1–3). Rome issued the Carthaginians with a blatantly bellicose ultimatum: either they abandoned their historic city and emigrated inland, or else the Romans would forcibly move them and destroy their city. The Carthaginians rejected the outrageous demand and dug in to defend their homes. But they could not withstand the Roman military machine. Carthage was annihilated, its survivors enslaved, and its territory converted into the Roman province of Africa (Diodorus Siculus, *Bib. hist.* 32.1–14, 22–26; Appian, *Punic Wars* 74–135; Livy, *Per.* 51.1–6; cf. Polybius, *Hist.* 38.3). Both Corinth and Carthage would lie desolate for a century, twin testaments to the towering power of Rome, which had swallowed up multiple states in a handful of years.[37]

News of these developments reached Ptolemy VI just as he placed the Seleucid diadem on his brow in late 146 BC. It gave him pause. Rome was perfectly capable of waging successful campaigns on multiple fronts[38] and had already demonstrated it would not tolerate a unitary empire in the eastern Mediterranean. Ptolemy must also have seen how brittle Seleucid sovereignty had become and how much would be required just to keep it intact. It was simply not worth tempting fate over a prize that was already half-broken. As Josephus puts it, since Ptolemy VI was "intelligent enough to calculate the future, he decided not to appear as one giving the Romans cause for animosity"

---

37. Settlement at Carthage and Corinth would eventually be revived by Julius Caesar.
38. Rome had also at this time waged the protracted Lusitanian War and Second Celtiberian War in Spain, showing dexterity in fighting on many fronts at the same time. See Sinnigen and Boak, *A History of Rome*, 129.

(*Ant.* 13.114). Accordingly, Ptolemy abdicated the Seleucid throne barely months after taking it.

Instead, Ptolemy offered the crown to the young invader, Demetrius II, along with the hand of his daughter, Cleopatra Thea, in marriage (1 Macc 11:9–12; *Ant.* 13.109–110).[39] The move afforded him control of the boy without the liability of directly ruling the fragile Seleucid kingdom under the nose of the Romans. But part of the deal included the transfer of Coele Syria to the Ptolemaic kingdom (Diodorus Siculus, *Bib. hist.* 32.9c). Young Demetrius II accepted Ptolemy's surprise offer. All that was left to do was hunt down Alexander Balas. Spoiling for the fight, Alexander Balas drew Ptolemy and Demetrius into battle near the Oenoparus River outside Antioch (September 145 BC), but he was comprehensively defeated. After the battle, Alexander Balas found refuge with an Arab chieftain who perfidiously had him murdered and sent his head back to the victors in Antioch.[40] Ptolemy VI, however, had been thrown from his horse during the battle and knocked senseless. When Alexander Balas's severed head arrived in Antioch, Ptolemy regained consciousness enough to understand what had happened, but just days later he himself succumbed to his injuries (Polybius, *Hist.* 38.19; cf. Strabo, *Geography* 16.2.8). Ironically, then, both Ptolemy VI and Alexander Balas met their fate within days of each other. The fifteen-year-old Demetrius II Nicator ("Victor") thus swept to sovereignty of the Seleucid kingdom (1 Macc 11:9–19; *Ant.* 13.109–119), while the Ptolemaic kingdom was inherited by Ptolemy VI's younger siblings, Cleopatra II and Fatso Ptolemy VIII.

Ptolemaic forces retreated from the coastal plain, leaving Coele Syria an open wound between the Ptolemaic and Seleucid realms. This left Jonathan as the local strongman, and he now attempted to bandage the wound with a new Jewish state. Technically he was back under Seleucid authority, but he made the most of the new situation by attempting to remove the Seleucid garrison from Jerusalem's Acra (1 Macc 11:20). It was a bid for complete Jewish independence from the Seleucids.

Word of Jonathan's plans quickly reached Demetrius II in Antioch.

---

39. Both 1 Maccabees and Josephus present Ptolemy's offer to Demetrius II before presenting the fact that he had taken the Seleucid crown. This non-linear presentation unfortunately affects some scholarly reconstructions.

40. There are three versions of Alexander Balas's death. The first is a summary account, which associates his decapitation with the battle against Ptolemy VI (Livy, *Per.* 52.11). In the second, the Arab chieftain named Zabdiel severs Alexander Balas's head while giving him shelter (1 Macc 11:15–17; *Ant.* 13.117–118). In the third, the chieftain is named Diocles, and his protective efforts are undermined by two of Alexander Balas's officers, who murder him (Diodorus Siculus, *Bib. hist.* 32.9d–10.1). "Diocles" is a viable Greek version of the Semitic name, "Zabdiel," so the identity of the chieftain can be certified. It seems the first two accounts summarize elements of Diodorus's more detailed third version.

If Judea gained independence, the young king would lose control of all Coele Syria. Demetrius was intoxicated with his new power, and his sense of diplomacy had all the hallmarks of an entitled teenager who had grown up with mercenaries.[41] Not wishing to see his newly won toy break overnight, Demetrius demanded a parley with Jonathan at Ptolemais-Acco. Jonathan agreed, but in a move of passive defiance, he refused to halt the preparations for siege against the Acra (1 Macc 11:21–24).

The conference at Ptolemais-Acco convinced Jonathan that Judea could not achieve independence easily. But it also showed young Demetrius that he could not simply boss Jonathan around as if he were one of his Cretan mercenaries. Jonathan was a hardened fighter and the high priest of an increasingly significant nation. Thus, Jonathan was the overall winner from the negotiations. He intimidated the swaggering youth into a formal confirmation of his high priesthood, as well as tax and land concessions resembling the promises the lad's alcoholic father had made a few years earlier. This included the annexation of three Samarian districts: Aphairema (Ephraim), where the Gophna Hills were located; Rathamin (Arimathea) in the lowlands, near Modiin; and Lydda on the coastal plain (1 Macc 11:24–37; cf. 10:25–45).[42] But the Acra and the *polis* remained fixedly Seleucid.

Content with the retention of Judea, Demetrius II returned to Antioch. But the stripling king's problems were just beginning. He soon came to a stark realization: his new kingdom was running out of money. After a failed campaign to retake Elymais,[43] Demetrius was forced into a move that was both humiliating and audacious: he retrenched the Seleucid standing army and retained only his Cretan mercenaries (1 Macc 11:38). The subsequent loss of pay for thousands of soldiers caused civic unrest as they dispersed throughout the realm. Riots erupted in Antioch itself, compounded by Demetrius's heavy-handed response (Diodorus Siculus, *Bib. hist.* 33.4–5a). The whole situation was then exploited by a military official named Diodotus Tryphon, who took custody of Alexander Balas's surviving infant son, Antiochus VI, and rallied disgruntled veterans to the infant's banner in a challenge to Demetrius (1 Macc 11:38–40). The Seleucid kingdom was descending into anarchy.

The retrenchment meant that the Seleucid garrison in Jerusalem's Acra technically became defunct. But rather than abandon their post, the soldiers remained defiantly in place, even going on occasional rampages, which harassed

---

41. Diodorus attributes Demetrius's "tyrannical cruelty and various lawless excesses" to both his own nature and the influence of his mercenary commander, Lasthenes (Diodorus Siculus, *Bib. hist.* 33.4).
42. Notably, the port city of Joppa was not included in the territory annexed to Judea.
43. Potts, *The Archaeology of Elam*, 384; Grainger, *The Fall of the Seleukid Empire*, 78.

the local population. Jonathan seized the opportunity and urged Demetrius to enforce the removal of the garrison. It was as good as an ultimatum for Jewish independence. Cornered by his kingdom's apparent devolution, Demetrius agreed on the condition that Jonathan send troops to Antioch to help contain the anarchy enveloping the Seleucid capital. Seeing this as an efficient quid pro quo, Jonathan complied and helped bring Antioch back under control, much to the offence of the Antiochenes. But no sooner had Demetrius regained control of the city than he reneged on his promise to Jonathan. In a bid to recover a revenue stream, he instead revoked the tax exemptions he had granted Judea (*Ant.* 13.143). Fed up with the lad, Jonathan broke ranks with him completely and began working openly towards the creation of an independent Jewish state (1 Macc 11:41–53).

Soon after, Diodotus Tryphon successfully chased Demetrius from Antioch (*Ant.* 13.144; 1 Macc 11:54–56), and civil war erupted throughout Syria (Livy, *Per.* 52.13; Diodorus Siculus, *Bib. hist.* 33.9). From 144 BC, two sets of currency were minted throughout the putative empire, one bearing the imprint of Demetrius II Nicator and the other of Antiochus VI Epiphanes Dionysus.[44] The fragile empire was fractured, with different regions declaring for the different claimants or even for their own independence.

Tryphon courted Jonathan with confirmation of his high priesthood, issued in the name of baby Antiochus VI, along with further status symbols, including the promotion of his brother, Simon Thassi, to general of the coast from Tyre to the border of Egypt. Jonathan was now every bit as powerful as Tryphon, but he acquiesced to the alliance out of resentment towards Demetrius II. He then began a campaign of conquest, which saw him bring the southern coastal plain under his control, before venturing into Galilee (1 Macc 11:57–62). Galilee was still mainly populated by Phoenicians, Syrians, and Greeks, with only small pockets of Jewish settlers. But with a hard-fought victory against Demetrius's mercenaries, Jonathan captured a few Galilean sites, including the Tyrian administrative town at Kadesh. While he did this ostensibly in the name of baby Antiochus VI, it turned Galilee into a no-man's land in the civil war, sparking the abandonment of many settlements. This paved the way for the promotion of Jewish settlement throughout Galilee.[45]

---

44. Chrubasik, *Kings and Usurpers*, 136–38. The images on the coins of Antiochus VI usually portray the king as a youth rather than a baby, except for one issue from Antioch (Newell 249), which clearly shows a smooth, pudgy-faced child.

45. Uzi Leibner, "Galilee in the Second Century BCE: Material Culture and Ethnic Identity," in Berlin and Kosmin, *The Middle* Maccabees, 142–44; Danny Syon, "The Hasmonean Settlement in Galilee: A Numismatic Perspective," in Berlin and Kosmin, *The Middle Maccabees*, 188–92.

Jonathan returned to Jerusalem to lay the diplomatic groundwork for a new Jewish state. Taking a leaf from this brother's book, he sent a delegation to Rome to renew the treaty of friendship. But the Roman Senate only provided the Jewish ambassadors with letters of safe conduct back to Judea (1 Macc 12:1–4), which meant Jonathan did not get all he wanted. Judea was not central to Rome's purposes, especially with Seleucid power being dulled by civil war. The Senate could afford to be as polite with Jonathan as it had with Judas: affirming ties but refusing an actual alliance.

Rome's hands-off approach did not put a Jewish state on the map, but neither did it prevent Jonathan from attempting to do so himself. He ventured into central Lebanon and fended off further attempts by Demetrius to curtail his activities (1 Macc 12:24–34).[46] With the breathing space this gave him, he attempted to rid Judea of every last vestige of Seleucid rule, including the garrison in the Acra (1 Macc 12:35–37). He redoubled the efforts to fortify Jerusalem and the wider country (1 Macc 12:38), which included the first defensive station atop the desert promontory of Masada (*J.W.* 7.285). He also appealed for support from Jewish communities abroad (2 Macc 1:7), especially in Egypt, though what kind of support was forthcoming is unknown.

Jonathan's asphyxiation of the Acra and the *polis* in Jerusalem was working. Sentiment among conservative Jews in Jerusalem must have been running high, as independence from foreign rule was within their grasp. The last time Judea had ruled itself as an internationally recognized state had been when the Davidic dynasty ruled Judah five centuries before. To prevent the inevitable, Tryphon raced to Palestine, arriving at the end of autumn 143 BC. The choice he faced was whether to use force or diplomacy to prevent Jewish secession. He brought his trusty veterans with him, but Jonathan met him at Scythopolis in the Jezreel Valley with an enormous force—40,000 men according to 1 Maccabees 12:41. Although this is undoubtedly an exaggeration, it still reflects the fact that Jonathan's forces were augmented by a huge volunteer militia, eager not to let independence slip from their grasp.[47] Tryphon realized that military intervention against such a hoard was unfeasible and opted to negotiate.

Jonathan was in the ascendant position and was not going to settle for anything less than Jewish independence. Tryphon surprisingly conceded.

---

46. First Maccabees 12:25 places the confrontation in the region of Hamath, which was not the primary city of that name in central Syria (Great Hamath [modern Hama]), but either Lebo Hamath (modern Laboueh?) or Hamath Zobah (Baalbek?) in Lebanon. See Julius Lewy, "The Old West Semitic Sun-God Ḥammu," *HUCA* 18 (1944): 429–88.

47. Since Jonathan's men could be dismissed to their homes (1 Macc 12:45), many of them did not belong to a professional standing army.

He agreed to give Jonathan control of Ptolemais-Acco, the administrative capital of Coele Syria. "I will hand it over to you, along with the remaining fortresses, the remaining forces, and all who are currently in the administration, and then turn around and withdraw," he pledged (1 Macc 12:45). With those words, Tryphon effectively revoked Seleucid sovereignty over southern Coele Syria.

News of the landmark agreement must have been greeted with sheer elation by Jonathan's men. It had been twenty-five years since Jonathan and his brothers had begun the struggle against Seleucid domination. Now Jewish independence was to become a reality. Jonathan was now in his fifties—a timeworn warrior and senior priest, with at least two sons of his own. He had become the champion of the Jewish nation, and now, as its high priest and elder statesman, he was to lead it to freedom. He dismissed most of his men, allowing them to return to Judea with the good news of the freedom of the Jews. He stationed 2,000 soldiers at Scythopolis and took 1,000 soldiers as a personal bodyguard, who escorted him and Tryphon to Ptolemais-Acco (1 Macc 12:45). Here the city's gates were opened to him, and Jonathan walked in as the lord elect.

Once inside the city, the gates were shut behind him. Jonathan was seized, and a mob surrounded his men. Tryphon had betrayed him. With cold malice, the Seleucid general ordered the execution of them all (1 Macc 12:48) and then dispatched his veterans to finish off Jonathan's troops at Scythopolis. But word of the treachery had already reached them, and outrage steeled them for the fight. The clear signs of resistance prompted Tryphon's men to back off, allowing the Jewish troops to hasten back to Judea. Thus, news throughout the region of the freedom of Judea was quickly followed by news of Tryphon's treachery (1 Macc 12:49–52).

In Jerusalem, an incensed Jewish Senate hailed Jonathan's brother, "Clever" Simon Thassi, as high priest and military leader (1 Macc 13:1–9).[48] He took a contingent of angry solders to the fortified town of Adida, near Joppa, to confront Tryphon as he headed south. When the Seleucid general saw the size and willingness of Simon's forces, he sent a delegation to negotiate (1 Macc 13:11–14).

To everyone's surprise, the delegation revealed that Jonathan was still alive. Tryphon was willing to release him on condition that Judea pay him (and toddler Antiochus VI) 100 silver talents in back taxes and submit two of Jonathan's sons as hostages to guarantee his docility (1 Macc 13:15–16). It was

---

48. Jonathan's eldest son, whose name we do not know, must have been too young to assume his father's mantle.

an ingenious ultimatum, for Jonathan's survival meant that Simon could not legally function as high priest and pitted Simon's relationship with his brother against the affairs of the state. If Simon refused Tryphon's terms, he would be signing his brother's death warrant. If he agreed, he would be robbing the temple treasury of the donations of the faithful to pay for Jonathan's release and selling out Jewish independence. He opted to pay Tryphon and hand over two of Jonathan's sons. But as the money and the boys were transferred, Tryphon reneged and failed to release Jonathan (1 Macc 13:17–19). Instead, he punched through Simon's defenses and thrust into the Judean highlands from Idumea. Simon scrambled to defend the country. If he failed, the entire bid for Jewish independence was done for (1 Macc 13:20).

It was by now late winter in 142 BC, and those trapped in the Acra and the *polis* were starving to death. If they succumbed, Jewish soldiers would gain control of the fortress and its citadel and perhaps be able to withstand Tryphon's onslaught. Tryphon needed a quick victory to prevent this and to free himself up to deal with Demetrius II elsewhere. He received messages from the beleaguered garrison urging him to approach Jerusalem from the east, via the Judean Desert. Tryphon stole a dash through the desert with his cavalry during the night, but an atypical snowstorm lashed the area and prevented his horses from making the ascent to Jerusalem. Finding himself freezing in a desolate location and cut off from supplies, Tryphon was forced to abandon his attempt to rescue the Acra. He fell back across the Jordan with Jonathan and sons in tow and decided to continue his campaign against Demetrius in Syria. Jonathan was now of no further use to him. And so, he murdered Jonathan and his two sons, disposing of their bodies in a town called Baskama in Gilead (1 Macc 13:21–23).

It is claimed that Simon retrieved his brother's remains and reinterred them in the family tomb at Modiin, but the claim is unverifiable. In any case, he erected seven elaborate funerary monuments at Modiin in honor of his parents, his four dead brothers, and himself. Each monument consisted of a pyramid atop a pillared structure (1 Macc 13:25–30). Though these monuments are no longer extant, the exact design can still be seen today in the so-called Tomb of Zechariah in Jerusalem's Kidron Valley—a funerary structure in memory of the priestly Hezir clan, built just a few years after Simon's funerary monuments.

Jonathan Apphus had continued the legacy of his brother, Judas Maccabeus, in the struggle to preserve conservative Judaism. The only way this could be achieved was with the loosening of Seleucid shackles, for the Seleucids empowered the liberal Jewish factions. Although conservative Judaism was itself soaked in Hellenism, it still advocated the distinctiveness of Jewish culture, whereas Hellenizing Jews were content to adopt the more cosmopolitan values of their Greek neighbors. Judas had led the struggle against this as a fundamentalist extremist—a polarizing outlaw. Though Jonathan was initially every bit as hardline as Judas, his impact comes from his attempt to gain independence as a recognized statesman. He brought the Maccabean resistance back from the brink of extinction in 160 BC and used the political instability around the Seleucid throne to great advantage. He converted the Maccabean resistance from extremist militia on the fringe of Jewish society to mainline conservative movement with a unifying appeal. This operational softening also saw him become the undisputed high priest in 152 BC, which he augmented with his political and military acumen to lead the Jewish nation to the edge of freedom.

Under Jonathan, the high priesthood also became an established Hellenistic office. He occupied the high priesthood on Seleucid terms but did so as a conservative. The cultural and political currents during his leadership enabled him to strike a balance between Jewish and Hellenistic expectations to such an extent that, thereafter, the Hellenistic trappings of the Jewish high priesthood were deemed mandatory even by conservatives. It demonstrated that the Maccabean struggle had not simply been about opposition to Hellenism. Rather, it had been a battle between conservative and liberal brands of Judaism for control over how (not if) Hellenism influenced Judaism. By eschewing fundamentalism and terror, Jonathan redirected Seleucid support towards the conservative agenda. Ironically, though, this also began the Hasmonean creep towards the liberal end of the spectrum. Jonathan the Trickster brought the Jewish nation to the threshold of independence, but he did not live to carry it across, being outsmarted by Tryphon's trickery. He had lived much of his life by the sword, and the sword ignominiously caught up with him.

3.7 JEWISH INDEPENDENCE

3.7.1 THE CLIENT STATE OF JUDEA

Simon, the last surviving Hasmonean brother, assumed the mantle of high priest and revolutionary statesman after Jonathan's death. He reached out to Tryphon's rival, young Demetrius II, in search of an accord that might mutually benefit them. Demetrius II responded favorably:

> King Demetrius,
> To Simon, high priest and friend of the king, and to the elders and nation of the Jews,
> Greetings.
> The crown of gold and the palm branch that you sent, we have received. We are ready to make a general peace with you, and to write to those in the administration to permit you exemption of taxes. All that we put in place for you still stands. Let the fortresses you have constructed belong to you. We pardon any errors and mistakes committed to the present day. The crown tax, and anything else levied in Jerusalem, is no longer to be levied. And if any suitable persons among you desire to be registered among our staff, let them be registered, and let there be peace between us. (1 Macc 13:36–40)

With this letter, Demetrius gave his imprimatur for Judea to become a self-governing client state. Jewish independence thus became a reality in May 142 BC. The moment was marked by the author of 1 Maccabees as follows:

> In the one hundred and seventieth year [of the Seleucid era], the yoke of the gentiles came off Israel, and the people began to write in their documents and contracts, "First year of Simon, Great High Priest, Generalissimo and Leader of the Jews." (1 Macc 13:41–42)

The titles attributed to Simon are critical for understanding both Judea's status and the theological significance of this moment. Simon was acknowledged as a religious, military, and civic leader, but he was not accorded the title "king" (Greek: *basileus*). Instead, the adjective "great" (Gk. *megalos*) was appended to the title "high priest" (Gk. *archiereus*), indicating that Simon ruled the Jewish state as high priest. This made the Jewish state a hierocracy rather than a kingdom.

Theologically, this posed a dilemma for Jews who remained committed to the idea that Israel was rightly ruled by a Davidic king. These included members of the Davidic family itself, many Pharisees, scribes, officials, and entrepreneurs. For them, rule by a high priest was an acceptable interim measure, as it had been when the high priest Joshua led the Jerusalem community during the absence of Zerubbabel (see 1.1.2 above). But even this was to last only until the return of the Davidic "Sprig," Zerubbabel (Zech 3:8; 4:8–10). They could accept Simon's leadership as a first step towards restoration but could not accept Hasmonean rule as a permanent norm. For them, the prophetic promises meant the Jewish nation could only be fully restored as a Davidic kingdom stretching from Lebo-Hamath to the border of Egypt (1 Kgs 8:65; 2 Chr 7:8; cf. Gen 15:18). And this implied the subjugation of the nations, not just their approval.

On the other hand, there were those who, like Ben Sira half a century earlier, saw the Davidic monarchy as a cherished fossil that posed no theological obstacle to the nation's evolution into a hierocracy. Indeed, the Torah stipulated that Israel was "a kingdom of priests and a holy nation" (Exod 19:6). This, they argued, made hierocracy of a higher order than monarchy, so that Simon's leadership was viewed as a return to the ideal that Israel experienced under Moses and Aaron. Since the Zadokite crisis, the Sadducees deemed it necessary to support a new priestly line, and the Hasmoneans, as Aaronide priests, met the requisite standards of Torah. Furthermore, Judea's *amicitia* with Rome mandated that the Jews be led by a high priest, not a king (Diodorus Siculus, *Bib. hist.* 40.2.1).

A Jewish edict from 140 BC testifies to this theological friction. The edict provides a prolix justification of Simon's leadership of the Jewish state, a full two years after it had begun, and concludes with the following stipulations:

> The Jews and the priests consented to Simon being their ruler and high priest in perpetuity (until a reliable prophet should arise) and being Generalissimo over them; as matters pertaining to the holy precincts concern him, for him to make appointments over their operations, over the country, over the military, and over the fortresses; and as matters pertaining to the holy precincts concern him, that he should be obeyed by all, and that all documents within the country should be written with reference to his name; and that he will

be clad in purple and wear gold. It is illegal for anyone among the laity or the priests to reject any of these conditions, or speak against what he has declared, or to gather an assembly within the country without him, or to be clad in purple or wear a golden buckle. Whoever acts against these conditions, or rejects any of them, will be liable. (1 Macc 14:41–45)

The edict, which was inscribed on bronze tablets and displayed at the temple (1 Macc 14:27, 48), gave Simon total authority over the Jewish nation.[1] But the legal clauses, especially their exclusions, hint that the two years following Jewish independence had seen considerable debate over the nature of Simon's powers.[2] Some, such as the Sadducees, were committed to Simon as head of state in perpetuity. Others, like certain Pharisees, scribes, and other Davidic loyalists, argued that Simon's prerogatives ultimately belonged to a king and, so, ongoing prophetic revelation would at some point necessitate the end of his leadership and a new mode of government. The only other scripturally warranted mode was Davidic kingship—something that was to be expected, since God had made a covenant "in perpetuity" with the Davidic dynasty (2 Sam 7:13). And yet, the total power of appointment and right to sport purple and gold were given to Simon alone, to the exclusion of any other possible arrangement. The wording of the edict, therefore, attests to political and theological friction, even alluding to the threat of breakaway assemblies in Judea. These threats were clearly credible enough to warrant both specific condemnation and concession in the edict—something that smacks of political compromise. Simon's detractors were prepared to support him only "until a reliable prophet should arise" (cf. 1 Macc 14:41). It was enough to preserve national unity under the high priest, but it fueled theological differences.[3]

The concession demonstrated that a critical mass of Jews believed that the prophetic voice had not fallen silent. It enshrined the notion that ongoing divine revelation and eschatology could still shape the nature of Jewish identity and its leadership; that the blessed, who were able to stand in the assembly of the righteous, were not just those who meditated on Torah (Ps 1) but who also found refuge in Yahweh's Davidic king. In fact, the rulers and judges of the whole earth were directed to serve him, lest they incur wrath (Ps 2). The pairing

---

1. Babota (*Hasmonean High Priesthood*, 256–58) argues that the edict did not make Simon's high priesthood hereditary. However, the Greek phrase *eis ton aiōna* ("in perpetuity") implies a hereditary priesthood, as indeed the high priesthood traditionally was. Furthermore, the author of 1 Maccabees prefaces the edict with a reference to the people seeking to thank "Simon and his sons" (1 Macc 14:25).
2. Babota, *Hasmonean High Priesthood*, 260.
3. See Sievers, *The Hasmoneans and Their Supporters*, 119–27.

of the first two psalms as a double-barreled introduction to the canonical Psalter may or may not have occurred in response to this moment of history, but at the very least it captured the sentiment of Davidic loyalists about what made for legitimate leadership in Israel. While Simon based his leadership on Moses's priestly role, Davidic loyalists emphasized Moses's prophetic role. They took the Deuteronomic hope that a *prophet* of the stature of Moses would one day arise in Israel to lead the nation (Deut 18:15; 34:10–12) and wedded this to the expectation of a restored Davidic kingdom. It was this expectation that led some in the first century to wonder whether John the Baptist or Jesus were "the prophet who is to come into the world" (John 6:14; cf. 1:21, 25; 7:40)—that is, the "reliable prophet" with the divine authority to reconfigure the governance of the nation and restore it to its Davidic fullness (cf. 1 Macc 14:41).

But for those committed to Hasmonean leadership "in perpetuity," like the Sadducees, the edict of 140 BC demonstrated a theological commitment against ongoing prophecy, for they would never have allowed a sunset clause on Simon's leadership if they honestly believed it could be triggered. By inserting the word "reliable" (Gk. *piston*) into the credentials of any so-called prophet, the composers of the edict took a sly jab at those who believed such a prophet might arise. This did not come, as is sometimes surmised, from a rejection of the Prophets as the second canonical collection of the Jewish Scriptures. Rather, it came from the premise that the age of prophecy, as with the age of Davidic monarchy, had ceased, which for them made the insertion of the prophet clause into the edict an innocuous, and therefore tolerable, concession.

The edict was, therefore, a victory for Simon's supporters, who came to see prophecy as a phenomenon of the past. It excluded from power those who held the prophetic traditions on equal footing with the Torah, who believed in ongoing prophecy, and deemed national restoration to be incomplete. It left them aiming to affect public policy and theological expectations from the sidelines, as their unrealized eschatology looked towards future change.

Thus, Judea effectively became a kingdom of priests. For Simon and his supporters, Zion theology was about the temple alone and no longer carried any Davidic connotation (cf. 2 Sam 5:7). The temple and its priesthood had inherited all royal prerogatives, and Simon was its human face. The priestly expropriation of royal messianic theology meant that God had installed his priest, not his Davidic son, on Zion, his holy hill (cf. Ps 2:6). It was a realized eschatology that required no further theological development. This was the logical endpoint of Maccabean belief: God ruled through his chosen priest rather than a king, and the people could only come to God through Simon the high priest. He became the means of national unity and divine favor.

3.7.2 SIMON THASSI AS HIGH PRIEST (142-134 BC)

Judea's new status imbued Simon with the dignity of a head of state and altered the political landscape. One of Simon's first orders of business was to reach out anew to Rome, to convert the existing *entente cordiale* into a more formal recognition of the Jewish state. The delegation arrived in Rome late in 142 BC, bearing a golden shield weighing a thousand minas as a gift.[4] The Roman Senate voted to recognize the Jewish state formally—a decision that was broadcast to other regional heads of state (1 Macc 14:16-24; 15:15-24). With Roman recognition, Judea definitively crossed a political threshold and could only be made to cross back through conquest.

As Simon presided over Passover festivities at the temple in April 141 BC, just yards away in the Acra and *polis*, Seleucid soldiers and Greek civilians were starving to death from the Jewish blockade. Just weeks later, they capitulated. On 2 June 141 BC, Simon triumphantly took possession of the Acra amidst joyous Jewish celebration.[5] The Acra and *polis* had finally fallen and with it the last vestige of Seleucid domination in Jerusalem. The gaunt garrison and residents were evicted and became refugees. As a symbolic gesture of the overthrow, Simon ordered the height of the Acra to be reduced, thus mitigating the structure's physical dominance, especially in comparison to the temple (*J.W.* 5.139).[6] The city of David was ritually cleansed, and Jerusalem once more became a unified city. Jews were brought in to repopulate the city of David, and Jewish soldiers occupied the Acra (1 Macc 14:7, 36, 49-52).

That same year, the Parthians under Mithridates I invaded and conquered Babylonia, with the aim of recreating the old Persian Empire.[7] The conquest amputated one of the Seleucids' richest provinces from the kingdom, crippling the war-torn realm even further. In a bid to recover the prosperous province, Demetrius II, now finally out of his teens, mobilized his mercenaries but a year later found himself in chains, a prisoner of Mithridates. The eastern provinces were definitively lost, and Demetrius was exiled to Hyrcania where he lived a life of relative comfort (Justin, *Epit.* 36.1.1-5).

Tryphon's own efforts took a sudden turn when the toddler king,

---

4. In modern terms, the shield, weighing half a ton, would be worth approximately US$18 million.

5. The date given is 23 Iyyar in year 171 of the Seleucid era. Babota (*Hasmonean High Priesthood*, 247) calculates this as 4 June (not 2 June) 141 BC.

6. Elsewhere, Josephus claims that Simon demolished the Acra (*Ant.* 12.252, 362; *J.W.* 1.50), but this is historically inaccurate. Archaeology has shown that the Acra persisted until the end of the second century BC (see 3.7.6).

7. See Józef Wolski, *The Seleucids: The Decline and Fall of Their Empire*, trans. Bruce D. MacQueen (Kraków: Nakładem/Polskiej Akademii Umiejętności, 1999), 104-8.

Antiochus VI, died in 140 BC (1 Macc 13:31; Diodorus Siculus, *Bib. hist.* 33.28; Appian, *S.W.* 68). Even if Tryphon orchestrated the boy's demise, as some sources claim (cf. Livy, *Per.* 55.11; Josephus, *Ant.* 13.218), it left him without a royal aegis under which to fight.[8] So Tryphon himself now assumed the Seleucid crown and began minting coins bearing the insignia, "King Tryphon Autocrat."[9] With Demetrius II in exile, Tryphon became the new Seleucid king.

Almost instantly, though, a new claimant to the Seleucid throne arose in the person of Antiochus VII, the younger brother of Demetrius II. After their father had whisked them out of Syria, Antiochus VII had been raised in the Pamphylian port of Side, from where he gained his nickname, "Sidetes." When the Parthians captured Demetrius II and Tryphon became undisputed ruler, Demetrius's queen, Cleopatra Thea (daughter of Ptolemy VI), urged eighteen-year-old Antiochus to intervene. When he landed at Seleucia-Pieria in 139 BC, he promptly married her (despite Demetrius still being alive, albeit in exile),[10] and portions of the kingdom began to declare in his favor (*Ant.* 13.221–222), reigniting civil war.

Antiochus VII Sidetes initiated a diplomatic relationship with Simon, which upheld the freedom of Jerusalem and the temple (1 Macc 15:1–9). Simon used this support to expand the frontiers of the Jewish state—the first step in acquiring all the covenant territory of Israel. He captured Gazara (Gezer) and nearby Joppa on the coastal plain and settled Jewish people in them (1 Macc 13:43–48; 14:5). With these acquisitions, the Jewish state acquired a Mediterranean port and a valuable customs post along the *Via Maris*, allowing for greater economic development and the enriching of Simon's coffers.

Simon was now in his late sixties, with four sons of his own: Judas, John, Mattathias, and another son whose name is unknown (cf. *Ant.* 13.247). Though the sources do not specify it, Judas was almost certainly given a position in the temple administration, since he would eventually succeed to the high priesthood. John was granted military command at Gazara (1 Macc 16:1–3). Simon also had at least one daughter who was married to Ptolemy Abubus, the governor of Jericho and the Jordan Valley.

---

8. The issue probably comes down to timing. If Antiochus VI's death occurred before Demetrius's capture, then it was quite possibly an accidental death during surgery. But suspicion escalates if the boy died after Demetrius's capture, as only the boy himself would have stood between the conniving Tryphon and the throne.

9. The last coins issued in the name of Antiochus VI come from 141 BC. See Chrubasik, *Kings and Usurpers*, 154–61.

10. The following year, Demetrius II married Rhodogune, the daughter of his captor, Mithridates I, while still in exile in Hyrcania.

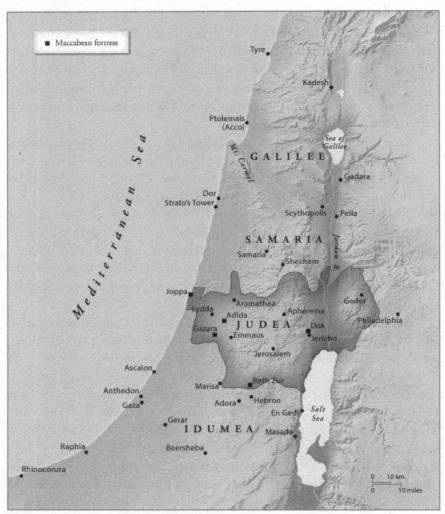

The State of Judea under Simon Thassi (142–134 BC).

Despite its cordial start, Simon's relationship with Sidetes soured after Sidetes gained the upper hand over Tryphon. Sidetes argued that Joppa, Gazara, and the *polis* in Jerusalem were Seleucid cities and threatened war if Simon did not relinquish them and pay 500 silver talents in compensation and a further 500 silver talents in back taxes. For Simon, Jerusalem was not up for negotiation. Instead, he offered Sidetes 100 talents of silver for recognition of Jewish sovereignty over Joppa and Gazara. But Sidetes rebuffed him and sent a general, Cendebeus, to harry the Jewish population. Simon put an army at the disposal of his son, John, who used imaginative tactics to rout Cendebeus's troops (1 Macc 15:25–16: 10). It was a momentous victory, for not only did it give Simon continued control over Gazara and Joppa, it also meant a decisive break with the Seleucid kingdom. From now on, Judea would not be a Seleucid client but would chart its own political course.

Yet Judea once again became vulnerable to attack after Sidetes won the Seleucid civil war against Tryphon in 136 BC (Strabo, *Geography* 14.5.2; Appian, *S.W.* 68; *Ant.* 13.224). Sidetes could at any time attempt to retake Joppa, Gazara, and the Acra in Jerusalem. To deal with the threat, Simon kept John at Gazara, and through most of 135 BC attempted to secure Judea's food supplies ahead of a Sabbatical Year beginning in September. When the Sabbatical Year began, Simon toured the country with his wife and two of his sons, Judas and Mattathias. Since Simon was in his seventies by this time and Judas had just attained the age of thirty, the tour provided a way of raising Judas's profile as the heir apparent to the high priesthood.

In February 134 BC, Simon and his family arrived at the fortress of Dok, outside Jericho, where they were welcomed by the local governor, his son-in-law, Ptolemy Abubus. But as they wined and dined, Ptolemy set his henchmen on them. Simon was murdered at the table, while his wife and two sons were taken hostage. Ptolemy then sent soldiers to assassinate John at Gazara and to persuade the soldiers there to join his *coup d'état*. He also dispatched men to take control of Jerusalem and do away with Simon's youngest (anonymous) son. Ptolemy is said to have sent a report of developments to Sidetes (1 Macc 16:11–20; *Ant.* 13.228), which means he had either been bought off by Sidetes or wanted to gain the high priesthood for himself and make Judea a Seleucid client again. Either way, Ptolemy Abubus brought down the last of the five Hasmonean brothers who had led the Maccabean resistance. Like Jonathan, Simon fell afoul of treachery. His time as Jewish leader had seen the momentous attainment of Judea's independence, and he had steered the ship of state into clearer waters by holding his nerve against Tryphon and Sidetes. However, his murder rained a storm of political instability down on Judea and threatened to drive the nation back towards the reefs of Seleucid rule.

3.7.3 JOHN HYRCANUS I AND THE SIEGE OF JERUSALEM (134/3 BC)

Simon's body was still warm when word reached his second son, John, at Gazara, about what had happened at Dok. It is likely that John and the rest of the country were mistakenly told that his mother and brothers had also been murdered, for his subsequent actions are predicated on that understanding.¹¹ John killed his would-be assassins (1 Macc 16:19–22) and then raced to Jerusalem before his brother-in-law could reach it.¹² While Ptolemy Abubus attempted to gain entry, John went about securing the high priesthood for himself. As Simon's second son, he was never meant to inherit the sacral office—that right should have fallen to his brother, Judas. But John was working on the assumption that Judas had perished, such that he needed to act with haste to prevent Ptolemy from capturing the Jewish state and handing it over to Antiochus VII Sidetes.

But taking the high priesthood was not a straightforward venture. Josephus refers to John as a "youth" (Gk. *neaniskos*) at this point (*J.W.* 1.55; *Ant.* 13.229), which means John was under the minimum thirty years of age for the office. In later years, questions over the legitimacy of John's high priesthood would surface (see 3.7.6 below). In any case, the conflict between John and Ptolemy Abubus dragged out for some months, and during this time John must have become aware that his mother and two brothers had not been murdered. Indeed, it was to Ptolemy's advantage to keep them alive and throw the priestly succession into confusion as Passover approached.

Nevertheless, John did secure the high priesthood (*Ant.* 13.230). He probably argued that his brother had never held the office, and was prevented from taking it up when the nation urgently needed a head of state to deal with the crisis threatening the nation's independence. The nation also needed a high priest to officiate at the upcoming holy days. Some might have argued for a separation of powers at this point (a suggestion that surfaced later), but John got his way and by Passover 134 BC he was declared high priest. Being under thirty, he set a precedent for future generations, so that henceforth the high priest did not have to be at least thirty years of age.

John attempted the rescue of his mother and brothers, but Ptolemy Abubus began torturing them on the battlements of Dok, before his very eyes. John could not bring himself to continue besieging Dok, so a stalemate developed. It dragged on until September when Antiochus VII Sidetes invaded Judea. John was forced to lift the siege and attend to the invasion, which gave Ptolemy a chance to escape across the Jordan and find refuge with the ruler of Philadelphia, Zeno Cotylas.¹³ Here he presumably hoped to sit out the

---

11. This is probably why 1 Macc 16:16 telescopes the deaths of Simon, Judas, and Mattathias.

12. First Maccabees finishes with John killing his would-be assassins and a summary reference to the remainder of his high priesthood (1 Macc 16:23–24). Hereafter, we are reliant on Josephus, the Dead Sea Scrolls, and numismatics for information about John.

13. Josephus calls Zeno the "tyrant" of Philadelphia, which might suggest that the city had a measure of independence. We do not know if Zeno was in any way connected to the Tobiads who, for generations, had ruled Philadelphia, up until at least the time of Hyrcanus (198 BC).

war in Judea and, after a Seleucid victory, return to be confirmed in the high priesthood by Sidetes.[14] Before he skipped Judea, though, he had John's mother and two brothers murdered (*Ant.* 13.230–236).

John had to lay aside the psychological impact of his family's murder and throw himself into the defense of the country he now headed. Sidetes had timed his invasion to take full advantage of Judea's low food supplies at the end of the Sabbatical Year (autumn 134 BC). He pillaged the Judean countryside, burning villages, supplies, and wild crops. By the winter, he had brought the country to its knees. He also knew that the Romans would not intervene, for they were facing their own threat of famine after a slave revolt (the First Servile War) broke out in Sicily, the breadbasket of Italy (Diodorus Siculus, *Bib. hist.* 34/35.2).[15] By early 133 BC Sidetes had pinned John and the Jewish army in Jerusalem. He built a siege wall north of the temple to prevent all movement in and out of the city (*Ant.* 13.237).[16] With null agricultural activity, the celebration of Shavuot (Weeks/Pentecost), the harvest festival, in May 133 BC must have been a most somber affair.

John faced a military and moral dilemma. Jerusalem was packed with people who had fled the decimation of the countryside for the safety of city walls. But with more mouths to feed, the city's supplies dwindled quickly. With famine taking hold, John decided to make supplies last longer by expelling all who were unable to participate in the defense of the city (*Ant.* 13.237–241).[17] We should not imagine that he reached this decision lightly. The personal and national trauma must have weighed on him heavily. His reticence to continue bombarding Dok when Ptolemy Abubus was torturing his family tells us that there was some tender nerve in him. But the masses were his compatriots, not his flesh and blood, and expediency overruled his compassion. His decision would have done nothing to endear him to the masses, many of whom were probably turning against him and calling for new leadership. But, short of assassination, there was little anyone could do to change the circumstances, especially as John was the most capable military leader in Judea. The choice was stark. They could liquidate John, capitulate to Antiochus VII Sidetes,

---

14. Grainger (*The Wars of the Maccabees*, 74) argues that Ptolemy Abubus's departure implies the surrender of his ambitions, but this is not necessarily so. Jason had found similar refuge when Menelaus ousted him from the high priesthood and returned from Transjordan to Jerusalem in an attempt to regain the office (see 3.2.3).

15. Sinnigen and Boak, *A History of Rome*, 129, 150–51.

16. The rest of the city's perimeter was marked by steep valleys, which Sidetes easily contained with seven troop detachments.

17. This tactic was also infamously employed by Vercingetorix during Caesar's siege of Alesia in 52 BC.

be subsumed back into the Seleucid realm, and perhaps accept Ptolemy Abubus as the subordinate Jewish leader, or else they could persist with a beleaguered John in the faint hope that a miracle might bring salvation.

Alas, no miracle occurred. The wretches whom John expelled spent the next months trapped between the city and the siege wall of Antiochus Sidetes. In this no-mans-land many starved to death, while others turned to skin and bone. Their plight demoralized their compatriots, until eventually they defied John and opened the gates to take them back in (*Ant.* 13.241). This occurred during the few days between the Day of Atonement and the Festival of Sukkot (mid-October 133 BC), when the city itself had almost run out of food. Opposition to John's leadership thus increased as morale plummeted.[18]

To boost spirits and save his flagging reputation, John petitioned Sidetes for a seven-day truce to celebrate Sukkot. With victory a foregone conclusion, Sidetes not only agreed to the request but also supplied the sacrificial bulls, along with aromatic spices. His gesture was designed to appeal to the hungry populace and allay their fears that he was anything like Antiochus IV Epiphanes, their nemesis of a previous generation, who had bluntly imposed the sacrifice of swine on Jerusalem's altar. It softened views of him by demonstrating his leniency, goodwill, and sensitivity to Jewish piety, in stark contrast to John, who had callously expelled the vulnerable just months earlier. Sidetes thus came across as a better patron of Judaism than the high priest himself. As a result, the people began referring to Sidetes as *Eusebēs*—Antiochus "the Pious," or in Hebrew, Antiochus the *Hasid* (*Ant.* 13.242–244)—a sidelong censure of John.[19]

The Seleucid king's piety took the wind out of the sails of Jewish independence. Continued resistance now seemed futile. Throughout Sukkot, pressure mounted on John to spare the nation further suffering by capitulating to Sidetes. John gave in and entered negotiations with the king. In return for reintegration into the Seleucid kingdom, John demanded that he be recognized as high priest and that Judea retain control over Gazara and Joppa. Sidetes insisted that John lease the cities from the Seleucid crown and that a Seleucid garrison be once more stationed in the Acra. John agreed to lease the cities but refused a Seleucid garrison in Jerusalem. Instead, he proposed the payment of 500 talents of silver and the offering of hostages as a guarantee of Jewish loyalty. Sidetes accepted, provided there was an immediate down payment of

---

18. Cf. Sievers, *The Hasmoneans and Their Supporters*, 139.

19. Grainger (*The Wars of the Maccabees*, 74–75) argues that the truce and gesture of Sidetes are pure fabrication. However, they make sense of the subsequent situation and why Sidetes, ostensibly an enemy, was remembered by the Jews with such a favorable epithet. Note that this epithet of Antiochus VII Sidetes should not lead to him being confused with the later "Pious" Antiochus X (Gk. *Eusebēs*).

300 talents and the walls of Jerusalem were demolished (*Ant.* 13.245–248; Diodorus Siculus, *Bib. hist.* 34.1; Justin, *Epit.* 36.1).

To pay Sidetes, John emptied the temple coffers, but this yielded insufficient funds. To make up the shortfall, he is said to have opened the tomb of King David and taken 3,000 talents of silver from one of its chambers (*Ant.* 7.393; 13.249). Since grave robbery was frowned upon by all cultures, such an action could not have been fabricated to achieve a popular political end.

But the incident is not as straightforward as reported by Josephus. In the time of Nehemiah (Neh 3:16), David's tomb was located in the city of David— that is, in the fortress of Zion (1 Kgs 2:10; cf. 2 Sam 5:7). By the first century BC, the tomb's location had been transferred to the Western Hill (cf. Acts 2:29), which is probably what facilitated its renaming to "Mount Zion." We can only speculate on the date and nature of this transfer, but a time shortly before John's surrender to Sidetes makes the most plausible scenario. The Acra and its *polis* were built just south of the temple and may have been erected over the original tombs, as their association with the "city of David" shows (1 Macc 1:33; 2:31; 7:32; 14:36; cf. Ezek 43:7–9; Song 4:4).[20] The capture of the Acra in 141 BC and the construction of a glacis shortly afterwards might have prompted the relocation of the Davidic tombs to the Western Hill. Such an event would have portrayed the Hasmoneans as the patrons of Israel's great past, the heirs of its royal prerogatives, and the keepers of Zion theology. It might also have been marked by the erection of external monuments (cf. Herod's later monument [see 4.5.5 below]) and treasures for the burial chamber. Such tokens would have been particularly meaningful to those who still valued the Davidic promises and believed in eschatological resurrection.

In support of such a scenario, we may proffer the fact that Simon erected funerary monuments for his own family at Modiin. Additionally, there is the funerary plaque dated to the first century BC or AD, which once marked the location where the bones of King Uzziah were reinterred:

Here were brought the bones of Uzziah, king of Judah. Not to be opened.[21]

---

20. Excavations have confirmed that at least part of the Acra was built along the same lines as earlier buildings dating to Iron Age IIC. See Yiftah Shalev et al., "Jerusalem in the Early Hellenistic Period: New Evidence for Its Nature and Location," in Berlin and Kosmin, *The Middle Maccabees*, 35.

21. The inscription was discovered in 1931 in the keeping of the Russian Orthodox "Eleona" Church on the Mount of Olives, so its original location in antiquity is unknown. See William F. Albright, "The Discovery of an Aramaic Inscription Relating to King Uzziah," *BASOR* 44 (1931): 8–10, https://doi.org/10.2307/1355511. Uzziah is said to have been buried in a plot outside Jerusalem because his leprosy precluded his burial inside the city (2 Chr 26:23; cf. 2 Kgs 15:7). It is doubtful, therefore, that Uzziah's remains were secondarily interred with David's remains.

Here, then, is proof of the reburial of a Davidic king's remains, along with a warning against disturbing his final resting place, albeit from a time after John. It is not beyond belief, therefore, that John stripped a recently relocated tomb of David of its associated treasures to pay off Sidetes. The odium of such a sacrilege might also explain the undoubted exaggeration in the story Josephus received, namely that John found a staggering 3,000 silver talents in the tomb.[22] It is far more likely that John stripped the tomb's riches (either from its inside or outside) to make up the shortfall in the 300 silver talents he needed to pay Sidetes, but this was quickly inflated by a fuming populace to 3,000 silver talents. Whatever the details, the incident shows that John was treading on political eggshells. That he could afford to tamper with the material legacy of David reveals just how impotent the Davidic descendants had become by this time. The entire incident is bizarre, and we may never know precisely what happened, but it reveals the desperate situation Jerusalem was in. At the end of it, John had enough to pay off Sidetes.

In late 133 BC, then, the Seleucid siege of Jerusalem was lifted, and Judea was reincorporated into the Seleucid realm. John had the indignity of inheriting an independent nation and surrendering it less than two years later. He now also bore the ignominy of being a tomb robber. He retained the high priesthood, but he was no longer a head of state in his own right. He was but a Seleucid appointee. Thus, it was in the name of Antiochus VII Sidetes that copper coins were minted in Jerusalem from 132 BC.[23] John also handed over the hostages to Sidetes, one of whom was his own younger brother (*Ant.* 13.247). Seleucid troops set about tearing down the city's fortifications, and when this was sufficiently accomplished, Sidetes left. Some Jews used the ensuing calm to leave the country. One of them was the grandson of Jesus ben Sira who migrated to Egypt in 131 BC where he translated his grandfather's book into Greek.[24]

3.7.4 JOHN HYRCANUS I IN THE SHADOW OF THE SELEUCIDS

John's popularity hit an all-time low. Perhaps the only thing saving him was his confirmation as high priest by Antiochus VII Sidetes and the lifetime tenure of

---

22. This would be the equivalent of US$4.5 billion today.
23. Grainger, *The Fall of the Seleukid Empire*, 97.
24. In the prologue to his translation, Ben Sira's grandson states that he arrived in Egypt in the thirty-eighth year of King Euergetes, who can only be identified with Euergetes II, the birthname of Fatso Ptolemy VIII. His first year would have been 168 BC, when he first became co-ruler with his siblings, Ptolemy VI and Cleopatra II.

his office. But he must surely have feared for his life, especially since his father had been recently assassinated. There was only so much vitriol he could deflect. John thus faced a massive task to regain public confidence.

The size of the Jewish army was impacted by the Seleucid invasion and the associated famine (cf. *Ant.* 13.246). But even some of the remaining Jewish soldiers walked away from John, unwilling to receive payment from the proceeds of tomb robbery.[25] This forced him to employ gentile mercenaries and pay them with some of the money looted from David's tomb (*Ant.* 13.249). The Jewish military thus began to operate in Greek, but this was also a logical outworking of the process begun by Jonathan Apphus, when he accepted the accolades of Alexander Balas. The Hasmonean high priest was like other high priests throughout the Hellenistic world.

John also attracted the epithet "Hyrcanus," the name by which Josephus predominantly refers to him. The theory that claims he received the moniker for accompanying Sidetes on campaign to Hyrcania (see this section below) must be ruled out, for there is no evidence that John (or Sidetes) ever reached Hyrcania, and the epithet appears in abbreviated form on coins minted in Jerusalem before that campaign anyway.[26] There are three other theories we may advance. The first is that the mercenaries John employed were originally from Hyrcania at the southeastern corner of the Caspian Sea, such that he became known as the Hyrcanian commander. Unfortunately, Josephus does not tell us where the mercenaries were from, so this remains speculation. The second theory is that "Hyrcanus" was a Greek name that Sidetes imposed upon John, while the third is that it was a Greek name John chose for himself for use in international contexts.

In 131 BC John marched out with his mercenaries and remaining Jewish soldiers to accompany Sidetes in his attempt to recover the eastern provinces from the Parthians. At one point, John prevailed on Sidetes to pause the campaign to allow the Jewish soldiers to observe Pentecost (Shavuot). Sidetes obliged, once again proving himself a benefactor of Jewish customs (*Ant.* 13.251–253). The campaign was initially a great success. Sidetes won back Babylonia and Media and installed his troops throughout the territories. But in the winter of 130/129 BC, the citizens themselves turned on Sidetes's troops and displaced them (Justin, *Epit.* 38.10). In despair at his losses, Sidetes committed suicide (Appian, *S.W.* 68), leaving the Parthians to take back control of Babylonia and Media. Whether John was party to Sidetes's

---

25. Cf. Grainger, *The Wars of the Maccabees*, 75.
26. Oliver D. Hoover, "The Seleucid Coinage of John Hyrcanus I: The Tranformation of a Dynastic Symbol in Hellenistic Judaea," *AJN* 15 (2003): 30, n.2.

downfall is unknown, but he survived the war and returned to Jerusalem. The political subordination of Judea also died with Sidetes. Thus, "John Hyrcanus" found himself heading an independent state again, four years after he had lost it. The reduced Seleucid kingdom now reverted to Sidetes's older brother, Demetrius II, whom the Parthian king, Phraates II (son of Mithridates I), had earlier released from exile.[27]

Spending almost two years away from Judea was a boon for John, and the recovery of independence gave the population reprieve from the burdens of Seleucid taxes. The threat of Ptolemy Abubus also receded.[28] It seems the whole of Judea breathed a collective sigh of relief, allowing John to begin a new chapter. There was now space for John to prove himself a better promoter of the Jewish nation than Sidetes had been.

The demise of Sidetes created a military vacuum, which John exploited. Josephus implies that he went on a conquering spree (*Ant.* 13.254–258), but this is a summary statement that camouflages some chronological complexity.[29] Rather than accomplishing everything on Josephus's list at this time, John's initial achievements were more modest. He regained sovereignty over Gazara and Joppa, thus securing control over the *Via Maris* and gaining unfettered access to the Mediterranean.[30] He also gained a similar controlling point on the King's Highway at Medeba in Transjordan, though this exacted a heavy toll on his forces.[31] Although Jews had lived here for centuries (e.g., the Tobiads), more began to move into the region over the next generations, and it soon acquired the name Perea ("Further" Judea). With these acquisitions, John tapped two rich veins of trade, putting Judea in a position to grow economically.

3.7.5 JUDEA AND INTERNATIONAL DEVELOPMENTS (133–123 BC)

The four years Judea spent subsumed back into the Seleucid kingdom (133–129 BC) saw some tumultuous developments throughout the Mediterranean world, which would have lasting repercussions. In 133 BC, Attalus III, the

---

27. See Wolski, *The Seleucids*, 112.
28. Ptolemy Abubus is never mentioned again. Zeno continued to rule in Philadelphia and was followed there by his son, Theodorus.
29. Jonathan Bourgel, "The Destruction of the Samaritan Temple by John Hyrcanus: A Reconsideration," *JBL* 135.3 (2016): 505–23, https://doi.org/10.15699/jbl.1353.2016.3129.
30. This is not mentioned in Josephus's list of John's conquests. However, John's later appeal to Rome necessitates his full control of them (see 3.7.5).
31. Sievers (*The Hasmoneans and Their Supporters*, 142) sees the acquisition of Medeba at this time as unlikely, but John's subsequent accumulation of wealth testifies to footholds on the trade routes.

bohemian king of Pergamum, died without leaving a son to succeed him. He saw Rome's expansion into the Greek east as inevitable and wished to spare his kingdom conflict. So, being the eccentric he was, he sensationally bequeathed his entire kingdom to the Roman Republic. A few years later, it was incorporated into the Republic as the province of Asia.

This novel bequest came to Rome in the throes of an economic crisis. The Roman military was still technically a militia, which drew predominantly on Italian farmers for its ranks. But Rome's growth had attracted many to the city, hampering the supply of troops and impoverishing agricultural production. This was exacerbated by the slave revolt in Sicily, which strangled the supply of grain to the rest of Italy. In 133 BC, a tribune of the plebs, Tiberius Sempronius Gracchus, proposed using the treasury of Attalus to pay for a redistribution of land to entice people back to farming and potential service in the army. But his proposal trod on the toes of wealthy patricians who drew much of their wealth from public lands. Tiberius pressed ahead with his reforms by legally circumventing the Senate, but he was soon lynched by his opponents and his body tossed into the Tiber (Diodorus Siculus, *Bib. hist.* 34/35.5–7).[32] The whole affair showcased how legal means could be used to undercut the authority of the Senate and the lengths patricians would go to in order to protect personal rather than national interests. It set precedents that, in time, would permit individuals to claim their own interests as those of the state and eventually rise above the state altogether. It also exposed the polarized nature of Roman society, which was split between the old-money *Optimates* ("Aristocrats") and the *Populares* ("Populists") who championed the people.[33]

In Egypt, the death of Ptolemy VI (145 BC) saw the throne pass to his brother, Fatso Ptolemy VIII,[34] who married his sister, Cleopatra II. Fatso Ptolemy was a sordid character whose list of pathologically savage acts included the butchering of his own son and the rape of Cleopatra II's daughter, Cleopatra III, by whom he fathered a son (Ptolemy IX). He subsequently deposed Cleopatra II and married Cleopatra III, but this sparked civil strife. The Jewish community of Egypt played a pivotal role in forcing Fatso Ptolemy to flee the country (Diodorus Siculus, *Bib. hist.* 34/35.18). Among the most prominent Jewish figures were two generals in the Ptolemaic army, Onias and Dositheus

---

32. Sinnigen and Boak, *A History of Rome*, 166–69; Mary T. Boatwright et al., *The Romans: From Village to Empire: A History of Rome from Earliest Times to the End of the Western Empire*, 2nd ed. (Oxford: Oxford University Press, 2012), 144–48.

33. These were unofficial terms used in the first century BC and were never indicative of any organized political party.

34. Ptolemy VII, a son of Ptolemy VI, never ruled in his own right and was murdered by Ptolemy VIII. Note that some scholars swap the enumeration of these two Ptolemies.

(*Ag. Ap.* 2.49–52), the former most likely being the Zadokite Onias IV, now in his fifties.[35] But by 130 BC, Fatso Ptolemy had returned and won back all of Egypt, except for Alexandria, where Cleopatra II held out against him.

In Syria, the fortunes of Demetrius II had changed remarkably after the death of his brother, Antiochus VII Sidetes. He remarried his first wife, Cleopatra Thea, who was none too pleased by the development. A few months later, he received a delegation from his (once again) mother-in-law, Cleopatra II, who urged him to come to her aid against Fatso Ptolemy. In exchange for his military assistance, she offered him nothing less than the throne of the Ptolemaic kingdom (Justin, *Epit.* 39.1). Lacking the political acumen that had caused Ptolemy VI to baulk at uniting the Ptolemaic and Seleucid realms (see 3.6.6 above), Demetrius intrepidly swung into action (Justin, *Epit.* 39.1). He marched an army south, violating Judea's control of Joppa and Gazara on the way. Whether he enlisted John Hyrcanus I's help is simply unknown. What we do know is that Demetrius totally underestimated the task of conquering Egypt, as his forces mutinied the moment they caught sight of Fatso Ptolemy's army at Pelusium. The campaign of the cocksure Demetrius thus unraveled before a sword was even swung.

Matters grew worse for him when he returned to a Syria set in rebellion against him. Its citizens recalled the rash diktats of his first reign (see 3.6.6 above) and, incited by Cleopatra Thea herself, rose up against his rule. Cleopatra Thea's position became even more powerful when her mother, Cleopatra II, arrived in Antioch. She had decamped from Alexandria with the Ptolemaic treasury, leaving Egypt to Fatso Ptolemy. This put the Seleucid capital under the control of powerful Ptolemaic women.

Then, in late 129 BC, Fatso Ptolemy injected a new claimant to the Seleucid throne: a man he named Alexander II. The cover story was that he was the son of Alexander Balas and grandson of Antiochus IV. Despite the charade, people in Syria were glad to have a king other than Demetrius II, so they readily accepted his claim, cheekily nicknaming him "Zabinas," an Aramaic word meaning "one who is bought" (*Ant.* 13.267–268; Justin, *Epit.* 39.1). His arrival prompted the two Cleopatras to abandon Antioch for Ptolemais-Acco. However, the apparent unity that Alexander Zabinas brought to Syria was ethereal, consisting primarily of hatred for Demetrius rather than support for Zabinas. Zabinas was an immature scamp—likeable but devoid of political vision. The clouds of civil war, which had never really departed from Syria, opened once again.

---

35. The nature of Josephus's testimony means this identification is not straightforward. However, the sons of Onias IV did hold high military rank in Egypt (*Ant.* 13.285–87).

The fresh storm that lashed the Seleucid realm gave John Hyrcanus space to secure Judea's borders. He dispatched an embassy to the Roman Senate, which argued that Rome's previous acknowledgement of Judea under his father, Simon, included Jewish sovereignty over Joppa and Gazara, making it illegal for Sidetes to have reclaimed them and for Demetrius II to have marched through them. In a session dated to February 127 BC, the Roman Senate agreed and issued an edict to that effect. It also recognized Jewish control of Perea in Transjordan and stated its intention to prevent future violations of Jewish borders (*Ant.* 13.259–266).[36]

The Senate's decision led Zabinas to recognize Jewish sovereignty over the relevant areas. John presumably reciprocated by recognizing Zabinas as sovereign over the Seleucid domains—a great snub to the precocious Demetrius, who spent the next two years trying to get back onto the front foot. It was to no avail, as Zabinas defeated him in battle near Damascus in late 126 BC. Soon afterwards, Demetrius was captured at Tyre and summarily executed (*Ant.* 13.268; Justin, *Epit.* 39.1). Thus, the life of the petulant young king, who had been responsible for granting Judea's initial independence as a client state, came to a pitiful end.

If Seleucid politics had not been farcical enough, they now degenerated even further. Cleopatra Thea's son by Demetrius II, sixteen-year-old Seleucus V, declared himself king. But Cleopatra Thea knew of the lad's hatred for her and, fearing for her own life, immediately had him killed (Livy, *Per.* 60.11). With the support of her mother, she then declared herself ruler of the Seleucid kingdom. Yet, in a chauvinistic world, her reign was utterly frowned upon. Cleopatra Thea was more than capable of reading the political temperature, so she raised her youngest son by Demetrius to rule with her. The boy's name was Antiochus, and he was ferried to Ptolemais-Acco from Athens, where he was being educated. The lad had such a beak of a nose that he came to be known as Antiochus VIII Hooknose (Gk. *Grypos* [Justin, *Epit.* 39.1]). Some of his coinage, which bears his profile, gives him a prominent but modest protrusion, while other coins bear franker testimony to the contours of his conk.

The death of Demetrius II handed Alexander Zabinas more power in Syria, and he broke ties with his erstwhile controller, Fatso Ptolemy VIII. To claw some power back, Cleopatra Thea struck a deal with her uncle, Fatso Ptolemy, to marry her son, Antiochus Hooknose, to his daughter by Cleopatra III, the young princess Tryphaena. As galling as this might have

---

36. See Zollschan, *Rome and Judaea*, 242–47. Cf. Duncan E. MacRae, "Roman Hegemony and the Hasmoneans: Constructions of Empire," in Berlin and Kosmin, *The Middle Maccabees*, 333–34.

been to the older Cleopatra II, she was a political pragmatist and supported the idea in order to oppose Zabinas. The marriage gave Fatso Ptolemy a new puppet in the Seleucid kingdom. He duly supplied his new son-in-law with troops, and Cleopatra II was permitted to return home to Alexandria, where she became co-ruler with Fatso Ptolemy and her other daughter, Cleopatra III (Justin, *Epit.* 39.2).

John Hyrcanus, now in his late thirties, suddenly found himself the elder statesman in the region. But though he supported Zabinas's claim, he let the two Seleucid claimants fight it out for themselves. A battle loomed in 123 BC, but the sources contradict each other on whether it actually took place (Justin, *Epit.* 39.2; Diodorus Siculus, *Bib. hist.* 34/35.28). What is clear is that, without the support of Fatso Ptolemy, Zabinas was bankrupt and unable to pay his troops—an ironically similar position to that which Demetrius II had faced. Rather than retrench his soldiers, he tried melting down statues in Antioch's temple of Zeus to mint coins instead, but this sacrilege turned all and sundry against him. He was chased from Antioch, captured, and brought before Antiochus Hooknose, who promptly executed him (Justin, *Epit.* 39.2; Diodorus Siculus, *Bib. hist.* 34/35.28).

This left Cleopatra Thea and young Antiochus VIII Hooknose jointly ruling the Seleucid kingdom. But Hooknose's misogyny outgrew even his beak, and he was soon attempting to shake off his mother's power. Ever attuned to a threat, Cleopatra Thea employed what was now classic Ptolemaic tactics: murder. She poisoned her son's wine, but he, quick to her game, forced her to drink it instead. Thus, Cleopatra Thea was outplayed by her own son and died of her own medicine in 121 BC (Justin, *Epit.* 39.2).

John Hyrcanus had made an enemy of Antiochus Hooknose through his support of Zabinas. However, Hooknose was unable to take any action against him, as his kingdom was crumbling around him. In fact, he was forced to grant independence to important pieces of his kingdom, retaining only a sham of sovereignty. Then, from 114 BC, he had to fend off a challenge from his half-brother, Antiochus IX Cyzicenus (the son of Antiochus VII Sidetes and Cleopatra Thea). It was yet another Seleucid civil war. The Parthian kingdom took advantage of this by swallowing up former Seleucid territories in northern Mesopotamia, inching closer to the Syrian heartland. As the Seleucid kingdom contracted under the triple pressure of Rome's eastward expansion, Parthia's westward growth, and the Ptolemies' meddling from the south, it was also cannibalizing itself through incessant internal strife. It meant the remainder of John Hyrcanus's life was relatively free from external pressure, which allowed Judea to flourish (cf. *Ant.* 13.272).

3.7.6 "JOHN THE HIGH PRIEST AND THE COMMUNITY OF THE JEWS"

Command of the vital economic centers at Joppa, Gazara, and Perea brought rich streams of revenue into John's coffers. It allowed him to mint his own coins sporting the inscription, "John the high priest and the Community of the Jews," in patriotic Paleo-Hebrew script.[37] Soon he was able to fund major construction works, one of the most pivotal being the reconstruction of Jerusalem's demolished walls. Jerusalem's Western Hill attracted more settlement, so John's walls incorporated it (including the relocated tomb of David) into the city. He also ordered the complete demolition of the Acra[38] and the extension of the temple campus southwards to erase part of its footprint (*Ant.* 13.215–217).

John also constructed palaces for himself, increasing his prestige. It was the act of someone who was becoming something more than a high priest. He increasingly took on the airs of a Hellenistic monarch, though he never claimed the title of "king." His primary residence was built on Jerusalem's Western Hill, next to the site that Jason's gymnasium had once occupied. The gymnasium was turned into a public square known as the Xystus (*J.W.* 2.344; cf. 1 Macc 1:14; 2 Macc 4:9, 12).[39] From here, John built a bridge across the Tyropean Valley to the temple precinct itself. He also built a luxurious winter palace outside Jericho, which included peristyles and pools, as well as a *miqveh* for ritual bathing.[40] From around this time, ritual baths (Heb. *miqvaot*) became commonplace throughout Palestine, probably under the growing influence of the Pharisees.

Despite the stability and prosperity that came to Judea, John still faced domestic opposition. Among his detractors were the Essenes, who had now developed into a monastic sect. What prompted their return from exile near

---

37. The Hebrew phrase *hbr yhdm* on John's coins can be translated either as "the community of the Jews" (a reference to the whole Jewish nation), or as "the Senate of the Jews." See Ya'akov Meshorer, *A Treasury of Jewish Coins from the Persian Period to Bar-Kochba* (Jerusalem: Yitzhak ben-Zvi, 1997), 30–39.

38. Josephus claims that Simon Thassi demolished the Acra (*Ant.* 13.215–17; *J.W.* 1.50), but he probably only reduced one of its towers (see 3.7.2). Archaeology shows that the Acra was dismantled in the late second century BC. See Zilbersetin, "Hellenistic Military Architecture," 45–47, 50–51.

39. The term "Xystus" refers to the peristyle or manicured garden surrounding the open training area of a gymnasium. The fact that the plaza in front of the Hasmonean palace was called by this Greek name is proof positive that the Greek gymnasium had been on this location. Once decommissioned, the open training area was repurposed as a public square, and the remainder cleared to make way for John's palace.

40. Eyal Regev, "The Hellenization of the Hasmoneans Revisited: The Archaeological Evidence," *Advances in Anthropology* 7 (2017): 177–82.

Damascus is unknown, but they settled on Jerusalem's Western Hill, creating a monastic enclave near the southwestern gate, which came to be known as the Essene Gate (cf. *J.W.* 5.145). Their mode of resistance to John was not violence but literary activity, prophecy, and piety. In their sectarian writings, they drew a comparison between John's building activities (in Jerusalem and Jericho) and the curse that the book of Joshua placed on the person who rebuilt Jericho:

> And at the time that Joshua finished praising and extolling with his psalms, he said, "Cursed be the man who rebuilds this city [Jericho]. With his firstborn will he found it, and with his youngest will he set up its doors." Here is a cursed man [John Hyrcanus], one of Belial, standing to become a fowler's snare to his people, and a ruin to all his neighbors. (4Q175, 21–24)[41]

Since the Essenes were a reclusive sect, their influence across the populace was limited. The public was far more influenced by the Pharisees, who were drawn largely from the laity. Their support for John was qualified and gave rise to considerable tension. Josephus gives the anecdote of a banquet at which a cantankerous Pharisee named Eleazar urged John to relinquish the high priesthood and content himself with civic leadership alone. The reason for the demand was that John's mother had been captured during the persecution under Antiochus IV Epiphanes. (*Ant.* 13.288–292). The anecdote bears the hallmarks of a well told tale,[42] but it does preserve something of the historical currents. Some of the Pharisees had come to accept John's civic leadership in lieu of viable Davidic leadership but questioned his legitimacy for the priesthood as they developed their Oral Law. The question was not just over John's parentage but his holiness. According to Torah, a priest could only marry an Israelite virgin or else his children would be defiled. Furthermore, the women of a priest's household could not be sullied by prostitution (Lev 21:7–9, 13–15). In developing their Oral Law, the Pharisees extended these tenets to encompass rape, leading them to conclude that even the mere possibility that John's mother had been raped during the Antiochene persecution compromised John's holiness and fitness for service.[43] The charge evidently could not be proved for lack of witnesses, but this was immaterial to the fundamentalist

---

41. This document (4Q175), known as Testimonia, is paleographically dated to the early first century BC. For a survey of interpretations of this text, see Eshel, *The Dead Sea Scrolls and the Hasmonean State*, 63–89. See also 3.7.8.

42. A different version of the tale is told in the Talmud (b. Qidd. 66a), where it is erroneously told of Alexander Jannaeus.

43. Christophe Batsch, "The Defiled Mother: Reappraisal of a Legal Innovation in Ancient Judea," trans. Anne Stevens, *Clio. Women, Gender, History* 44 (2016): 21–43.

Pharisees, for it was the unverifiable nature of the situation that jeopardized John's holiness in their eyes. John might have challenged the charge by claiming he was born after Antiochus IV's reign, but this simply drew attention to the fact that he had been a "youth" (under thirty years of age) when he acquired the high priesthood (*J.W.* 1.55; *Ant.* 13.229), compromising the legality of his station even further. John did not back down, and this fueled his tension with the Pharisees.

The Pharisees' Oral Law might have held appeal for fundamentalist laity, but it posed restraints on the high priest over and above the dictates of the written Law. Neither John nor his staunch Sadducee supporters were going to countenance such strictures. The Sadducees are sometimes characterized as rejecting the canonical prophets and holding only to the authority of the Torah, but this is a misunderstanding of the evidence. The Sadducees recognized only the written Torah in express denial of the authority of the Pharisees' Oral Torah (*Ant.* 13.297; 18.16). Their rejection of prophecy was not a rejection of the prophetic canon, which was necessary to the claim of Jerusalem's primacy, but a conviction that the phenomenon of prophecy had ceased. They were, in other words, Jewish cessationists specifically opposed to the fundamentalist Pharisees and their traditions. They thus were moving towards a progressive outlook.

Josephus claims that the friction between John and the Pharisees led to an uprising, though he furnishes no specifics other than John's success in quelling it (*Ant.* 13.299). The nature of this "uprising" is probably to be gleaned from the rhetoric employed in the "Hanukkah Letter," written by the authorities in Jerusalem in 124 BC, preserved in 2 Maccabees 1:1–9:

> To the brethren who are Jews throughout Egypt, greetings.
> From the brethren who are Jews in Jerusalem and the country of Judea, earnest peace.
> May God do you good and remember his covenant with Abraham, Isaac, and Jacob, his faithful servants. May he give you all a heart to revere him and do his will with a generous heart and willing spirit. May he open your heart to his law and to the ordinances and enable peace. May he hear your petitions and be reconciled to you. May he not abandon you in an evil time. We are now praying for you here.
> While Demetrius reigned, in the 169th year [143 BC], we Jews had written to you at the height of our distress, which had come upon us in the years after Jason (and those with him) had left the holy land and the kingdom, burned the gate, and shed innocent blood. We petitioned the Lord

and were heard. We offered sacrifice and flour, lit the lamps, and set out the bread. And now, we write that you should observe the days of booth-making in the month of Kislev [i.e., Hanukkah].

Year: 188th [124 BC]

This letter told the Jews of Egypt that they still owed their allegiance to the temple in Jerusalem and, by inference, not to the temple of Onias IV at Leontopolis. While there is no indication that Onias's temple became anything more than a marginal accessory to Jewry in Egypt, the influence of Onias IV's family persisted. Onias's sons, Hilkiah and Ananias, became generals of Jewish cohorts in the Ptolemaic army (*Ant.* 13.284–287). In 124 BC, Onias would have been in his sixties. It could be that his death was the occasion for the Hanukkah Letter, but even if Onias was still alive, his senior years and the rising importance of his sons raised the issue of the future of the Zadokite line. Would it be possible for one of Onias's sons to return to Jerusalem to reinstate the Zadokite priesthood there? This prospect might have lain behind the Pharisaic suggestion that John surrender the priesthood and confine himself to civic authority. After all, if John had done so, the question arising would have been who was to succeed him as high priest. Irrespective of the Pharisaic objections to John's priesthood, the survival of the Zadokite line beyond Onias IV must have raised questions about the ongoing legitimacy of the Hasmonean priesthood, which had filled the breach left by the Zadokite priesthood in Jerusalem (see 3.5.8 above). Since the Zadokite line had survived in Egypt, could or should it be reinstated in Jerusalem?

The answer given by the Hanukkah Letter was a resolute "no." It makes no overt reference to Onias or his sons, but this is not surprising, since that would be to accord them some dignity. Instead, the letter mentions Jason, the uncle of Onias IV and the last Zadokite high priest to actually serve at the Jerusalem temple. He is held up for his iniquities and ultimate departure from "the holy land," implying that he was the reason for the downfall of the Zadokite line, even before Onias IV had built his temple. In contrast, the Hasmoneans are held up as the ones who endured the full force of the dystopia that descended on Judea from 167–142 BC, who successfully resisted it, cleansed the Jerusalem temple, reinstituted the cult, and were the ones whose prayers the deity heard. The first person ("we") of the letter is identified with the Jewish people as a whole, but a Hasmonean voice is clearly discerned in the rhetoric. The letter thus portrays the Hasmoneans as the ones through whom divine blessing flowed to the covenant people.

This Hanukkah Letter demonstrates that in 124 BC opposition to John

Hyrcanus's priesthood was piquing in the light of a potential revival of the Zadokite line. There was at least passive resistance to John in Egypt, which implies more active resistance in Judea itself. What form such resistance might have taken is unknown, since Josephus gives no details of the apparent "uprising." But, the Jewish leadership in Jerusalem, consisting primarily of Sadducees, was firmly behind John. This was quite telling, since the Sadducees, as the spiritual heirs of the Zadokites in Judea, could have revoked their support for him and helped reinstate the Zadokite line. The Essenes, who opposed Hasmonean priesthood altogether, might have hoped for this, but the pacifist expression of their apocalyptic hopes did not make for an uprising. Any actual violence must have come from the Pharisees or a groundswell among the populace. The tensions, therefore, represent a widening breach between the upper crust of Jewish society who were aligned with John Hyrcanus and the more common elements generally aligned with the Pharisees. John might have used force to quell opposition, but a highly effective way to combat it in the longer term was to cultivate cultic practice that promoted the necessity of the Hasmonean priesthood over against Zadokite priesthood. The promotion of Hanukkah in both Judea and the diaspora was a means of achieving this.

The Hanukkah Letter was followed by a second letter (2 Macc 1:10–2:18), also treating the issue of Hanukkah. Its authenticity is suspect, but its argument is clear: God raised particular individuals for the survival of the cult, and Judas Maccabeus, who founded the Hasmonean priesthood, was the latest of these. The two Hanukkah letters were then prefixed to an abridged version of Jason of Cyrene's account of the Maccabean resistance led by Judas, ending with the commemoration of Judas's defeat of Nicanor (see 3.5.9 above)—that is, the remainder of 2 Maccabees (2 Macc 2:19–15:38). What's more, the account includes characters who profess belief in eschatological resurrection, as the Pharisees did, thereby depicting the Hasmoneans as the champions of those who express such belief, even though the Hasmoneans themselves did not believe in resurrection. It therefore subverted the theological platform of the Pharisees by showcasing how even conservatives and fundamentalists could and should support the Hasmonean priesthood.

Tensions over John's priesthood focused attentions on whether it was right for one person to be both civic governor and high priest. Historically, this combination of lay and sacred offices first surfaced with the high priest Joshua (late sixth century BC), received impetus in the time of Jaddua (fourth century BC), and became an enshrined institution by the time of John Hyrcanus I. The author of 1 Maccabees, who was a Sadducee supporter of John, argued that Hasmonean leadership was the most appropriate response to the internal and external challenges that threatened the existence of the Jewish nation. He held up the biblical figure of Phinehas as the model for Hasmonean leadership.[44] Phinehas was of priestly pedigree, but it was his zeal for the Law, demonstrated by his killing of the apostate, Zimri (1 Macc 2:23–26; cf. Num 25:6–15), which induced God to grant him perpetual priesthood. Phinehas, therefore, combined the roles of lay warrior and sacred priest and received God's imprimatur for his zeal. The argument of 1 Maccabees was that the Hasmoneans demonstrated this same requisite zeal for the Law by ousting the "lawless" (e.g., 1 Macc 1:11).[45] It was appropriate, therefore, that the civic and priestly offices be combined in Hasmonean hegemony, expressed in the leadership of John Hyrcanus (1 Macc 16:23–24).

3.7.7 THE CONQUESTS OF JOHN HYRCANUS I

As Antiochus VIII Hooknose and Antiochus IX Cyzicenus jabbed and feinted lethargically at each other, John Hyrcanus I pushed the borders of Judea outward. First up was the conquest of Idumea to Judea's south (ca. 114 BC).[46] As demonstrated by the Pentateuchal narratives of Jacob and Esau, Jews saw Idumeans as close relatives—an affinity furthered by the likelihood that Idumeans believed their patron deity, Qos, was the same god as Yahweh. Whether Jews reciprocated this belief is not clear, but Idumeans had historically circumcised their male children. This had, however, fallen out of practice as Idumeans embraced progressive Hellenism and came to identify their deity with Zeus.

In conquering Idumea, John followed a Judaizing policy, which allowed those who consented to circumcision and pledged to follow Jewish laws to remain in the land (*Ant.* 13.257–258). The implication was that the land belonged to Yahweh and thus only Yahweh's covenant people, Israel, could remain in it. It was a recapitulation of Joshua's conquest, which perhaps led the Essenes to draw the ironic comparison that John was himself under the curse that Joshua had imposed on the one who rebuilt Jericho (4Q175, 21–24; cf. Josh 6:26; see 3.7.6 above). This Judaizing policy became a standard part of John's conquests. In this case, it recognized Malachi's statement that Yahweh

---

44. Cf. Babota, *Hasmonean High Priesthood*, 279–84.
45. Harold W. Attridge, "Historiography," in *Jewish Writings of the Second Temple Period: Apocrypha, Pseudepigrapha, Qumran Sectarian Writings, Philo, Josephus*, Compendia Rerum Iudaicarum ad Novum Testamentum 2 (Assen/Philadelphia: Van Gorcum/Fortress, 1984), 173.
46. Berlin, "Between Large Forces," 7–8. Josephus, who telescopes all John's conquests into a single campaign (*Ant.* 13.254–258), does not necessarily list them in chronological order. The order argued for here is based on the geopolitical realities gleaned from a variety of sources.

"loved Jacob," but it did not press the statement that he "hated Esau" to its fullest extent (Mal 1:2–3). Instead, it followed the command of Deuteronomy 23:7 ("Do not despise an Edomite, for he is your brother") and allowed the possibility for Esau (Idumea) to become Jacob (Israel).

By converting people through forced circumcision, John was operating under a model that tied ethnic identity to active culture over passive ancestry. This was a significant milestone on the way to prizing apart ethnicity and faith—a process that would only be completed when the early church recognized gentiles as full members of the body of believers without ethnic change. The Judaizing Christians of the early church followed a similar policy to that of John Hyrcanus when they demanded that gentiles could only worship God through Jesus by first joining the covenant people of Israel through circumcision. This was deemed possible because ancestry had been loosed from the equation of religious identity. But there was still a notion that religion was tied to culture, such that worshipping the Jewish messiah necessitated adopting Jewish culture. The apostle Paul railed against this in his letter to the Galatians, insisting that Christian identity was formed on the basis of faith rather than culture (Gal 2:15; 3:1–6). This led to one of his most famous statements:

> There is neither Jew nor Greek, there is neither slave nor free, there is neither male nor female; for you are all one in Christ Jesus. If you are of Christ, then you must be the seed of Abraham, and heirs according to the promise. (Gal 3:28–29)

In the second century BC, however, belonging to the covenant people was about circumcision, zeal for a culture of Torah, and connection to the promised land. In other words, religion was primarily an issue of conscious state and cultural allegiance over ancestry.

The religious similitude between Jews and Idumeans means Idumean conversion was probably not as radical as might initially seem. The Idumeans had been considered a de facto part of Israel when Sanballat II had tried to form an Israelite coalition two centuries earlier (see 1.7 above). More conservative Idumeans probably never stopped circumcising their children, enabling an easy integration into the Jewish nation. Those who had stopped and were unwilling to undergo the procedure would have been forced to leave the territory, though how stringently this was enforced is unknown. John's conquest was as much about the acquisition of traditionally Israelite territory as it was the Judaization of its inhabitants. Idumean newborns were circumcised from this time, ensuring that within a generation all Idumeans had become religiously

Jewish. Idumeans and Jews also shared Abraham as a common ancestor, and indeed the traditional burial site of Abraham, the Cave of Machpelah, was at Hebron in Idumean territory. John Hyrcanus built a pilgrimage shrine at the cave, presumably to foster the integration of Idumeans into the Jewish nation.[47]

John then turned north to Samaria, which was still a contiguous component of the Seleucid kingdom. He invaded in 111 BC,[48] his prime target being the Samaritan temple on Mount Gerizim. In John's day the Samaritan temple was an impressive citadel on the summit, roughly the same size as the Acropolis of Athens. It was approached from the valley below by a grand stone staircase of around 1,500 steps and had a large adjacent administrative complex and residential area (800 × 500 meters). It was a monumental holy city and pilgrimage site, as evidenced by numerous dedicatory plaques at the site (*TAHNDT* A:118, B: 345–57). Similar plaques found on the Greek island of Delos, which mention "Israelites [i.e., Samaritans] who make offerings at the temple of Argarizein" (from Heb., *har Gerizim*, "Mount Gerizim"), demonstrate its international renown.[49]

There is no literary account of the conquest beyond Josephus's most summary of statements, which itself contains known inaccuracies (*Ant.* 13.255–256).[50] So, we are reliant on archaeology and topography to provide much of the picture. John's conquest included the obliteration of Shechem at the foot of the mountain[51] and a blockade of the settlement at the top, which must have lasted months. On 12 December 110 BC, the defenders of Mount Gerizim capitulated, and Jewish forces ascended to take control of the site.[52] John had the temple razed in a conflagration that consumed the entire complex and its residential area.[53] When the embers cooled and winter set in, he posted a gar-

---

47. See Noam Arnon and David Ben-Shlomo, "Iron Age Pottery from the Cave of the Patriarch at Hebron," *IEJ* 70.1 (2020): 50. Though we cannot be totally sure that John Hyrcanus I built this shrine, it was certainly constructed in the Hasmonean era, with John Hyrcanus's policies providing the most logical context for its construction.

48. The campaign against Mount Gerizim and Shechem is often erroneously placed in the 120s BC, but this is on the basis of Josephus's confused chronology (*Ant.* 13.254–258). The archaeological record has shown that it occurred in 111/10 BC immediately before the campaign against the *polis* of Samaria.

49. Gary N. Knoppers, "Aspects of Samaria's Religious Culture during the Early Hellenistic Period," in *The Historian and the Bible: Essays in Honour of Lester L. Grabbe*, ed. Philip R. Davies and Diana Vikander Edelman, LHBOTS 530 (London: T&T Clark, 2010), 159–74; Reinhard Pummer, *The Samaritans: A Profile* (Grand Rapids: Eerdmans, 2016), 80–88, 92–95.

50. Josephus states that the Samaritan temple stood for 200 years, but this is based on his erroneous dating of its foundation to the time of Alexander the Great (332 BC) rather than to its actual foundation in ca. 447 BC (see 1.7.3). He also amalgamated all John's conquests into a single campaign, mistakenly placed in ca. 128 BC.

51. One of the handful of tiny villages, which emerged from the rubble, was Sychar (cf. John 4:4).

52. The precise day, 21 Kislev, is recorded in Ta'anit, and the year can be confirmed archaeologically.

53. Yitzhak Magen, *The Samaritans and the Good Samaritan*, trans. Edward Levin, Judea and

rison to prevent anyone from attempting to use the site in a cultic way. And thus, the temple to Yahweh, which Sanballat I founded in ca. 447 BC, was destroyed, after standing for a third of a millennium.

The magnitude of the moment is hard to understate. For the Samaritans, it was a catastrophe akin to what the Babylonian conquest of Jerusalem in 586 BC had been for Judah. From John's perspective, he eradicated the most potent rival to the Jerusalem temple, making him the one and only true priest in all Israel. He could now bring the Israelite nation together in worship at one temple in Jerusalem. In theory, therefore, the fall of Mount Gerizim opened the way for John to stitch the pieces of Israel back together—a feat that Sanballat II had failed to achieve.

For Davidic loyalists, this was a welcome prospect, particularly since the prophets of old had mandated the reunification of all Israel. But this prospect was ultimately frustrated by the lack of Davidic leadership and the fact that the Jerusalem temple had been emptied of its Davidic import. For those Jews who had transferred the prerogatives of Davidic leadership to the priesthood, John Hyrcanus's conquest of Mount Gerizim signaled a cleansing of the nation and an opportunity to reunite it.

But no substantive reunification occurred. The Samaritans were nominally enfolded into the Jewish state under John Hyrcanus, which obliged them to worship under his cultic leadership in Jerusalem. While some may have done so, the vast majority did not. Instead, Samaritans viewed John as a new Nebuchadnezzar—a foreign conqueror who had committed the worst atrocity imaginable. They could not, therefore, accept his leadership or worship at his temple. Thus, an even greater chasm between Jews and Samaritans developed. The enmity that had simmered between them since the early Hellenistic era boiled up into sheer hatred. John's attempt to reunite the nation had deeply offended and wounded the Samaritans. As long as there was need for a single physical temple in a particular territory, there could be no peace between Jew and Samaritan—only the subjugation of one community by the other.

In response to the catastrophic events of 110 BC, the Samaritans developed their own notion of an eschatological messiah. This figure was known as the *Taheb*, an Aramaic term meaning "restorer."[54] He was to be a prophet like

---

Samaritan Publications 7 (Jerusalem: Israel Antiquities Authority, 2008), 25–28; Knoppers, *Jews and Samaritans*, 212–13.

54. Many of the texts on which our knowledge of the *Taheb* is based are from centuries later, but we can trace their trajectory through Josephus and the New Testament to understand how and when the essential tenets evolved. See Ferdinand Dexinger, *Der Taheb: Ein "Messianischer" Heilsbringer Der Samaritaner*, Kairos Religionswissenschaftliche Studien 3 (Salzburg: O. Müller, 1986).

Moses (cf. Deut 18:15), who would restore the tabernacle on Mount Gerizim, and until his coming the world would live in a time of divine displeasure. These beliefs prevailed into the first century, as reflected in the episode of Jesus's interaction with the Samaritan woman (John 4:19–26). The early church built on these expectations to welcome Samaritans who recognized Jesus as Messiah, though this entailed the adoption of a Jewish conceptuality (cf. John 4:22). Nonetheless, the early church viewed Samaritan conversions as the fulfilment of the prophetic hopes for the restoration of Israel under a Davidic king (Acts 8:14–17; cf. 1:6–8). This was probably bolstered after the destruction of the Jerusalem temple in AD 70, when the early church developed a theology of the heavenly priesthood of Jesus—a notion more compatible with native Samaritan sensibilities. The willing unity between Jews and Samaritans in the early Christian community was something that John Hyrcanus was unable to achieve.

After subjugating the Samaritans, John moved to besiege the Greek *polis* at the city of Samaria (109 BC).[55] The siege was conducted on an enormous scale, which included the construction of a circumvallation around the walls. But John did not stay to oversee the protracted siege. He departed for Jerusalem to officiate at a festival (probably the Day of Atonement) and left the siege in the hands of his two eldest sons, Judas Aristobulus and Antigonus (*J.W.* 1.64; *Ant.* 13.275–276). John had another three sons—Alexander Jannaeus, Absalom, and the youngest, whose name is unknown (*Ant.* 13.323; 14.71)—but they are never mentioned in relation to this campaign.

The siege of Samaria attracted the attention of Antiochus IX Cyzicenus, who at this moment was ascendant in the Seleucid civil war. The young king came to rescue the Greeks of Samaria, but Judas Aristobulus and Antigonus successfully repelled him. It is said that the rout occurred on the same day that their father, John, was offering incense inside the temple at Jerusalem, and that the divine voice spoke audibly to him informing him of their victory. John allegedly emerged from the temple and relayed the divine pronouncement to the waiting crowds. When the victory was confirmed, John's supporters acclaimed him as having the gift of prophecy (*J.W.* 1.68–69; *Ant.* 13.282–283). The story conveniently portrays John as rightly holding the office of priest, judge, and prophet, so it was probably a piece of propaganda that his supporters spread to legitimize him holding multiple offices, while fending off any attempts by discordant prophetic figures claiming to be the "reliable prophet" who might put an end to Hasmonean rule (cf. 1 Macc 14:41).

---

55. Grainger, *The Wars of the Maccabees*, 87.

Cyzicenus did not give up on Samaria, even receiving military assistance from Ptolemy IX. This Ptolemy, who went by the puckish nickname "Chickpea" (Gk. *Lathyros*), perhaps because of a cleft chin, had broken ranks with his mother, Cleopatra III, who ruled after the deaths of Fatso Ptolemy VIII and Cleopatra II (116 BC and 115 BC respectively). But no matter what Cyzicenus tried, his efforts came to nothing. John Hyrcanus returned to see the siege to its inevitable end. On 24 November 108 BC, the *polis* fell.[56] The population was enslaved, and the city was methodically destroyed.[57] The victory cleared the path for John to establish sovereignty over all the highlands up to Mount Carmel on the coast. One of Cyzicenus's commanders was also bribed into surrendering Scythopolis in the Jezreel Valley, which was subsequently sacked (*J.W.* 1.65; *Ant.* 13.279–283).[58]

The annexation of these territories was laden with biblical substance. John Hyrcanus had united the heartland of Israel under a Jerusalem-based banner for the first time since the celebrated ancient kings, David and Solomon. Parts of the coastal plain, Galilee, and Transjordan still lay beyond the Hasmonean borders, but they were peripheral to the biblical heartland. John undoubtedly made much of his accomplishments, and they probably boosted the legitimacy of his leadership within Judea. Davidic loyalists might have vaunted his achievements (despite the disturbance to the bones of David early in his rule), even as they excited apocalyptic hope for a Davidic king. Even the Pharisees must have celebrated the moment. It is likely that the victory provided John with the opportunity to attempt a détente with the Pharisees by having his eldest son, Judas Aristobulus, marry Shelomzion, the daughter of an eminent Pharisee named Shetach ben-Yossi. She is better known to us as Salome Alexandra.[59]

The book of Judith was probably written in Pharisee circles at precisely this time. The heroine, Judith, whose name means "Jewish," is an embodiment of the Jewish state. The story, set in a fictitious past, depicts Judith's cunning

---

56. The precise day, 25 Heshvan, is recorded in Ta'anit, and the year can be confirmed by alignment with other known events.

57. Evidence of the destruction is seen in the archaeological record. See John W. Crowfoot, Kathleen M. Kenyon, and Eleazar L. Sukenik, *The Buildings at Samaria (Samaria-Sebaste I)* (London: Palestine Exploration Fund, 1942), 28–31, 121; Sievers, *The Hasmoneans and Their Supporters*, 144–46.

58. Bourgel, "The Destruction of the Samaritan Temple by John Hyrcanus," 513–14. The event is commemorated in Ta'anit, which dates the exile of the gentile inhabitants of Scythopolis to 15–16 Sivan (8–9 June 107 BC).

59. Atkinson argues that, since Salome Alexandra was considered a royal, her father must have been part of the wider Hasmonean family; see Kenneth Atkinson, *Queen Salome: Jerusalem's Warrior Monarch of the First Century B.C.E* (Jefferson, NC: McFarland, 2012), 61. However, no source confirms this. On the contrary, her royalty is always seen with respect to her marriages, her sons, and the fact that she eventually ruled the Jewish state as its queen. Her father's descent was immaterial to this. Furthermore, rabbinic sources imply she was sister to Simeon ben-Shetach, though some have questioned this connection.

defeat of the gentile general Holofernes, using tropes found in the biblical narratives of Jael's triumph over Sisera (Judg 4) and David's slaying of Goliath (1 Sam 17). The book reflects high Jewish nationalism and triumphalism, the sway of Jerusalem over the Samarian highlands, and expressions of Pharisaic piety.[60]

As John was securing control all the way to Scythopolis, Cyzicenus took back Joppa and the whole coastal plain, depriving the Jewish state of its Mediterranean port.[61] John did not hurry to recover them, as the following year (107/6 BC) was a Sabbatical rest for the land. But when the year was out, he sent a diplomatic mission to Rome (106/5 BC),[62] requesting the Roman Senate to uphold upon its decree of 127 BC (see 3.7.5 above) and order Cyzicenus out of Joppa and its environs. The Roman Senate complied, and the ruling council of Roman Asia at Pergamum (the closest Roman territory to Judea) vowed material support for the Jewish cause (*Ant.* 14.247–255).[63] The political pressure was enough to see Cyzicenus evacuate (105/4 BC), opening the way for Jewish forces to take back Joppa and Gazara.

However, John did not live to see the reoccupation, for he passed away before reaching the age of sixty. Notwithstanding the shaky start, setbacks, and dissent to his rule, he had become a famed Hellenistic leader. He governed a Jewish state in a Greek world in which he was eminently comfortable. We see this by the mix of Semitic and Greek names he gave his sons, their Greek education,[64] and his kindly attitude towards the people of Athens, which earned him official accolades, including a brass statue at a public temenos and acclaim at Athenian religious festivals (*Ant.* 14.149–155).[65] John thus straddled both the Jewish and Greek worlds in a way that did not undermine his Jewishness in the opinion of most. His conquests and the political acuity of his later years allowed him to reach a détente with the influential fundamentalist Pharisees, sealed with the marriage of his eldest son to the daughter of a prominent Pharisee.

---

60. The book of Judith probably had an oral history going back to the late Persian era and subsequently developed in several stages before reaching its final form late in the time of John Hyrcanus I. See Carey A. Moore, "Judith, Book Of," *ABD* 3:1117–25.

61. Numismatic evidence proves Cyzicenus's control of the coast until 104 BC. See Zollschan, *Rome and Judaea*, 257.

62. *Pace* MacRae ("Roman Hegemony and the Hasmoneans," 334–35), who dates this embassy to 113/2 BC.

63. Josephus mistakenly assigns the decree to the era of John Hyrcanus II. But the decree's reference to "King Antiochus, son of Antiochus" can only be to Antiochus IX Cyzicenus, son of Antiochus VII Sidetes, meaning its reference to "Hyrcanus" must be to John Hyrcanus I. See also Zollschan, *Rome and Judaea*, 254–58.

64. Grainger, *The Wars of the Maccabees*, 94–95.

65. These plaudits were recorded in Athens in April 105 BC as John's ambassadors made their way from Rome to Pergamum. Josephus preserves the script of the official vote of thanks, though he mistakenly attributes them to John Hyrcanus II. See VanderKam, *From Joshua to Caiaphas*, 355.

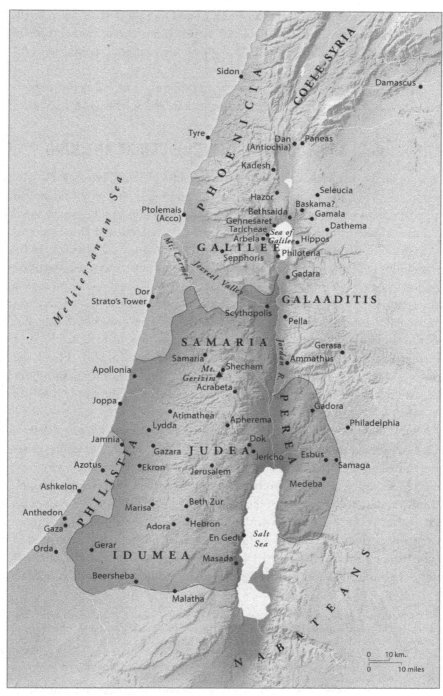

Judea after the Conquests of John Hyrcanus I (134–104 BC).

John had become a centrist, but he and his Sadducee supporters were clearly moving towards a progressive outlook. He lasted thirty years at the helm of the new Jewish state, extending it in size, bringing it international recognition, and growing the prestige of Hasmonean rule.

Just before he died, John did something that most probably did not see coming: he bequeathed his Hellenistic Jewish state to his wife (*Ant.* 13.302).

3.7.8 JUDAS ARISTOBULUS I (104 BC): PRIEST AND KING

Unfortunately, history has not preserved the name of John Hyrcanus I's wife. Leaving the Jewish state in her hands was an enormous vote of confidence in her, particularly since many would have opposed her simply for being a woman in a man's world. John's sons were all born to privilege, and this seems to have stirred in them a sense of entitlement and immaturity. The eldest, Judas Aristobulus (whom we will refer to simply as Aristobulus), was in his twenties, and John knew what it was to have national leadership thrust upon him at that age. Aristobulus was a capable military leader but steering the ship of state was a more delicate task. He shared a camaraderie with his next brother, Antigonus, but the same cannot be said for the other three sons. John himself had become estranged from his third son, Alexander Jannaeus (*Ant.* 13.322), though the true reason for this breakdown has been lost to legend.[66] Rather than submit the state to the impulses of brash youth, John placed it in the steady hands of his wife.

But things did not go steadily. Aristobulus was anointed high priest despite being technically underage and not head of state. His father's age at his consecration had set a precedent that soon led to the tradition that the high priest could be as young as twenty, probably in line with the youngest age at which a Levite could receive a share of the tithes (2 Chr 31:17).[67] Then, Aristobulus led a palace coup that resulted in the imprisonment of his mother and three youngest brothers. He spared Antigonus because of their close relationship and relied on him as military chief. In the months that followed, their mother succumbed to starvation. With the immediate challenges to him duly dealt

---

66. As the backstory to this estrangement, Josephus claims that John Hyrcanus asked God to show him which of his sons should succeed him. When God pointed out Alexander Jannaeus, rather than one of his two eldest sons, he was grieved because he did not like his third son and therefore banished him to Galilee. The story is a midrash of sorts, probably arising after John's death, and exhibiting tropes evident in dramatic Greek literature. See Joshua Efron, *Studies on the Hasmonean Period*, Studies in Judaism in Late Antiquity (Leiden: Brill, 1987), 167.

67. This minimum age of twenty is preserved in subsequent Jewish tradition (b. Ḥul. 24b; cf. Maimonides, *Klei haMiqdash* 5.15), but note the even younger age of Aristobulus III (see 4.5.1 below).

with, Aristobulus placed a diadem on his own head and declared himself king of the Jews (*Ant.* 13.301–302). It was the first time since the fall of Jerusalem in 586 BC that Judah had a Judean king.[68]

While this was not an unexpected development, given the surge in international prestige of the Hasmoneans, it crossed a decisive political and theological threshold. The supporters of the Hasmoneans, such as the Sadducees, identified the kingdom of Aristobulus with the kingdom of God himself. Israel had truly now become a kingdom of priests (cf. Exod 19:6)—or, rather, the kingdom of *a* priest. For Davidic loyalists, it was a step too far. In their eyes, the crowning of Aristobulus was as good as the appointment of King Saul (1 Sam 9–10). And since Aristobulus sported the epithet "Philhellene" (*Ant.* 13.318), marking him out as a progressive Hellenizer, he instantiated exactly what had been wrong with the kingship of Saul: he was a king such as those the other nations had. This added fuel to the fire of their apocalyptic hope that God would himself step into history and make good on his ancient promises to raise a son of David to rule as son of God.

The Pharisees might initially have been onside with Aristobulus by virtue of his marriage to Salome Alexandra. Her brother, Simeon ben-Shetach, was an upcoming luminary in Pharisee circles and a member of the Jewish Senate. But the ruthlessness of Aristobulus's power grab did not endear him to them. Many Pharisees still hoped for a Davidic kingdom, though their political hopes were being increasingly shaped by a desire to see their Oral Law become as ascendant as the written Law (Torah). Thus, they continued to hold to the expectation that "the Prophet" would arise to steer the nation in a new direction (1 Macc 14:41; cf. Deut 18:15; John 1:24), making for an uneasy relationship with Aristobulus.

For the Essenes, Aristobulus's move was simply confirmation of the illegitimacy of the Hasmoneans. One particular Essene, a prophetic figure named Judas, even predicted that Aristobulus's brother, Antigonus, would die on a certain day after the Festival of Sukkot in October 104 BC, at Strato's Tower, a small coastal town (*Ant.* 13.311–312).

After his palace coup, Aristobulus continued his father's campaign of conquest by pushing north. With the aid of Antigonus, he conquered the Itureans (*Ant.* 13.318), a tribe that had emerged from the Anti-Lebanon Mountains to seek independence from the Seleucids and that eventually settled in Galilee

---

68. Zerubbabel probably declared himself king in Jerusalem in December 520 BC, as the temple was being built, but the Persians removed him from the position just weeks later (see 1.1.2). His maneuver ultimately failed, meaning the last recognized king of Judah was Zedekiah in 586 BC.

and Gaulanitis (biblical Golan).[69] Aristobulus forced circumcision upon them and placed them in emerging Jewish settlements throughout Galilee and Gaulanitis, especially around the Huleh Valley and along some of the main thoroughfares.[70] The subjugation of the Itureans, therefore, opened the door for Jewish control of Galilee. Actualizing this control over the whole region would require further military operations, but it was now clear that the Galilean bough was about to break off the Seleucid tree.

Aristobulus returned to Jerusalem to discharge his duties as high priest at the autumnal festivals for the first time, leaving the Galilean campaign to Antigonus. His brother was eminently successful, but reports of this incited Aristobulus to jealousy. Despite his affection for his brother, Aristobulus was an insecure character, and his actions towards the rest of his family revealed his lust for power. This now morphed into paranoia.

Immediately after the Day of Atonement, Aristobulus fell gravely ill and was unable to preside at the Festival of Sukkot. Antigonus himself returned to Jerusalem and during the festival acted as his brother's deputy and led public prayers in the temple for his recovery. The fact that he was the logical heir to the throne (Aristobulus had no children yet) probably motivated him to make a showy display of support for his brother and thus deflect any suggestion that he might be hoping for his demise (*Ant.* 13.303–306).

The gesture had the opposite effect, however, and Aristobulus felt that Antigonus had stolen the limelight at the first opportunity. Accordingly, Aristobulus ordered his brother to report to him unarmed, probably for a dressing down. Fearing that Antigonus would show up armed anyway, Aristobulus instructed his guards to be on alert and strike down Antigonus if he was armed. It is reported, however, that the queen, Salome Alexandra, told Antigonus to come dressed in his new battle armor. This was probably a completely innocent suggestion, since she was probably not privy to Aristobulus's paranoid plot, but circumstance and gossip seem to have overblown her role into a conspiracy (*Ant.* 13.308). In any case, the unsuspecting Antigonus did have his armor on as he headed to his brother's side. On his way, he happened to pass Judas the Essene, who had foretold that Antigonus would die that very day at Strato's Tower. Judas admitted that he must have been wrong because there was not

---

69. Grainger, *The Fall of the Seleukid Empire*, 146, 159–60, 180. There is debate about whether the Itureans were originally an Arab or Aramean tribe.

70. Mordechai Aviam, "The Transformation from Galil Ha-Goyim to Jewish Galilee: The Archaeological Testimony of an Ethnic Change," in *The Archaeological Record from Cities, Towns and Villages*, ed. David A. Fiensy and James R. Strange, vol. 2 of *Galilee in the Late Second Temple and Mishnaic Periods* (Minneapolis: Fortress, 2015), 9–21.

enough time for Antigonus to reach Strato's Tower—a coastal location that was probably next on the list for conquest. Antigonus pressed on and arrived for his interview. But the guards had seen him in full armor and set upon him in a dark passage of a wing known colloquially as "Strato's Tower." Thus, Antigonus died by his brother's paranoia, and the prediction of Judas the Essene was declared to have come true (*Ant.* 13.307–313).[71]

Aristobulus was struck with grief at his brother's demise. His condition rapidly worsened with severe abdominal pain, widely deciphered as divine retribution for his brother's murder. Just days later, Aristobulus himself was dead (*Ant.* 13.314–317). He had been in power for just ten months. In a document written a handful of years later (4Q175), the Essenes interpreted the deaths of Aristobulus and Antigonus as divine confirmation that they and their father, John, were under divine curse:

> [The cursed man's] sons will arise, both of them, to become instruments of violence. They [John and his sons] will rebuild this city, set up a wall for it with towers to make a fortress of wrongdoing, a great evil in Israel, and an atrocity in Ephraim and Judah. They will make a blasphemy in the land, a great disgrace among the sons of Jacob, and shed blood like water upon the ramparts of Daughter Zion, within the perimeter of Jerusalem. (4Q175, 24–30)[72]

The geographer, Strabo, described Aristobulus with the Greek word *epieikēs* (*Ant.* 13.319)—a word with meanings such as "fair," "competent," and "proper."[73] This was an outsider's perspective, highlighting the young man's Hellenistic upbringing and adroitness in military matters. In most Jewish eyes, he died in a spasm of divine retribution. His personal insecurities towards his family got the better of him, and both he and they suffered as a result.

3.7.9 THE EARLY REIGN OF ALEXANDER JANNAEUS

Salome Alexandra suddenly found herself widowed and holding the future of the Hasmonean dynasty in her hands. The actions she then took reveal that she

---

71. It is also possible that the colloquial name of "Strato's Tower" was given to this passageway after Antigonus's murder, in light of Judas's prediction.

72. The identity of the cursed man and his two sons has been debated, but by far the best candidates are John and his sons, Aristobulus and Antigonus. See Eshel, *The Dead Sea Scrolls and the Hasmonean State*, 63–89. Note also the reference to "Ephraim and Judah," which is suggestive of the recent annexation of Samaria to Judea. We cannot rule out the possibility, though, that the Essenes were referencing Aristobulus and John's youngest (anonymous) son, rather than Antigonus. See 3.7.9 below.

73. Josephus quotes Strabo, who was relaying the opinion of the Greek writer Timagenes.

possessed conservative convictions. After all, she came from a fundamentalist Pharisee family, and her brother, Simeon ben-Shetach, might have influenced her to some extent. Her first autonomous act was to release Aristobulus's three surviving brothers from prison and submit to the law of levirate marriage. This saw her marry the eldest surviving brother, twenty-four-year-old Alexander, who was thirteen years her junior.[74] Alexander's Hebrew name was Jonathan, or Yannai in colloquial Aramaic, Hellenized to "Jannaeus." To the Hellenistic world he became King Alexander, while within Judea he was King Jonathan.

The marriage might have raised some eyebrows because a priest was restricted by Torah to marrying a virgin (Lev 21:13–15).[75] The Pharisees had, after all, disparaged the legitimacy of John Hyrcanus over the questionable status of his mother. However, two factors contributed to the issue being overlooked in the case of Salome Alexandra. First, Aristobulus had died without an heir, and so the need to continue the high priestly succession was paramount. His brother, Alexander Jannaeus, could have fulfilled this by simply marrying another woman. But, secondly, Salome Alexandra was the Pharisees' foot in the door to the corridors of power. She was, after all, from a prominent Pharisee family and would be remembered as their great benefactor. Thus, Hasmonean and Pharisaic goals converged at this point, and the marriage went ahead.

Alexander Jannaeus's succession to power was not without dispute, though. While his next brother, Absalom, is said to have enjoyed a life free of political enterprise, the same cannot be said for his youngest brother, whose name has not been preserved. This youngest brother's challenge might have come at some point later in Alexander's reign (see this section below), but whatever the details, we do know that Alexander responded in kind: he had his youngest brother executed (*Ant.* 13.323).

This maneuver reveals something of the drive and ruthlessness that would characterize Alexander's reign. His two older brothers had outshone him and then imprisoned him. Incarceration had claimed the life of his mother, so he appears to have exited his prison cell determined to cut down any threat to his

---

74. Salome Alexandra's age is determined by details relating to her own death and that of Alexander (*Ant.* 13.404, 430).

75. Atkinson (*Queen Salome*, 62–64; cf. 96–102) argues on this basis that Salome Alexandra could never have been married to Aristobulus. Instead, he argues that Aristobulus had been married to one "Salina Alexandra," whom Atkinson differentiates from Salome Alexandra. However, there is an identification implied between Aristobulus's wife, "Salina . . . called by the Greeks, 'Alexandra,'" (*Ant.* 13.320), and the "Alexandra" who is named without further introduction as the wife of Alexander Jannaeus (*Ant.* 13.405). Furthermore, the Semitic name Shelomzion is abbreviated and transcribed into Greek in various ways (e.g., Salina, Salome). This underscores the fact that the wife of Aristobulus and the wife of Alexander Jannaeus were one and the same woman.

life and power. He was a survivor bent on asserting his authority and leaving his mark.

He began his reign by reoccupying Joppa in early 103 BC. He then went for the regional Seleucid capital at Ptolemais-Acco. That he even attempted this was a sign of how impotent the Seleucid claimants, Hooknose and Cyzicenus, had become. As Josephus puts it, the two kings "endured like athletes who, energy depleted, yet too embarrassed to yield, carried on the contest through lull and pause" (*Ant.* 13.327). Capturing Ptolemais-Acco would open all of Galilee and the coastal plain to Jewish control.

Like all gentile residents of the region, the people of Ptolemais-Acco did not desire Jewish suzerainty or the Judaizing blade that came with it. They sent various maydays, including to Ptolemy IX Chickpea. This cunning Ptolemy had burnt his bridges with his mother, Cleopatra III, and made himself king of Cyprus. He relished the opportunity to become the Ptolemy who took back Coele Syria, so he initiated a full-scale invasion of the Levant. His arrival made Alexander think twice. Rather than confront Ptolemy Chickpea, he entered negotiations with him and successfully bargained for control of Strato's Tower and Dor to the south. But Alexander knew he could not trust Ptolemy Chickpea, whose purpose was clearly domination of the whole region. So, while he was subduing Strato's Tower, he also sent envoys to the rogue's mother, Cleopatra III, in Alexandria. She secretly agreed to launch a counter-invasion with the purpose of defeating her recalcitrant son once and for all. Thus, Alexander was drawn into an internecine Ptolemaic war (*Ant.* 13.328–36).

When Ptolemy Chickpea discovered that Alexander was double dealing, he was infuriated and went on the rampage. He invaded Galilee, ransacked Jewish towns, and pursued Alexander all the way to the Jordan Valley. Here Ptolemy Chickpea inflicted a serious defeat on him.[76] Alexander was lucky to limp back to Jerusalem. As Ptolemy Chickpea pursued him south, he terrorized villages along the way (*Ant.* 13.336–347). The Essenes interpreted Ptolemy Chickpea's warpath as a sign of the impending "last of days," recapitulating Isaiah 10:24–34, which was originally about Sennacherib's invasion of Judah in 701 BC (4QpIsa^a [4Q161]).[77]

Cleopatra III's counter-invasion began when her other son, Ptolemy X

---

76. Josephus gives the place of the defeat as Asophon (*Ant.* 13.338), which should be equated with Zaphon, midway between Lake Galilee and the Dead Sea. See Eshel, *The Dead Sea Scrolls and the Hasmonean State*, 93, 95.

77. The Pesher of Isaiah (4Q161) provides insight into how the Essenes read their own times as part of an eschatological countdown to the "last of days." See Eshel, *The Dead Sea Scrolls and the Hasmonean State*, 91–100.

Alexander, landed at Ptolemais-Acco with a force that included Jewish soldiers from Egypt under the command of Hilkiah, son of Onias IV. They raced in pursuit of Ptolemy Chickpea, who was thus forced to give up any notion of besieging the city. When he learned that his mother had also left Egypt and arrived at Ptolemais-Acco, he decided to take a run at Egypt instead, in the hope that the country would have been left vulnerable by the absence of so many troops (*Ant.* 13.347–351).[78]

Hilkiah's arrival in the region must have caused a sensation, especially among Jews averse to Hasmonean leadership. Alexander Jannaeus had been duplicitous, suffered an amateurish defeat that caused prolific loss of life, invited atrocities into rural Judea, and brought Jerusalem to the brink of disaster again, all within the first year of his reign. Hilkiah, a Zadokite descendant, however, had heroically come to the holy city's aid and warded off its assailant. Alexander's reign had barely started and there must surely have been many crying for his abdication and replacement. Even his Sadducee supporters, the self-proclaimed heirs of the Zadokite legacy, must have been in a quandary. As it turned out, they were to be disappointed. Hilkiah continued with Ptolemy X in pursuit of Ptolemy Chickpea and checked his advances into Egypt, but in the process he lost his life (*Ant.* 13.351). Opposition to Alexander Jannaeus probably reached a new pique. It might have been at this time that his youngest brother attempted to wrest the kingdom from him, but even so, it was to no avail (see this section above).

Alexander only just clung to power, and it might have slipped away from him completely at this moment. Cleopatra III conquered Ptolemais-Acco,[79] and the entire region now lay at her feet. She brought an army under the command of Ananias (Hilkiah's brother) across to Scythopolis, thus effecting Ptolemaic control over the trunk road through the Jezreel Valley. This curtailed Alexander's reach into Galilee and Gaulanitis and made him vulnerable to Cleopatra sweeping south and taking the Jewish state for herself. Realizing this, Alexander hurried to beseech her at Scythopolis. Here he came face to face with Ananias, the surviving son of Onias IV and one of his greatest living rivals. While most of Cleopatra's tacticians encouraged her to press ahead into Judea, her hand was staid by none other than Ananias himself. He argued that attacking Judea risked offending the entire Jewish community in Egypt, including within Alexandria itself, where Jews made up at least a quarter of the population. We can only speculate as to Ananias's personal motivation for counselling

---

78. On the timing of events, see Hölbl, *A History of the Ptolemaic Empire*, 209.

79. An eyewitness account of the city's conquest appears on the funerary statue of Petimuthes, one of Cleopatra III's generals. See Hölbl, *A History of the Ptolemaic Empire*, 209.

such moderation, since, as a Zadokite, he would almost certainly have emerged as a powerbroker if Alexander were deposed. But it was wise counsel since Judea also enjoyed *amicitia* with the Roman Republic. Rome had overcome its earlier difficulties. Its celebrated consul, Gaius Marius, had recently defeated the wolfish King Jugurtha in Numidia, demonstrating how Rome could intervene in localized conflicts. Cleopatra was thus dissuaded from proceeding and instead agreed to an alliance with Alexander (*Ant.* 13.352–355). It did not amount to much in the end, for Cleopatra returned to Egypt with Ptolemy X, only to be murdered by him the following year (101 BC).[80]

Alexander thus survived a tumultuous start to his reign and surprisingly found himself in possession of the northern coastal plain between Joppa and Mount Carmel. The anchor that appears on some of his coins probably celebrates these coastal acquisitions.[81] Since the sea was also a biblical image symbolizing chaos and political turmoil (cf. Gen 1:2; Ps 46:2; Isa 5:30; Dan 7:2–3), the anchor also represented Alexander's claim to have achieved stability and expressed the aspiration that the Jewish king might rule from sea to sea (cf. Ps 72:8). In this regard, the acquisition of this stretch of the *Via Maris* (the "Way of the Sea") had considerable biblical portent:

> Yet there is no more gloom for the perturbed.
> That first time,
> he denigrated the land of Zebulun and the land of Naphtali.
> But this latest time,
> he has honored the Way of the Sea, Transjordan, and Galilee of
>   the gentiles.
> The people walking in darkness have seen a great light;
> on those residing in the land of deathly shadow, a light has shone.
> "You have enlarged the nation.
> Have you not also heightened the celebration?
> They celebrate before you like the celebration of the harvest,
> as they rejoice when dividing plunder."
> ... For a child was born to us;
> a son was given to us.
> The government was on his shoulders,
>   and he was named, "Miracle, Counsellor, Divine Warrior, Perpetual
>   Father, Prince of Peace."

---

80. Hölbl, *A History of the Ptolemaic Empire*, 210.
81. Regev, "The Hellenization of the Hasmoneans Revisited," 186.

> Of the increase of sovereignty and peace,
> there will be no end,
> on the throne of David and over his kingdom,
> to establish it and stabilize it
> with justice and righteousness,
> now and forever.
> The zeal of Yahweh of Ranks will achieve this.
> (Isa 9:1–3a, 6–7[8:23–9:2a; 9:6–7 MT])

This prophecy from Isaiah identified the conqueror of the *Via Maris*, Transjordan, and Galilee (the lands of Zebulun and Naphtali) as the one who had the right to rule David's ancient kingdom. Jewish rule over Perea in Transjordan had been internationally recognized since the time of Alexander's father (John Hyrcanus I). Aristobulus's defeat of the Itureans raised the prospect of the conquest of Galilee. With Alexander's sudden acquisition of the *Via Maris* north of Joppa, the stars were beginning to align as per the Isaianic prophecy, allowing Alexander to position himself as the fulfiller of divine prophecy. And so, Alexander set about trying to make that a reality.

Up to this point, Lower Galilee "faced" west towards Ptolemais-Acco, as the coastal city's hinterland, while Upper Galilee was the territorial interior of Tyre.[82] Cleopatra III's conquest of Ptolemais-Acco had given the Ptolemies a bridgehead in Coele Syria, but it also detached its hinterland (Lower Galilee) from the city's authority, making the region ripe for Alexander's picking. He took back control of Scythopolis in the Jezreel Valley and conquered the *polis* of Gadara, southeast of Lake Galilee.[83] This effectively gave him control of Lower Galilee to the west of the lake and Gaulanitis and Batanea to its east. Josephus never mentions whether Alexander Judaized the population, but it is a safe assumption. The idyllic *polis* of Philoteria on the southwestern shore of Lake Galilee witnessed an abrupt end to its Greek culture at this time—evidence of an exodus of gentiles.[84] Alexander then pushed south and consolidated control over Perea (*Ant.* 13.356, 374). These campaigns were costly,

---

82. Cf. Berlin and Herbert, "The Achaemenid–Ptolemaic Transition," 145–46, 153.

83. Gadara had been the birthplace of the Greek satirist, Menippus (third century BC), whose techniques David Valeta argues were influential over the composition of the Dan 1–6. See *Lions and Ovens and Visions: A Satirical Reading of Daniel 1–6* (Sheffield: Sheffield Phoenix Press, 2008). The philosophers Philodemus and Meleager were also born at Gadara and might even have been directly impacted by Alexander Jannaeus's conquest of the city in ca. 100 BC.

84. Miriam Pines et al., "Heads or Snails? A Rustic Feast at Hellenistic Philoteria (Tel Bet Yeraḥ, Israel), circa 150 BCE," *JEMAHS* 8.1 (2020): 79–93, https://doi.org/10.5325/jeasmedarcherstu.8.1.0079.

but they yielded control over Galilee and a long stretch of the lucrative King's Highway in Transjordan.

Alexander could now claim to have fulfilled Isaiah's prophecy (Isa 9:1–7[8:23–9:6 MT]), giving him the legitimacy to rule David's ancient kingdom. Accordingly, he minted coins carrying his royal title and the emblem of a star surrounded by a royal diadem, alluding to the blessing of Balaam that carried messianic expectation: "A star has journeyed from Jacob, a scepter has risen out of Israel" (Num 24:17).[85] These developments must have presented a serious challenge to all who held the classic expectation of a Davidic messiah, for Alexander had ostensibly earned all the Davidic plaudits by his conquests. But the development of apocalyptic messianism meant that those who continued subscribing to the classic beliefs could not identify Alexander as the longed-for messiah, for not only was he not of David's line, but he had also arguably failed to bring about the eschatological judgment day, which would prompt the resurrection of the dead and establish the reign of God on earth. Alexander's successes, therefore, challenged the immediacy of messianic expectation but did not deter those who framed their expectation with apocalyptic eschatology.

Alexander built several fortresses throughout the Jordan Valley as a military spine for his kingdom. Among them were Alexandrium (named after himself), guarding the approach to Samaria; Hyrcania (named after his father), guarding the approach to Jerusalem; and Machaerus (from Gk. *machaira*, meaning "blade"), overlooking the Dead Sea in Perea.[86] To mirror Machaerus on the Judean side of the Dead Sea, he improved the fortifications at Masada. He also completely renovated the site of his father's palace outside Jericho, building a fortress atop a huge artificial mound and a palatial complex that included sumptuous living quarters, twin pools, bathhouses, and pleasure gardens.

The expansion of Alexander's kingdom ruffled the feathers of the Nabatean Arabs. The Nabateans occupied the fringes of habitable territory from Damascus in the north, down through eastern Transjordan, and around the southern edge of the Dead Sea into the Negev. Their capital lay at Petra, midway between the Dead Sea and the Gulf of Aqaba. They dominated trade between the Red Sea and the Mediterranean, exerting considerable influence over the port of Gaza and the regional entrepot at Damascus.[87] But Alexander Jannaeus's

---

85. Meshorer, *Persian Period through Hasmonaeans*, 60–61; Regev, "The Hellenization of the Hasmoneans Revisited," 187. This imagery was also pivotal in the rise of Simon bar-Koseba, who claimed to be the Jewish messiah and was hailed by his supporters as Simon bar-Kochba ("son of the Star").

86. Machaerus is the site where, over a century later, Herod Antipas imprisoned and beheaded John the Baptist.

87. See Berlin, "Between Large Forces," 24–25.

conquests in Transjordan diverted tolls and sales away from Nabatean coffers towards Jerusalem's. This caused political friction and forced the Nabateans to focus their economic efforts on Gaza, which lay outside their own territory.

The tension escalated when Alexander Jannaeus besieged and occupied Gaza in 99/8 BC (*Ant.* 13.357–364). In fact, he took control of the entire coastal plain, leaving only Ashkelon as an autonomous city of "holy asylum" for gentiles.[88] The capture of Gaza opened the floodgates of economic prosperity to the Jewish state but at the expense of the Nabateans.

At this point, Alexander Jannaeus controlled almost the entire covenantal territory of Israel, putting him alongside the famed ancient kings, David and Solomon. One could have argued that Alexander had fulfilled the promises of God to restore the nation, for they were now an independent state under the authority of a native king who exercised sovereignty over practically the entire promised land. But while most Jews held a special love for their fabled ancient kings, they did not necessarily hold Alexander in equal esteem. The Hasmoneans were not the Davidic dynasty, and therefore keen theological questions arose as to the nature of prophetic fulfilment. This was no problem for the Sadducees, who believed God had moved on from any promises issued in the foggy distant past of nine centuries before. What mattered was the here-and-now, and Alexander had just recovered Jewish sovereignty over the promised land. Israel as a kingdom of priests had become a reality (cf. Exod 19:6). But the Pharisees had mixed feelings, as they viewed Alexander taking on the proud airs of a liberal Hellenistic monarch rather than committing himself to observance of the Law and the tenets of their Oral Law. Alexander may have achieved important biblical milestones, but many felt he was blurring the distinctiveness ("holiness") of the Jewish nation.

The Nabateans responded a few years later. King Obodas, who succeeded Aretas II in 96 BC, harried Alexander's defenses in Transjordan and in ca. 94 BC inflicted a humiliating defeat upon him along the banks of the Yarmuk River near Gadara (*Ant.* 13.375; *J.W.* 1.90). Whether the Nabateans won back some control of the King's Highway is unknown, but Alexander was unable to fight back. Thanks to his hubris and lack of diplomacy, many Jewish sons lay dead along the Yarmuk, prompting fresh waves of opposition to him in Judea. The fundamentalist Pharisees became his most vocal adversaries, and they created a groundswell of opposition to him throughout the kingdom.

---

88. An abbreviation for "holy asylum" appears on Ashkelon's coins from 106/5 BC, perhaps indicating that Ashkelon had offered refuge to gentiles who refused to undergo Judaization. See Oren Tal, "Greek Coinages of Palestine," in Metcalf, *Oxford Handbook of Greek and Roman Coinage*, 267–68; Grainger, *The Wars of the Maccabees*, 105.

3.7.10 ALEXANDER JANNAEUS AND THE JEWISH CIVIL WAR

Opposition to Alexander Jannaeus reached a critical crescendo at the Festival of Sukkot in ca. 94 BC. According to Torah, Sukkot (and the other major festivals) required the presentation of food and drink offerings upon the altar of Yahweh (Lev 23:33-38). The only kind of drink offering stipulated in Torah was wine (Lev 23:13). But the Pharisees had developed a tradition that required the drawing of water from Jerusalem's Pool of Siloam to pour on the altar along with the wine. This was seen as a literal enactment of the poetic sentiments in Isaiah 12:1-6, which mentions the drawing of water from the wells of salvation in thanksgiving for Yahweh's saving acts. The tradition attests to the hyper-literal hermeneutic of the fundamentalist Pharisees. The priests who belonged to the Sadducee party saw it as entirely unnecessary. During this particular Sukkot, the people had gathered in the temple courts, bearing palm branches and citrons, as per the festivities. Alexander was presiding at the altar when he was handed a water bowl to offer water in accordance with the Pharisaic stipulation. But instead of complying, Alexander poured the bowl's contents contemptuously on the ground. Rankled by this supreme affront, the Pharisees and their sympathizers began pelting Alexander with their festive citrons and flinging the charge that had been leveled at his father, namely that he was descended from a prisoner of war and therefore unfit for priestly service (*Ant.* 13.372; m. Sukkah 4:9). Josephus gives the impression that a massacre of 6,000 people ensued (*Ant.* 13.373). This is hardly likely, though we cannot completely discount the possibility that Alexander enacted some kind of lethal reprisal.

From this point on, Alexander was actively hostile towards the Pharisees and anyone who opposed him.[89] He subsequently erected a wooden palisade around the sanctuary, creating a dedicated court of priests, which excluded Jewish laity from its confines and screened off all cultic proceedings. This only distanced Alexander from them and embittered the population towards the Sadducees. Inadvertently, then, Alexander helped to promote the popularity of the fundamentalist Pharisees, whose homespun piety could be kept by any commoner in day-to-day life.

Thereafter, he began a reign of terror that sought to obliterate all his opponents. It is likely that this was the occasion for the departure of most Essenes from Jerusalem. Some fled to Egypt,[90] but as the archaeological record shows,

---

89. Efron (*Studies on the Hasmonean Period*, 168) claims that this tension was projected back onto this time from a later period. However, the severity of the hostilities that erupted immediately afterwards speaks against this.

90. Philo's *Contemplative Life* studied the enigmatic "Therapeutae," whom he knew from the

many fled to Qumran in the Judean desert and established a monastic community.[91] To the Essenes, Alexander's reign of terror must have felt like the purge of Alcimus in 162 BC (see 3.5.4 above). But their pacifist ethic prevented them fighting back. They dealt with his hostility through withdrawal to the desert to await the eschatological intervention of God. We do not know whether any of the Essenes fell victim to the terror. Interestingly, one of the documents found at Qumran (4Q448) is a prayer specifically about "Jonathan the king" (i.e., Alexander Jannaeus). Its tenor appears salutary, but its expression is ambiguous at the critical point of reference, making it difficult to discern whether the prayer cries, "Awake, O Holy One, *for* Jonathan the king," or "Awake, O Holy One, *against* Jonathan the king" (4Q448 II, 1–2). If a positive view is taken, it might show that the Essenes had once warmed to Alexander, although it is also possible that, despite ending up among the cache of Essene texts, the document originated outside Essene circles.[92]

The Pharisees, however, were Alexander's prime target, and since their influence had leavened throughout the whole populace, much of the country turned against him. The persecution put Alexander's own brother-in-law, Simeon ben-Shetach, in the line of fire. Many leading Pharisees, such as Joshua ben-Perachiah,[93] fled to Alexandria, but Simeon braved the threat in Judea. A later tradition claims that his sister, Queen Salome Alexandra, helped him go into hiding (b. Sotah 47a; b. San. 107a). Her husband's tyranny must have put considerable strain on the marriage. This must surely have been exacerbated when Alexander began to act the part of an oriental despot by taking concubines, which was expressly taboo for any priest (Lev 21), and polluted the sanctuary. This had been one of the primary issues of the Manasseh Affair in 350 BC (see 1.7.3 above). But whereas Simon Thassi's civic authority had been subsumed within his priesthood, Alexander's priesthood was subsumed within his kingship, putting him over and above the sacral institution. In this, he made himself a true liberal Hellenistic monarch after the likeness of the Ptolemies and Seleucids, with only one difference: he never seems to have demanded worship as a god.

---

environs of Alexandria. It was paired with a now lost study of the Essenes, suggesting he had firsthand knowledge of them in the first century AD (cf. Philo, *Vita* 1).

91. Magness, *Archaeology of Qumran*, 68.

92. See Eshel, *The Dead Sea Scrolls and the Hasmonean State*, 101–15.

93. The Talmudic references to Joshua ben-Perachiah mention that he had a student known as Jesus the Nazarene, who accompanied him to Alexandria but whom he later castigated for being a lecher, an idolater, and for leading Israel astray. It is entirely possible that Joshua had a student named Jesus, but even so, later rabbinic traditions denouncing Jesus of Nazareth have been dissolved into those of the student of Joshua ben-Perachiah, resulting in a homogenized anachronism.

A protest against this subordination of the priesthood to kingship is evident in the Testaments of the Twelve Patriarchs. This pseudepigraphal work shows evidence of later Christian redaction, but its original core reaches back to the Hasmonean era. Within this composite work, the Testament of Judah has the eponymous patriarch make the following statement:

> So now, children, love Levi, so that you endure. Do not rise up against him, so that you are not annihilated. For the Lord gave the kingship to me, and the priesthood to him, but subordinated the kingship to the priesthood. To me he gave all that pertains to the earth, and to him all that pertains to the heavens. Just as the heaven surpasses the earth, so also the priesthood of God surpasses all that pertains to kingship on the earth, unless through sin it falls away from the Lord and is dominated by earthly kingship. (T. Jud. 21.1–4)

This statement seeks to dissuade violence against the priesthood on pain of divine retribution. However, it also demanded a clear demarcation between the sacral and the secular, which then absolved action taken against anyone, like Alexander Jannaeus, who eradicated the distinction. This was a novel development, for the priesthood had been subordinate to the royal office when Judah had been ruled by Davidic kings. The Chronicler, writing in the late fourth century BC, argued that the Davidic kings were the builders and patrons of the Jerusalem temple because they "sat on the throne of Yahweh" (1 Chr 29:23). But the rising power of the priesthood turned that on its head and erased the royal content of Zion theology. As far as classic theology went, Alexander's crime was that he was not a Davidic king. As far as more recent ideological development went, Alexander's crime was that he had chosen to act more as a king than a priest, privileging the secular over the sacred. For the Pharisees, Alexander's actions and attitudes disqualified him from the high priesthood and might even have alienated some of the Sadducees, who were, for the most part, priests. It would lead the rabbis of a later era to look back on this point of history as a time when Alexander was filled with heresy, when all the Jewish sages were killed, and when the world was desolated (b. Qidd. 66a).

The Jewish state was plunged into civil war. According to Josephus, the conflict lasted six years (ca. 93–87 BC) with a death toll upward of 50,000 people (*Ant.* 13.376; *J.W.* 1.91). Even if the figure is exaggerated, it testifies to the perceived magnitude of the strife. The recent war casualties meant Alexander had to employ mercenaries from Pisidia and Cilicia to replenish his army (*Ant.* 13.374), which only goaded the popular perception that he had essentially become a Greek king. There were moments of attempted negotiation, but these never achieved anything. According to Josephus, when Alexander asked his opponents what they expected him to do, they urged him to kill himself (*Ant.* 13.376; *J.W.* 1.92).

According to Talmudic sources, Alexander's brother-in-law, Simeon, was known to Parthian ("Persian") dignitaries as an intelligent man with whom they had dealings within Judea—a situation that would later cause friction between Simeon and Alexander (y. Naz. 54a; cf. b. Ber. 48a). If there is any kernel of historicity behind this, it might indicate that Simeon was involved in a kind of underground political resistance that went as far as contacting foreign regimes.[94] We do know that Alexander feared the intervention of the Nabateans (*Ant.* 13.382) and that his opponents reached out to the Seleucids. It might also indicate that his queen, Salome Alexandra, was clandestinely working against him.

The Seleucid civil war had reached a resolution of sorts in 97 BC when Antiochus VIII Hooknose was assassinated by one of his staffers (*Ant.* 13.365). The assassin appears to have been motivated to end the lethargic conflict as Rome's tentacles spread eastward. The Romans were taking a greater interest in the Seleucids' northern neighbors in Pontus, Armenia, and Cappadocia. They had also taken it upon themselves to deal with the pirates who had begun to operate out of Cilicia and who were disrupting trade to Italy (Livy, *Per.* 68).[95] This anti-piracy campaign resulted in the Roman annexation of western Cilicia, which made the Romans direct neighbors of the Seleucids. If the Seleucids could not impose order on the northeast corner of the Mediterranean, there was nothing preventing the Romans from sweeping the Seleucids aside and doing it themselves. Thus, in 97 BC Hooknose was murdered, and his half-brother, Antiochus IX Cyzicenus, became the sole Seleucid ruler.

It was a short-lived peace, however, as Seleucid politics descended even deeper into violent, fractious farce. Hooknose left behind five bumptious sons and at least one daughter by his Ptolemaic wife, Tryphaena. The eldest son, Seleucus VI, whom Appian described as "violent and tyrannical" (Appian, *S.W.* 69), killed his uncle, Cyzicenus in 95 BC, and took over Antioch. He was immediately challenged by Cyzicenus's teenaged son, "Pious" Antiochus X (Gk. *Eusebēs*), who drove him out of the capital.[96] Just a few months later, Seleucus VI met his fate at the hands of an angry mob in Mopsuestia (Appian, *S.W.* 69; *Ant.* 13.366–368). Twins, Antiochus XI and Philip, tried to avenge the death of their eldest brother,

---

94. The Talmud puts this in the context of previous state visits to Jerusalem made by the Persians (i.e., Parthians). This is possible, though Simeon's role in any such visits is questionable.

95. Grainger, *The Fall of the Seleukid Empire*, 167–68.

96. "Pious" Antiochus X was Cyzicenus's son by Cleopatra IV (daughter of Fatso Ptolemy VIII and Cleopatra III, and sister to Ptolemy IX Chickpea, Ptolemy X Alexander, Cleopatra Selene, and Tryphaena). On the derivation of his nickname, see 3.7.12.

but the first twin died in the attempt in 93 BC (*Ant.* 13.369).⁹⁷ Meanwhile, one of Hooknose's other sons, Demetrius III Eukairos ("Opportunist"), took charge of Damascus and fended off dogged Nabatean attempts to take control of the city.⁹⁸ The situation left Syria segmented into three bands: "Pious" Antiochus X controlling Antioch and the north, Philip controlling Berea and central Syria, and Demetrius controlling Damascus and the south.

It was to young Opportunist Demetrius III that the opponents of Alexander Jannaeus appealed (*Ant.* 13.376; *J.W.* 1.92). The invitation for a Seleucid to invade reveals how desperate the cry against Alexander had become. Young Demetrius was keen to bolster his territory. What's more, the Romans were at this time enveloped in a critical fight against their own allies in Italy, who were disgruntled over not being granted the rights of Roman citizenship (the Italic War).⁹⁹ They were, therefore, unable to fulfill their treaty obligations and come to the aid of the Jewish kingdom. So, when Alexander's detractors approached him, Opportunist Demetrius jumped at the opportunity.

The invasion came in 89 BC. Josephus's accounts of the war (*Ant.* 13.377–379; *J.W.* 1.92–95) are riddled with inaccuracies and implausibilities, but we know that Demetrius penetrated as far as Shechem at the foot of Mount Gerizim. He apparently had with him many citizens of the Jewish state, and one cannot help but wonder whether most of these were Samaritans hoping to break free of Jewish control. Alexander confronted Demetrius at Shechem, but Demetrius annihilated his mercenary ranks and put Alexander to flight. Alexander's opponents must have reveled in the result, as it now became clear that Alexander was on borrowed time.

But history is filled with curious twists, and another occurred at this juncture. The king of Pontus, Mithridates VI,¹⁰⁰ desired to dominate Asia Minor.

---

97. Robert E. G. Downey, *A History of Antioch in Syria from Seleucus to the Arab Conquest* (Princeton, NJ: Princeton University Press, 2015), 133–34.

98. Josephus's chronology, which sees Demetrius III installed in Damascus only some years later, is mistaken, as numismatic evidence proves. See Kenneth Atkinson, "Historical and Chronological Observations on Josephus's Account of Seleucid History in *Antiquities* 13.365-371: Its Importance for Understanding the Historical Development of the Hasmonean State," *Scripta Judaica Cracoviensia* 14 (2016): 10, https://doi.org/10.4467/20843925SJ.16.001.5660. There was a sudden year-long suspension in the minting of Demetrius's coins in Damascus in 93 BC, which indicates that he probably lost control of the city momentarily to the Nabateans (see Atkinson, "Historical and Chronological Observations," 10, 13, 17). Atkinson believes Alexander Jannaeus probably took Damascus at this time, but this is unrealistic since he was defeated by Obodas that year at the Yarmuk River. It is far more likely that Obodas himself occupied Damascus.

99. Sinnigen and Boak, *A History of Rome*, 185–87; Le Glay et al., *A History of Rome*, 130–32; Boatwright et al., *The Romans*, 171–75. The Italic War is sometimes called the Marsic or Social War.

100. He is not to be confused with any of the four other distinct persons bearing the name Mithridates in historical and geographical proximity at this time. All told, the five relevant Mithridatoi were: (1) Mithridates II of Parthia; (2) Mithridates III of Parthia (probably a son of Mithridates II);

With Rome focused on fighting the Italic War, he saw a chance to further his ambition. In late 89 BC he invaded Cappadocia to his south and deposed its Roman-backed king, Ariobarzanes. The maneuver brought Mithridates VI to the threshold of the Seleucid realm and its client kingdom, Commagene. Commagene's own king, Mithridates I Callinicus, was married to Laodice Thea, the sister of both Demetrius III and Philip.[101] She appealed to her brothers and also to her cousin, "Pious" Antiochus X, for military aid against the Pontian king. "Pious" Antiochus was the first on the scene but was killed for his efforts (*Ant.* 13.371). Demetrius III was preparing to issue the *coup de grâce* to Alexander Jannaeus when news of "Pious" Antiochus's fate reached him. His primary rival in Syria was now dead, and Antioch was vacant. If he persisted with his campaign against Alexander, he risked Mithridates VI of Pontus snatching Antioch for himself and dealing a potential lethal blow to the Seleucid kingdom. Alternatively, his brother Philip might take the city and become the dominant power in Syria. So, Demetrius immediately aborted his efforts against Alexander and bolted for Antioch. His haste was rewarded, as he was the first one there.[102]

Demetrius's inopportune departure from Judea was probably what led the Jews to remember him not as *Eukairos* ("Opportunist") but as *Akairos* ("Untimely").[103] Though Alexander's forces had been decimated, his opponents were left without any shield against him. Some who realized this capitulated quickly.[104] Seeing the pragmatic side of this, Alexander seems to have

---

(3) Mithridates Sinaces, a local Parthian governor; (4) Mithridates I Callinicus of Commagene; and (5) Mithridates VI of Pontus. The plethora of Mithridatoi has led to an understandable tangle of persons, events, and dates in both the ancient sources and modern history books. Josephus himself mistook Mithridates VI of Pontus for Mithridates II of Parthia, leading him to erroneously attribute this strange twist to "the Parthians" in 92 BC (*Ant.* 13.371) rather than "the Pontians" in 89 BC. This mistake led him to a rather acrobatic explanation for what compelled Demetrius to abandon his campaign against Alexander, and this mistake has rippled through the centuries. The mistakes are only undone by carefully isolating each personage, determining chronologies through numismatic evidence, and weighing up written sources in their original languages.

101. Josephus calls Laodice "queen of the Samenes" and says she was at war with the Parthians (*Ant.* 13.371). This has puzzled many and given rise to the erroneous suggestion that Laodice was queen of an otherwise enigmatic Arabian tribe. Whiston's translation of Josephus even posits the opaque translation, "queen of the Gileadites," on the surmise that Laodice was not a queen but the leading city in Gilead—a geopolitically preposterous interpretation. The term "Samenes" is derived simply from Sames, who reigned over Commagene in the previous generation and who was the father of Laodice's husband, Mithridates I Callinicus. In the same way, then, that one might refer to Syria as the land of the "Seleucids," so also one might refer to Commagene as the land of the "Samenes."

102. Cf. Atkinson, "Historical and Chronological Observations," 7–21.

103. Josephus gives this as Demetrius's epithet (*Ant.* 13.370, 376; *J.W.* 1.92), but its pejorative edge is probably a deliberate adulteration of a more congenial original.

104. This is the best explanation for what Josephus implausibly portrays as a defection of Jews to Alexander, motivated by pity for his change of fortune (*Ant.* 13.379). He also mistakenly placed this defection before Demetrius's departure, leading him to extrapolate the false conclusion that Demetrius

been conciliatory towards them. But there were many who continued to defy him, and he now hounded them with renewed ferocity.

With Demetrius gone and Alexander's forces depleted, Obodas of the Nabateans seized the chance to win back territory in Transjordan. Alexander understood the threat, so he ceded control over a portion of the King's Highway. This was enough to placate Obodas and allowed Alexander to zero in on his domestic enemies.

This he did by cornering the defiant rebels in a town whose name has unfortunately not been uniformly preserved.[105] Alexander successfully besieged the town and took approximately 800 rebels captive, along with their families (ca. 87 BC). He brought them to Jerusalem, determined to make an example of them. To that end, he passed a most barbaric sentence against them, which scarred the Jewish psyche: he had all 800 rebels crucified in full view of the residents of Jerusalem and had their wives' and children's throats cut as the crucified men watched on. While the bloody executions were carried out, Alexander wined, dined, and frolicked nearby with his concubines (*Ant.* 13.380–381; cf. 13.410; *J.W.* 1:97).

The calculated savagery of Alexander's revenge suggests that many of these 800 victims were fundamentalist Pharisees. At the moment of their execution, he deliberately acted out some of the very excesses that had drawn their criticism. His queen, who came from a notable Pharisee family, was notably absent from the macabre event. By hanging his victims on crosses, Alexander sent a clear message through the precedent of Deuteronomy 21:22–23: he, as high priest, had enacted judgment upon those deemed accursed by God himself. The public executions put an end to all resistance, as all remaining rebels fled the country (*J.W.* 1.98). The civil war thus came to an end.

Alexander broke the spirit of his country with this gruesome display of tyranny. He, the high priest, had abused his own compatriots. Crucifixion was an exceptional form of execution even among gentile states, being reserved for renegade slaves, traitors, and the vilest of criminals. The violation of life and limb inflicted excruciating pain and humiliation on its stripped victims, such that it was scarcely mentioned in polite Roman company (cf. Cicero, *Rab. Perd.* 5.16). The sheer scale and ferocity of Alexander's mass crucifixions is, therefore, indicative of how he perceived both himself and his enemies. His shocking actions saw him branded as a "Thracian" (Gk. *Thrakidēs*)—the

---

left because he was discouraged by Alexander's new support. But Josephus was unaware that Antiochus X's death was the real spark for Demetrius's departure.

105. Josephus calls it both Bethomme and Bemeselis (*Ant.* 13.380; *J.W.* 1.96). Its location is unknown.

epitome of wanton, uncivilized cruelty, worse even than the worst gentile rulers who savagely lorded it over their own subjects with godlike impunity.[106]

Alexander's cruelty induced an outpouring of public sympathy for the Pharisees, most of whom were now abroad in Alexandria. He recognized that his heavy hand now demanded a rapprochement of sorts, particularly with members of the Jewish Senate. His most consequential ally became his queen, Salome Alexandra, with her familial Pharisee connections and widespread public support (*Ant.* 13.407). She brought her brother, Simeon, out of hiding and brokered a tense but civil accord between him and Alexander (cf. y. Naz. 54a; cf. b .Ber. 48a).[107] Simeon was restored to the Jewish Senate, a position he then used to facilitate the return of other Pharisees from Alexandria, such as Joshua ben-Perachiah (b. Sotah 47a). In this way, the Pharisees began to regain some of the political standing they had lost. Nonetheless, Alexander had lost the loyalty of the country. Although no one arose to challenge him directly, popular resentment against the Hasmonean dynasty simmered broadly.

3.7.11 THEOLOGICAL RESPONSES TO ALEXANDER JANNAEUS

Alexander Jannaeus was squarely in the crosshairs of the authors of the Testaments of the Twelves Patriarchs:

> For those who reign will be like sea monsters,
> swallowing men like fish.
> Free daughters and sons they will enslave.
> Homes, fields, flocks, and funds they will seize,
> and the flesh of many they will unjustly give to the ravens and ibises.
> They will excel in evil, priding themselves on ambition.
>   (T. Jud. 21:7–8)

> You will raid the offerings of the Lord, steal from his portions, and take the choice portions from what is sacrificed to the Lord, while derisively eating with whores, and teaching the commands of the Lord in arrogance. You will violate married women, you will defile the virgins of Jerusalem, and with whores and adulteresses you will collude. You will take the daughters of gentiles as wives, purifying them but with illegal purification. Your intercourse with them will rival Sodom and Gomorrah for its irreverence. You will grow

---

106. Cf. Cicero's use of "Thracian" as a stereotype for wanton murder (*On the Consular Provinces* 4.9).
107. The Talmudic sources focus on the issue of pronouncing a grace after a meal, but underlying the halakhic discussion is Simeon's re-emergence into public life.

puffed up over your priesthood, rising up against men. Not only that—growing puffed up against the commands of God, you will mock all that is holy, while laughing in contempt. (T. Levi 14:5–8)[108]

The Essenes' condemnation of John Hyrcanus and his sons now included Alexander, recognizing him as one who would "shed blood like water upon the ramparts of Daughter Zion, within the perimeter of Jerusalem" (4Q175, 24–30). In the Pesher of Nahum (4Q169), composed in the mid-first century BC, Alexander and his foe, Demetrius III, are both depicted as lions in what was seen as a recapitulation of Nahum's prophecy:

"Wherever the lion goes to enter,
there the lion's cub goes without fear." [Nah 2:11b]

Its interpretation: this is about Demetrius [III], the Greek king, who sought to enter Jerusalem on the bidding of those who seek easy answers [i.e., the Pharisees]. [But Jerusalem was not put into] the hand of the Greek kings, from Antiochus until the rise of the rulers of the Kittim [the Romans]. But afterwards, it will be trampled . . .

"The lion preys sufficiently for its cubs,
and it strangles prey for its lionesses." [Nah 2:12a]

Its interpretation: this is about the Lion of Rage [Alexander Jannaeus], who attacked his own nobles and the men of his own counsel . . .

["Then he fills his] lair [with prey],
and his den with game." [Nah 2:12b]

Its interpretation: this is about the Lion of Rage [who took] vengeance on those who seek easy answers, when he would hang men alive, [as was done] in Israel in former days, for this applies to anyone hung alive on a tree. (4QpNah [4Q169], frags. 3–4, col. I, 1–8; cf. 4QpHos[b] [4Q167], frag. 2, 2–4)

While the Essenes reserved some sympathy for the plight of the crucified Pharisees, their fate was also seen as a consequence of them "seeking easy

---

108. All the second person pronouns here are plural, giving the pronouncements a generic, proverbial feel. However, given the date of the original compositions, allusions to Alexander Jannaeus must have guided the author(s).

answers"—a pejorative term the Essenes used for all fundamentalists, but especially the Pharisees.[109]

In reaction against Alexander, the Essenes developed a theology of two eschatological messiahs—one "from Aaron" and one "from Israel"—who would bring an end to the current age of wickedness (CD 20:1; cf. 1:7; 12:23–13:1; 14:19; 19:10–11).[110] The Aaronic messiah was a priestly figure, while the messiah "from Israel" was a Davidic figure. In the Pesher of Isaiah (4QpIsa [4Q161]), the Essenes expressed the expectation that the Davidic "Sprig" would arise in the last of days to receive a glorious throne (4QpIsa [4Q161], frag. 8, col. X, 17–19). Whether they thought he would be an actual Davidic descendant or a non-Davidide who received royal prerogatives cannot be definitively determined. In any case, this theology expressed the Essenes' conviction that priestly and civic leadership should never be combined, for it would stain the cult. Alexander had subsumed the priesthood into the kingship—an unacceptable situation to the Essenes, who were concerned about preserving the holiness of Israel through proper priestly function.[111]

Both the Essenes and Pharisees approached their desire for an end to the Hasmonean dynasty in a similar way: they each observed their sectarian traditions, which they saw as complements to Torah observance. The Essenes developed their monastic traditions, seen chiefly in their Manual of Discipline (1QS), while the Pharisees developed their Oral Law. Both sects viewed their efforts as wholly in keeping with the dictates of the deity, "just as he commanded via Moses and via all his servants the prophets" (1QS 1:2–3). It was all part of a theology that believed covenantal obedience would speed the dawn of the eschatological age and the advent of a new and divinely ordained "king of the Jews." It was the same impetus that led John the Baptist and Jesus a century later to urge their fellow Jews to repent, and for their covenantal righteousness to exceed that of the Pharisees and teachers of the Law, so that they might see the arrival of the kingdom of heaven (Matt 3:1–2; 4:17; 5:20).

Some of Alexander's Sadducee supporters who did not necessarily believe in eschatological deliverance were probably alienated by his savagery also. One example of this pertains to a certain Lysimachus, son of Ptolemy, a resident of

---

109. Before it became a standard pejorative for the Pharisees, the Essenes had used the same basic term to describe the fundamentalist Maccabees (see 3.5.8).

110. Although the Damascus Document has an origin in the mid-second century BC, when the Essenes began to crystallize as a distinct sect in exile from Judea, the importance of the work for Essene identity and theology meant it was redacted in subsequent decades, especially as the Essenes adapted to new situations.

111. John J. Collins, *The Scepter and the Star: Messianism in Light of the Dead Sea Scrolls*, 2nd Ed. (Grand Rapids: Eerdmans, 2010), 79–109.

Jerusalem (perhaps a priest), who translated the book of Esther from Hebrew into Greek. The book of Esther had originally been composed in Hebrew during the late Persian or early Hellenistic era and told of the origins of the Festival of Purim. Lysimachus's version was a dramatic retelling of the story in Greek with additions to the original Hebrew plot, which made the role of God more overt. This Greek version was brought to Egypt in 76 BC by two Jewish priests, Dositheus and his son, Ptolemy (seemingly unrelated to the translator, Lysimachus). This fact was appended as a colophon to Lysimachus's Greek version and preserved in what has come to be known as the Greek Additions to Esther.[112] The book itself tells the story of Esther, a Jewish queen who, with the help of her kinsman, Mordecai, manages to influence her wanton husband, the Persian King Ahasuerus, to put an end to the potential slaughter of the Jewish people. The story finishes with a surprising and decidedly non-eschatological reversal of fortunes, as the Jews take vengeance upon their would-be attackers, resulting in the Festival of Purim as an annual commemoration.

The parallels between the book of Esther and the reign of Alexander are stark: Queen Salome Alexandra resembles Queen Esther in her surreptitious activities to stem the slaughter of her people; Salome Alexandra's brother, Simeon, resembles Esther's kinsman, Mordecai, in rising to prominence and becoming a lynchpin in resisting the attacks upon the Jewish people; and the gentile king, Ahasuerus, resembles the practically gentile Alexander in being a womanizer and winebibber who wielded wide-ranging power. The timing of the translation and the way its story resonates with the people and events of this time suggest that Esther was being read to satirize Alexander and promote resistance to the excesses of Hasmonean power. Because the book of Esther was composed before the Hasmonean era, the parallels are neither exact nor exhaustive. For example, the arch-villain of the book, Haman the Agagite, does not have any historical parallel of whom we know. However, even the inexactitudes provide fuel for resistance. Ahasuerus is a purely royal figure, unassociated with the priesthood, which again resonates with the desire of many Jews that the Hasmoneans relinquish sacral authority and confine themselves to civic rule. Finally, the reversal of fortunes at the end of the book gave readers the chance to imagine a different outcome to the slaughter that Alexander inflicted and celebrate such an imagined outcome during Purim. The festival coincided with the Hasmonean "Day of Nicanor," which commemorated Judas Maccabeus's defeat of the Seleucid general in 160 BC (see 3.5.9 above).

---

112. The dating is derived from the reference to the "fourth year of the reign of Ptolemy and Cleopatra," who are to be identified as Ptolemy XII and Cleopatra V. It is less likely that the royal couple mentioned are Ptolemy IX Chickpea and Cleopatra Selene (or even Cleopatra III).

By promoting the observance of Purim, Dositheus the priest may have been trying to crowd out the observance of the Day of Nicanor and thus undermine the regalia of Hasmonean power. If so, then the colophon attests to disquiet against Alexander even among the priestly ranks.

3.7.12 THE LATTER REIGN OF ALEXANDER JANNAEUS

The unending game of snakes and ladders among claimants to the Seleucid throne had repercussions for the Jewish state. Antioch declared itself a neutral zone belonging to no claimant, which saw the battle to control Syria focus on Damascus instead. Demetrius III attempted to eliminate his brother, Philip,[113] who appealed to the Parthians for help. Eager to step into Syria itself, the Parthians obliged, and in 87 BC they captured and exiled Demetrius to Parthia, where he died soon after (*Ant.* 13.384–386). But their intervention made Philip a de facto client king of their swelling empire. Philip's youngest brother, Antiochus XII Dionysus, gained control of Damascus,[114] but in 86 BC he went campaigning against the Nabateans, whom he perceived as his greatest threat. He died attempting to outflank them in the Negev (*J.W.* 1.99–102; *Ant.* 13.387–92).[115] Damascus was then occupied by Cleopatra Selene, the longsuffering daughter of Fatso Ptolemy VIII and Cleopatra III.[116] She had been wife to five separate monarchs and was mother to two of "Pious" Antiochus X's sons.[117] She declared the eldest son, nine-year-old Antiochus XIII, king, and ruled in his name while he was ensconced in Roman Asia (he was later given the nickname "Asiaticus").

At this point, an Iturean strongman named Ptolemy Menneus took

---

113. *Pace* Grainger (*The Fall of the Seleukid Empire*, 177–79), who overlooks the significance of Antioch's neutrality for Demetrius's position.

114. *Pace* Grainger (*The Fall of the Seleukid Empire*, 182, 224 [n. 7]), who assumes the brothers were working in concert, despite the contradiction this entails for the events that followed.

115. Josephus's account of Dionysus's campaign involves a curious episode in which Alexander Jannaeus attempted to halt his advances in the coastal plain. The historicity of the incident is rightly questioned. See Alexander Fantalkin and Oren Tal, "The 'Yannai Line' (BJ I, 99–100; AJ XIII, 390–91): Reality or Fiction?," *PEQ* 135.2 (2003): 108–23.

116. Cleopatra Selene's control of Damascus is known by the coins issued there in her name and her son's, but the date of these coins is unclear. Her control must have been brief. Politically, 86 BC is the most likely moment in which it occurred.

117. Cleopatra Selene was married to and divorced by two of her own brothers (Ptolemy IX Chickpea and Ptolemy X Alexander), before her mother married her off to Antiochus VIII Hooknose. When Hooknose was assassinated, his half-brother, Cyzicenus, married her. After Cyzicenus was killed by Seleucus VI (son of Hooknose), Cyzicenus's own son, "Pious" Antiochus X, married her. A son marrying his father's wife was deemed impious even in Hellenistic society (cf. 1 Cor 5:1), with Appian theorizing that the Syrians gave Antiochus X the nickname "Pious" in sarcasm (Appian, *S.W.* 69).

advantage of the cannibalization of the Seleucid dynasty. He had carved out a new state for himself, centered on the city of Chalcis in the Lebanese Bekaa Valley. It extended from Heliopolis (Baalbek) in the north to the Huleh Valley of Galilee in the south. He now made a successful grab for Damascus, too, forcing Cleopatra Selene to retreat to Ptolemais-Acco. He then incorporated the Transjordanian regions of Gaulanitis and Batanea into his nascent realm—lands Alexander had ceded to the Nabateans.

This new splash of political paint caught the attention of Alexander. Before the paint dried, he mobilized forces to regain the territories he had lost and even challenged Ptolemy Menneus for sovereignty over Damascus. After three years of warfare (ca. 85–83 BC), he had wrested Upper Galilee and most of Transjordan off Ptolemy Menneus, allowing for the promotion of Jewish settlement in these areas once again (*Ant.* 13.393–394). He enforced a policy of Judaization, which led to the destruction of Pella for its refusal to comply (*Ant.* 13.397). For Galilee in particular, this completed a critical political and cultural reorientation, as it pivoted away from the Hellenistic centers of Tyre and Ptolemais-Acco to its west, towards Jerusalem in the south.[118] Within a few decades, "Galilee of the Nations" would become majority Jewish.[119] Alexander's victories thus brought almost the entire covenantal land of Israel under his control. The only territories eluding him were Ptolemais-Acco and Ashkelon.

Alexander was now in prime position to win sovereignty over Damascus, whose citizens did not welcome the prospect of the circumcision blade, which came with Jewish sovereignty. But Alexander had to redeploy his troops when the Nabatean king, Aretas III, invaded the Jewish kingdom from the south (83 BC). Aretas gained control of Gaza and Ashkelon and then defeated Alexander near Adida on the *Via Maris*, east of Joppa (*Ant.* 13.392). Alexander now used Damascus as a bargaining chip to propose a three-way peace deal: Aretas III would evacuate the coastal plain, giving the Jewish kingdom sovereignty over its entirety; Alexander would cede Batanea to Aretas III; and Damascus would accept Nabatean sovereignty. All three parties agreed. By subsequently minting coins at Damascus with a Greek inscription styling himself as "King Aretas Philhellene," Aretas allayed the cultural fears of the Damascenes.[120]

---

118. Lower Galilee had already begun this pivot after Cleopatra III conquered Ptolemais-Acco (102 BC).

119. Morten Hørning Jensen, "The Political History in Galilee from the First Century BCE to the End of the Second Century CE," in *Life, Culture and Society*, vol. 1 of *Galilee in the Late Second Temple and Mishnaic Periods*, ed. David A. Fiensy and James R. Strange (Minneapolis: Fortress, 2014), 55–57.

120. Aretas began minting coins in Damascus in 83 BC. See Glen W. Bowersock, *Roman Arabia* (Cambridge, MA: Harvard University Press, 1994), 25–26.

482   THE HASMONEAN ERA (167–63 BC)

The Hasmonean Kingdom of Alexander Jannaeus.

In turn, Alexander minted coins in his twenty-fifth year (79/8 BC), which styled him as "King Alexander" in Aramaic—the dominant language of Syria and Galilee.[121] These coins also demonstrated his preference for the royal title over his priestly title.

---

121. Aramaic was widely spoken, including in Judea. However, official affairs were usually conducted in Hebrew or Greek, making the use of Aramaic on these coins unique. Cf. VanderKam, *From Joshua to Caiaphas*, 334.

It is likely that Antipater, Alexander's commander in Idumea, was pivotal in brokering the peace agreement. Antipater was the son of native Idumeans who had undergone Judaization under John Hyrcanus but continued to be liberal Hellenists. He was well connected (*Ant.* 14.10), with his wife, Cypros, being a relative of Aretas himself.[122] As a result of the agreement, hostilities with the Nabateans came to an end.

Alexander soon began to suffer the effects of his alcoholism (*Ant.* 13.398). In 76 BC he was besieging a fortified town called Ragaba, whose location is disputed,[123] when it became clear that he was dying. Queen Salome Alexandra hurried to him, and Alexander made her his successor—a testament to her standing in the kingdom. He advised her to offer positions of power to the fundamentalist Pharisees to stabilize the kingdom but also to prevent the potential desecration of his body as backlash for having crucified so many of them. He died at Ragaba, aged fifty-one, after a reign of twenty-seven years (*Ant.* 13.399–404; *J.W.* 1.107).[124]

3.7.13 QUEEN SALOME ALEXANDRA

Queen Salome Alexandra was a senior stateswoman of sixty-four years of age when she took over the governance of the Jewish kingdom in 76 BC. After Alexander's lavish funeral, she made two key political moves. The first was the appointment of John Hyrcanus II, her eldest son by Alexander, to the high priesthood (*Ant.* 13.408). John was in his mid-twenties at the time, so the new tradition that the high priest could be less than thirty years of age was further ingrained within the sacral institution. By retaining civic rule for herself, Salome Alexandra separated the priesthood from civic authority. This would not have placated those who were resolutely opposed to the Hasmonean priesthood were it not for her second political move: Joshua ben-Perachiah was made president (Heb. *nasi'*) of the Jewish Senate, and her brother, Simeon, became his vice president (cf. y. Ḥag. 2.2; y. Sanh. 6.6).[125] This appears to have

---

122. We do not know exactly when Antipater married Cypros, but they began having children within a few years of this peace agreement.

123. Ragaba is sometimes identified with Argob in Transjordan, in which case Alexander flagrantly broke his treaty with the Nabateans. It is possible, however, that he was not besieging the city but fortifying it. Alternatively, Ragaba might have been near the confluence of the Jabbok and Jordan Rivers (cf. *BAGRW* 69-C5).

124. Josephus undoubtedly used some license in recreating the instructions of the dying Alexander to Salome Alexandra. But the events that followed show that he was depicting reality dramatically rather than fabricating it entirely. Cf. VanderKam, *From Joshua to Caiaphas*, 331–32.

125. No Talmudic source states this overtly, but it is deduced from a set of other attested facts: (1) in the days of John Hyrcanus I and Alexander, the Sadducees dominated the Jewish Senate; (2) Salome

been an innovation, since the high priest had been the *ex officio* head of the Jewish Senate before this time, as Hasmonean coins demonstrate. Salome Alexandra broke with this tradition and placed the chief political assembly of the Jewish nation in the hands of the hugely popular fundamentalist Pharisees. Many of them who had found refuge in Alexandria now returned to the Jewish kingdom and began taking up seats in the assembly, transforming it from a senate of elders (*gerousia*) advising the high priest into a council of politicians (*synedrion*)—what would come to be known as the Sanhedrin—with a raised profile as a religious court. This promoted ongoing legal reflection by the Pharisees, and the development of increasing legal rigor in their Oral Law—a natural graduation with the legislative and political power they now received. It gave considerable ideological momentum to the Pharisaic movement. The tide of power thus began to flow towards the fundamentalist Pharisees, as it ebbed away from the increasingly progressive Sadducees.[126]

Joshua ben-Perachiah died not long after his appointment to the Jewish Senate's presidency, which allowed Salome Alexandra's brother, Simeon, to take up the role in his place.[127] He applied Pharisaic logic to the decisions of the Jewish Sanhedrin with evangelical zeal. Later rabbinic tradition credits him with reinstating the Torah in Israel (b. Qidd. 66a), by which is meant that the Pharisees gained political dominance and enforced their Oral Law upon Jewish society. In demonstration of his puritanical approach, Simeon is said to have crucified eighty women of Ashkelon for practicing sorcery (b. Sanh. 45b–46a; cf. Exod 22:18).[128] This was probably a showcase of newly acquired Jewish sovereignty over the city, which had been a city of holy asylum for gentiles. Ironically, the relatives of the executed women (presumably gentiles who were nominally Judaized) got their revenge by successfully bringing capital charges against Simeon's son through the very system of Jewish justice that he himself represented (y. Sanh. 6.3).[129]

Alexandra promoted the Pharisees to power; (3) Joshua ben-Perachiah returned to Judea from refuge in Alexandria (b. Soṭah 47a), and is attested as its president; (4) Simeon ben-Shetach is attested as president of the Jewish Senate later in his sister's reign, and he was succeeded by his deputy, Judah ben-Tabbai (Gemara on b. Ḥag. 16b).

126. The Pharisees saw the power they gained at this time as ideal for the governance of the Jewish nation: a monarch and high priest led by the advice of the Jewish Sanhedrin, guided by the sagacity and piety of the Pharisees and their traditions. It would lead them eventually to project this ideal back onto monarchic Israel (e.g., b. Sanh. 107a).

127. One could argue that this was Salome Alexandra's intention all along, and that the appointment of the elderly Joshua helped avoid the direct charge of nepotism.

128. Later Pharisaic tradition prohibited the capital sentencing of more than one person on a single day, and thus Simeon's execution of eighty women was seen as exceptional and not to be used as a legal precedent.

129. The rabbinic tradition states that the charges against Simeon's son were false, but Pharisaic

The Essenes saw the ascendancy of the fundamentalist Pharisees ("those who seek easy answers") as a time of puritanical terror, which recapitulated the prophecy of Nahum (see 4QpNah [4Q169], III.4.3–10a). They also blamed Salome Alexandra for facilitating it, characterizing her as the embodiment of "the whore" who is a "mistress of sorcery" in Nahum 3:4. Despite the quiet antipathy of the Essenes, she was generally liked by the people. From her reign onwards, the name "Salome" became the second most popular name for Jewish girls (after "Mary/Miriam").[130]

But Salome Alexandra was still a woman in a world dominated by men and their expectations of power. Her eldest son, John Hyrcanus II, lacked initiative and vision, making him ill-suited to politics and leadership. Initially, this served his mother's purposes well, since his passivity gave the Pharisees enormous latitude (*Ant.* 13.408; *J.W.* 1.109). But this allowed certain Pharisees to take revenge on some of the Sadducees and other royal advisors who had been instrumental in their persecution under Alexander Jannaeus. This deepened the chasm between the two parties. Although Judaism's most important institution, the temple cult, was still predominantly the domain of the Sadducees, the high priest himself was now a lackey of the Pharisees. This understandably made the Sadducees politically skittish.

The Sadducees rallied to petition the queen for change. Among their chief spokesmen was the queen's younger son, Judas Aristobulus II, who was very much in the mold of his father: a political animal with a fiery temperament (cf. *J.W.* 1.109). Aristobulus castigated his mother for ambitiously holding power as a woman when there were men in the prime of life suitable for leadership. The clear insinuation was that he himself ought to be the civic ruler of Judea. The Sadducees argued that the queen was acting unwisely and even threatened to offer themselves as mercenaries to enemy states, such as the Nabateans. In response, Salome Alexandra permitted the Sadducees to take control of the kingdom's defenses and made Aristobulus an army commander. But she retained civic governance of the kingdom and kept three fortresses (Hyrcania, Alexandrium, and Machaerus) for her personal use (*Ant.* 13.409–418). Sensing the potential rivalry between her two sons, but willing them to work together, she ordered the construction of twin residences for them at the Hasmonean estate outside Jericho.[131] The luxurious residences were semi-detached mirror images of each other, with a central line of chambers dividing them—a

---

tradition prohibited the recanting of prior testimony. This fact might lie behind the saying attributed to Simeon in which he urged thorough cross-examination of witnesses (m. 'Avot 1:9).

130. Atkinson, *Queen Salome*, 22.
131. Berlin, "Between Large Forces," 35, 42.

premonition of the divide that was growing between the brothers and the sects that lay behind them.

3.7.14 ROME, PONTUS, ARMENIA, AND THE END OF THE SELEUCID KINGDOM

Resentment against Roman rule in Asia had grown over the decades, particularly as Roman moneylenders issued extortionate loans to locals and then foreclosed when they could not be repaid (Memnon, *Hist. Her.* 27.5–6). The result was a rapid transfer of property to Roman owners and an influx of Romans and Italians into the region. Mithridates VI of Pontus used the regional discontent to his advantage. After his invasion of Cappadocia in 89 BC, he secretly organized a coordinated attack on Romans throughout major cities of Asia, resulting in the massacre of thousands on a single night (Appian, *M.W.* 22–23)—an event the Romans dubbed the "Asiatic Vespers" (88 BC). Similar anti-Roman sentiment gripped the western side of the Aegean. So, when Mithridates sent an army to Greece itself, he was hailed as the ostensible liberator of Greek civilization.

Rome now rose to his threat. The Republic had just brought the four-year Italic War against its erstwhile Italian allies to a resolution. As consul in 88 BC, Lucius Cornelius Sulla was given command of the response to Mithridates. But his deployment was delayed when his former mentor, Gaius Marius, attempted to take command off him. The breach between the two men was symptomatic of a larger friction between the patrician faction of the *Optimates*, which Sulla represented, and the plebeian faction of the *Populares*, championed by Marius. Sulla marched on Rome with Roman armies, violating its sacrosanct status in the minds of all Romans. It was a pivotal moment that redefined Roman politics, for Sulla blatantly disregarded the Republic's hallowed traditions but did so ostensibly in defense of the Republic itself. It was a shot across the bows of Roman political process. Sulla's unscrupulous maneuver caught Marius completely by surprise and allowed Sulla to defeat him (Plutarch, *Sull.* 8.1–10:4).

Having stamped his ascendancy on Rome, Sulla set off for Greece. In 86 BC he besieged and captured Athens and engaged in a program of opportunistic pillaging and ransacking of temple treasuries. After punching Greece into submission, Sulla pushed Mithridates's army back to Asia Minor. But back in Rome, Sulla's enemies had rallied against him, prompting him to make a quick peace with Mithridates so that he could return to Rome. This saved Mithridates from total defeat. Although he was forced to evacuate all territories he had previously occupied, he emerged from the fray with a treaty of *amicitia* with the Republic (Plutarch, *Sull.* 12.1–25.2).

But Mithridates's ambitions had not been curtailed, and he indomitably continued to build up his military. This sparked a rogue intervention by a Roman commander in 83 BC (the Second Mithridatic War), which ended embarrassingly for the Romans when Sulla ordered a halt to the operation. It left Mithridates in an even stronger position, with dynasts throughout Asia Minor clamoring to his side, railing against Rome's iron fist.

One dynast already allied to him through marriage was Tigranes II of Armenia. Tigranes was originally a client king of the Parthians, but with the Parthian Empire descending into civil strife in the 80s BC, he had a growing sense of independence and filled the vacuum the Parthians were leaving. By 78 BC, he had annexed all the former Seleucid client kingdoms in northern Mesopotamia, taken control of Media, struck into Cappadocia, and occupied eastern Cilicia. This stretched Tigranes's domain from the shores of the Caspian Sea to the Mediterranean, making him even more powerful than his father-in-law, Mithridates.

Philip's moribund Seleucid kingdom now consisted solely of northern Syria, making it just another minor regional state. Three years later (75 BC) Philip died, though exactly how is unknown.[132] With him, Seleucid power practically sputtered out. Philip was survived by his son, Philip II, but the senators of Antioch chose not to recognize his claim or the claims of Cleopatra Selene and her son, Antiochus XIII Asiaticus. Instead, they invited Tigranes to reign, figuring that he would otherwise invade but also that his dynasty could bring much-needed stability to the region.[133] And so, the Armenian king swallowed up the last vestige of the Seleucid kingdom (Justin, *Epit.* 40.1).

Cleopatra Selene still ruled in Ptolemais-Acco on behalf of her son, Asiaticus. But he was probably still in Roman Asia, and the Seleucid dynasty he represented was now practically dead in the face of Tigranes's rise. Whether in understanding or denial of the dire political reality, Selene sent Asiaticus along with his younger brother, Seleucus VII, to the Roman Senate to seek endorsement for their claim to the Seleucid throne. The Senate acknowledged the claim of both boys (Cicero, *Ver.* 2.4.61) but knew that they were endorsing ownership of a political corpse. The only significance in the decision was that it told Tigranes that he was now on the wrong side of the Roman ledger.

---

132. The ancient sources are scant, so we are dependent on numismatics to provide chronological stakes in the ground.

133. Grainger, *The Fall of the Seleukid Empire*, 189.

Yet Selene, a daughter of the Ptolemaic dynasty, sought the Senate's approval for her sons' claims to the Ptolemaic kingdom as well. Her basis for this was that one of her older sons, Ptolemy XI Alexander II, whom she had borne to Ptolemy X Alexander, had taken the Ptolemaic throne in 80 BC as Rome's expressly endorsed candidate, only to be lynched by a maddened mob in Alexandria. In his stead, Egypt was now ruled by Ptolemy XII Auletes ("Flautist"), an illegitimate son of Ptolemy IX Chickpea and stooge of Mithridates VI of Pontus who was opposed to Roman rule.[134] Selene put her two boys forward as legitimate scions of the Ptolemaic dynasty, with both of them holding pro-Roman loyalties.[135] However, the Roman Senate denied Selene's claim and chose instead to deal directly with Ptolemy the Flautist. If the Romans displaced him, they would give both Egypt and Mithridates a *casus belli* against them, with the potential of uniting the whole eastern Mediterranean (except for the Hasmonean state) against them. It was a safer bet to uphold Ptolemy the Flautist's rule in Egypt while trying to dissolve his allegiance to Mithridates. The denial of Selene's claim left her politically isolated. Though she and her sons survived, Rome's decision practically confirmed the death of the Seleucid kingdom.

An historical autopsy reveals that the primary cause of the Seleucid kingdom's death was squabbling over the throne. The dynastic feuds had been set in motion a century earlier, when Rome traded the young crown prince, Demetrius I, as hostage for his uncle, after Seleucus IV's failure to pay war reparations (see 2.8.8 above). Demetrius's uncle usurped the Seleucid throne as Antiochus IV, creating a rival line within the dynasty. The excessive ambitions of both lines fueled a century of internecine fighting, which fractured the once vast empire. It led to the secession of the Jewish state and the sclerosis of popular sentiment against Seleucid rulers. The kingdom's lack of internal integrity meant it was unable to withstand the external pressures of Ptolemaic meddling from the south, Parthia's encroachments from the east, and the towering shadow of Roman influence from the west. It is almost ironic, then, that the final *coup de grâce* was delivered by Tigranes II from Armenia in the north.

---

134. Ptolemy IX Chickpea had taken back control of Egypt in 88 BC and reigned until his death in December 81 BC, leaving the throne to his daughter, Berenice III. Rome then appointed Cleopatra Selene's son, Ptolemy XI, to rule as Berenice's husband. But Ptolemy XI murdered Berenice for which he was lynched just weeks later. Passing over the other sons of Cleopatra Selene, the Alexandrian elite opted instead to grant the throne to Ptolemy the Flautist, an illegitimate son of Chickpea, and gave Cyprus to his younger brother, Ptolemy of Cyprus. See Hölbl, *A History of the Ptolemaic Empire*, 213–14, 222.

135. The father of the boys had been "Pious" Antiochus X, who, although a Seleucid, was of Ptolemaic descent by both his mother (Cleopatra IV) and paternal grandmother (Cleopatra Thea).

3.7.15 TIGRANES II AND THE JEWISH STATE

As the borders of Tigranes II's Armenian empire distended southwards, the Nabateans promptly abandoned Damascus. This sparked a conflict between Salome Alexandra and Ptolemy Menneus for control of the city, with Salome Alexandra dispatching her son, Aristobulus, to fight the Iturean king. But Tigranes denied them both by establishing his own sovereignty over Damascus in 72 BC (*Ant.* 13.418). Most of Syria was thus folded into the Armenian Empire, and Ptolemy Menneus became a submissive client king.[136] It had been many decades since a political and military force as large as Tigranes's had united the region. The Jewish state suddenly found itself as the novel empire's immediate southern neighbor—a threatening proposition for Salome Alexandra after her failed dash for Damascus.

Tigranes was, however, more interested in Cleopatra Selene than Salome Alexandra. Selene had made herself Tigranes's enemy when she petitioned Rome to recognize her sons' claim to the Seleucid domains. But having been wife to five monarchs of Ptolemaic and Seleucid pedigree, Selene had become a political baton of sorts. Tigranes probably intended on marrying her to cement his rule over Syria and potentially open the door to claims over Egypt. So he marched across Galilee (now part of the Jewish state) to Ptolemais-Acco, where he began to besiege Selene in 71 BC (*Ant.* 13.419–20).

This maneuver signaled that Tigranes was unlikely to leave the Jewish state unmolested in his grander plans. Food in the Hasmonean kingdom was in low supply after a Sabbatical Year (72/1 BC). Being in such a vulnerable position, Salome Alexandra dispatched gift-laden envoys to Tigranes, who responded with assurances about the Jewish state's security (*Ant.* 13.419–21). This probably meant that he intended to make the Hasmoneans his clients, as he had done with Ptolemy Menneus. Thus, while the embassy secured the survival of the Hasmonean kingdom, it could not guarantee its ongoing independence (cf. Appian, *S.W.* 48). The question was what Tigranes would do after the siege of Ptolemais-Acco.

Tigranes captured the city early in 70 BC and took Cleopatra Selene into his custody. This finally eradicated the charade of Seleucid rule and abolished the Ptolemaic bridgehead in the Levant.[137] Next, Tigranes probably planned

---

136. Grainger, *The Fall of the Seleukid Empire*, 195.
137. We must remember that Cleopatra Selene was both a Ptolemaic princess and a member of the Seleucid dynasty. She ruled Ptolemais-Acco as a member of the Ptolemaic dynasty and on behalf of her Seleucid son, Antiochus XIII Asiaticus. The political status of Ptolemaic-Acco is testament to just how intertwined the Ptolemaic and Seleucid dynasties had become.

on advancing into the Hasmonean kingdom. But as had been the case on previous occasions, the quirks of international politics intervened to give the Jews a reprieve. The Romans had dished out a bevy of embarrassing defeats to Tigranes's father-in-law, Mithridates VI of Pontus, who subsequently took refuge in Tigranes's Armenia (Memnon, *Hist. Her.* 27.7–31.1; Appian, *M.W.* 82). Fearing that the Romans would now invade his territory, Tigranes shelved any plans regarding the Jewish state and headed back to his homeland with Cleopatra Selene in tow (70 BC). When he refused the Romans' demand to surrender Mithridates to them (Memnon, *His. Her.* 31.2–3), the Romans invaded. Over the next three years (69–67 BC), they defeated Tigranes in open battle and reduced his empire to the Armenian heartland (Memnon, *Hist. Her.* 38.2–7). Tigranes was only spared a complete defeat when the Roman general, Lucius Licinius Lucullus, was stymied by a mutiny among his own men (Plutarch, *Luc.* 30.3–4). Thus, Tigranes survived the campaign and Mithridates even managed to retake Pontus. But Tigranes had been cut off from his recent acquisitions, plunging Cilicia and Syria into political limbo. Cleopatra Selene might have been able to make something of this but as she was of no more use to Tigranes, he had her executed.

Salome Alexandra thus never had to face Tigranes directly. The Hasmonean kingdom kept its independence and friendship with Rome, while the major centers of Syria were left in a political vacuum.

3.7.16 THE DEATH OF SALOME ALEXANDRA

In 67 BC Salome Alexandra fell sick. Her younger son, Judas Aristobulus, feared that his older brother, John Hyrcanus II, would inherit civic power in addition to the high priesthood, and that this would give the fundamentalist Pharisees free rein throughout the country, disenfranchising the progressive Sadducees even further. He and the Sadducees sprang into action and, within two weeks, secured most of the fortifications throughout the country, ensuring that Hyrcanus was confined to Jerusalem. Salome Alexandra was in no position to stop him, but from her sickbed she ordered the arrest of Aristobulus's family. He had married the daughter of his uncle, Absalom, and had four children with her: two sons, Alexander and Mattathias Antigonus (then teenagers), and two daughters. The four children, along with their mother, were detained in the Baris fortress at the northwest corner of the temple complex. Though this did not prevent Aristobulus's political growling, it did muzzle his military bite (*Ant.* 13.422–429).

Not long after, Salome Alexandra succumbed to her illness, having reigned for nine years (*Ant.* 13.430). She was only the second woman to rule in Jerusalem—the first being Queen Athaliah (daughter of the Israelite King Ahab), who had become sole ruler of Judah some eight centuries earlier. Salome Alexandra had restored a sense of equilibrium to the Jewish state after the ferocious excesses of her husband. But that equilibrium was perilously fragile, threatened by the intense rivalry between the fundamentalist Pharisees and progressive Sadducees, the mismatched drive of her two sons, and the persistent volatility in Syria. With her passing, the state diadem fell to the weak-willed John Hyrcanus II, with the strongminded Aristobulus ready to pounce.

3.7.17 THE FRATERNAL CIVIL WAR (67–63 BC)

As soon as John Hyrcanus II inherited the title of "king," he was challenged by his brother, Aristobulus. Their fraternal conflict was, however, a front for a deeper battle between the Pharisees and Sadducees for control of the nation. It now erupted into civil war.

The conflict had been brewing ever since Jewish independence in 142 BC. The Sadducees were drawn mainly from the priestly classes and so represented the upper crust of Jewish society with a traditional right to wield power (cf. the Roman *Optimates*). Socially, this made them conservative, but they had shifted over time and become culturally eclectic and politically progressive. The Pharisees were an equally peculiar mirror image. As a lay movement, their popular social base would have made them progressive (cf. the Roman *Populares*), but they were culturally and politically ultra-conservative. This mismatch between social makeup, religious conviction, and political outlook gave Judea a unique dynamic, complicated by the incongruent role of John Hyrcanus II at the center of it all. As high priest, and now also king, one would have expected him to be aligned with the priestly Sadducees. But he was weak-willed—a pushover for those already holding most of the power in Judea, namely the Pharisees. The differences between the parties had become politicized the moment Salome Alexandra began making room for Pharisees in the highest echelons of Jewish society, disgruntling the Sadducees who had been there first. Neither party was willing to concede ground. Thus, in Aristobulus's challenge to John Hyrcanus II, we also see the Sadducees vying to retake the control they believed was theirs by divine right. They believed that if Judaism was to be a theocracy, as Torah advocated, then the high priest was to be part of a sacred fraternity, distinct from the people. But since John Hyrcanus II did not have the will to alter the current situation, he would have to be dislodged. Aristobulus was, therefore, not merely trying to grab power for himself but aiming to recover the nation's leadership for those who felt they held a divine right to it.

The brothers immediately went to war. Aristobulus and his Sadducee supporters were in the dominant position, and Hyrcanus was too squeamish for a proper fight. So when Aristobulus surrounded Jerusalem, Hyrcanus capitulated before a siege could begin. He readily agreed to abdicate both the high priesthood and the kingship to Aristobulus, release his brother's family from the Baris fortress, and then retire from public life. The brothers took oaths, swapped residences in Jerusalem, and Aristobulus II took up the national leadership (*Ant.* 14.4–7). The rapprochement probably occasioned the marriage of Aristobulus's eldest son, Alexander II, to Hyrcanus's daughter, Alexandra II, binding the two sides of the family in a marriage typical of Hellenistic royalty.[138] To further cement his new authority, Aristobulus immediately began extending his twin mansion at the Hasmonean estate outside Jericho and started minting his own coins.[139]

The fact that John Hyrcanus II lay down his leadership so quickly demonstrates his flaccid political will. His abdication must have sparked a constitutional crisis, since Torah demanded that the high priestly office be held for life (cf. 2.6.2; 3.5.9). The Pharisees challenged the legality of Aristobulus II's high priesthood and not just because of its political implications for them. Aristobulus presumably foresaw this objection, which is why he made his brother take an oath in the temple itself. Of course, this raised the legal question of whether a biblical directive regarding primogeniture and the lifelong tenure of the high priest could be overturned by an oath in the divine name. Thus, the change in leadership did not settle matters.

Hyrcanus's retirement did not put an end to the civil war either. His lackluster character was now offset by the vivacity of Antipater, the governor of Idumea. Far from a fundamentalist, Antipater was a self-confessed Hellenist, which should have aligned him with Aristobulus and the Sadducees. However, as time would show, he was clearly devoted to Hyrcanus and certainly no friend of Aristobulus, though exactly why is unknown. Whatever his motives, he now impelled Hyrcanus not to give up on his claim to the Jewish leadership. Instead, he devised a strategy of creating a covert alliance between Hyrcanus and the Nabatean king, Aretas III, to whom Antipater was related by marriage.

---

138. No source tells us when this marriage took place, but it had occurred before 65 BC. The ages of all the persons involved (John Hyrcanus II was about thirty-six, Aristobulus II about thirty-four, and their children were young teenagers) and the political implications point to this time as the only viable occasion for it.

139. Meshorer, *Ancient Jewish Coinage. Volume I: Persian Period through Hasmonaeans*, 46–47, 84.

At Antipater's bidding, Hyrcanus absconded from Jerusalem with his family in ca. 65 BC and took refuge at Aretas's court in Petra. Antipater also brought his own wife, Cypros (a relative of Aretas), and their five children, all aged under twelve: Phasael (or Faisal), Herod (aged nine at the time), Joseph, Pheroras, and a daughter, Salome.[140] Through Antipater's mediation, Hyrcanus came to an agreement with the Nabatean king to cede portions of Perea, the Negev, and Idumea to Aretas in exchange for armed support that would return him to the Jewish leadership (*Ant.* 4.12–17; *J.W.* 1.123–26).

But before the campaign could get going, an ecological hurdle faced them. During the winter of 66/5 BC, the rains throughout the region failed and agricultural production plummeted. As the upcoming year (65/4 BC) was a Sabbatical rest for the land, famine became a serious risk, making a military campaign too risky. Since drought was a classic warning sign of covenantal breach (Deut 28:22–23), the Pharisees probably interpreted conditions as divine judgment upon Aristobulus and the Sadducees. In the Pesher of Hosea, the conservative Essenes interpreted it as a recapitulation of Hosea 2:10–12—a judgment for the apostate reign of Salome Alexandra, who had privileged the fundamentalist Pharisees and led the nation astray (4QpHos^a [4Q166], col. II, 1–14).

During Passover in 65 BC, a prophet named Onias (or "Honi") was called upon to pray for rain (m. Ta'an. 19a; 23a).[141] Circumstantial evidence suggest Onias was a Galilean, who was in Jerusalem either as a migrant resident (cf. Anna [Luke 2:36–38])[142] or a Passover pilgrim.[143] He had a reputation as a righteous man, beloved of God (*Ant.* 14.22), and worker of miracles, though we have no details of how this reputation developed. His epithet of "Circle-Drawer" derives from a rabbinic tradition, which relates that, in response to the appeal for him to pray for rain, Onias drew a circle on the ground and placed himself inside it. He vowed not to step out until God had given his people the right kind of rain, and God eventually obliged after Onias kept badgering him.[144] Simeon ben-Shetach, who was president of the Sanhedrin at this

---

140. The names of Antipater's children reveal his own cosmopolitan character, as they have Arab, Greek, and Jewish derivations.

141. Onias is often known by the Semitic form of his name, Honi, which is a diminution of Johanan ("John").

142. Anna's Galilean heritage is shown by her affiliation with the tribe of Asher, which had its traditional territory along the Galilean coast around Ptolemais-Acco. It is unknown how or if she was affected by Tigranes's siege and capture of the city in 71–70 BC.

143. Geza Vermes, *Jesus the Jew: A Historian's Reading of the Gospels* (New York: Macmillan, 1973), 72.

144. The incident makes use of a motif familiar from Antiochus IV's confrontation with Gaius Popilius Laenas near Alexandria (see 3.2.4).

time, had wanted to prosecute Onias for presumptuously issuing the deity with an ultimatum, demonstrating the puritanical hold that the Pharisees had over expressions of Jewish faith. But Simeon could not deny the benefit of the rains that had come after Onias's prayer. He thus concluded that Onias had related to God like a nagging son, and that God, as a fatherly figure, had overlooked his insolence (cf. Luke 11:5–13). The incident earned Onias an Elijah-like reputation (cf. Gen. Rab. 13.7), as the ancient prophet had also brought an end to a devastating drought (2 Kgs 18:41–46). The divine promise to send an Elijah-like figure before the day of Yahweh (Mal 3:23[4:5 MT]) must have imbued the moment with eschatological expectation, just as the appearance of John the Baptist would a century later.

One of the eighteen so-called Psalms of Solomon was probably composed in response to this incident. It reflects on God's provision at the psalmist's request and concludes with an assertion of God's kingship—a poignant comment in the context of the Fraternal Civil War.

> When we are in trouble,
> we will call upon you for help,
> and you will not turn away our plea,
> for you are our God.
> Do not make your hand heavy against us,
> so that we do not sin out of need.
> And if you do not restore us, we will not desist,
> but to you we will come.
> For if I hunger, to you I will cry out, O God,
> and you will provide for me . . .
>
> You feed the kings, rulers, and the peoples, O God.
> And who is the help of the poor and needy,
> if not you, O Lord?
> And you will hear,
> for who is kind and gentle but you,
> cheering the soul of the humble
> with an open hand of mercy? . . .
>
> May they who fear the Lord be cheered with good things,
> and your kindness over Israel in your kingdom.
> The glory of the Lord is blessed,
> for he is our king. (Pss. Sol. 5:5–8, 11–12, 18)

With a harvest secured by late rains, Aretas III and John Hyrcanus II launched their invasion of the Jewish state in spring 64 BC. Aristobulus was put on the back foot. Many of Jerusalem's elite realized that a siege of Jerusalem was inevitable and quit the country for Egypt. Others simply defected to Hyrcanus. The balance in the fraternal conflict thus swung away from Aristobulus. Hyrcanus marched on Jerusalem (with Aretas and Antipater), and the city surrendered to him without a fight. Aristobulus, however, remained holed up with his priestly supporters inside the fortified temple complex. And so, a blockade of the temple ensued (*Ant.* 14.19–21).

At this point, Onias the Circle-Drawer features once again. Hyrcanus's men tracked the prophet down and demanded he call down a divine curse upon Aristobulus and his embattled priests (cf. Num 22–23). This probably betrays the public relations nightmare Hyrcanus now faced. He may have been the toff of the populist Pharisees, but he was now attacking the sacred precincts at the heart of the nation's identity. He not only risked damage to Yahweh's temple, but he could be about to kill sacrosanct Jewish priests and Levites. What's more, he had taken an oath in the divine name to abdicate to his brother, and thus a direct attack upon him risked divine retribution for the breaking of an oath. Aristobulus must surely have broadcast these facts to portray his brother as devoid of will, authority, and rectitude—a puppet of Antipater and the gentile horde of Aretas. By imposing the popular Onias into the fray, Hyrcanus was looking to recover support for his cause and even perhaps to make someone else the instrument of Aristobulus's downfall.

Onias, however, remained doggedly neutral. Rather than comply with the demand to curse Aristobulus and the priests, Josephus depicts Onias praying, "O God, king of all, since those standing here with me are your people, and the besieged are your priests, I beg you neither to listen to these here against those there, nor to fulfil what those there request against these here" (*Ant.* 14.24). If this tradition captures anything of the historical reality of Onias's centrist attitude, it demonstrates that some placed more stock in essential ethnic identity than in any political affiliation. No Jew was beyond the pale, for every Jew was a member of the indivisible covenant nation, regardless of their faction. Even as this attitude acknowledged the sacred status of the priests, it condemned the conflict that cut such a deep national divide and menaced the country by war. By thus imploring God not to listen to his people, Onias issued a stinging prophetic critique of all the nation's leaders, blaming them for imperiling the nation and being out of touch with God himself. It was a critical estimation that Jesus would also issue a century later, but with an apocalyptic urgency that demanded national repentance, an end to the old order, and the birth of a new kingdom.

At this point, Onias disappears from the historical record. Josephus claims he was immediately stoned to death for his failure to comply (*Ant.* 14.24). In all likelihood, Onias did meet a sinister end at the hands of Hyrcanus's men, who then tried to cover up the deed. But Onias's mysterious disappearance led to a public outcry, followed by speculation over the manner of his disappearance. This reconstruction of events accounts for the popular comparison of Onias to Elijah as a prophet who brought an end to a devastating drought (see immediately above) and then went missing. It also provides the necessary room for the emergence of a later tradition that Onias fell asleep for seventy years (m. Taʿan. 23a), like an ancient-day Rip Van Winkle. Whether Hyrcanus was complicit in Onias's demise cannot be determined, but the Elijah-like stature of Onias must have fueled eschatological fervor. Anger at Hyrcanus and sympathy for Aristobulus now rebalanced the national conflict, showing how pivotal a prophetic figure could be in Jewish politics.

The blockade of the temple continued as Passover loomed in mid-April 64 BC, but this hampered access for pilgrims and prevented the procurement of livestock for sacrifice. Aristobulus saw this as an opportunity. From atop the temple fortifications, he requested access to livestock to enable the festival to go ahead. Any refusal by Hyrcanus would now paint him in yet more sinister colors for hindering the nation's religious duty. But Hyrcanus was unwilling to ease the blockade. He lacked the insight to demand access to the temple to offer the sacrifices in his brother's stead. Instead, he demanded an exorbitant price for each animal (*Ant.* 14.25–26), probably hoping that Aristobulus would refuse to pay. But Aristobulus called his bluff. He sent payment over the wall to Hyrcanus's men, thereby appearing as the party most committed to facilitating the nation's piety, even at great personal expense. The move instantly trumped Hyrcanus, who then reneged on his offer. The public observation of Passover was thus compromised, and Hyrcanus's reputation nosedived.

According to Josephus (*Ant.* 14.27–28), a violent windstorm blew across the region soon after and stripped the country of its crops (bearing in mind that it was a Sabbatical Year). The incident was interpreted as divine wrath against Hyrcanus. This was probably the popular perception of a violent earthquake, which hit Syria at precisely this time (Justin, *Epit.* 40.2; Orosius, *Hist. Ag.* 6.5.1) and which was large enough to have damaged crops in Judea.[145]

---

145. This is earthquake "008" in the list compiled by Mohamed Reda Sbeinati, Ryad Darawcheh, and Mikhail Mouty, "The Historical Earthquakes of Syria: An Analysis of Large and Moderate Earthquakes from 1365 B.C. to 1900 A.D.," *Annals of Geophysics* 48.3 (2005): 347–435, https://doi.org/10.4401/ag-3206. In Syria, it was approximately 6.5 on the Richter Scale, which would have caused

It certainly must have added to the eschatological atmosphere of the time, especially as it affected food supplies once more. The Essenes interpreted the food shortages and mourning as a confirmation of God's anger at the Hasmonean regime and the Pharisees (4QpHos^a [4Q166], col. II, 1–19). There was, therefore, a growing sense throughout the country of divine displeasure with all Hasmonean leadership.

The loss of crops must have affected Aretas's resolve to carry on the blockade. Antipater's plans for the restoration of Hyrcanus were clearly unravelling. But outside intervention soon changed the whole course of the war and placed the Jewish state in an entirely new situation (see Part Four below).

---

considerable structural damage. In Jerusalem, it was felt at a magnitude of 5.4, which would cause visible swaying of trees and minor structural damage (see "Earthquake Intensity Scales," Sizes.com, February 1, 2010, https://www.sizes.com/natural/quakintens.htm). Cf. Iaakov Karcz, "Implications of Some Early Jewish Sources for Estimates of Earthquake Hazard in the Holy Land," *Annals of Geophysics* 47.2/3 (2004): 759–92.

3.8 CONCLUSION

The early Hasmonean era (167–142 BC) was characterized by the Maccabean Revolt and the gradual separation of the Jewish people from their Seleucid overlords. The period could just as easily be considered part of the Seleucid era. At its heart, the revolt was an intra-Jewish civil war between conservative-fundamentalist factions committed to traditional modes of cultural and religious expression, and progressives keen to embrace Greek ideals and integrate the Jewish people more fully into the Hellenistic world. In many ways, this was friction between a protective isolationist posture (cf. Nehemiah in the Persian era) and an ancient form of globalism. It is a mistake to think that Jewish conservatives and fundamentalists resisted Hellenism completely, for they easily and perhaps imperceptibly adopted many elements of Greek culture and thought, such that, by the time of the Maccabean Revolt, Judaism was very much Hellenized already. The bone of contention was the degree of Hellenization and who had the right to determine it. Even with the development of various Jewish schools of thought, Jews still believed in the oneness of Israel on the basis of the Torah's covenant theology. This necessitated a centralized, communal approach to Jewish identity, which pitted competing factions against each other to become the gatekeepers of that singular identity. Jews were, on aggregate, conservative in comparison to Greeks. So, when the Seleucids empowered the progressives as the Jewish gatekeepers, Jewish conservatives and fundamentalists reacted against it. In their eyes, Antiochus IV's revocation of the Jews' ethnic status within the Seleucid kingdom led to the annihilation of Jewish distinctiveness ("holiness"). Thus, the Seleucids added an external spark that ignited a highly combustible internal matter.

Jewish independence was only achieved in 142 BC, aided in large measure by Jonathan Apphus's abandonment of extremism and his adoption of more diplomatic methods. This was augmented by the intrigues that would eventually poison the Seleucid kingdom itself. Independence in theory made possible the recovery of national holiness as per the mandate of Torah. However, many quarters of Jewish society believed that such holiness had not been recovered under the Hasmoneans, who had replaced the Zadokite priesthood and who, as time went on, began to resemble exactly the kind of leadership against which the nation had revolted. This was especially the case after Aristobulus I added a royal diadem to his high priestly brow in 104 BC but gained notorious momentum under Alexander Jannaeus (104–76 BC).

For their part, the Hasmoneans legitimized their leadership through seven strategies. The first was international recognition, of which solidarity with the powerful Roman Republic was a key feature. The second was securing the hereditary high priesthood, which concentrated power within the Hasmonean family and in time developed into a royal dynasty. The third was the promulgation of cultic and cultural practices associated specifically with Hasmonean power. The festival of Hanukkah, which commemorated the rededication of the temple under Judas Maccabeus in 164/3 BC, was the most prominent of these, quickly achieving a kind of canonical status alongside Passover, Pentecost (Shavuot), and Sukkot. The fourth strategy was the composition of propaganda, of which the books of 1 and 2 Maccabees take pride of place.

The fifth strategy was the subversion of the prophetic voice. The Jewish Edict of 140 BC made Simon Thassi the head of state as high priest "until a reliable prophet should arise" (1 Macc 14:41). This was a concession to those who saw Hasmonean leadership only as an interim measure. But a generation later, the supporters of John Hyrcanus I acclaimed him as possessing the gift of prophecy, thereby placing the prophetic check of the Hasmoneans in the hands of the Hasmoneans themselves. Even though prophetic figures continued to arise, they were exploited and suppressed by the temple institution, so that the status quo of Hasmonean leadership could not be dislodged. In the eyes of the temple elite, God's purposes had reached their fulfilment in a Hasmonean priestly kingdom, making further divine revelation obsolete. This attitude would persist among priestly circles into the first century and then be employed in later centuries by the rabbinic heirs of the Pharisees to counter the claims of early Christianity. It permitted the temple institution to dictate the shape of the Jewish Scriptures, which privileged the Torah above all, ossified the prophetic canon, and permitted a collection of Psalms (see also 4.2.2 below). It was not until after the destruction of the temple in AD 70 that questions were again raised about the extent of the Hebrew Scriptures, and by this time Christians were developing their own set of sectarian writings (the New Testament) out of a conviction that God had indeed revealed and done more in the person of Jesus.

The sixth strategy of Hasmonean legitimization was the creation of infrastructure that facilitated Jewish life and promoted Hasmonean prestige. Jerusalem boomed as a holy city and site of pilgrimage under Hasmonean leadership, especially when John Hyrcanus I enlarged and fortified the temple complex. The creation of a fortification system throughout the Hasmoneans' territories enhanced military and economic control, while the construction of palatial residences gave them imperial eminence.

The final Hasmonean strategy was the recovery of the territory traditionally associated with covenantal Israel. Hasmonean conquests brought them fantastic wealth that funded their infrastructure projects. The borders of Hasmonean rule were perennially elastic, but the dynasty won most of the land between Upper Galilee and Idumea ("from Dan to Beersheba"), along with tracts in Transjordan. In this way, they viewed themselves as the restorers of Israel and the means of national unity and bolstered social cohesion through a policy of Judaization. Integral to this was the destruction of the Samaritan temple on Mount Gerizim (110 BC). On one level, this seemed to fulfil the classic prophetic hope for the reunification of all Israel. But it was merely a political patchwork rather than an organic reconciliation of the Jewish and Samaritan communities. The sack of Mount Gerizim damaged the Samaritan psyche and froze Jewish-Samaritan relations thereafter in cold antipathy.

Despite these achievements, Hasmonean leadership was never a settled matter. For some, like the Pharisees and Davidic loyalists, it was provisional leadership at best, while for others, like the Essenes, it was an abomination. Only the Sadducees, as heirs of the Zadokite legacy, appear to have been full supporters of the dynasty. The Essenes would eventually withdraw from the political heat and spawn an ascetic monasticism that awaited the red-hot fury of God's apocalyptic wrath. Yet, even in their seclusion at Qumran, they continued to reflect on political power, trying prophetically to perceive the will of God within history. Davidic loyalists no longer formed a distinct group, as the Davidic family had long since lost any official place in society. But there were Jews in various quarters of society who still clung to classic prophetic hopes, believing that God had not departed from his ancient promises to David or altered his steadfast character. Like the Essenes, they looked for people and events that might further revelation and activate God's promises for salvation from the ravages of incompetence, sin, and death. The Pharisees, who initially developed their brand of lay piety away from the flame of power, were scorched by the opposition of Alexander Jannaeus and his Sadducee supporters. Unlike the Essenes, though, they attained political power under Salome Alexandra, which graduated their lay movement into a sophisticated political party that controlled the Sanhedrin. This added rigor and legal authority to their fundamentalist piety, creating a puritanical ethos throughout the nation, which kept alive their conflict with the more progressive Sadducees. These groups developed eschatological hopes for change in line with their apocalyptic frameworks. They looked forward to the advent of a Davidic messiah and/or the Prophet who would reveal God's will, demote the Hasmoneans to a more modest place, and bring about the full redemption of Jerusalem (cf. Luke 2:38).

As the Hasmoneans increasingly took on the trappings of prosperous Hellenistic monarchs, so their dysfunction grew, and they became more distant from the generally conservative people they ruled. They had, to be sure, brought benefit to the Jewish people, but now their power and prestige were encroaching on the safety of their subjects. The dynasty suffered as a result. With the Fraternal Civil War, the progressive Sadducees and fundamentalist Pharisees each lined up behind their favored Hasmonean candidate. For the Sadducees, this was an ideological struggle for priestly privilege; for the Pharisees, it was a pragmatic endeavor to protect the power and influence they had acquired—a battle between the Jewish *Optimates* and *Populares*, as it were. Around them, Judaism was a pot simmering with apocalyptic expectation, its flame fueled by political uncertainty, theological disputation, Jewish nationalism, Hellenistic globalism, and a sense of divine displeasure with the covenant people. And now the Romans, who had been drawing ever nearer throughout the preceding century, stood poised to upend the pot.

PART 4
THE ROMAN ERA (63–4 BC)

4.1 ROMAN CONQUEST

4.1.1 POMPEY THE GREAT

On a Sabbath day in June 63 BC, the Roman general Gnaeus Pompeius Magnus strode triumphantly into the inner sanctum of Yahweh's temple in Jerusalem after a three-month siege to take the city.[1] His bold entry ritually desecrated the temple grounds, brought the Fraternal Civil War between John Hyrcanus II and Aristobulus II to an end, and reduced the Jewish state to a conquered tributary of Rome.

Pompey Magnus, as he is better known, was an arriviste, representing the new breed of Romans seeking to forge their own reputation in the opportunities afforded them by Rome's growing ascendancy. This made him predisposed to the *Populares* faction. But Pompey was a maverick among mavericks and made his reputation in the service of Sulla, one of the *Optimates*. When Sulla returned from the First Mithridatic War in 83 BC, he found the *Populares* in control of the Republic. Sulla stepped in to take the Republic back from them and set a young Pompey against their ranks in Sicily and Africa. Pompey pounced on them so agilely that Sulla gave him the epithet *Magnus* ("Great") in imitation of Alexander the Great. It was a compliment Pompey cherished and took to fulfilling with glitz and gusto. Sulla went on to become dictator of Rome (82–79 BC) with the ostensible aim of rebuilding the Republic after the damage done to it by the *Populares*. The reign of terror he unleashed on them was clearly a personal vendetta as much as a political antidote, showing how one could align the interests of the state with one's own ambitions. It was a lesson that served Pompey well, long after Sulla died in 78 BC.

---

1. Pompey's conquest of Jerusalem occurred "in the third month, on the day of the fast" during the consulship of Gaius Antonius Hybrida and Marcus Tullius Cicero (*Ant.* 14.66, 68). There is ambiguity about whether the third month refers to the length of Pompey's siege or the calendar month in which the city was taken. If, as seems likely, Pompey's siege began in the spring, both possibilities coincide to yield a date in June. This corroborates with the calculation that Pompey's victories became known in Rome by late summer 63 BC, when a peace-time augury was taken. Some have surmised that "the fast" was the Day of Atonement (October). However, Strabo refers to the Jewish Sabbath as a "day of fasting" specifically in reference to Pompey's siege (*Geography* 16.2.40), eliminating the need for the improbable suggestion that Pompey's conquest occurred in autumn of 64 BC; *pace* Duncan Cameron, "Towards a Re-Dating of Pompey's Conquest of Jerusalem," *JJS* 69.2 (2018): 225–47, https://doi.org/10.18647/3370/jjs-2018. Allowing at least four weeks for news to reach Rome, Jerusalem was captured either on 6 or 13 June of 63 BC.

Through competence, opportunism, and a healthy dose of luck, Pompey climbed the military and political ladder earlier than anyone before him. But he soon garnered a reputation for progressing his own agenda and riding the coattails of others. For example, when the richest man in Rome, Marcus Licinius Crassus, suppressed the slave revolt of Spartacus (73–71 BC), Pompey conducted a mop-up operation and then took all the plaudits for himself. In 67 BC, he was given a three-year command to tame the Cilician pirates, who were menacing trade and the grain supply to Italy. Pompey's authority stretched across the entire Mediterranean Sea and up to fifty miles inland. Never before had the Senate granted one man such sweeping powers for so long, setting a precedent that would eventually lead to the eclipse of the Senate itself. Pompey took just three months to deal with the pirates, partly by making them his personal clients. The following year, he was given command of the Third Mithridatic War. A soldiers' mutiny had prevented Lucius Licinius Lucullus from dealing the death blow to Mithridates VI of Pontus and Tigranes II of Armenia (see 3.7.15 above), but he had softened them up enough for Pompey to score crucial victories against them. It prompted Lucullus to liken Pompey to a lazy vulture that fed on carrion slain by others (Plutarch, *Pomp.* 31.6).

Pompey annexed Pontus, but rather than pursue Mithridates, he went on a conquering spree in Cappadocia, Cilicia, and Syria. In doing so, he filled the vacuum left by Tigranes after his withdrawal (see 3.7.15 above) and prevented the formation of an anti-Roman bloc in the eastern Mediterranean. But these conquests also brought Rome to the doorstep of the Parthians who controlled Mesopotamia and lands further east. The Parthians were not enemies of Rome (cf. Appian, *M.W.* 101–102), but they had recently emerged from civil strife and eyed lands closer to the economic hub of the Mediterranean. Pompey rankled them by depriving them of these lands (Appian, *M.W.* 101–2, 114; *S.W.* 50; Justin, *Epit.* 40.2).[2]

In mid-64 BC Pompey arrived in Syria. If Tigranes II had dealt the death blow to the Seleucid dynasty, it was left to Pompey to bury it. Pompey did not take the risk of establishing a client state for that would invite the competing claims of Philip II and Antiochus XIII Asiaticus. Instead, he annexed what remained of Cilicia and created the new Roman province of Syria (Diodorus Siculus, *Bib. hist.* 40.1a–b; Appian, *S.W.* 49). Asiaticus was probably executed, and Philip II fled.[3] The corpse of Seleucid sovereignty was thus buried in a Roman tomb, and Rome became the neighbor of the Hasmonean kingdom.

---

2. Boatwright et al., *The Romans*, 207.

3. No source ever mentions the fate of Asiaticus, but he is never heard of again. His execution is, therefore, assumed rather than verified.

4.1.2 THE ROMAN CONQUEST OF JERUSALEM (63 BC)

While Pompey was subduing northern Syria,[4] he dispatched his tribune, Aemilius Scaurus, to deal with the strife splitting the Hasmonean kingdom, which was still in formal friendship with Rome. Scaurus arrived at Jerusalem in September 64 BC in the midst of John Hyrcanus II's siege of the temple (see 3.7.17 above).[5] Both Hyrcanus and Aristobulus petitioned him with bribes, which Scaurus shamelessly accepted. In the end, Scaurus's aristocratic roots led him to favor Aristobulus, who was supported by the priestly establishment. Scaurus ordered the dispersal of Nabatean troops, and so Hyrcanus's siege of the temple came to an end. As Scaurus returned to Syria, Aristobulus opportunistically sprang a revenge attack on his brother and the retreating Nabateans near a town called Papyron, probably on the outskirts of Philadelphia. Hyrcanus, Aretas, and Antipater survived the skirmish, but Antipater's brother, Phalion, did not, driving a further wedge between the Idumean governor and Aristobulus (*Ant.* 14.29–33; *J.W.* 1.127–130).

Hyrcanus might simply have retired at this point, but the feisty Antipater took him to bargain directly with Pompey at Damascus. There, Antipater smeared Aristobulus as an enemy of Rome, with alleged ties to piracy and Mithridates VI of Pontus. The accusations forced Aristobulus to come personally to Damascus. He argued that he had seized power in Judea because of his brother's ineptitude rather than any plot to align the Jewish state with an anti-Roman axis. But Aristobulus's hauteur was such that he also felt it beneath his own station as a monarch to be defending himself before a gentile general. He sanctimoniously quit Damascus and offended Pompey in the process. At the same time, another Jewish embassy arrived to request that Pompey recognize neither Hyrcanus nor Aristobulus but rather to let the nation revert to a hierocracy led by priests. This embassy might have been sent by Essenes, sensing an opportunity to divest the Hasmonean dynasty of its power, or else by priests and scribes who had become disenchanted with the Hasmoneans for absorbing the high priesthood into the monarchy.[6] Whatever the case, the embassy appealed to the Roman Republic's famous distaste for kings. It forced

---

4. Among those Pompey subdued was the tyrant of Lysias (near Apamea), named Silas the Jew (*Ant.* 14.40). Unfortunately, nothing more is known about him.

5. Scaurus is one of the few people specifically named in the Dead Sea Scrolls. He is mentioned twice in a calendrical text (4Q333), which implies that he was in Jerusalem during September-October of 64 BC, including the Festival of Sukkot (9–15 October).

6. Grainger (*The Wars of the Maccabees*, 144–45) makes the case that it was a delegation from the Pharisees, but this is unlikely since the proposal to be ruled by priests would effectively place power in the hands of the Sadducees, who were rivals of the Pharisees.

Aristobulus's representatives to appeal to the Roman penchant for tradition by arguing that Aristobulus had merely inherited the form of government practiced by his father (*Ant.* 14.37–45; *J.W.* 1.131–33).

Even though Pompey was no stickler for tradition, he did not want to risk digging a political hole for himself by acting precipitously against a state with a treaty of *amicitia* with Rome. He had already put many in Rome offside, including some of his powerful *Optimates* supporters, by chasing fame and fortune rather than Mithridates VI. A change of government in the Jewish state, be it either in pattern or personnel, could destabilize the region yet further and bog Pompey down in an anti-Roman conflict that could spread to the neighboring Nabateans and Ptolemies. This would draw even further ire from Pompey's vocal detractors in Rome.

But the Jewish embassies were not the only ones Pompey received in Damascus. Ptolemy (XII) the Flautist sent a delegation from Alexandria to recognize Roman rule in Syria (*Ant.* 14.34–35). Ptolemy was formally acknowledging the death of his dynasty's nemesis, the Seleucid state. He was also acting expediently, since his anti-Roman mentor, Mithridates VI, was now a fugitive in the Crimean Peninsula, while Pompey was within striking distance of Egypt itself. Ptolemy thus came out as overtly pro-Roman, dousing any possibility of a wide anti-Roman conflagration in the eastern Mediterranean. Pompey could now deal with the troublesome Aristobulus and still contain any subsequent conflict within the Jewish state itself. Pompey was now an unchallenged powerbroker, making or breaking kings on Rome's behalf, and he stood poised to bring stability to the entire eastern Mediterranean—an achievement even his fiercest critics could not decry.

Pompey dismissed all the Jewish delegations from Damascus. Then, in the early spring, he brought his legions south and turned the screws on Aristobulus by demanding he turn over possession of certain fortified cities (*Ant.* 14.46–51; *J.W.* 1.133–136).[7] Subsequent developments suggest that this was a demand to liberate the Greek cities that Alexander Jannaeus had conquered and Judaized, such as Scythopolis and Pella. Aristobulus's acquiescence would mean ceding control of valuable economic centers on trade routes and relinquishing the program of Judaization over the locals, allowing their gentile culture to rebound. Perhaps seeing the writing on the wall, Aristobulus unceremoniously begged Pompey for his own position, agreeing to client status and tributary payments. But when Pompey also demanded possession of Hasmonean fortresses as an

---

7. The testimony of Josephus at this point is somewhat garbled, perhaps because he was trying to harmonize his sources. The outline given here represents what can be corroborated between Josephus's testimony and other sources and what is likely to have transpired based on the known political currents.

act of good faith, Aristobulus dithered (*Ant.* 14.52; *J.W.* 1.137). His mother had given him and his Sadducee supporters control of these fortresses. If Aristobulus handed them over to Pompey, he would be selling out his own supporters and disarming his own kingdom. Pompey's desire to remove him from power was now clear for all to see.

As Pompey moved his legions to Jericho, Aristobulus gave him a verbal commitment to welcome him into Jerusalem and thus formally submit the Jewish kingdom as a client state of Rome. But two events hampered the execution of this commitment. The first was word reaching Pompey of the death of Mithridates VI of Pontus in the Crimean Peninsula (*Ant.* 14.53; *J.W.* 1.138; Appian, *M.W.* 101–12; Dio Cassius, *Hist. Rom.* 37.11–13). There were no longer any loose ends for Pompey to deal with in the far north, meaning he was free to act here in the south as he saw fit. The second was that Aristobulus's supporters refused to turn over their fortresses to Pompey. This gave Pompey his *casus belli*. He took Aristobulus into custody and made the ascent to the Jewish capital (*Ant.* 14.54–57; *J.W.* 1.139–41). Barely six months after the Nabatean siege had ended, Jerusalem was once again facing siege.

Jerusalem's residents, however, opened the gates to Pompey. He occupied the residential parts of the city and then began to besiege the temple compound, where Aristobulus's supporters were again holed up (*Ant.* 14.58–60; *J.W.* 1.141–44, 148). In June, Pompey brought in his siege engines, which brought down one of the towers of the Baris fortress and breached the temple's northern wall. Troops poured in and ran amok, slaughtering hundreds who, because it was the Sabbath, put up practically no resistance. Pompey secured the complex and then ordered the Baris fortress and the northern wall to be razed (*Ant.* 14.61–71; *J.W.* 1.145–51; Strabo, *Geography* 16.2.40).

Pompey was filled with awe at the famed Jewish temple. Eager to tread where few had trod before, he took a small entourage of men and entered Yahweh's holy of holies. While he could have plundered the temple's treasury, he saw it as counterproductive to his desires for the country. Besides, the rest of his campaign had already paid him and his troops handsomely. Thus, he left the compound and permitted the surviving priests, under the direction of Hyrcanus, to perform the necessary cleansing (*Ant.* 14.72–73; *J.W.* 1.152–53).

We must not underestimate the trauma that Pompey's capture of Jerusalem inflicted on its inhabitants. The people opened the city gates to him, not because they desired to welcome him but to avoid deprivation and destruction. Although Rome had for a century been a distant guarantor of sorts, Pompey brought with him the weight of Roman imperialism and inflicted damage on Judaism's sacred temenos. Since the priests and defenders were not going to fight back on a Sabbath, he could have taken control of the temple without the ensuing slaughter, but he permitted the bloodshed nonetheless. And although he did not pillage the temple, his entry into the inner sanctum was a most odious sacrilege to all Jews. At every opportunity, Pompey sought to satisfy his own whim in pursuit of Alexander-like glory and to shape Roman policy around his own persona. Jerusalem was not destroyed nor was there a crisis of the same magnitude as that initiated by Antiochus IV. Yet, Pompey still thwarted Jewish independence and rode roughshod over Jewish sensibilities.

One of the Psalms of Solomon ruminates over Pompey's attack (and other events over the following fifteen years). The psalmist interprets the loss of independence as a divine judgment upon "the sons of Jerusalem" for profaning God's offerings—an allusion to the Hasmoneans and their supporters, especially after their warring compromised the observance of Passover in 64 BC:

> When the sinner [Pompey] set himself up proudly,
> with battering ram he brought down fortified walls,
> and you [God] did not prevent him.
> Foreign nations climbed your altar,
> trampled it proudly underfoot,
> because the sons of Jerusalem defiled the holy things of the Lord;
> they profaned the offerings to God with lawlessness.
> Because of these, God said, "Cast them far from me,
> I have no pleasure in them."
> The beauty of its glory was disdained before God—utterly devalued.
> The sons and daughters were in terrible captivity,
> their neck in a collar, a spectacle among the nations.
> You [God] acted as their sins deserved—
> for he left them in the hands of their conquerors.
> He turned his face away, not pitying them—
> young and old and children alike,
> for they all alike practiced evil, so that they did not listen.
> Heaven grew indignant, and the earth was disgusted at them,
> for no man had ever done as they did.
> Yet the earth will acknowledge all your righteous judgments, O God.
> They made the sons of Jerusalem a joke in place of the whores
>   within her;
> every passerby entered [the temple] in broad daylight.
> They were mocking such lawlessness,
> even as they themselves were doing the very same....

> Removed was the crown of glory, which God had placed on her
> [Jerusalem].
> In dishonor her beauty was cast to the ground.
> I both saw and begged the face of the Lord and said,
> "Long enough, O Lord, has your hand been heavy upon Jerusalem,
> with the attack of nations.
> For they mocked, and in rage and anger they never let up their wrath.
> They will annihilate us, unless you, O Lord, reprimand them in
> your anger.
> For they have not acted in zeal, but out of personal lust,
> pouring out their anger upon us to pillage us.
> Do not delay, O God, to repay them on their own heads,
> to turn the pride of the dragon to ignominy." (Pss. Sol. 2:1–12, 22–25)

The psalmist portrays the Hasmoneans (past and present) as entering the temple with the same flippant attitude as Pompey and his troops. In this way, he depicted the Roman conquest as appropriate retribution against the Hasmoneans, even though it caused wider suffering. The psalmist, therefore, was evidently a scribe who shared the ideological perspective of the delegation that had asked Pompey to let the Jewish state revert to non-monarchic leadership. Yet, he depicts Pompey as either the pride of the dragon, with the dragon representing Rome, or as the dragon itself—the beast that classically set itself in opposition to God.

4.1.3 THE CLIENT STATE OF JUDEA

With the conquest of Jerusalem, the Hasmonean kingdom was transformed into a Roman client state. Pompey restored John Hyrcanus II as high priest, thus reinstituting foreign control over the sacerdotal office—a situation last seen when Alexander Balas had confirmed Jonathan Apphus as high priest in 152 BC. But Pompey also deprived Hyrcanus of royal title. The Hasmonean kingdom had come to an end.

Pompey also liberated many cities that the Hasmonean dynasty had conquered and divested the Jewish state of all its major trade routes. The entire coastal plain of *Palaestina*, as the Romans called it, was removed from Jewish sovereignty, and each of its major cities (including Marisa in Idumea) made clients of Rome.[8] Scythopolis in the eastern Jezreel Valley and the Greek cities

---

8. The term "Palestine," derived from the name of the Philistines, was known well before this

of the Transjordanian hills were likewise detached from Jewish control and placed under the headship of Damascus in a common league that would come to be known as the Decapolis—the "Ten City" league (cf. Pliny the Elder, *Nat.* 5.16).[9] This also had the effect of curtailing the territorial reach of the Nabateans. The city of Samaria was also given client status.[10] These losses confined the Jewish state to the hills of Galilee, Samaria, Judea, Idumea, and the region of Perea in Transjordan. The Romans named the rump state "Judea" (Lat. *Iudaea*; Gk. *Ioudaia*) to reflect its ethnic heartland and leadership—the biblical term "Israel" was meaningless to the Romans. Thus, Judea, along with the new city-states spawned from its amputations, were enlisted as satellites of the new Roman province of Syria, governed by Aemilius Scaurus (*Ant.* 14.74–79; *J.W.* 1.155–57).

The loss of ports and international highways economically emasculated the Jewish state, but not to the extent that it could no longer function as a viable tributary to Rome. The Roman silver denarius entered the currency pool of Judea for the first time, albeit modestly at first.[11] Over the subsequent years, private contractors arrived with the authority to farm taxes for Rome, gather tribute, issue loans, and foreclose on properties from those who could not repay their loans. Some tax farmers even arose among the Jews themselves, earning the hatred of their compatriots. According to Josephus, the Romans exacted over 10,000 talents of silver from the state's population over the next few years (*Ant.* 14.78).[12] Where he pulls this figure from is unknown, but it is not farfetched if it pertains to the overall economic impact. As Roman taxes were imposed, those without liquid assets to pay would have been forced to sell their animals or small plots, often to wealthier landowners, such as priests (cf. Matt 18:25). While this would also mean inheriting outstanding debts, the wealthy buyers could offset these debts by renting out the property to tenant farmers

---

time. Herodotus (fifth century BC) referred to the inhabitants of the coastal plain as "the Syrians called Palestinians" (*Hist.* 3.5.1), and Aristotle (fourth century BC) called the Dead Sea "a lake in Palestine" (*Meteorology* 2.3.19). After Pompey's conquest, the term was used more frequently to denote the coastal plain (cf. Plutarch, *Pomp.* 45.1) and eventually became an official provincial name in the time of Hadrian.

9. Subsequent history would see these cities loosened from the headship of Damascus, but they still remained a subregional league. See Peter Richardson, *Herod: King of the Jews and Friend of the Romans* (Columbia: University of South Carolina Press, 1996), 88–91.

10. Grant and Jensen surmise that Pompey removed the whole region of Samaria from Jewish control. See Michael Grant, *Herod the Great* (London: Weidenfeld and Nicolson, 1971), 31–32; Jensen, "Political History in Galilee," 58. But there is no explicit claim to this effect in any of the sources. The fact that the Samaritan temple was not rebuilt suggests that Jewish control continued to prevail over the Samaritan community, and that only the city of Samaria was removed from Jewish oversight.

11. Meshorer, *Persian Period through Hasmonaeans*, 59.

12. In modern terms, this would be the equivalent of approximately US$15 billion.

(quite often the previous landowners). Then there were those on the poverty line who simply could not afford taxes or rents and so hired themselves out as day laborers or sold themselves and family members into slavery—all economic realities that feature in the parables of Jesus. Thus, a significant redistribution of wealth occurred. Rome was no longer the protector from across the sea but the new Babylon who forced many from their land and took away Jewish independence because of the sinfulness of the Jewish leaders.

4.1.4 THEOLOGICAL RESPONSES TO THE ROMAN CONQUEST

The Essenes equated the Romans with the ancient Babylonians, as seen in their Pesher of Habakkuk (1QpHab), written in the late first century BC. They referred to the Romans as "Kittim," borrowing the biblical term that had come to denote seafaring peoples from the Mediterranean coastlands (cf. Gen 10:4; Dan 11:30).

> "For I am about to raise up the Babylonians,
> that bitter and rash nation." [Hab 1:6a]

> Its interpretation: This is about the Kittim [the Romans], who are swift and mighty enough in war to destroy so many, that the whole earth comes under the sovereignty of the Kittim. They occupy many countries, yet do not trust the regulations of God.

> "They march across the regions of the earth
> to possess settlements not their own." [Hab 1:6b]

> Its interpretation: This is about the Kittim, who . . . cross the plain to attack and raid the cities of the earth . . .

> "At every fortress, he laughs.
> He heaped up dirt and captured it." [Hab 1:10b]

> Its interpretation: This is about the commanders of the Kittim, who raided the fortresses of the people, and laughed in ridicule at them. With a great many people, they surrounded and seized them. With terror and fear, they were put into their hand, and they demolished them because of the guilt of those who dwell there. (1QpHab 2:10b–3:1; 4:3b–4:9a)

The Essenes were not alone in making such an assessment of the Romans and the Jewish leadership. Many recognized that, for all their faults and foibles, the Hasmoneans had carved out an independent kingdom, unified the covenantal lands of ancient Israel, and centralized the national leadership in Jerusalem—all theologically orthodox notions consonant with Torah and prophetic expectations. They had, in part, helped create circumstances that could promote covenantal holiness, which might lead in time to the fulfilment of prophetic hopes. But they themselves then became an encumbrance to such holiness and hope and were seen to have led the nation into sin. They had become just like the leaders of other nations around them—Hellenistic monarchs driven by hubris, squabbling for their own power. They had compromised the integrity of the Jewish state, and the Roman military fist knocked the breath out of the nation. Admittedly, Rome had not beaten Judea to a pulp, as it would in AD 70. But the guarantor of national holiness, the high priest John Hyrcanus II, was now a Roman appointee, and he was being controlled locally by his cosmopolitan adviser, Antipater the Idumean—a man religiously Jewish but with one foot in the Greek world and the other in the Nabatean. The program of national restoration in fulfilment of Torah and prophetic hopes had been utterly compromised.

As sons of Alexander Jannaeus, John Hyrcanus II and Aristobulus II embodied the biblical motif of the two wayward sons of a prominent man. The most cogent exemplars of this motif were Nadab and Abihu, the sons of Aaron, who offered unauthorized fire on the altar and were immolated by a divine flame (Lev 10:1–2); and Hophni and Phinehas, the sons of Eli, who had shown contempt for Yahweh's offerings, abused the people under their care, and lost their lives and the ark of the covenant in battle against the Philistines (1 Sam 2:12–17, 34; 4:4–11). With such priestly precedents, one can understand the sense of dread felt by the Jewish nation at the brothers' infighting, the expectation of divine judgment, as well as the desire for a prophet to set the nation aright and a messiah to rule the people in righteousness. Just as David had been the king of Yahweh's choosing to rescue the nation floundering under the corruption exemplified by Eli and his two sons, so the hope of many was for a new David to rescue the nation from the mess the Hasmoneans had manufactured and the oppression of foreign nations.

One of the Psalms of Solomon aptly captures this sentiment, picking up the imagery of Psalm 2 and alluding to various events of the Hasmonean era:

> You, Lord, chose David as king over Israel,
> and you swore to him about his offspring,

that his kingdom would never fail before you.
But in our sins, sinners rose up against us.
They took hold of us and expelled us in ways I can scarcely express.
They seized us by force and did not honor your precious name.
To their own glory, they established a kingdom of their own eminence.
They ruined the throne of David in arrogant exchange . . .

But the sons of the covenant, who were mingled amongst them,
    outperformed them.
There was not one of them in Jerusalem who practiced mercy or truth.
Those who loved the gatherings of the pure managed to flee
    from them,
like birds thrown from their nests.
They roamed in deserts to save their lives from evil,
and precious in the sight of these exiles
was the life of anyone who was saved from them.
They were scattered by the lawless over the whole earth,
for the sky ceased to drop its rain upon the earth.
Eternal springs rising from the deep and down high mountains were
    stopped,
for among them there was none who practiced righteousness or justice.
From their leader down to the least of people, all were in sin—
the king in illegality, the judge in inconsistency, and the people in sin.
Look, Lord, and raise up for them their king,
the son of David, in the time that you have chosen,
your child to reign over Israel.[13]
Equip him with strength to shatter unrighteous rulers,
to cleanse Jerusalem of the nations that destructively tread her down;
in the wisdom of righteousness, to expel sinners from your property;
to crush the pride of the sinner like a clay vessel;
with an iron rod, to crush their whole basis;
to eradicate unlawful nations with the word of his mouth;
at his rebuke, to make nations flee from his presence,
and reprimand sinners for the thought of their hearts.
He will gather a holy people, whom he will lead in righteousness;
he will judge the tribes of the people sanctified by the Lord their God.

---

13. Alternatively, "to reign over Israel, your child."

> He will be a righteous king over them, taught by God,
> and there will be no unrighteousness among them in his days,
> for all will be holy, and the king will be the Lord's messiah.
> For he will not trust in horse or rider or bow,
> nor raise gold and silver for war,
> nor lead many people in hope of a day of battle.
> The Lord himself will be his king,
> the hope of him fortified with hope in God.
> He will have mercy on the nations in fear before him,
> for he will strike the earth with the word of his mouth forever.
> He will bless the Lord's people in wisdom with gladness.
> He will be innocent of sin, to rule a great people,
> reprimanding rulers and removing sinners with the power of his word.
> He will not weaken from God in his days,
> for God will make him strong with the holy spirit,
> and wise with intelligent counsel
> —with power and righteousness. (Pss. Sol. 17:4–6, 15–26, 32–37)

The psalm describes the Davidic messiah as the antithesis to the Hasmoneans, their counsellors, and the foreign powers that had ruled the Jews. The imagery is prophetic insofar as it depicts the king as God's chosen vessel to enact judgment and establish righteousness in fulfilment of the promises to David. It is apocalyptic insofar as it sees the messianic king repudiating military force and wealth and establishing righteousness through the power of the divine word. It is eschatological insofar as it foresees a sharp discontinuity between the previous age of sin and the future age of blessing. The notion that God had already chosen a time for the messiah's rise makes his advent inevitable, producing messianic expectation and pious patience—ideas consonant with the ethic propounded in the book of Daniel. Of course, certain quarters of Judaism no longer cared for prophetic fulfilment. Davidic hopes had perished from the ranks of the Sadducees and other Jewish nobility. But it was still very much a factor influencing the religious hope of many in their new situation under Roman sovereignty.

4.2 THE DEVELOPMENT OF JUDAISM

4.2.1 THE PHARISEES, SCHOOLS, AND SYNAGOGUES

The blow to national holiness that Hasmonean leadership and the Roman conquest engendered made the Pharisees more desperate to disseminate their own brand of holiness throughout the Jewish state. To that end, they pursued two strategies. The first was to gain as much power in the Jerusalem Sanhedrin as they could. Simeon ben-Shetach was still its president, and as uncle to John Hyrcanus II, he had some sway over the high priest. But Simeon was now elderly, and Hyrcanus was increasingly beholden to the indefatigable Antipater, who was keen to collaborate with the Romans. The Pharisees therefore focused on stacking the Sanhedrin with as many of their members as they could. Many Sadducees had also lost their lives in support of Aristobulus II when the Romans conquered the country (cf. *Ant.* 14.74; *J.W.* 1.154), which allowed the Pharisees to fill important vacancies more easily. When Simeon ben-Shetach eventually died (we are not sure exactly when this was), the presidency passed to his Pharisaic deputy, Judah ben-Tabbai (Gemara on b. Ḥag. 16b).

The second strategy of the Pharisees was the development of schools. Simeon ben-Shetach had encouraged the education of children, and it now became a more deliberate effort (y. Ketub. 8:11, 32c; cf. B. Bat. 21a). This took the models of the Greek gymnasium and philosophical tradition, especially Plato's Academy (recently destroyed by Sulla [86 BC]), and baptized them into Judaism. This obviated the need to rely on foreign institutions for education and helped to foster distinctive Jewish culture, particularly of the fundamentalist Pharisaic brand.[1] The curriculum did not involve training for war or sport, or the study of Greek literature and philosophy (as far as we know). Rather, it concentrated on the study of Scripture, especially the Torah. The Pharisees took their mandate from Torah's insistence that parents teach their children in the ways of Yahweh, which would result in divine blessing (Deut 6:1–3, 7; 11:19–21). The Pharisees were not content to leave this task in the hands of parents, especially in the social dislocation following the Roman conquest. Economic upheaval drew the deprived into desperate circumstances,

---

1. Cf. Elisa Uusimäki, "The Rise of the Sage in Greek and Jewish Antiquity," *JSJ* 49.1 (2018): 1–29.

with religious devotion becoming a potential casualty. The danger was further covenantal breach and consequent divine judgment. As avowed Torah experts, the fundamentalist Pharisees viewed themselves as best placed to offer the right education. Indeed, the development of schools presented the Pharisees with the opportunity to promote the reading and discussion of Scripture, which would increase religious awareness and devotion throughout the country with concomitant covenantal blessing. It also had the potential to increase literacy, which could thereby improve socio-economic prospects (even if the focus was primarily on scriptural learning).

The Pharisees may have taken a leaf out of Essene practice, which had developed a process of education for the youngsters in their own community:

> This is the rule for all who are duty-bound to the congregation, for every citizen in Israel:
>
>> From his youth, he is to be taught from the meditation manual. As he gets older, he is to be educated in the regulations of the covenant, and to receive instruction in their customs. For ten years, he will come through childhood. At age twenty, he may graduate to the initiates and come to membership within his clan, belonging to the community in the holy congregation. (Rule of the Congregation [1QS^a] 1:6-9)

The aim of the Pharisees' schools was to produce a class of "saints" (holy ones) or "sons of the commandment"—educated Jews who were devoted to piety, qualified to be gatekeepers of the community, and heirs of God's coming kingdom, which would one day crush the kingdoms of the earth, as per the vision of Daniel 7. Some of these educated people would become the rich young rulers of districts, while others would swell the ranks of the Pharisees and help them impose their ultra-conservative vision upon the Sanhedrin and the nation. In this way, Pharisaic thinking was akin to Plato's argument that the best form of government was one in which philosophers ruled, for their love of wisdom made them the most competent to take charge of public affairs (*Republic* V–VII). It is why the Pharisees and teachers of the Law came to be viewed as community leaders of exceptional righteousness and harbingers of the coming kingdom of God (cf. Matt 5:20; Phil 3:4–6).

To call these schools a public school system is an overstatement, as they were not centrally funded, and there is little evidence that they became ubiquitous.² They were ad hoc, being famed more for the teachers themselves (e.g., Hillel, Shammai) than for the schools as a phenomenon. If literacy did increase, it was modestly, for the majority of the population remained illiterate—"people of the land" (Heb. *'am ha'arets*), as the Pharisees disparagingly called them. Although widespread education of the population might have been an aspirational goal, few could spare the time or expense to educate even a single son. This is not to imply that teachers grew rich from charging for their tuition—they often had a reputation for poverty and needed to work in other professions for most of the year to make a living, leaving them to teach only in particular seasons. Payment for their services amounted to little more than a stipend to compensate for time lost in their other work.³

This means there was no such thing as fixed enrolment or a set curriculum. The program of study was defined by the teacher in each individual school and shaped by the needs of his students present. However, the reading of the Scriptures was almost certainly universal. This increased the work and profile of scribes who could copy the Scriptures and spawned a new class of teachers of the Law, whose ranks persisted into the first century, as reflected in the Gospels. Not every such teacher of the Law was a Pharisee, for any person could in theory start a school if they had a reputation for instruction and opportunity to conduct lessons. Nevertheless, the Pharisees were the prime movers, especially as such schools presented them with the means of promoting their own puritanical interpretation of Torah, as reflected in their Oral Law. Jesus viewed the Oral Law as aberrant, since it went beyond the written Scriptures and claimed equal authority with it (cf. Deut 4:2; Matt 15:1–14), but this did not stop him engaging with schools. As the schools increased, so did the socio-political influence of the Pharisees, and Jesus was a vocal critic of this.

Pharisaic piety and ethics, based as it was on very literal interpretations of the Law, gained widespread currency. We begin to see, for example, increased use of *tefillin*—tiny extracts of Torah placed in small receptacles that were strapped to the forearm and forehead, in hyper-literal fulfilment of the injunction to bind the commandments on the arm and to have them dangle before the eyes (Deut 6:8). Similar amulet-like extracts (*mezuzot*) were placed in doorjambs to fulfil the command to write the Law on the posts of one's

---

2. The later rabbinic claims that the schools abounded is an exaggeration or a retrojection. See Catherine Hezser, *Jewish Literacy in Roman Palestine*, Texts and Studies in Ancient Judaism 81 (Tübingen: Mohr Siebeck, 2001), 50.

3. Hezser, *Jewish Literacy in Roman Palestine*, 57.

house (Deut 6:9).[4] A concern for ritual purity saw the development of rigorous washing disciplines and the installation in domestic dwellings of ritual baths (*miqvaot*) and stone storage vessels which, according to the Oral Law, could not be ritually contaminated. Innovative doctrines also emerged, such as the notion that God had imparted the Law to Moses via angels, as a means of preserving his absolute transcendence and holiness vis-à-vis sinful humans.

It was not just children who came to the schools for elementary instruction. The reputation of some teachers grew so great that they were recognized with the honorific title of *rabbi* ("grand master"). They attracted older students—disciples—who continued their education through ongoing discussion of the Scriptures and a program of mentorship, not dissimilar to some of the Greek philosophical schools. The expectation was that these disciples would, in turn, become the teachers, rabbis, politicians, and community leaders of the future, perpetuating the traditions of their rabbi. That the title "rabbi" was frequently given to Jesus of Nazareth suggests that he was a highly recognized teacher of adult disciples. Although there is no overt claim that Jesus educated children, there is circumstantial evidence that he might have or that people desired him to do so. For instance, he is said to have placed a young child among his adult disciples and told them to become like the child in lowliness in order to be great in the kingdom of God (Matt 18:1–5). If this visual illustration was specific to discipleship, then the child embodied a novice keen to learn, in contrast to the opinionated, argumentative students that Jesus's disciples had become. People also brought their children to Jesus, much to the chagrin of his disciples, which drew Jesus's statement that the kingdom of God belonged to such children (Matt 19:13–15; cf. 11:25).

Most schools probably operated out of the houses of wealthy individuals (cf. Mark 2:1–4) or in makeshift quarters, like open squares, city gates, or groves (cf. Acts 16:13). Only a few schools met in dedicated study halls. But the growth of the school movement increased the demand for such study halls. The result was the proliferation of synagogue buildings that could host elementary tuition, act as lecture theaters for rabbis and their disciples, host halakhic debate, provide secure storage of expensive scrolls of Scripture, and hold larger public gatherings at which the Scriptures could be read, the citizenry instructed, and prayers offered.[5] Average citizens keen to practice their culture would gather with teachers and rabbis for public worship wherever they could

---

4. This was not completely novel, as religious amulets were popularly used throughout the Mediterranean and ancient Near East for millennia beforehand.

5. It is wrong to assume that a building would function solely as a study hall, especially when schooling probably occurred only during certain seasons of the year. The proliferation of multi-purpose

find space, but this increasingly occurred in dedicated synagogue buildings. Indeed, the Greek word *synagōgē* implies a gathering of people rather than a specific building.[6] In this way, the Jewish school essentially merged with the prayer house of diaspora Jewry to fuel the growth of synagogues throughout Palestine.[7]

The Theodotos Inscription from Jerusalem provides a pivotal piece of evidence for this. This dedicatory plaque, written in Greek, once stood within a late first century BC synagogue in Jerusalem's city of David quarter:

> Theodotos, son of Vettenus, priest and synagogue ruler, son of a synagogue ruler, grandson of a synagogue ruler, built this synagogue for the reading of the Law and the teaching of the commandments, as well as the salon, the rooms, and the water fixtures, as a guesthouse for those in need from abroad. It was founded by his fathers, and the elders, and Simonides. (*CIJ* 2:1404)

Since Theodotos's father and grandfather had been heads of the synagogue before him, it must have existed in the mid-first century BC even before there was a dedicated building.[8] As a priest, Theodotos was probably not a Pharisee, which shows that the school movement caught on beyond Pharisee circles. By the following century, synagogues were found across Judea, Transjordan, and Galilee, and indeed throughout the world of the diaspora, and even among Samaritan communities.

In Jerusalem, some schools met within the outer grounds of the temple. The Lucan depiction of the twelve-year old Jesus interacting with teachers in the temple courts (Luke 2:41–50) aptly captures this historical reality, showing a youngster keen to learn, even without his parents' knowledge.[9] What other formal education Jesus might have undergone is not known for certain (cf. Matt 13:54; Mark 6:2), though his ability to read the Scriptures and discuss them suggests some exposure to education. He himself is known to have taught in the temple precincts (Matt 21:23; 26:55; John 7:14, 28; 8:20), and the early church also met there (Acts 2:46).

---

synagogues, as well as larger domestic dwellings, is evidence enough that ad hoc schooling took place. Cf. Hezser, *Jewish Literacy in Roman Palestine*, 51–56.

6. We find a similar phenomenon with the idea of "church" (Greek: *ekklēsia*), which originally denoted a political gathering of people but eventually came to be used of the building in which Christian gatherings took place.

7. Many prominent Pharisees of the first century BC had spent time in Egypt, often to escape persecution. The growth of school-synagogues after their return to the Jewish state suggests the influence of the prayer houses of Egypt upon their vision.

8. John S. Kloppenborg Verbin, "Dating Theodotos (*CIJ* II 1404)," *JJS* 51.2 (2000): 243–80.

9. Géza Vermès, *The Nativity: History and Legend* (London: Penguin, 2006), 152.

Many average citizens who came to worship at the synagogues could not necessarily understand all the archaic Hebrew of the Scriptures, since their first language was Aramaic. To promote understanding and facilitate discussion, the Scriptures were translated and paraphrased into Aramaic. By the end of the first century BC, these were being committed to writing and came to be known as targums (from an Aramaic word meaning "interpretation"). The most famous were Targum Onkelos (Torah) and Targum Jonathan (Prophets).[10]

4.2.2 CANONS OF SCRIPTURE

The growth of Jewish school-synagogues precipitated a heightened awareness of scriptural canons. The Torah and Prophets had long since been closed as authoritative corpora (cf. Matt 5:17), and the Psalter was also recognized as an authoritative collection (cf. Luke 24:26, 44). These were staples for reading within the school-synagogues. But this raised questions about whether any other Jewish literature might viably be studied and read publicly. There was an abundance of other Jewish writings, some centuries old (e.g., Lamentations, Chronicles, Job), and others of more recent vintage (e.g., Ben Sira, Song of Songs, Psalms of Solomon, Assumption of Moses). While these were all read widely, and some even translated into Greek, the question of whether some could sit alongside the Psalms in a third canonical collection gained traction. It was important for students and disciples to discern which books could be prized as divinely inspired, which were simply beneficial for critical reading, and which books were of dubious value.

The question was not framed with specific clarity in the first century BC, but it emerged out of the fact that laity (and not just priests) were handling scriptural scrolls in the school-synagogues. Consideration of the issues enabled the Pharisees to define the scope of the Jewish Scriptures, especially over and against the competing claims of the Sadducees and Samaritans, and thus help shape Jewish identity. Books that were of divine origin were deemed holy and, as the rabbis eventually couched it, would defile a lay person who handled them ("make the hands unclean" [m. Yad. 3:5]).[11] It was not until the late first century that there was general agreement over which books deserved a place

---

10. Targums on the books that would come to be part of the Writings (*Ketubim*) were less fixed and poorly preserved. This helps us discern something of the canonical consciousness of Judaism and trace the late development of the Writings.

11. For a discussion on the meaning of this perplexing principle, see Timothy H. Lim, "The Defilement of the Hands as a Principle Determining the Holiness of Scriptures," *JTS* 61.2 (2010): 501–15.

alongside the Psalms, and these solidified into the third Hebrew canon, known as the Writings (cf. *Ag. Ap.* 1.38). Its compilation and closure can be largely attributed to the proliferation of school-synagogues.

Over the course of time, the Pharisaic penchant for the utmost literalism led to the redefining of certain canonical issues. For example, the claim that Qoheleth was "son of David, king in Jerusalem" (Eccl 1:1) led to the equation of Qoheleth with King Solomon (cf. t. Yad. 2:14). A view developed that only prophets known from biblical texts could have been inspired by God to write Scripture, despite the lack of overt statements of authorship in many biblical works (e.g., Genesis). This flattened rhetorical understanding and authorship issues. It attached the concept of divine inspiration to a closed set of individuals from the far distant past and eliminated the reality of redaction and literary development almost completely from the understanding of biblical books. This led, for example, to the notion that Moses wrote practically the entire Torah; that Samuel authored the books of Judges, Samuel, and Ruth; that Jeremiah authored Kings and Lamentations, in addition to his own prophetic book (cf. B. Bat. 14b–15a); and that Isaiah had composed the whole book bearing his name, despite portions of it being relevant only centuries after his lifetime. Yahweh's punctiliar delivery of the Ten Commandments to Moses became the paradigm for how the divine inspiration of Scripture was understood. Biblical authors became mere conduits of the divine word—postmen, as it were, rather than active spokesmen on the deity's behalf who might give essence and shape to the divine word. This flattened view of literary development and rhetorical artistry arose out of the pairing of Pharisaic hyper-literalism and the belief in the sovereignty of God over all history. Thus, for example, the Pharisees proposed that Isaiah was able to prophesy about the exile in Babylon and the return from it, even though he lived one to two centuries earlier because God, as the author of history, revealed it to him ahead of time. The issue of whether such knowledge was relevant to audiences in Isaiah's own day, which would enable them to respond adequately to it, was completely overshadowed by a fetishistic commitment to hyper-literalism and a puritanical concern for God's sovereignty over history.

It is not hard to understand how this concern arose in the context of the failure of Jewish sovereignty and the escalating hope for the eschatological kingdom of God. But this reframing of authorship issues had two critical long-term effects. The first was to relegate revelation to the far distant past as a completed phenomenon. The Hasmoneans and Sadducees had effectively made this move some decades earlier, but the Pharisees now began to move in a similar hermeneutical direction. Prophetic figures were still acknowledged in broader Judaism for a further century or more, and prophetic activity was still expected and encouraged in the early church. But by the end of the first century, Josephus asserted that prophetic activity practically ceased at the time of Artaxerxes I (465–424 BC) and that all Jewish writings since then suffered "because there had not been an exact succession of prophets" (*Ag. Ap.* 1.41). The second effect was to enshrine the Pharisaic Oral Law as divinely inspired and, therefore, on par with the written Torah. With divine inspiration being confined to the distant past, this necessitated the claim that God had committed the Oral Law to Moses at Sinai through the agency of angels, along with the written Torah. This was a theological necessity if the fundamentalist Pharisees were to avoid the charge that they had added to the Law in contravention of their own interpretation of Deut 4:2. This claim did not achieve full definition until after the fall of the temple in AD 70, but it demonstrates the increasing profile of the Oral Law as Pharisaic influence within Judaism grew.

4.2.3 HILLEL THE ELDER

Hillel the Elder was one of the most influential rabbis of Second Temple Judaism. His stature was so significant that memory of his life was schematized to conform to the pattern of Moses's life. Discerning fact from pious fiction in his curriculum vitae is, therefore, difficult. Hillel was probably born ca. 80 BC under Parthian rule in Mesopotamia[12] and was of ostensibly Davidic descent.[13] He had at least one brother, Shebna, who became a wealthy merchant (b. Sotah 21a). At some point, the brothers migrated to Jerusalem, though whether this was as children or as adults is not clear.

Hillel opted against pursuing business and devoted himself to the study of Torah. He became a pupil of some leading lights with significant political careers, such as Abtalion, the disciple and successor of Judah ben-Tabbai (president of the Sanhedrin, ca. 60–54 BC). Judah was known to major more on scriptural exegesis than the Oral Law, which was a trait he passed down to Abtalion and thence to Hillel.[14] He also studied under Menahem the Essene,

---

12. Hillel's death is usually dated to ca. AD 10, and his birth is then backdated to ca. 110 BC on the basis of deliberate Mosaic schematization. It is far more likely that Hillel was born decades later and died slightly earlier than the traditional dates assigned.

13. Hillel's Davidic lineage is gleaned from a later tradition, which traces the ancestry of his prominent descendant, Judah ha-Nasi (the compiler of the Mishnah), allegedly back to David via his son Shephatiah (b. Ketub. 62b; cf. 2 Sam 3:4; 1 Chr 3:3).

14. There is a much later tradition that Judah ben-Tabbai was the founder of Karaite Judaism, which recognized the authority only of the written Torah and rejected the Oral Law that characterized rabbinic Judaism. However, there is no way to verify this tradition.

who was at one time the vice president of the Sanhedrin. Hillel even succeeded Menahem as head of his school. From an early stage, he cultivated a reputation as a problem solver and competent exegete, developing seven principles of exegesis (t. Sanh. 7:5). His halakhic hermeneutic tended to show more latitude than some of his peers—a tendency that differentiated him from his later halakhic competitor, Shammai.

Hillel became one of the most distinguished scholars of his generation and attracted several disciples. There may even have been growing anticipation over whether he, a Davidic descendant, might become a messianic figure. The later tradition that he became president of the Sanhedrin (b. Pesaḥ. 66a; b. Šabb. 31a) is fallacious, but it is plausible that he attained membership of the Sanhedrin. Even if many pinned political or messianic hopes on him, though, Hillel himself deflected these in preference to a salubrious life of study.

Hillel influenced Judaism through his irenic character and teachings, which sometimes softened the hard edge of Pharisaic legalism. Three didactic contributions stand out. The first was a maxim remembered in a later rabbinic parable (b. Šabb. 31a). According to the tale, a potential gentile convert asked Hillel to explain the whole Torah to him in the time it took him (the gentile) to keep balance on one foot. Hillel produced the maxim, "Do not do to others what is hateful to you. That is the complete summary of the Torah. The rest is its commentary. Go, apply yourself." The similarity with Jesus's own "Golden Rule" ("Do to others as you want them to do to you" [Luke 6:31]) is apparent, and Hillel's maxim almost certainly influenced Jesus's formulation. Both encouraged brotherly love in fulfilment of the Law (cf. m. 'Avot 2.4). Jesus's version developed Hillel's thought further by taking a default attitude of positive engagement ("Do . . .") over Hillel's attitude of benign disengagement ("Do not do . . ."). One wonders whether, as a child, Jesus ever had any direct encounters with the elderly Hillel (cf. Luke 2:46).

Hillel's second major teaching was about whether the Passover could be sacrificed on a Sabbath without contravening the command to desist from work. This conundrum probably arose in the late 40s BC, after Passover coincided with the Sabbath three times in eight years (50, 47, 43 BC).[15] He argued that, on analogy with the daily sacrifices, which were still offered every Sabbath, the Passover sacrifice took precedence over the cessation of work (b. Pesaḥ. 66a). The nature of the controversy shows how concerned the Pharisees and other Jewish leaders were for legal literalism and precision. Hillel's approach provides

---

15. Passover fell on the Sabbath also in 23, 19, 16, and 3 BC, which all ostensibly occurred in Hillel's lifetime. However, the tradition relating to Hillel's solution suggests he formulated it in his younger days.

an interesting yardstick to Jesus's own appeal to the work of God and priests on the Sabbath as a means of discerning ethical priorities and his own authority to perform particular acts and make halakhic pronouncements (Matt 12:1–8; John 5:16–18).

The third major contribution of Hillel was the invention of the *prozbul* custom. According to the Sabbatical laws of Deuteronomy 15, all debts between fellow Israelites were to be cancelled every seven years. In the wake of the economic strain that Roman conquest foisted upon Judea, many people were unable to meet their financial obligations within the standard six-year period. Creditors, therefore, were having to forego the recovery of their loans, rendering their lending services economically untenable. Moneylenders were understandably reluctant to provide loans to those who desperately needed funds to develop or hold onto their livelihoods. This situation encouraged unscrupulous behavior by creditors who either ignored the Sabbatical dictates in order to protect their own finances or used violence to foreclose on loans, driving the most vulnerable out of the country or to criminal behavior themselves. It also restricted the responsibly minded to procuring loans from foreign creditors not subject to the Sabbatical law, but this meant they had to mortgage their property within the covenant land to gentiles. These circumstances were the very antithesis of the Sabbatical Year's purpose, which was to curb poverty, encourage generosity and financial responsibility, and prevent Israelites from becoming dependent on gentiles. The result was economic mayhem that compromised the observance of Torah, damaged the social fabric of Judaism, promoted classism, increased foreign ownership of Jewish land, and consigned some Jews to slavery.

Hillel's solution was to arrange for creditors and debtors to make any outstanding loan over to the Jewish community at large ahead of any Sabbatical Year, for the duration of the Sabbatical Year. This effectively turned the loan into a public "endowment" (Heb. *prozbul*, from Gk. *prosbolē*) and therefore not liable to either cancellation or repayment while the Sabbatical Year was in force. Community judges held the "endowments" in trust for the relevant parties, and once the Sabbatical Year was over, the "endowment" reverted to a loan again, with all previous conditions intact (m. Šeb. 10). In this way, the Sabbatical Year became effectively a hiatus in the period of the loan. Hillel's innovation was for "the protection of society" (m. Giṭ. 4.3) in a period of economic disarray. Yet the *prozbul* appealed to the hyper-legal inclination of his fellow Pharisees because the loophole still allowed for the technical observance of the Sabbatical laws, even though it effectively subverted them. The innovation soon became a standard, rather than exceptional, condition of loans.

It is in this socio-economic context that Jesus proclaimed himself the anointed harbinger of the Jubilee (Luke 4:18–21), taught Simon the Pharisee about the free cancellation of large debts that could not be repaid (Luke 7:36–50), and taught his own disciples to petition God for the forgiveness of their debts, as they themselves forgave their debtors (Luke 11:4). While these statements included symbolic allusions to sin as debt, they were not solely symbolic. Jesus criticized obedience by loophole, or purely external piety that did not come from the heart. It led him to bemoan the fate of the Jewish nation (Matt 23:1–39) and to seek the establishment of an entirely new eschatological order (Matt 16:27–28; 24:27–44; 26:61).

Hillel lived a very long life, dying probably in his eighties in the early years of the first century. His grandson, Gamaliel I, continued his tradition, becoming a leader of the Pharisees in the first century and sitting on the Sanhedrin. In this capacity, Gamaliel featured pivotally in the trial of Jesus's apostles (Acts 5:33–40). He was also a prominent rabbi, among whose students was Saul of Tarsus (i.e., Paul [Acts 22:3]).

4.2.4 GODFEARERS AND CONVERTS

In their pursuit of virtue, the Greek philosophers had promoted a kind of humanism that sought to apprehend reality without reference to the capricious Greek gods. The Greek notion of the *logos* as an ordering principle of the universe began to break down the impulse to honor deities with baser instincts, who did nothing for promoting virtue or order. The *logos* thus found a distinct parallel with the Jewish understanding of Yahweh as a transcendent and righteous creator. Platonic philosophy especially, with its emphasis on apprehending "the good"—the ideal that lay behind all reality—provided a clear conduit between Greek and Jewish thought (cf. 2.4.3 above). The *logos* was also understood as the process of rational thought, which led to reason, wisdom, and virtue (cf. the modern term "logic"). This found parallel in the Jewish concepts of divine revelation and discourse over the Scriptures, which took place in the school-synagogue. What's more, the growth of school-synagogues made Judaism more visible and accessible to gentiles. Just as Greek thought provided robust structures for Jewish theology, so Jewish wisdom and ethics provided an appealing model of the virtuous life for philosophically minded Greeks.

Consequently, some gentiles found Judaism philosophically and ethically appealing. Such gentiles frequented Jewish synagogues, listening to and engaging in discussion of the Scriptures. For a minority, the appeal was so complete that they became proselytes by undergoing circumcision. For the majority, though, the attraction did not anesthetize them to the circumcision blade. Instead, it commended a generic monotheism with Yahweh as the universal lord of creation. It repudiated the fickle deities of the Greek myths, along with their idols and cults. Instead, it encouraged ethical discourse and the pursuit of virtue and sexual continence. Such gentiles came to be known as "Godfearers." They were never accepted as full members of the Jewish community, even in diaspora contexts. Yet, because their attachment to the God of Israel was voluntary and countercultural, their knowledge of the Jewish Scriptures was sometimes more complete than that of native Jews. Such devotion earned them Jewish respect as righteous gentiles. In the first century, the preaching of the Christian gospel in synagogues would win over many such Godfearers. Although there was confusion in the first decades of the early church over whether gentiles needed to Judaize to become full members, the question was soon settled in the negative. It paved the way for the development of a culturally mixed church, which gentiles would come to predominate. This is not to take away from the fact that pagan Greeks were converted to Christianity, too. However, Godfearers provided a critical cultural platform for Christianity's success in the early years (cf. Acts 10:2, 22; 13:26; 17:4).

4.3 ROMAN HEGEMONY

4.3.1 POMPEY'S RETURN TO ROME

As Pompey journeyed back to Rome, he took with him Aristobulus II, Aristobulus's four children, and Aristobulus's father-in-law, Absalom (son of John Hyrcanus I). Pompey intended to feature them as prisoners in his triumphal procession through Rome. But along the way, Aristobulus's eldest son, Alexander II, slipped his captor (*Ant.* 14.79; *J.W.* 1.158), and Pompey was unable to recapture him. In order not to draw attention to his escape, Pompey featured only Aristobulus in the procession, which occurred on Pompey's forty-sixth birthday (29 September 61 BC [Plutarch, *Pomp.* 45.4).[1]

Pompey boasted that he received Asia as the remotest of Rome's provinces, and his conquests had put it in the middle (Pliny the Elder, *Nat.* 7.27). He increased Rome's total annual tributary income by 70 percent, deposited some 20,000 talents of silver and gold into Rome's coffers,[2] paid each of his soldiers over thirteen years of wages for their five years of service, and still had enough left over to surpass the wealth of Rome's previous richest man, Marcus Licinius Crassus. He had now celebrated a triumphal procession for victories on each of the three known continents: Africa, Europe, and Asia (Plutarch, *Pomp.* 45.3–5). To cap off his achievement, he financed the construction of an entertainment complex overlooking the Field of Mars, just outside Rome's walls, where annual elections were held. Built ostensibly as a temple to Venus, the enormous structure contained, amongst other things, a theater and assembly chamber, complete with a statue of Pompey himself. The palatial complex was a monument to Pompey's glory and testament to how he was molding Roman society into his own likeness. It was accordingly dubbed "Pompey's Theater."[3]

Despite his successes, Pompey found himself rebuffed by the *Optimates* in the Senate, who did not rubber-stamp his arrangements in the east. They were threatened by the enormous influence he now wielded and feared that he had become bigger than the state itself. Although the Republic had created

---

1. In his list of the paraded captives, Plutarch mentions Aristobulus without reference to his other family members. This is conspicuous, since Plutarch mentions the families of other notable captives.
2. In modern terms, this is the equivalent of US$30 billion.
3. Boatwright et al., *The Romans*, 219.

laws to prevent such a thing from happening, Sulla's dictatorship (82–79 BC) had shown that these laws could be exploited, and the Republic had been destabilized ever since. Pompey had amassed his colossal wealth and power legally, effectively becoming a personal franchise of the Roman state itself. Furthermore, the conspiracy of Catiline (63 BC), who had plotted a *coup d'état* that was only foiled in the late stages by Cicero, spooked Roman society. There was a heightened suspicion that unscrupulous individuals might take the state hostage to their own ambition. The *Optimates* thus kept obstructing Pompey's goals, while the *Populares* were being drawn ever closer to him. As long as his configuration of the east remained unratified, there was potential for instability to creep back into the east. The fact that Aristobulus II's son, Alexander II, remained at large contributed to this. Rome was thus bifurcated between the standard machinery of state, represented by the patrician *Optimates*, and the virtual "state" of Pompey, backed by the *Populares*.

4.3.2 THE FIRST TRIUMVIRATE

In the same year that Pompey conquered Jerusalem and restored John Hyrcanus II as high priest (63 BC), Rome also received a new high priest. The position of *Pontifex Maximus* went to Gaius Julius Caesar. Caesar was a patrician by birth, but his family had fallen into financial difficulty (by patrician standards). Consequently, Caesar did not grow up on Rome's exclusive Palatine Hill but in the infamous Suburra district. He could therefore mix affably with commoners, putting him in the unique position of straddling both the high patrician and low plebeian classes. When Caesar's aunt married Gaius Marius, the paragon of the *Populares*, Caesar's fortunes improved notably. This all changed during the dictatorship of Sulla, which wreaked havoc on all who were connected to Marius. Caesar survived Sulla's proscriptions and pursued a successful career in the military. He was a Machiavellian personality: brave, unyielding, opportunistic, enterprising, and a flagrant womanizer. But he was still in need of wealthy patrons to get him into key political positions. One of Rome's richest men, Crassus, came to his aid, helping Caesar to clear his debts and forming a political bond with him.

In 61 BC, Caesar took a military command in Further Spain where he ingratiated himself with his troops and amassed enough wealth to recover some financial independence. For his victories, the Senate awarded him the supreme honor of a triumph. The honor was significant for two reasons: first, it was bestowed very rarely; second, the triumphing commander was visibly presented as the embodiment of Jupiter. The divine and the human met in his person, suspending for a fleeting moment Rome's distaste for the glory of one man. It is why a slave always accompanied the triumphing commander and whispered in his ear, *"Memento, mori"* ("Remember, you are mortal"). Pompey had enjoyed the privilege an unprecedented three times. The problem for Caesar, however, was that he wanted to stand for election as consul, Rome's highest civic office, which would require him to lay down his military command and forfeit his triumph. The Senate refused to let him have both. Caesar surprised everyone by foregoing his triumph and running for consul instead.

As part of his election strategy, Caesar gave his daughter, Julia, in marriage to Pompey, to cement an alliance with him. He then convinced Pompey and Crassus to put aside their personal differences in the interests of an "off the books" political alliance, which could serve each of their political ends, especially if Caesar were elected consul. Caesar brought political wile to the monumental resources of Pompey and Crassus, creating a pact that could work within the state at the same time as undermining it. Thus, the "First Triumvirate" of Caesar, Crassus, and Pompey was born (Plutarch, *Pomp.* 47.1–6). Caesar was duly elected consul for 59 BC, and violence became a frequent feature of Roman political life. He passed legislation that landed enough blows on the Senate to leave it politically limp. Among his achievements was the ratification of Pompey's settlement in the east, which included his reconfiguration of Judea.

When the year of his consulship came to an end, Caesar had himself appointed to an unparalleled five-year term as governor of Rome's Gallic provinces. That way, he could be away from Rome long enough to escape immediate prosecution by his enemies while giving himself the opportunity to compile a reputation and fortune as great as Pompey's. There were rumblings of rebellion in Gaul and opportunities aplenty among the tribes on the frontiers. So, as Rome descended into political anarchy behind him, Caesar embarked on the conquest of the entirety of Gaul, pushing Roman control from the Mediterranean coast all the way to the North Sea and from the Rhine River in the east to the Atlantic in the west. It was a campaign that exterminated several tribes and culminated years later in his brutal victory at Alesia in which he received the surrender of the Gallic chieftain Vercingetorix (52 BC).

4.3.3 THE UPRISINGS OF ALEXANDER II AND ARISTOBULUS II

After Pompey's conquest, John Hyrcanus II ruled once again as high priest of the Jews, though it was Antipater who ran the affairs of state. Antipater kept Pompey's political reconfiguration in place for the four years it remained unratified by the Roman Senate (63–59 BC), proving himself a dependable ally of the Romans.

Aristobulus II, however, had never been executed in Rome but was kept under permanent house arrest. His eldest son, Alexander II, was also still at large. We know nothing of his whereabouts until he shows up in Judea in 58 BC, drumming up support among the Sadducees, who had been politically marginalized by the growing power of both Antipater and the Pharisees. Alexander had the general approval of the Jewish public, who had grown to dislike Hyrcanus and his wily executive, Antipater, as beneficiaries of the Roman conquest. Alexander also leveraged anti-Roman sentiment among his former enemies, the Nabateans. Their political hatred focused on Antipater, who had not only become a Roman collaborator but had even tried to help the Romans turn the Nabateans into a client kingdom (*Ant.* 14.80–81; *J.W.* 1.159). Alexander was now in his mid-twenties and not short on daring and drive. The question was how he could possibly achieve a takeover that was so flagrantly anti-Roman under the very nose of the Romans themselves.

His opportunity came in 57 BC. His move coincided with the arrival of the new Roman governor of Syria, Aulus Gabinius.[4] Hyrcanus and Antipater appear to have been absent from Jerusalem, presumably welcoming Gabinius in either Antioch or Damascus. The Roman garrison in Jerusalem did not initially realize that a *coup d'état* had taken place in the city. The priests and aristocracy must therefore have been complicit in transferring power peacefully to Alexander. But Alexander then revealed his hand when he began repairing the temple's northern wall. The Roman garrison kicked into action and prevented him from completing the fortification—a major setback to his cause. Nevertheless, Josephus states that Alexander gathered an army of 10,000 men and 1,500 horses from outside the city—numbers that, even if exaggerated, still reveal a country disaffected with the lethargic Hyrcanus and his controller, Antipater. It might even reveal the participation of Nabateans in the *coup d'état*. Alexander then took control of the fortresses at Alexandrium, Hyrcanium, and Machaerus, in preparation for the military showdown with the Romans, which was sure to come (*Ant.* 14.82–83; *J.W.* 1.160–61).

When the coup became known to Hyrcanus and Antipater, they appealed immediately to Gabinius. As an avid supporter of Pompey, Gabinius was

---

4. Aulus Gabinius had been consul in Rome the previous year (58 BC). He is perhaps most famous for having proposed the *Lex Gabinia*, the law that granted Pompey control over all the sea and its coasts in order to defeat the Cilician pirates (67 BC).

disinclined to give any quarter to the young man who had escaped Pompey's custody. He marched south with new recruits and dealt Alexander a series of defeats. One of the Roman officers who distinguished himself in the campaign was the twenty-six-year-old cavalry commander, Mark Antony. Aided by Antipater, Antony was pivotal in capturing the fortress of Alexandrium, after which Alexander capitulated. Alexander's life would surely have been forfeited also had it not been for the intervention of his mother who had not been taken to Rome by Pompey with the rest of her family. She appealed to Gabinius for her son's life, and the governor surprisingly acquiesced. Alexander's survival was certainly not in Roman interests, so it is likely that Gabinius was bribed, perhaps with a personal liaison in addition to silver.[5] Either way, Alexander was chastened but permitted to go free (*Ant.* 14.84–90; *J.W.* 1.162–68).

Gabinius now took a hands-on approach to Judea. He broke down the Judean fortresses and bolstered the infrastructure of the gentile cities around the edges of the Jewish state, which were loyal to Rome. He then reinstated John Hyrcanus II as high priest and divided the country into five regions, each with its own Sanhedrin. These were based in Jerusalem (governing Judea and Idumea), Gadara (governing Gaulanitis),[6] Amathus (governing Perea), Jericho (governing the Jordan Valley and the Samaritans), and Sepphoris (governing Galilee). In doing so, Gabinius truncated the power of the Jerusalem Sanhedrin, which was under the sway of the fundamentalist Pharisees. He probably did this to mollify the more progressively minded Sadducees and the aristocracy, who were the most discontent at Pharisaic power. This also limited the political power of the high priest, making him little more than a titular communal head—a notable fall from the heyday of the Hasmonean monarchy. On the surface of it, this appeared to curb Antipater's power also, but it actually gave him the latitude to wheel and deal independently of John Hyrcanus, which might have been Gabinius's purpose all along (*Ant.* 14.91; *J.W.* 1.168–70). Indeed, Antipater may well have had a hand in the shape of the shake-up.

---

5. In Rome, Cicero was particularly fierce in assassinating Gabinius's character by pointing out his penchant for bribery (e.g., Cicero, *Sest.* 43.93). Gabinius was later convicted on extortion charges in Rome (see 4.3.4).

6. Gadara was a predominantly gentile city southeast of Lake Galilee, which had been given its independence from Jewish rule by Pompey in 63 BC. Gabinius evidently repealed this, thus allowing Jewish rule of the Gaulanitis region east of Lake Galilee. The naming of Gadara as one of the five regional capitals is sometimes viewed as a mistake for Adora, one of the main centers of Idumea (e.g., Yohanan Aharoni et al., *The Macmillan Bible Atlas*, 3rd ed. [New York: Macmillan, 1993], 161). However, the later incorporation of Gadara into Herod's kingdom suggests no such mistake.

This was not the end of the matter, though. Word of Alexander II's rebellion quickly reached Rome, prompting Aristobulus II to escape his confinement and return to Judea, accompanied by his younger son, Mattathias Antigonus. Gabinius was in the throes of preparing a campaign against the Parthians, but he shelved these plans as Aristobulus expeditiously appeared in Judea and began refortifying the country (56 BC). The Fraternal Civil War between John Hyrcanus II and Aristobulus II thus reignited, with many of the country's leaders happy to throw in their lot with Aristobulus, who presented them with the best chance of ridding Judea of the Romans and ratting out the collaborators, most notably Antipater.

But Aristobulus had never proven himself a military strategist. He was quickly thwarted by the Romans, who hounded him to the fortress at Machaerus, where he surrendered after just two days. The Fraternal Civil War was thus doused almost as quickly as it had caught alight. Aristobulus was carted off to Rome a second time, along with his younger son. But, at his wife's request, Gabinius petitioned the Roman Senate to release all of Aristobulus's children. Once again, we are left with the likelihood that Aristobulus's wife bribed Gabinius. In any case, the Roman Senate granted her request. So, Mattathias Antigonus and his two sisters left the imperial capital and settled with their elder brother, Alexander, and their mother at Ashkelon (*Ant.* 14.92–97; cf. 14.126; *J.W.* 1.171–74; cf. 1.185–86). Aristobulus, however, was left incarcerated in Rome. The only thing saving his skin was probably the fact that the Romans considered his person inviolate since he was a former high priest.

On the one hand, by showing leniency to Aristobulus and his children, Rome showed magnanimity to the dynasty of an erstwhile friendly state. On the other hand, it meant that matters in Judea would not settle. Rome had no ideological interest in who ran the country. What it wanted was a compliant client state that paid its taxes and fell into line diplomatically. From that perspective, an easier solution for Rome would have been to remove the Hasmonean dynasty completely and turn the government over to a trusted lackey like Antipater. But the importance of the high priesthood was now so ingrained into Jewish identity that the Hasmoneans could not be so easily sidelined without inciting the entire country. As malleable as Gabinius was with bribes, he was still diplomatic enough to recognize that any further meddling in the dynasty would touch a raw nerve in a society that had quickly become anti-Roman.

While Judea simmered, the Ptolemaic kingdom was thrown into disarray. Ptolemy (XII) the Flautist had been losing control of Egypt and sent the country hurtling towards bankruptcy with all the bribes he expended to maintain Roman support for his rule. In 57 BC he was overthrown by his own daughter, Berenice IV. Ptolemy took his younger daughter, Cleopatra VII (then just twelve years old), and found asylum at one of Pompey's Italian villas. From there he petitioned the Roman Senate to return him to his throne, but the opponents of the Triumvirate blocked his request. The following year (55 BC), however, the Triumvirate exploited the annual election, so that Pompey and Crassus emerged as consuls, while Caesar extended his term in Gaul.[7] Pompey then snubbed the Senate by giving Gabinius a direct order to restore Ptolemy to his throne. Ptolemy promised his patrons 10,000 talents of silver for their backing,[8] though it is questionable how he could ever have made good on his promise. But Pompey was more interested in having the whole of Egypt as his personal client to worry about such details. Gabinius duly marched into Egypt, aided by his cavalry commander, Mark Antony, and also by troops and supplies from Antipater (*Ant.* 14.98–99; *J.W.* 1.175). Ptolemy the Flautist was thus returned to his throne, and Berenice IV was executed.

But while Gabinius and Antipater were in Egypt, Aristobulus's son, Alexander, sprang into action once more. The Jewish aristocracy appeared only too happy to support him again, as did the average Jew whose life had been economically upended by Roman hegemony. In no time, Alexander was commanding a makeshift army of up to 30,000 men from all over the country, intent on full scale revolt.[9] The mob turned against all symbols of Roman domination and slaughtered as many Romans as they could. Their lightning success seems also to have sparked similar mob uprisings in Syria (*Ant.* 14.100; *J.W.* 1.176). Gabinius dispatched Antipater back to Judea, where he convinced many in the aristocracy to withdraw their support from Alexander. This took the wind out of the sails of revolt, though violence was still rampant throughout the country. When Gabinius himself returned from Egypt, he found Roman forces pinned on Mount Gerizim by Alexander's unruly mob. Alexander retreated at the sight of Gabinius, who chased him north to Mount Tabor in Galilee. Most of Alexander's mob deserted him along the way, while those who stood to fight were massacred.

Once again, Alexander surprisingly survived his defeat, probably through yet more bribery of Gabinius. He slunk off to a comfortable existence, and two

---

7. The Triumvirate's strategy was hammered out during their (open) secret conference in Lucca (56 BC).

8. In modern terms, this is the equivalent of US$15 billion.

9. The number of men is improbably large for an organized force. It almost certainly reflects a reaction against Roman rule at a more grassroots level.

years later (53 BC) his wife, Alexandra II, gave birth to a son, whom he named Jonathan Aristobulus III. This was the second child she bore Alexander—the first had been a daughter, Mariamme, born in ca. 63 BC.[10] The birth of Aristobulus III was momentous, for he was the grandson of John Hyrcanus II through his mother and of Aristobulus II through his father—a potentially unifying persona, as was no doubt intended by the marriage of his parents. There is no indication that Hyrcanus had any son who might succeed to the high priesthood after him. This meant that his brother and nephews had been his rightful heirs up to this point. But upon his birth, Aristobulus III became John Hyrcanus's direct natural heir, supplanting all other males in Aristobulus's line from the succession. This made Aristobulus II and his two sons dispensable to the sacerdotal succession and, therefore, to Roman policy. This, in turn, only made them more desperate to attain power for themselves. Standing in their way, though, was the Triumvirate, who supported Hyrcanus and his executive, Antipater.

4.3.4 JUDEA AND THE CAMPAIGN OF CRASSUS

As governor of Syria, Aulus Gabinius proved insensitive, inept, and monumentally corrupt. So, when his protectors, Pompey and Crassus, finished their term as consuls at the end of 55 BC, Gabinius was recalled to Rome, where he was convicted of extortion and exiled (Dio Cassius, *Hist. Rom.* 59.1–60.1; 63.1–5). His cavalry commander, Mark Antony, was also recalled, but found reassignment in Gaul on the staff of Julius Caesar.

Crassus himself replaced Gabinius as governor of Syria, in the hope of forging a military reputation to rival Pompey's and Caesar's. To that end, he set his sights on conquering the Parthian Empire. A confrontation between Rome and the Parthians was practically inevitable, as each empire was expanding in the direction of the other and now shared a border along the Euphrates. But Crassus intended on launching an unprovoked attack.

Crassus proved even more flagrantly corrupt than Gabinius. To finance his campaign, he raided the temple in Jerusalem, stripping it of its gold and confiscating its treasury (*Ant.* 14.105–109; *J.W.* 1.179). Not only was this sacrilege against God, to whom the treasury belonged, but it also robbed Judea of its

---

10. The guardian role Mariamme would take in her brother's life points to her being the older sibling. But the difficulty in pinning down her father's (and even her mother's) whereabouts for large swathes of time make it hard to know exactly when she was born. The most likely time was between her parents' marriage (ca. 65 BC) and her father's initial arrest by Pompey in 63 BC, *pace* Richardson, *Herod*, 121, n.105.

central bank, plunging the country into yet more fiscal misfortune. So Jewish animosity at Roman hegemony boiled over. There was little John Hyrcanus II and Antipater could do to stop Crassus, even if they had wanted to. As the chief collaborators with Rome, they too became objects of the general animus. Thus, as Crassus launched his Parthian campaign in 53 BC, another uprising ensued in Judea.

This was the fourth Jewish uprising in four years, and the third attempt of Alexander II to wrest power from Hyrcanus and Antipater. It might have gone the way of all the other uprisings were it not for Crassus's supreme incompetence on campaign. Crassus consistently ignored strategic advice and marched his heavy infantry across the arid steppe of northern Mesopotamia. His sapped legions, on the verge of mutiny, eventually came within sight of Carrhae (biblical Haran), where they were annihilated under a deadly rain of volleys from mounted Parthian archers. Crassus was himself killed shortly after the battle (*Ant.* 14.119; *J.W.* 1.179). So complete was his defeat that Carrhae cut a gash across the Roman psyche to match the one inflicted by Hannibal at Cannae in 216 BC. Crassus's fate even took on the proportions of tragic myth, as the story developed that the Parthians decapitated him and either used his head as a prop in a play or poured molten gold into his mouth to satisfy his legendary hunger for wealth (Dio Cassius, *Hist. Rom.* 40.27; cf. Plutarch, *Crass.* 33.1–4).[11]

The death of Crassus came at a time of political upheaval for Rome. Not only did it unbalance the Triumvirate, but it undid Pompey's conquests of a decade earlier, leaving Syria ungoverned and exposed to Parthian attack. Roman hegemony over Judea collapsed, giving Alexander the opportunity to take control of the country away from his uncle and Antipater and reinstate the Hasmonean monarchy in his father's name.

Our sources are meager, but it seems Alexander had some success. Yet, he soon ran into a roadblock: Crassus's commander, Gaius Cassius Longinus, survived Carrhae and took it upon himself to bring the surviving troops back to Syria in an attempt to maintain Roman ascendancy. Galilee had become a hotbed of anti-Roman fervor (see 4.3.10 below), but Cassius defeated a contingent of Alexander's forces at Taricheae, better known as Magdala, on the western shore of Lake Galilee. According to Josephus, Cassius's victory was followed by the enslavement of 30,000 Jews (*Ant.* 14.119–20; *J.W.* 1.180; cf. Plutarch, *Brut.* 43.7). Alexander, however, was spared for the third time after

---

11. David Braund, "Dionysiac Tragedy in Plutarch, Crassus," *The Classical Quarterly* 43.2 (1993): 468–74.

defeat. This time it was not down to bribery but to the intervention of his uncle, Hyrcanus, who did not want to take the hard decision of recommending the execution of his daughter's husband and the father of his sacerdotal heir. Alexander thus returned to the *polis* of Ashkelon, where the rest of his family resided and resumed life as a private citizen.

Cassius returned to Syria where he defended Roman interests against Parthian incursions for the next two years. His successes helped Antipater keep a volatile Judea leashed to Roman hegemony, fragile though it was. The country was still reeling from Crassus's raid on the temple, and his defeat was understood as divine retribution. It also demonstrated that Rome was not invincible. With the Parthian Empire now casting shadows across Roman Syria, Jews continued to hope that Roman hegemony might still be broken. The veneer of stability in Judea was paper-thin.

4.3.5 THE ROAD TO ROMAN CIVIL WAR

The Triumvirate of Pompey, Crassus, and Caesar was a delicately poised political tripod. Together, they outmaneuvered all legal means to curb their power, becoming a veritable parallel state to the Roman Republic. But in 54 BC Pompey's wife, Julia, died in childbirth, removing the familial connection between Pompey and Caesar. Then, Crassus's death at Carrhae in 53 BC unbalanced the tripod completely, causing a political reset between Pompey and Caesar. Furthermore, the political chicanery, which had allowed the Triumvirate to outflank the Senate, had the unintended effect of encouraging others to use similar tactics. The result was political mayhem in Rome fueled by personal ambitions and violence, which legal process was unable to stop. This was exacerbated the same year by the suggestion that Pompey be granted a dictatorship to bring the Republic back under control (Plutarch, *Pomp.* 54.2–5). The turmoil in Rome reached such fever pitch that the annual consular elections in 53 BC were postponed, which only marginalized political process even more and further weakened the Senate's ability to impose order (Dio Cassius, *Hist. rom.* 40.17.2).

A tipping point was reached in January 52 BC with the murder of Publius Clodius Pulcher. Clodius was a scandalous figure—a patrician who gave up his aristocratic heritage to become a commoner, so as to use the Plebeian Assembly (thus bypassing the Senate) to get back at his rivals among the *Optimates*. After Clodius's murder at the bidding of *Optimas* Titus Annius Milo, Clodius's outraged supporters conveyed his corpse to the Senate House, which they set on fire as both a cremation of Clodius's body and a protest against the obnoxious conservatism of the *Optimates*. The city then erupted in violence.

A hamstrung Senate, which had no elected consuls to take control, could only watch as rioting took hold. The only ones powerful enough to restore order were Pompey and Caesar. But with the Triumvirate now dissolved, the state of affairs between them was uncertain. Both Caesar and Pompey were technically provincial governors at this point. But while Caesar was physically in his province of Gaul, Pompey was governing his assigned province of Spain from Rome itself.[12] The *Optimates* were alarmed by the extreme popularity that Caesar had won among the *Populares*, and feared that, if he were recalled to Rome, he would take the emergency powers of a dictator to deal with the disorder. Emergency powers were precisely what the Roman Republic needed in the midst of the anarchy, but the *Optimates* could not brook giving Caesar, the darling of the *Populares*, power. So, the conservative Senators approached Pompey as the lesser of two evils and asked him to take control. Pompey was appointed sole consul—an unconstitutional move aimed at avoiding a formal dictatorship, but this is effectively what Pompey was given. He now had the novel solitary power of supreme civic office and military governance, setting a new precedent that would shape Roman politics for centuries to come: the role of *Princeps* ("first" man in Rome).[13]

Pompey restored order and, in the spirit of the Triumvirate, continued to support Caesar's political aims. Chief among these was the ability for Caesar to seek public office while being absent from Rome and in possession of military command. The prospect of Caesar at the head of an army also taking civic power spooked his opponents, so they actively worked to thwart him and turn Pompey against him. They succeeded in passing other laws that would strip Caesar of his provincial governorship and force him to present himself in Rome without military command. But Caesar's supporters decried the double standard since these restrictions had not also been imposed on Pompey. Any sense of common purpose between Caesar and Pompey now dissolved completely. In a letter to the Senate, Caesar suggested that both he and Pompey resign their provincial offices and give up command of their respective legions, returning to a constitutionally legal situation. But Pompey was unwilling to surrender

---

12. Pompey stayed in Rome ostensibly to execute his office as Grain Commissioner.

13. The concept of the *Princeps* found chief expression in the Imperial Age from Augustus onwards, but its legacy continued into the Byzantine era and, one may argue, only ceased with the fall of Czarist Russia during the Russian Revolution of 1917.

his troops. A showdown between the two for supremacy in Rome was now unavoidable.[14]

Stirring the pot yet further was the likelihood of conflict with the Parthians. Cassius and his replacement, Bibulus (an avowed enemy of Caesar),[15] had been valiantly holding Syria against the Parthians with the meager remnants of Crassus's defeated legions, and these desperately needed reinforcing. A deal was struck for Caesar and Pompey to each contribute one legion to the defense of Syria. But Pompey had lent one of his legions to Caesar for use in Gaul, and Pompey now volunteered that legion for Syria. The deal meant that Caesar effectively lost two of the legions under his command while Pompey lost none. Furthermore, Pompey never dispatched the legions to Syria but rather held them in Italy to use against Caesar. The stage was thus set for a cataclysmic military conflict.

By this point (December 50 BC), the Roman Republic was in its death throes, as all its political processes had become irrelevant before Pompey and Caesar. Roman tradition, which had been forged in the conviction that no one man should ever hold supreme power, was being crushed under the weight of two rivals who had each grown bigger and mightier than the Republic itself. Even as the conservative *Optimates*, champions of Roman tradition, lined up behind Pompey, their vision of restoring the Republic's integrity was in tatters. The *Populares* who lined up behind Caesar hoped to overthrow the corrupt old guard and set up a new order under the regime of a man who knew them and shared with them the benefits of his stellar success.

Caesar moved the one legion he had on hand (the rest were still in Gaul) just north of the border of Italy along the Rubicon River. He hoped that the threat of war might convince Pompey to seek a détente. But instead, Caesar was declared an enemy of the state on 7 January 49 BC (Caesar, *Civ.* 1.5). News of this reached him three days later, leaving him with a pivotal choice: he could deny the charge against him by withdrawing to the safety of Gaul and perhaps living to fight another day; or he could advance into conflict with fellow Romans, but with the goal of remaking the state that had alienated him. He wasted no time. At sunset on 10 January 49 BC, Caesar crossed the Rubicon and ignited the Roman Civil War (Caesar, *Civ.* 1.8.1; Plutarch, *Caes.* 32.8; Suetonius, *Caes.* 32.1; Appian, *Bell. civ.* 2.35).

---

14. Charles Freeman, *Egypt, Greece, and Rome: Civilizations of the Ancient Mediterranean* (Oxford: Oxford University Press, 2014), 430–32.

15. Marcus Calpurnius Bibulus had been co-consul alongside Julius Caesar in 59 BC but was so politically outwitted by Caesar that he locked himself away and refused to participate in government. His complete ineffectiveness drew the snide remark that the two consuls that year had been "Julius and Caesar."

Several historical forces led Rome to this explosive moment. The precedent of Alexander the Great, who had conquered much of the known world in the fourth century BC, cast an avid spell over every military commander after him, including Pompey and Caesar. But Alexander's example promoted autocratic monarchy, whereas Rome's republic had sprung from an overthrow of autocracy. This produced ambitions in Rome's commanders that were at odds with its traditional ideals. Rome's political processes had also been generated when it was but a modest city-state occupying the Latin hills of central Italy. These processes were ill-equipped to govern an entire empire stretching across multiple territories on three continents. Even when Rome tried to fit its republican ideal on these territories by imposing provincial government, the provinces themselves functioned as adjuncts to the Republic rather than as integrated parts of it. They were sandboxes of autocracy, allowing Roman governors and generals, like Pompey and Caesar, to act as practical monarchs in the provinces and cultivate autocratic instincts.

The dictatorship of Lucius Cornelius Sulla (82–79 BC) also exposed the loopholes in Roman law and governance. As an *Optimas*, Sulla forced his way to the dictatorship to put the *Populares* back in their place. But his reign of terror demonstrated how the loopholes could be genuinely exploited by someone to achieve personal ambitions. His fractious dictatorship only embittered the *Populares* even more against the status quo and provided the template for how someone with the will and the wile might use both political process and the military to circumvent the Senate. Pompey, Crassus, and Caesar were three such individuals. Thus, when Sulla retired and died soon after, the political game was restarted with renewed vigor.

These developments turned the Roman Senate into a self-important anachronism—an oligarchic form of government overseeing a jigsaw of provincial pieces but that was only really interested in its own piece of the puzzle. This translated into a fatal inertia—a failure to deal with loopholes and adapt its processes to the rigors of empire. The result was bitterness and instability within Rome and among its provinces and clients (Aristobulus II and Alexander II being cases in point). It also created the opportunity for someone with a vision for centralization to deal with the disparate pieces as a collective whole, even if this meant subverting the traditional but powerful oligarchy. The First Triumvirate had initially taken this opportunity for more holistic governance, before Crassus's catastrophic Parthian campaign unraveled its efforts. Yet, it set in motion political forces that could not be stopped without wholesale reform, and the Senate had neither the will nor the flexibility to undertake such reforms. Loopholes and tradition sapped Roman government of its strength.

Amidst this flux, one facet of Roman power did adapt to the rigors of empire: the Roman military machine. It grew and evolved into a professional army that could maintain Rome's imperial jigsaw around the Mediterranean. But as it did so, it outgrew the control of the traditional oligarchy in Rome, handing more power to the generals who commanded its legions. By 52 BC, the power and celebrity of Rome's generals, Pompey and Caesar, eclipsed the power of its politicians. When political power was then handed to Pompey as sole consul in 52 BC, civil war was practically guaranteed. The spark that ignited the war came in the chaos of January 49 BC. And since Roman authority stretched across the Mediterranean Basin and beyond, the Roman civil war would effectively be a world war, affecting Judea too.

4.3.6 THE FATE OF ARISTOBULUS II AND ALEXANDER II

After Caesar crossed the Rubicon, Pompey evacuated his legions from Italy to Greece, along with the leading figures of the Senate. From Greece Pompey planned to use his vast connections and wealth to bolster his armies and crush Caesar. Among these connections were his Jewish clients, Antipater and John Hyrcanus II.

In Italy, Caesar's legions from Gaul reached him, but Caesar was not yet in possession of ships to ferry them across the Adriatic. Furthermore, he now feared that Pompey's legions in Spain would occupy Gaul behind him and attack him from there. Faced with the prospect of war on two fronts, Caesar implemented three strategies. The first was to secure control of Italy, for which Mark Antony's appointment as lieutenant was pivotal. The second was an attempt to open another front to Pompey's rear in the east, so as to rebalance the stakes. This he planned to do by releasing Aristobulus II from incarceration in Rome and sending him back to Judea with two legions to challenge Hyrcanus and Antipater (*Ant.* 14.123; *J.W.* 1.183). If Aristobulus could gain control in Judea, he could attack Pompey from the rear and thus keep him bogged down in the east. The third strategy was to eliminate the threat to his own rear by defeating Pompey's legions in Spain. If Caesar could do all this, he would gain the strategic advantage by trapping Pompey in Greece or Asia Minor while he himself was in possession of Rome.

As Caesar departed for Spain, he ordered the release of Aristobulus. Yet, Aristobulus was unable to embark on his mission, for Pompeian loyalists poisoned him while he was still in Italy. Since Aristobulus had been a high priest, his murder was sacrilegious even in Roman eyes. This explains why Mark Antony had Aristobulus's body preserved in honey and eventually sent to

Judea for burial, despite having defeated him at Machaerus seven years earlier (*Ant.* 14.124; *J.W.* 1.184).[16]

The murder of Aristobulus would have caused consternation in Judea, for most of the aristocracy and priestly caste had been on his side. They once again found themselves looking to Aristobulus's son, Alexander II. The majority in Judea viewed Pompey as the aggressor who had taken away Jewish independence and brought the Roman tax farmers—a situation made more acute by Pompey's new governor in Syria, Metellus Scipio, who was extracting taxes at alarming rates to finance Pompey's war effort (Caesar, *Civ.* 3.31–33).[17] Most Jews, then, were ready to back Caesar, not out of conviction for his cause but out of distaste for Pompey and the prospect of concessions to ease their plight.

Pompey was no fool, for he realized that Alexander could simply replace Aristobulus in Caesar's plan. So, he ordered Metellus Scipio to deal with the Hasmonean prince once and for all. Alexander was arrested and brought to Antioch, where there would be no fourth reprieve. This time, Alexander was beheaded (*Ant.* 14.125; *J.W.* 1.185). His execution still left his younger brother, Mattathias Antigonus II, in Ashkelon to keep alive Aristobulus's line. But he, along with his sisters and mother, were whisked away to Lebanon into the custody of the Iturean king, Ptolemy Menneus. Pompey had once again made himself an aggressor towards the Jews. It jaundiced the nation against him and his local lackeys, Hyrcanus and Antipater.

4.3.7 CONCLUSION OF THE ROMAN CIVIL WAR

The deaths of Aristobulus II and Alexander II meant that Judea remained in the hands of John Hyrcanus II and Antipater as Pompeian loyalists. Since this ruined Caesar's plan to open a new front to Pompey's rear, the need for Caesar to neutralize Pompey's forces in Spain and Gaul became more urgent. Caesar achieved this with alacrity, and by December 49 BC he was back in Rome where the emergency powers of a dictator were conferred upon him. He was, however, at pains to make every political step he took constitutionally legal. So he laid these powers down within days and held elections, which saw him legally voted in as consul for 48 BC (Caesar, *Civ.* 2.21; 3.1).

The following month (January 48 BC) Caesar ferried his troops across the

---

16. Josephus does not specifically mention where Aristobulus was murdered, but since his body was preserved by Mark Antony, who was in Italy, and returned to Judea for burial, Aristobulus must have been murdered while he was still in Italy. *Pace* Grainger, *The Wars of the Maccabees*, 157–58.

17. Cassius, who had defended Roman interests in Syria after the disaster of Carrhae, was a supporter of Caesar. The Pompeian Senate removed him and replaced him with Scipio.

Adriatic. Pompey advanced and hemmed Caesar in at the port of Dyrrachium, but a few months later Caesar busted out of the vice and headed south to Thessaly. Pompey now had the opportunity to let his forces grind down Caesar's army through a war of attrition while he beelined for Rome to retake control of the government. Instead, he followed Caesar into Thessaly, and on 9 August 48 BC joined battle with him near the town of Pharsalus. The battle was an unmitigated disaster for Pompey, as Caesar decimated his larger armies with superior tactics. As Pompey fled, Caesar showed clemency to the surviving forces who surrendered to him, and the pendulum of war swung manifestly towards him (Caesar, *Civ.* 3.80–99).

Pompey needed to replace his lost armies, and his best prospects for this lay in the east. However, news of the outcome at Pharsalus preceded him and emboldened the residents of Antioch to prevent him from setting up an operations center there (see also this section below). Pompey was forced to collect as much money as he could from his eastern connections, including John and Antipater, and then flee south towards Egypt.

But Pompey was sailing into an incendiary situation. When Aulus Gabinius had restored Ptolemy (XII) the Flautist to the Ptolemaic throne (55 BC), he left troops behind to guarantee his rule. But since Egypt was an independent realm, these *Gabiniani*, as the troops came to be known, were outside all Roman accountability structures and became a law unto themselves, wreaking havoc in Alexandria and embittering the local population. Ptolemy the Flautist then died in 51 BC and bequeathed the throne jointly to his eighteen-year-old daughter, Cleopatra VII, and ten-year-old son, Ptolemy XIII. Cleopatra had a marvelous intuition for administration and was a highly educated polyglot. She took the lead in government with the aim of repairing the damage her prodigal father had inflicted on the stressed Ptolemaic kingdom and reining in the *Gabiniani*. Her endeavors were challenged by both the failure of the Nile's annual flooding in 49 BC[18] and her brother's minders, who found such initiative from a young woman unacceptable. A civil war between the siblings thus broke out, with Pompey and the *Gabiniani* supporting Ptolemy XIII. Cleopatra was forced to flee Egypt and raise an army in the Levant to challenge her brother (Caesar, *Civ.* 3.103).[19] Roman control of Syria

---

18. See Duane W. Roller, *Cleopatra: A Biography*, Women in Antiquity (Oxford: Oxford University Press, 2010), 54.

19. Cleopatra probably had three reasons for canvassing Syria. The first lay in the historic familial connections between the Ptolemies and Seleucids. Even though the Seleucids were no longer in power, the last figures of the dynasty stood to benefit from the internecine strife in Egypt (Roller, *Cleopatra*, 59). The second reason was the unrest that had been gripping Syria since the time of Gabinius. Alexander II's third

had all but collapsed, and the fear of a Parthian invasion was grave. Gaza and Ashkelon had already opted for the security of Cleopatra's hegemony in previous years,[20] and other polities were now emboldened by her activism. Indeed, it was she who put lead into the spine of Antioch's leaders to prevent Pompey from landing in Syria.

Thus, when Pompey arrived off the shore of Pelusium in Egypt on 28 September 48 BC (the day before his fifty-ninth birthday), he was literally wading into the midst of someone else's civil war. Young Ptolemy XIII, now aged thirteen, was in Pelusium to check the advance of Cleopatra, who was returning at the head of her Levantine army, consisting of troops that she had prevented Pompey from recruiting. If Pompey wanted to get enough forces to challenge Caesar, he would have to interpose himself into the Ptolemaic civil war on the side of young Ptolemy XIII. But since Caesar's victory at Pharsalus, the boy king's minders feared Caesar more than Pompey. So, they acted decisively. When Pompey requested an audience with the young king, he was ferried to shore in a small craft, but he never reached the shore alive. He was murdered on the boat, and his head removed from his shoulders (Caesar, *Civ.* 3.104; Plutarch, *Pomp.* 77.1–80.4). In hot pursuit, Caesar arrived in Alexandria three days later and was presented with Pompey's head as a trophy. The Roman Civil War was over, and Julius Caesar was the undisputed master of Rome.

In Judea, the death of Pompey, "the dragon" (Pss. Sol. 2:25), was celebrated as divine retribution for his sacrilege of 63 BC:

> Do not delay, O God, to repay upon their heads,
> to turn the pride of the dragon to ignominy.
> I did not wait long until God showed me that hubris,
> massacred on the hills of Egypt,
> despised beyond even the least thing on land and sea,
> his corpse ferried over the waves in much hubris,
> but with none to bury him,
> for he despised him [God] in ignominy.

---

anti-Roman uprising in Judea (55 BC) had infected the Syrians with similar sentiments, especially after the hefty economic burden Rome had laid across their shoulders. The third reason was the Roman Civil War itself, which had weakened Rome's hold over Syria. Cleopatra adroitly used this, probably playing on local fears of an imminent Parthian invasion as well and invoking historic Ptolemaic claims to Coele Syria.

20. Coins bearing Cleopatra's emblems come from both cities. See Roller, *Cleopatra*, 59; Yoav Farhi, "Cleopatra in Gaza(?): A Hitherto Unpublished Coin Type from Gaza and the First Year of Coinage in Gaza under Roman Rule," *AJN* 27 (2015): 141–54.

>   He did not consider that he was but a man,
>   nor consider his ultimate end.
>   He said, "I will be lord of land and sea,"
>   and did not recognize that God is great,
>   sovereign in his great might.
>   He is king over the skies,
>   judging kings and rulers. (Psalms of Solomon 2:25–30)

4.3.8 JULIUS CAESAR IN EGYPT

Although Julius Caesar won the Roman Civil War, it had at the last moment become intertwined with the civil war in Egypt. Initially, he insisted that the siblings, Cleopatra VII and Ptolemy XIII, reconcile themselves to ruling together. But the canny Cleopatra conspired to exploit Caesar's infamous womanizing proclivities. She snuck into the royal palace at Alexandria, allegedly concealed in a rolled-up carpet, and there she seduced the consul. Caesar was over thirty years her senior and, as master of Rome, able to manipulate the political configuration of Egypt. Her competence gave her good reason to govern Egypt in her own right, and the best way she figured of achieving this was not just by coaxing Caesar to her cause but by bearing him a son. This would enable her to co-rule with a male relative who was not her brother while ensuring the lasting support of Caesar. Even more audaciously, if Caesar were to transform the Roman Republic into a monarchy, as many were convinced he now would, then any son she bore him potentially stood to inherit a united kingdom of Egypt and Rome.

Her ploy worked. Caesar was won to her cause and remained in Alexandria to uphold her claim. This was no easy task, as fighting between the two sides continued, and Caesar came close to losing his life in Alexandria's Great Harbor (Caesar, *Alex.* 21.2–3; Dio Cassius, *Hist. rom.* 40.3–5).[21] But he survived and took the battle to young Ptolemy in the Nile Delta. After the decisive battle (13 January 47 BC), young Ptolemy XIII fled to a ship on the Nile but drowned when it capsized (Caesar, *Alex.* 31.6).

Surprisingly, one of the most significant people to feature in Caesar's victory was Antipater. After Pompey's death, both Antipater and John Hyrcanus II had to repair the political damage of their association with

---

21. In December 48 BC the conflict saw much of the priceless collection in the Museum's Royal Library go up in flames. The surviving volumes were relocated to the temple of Serapis. It is possible that the Royal Library's collection had grown too big for the museum and that the temple of Serapis was used as a kind of stack even before the fire of December 48 BC.

Pompey. Their opportunity came when one of Caesar's allies, Mithridates of Pergamum, marched reinforcements through the Levant on the way to aid Caesar in Egypt.[22] Antipater mustered 1,500 Jewish troops to join them.[23] This force proved pivotal in helping Caesar clinch victory (*Ant.* 14.127–36; *J.W.* 1.187–93). Antipater himself, now in his late sixties, even distinguished himself with bravery on the battlefield. He thus returned to Judea having proved his value and loyalty to Caesar.

Caesar's victory left a pregnant Cleopatra as Egypt's indisputable sovereign, and together, the two of them took a month-long celebratory cruise up and down the Nile (Appian, *Bell. civ.* 2.90). However, according to the terms of her father's will, which Caesar was bound to uphold, Cleopatra had to reign with a male relative. Accordingly, her pliant youngest brother, eleven-year-old Ptolemy XIV, was elevated to the throne alongside her. His position, however, was purely illusory, especially after Cleopatra gave birth to Caesar's son (23 June 47 BC), whom she named Caesarion ("Little Caesar"). Caesar had not waited around for his birth, though. He had departed Egypt four months earlier.

4.3.9 JEWS AND THE CAESAREAN SETTLEMENT

Roman sovereignty in Syria and parts of Asia Minor was hemorrhaging after Pompey's downfall, so Caesar headed there to stem the flow. On his way, he passed through Judea, where he was welcomed by John Hyrcanus II and Antipater. However, Aristobulus II's surviving son, Mattathias Antigonus II, came out of hiding in Chalcis to denounce them to Caesar. Antigonus made a compelling case. Hyrcanus and Antipater had sided with Caesar's enemy, Pompey, so their new loyalty to Caesar was a sham. They had conspired multiple times against Antigonus's father and brother, who had been so useful to Caesar's cause. Caesar should not, therefore, trust them. The leadership of Judea rightly belonged to him as the heir of Aristobulus II, and Caesar could rely on his unquestioned allegiance.

But Antipater, ever the savvy politician and quick wit, parried Antigonus's claims with a clever bit of theater: he bared his flesh to show Caesar the scars he had sustained fighting for him in Egypt. This visibly demonstrated that he

---

22. This Mithridates was the son of Mithridates VI of Pontus and a Galatian princess and had been educated in Pergamum.

23. Josephus initially states that Antipater raised 3,000 Jewish troops (*Ant.* 14.128), but when he later quotes a document by Caesar (*Ant.* 14.193), the number is 1,500 troops. This latter figure, coming from a primary source, is taken as more reliable.

had always been faithful to Rome itself and invested that faith in whomever embodied Rome to Judea. He also pointed out that Antigonus had escaped Roman custody with his father to lead an insurrection against Rome (*Ant.* 14.140–42; *J.W.* 1.195–98). Antipater won the argument. Further weakening Antigonus's claim was the fact that his brother's son, Aristobulus III, now a child of six, was still the rightful heir of both Hyrcanus and Aristobulus, and so Antigonus himself was dispensable. But Caesar did not get rid of him. If Hyrcanus and Antipater swerved from their newfound loyalty, they could always be replaced by Antigonus II, who still had a reasonable claim to the Jewish leadership.[24]

Caesar confirmed Hyrcanus as high priest and granted him the title of Ethnarch of the Jews (*Ant.* 14.190–99). He also had synagogues in Rome classified as *collegia*—legally recognized societies with the right to own property, hold gatherings, and enforce rules upon constituents. As *Pontifex Maximus*, Caesar was head of the *collegium* of Roman high priests, so his decision to incorporate synagogues as *collegia* was no token gesture. It gave legal protection to Jews in the imperial capital to carry on the same activities as their compatriots in Judea (see 4.2.1 above). In time, this would provide the arena into which the followers of Jesus would make the explosive claim that he was Israel's messiah—a claim that would polarize the synagogue, resulting in riots and the expulsion of Christian Jews from Rome in AD 49 (cf. Suetonius, *Claud.*, 25; Acts 18:2). This spawned the establishment of house churches with predominantly gentile congregants (Godfearers), since their Christian beliefs were no longer welcomed in the Jewish synagogue. It also prompted the apostle Paul to write to these gentile Christians in Rome (AD 55/6) to return to the synagogue and submit themselves to its legal authority as *collegia* (Rom 13:1–5), so that, like Jesus himself, they could become servants of the circumcised on behalf of God's truth (Rom 15:7–8).[25]

Caesar bestowed hereditary Roman citizenship upon Antipater, as well as the title of "Procurator" (Gk. *epitropos*). This confirmed Antipater's charge over all secular affairs of the Jewish state, independent of Hyrcanus, making him the *de facto* ruler of Judea. Caesar also allowed the repair of the temple's walls (*Ant.* 14.144) and redrew the borders of the Jewish state, reinstating its sovereignty over Joppa and the northern course of the *Via Maris* (*Ant.* 14.205–209).

---

24. Grainger, *The Wars of the Maccabees*, 158.

25. This is similar to the argument of Mark Nanos in *The Mystery of Romans: The Jewish Context of Paul's Letter* (Minneapolis: Fortress, 1996).

If many Jews had been hoping for greater autonomy and exemption from taxes, they were sorely disappointed. An annual tax of 25 percent of the country's agricultural product was imposed, with an exemption accorded only for the Sabbatical Year. This tax was "for the city of Jerusalem" (*Ant.* 14.202–203)—a clear announcement that Jerusalem was now considered Roman and, as such, was effectively leased back to the Jews. This, along with the power of appointment over the high priest, confirmed that the Romans were here to stay and that Jewish independence was off the table. As if to soften the blow, the territory belonging to Joppa (the northern coastal plain) was exempted from tax to Rome but required to pay an annual tribute of 34 silver talents to the high priest instead.[26] In practice, all this did was enrich Hyrcanus—a fact attested archaeologically by the renovations he undertook to the Hasmonean estate outside Jericho. On top of these taxes, Jews were still expected to pay the standard tithes to the temple (now recognized by Roman law [*Ant.* 14.203]), producing a priestly caste that was astronomically wealthier than the population it served. Only Antipater was exempted from paying any tax at all. Since the biblical tithing system was in place as a sign of the sovereignty of Yahweh over his covenant nation, the imposition of Caesar's tax placed Rome on equal footing with God. This made the question posed to Jesus eighty years later so provocative: "Is it right to pay tax to Caesar or not?" (Matt 22:17)

While these new revenue streams could have moved the priestly aristocracy to mandate a reduction in tithes to ease the financial burden on the average Jew, this was simply not possible in a climate of Pharisaic dominance or when most priests no longer believed in new prophetic revelation. The monolithic and fastidious attitude towards the interpretation of Torah, which the fundamentalist Pharisees had promulgated for generations, left no room for such measures and was smothering prophetic instincts that might suggest new approaches. Torah mandated the payment of tithes as both a tribute to Yahweh (Lev 27:30) and for the support of his ministers (Num 18:24–28), and both the priests and Pharisees upheld this literally at all costs, even if it meant people had to give up all that they had to live on (cf. Mark 12:41–44; Luke 21:1–4). It was this kind of religious entrapment that Jesus denounced:

> [The teachers of the Law and the Pharisees] tie up heavy loads and lay them on the shoulders of people, but they do not want to lift even a finger to move them. (Matt 23:4)

---

26. Josephus's source states that Joppa's annual tribute to the high priest was "20,675 modii [of wheat]" (*Ant.* 14.206). This calculates to just over 34 silver talents (approximately US$50 million).

A vital dilemma developed: relief from religious obligation was desperately needed in the conditions of Roman domination, but how could one possibly be a faithful Jew and not obey God's Law? The desire for change, be it in the political situation or covenantal obligation, flowed strongly, but still the bulwark of the national covenant resisted it, and it was now buttressed by Roman law and legions. There were two possible ways that change could occur: either people took up the sword to battle against those who imposed the Caesarean Settlement, or they waited for the rise of "a reliable prophet" (1 Macc 14:41) who could point the nation in a new direction and a messiah who could enact a new covenant (cf. Jer 31:31–34) and overcome the gentiles. In the first century, Christians would claim that John the Baptist was that prophet, that Jesus was that messiah, that Jesus was lord even over Caesar, that a new covenant had been forged, and that the gentiles could be overcome by conversion.

The imposition of Roman taxes fueled anti-Roman sentiment among Jewish ultra-nationalists. Caesar understood this, which is partly why he exempted Jews from service in the Roman legions and from needing to supply or quarter Roman soldiers—a unique provision among Roman provinces and client states (*Ant.* 14.195, 204, 225–67). In part this was a practical measure, for most Jews would not work or fight on the Sabbath or take up arms during a Sabbatical Year. But the exemption was more judicious, for it gave the Jews a sense that Rome appreciated their religious scruples. It would be enough to keep them from joining Caesar's enemies, who had survived Pompey's death and were still baying for Caesar's blood. All in all, this Caesarean Settlement was a positive development for Jews of the diaspora, who would remember Caesar fondly as their patron. But for Jews in Judea itself, the Settlement's concessions did not undo its political and economic burdens.

Caesar passed most of these measures through the Roman Senate once he returned to Rome. But this was not until October 47 BC. In the intervening months, he travelled to Syria where he appointed his cousin, Sextus Julius Caesar, as governor. He then hurried north to Pontus to deal with Pharnaces II, another son of Mithridates VI of Pontus. Pharnaces, who ruled the Bosporan kingdom in the Crimean Peninsula, had journeyed south and was creating disquiet in Pontus and Armenia. Fearing a repeat of the trouble that Pharnaces's father had caused Rome, Caesar determined to deal swiftly with him and defeated him at the Battle of Zela on 1 August 47 BC. After the battle, Caesar sent the briefest of reports to the Roman Senate: "I came. I saw. I conquered." (Lat. *Veni. Vidi. Vici.*)

4.3.10 THE DEVELOPING DYNASTY OF ANTIPATER

By granting Antipater sweeping powers as Procurator, Caesar confined the lackluster John Hyrcanus II to moral and ceremonial authority. This is seen by the fact that it was Antipater who executed Caesar's order to rebuild the temple's walls. This act pacified detractors somewhat in and around Jerusalem, but Antipater still needed to use his diplomatic skill to convince as many people as possible that submitting to the Caesarean Settlement was in everyone's best interests (*Ant.* 14.156–57; *J.W.* 1.201–2).

As part of this effort, Antipater restructured the governance of the Jewish state in a way that grew his own authority and paved the way for a dynasty to develop. For the tumultuous previous decade (57–47 BC), Judea had been governed by the five regional Sanhedrins established by Gabinius (see 4.3.3 above). Antipater abolished all of them except the Jerusalem Sanhedrin. The man who became its president at this time was the Pharisee Abtalion, one of Hillel's teachers. Like Antipater, Abtalion was a son of converts and perhaps even of Idumean origin, as was his vice president, Shemaiah.[27] It is tantalizing to see Antipater's hand in both their appointments, especially when we realize that Abtalion had not held the vice presidency before his appointment, as was usually the case. That office had been held by Menahem the Essene (another teacher of Hillel), who left the Sanhedrin and the ascetic lifestyle of his sect to pursue a gainful role in secular government, almost certainly at the coaxing of Antipater.[28]

But any pleasure the members of the Jerusalem Sanhedrin might have gained from the restructure was offset by Antipater's appointment of his eldest son, Phasael, as governor of Jerusalem (*Ant.* 14.158; *J.W.* 1.203). This meant that the Pharisees, who had dominated the Sanhedrin since the time of Salome Alexandra, had to cede a huge portion of their civic authority to Phasael. Antipater was clearly grooming his eldest son to succeed him, and Phasael proved to be a competent administrator. His effectiveness shrank the Sanhedrin's authority even more, stoking its displeasure, as later rabbinic traditions imply.[29]

---

27. Midrash Tanhuma-Yelammedenu (Vayakhel, 8) states that Abtalion and Shemaiah were Kenites, like the father-in-law of Moses. If so, they were originally from peoples associated with the Negev and Sinai regions and, therefore, either Idumean or Nabatean. Shemaiah is usually cited before Abtalion in rabbinic literature, but Josephus clarifies that Abtalion ("Pollion") was the senior of the two and that Shemaiah ("Samaias") was "his disciple" (*Ant.* 15.3).

28. Rabbinic literature claims that Menahem "went out" of the Sanhedrin and was replaced by Shemaiah (b. Ḥag. 16b). This was interpreted in various ways, but the most likely explanation is that Menahem agreed to an appointment in secular government, which resulted in him renouncing Essene strictures and embracing the benefits of office.

29. One tradition relates that, after performing the Day of Atonement rituals, the crowds following the high priest suddenly saw Abtalion and Shemaiah and were drawn to follow them instead, leading

Antipater also appointed his second son, Herod, as governor of Galilee (*Ant.* 14.158; *J.W.* 1.203). Herod was then twenty-seven years old[30] and married to an Idumean woman named Doris, with whom he had an infant son, Antipater II (born ca. 48 BC).[31] Antipater showed remarkable faith in Herod to manage the rage rolling through Galilee in the wake of the Caesarean Settlement. The chief dissenter was a warlord named Hezekiah, of whom we know precious little, apart from the fact that his militia's activities were violent and spilled over into Syria. This suggests that Hezekiah was targeting gentiles and Roman collaborators—an operation not dissimilar from those of the early Maccabean resistance. Hezekiah was the beginning of a groundswell movement, especially in Galilee, promoting the rise of warlords and brigands, which ultimately spawned the Sicarii and Zealot movements of the first century. From later statements made about Hezekiah's descendants, there is a possibility that he was of Davidic descent, which would add a messianic dimension to his movement.[32] Nevertheless, his uprising failed, for Herod had inherited his father's military prowess and dealt with Hezekiah with exceptional efficiency. The warlord and most of his men were hunted down and summarily executed, drawing the praise of Sextus Julius Caesar, the Roman governor of Syria, and of the Syrians themselves (*Ant.* 14.159–60; *J.W.* 204–205).

But Herod's swift justice provoked the supreme ire of the Jerusalem Sanhedrin, who saw in his freewheeling implementation of capital punishment a dangerous usurpation of their authority. Herod's initiative smacked of royal prerogative. What made this yet more unpalatable for some was the fact that the Caesarean Settlement had failed to reinstate Hasmonean monarchy, and now it appeared that Antipater and his family were taking advantage of this to further their own dynastic aspirations, with the pusillanimous Hyrcanus disinclined to stop them. So, while Herod's martial success had tamed Galilee

---

the high priest to spitefully denounce the two men. The trite incident highlights the jealousy of the high priest (b. Yoma 71b), but the reality behind it suggests a sense of the Sanhedrin's importance in the face of dissatisfaction with Hyrcanus and Antipater. Telling also is the fact that Shemaiah was remembered for the maxim, "Do not become too familiar with the ruling authority" (m. 'Avot 1.10), which insinuates his rising dissatisfaction with Antipater's ways.

30. Josephus mistakenly gives his age as fifteen years (*Ant.* 14.158).

31. Antipater II is sometimes enumerated as Antipater III because Herod's father and grandfather were both named Antipater. Herod's grandfather held office in Idumea and is sometimes simply called Antipas. For our purposes, he is passed over in our enumeration.

32. Hezekiah's son, Judas, also led an uprising and claimed to have royal pretensions (see 4.5.10). If Judas is to be equated with Judas the Galilean (plausible, but not certain), then he had three sons: James, Simon, and Menahem. Menahem became a royal claimant and leader of the Sicarii during the Jewish Revolt in AD 66, alongside his kinsman, Eleazar ben-Yair, who is noted for his last stand at Masada. In rabbinic literature, Menahem is associated with Hezekiah, and messianic notions are attached to him, though some of these seem garbled with traditions regarding Jesus (b. Sanh. 98b; y. Ber. 2:4). Cf. Jeremias Joachim, *Jerusalem in the Time of Jesus: An Investigation into Economic and Social Conditions during the New Testament Period*, trans. F. H. Cave and C. H. Cave (London: SCM Press, 1969), 276–77.

and neighboring Syria, it created a jurisdictional crisis within Judea (cf. *Ant.* 14.163–67; *J.W.* 1.208–209).

The Pharisee-stacked Sanhedrin badgered Hyrcanus to prevail upon Antipater to recall his son to face trial for alleged excesses against Hezekiah. Hyrcanus complied, which put him in the dire circumstance of betraying the family of his trusted executive in order to do the Sanhedrin's bidding. This effectively asserted the Sanhedrin's authority over any appointment Antipater made. But to make matters worse for Hyrcanus, Sextus wrote urging him to exonerate Herod of any wrongdoing because Herod's actions had been both justified and effective. Hyrcanus was a man torn by the will of others competing amongst themselves.

Herod had no intention of appearing meek or contrite at his trial. He appeared before the Sanhedrin dressed in purple and with an armed retinue. In this brazen show, he may have been motivated not just by the support of Sextus but also by a prediction of Menahem the Essene. Josephus tells the anecdote of how Menahem, presumably in the days of his vice presidency, had once crossed paths with a younger Herod and acclaimed him "king of the Jews," predicting that he would reign over the nation for some thirty years (*Ant.* 15.373–78). The young Herod had been amused by this, but now with his father's dynastic pretensions, the prediction no longer seemed abject fantasy.

Herod's ostentation had the desired effect, and his detractors were intimidated into silence. However, the Sanhedrin's vice president, Shemaiah, shamed his colleagues for their timidity and made a prediction of his own: if they did not condemn Herod now for murder, they would be granting him license to act against them and their king in the future because he was more concerned for his own power than the rightful rule of Jewish Law (*Ant.* 14.168–74; cf. *J.W.* 1.210–11). In relating the scene, Josephus has Shemaiah refer to Hyrcanus as "king." Since Caesar had not granted him such royal title, this probably reflects the fact that John Hyrcanus had once been king and that latent Jewish hopes for a future restoration of a native Jewish monarchy were still prevalent. But Shemaiah's intervention reveals that Herod's trial was a showdown between Antipater and the Pharisee-stacked Sanhedrin for control of the Jewish nation, and perhaps even to determine who a future Jewish king might be.[33]

It is ironic, then, that the passive Hyrcanus sabotaged the trial by showing some initiative. He adjourned it and privately advised Herod to escape Jerusalem (*Ant.* 14.177). This prevented a final verdict and handed victory

---

33. In Richardson's estimation, the account in *Antiquities* at this point is hardly reliable (*Herod*, 108–13). However, while Josephus almost certainly displays some rhetorical flourish, the historical dynamics they encapsulate make perfect sense of the wider socio-political currents at play.

to Antipater's family, for it ensured that Herod survived and the Sanhedrin did not get its way. In yet further irony, Hyrcanus's unanticipated initiative would undermine his own authority by guaranteeing that he would never be supported for a future royal role by the Sanhedrin.

Herod fled to Damascus, where Sextus commissioned him as commander of southern Syria, and the *polis* of Samaria. This gave Herod immense firepower, and he now plotted an invasion of Judea, motivated by revenge against the Jerusalem Sanhedrin. Had he actually carried out his plan, other warlords of Hezekiah's ilk might have been galvanized into action, and the country would have been torn apart by a new civil war. But Herod's diplomatically minded father dissuaded him from following through, and the country was spared a wider conflict (*Ant.* 14.178–84; *J.W.* 1.212–15).

Nonetheless, the country teetered on the edge of violence, with the tension between Antipater and the Sanhedrin threatening to push it off. Had Hyrcanus been a more commanding figure, he might have brought greater unity to the country and the prospect of a reinstatement of native Jewish monarchy. But he lacked the political spine and competence to be anything other than the puppet of those who had their own vision for the governance of Judea and the will to put it into action. Hyrcanus's political atrophy intensified the volatility of the country. For the Pharisees of the Sanhedrin, Jewish self-government was about maintaining the nation's purity in covenantal obedience to God. For the Sadducees, self-government was about maintaining the divine election of the priesthood to leadership of the nation and its temple. For the likes of the warlord Hezekiah, self-government seems to have been about the preservation of Jewish culture and resistance to economic oppression. For Antipater and his sons, government was about securing the place of Judea in a Roman world and making sure that a qualified hand was on the political tiller. For Julius Caesar, the government of Judea was about keeping the Jews aligned with his own interests. In the midst of all this, a substratum of Jewish society—Essenes and Davidic loyalists—waited for the intervention of God himself to fix everything that was wrong in both Judea and the world.

4.3.11 JULIUS CAESAR: MASTER OF ROME

During the period 48–44 BC, Julius Caesar held the consulship four times,[34] extinguished the social and political fires that civil war had ignited, passed

---

34. These were 48, 46, 45 (sole consul), and 44 BC, which were in addition to his first consulship in 59 BC.

into law the measures he had promised the Jewish nation (*Ant.* 14.185–216), defeated Pompey's surviving supporters in Africa (Caesar, *African War*), celebrated four separate triumphs, and provided lavish festivities for the citizens of Rome. In 46 BC he altered time itself by instituting a solar calendar of 365 days, with the addition of one extra day every four years (Suetonius, *Caes.* 40.1–2). The recalibration from the old system resulted in each subsequent new year beginning in January rather than March.

Although the Senate was compliant to Caesar's will, he was not without detractors. In 48 BC, Roman Asia officially recognized him as "a god made manifest" (Gk. *theon epiphanē*) and "common savior of human life" (*SIG* 760). Prior to this, no Roman had ever been acclaimed as a god, so this imbued Caesar (at least in Asia) with the kind of divinity associated with Hellenistic autocracy, much to the vexation of the *Optimates*.[35] Then, in 46 BC Cleopatra VII arrived in Rome with her infant son, Caesarion, and lodged in one of Caesar's villas (Dio Cassius, *Hist. rom.* 43.27; Suetonius, *Caes.* 52.1–2). Those who still defended the ideals of the Republic found the relationship scandalous; Caesar was cavorting with a foreign queen, considered a goddess in her own country, by whom he had fathered a son. What's more, that son represented what many Romans saw as the outlandish customs of Egypt, and yet he stood to inherit much within Rome itself. The presence of Cleopatra and Caesarion cast the shadow of divine monarchy across the tattered Republic and played upon the xenophobic reflex of many native Romans.

Furthermore, two new threats to Caesar arose that year. One came from Pompey Junior, the eldest son of Pompey Magnus, who was raising forces in Spain to challenge Caesar. The second threat came from Syria, where Caesar's cousin, Governor Sextus Julius Caesar, was assassinated at the instigation of an old Pompeian supporter named Caecilius Bassus. Antipater sent Herod, and perhaps Phasael also, to attack Bassus, who bunkered down at Apamea in northern Syria. A prolonged siege unfolded (*Ant.* 14.268–69; *J.W.* 1.216–17; Dio Cassius,. 47.27), which was actually a godsend for Antipater, as it took Herod out of the spotlight in Judea. From Caesar's perspective, it helped arrest the momentum of Bassus's challenge in Syria.

Caesar hurried to Spain and defeated Pompey Junior within seven months (Caesar, *Spanish War*). Towards the end of the campaign, he was joined by his grand-nephew, Octavian. The boy had been born in 63 BC and raised primarily by his grandmother, Julia, the youngest sister of Caesar. It was during Octavian's time in Spain that Caesar's affection for him grew to the

---

35. Freeman, *Egypt, Greece, and Rome*, 437.

point where he designated Octavian as his heir (Velleius, *Roman History* 2.59; Nicolaus of Damascus, fr. 127.23–26). Caesar was politically powerful enough to be flagrant in keeping his relationship with Cleopatra, despite his marriage to his third wife, Calpurnia. But he was also Roman enough to realize that Caesarion would never be accepted in Rome. Caesar saw in Octavian great potential for native Roman leadership. So, upon returning to Rome in 45 BC and celebrating yet another triumph, Caesar wrote Octavian into his will and sent him to further his education in Illyria.

By the beginning of 44 BC, Caesar's stranglehold on Roman government had increased appreciably. He had acquired the right to make government appointments, direct discussion in the Senate, control public funds, command armies without Senatorial approval, dress in triumphal garb at will, and sit on a golden throne. These powers practically consigned the Senate to irrelevance and created a pantomime of republican government.[36] The old guard, whom Caesar had pardoned after the civil war, were offended but powerless. To make matters worse, Caesar's birthday was celebrated with public sacrifice, his statue was placed in every temple, and plans were afoot to build a temple in his honor, with Mark Antony as his priest (Dio Cassius, *Hist. rom.* 44.4–6). Even the general public was starting to become conflicted: though they loved Caesar's achievements and the festivities he lavished on them, his all-pervasive power was becoming unnerving.

At this stage, Caesar was planning a grand campaign against the Parthians in the east (Plutarch, *Caes.* 58.4–7). As part of the propaganda for it, Caesar's stooges claimed that the sacred Sibylline Books predicted that Rome would defeat Parthia under the leadership of a king.[37] The claim gave the impression that monarchy in Rome was inevitable and that Caesar's ambitions were backed by the gods. Conservative senators grew ever more alarmed.

That alarm turned to panic in late January 44 BC when Caesar celebrated the annual Latin Festival on the Alban Mount, a site southeast of Rome, associated with Rome's ancient kings. As he was returning to Rome, he was hailed by someone in the crowd as "king" (Plutarch, *Caes.* 60.1–3; Dio Cassius, *Hist. rom.* 44.10). Though he demurred the title, the incident frightened those still committed to a Roman Republic. Caesar's critics figured that, if they did not act soon, he would keep extending his powers by steady degrees until he attained autocratic power.

---

36. Sinnigen and Boak, *A History of Rome*, 222.
37. The Sibylline Books are to be distinguished from the Sibylline Oracles (cf. 3.5.5). The original Sibylline Books had been lost in a fire that destroyed Rome's temple of Jupiter in 83 BC. Sulla sponsored the temple reconstruction, and the books were replaced by consulting oracles around the Mediterranean.

In early February 44 BC, a stacked Senate met without Caesar and voted to bestow yet more honors upon him. As senator tried to outdo senator, the list of accolades grew and included such statutes as renaming Quintilis, the month of his birth, "July" in his honor. The most significant distinction granted to him was the office of Dictator for Life. This was not monarchy, but it was as close to it that Rome had come since the overthrow of its ancient kings in the late sixth century BC. Despite this, some of Caesar's opponents saw a strategic opportunity. By heaping inordinate kudos upon him, they might be able to expose just how deeply his ambitions ran and perhaps turn sentiment against him—rapid change that might make people notice more starkly what was going on. It was a dangerous strategy, for if it backfired, Caesar would emerge as the practical monarch he seemed intent on becoming. This itself was confirmed when the Senate's representatives met with him to convey his new privileges. Caesar did not stand to greet them, as was the traditional token of respect for government officeholders. His enemies interpreted his laxity as a sign that he considered himself above Rome's governing institutions (Suetonius, *Caes.* 76.1; Dio Cassius, *Hist. rom.* 44.4–8).

Now, as Dictator for Life, Caesar seems to have engineered a stunt to take the temperature of popular sentiment towards him. On 15 February 44 BC, he was watching proceedings during the Lupercalia festival when Mark Antony, his co-consul for the year, offered him a royal diadem. Caesar humbly refused it, and the crowds applauded his action. Had they not done so, he might have taken the diadem when Antony offered it to him a second time. But he refused it the second time, too. Despite this theater, a diadem soon appeared on his statue in the Roman Forum, and when two magistrates removed it, Caesar had them stripped of their positions (Plutarch, *Caes.* 61.1–10; Dio Cassius, *Hist. rom.* 44.9). The incident demonstrated the affection that people had for Caesar but also their disavowal of monarchy.

The incident jogged Caesar's enemies into action. A cabal was formed by senators Gaius Cassius Longinus, the survivor of Carrhae, and Marcus Junius Brutus, the son of a former lover of Caesar's. Brutus had the symbolic distinction of being descended from the man chiefly responsible for overthrowing the last king of Rome in 509 BC. Their conspiracy won over scores of disaffected senators committed to preventing Rome's slide into tyranny. Their plot would demonstrate that Caesar's downfall was not the act of a lone wolf but the collective action of Rome's most responsible stakeholders (Appian, *Bell. civ.* 2.113–15).

On the morning of Sunday, 15 March 44 BC, just days before his planned departure for the east, Caesar arrived at Pompey's Theater where the Senate had been meeting since the destruction of the old Senate House eight years earlier. On his way to the chamber, he was accosted by members of the cabal and stabbed twenty-three times. According to Appian, his dead body fell before a statue of Pompey (Appian, *Bell. civ.* 2.117). With Caesar's corpse still warm, the assassins hurried to the Forum and proclaimed that they had liberated the Republic (Dio Cassius, *Hist. rom.* 44.19–20).

However, while the conspirators felled the tyrant, they failed to plan a subsequent takeover of the state. They had assumed the state would revert to its classic republican dynamics, but the Republic had been rendered impotent after decades of manipulation. It had no more elasticity with which to spring back. This is what Mark Antony, as Caesar's co-consul, exploited two days later when he convinced the Senate to pardon Caesar's assassins but agree to maintain all the dictator's prior appointments and execute his will. This ensured that the power structures Caesar had imposed remained intact. The Senate ironically voted for its own marginalization. What the "Liberators" succeeded in achieving was an assassination, but not a *coup d'état*.

Antony then found it easy to stoke public sentiment against them. In his will, Caesar left a monetary gift to each Roman citizen and donated one of his personal estates as public parkland. The public was soon viewing Caesar as a martyr who had fallen prey to the oligarchic interests of the *Optimates*. Sentiment boiled over into angry protest during Caesar's funeral in the Roman Forum, and the "Liberators" who had assassinated him promptly quit Rome (Appian, *J.W.* 2.126–48).

In his will, Caesar retrospectively adopted his grand-nephew, Octavian, as his son, and designated him his heir (Appian, *J.W.* 2.136). This surprised Mark Antony, who had fancied himself in the prime position to inherit Caesar's legacy. Antony figured he could simply dominate the boy, who was still in Illyria undertaking his education. Accordingly, Antony began using funds from Caesar's estate to further his own aspirations. But Octavian quickly learned of Caesar's death and landed back in Italy to take possession of his inheritance.

Antony could not see in Octavian what Caesar had seen: his intelligence. Even at just eighteen years of age, Octavian recognized that the Roman Republic was dead but that conservative *Optimates* senators refused to acknowledge it. He exploited their delusion and the assumption of his naivety to great advantage. When he won over some of Caesar's troops and denounced Antony as a threat to the Republic, mature senators, such as Cicero, saw in him a potential weapon to wield against Antony in their bid to repair the Republic (Appian, *J.W.* 3.47–48). So, they gave Octavian honorary consular powers for 43 BC. What the senators failed to recognize was how the death of the Republic allowed Octavian to wield them as his own weapon. When both elected consuls died trying to bring Antony to heel, Octavian emerged with actual consular command. Even at this stage, though, the senior senators still underestimated his ambition and ability.

4.3.12 THE DEMISE OF ANTIPATER

Caesar's assassins—the "Liberators"—remained committed to their cause. Young Octavian's opposition to Antony even gave them hope for restoring the Republic. This sent them on a quest to raise funds and troops to empower their efforts. To that end, Cassius came knocking on Judea's door (43 BC). His savage treatment of the Galileans nine years earlier at Magdala-Tarichiae (52 BC) intimidated John Hyrcanus II and Antipater into acquiescing to his demands. Cassius used their support for Caesar in Egypt as a pretext for demanding a punitive 700 talents of silver from the Jewish state.[38] Some of this was raised by enslaving whole towns that could not otherwise pay an adequate portion (*Ant.* 14.271–76; *J.W.* 1.218–22). Cassius's treatment demonstrated to the Jewish population that all they could expect from the Romans was insult and injury.

Herod saw in the shifting political tides an opportunity to further his own ambitions. He exacted his portion of Cassius's money from Galilee, which can only have embittered the already economically battered region even more. But in return, he received from Cassius a confirmation of his military command in Coele Syria and the promise of appointment as king of the Jews after the Liberators restored the Republic (*Ant.* 14.280). The prediction of Menahem the Essene was inching closer to reality.

After Cassius moved on, court intrigue beset Judea. Over the years, Antipater had developed an intense rivalry with a Jewish lieutenant named Malichus, who had once supported the cause of Aristobulus II. In 43 BC, Antipater was unexpectedly found dead at the age of seventy, and Malichus was blamed for poisoning him (*Ant.* 14.280–93; *J.W.* 1.225–35). Whether he did or not is unclear, but Herod schemed to ensure Malichus took the fall.

Antipater's career was a critical fulcrum in moving Judea from a troubled independent kingdom to a subordinate client state of Rome. His charisma and capabilities commended him initially to Salome Alexandra and then made him indispensable to the spiritless John Hyrcanus II. He was a cosmopolitan character, at home in whichever arena he happened to be. We might say that to the Jews, he was as a Jew; to the Nabateans, he was as a Nabatean; to the Greeks,

---

38. In modern terms, this is just over US$1 billion.

he was as a Greek; and to the Romans, he was as a Roman. This chameleon-like adaptability made him a survivor, always with a finger on the pulse of the wider political situation. He was a politician, a diplomat, a financier, a commander, a builder, and finally also an emerging dynast. As Procurator towards the end of his life, his authority over Judea easily eclipsed that of the high priest—a circumstance born over time by Hyrcanus's political vertigo. Yet, Antipater never sought to replace him. Whether this was because he was always the loyal servant of the Hasmoneans or simply a realist who saw the benefit of defraying power through a puppet, cannot be known. In either case, he was an industrious politician who bequeathed to his sons many of his own personal traits, as well as the opportunity to capitalize on Roman fractiousness and Jewish exhaustion.

4.3.13 THE SECOND TRIUMVIRATE

Mark Antony and Octavian were natural rivals for the legacy of Caesar: Antony, the seasoned soldier and brash deputy of the dictator, now almost forty years of age; Octavian, the young and demure novice, half Antony's age. Octavian weaseled his way into the corridors of power, ostensibly as an ally of the *Optimates* senators. In that capacity, he had Antony branded an enemy of the Republic. By mid-43 BC, the old senatorial guard, headed by Cicero, woke to the realization that they could not control Octavian and that he had outwitted them all. Antony found himself politically and militarily on the backfoot and realized that he could not overcome the Senate's opposition or the growing forces of the Liberators without Octavian's support. Despite their differences, the two of them had three things in common: they admired Caesar, they wanted to bring his assassins to justice, and they were realistic about the future of the Roman Republic. Accordingly, Antony entered negotiations with Octavian, and in November 43 BC the Second Triumvirate was proclaimed, consisting of Octavian, Antony, and Marcus Aemilius Lepidus (the man who succeeded Caesar as *Pontifex Maximus*). To cement the alliance, Octavian married Antony's stepdaughter, Clodia.[39] The Triumvirate was given full state powers, which guaranteed another Roman civil war, this time between the Triumvirate and the Liberators.

Within days of the Triumvirate's formation, Cicero was proscribed and executed, and with him died the last figment of the Roman Republic. The only

---

39. Clodia was the daughter of Clodius, whose murder sparked the burning of the Senate House in 52 BC. Clodius's wife, Fulvia, subsequently married Antony and retained her status as one of the most powerful women in Rome.

ones now left to champion the old order were the Liberators, who were raising their forces in the provinces. But even if they could defeat the Triumvirate, Rome could not revert to the Republic it once was. The First Triumvirate, which had initially been a private alliance, put too big a dent into the Republic. The fact that the Second Triumvirate became a reality through official means shows that the Republic was now a write-off. Men could now themselves become the state, making the other traditional offices of government mere illusions.

To cap matters off, the Second Triumvirate deified Julius Caesar. Four months after Caesar's assassination (July 44 BC), a bright comet was seen streaking across the day sky in Rome. At the time, Octavian proclaimed it to be his adoptive father, Julius Caesar, being raised to the heavens as a god. Also at this time, atmospheric conditions made for "a cloudy year," which obscured both the sun and moon and reduced crop yields for the next two years (Tibullus, *Elegies* 2.75–78; cf. *Ant.* 14.309; Plutarch, *Caes.* 69.4–5; Ovid, *Metam.* 15.785–90). We know today that these conditions were the result of two volcanic eruptions, but they were widely interpreted at the time as divine displeasure over the assassination of Caesar.[40] Two years later, the cult of *Divus Julius* was officially formed with a shrine in the Roman Forum (Dio Cassius, *Hist. rom.* 47.18–19). Caesar, who had succeeded in rising above the law in his lifetime, now rose to the plane of deity, to be worshipped in the operation of the Roman state. This chain of events probably lies behind the imagery in Revelation 9:1–6, though Revelation ironically reverses the import of the imagery to portray divine displeasure at the Roman imperial cult.[41] Octavian duly designated himself the son of a god. Although this was different to the Jewish notion that the Davidic king became God's adopted son at his enthronement (cf. 2 Sam 7:14), there was enough conceptual similarity that the later Christian claim about Jesus being Son of God would resonate with gentiles in a Greco-Roman world. The idea that a human being could be translated to the

---

40. The two volcanoes were Mount Etna in Sicily (44 BC) and the Okmok volcano in Alaska (43 BC). The catastrophic eruption of Okmok reduced temperatures in the Mediterranean Basin by up to 7°C during the affected two years and left an indelible mark on the ecological stratigraphy of the entire northern hemisphere. See Richard B. Stothers and Michael R. Rampino, "Volcanic Eruptions in the Mediterranean Before A.D. 630 from Written and Archaeological Sources," *JGR* 88.B8 (1983): 6358–60; Michael R. Rampino, Stephen Self, and Richard B. Strothers, "Volcanic Winters," *AREPS* 16 (1988): 88–89; Joseph R. McConnell et al., "Extreme Climate After Massive Eruption of Alaska's Okmok Volcano in 43 BCE and Effects on the Late Roman Republic and Ptolemaic Kingdom," *PNAS* 117.27 (2020): 15443–49.

41. Interestingly, this part of Revelation goes on to describe the invasion of an ominous army from east of the Euphrates, which is exactly what happened when the Parthians invaded Syria in 41/40 BC (see 4.4.3 below).

heavens after death was not novel in the first century. Where the early church differed to the cult of *Divus Julius* was in the conviction that Jesus was preexistent—God who had come down from the heavens to become human—and that Jesus's body, pierced though it was like that of the assassinated Caesar, had actually been resurrected from death.

The Triumvirate decided that Lepidus would remain in Italy to hold the home front while Antony and Octavian deployed to the provinces to confront the Liberators. The two sides met in October 42 BC outside the Macedonian city of Philippi. The strategic advantage lay with the better supplied forces of Cassius and Brutus. Cleopatra, who had returned to Egypt after Caesar's assassination, sent ships with reinforcements for the Triumvirate's armies, but stormy conditions prevented their arrival. The first battle between the two sides was indecisive, but Cassius received the false report that Brutus had been overwhelmed. On hearing this, Cassius believed that all was lost and committed suicide. But Brutus had not been defeated. He had survived, and all he needed to do now was not engage the enemy but wait for hunger to grip their poorly supplied armies. But after waiting many days, his own troops were on the verge of desertion. Fearing this outcome, Brutus finally attacked on 23 October 42 BC. He was overwhelmed and subsequently committed suicide. The Liberators had been defeated, and the Roman Empire belonged to Octavian, Antony, and Lepidus.[42]

After the battle, the Triumvirate permitted some of their soldiers to settle in Philippi, which was given the status of a Roman colony. They then proceeded to divide the Roman territories between themselves. Antony took command of the eastern provinces, with the goal of launching a campaign against the Parthians. Octavian was given command of the western Mediterranean, and Lepidus was granted nominal command of the African provinces.

---

42. Sextus Pompey, the younger son of Pompey Magnus, still held out against the Triumvirate in Sicily, but the defeat of the Liberators damaged his cause.

4.4 PARTHIAN HEGEMONY

4.4.1 HEROD AND MARK ANTONY

With the death of Antipater, his two sons, Phasael and Herod, stepped into the breach. Yet, the Jerusalem Sanhedrin still stood staunchly opposed to them. The last surviving son of Aristobulus II, Mattathias Antigonus II, might have capitalized on the new political conditions after Caesar's assassination, but the Second Triumvirate's victory at Philippi maintained the Caesarean Settlement in Judea and ensured his ongoing marginalization.

Herod, now thirty-two years of age, saw at this moment an opportunity to plant himself near the center of Jewish power and alienate Antigonus even further. He divorced his Nabatean wife, Doris, and was betrothed to the twenty-two-year-old Mariamme (*Ant.* 14.300), granddaughter of both John Hyrcanus II and Aristobulus II. She was also the older sister of young Aristobulus III, heir to the high priesthood of John Hyrcanus II. The engagement proved popular with some, but the members of the Sanhedrin rankled at the match. They sent repeated embassies to Mark Antony, requesting the removal of both Antipater's sons from power. Herod, however, was as attuned to their agenda as they were to his. He went personally to Antony to congratulate him on his victory at Philippi and to present a gift that would cement Herod as Antony's client. Satisfied with this bribe, Antony confirmed Herod and Phasael as "tetrarchs" in Judea under the ongoing titular headship of Hyrcanus and ordered the emancipation of all Jews whom Cassius had enslaved (*Ant.* 14.324–29; *J.W.* 1.242–47). Herod thus came across as a redeemer of the Jews.

This outcome enraged the Sanhedrin, who felt their relevance within Jewish government slipping inexorably before Antipater's sons. In some ways, this mirrored the plight of the Roman Senate over the previous decades. But the issue for the Sanhedrin, and for most Jews, was not the move towards autocracy but the assertion of Rome's imperial claims over all Jewish power structures. Judea was no longer the independent entity it had briefly been and that its divine national covenant called for. Antipater's two sons were Roman lackeys, and Judea was little more than Rome's pawn.

4.4.2 MARK ANTONY AND CLEOPATRA

Mark Antony moved around the eastern Mediterranean undoing the previous work of Cassius and seeing to the logistics of his upcoming Parthian campaign. As part of this effort, he needed to secure the support of Cleopatra VII and her Ptolemaic armies. He therefore invited her to the Cilician capital of Tarsus to negotiate. Although Cleopatra had tried to support both Antony and Octavian against the Liberators at Philippi, she saw Octavian, Caesar's heir, as a threat to her own son, Caesarion, the biological son of Caesar. On the precedent of the First Triumvirate, she figured that the Second Triumvirate was bound to have a limited lifespan and that she needed to back Antony against Octavian in the long term. So, Cleopatra arrived at Tarsus in October 41 BC aboard her magnificent state barge and, after reciprocal banquets, promptly seduced Antony (*Ant.* 14.324; cf. *J.W.* 1.243; Plutarch, *Ant.* 25.1–26.4).

Antony became smitten with Cleopatra, and indications are that she too fell for him. As Antony was from an originally plebeian family, he had only the most distant familial ties to Roman aristocracy. He therefore held little loyalty to the old Roman order and felt at home in the Hellenistic world that promoted autocratic rulers. His relationship with Cleopatra was, in many respects, simply the convergence of these dynamics. So enamored with Cleopatra did Antony become that, after she returned to Egypt, he followed her there and spent the winter of 41/40 BC in Alexandria. Before long, Cleopatra fell pregnant to him, and later in 40 BC she bore him twins: Alexander Helios and Cleopatra Selene II.

Antony's tryst scandalized Rome, just as Caesar's had before him. But whereas Caesar had maintained martial sensibility through his marital insensitivity, Antony did not. For, while he was ensconced in Alexandria, the Parthians invaded Syria. When he learned of this, he scrambled to Syria to deal with the situation.

4.4.3 MATTATHIAS ANTIGONUS II AND THE PARTHIAN INVASION

In the lead up to the Battle of Philippi, the Liberators Cassius and Brutus had sent a representative, Quintus Labienus, to the Parthians. His mission was to secure military reinforcements for their cause against the Second Triumvirate. This attempt to inject the Parthians into Roman political conflict reveals how fractious Roman politics had become. The Parthians stalled, and the Roman conflict reached its resolution at Philippi without them. But the Triumvirate's victory left Labienus stranded among the Parthians, and Antony's subsequent activities in the east convinced them that a Roman invasion was imminent. The Parthian king, Orodes II, and his son, Pacorus, were keen to prevent this. They had also not given up the long-term Parthian ambition of expanding to the shores of the Mediterranean. So, as Antony whiled away the winter of 41/40 BC with Cleopatra in Egypt, the Parthians launched a preemptive strike into Syria. Leading their troops across the Euphrates were the Parthian general Barzapharnes, the crown prince Pacorus, and Labienus. Memory of this event, and perhaps a fear of its repeat in the late first century, are probably reflected in Revelation 9:13–21 (cf. 4.3.13 above).

Labienus's involvement made the Parthians players in the internal disputes that continued to plague Rome even after Philippi. Labienus won over the Roman legions in Syria, after which the Parthians quickly overran the Syrian heartland and reached the Mediterranean Sea. The Syrian populace was still smarting from Rome's heavy-handed hegemony, so while they were swapping one imperial overlord for another, the hope was that the Parthians might prove the more benign rulers. After securing Syria, Labienus took his forces into Asia Minor in the hope of turning back the tide of the Triumvirate's supremacy. He was, however, to be thwarted the following year.

Meanwhile, Barzapharnes and Pacorus plunged south towards Judea. Their march raised the prospect that the Jews might be able to lift the burdensome Roman yoke from their shoulders. The spotlight fell on Mattathias Antigonus II, the last surviving son of Aristobulus II, to leverage the Parthians against Roman sovereignty in Judea. He was about thirty-five years old and still residing outside Judea in the Iturean kingdom of Chalcis in southern Lebanon.[1] Not only was he resolutely anti-Roman, but he also possessed the Hasmonean pedigree to replace his uncle as high priest. He struck a deal to pay the Parthians 1,000 silver talents of and 500 women (among them, the women attached to Hyrcanus and the sons of Antipater) for their aid in installing him as king. And so, Antigonus came down the coast with a contingent of Parthians to claim the Jewish state for himself (*Ant.* 14.330–32; *J.W.* 1.248–50).

The Jewish state was radiating rebellion against Rome, so Antigonus's arrival induced many to declare immediately for him. During the Festival of Pentecost (June 40 BC), he entered Jerusalem with a veritable army of pilgrims (cf. Matt 21:6–11; Mark 11:6–11; Luke 19:35–40; John 12:12–19), in addition to his band of Parthians. However, here he came up against resistance from

---

1. Philippion, the son of the kingdom's founder, Ptolemy Menneus, had fallen in love with Antigonus's sister, Alexandra. But Ptolemy Menneus murdered his own son in order to marry Alexandra himself (*Ant.* 14.126).

Phasael and Herod, who were now literally fighting for their lives. Fighting erupted in the streets, and a stalemate soon developed. Hyrcanus and Phasael realized that, with the popular opposition to their rule, their only chance for survival was to appeal directly to the Parthian general Barzapharnes, who was in Galilee. Herod, however, was convinced that their cause was lost and refused to go. His intuition was correct, for when Hyrcanus and Phasael met with Barzapharnes in Galilee, they were arrested. When news reached Jerusalem, Herod hastily got his family together, including his fiancée, Mariamme, and her mother, Alexandra II, and fought his way out of the city. He left his immediate family and fiancée atop the desert fortress at Masada and dispersed the rest of his guard throughout Idumea. He then fled the country (*Ant.* 14.333–62; *J.W.* 1.263–67). There was now nothing stopping Antigonus from taking over Judea.

Barzapharnes brought Hyrcanus and Phasael to Jerusalem in chains. The Hasmonean palace was sacked, along with the houses of their supporters. Idumea was also liberally pillaged and its chief city, Marisa, destroyed, probably because it was the hometown of Antipater and his sons. The Parthians then installed Antigonus II as king of the Jews under their suzerainty (*Ant.* 14.363–64; *J.W.* 1.268–69), thus formally ending Rome's hold over the entire Levant. The Hasmonean kingdom was once more a reality, this time as a client state of the Parthians.

As the new head of state, Antigonus faced a serious quandary about what to do with the incumbent high priest, his uncle, Hyrcanus. He could not simply execute him, for this would be a sacrilege of the highest proportions. Hyrcanus was hugely unpopular, but popular respect for the office of high priest stayed Antigonus's hand. He did not want to set a precedent that would come back to haunt him once he himself attained the high priesthood. Hyrcanus, now sixty-three years old and seemingly in good health, might continue in the sacerdotal role for many years to come. And by then his grandson and heir, Aristobulus III (Antigonus's nephew), might be old enough to fill the position after him. Antigonus, therefore, needed to act sooner than later to secure the high priesthood for himself. But merely replacing Hyrcanus was insufficient, since the high priesthood was a lifelong office, and having two living high priests would create ritual and political ambiguity.

In the midst of this dilemma, Antigonus happened upon a solution: he had Hyrcanus's ears mutilated (*Ant.* 14.366). According to one of Josephus's accounts, Antigonus personally bit his uncle's ear off with his own teeth (*J.W.* 1.270), but this is undoubtedly a sensationalist embellishment. The mutilation rendered Hyrcanus irreversibly unfit for the high priesthood, for the Torah required every priest to be without physical defect or else they would desecrate the sanctuary (Lev 21:17–23). This striking incident casts a shadow over events some seventy years later when Jesus was arrested by the temple guard just days after being popularly hailed as king when he entered Jerusalem. In the skirmish that broke out in Gethsemane, Jesus's disciple, Simon Peter, severed the ear of Malchus, the personal servant of the high priest Caiaphas (Matt 26:51; Mark 14:47; Luke 22:50; John 18:10). Far from simply a wild swing, Simon Peter's action was highly symbolic of the perceived illegitimacy of the entire temple institution, which Jesus had condemned just days before (Matt 21:12–13; 23:37–24:2; Mark 11:15–17; 13:1–2; Luke 19:45–46; 21:5–6; John 2:13–22).[2]

After his mutilation, Hyrcanus was exiled to Parthia. A couple of years later, he was released by Phraates IV (successor of Orodes II) and allowed to settle among the Jewish community of Babylonia, where he was accorded great dignity (*Ant.* 15.11–15; *J.W.* 1.273). Phasael, however, did not fare so well. Since he possessed no sacred status, he faced the prospect of torture and execution. Rather than endure this, he inflicted a mortal head injury on himself, probably by throwing himself from a window.[3] He was subsequently euthanized by Antigonus's surgeon (*Ant.* 14.367–69; *J.W.* 1.271–72).

4.4.4 THE FLIGHT OF HEROD

Herod initially fled Judea towards the Nabateans, but the Nabatean king's reticence to get involved in Judea's change of regime induced Herod to head towards Egypt instead. En route, he learned of the elevation of Antigonus II to the throne, his brother's death, and Antigonus's attempts to capture his family atop Masada. But with rain replenishing the stronghold's water supply, the fortress's topography guaranteed his family's safety for the short-term (*Ant.* 14.370–74; *J.W.* 1.273–78).

Herod arrived in Alexandria, where Cleopatra VII, pregnant with Mark Antony's twins, received him enthusiastically as a Roman ally. Antony himself had recently departed the city to confront the Parthians in the Levant. However, no sooner had he arrived there than he was forced to return to Italy to deal with the fallout from a war between his wife, Fulvia, and Octavian

---

2. Luke's portrait of Jesus healing the servant's ear (Luke 22:51) should not be seen as a show of support for Caiaphas and the temple institution or a demonstration of the miraculous but as a claim that Jesus had the authority and ability to fix what the temple authorities could not.

3. Josephus states that Phasael dashed his head on a stone. He was in custody at the time, so it is possible that he bashed his head against his cell wall, but it is more likely that he jumped headlong from a window.

(the Perusine War). Octavian had won this conflict and was riding high on popular indignation at Antony's dalliance with Cleopatra. The situation threatened to undermine Antony's position in the Second Triumvirate and hand full power to Octavian. He thus clambered to rescue his political career and keep a foothold in Italy itself. While Antony was sailing back to Italy, his wife, Fulvia, died, which potentially gave him the freedom to marry Cleopatra. However, his relationship with Cleopatra was politically poisonous in Rome, so he agreed to a pragmatic solution: Antony was betrothed to Octavian's half-sister, Octavia, which allayed Roman resentment against him and upheld the Triumvirate (Plutarch, *Ant.* 30.1–31.3). The match rescued Antony's career but also put him in a bind, since it rendered his relationship with Cleopatra even more politically toxic.

Herod realized that an association with Cleopatra was potentially awkward, even though she was in the network of Roman allies. A wiser course of action was to seek the direct support of the Triumvirate. Herod also had bargaining power, for in seeking the Triumvirate's backing, he would be furthering Rome's efforts to win back Syria and Judea from the Parthians. According to one of Josephus's pro-Herodian sources, Herod had no intention of putting his own claim to kingship ahead of young Aristobulus III's (*Ant.* 14.386–87), but this is altruistic propaganda. Herod sailed to Italy to solicit the support of the Triumvirate and the Senate for his own cause.

He arrived in Rome in late 40 BC, where he was received by his patron, Mark Antony. If Antony had not made peace with Octavian just weeks before, one suspects that Herod's petition might have fallen through the cracks as Italy fractured into civil strife. Instead, the political planets aligned, and Herod found enthusiastic support among all parties, who recognized his loyalty and the good standing of his late father, Antipater. Antony brought him into the midst of the Senate and argued that it was in Roman interests to appoint Herod as king of the Jews and support his efforts to oust Antigonus from Judea. The resolution was duly passed, and Herod exited the Senate, flanked by Octavian and Antony, as *Rex Iudaeorum*—king of the Jews (*Ant.* 14.376–87; *J.W.* 1.279–85; cf. John 19:19–22). Herod's week in Rome had turned him into royalty and fulfilled the prediction of Menahem the Essene.

4.4.5 THE RETURN OF HEROD

Herod was thirty-three years old when the Romans named him king of the Jews. But Judea still belonged to Mattathias Antigonus II, whose elevation by the Parthians had won popular acclaim for undoing over two decades of Roman interference. There was also the bonus of the resurrection of the Hasmonean dynasty. As hated as the dynasty had become during the tyranny of Alexander Jannaeus, it was still a native Jewish dynasty intimately tied to Judaism's cherished temple institution. Herod had no such pedigree. Thus, not only did Herod's appointment place him in the vortex between the Romans and the Parthians, he also had his work cut out for him in winning over the Jewish people.

He also had to sell the merits of his appointment to the family of his Hasmonean fiancée, Mariamme, especially since he had denied his young brother-in-law-to-be, Aristobulus III, of a throne. At the same time, Mariamme stood to become a queen—a prospect she had never faced before. Their upcoming nuptials now became increasingly important as a means of grafting Herod into the broader Hasmonean family and giving his leadership a veneer of legitimacy. This made his need to rescue the family from their confinement at Masada more urgent.

Meanwhile, Antigonus worked hard to cement his place as king and high priest. He minted coins that styled him "Mattathias the high priest" in Hebrew, and "Antigonus the king" in Greek. We see in this the revival of the twin titles reminiscent of his Hasmonean predecessors and confirmation that he viewed himself as a Hellenistic king who held the Jewish high priesthood. But as diligent as Antigonus was in consolidating his leadership, his Achilles' heel was the Parthians. They had put him on the throne, so he was technically subservient to them. Without their military backing, he was vulnerable to Herod and the Romans. But the ultimate goal of the Jews was, of course, complete independence. Nationalism, fueled by religious devotion, meant that the Parthians would one day have to go. The question was whether Antigonus, who still needed their support, could get to a point of viably freeing himself of them. The Parthians themselves would not simply step aside, so he either had to challenge them eventually or try to play the Romans off them to his own advantage.

In the summer of 38 BC, things began to swing against Antigonus. Mark Antony commissioned Publius Ventidius Bassus with the counterattack against the Parthians in the east. Ventidius was most successful, earning the scalps of both Labienus and Pacorus, for which he was awarded a triumph in Rome. His victories put a massive dent in Parthian hegemony over the eastern Mediterranean and isolated Antigonus in Judea. But Antigonus's bribery of a middle-ranking Roman officer named Silo prevented the Romans from making further gains in Judea (*Ant.* 14.392; *J.W.* 1.291–92). Thus, when Herod landed at Ptolemais-Acco to begin the process of claiming his kingdom, he had practically no further purchase than when he had fled.

Nevertheless, he adapted resourcefully by gathering support from the region's gentiles, his native Idumea (*J.W.* 1.290), and some of the Jewish military stationed in Galilee, where he had been governor. This allowed him to gain control over Galilee, despite stiff resistance from local warlords and brigands. He then secured the coastal plain, including the crucial port of Joppa, before acquiring Idumea with relative ease. In this task he was aided by his younger brothers, Joseph and Pheroras. He then successfully extricated his family from Masada (*Ant.* 14.394–400; *J.W.* 1.290–93). With custody of them and the territories he had gained, Herod had taken the challenge to Antigonus by confining him to the Judean Highlands.

Herod then marched on Jerusalem. Rather than put the city under siege, he tried to convince the population of his own leniency and that they should oust Antigonus. Antigonus countered by pointing out that even if he himself were ejected, Herod was not a Hasmonean and so could not rightly possess the Jewish throne (*Ant.* 14.400–404; *J.W.* 1.294–6). Herod realized that the only way for him to win Jerusalem was by conquest, and for this he would need the help of the Romans.

But Herod was unable to lay siege to Jerusalem. Unrest broke out again in Galilee, inducing him to leave his family in Samaria and return to deal with the hotbeds of hostility. He took control of the Galilean capital, Sepphoris, during a snowstorm, and had trouble dealing with warlords who had gone to ground in inhospitable areas—the same areas where, decades later, disadvantaged people would flock to Jesus and seek to make him their king, despite the rule of the Herodian family (cf. Matt 14:13–22; Mark 6:30–45; Luke 9:10–17; John 6:1–15).[4] Antony eventually sent Herod more support, but the Roman officer in charge proved so rash that he even inflicted damage upon Herod's supporters. Herod suspended his campaign and went to complain directly to Antony, who was fighting the Parthians and their allies on the Euphrates (*Ant.* 14.406–39; *J.W.* 1.297–321).

Herod's departure gave Antigonus much needed breathing space. His general, Pappus, fell upon some of Herod's army and killed its commander—none other than Herod's brother, Joseph. Pappus cut Joseph's head from his corpse and sent it to Herod's other brother, Pheroras. This action, which emulated Judas Maccabeus's treatment of Nicanor's corpse (160 BC; see 3.5.9 above), portrayed Antigonus as the rightful heir of the Hasmonean legacy and Herod as a foreign intruder akin to the Seleucids. The gesture incited more violence

---

4. Richardson (*Herod*, 156 nn.14, 250–52) points out the probability that most Galilean opposition to Herod came from the socially and economically disadvantaged, especially dispossessed landholders who had been exploited by the upper class.

in the north. Herod's supporters amongst the nobility were systematically rounded up and drowned in Lake Galilee (*Ant.* 14.448–50; *J.W.* 1.323–26).

Herod ended up aiding Antony against the Parthians in Syria. Together, in 38 BC, they defeated the Parthians and their clients, snapping the spine of Parthian hegemony in the Levant barely two years after it began (*Ant.* 14.439–47; *J.W.* 1.327). As Herod returned south, Antigonus was totally isolated, with only his meager military forces and spontaneous militias to resist Herod and the Romans.

4.4.6 HEROD'S SIEGE OF JERUSALEM (37 BC)

Herod returned to the Jewish state with two of Mark Antony's legions and some Syrian militias in early 37 BC. Antigonus's soldiers were unable to prevent him taking control of Galilee again. He then stormed down the Jordan Valley to Jericho, and from here repelled an ambush by some of Antigonus's soldiers coming down from the mountains. Herod had two near misses during this stage of his campaign. The first occurred when, the evening before the ambush, the roof under which he had just dined with local supporters collapsed. The second came in the form of an arrow that wounded his side during the skirmish. According to Josephus, Herod's survival of these close calls convinced many that he was favored by God (*Ant.* 14.451–56; *J.W.* 1.328–32).

Herod then marched into the highlands. With the aid of a supporting Roman force, he trapped Antigonus's commander, Pappus, in a pincer movement in Samaria. Pappus died in the battle, and Herod decapitated him, sending his head to his brother Pheroras as a trophy of revenge for the treatment of their brother, Joseph (see 4.4.5 above). After the battle, Herod had another close call. He was practically alone and had removed his armor to bathe when he inadvertently stumbled upon several enemy soldiers. They were, however, too panicked by their defeat to do him harm (*Ant.* 14.457–64; *J.W.* 1.333–42).

By summer of 37 BC, Herod cornered Antigonus in Jerusalem. He left his forces to besiege the city while he himself departed for Samaria, where he finally wedded Princess Mariamme, the granddaughter of John Hyrcanus II and Aristobulus II. He thereby successfully grafted himself into the Hasmonean family, ensuring that any children that came from the marriage legitimately bore the legacy of both strands of the Hasmonean dynasty, in addition to his own (*Ant.* 14.465–67; *J.W.* 1.343–44). Even Antigonus could not rival such a claim.

When Herod returned to Jerusalem, he concentrated his efforts on the northern wall of the temple. He was backed by a force of 30,000 soldiers, including Roman legionaries led by Antony's new governor of Syria, Gaius Sosius (*Ant.* 14.468–69; *J.W.* 1.345–46). With the upcoming year (37/6 BC) a Sabbatical rest for the land, Antigonus did not have the supplies to withstand a long siege. People within Jerusalem broke into several factions. Some prophetic figures predicted the defeat of Herod (*Ant.* 14.470; *J.W.* 1.347–48), while others urged Antigonus to surrender. Ironically, two of Herod's most vocal advocates inside the city were his erstwhile critics: Abtalion and Shemaiah, the president and vice president of the Sanhedrin (see 4.3.10 above). With Herod's victory becoming increasingly apparent, their support for him was probably more pragmatic than principled.

In July 37 BC Herod's forces scaled the north wall of the temple and took over the precinct.[5] The rest of the city followed a couple of weeks later. The Roman troops who stormed into Jerusalem began to kill and plunder indiscriminately and even tried to enter the inner courts of the temple, as Pompey had done twenty-six years before. However, Herod intervened, convincing Sosius to restrain his soldiers by promising to handsomely compensate every soldier, including Sosius. His promise worked.[6]

Antigonus was clapped in chains and carted off to Antony for judgment (*Ant.* 14.471–87; *J.W.* 1.349–57). Herod feared that if Antony took Antigonus for trial in Rome, he might escape execution and continue to threaten his own rule of Judea. Herod therefore bribed Antony, and Antigonus was summarily executed either by beheading (*Ant.* 14.488–90; *J.W.* 1.357) or crucifixion (Dio Cassius, *Hist. rom.* 49.22).[7] The execution of the Jewish high priest did little to endear Rome or Herod to the population. Furthermore, it signaled the formal end of the Hasmonean dynasty and the re-establishment of Roman hegemony over Judea. In demonstration of this, Herod enlarged the Baris fortress to accommodate a larger garrison and renamed it "Antonia" in honor of his patron, Mark Antony (*Ant.* 15.403–409; 18:91–92; *J.W.* 1.401; 5.238–46).[8]

---

5. Josephus states in *J.W.* 1.351 that the siege lasted five months, while in *Ant.* 14.476 he implies it lasted two months (cf. Richardson, *Herod*, 159).

6. On 3 September 34 BC Sosius celebrated a triumphal procession in Rome for his conquest of Jerusalem. See Richardson, *Herod*, 160.

7. The head of Antigonus might have been brought back to Jerusalem secretly for burial and his remains rediscovered in modern times. See Yoel Elitzur, "The Abba Cave: Unpublished Findings and a New Proposal Regarding Abba's Identity," *IEJ* 63.1 (2013): 83–102.

8. Ehud Netzer and Rachel Laureys-Chachy, *The Architecture of Herod, The Great Builder* (Grand Rapids: Baker Academic, 2008), 120–26.

4.5 THE AUGUSTAN-HERODIAN ERA

4.5.1 HEROD AND THE HIGH PRIESTHOOD

Herod became undisputed ruler of Judea (on behalf of the Romans) in 37 BC at the age of thirty-seven. He backdated the start of his reign to late 40 BC when the Roman Senate had bestowed the title upon him. Thus, the first coins he minted after capturing Jerusalem were marked with "Year 3" in their inscription.[1] This was part of a concerted program to wipe the reign of Mattathias Antigonus II from the record. But Herod's agenda was much bigger than that. Although he was nominally Jewish, he was ethnically Idumean through his father and Nabatean through his mother. Therefore, while he had gained the royal diadem from Antigonus, he was ineligible to assume the high priesthood also.

To deal with this, Herod created an entirely new aristocratic order beholden to him, not the Hasmoneans. Soon after capturing Jerusalem, he purged the Jewish aristocracy by executing forty-five prominent men, including members of the Sanhedrin who were connected to Antigonus. It was an iron-fisted approach, which saw the murder of Pharisees and Sadducees. In this way, Herod fulfilled the predictions of Abtalion and Shemaiah (see 4.3.10 above), though he spared them both for having tried to induce the city to surrender to him (*Ant.* 15.1–6; *J.W.* 1.358). The progressive courtiers, priests, and wealthy citizens who supported him soon came to form a disparate group that the New Testament calls "Herodians" (cf. Matt 22:16; Mark 36; 12:13).[2] They were awarded prominent estates with fortified manors and agricultural infrastructure, as was common throughout the Hellenistic world.[3] Indeed, it was this

---

1. Alla Kushnir-Stein, "Coins of the Herodian Dynasty," in *The World of the Herods: Volume 1 of the International Conference The World of the Herods and the Nabataeans Held at the British Museum, 17–19 April 2001*, ed. Nikos Kokkinos, Oriens et Occidens 14 (Stuttgart: Franz Steiner Verlag, 2007), 55–56; Donald T. Ariel, "The Coins of Herod the Great in the Context of the Augustan Empire," in *Herod and Augustus: Papers Presented at the IJS Conference, 21st–23rd June 2005*, ed. David M. Jacobson and Nikos Kokkinos, IJS Studies in Judaica 6 (Leiden: Brill, 2009), 113–26; David M. Jacobson, "Herod the Great, Augustus Caesar and Herod's 'Year 3' Coins," *Strata* 33 (2015): 89–118.

2. Richardson, *Herod*, 259–60. The Herodians were not an organized political party or order but simply the elite in society who viewed Herod and his dynasty as the most appropriate and viable rulers of Judea in the wider Roman context.

3. For example, one of these, a courtier named Ptolemy, received an estate of about a thousand acres in Samaria. See Hirschfeld Yizhar, "Fortified Manor Houses of the Ruling Class in the Herodian Kingdom of Judaea," in Kokkinos, *The World of the Herods*, 198–226.

landed aristocracy that featured in some of Jesus's parables (cf. Matt 13:24–30; Luke 12:16–21, 42–48; 14:28–30; 15:10–16:12).

The most significant dilemma facing Herod in this new order was his sixteen-year-old brother-in-law, Jonathan Aristobulus III. As grandson of both John Hyrcanus II and Aristobulus II, the lad was the rightful heir to the high priesthood and the entire Hasmonean patrimony. If Herod installed him as high priest, he would win favor with pro-Hasmoneans, but this was risky, for Aristobulus might be able to re-establish the Hasmonean dynasty and potentially regain the royal diadem as well. Herod could not simply have Aristobulus executed either, for that would destabilize the new order he was trying to create (cf. *Ant.* 15.30). The only way forward for Herod was to find some means of sidelining Aristobulus until a son from his union with Mariamme (Aristobulus's sister) could inherit both civic and religious leadership after Herod.

Two factors gave Herod some purchase on the situation. The first was Aristobulus III's youth. Although the minimum age for the high priesthood (once thirty years of age) had become moot since the days of John Hyrcanus I, Aristobulus was only sixteen in 37 BC—still excessively young for the senior-most clerical role in all Judaism (cf. *Ant.* 15.34). The second factor was Herod's status as king of Judea. Rather than follow the political legacy of the Hasmonean priest-kings, he chose instead to model himself on the more ancient legacy of the Davidic dynasty, which not only separated the royal and cultic offices but subordinated the high priest as an employee of the king. Underlining this point was the precedent of King Solomon, who had removed Abiathar from the high priesthood and appointed Zadok in his place (1 Kgs 2:35). Herod could not leverage the notion of a divine covenant to bolster his own legitimacy, but Solomon's precedent gave him enough political scope to remodel the high priesthood by putting an entirely neutral figure into the position.

The man he chose was Hananel (or "Ananelus"), a Jew born and raised in the Jewish diaspora of Babylonia (still under Parthian rule).[4] Hananel was apparently of high priestly heritage (*Ant.* 15.22, 39–40), though whether this means he was of Zadokite descent is simply unknown.

Herod may have enlisted the help of Hyrcanus in the selection of Hananel. The politically allergic former high priest was enjoying his retirement in

---

4. Hananel is almost certainly the same person as "Hanamel the Egyptian" mentioned in m. Parah 3:5. The epithet "Egyptian" is perhaps misplaced from its proper attachment to the person of Phiabi. See Peter Richardson, *Building Jewish in the Roman East*, Supplements to the Journal for the Study of Judaism 92 (Leiden: Brill, 2004), 290–91; VanderKam, *From Joshua to Caiaphas*, 397–98.

Babylonia, but he still longed for his homeland. Upon hearing of Antigonus's demise, he petitioned Herod to be allowed to return to Jerusalem, and Herod made it happen (*Ant.* 15.14–22). Herod was presumably banking on Hyrcanus's superlative passivity and poor reputation in Judea to prevent him becoming a potential rallying point for anti-Herodian sentiment. He may also have figured it better to keep the former high priest close to him than beyond his control.

The appointment of Hananel irked Mariamme, who pressured Herod to annul the appointment and put her brother, Aristobulus, into the position instead. It is possible that Mariamme threatened to denounce Herod or even walk away from the marriage. Her status as a Hasmonean princess certainly gave her prestige enough to become a rival for royal authority in her own right. After all, her great grandmother, Salome Alexandra, had ruled as queen four decades earlier. Herod could only prevent this by keeping her firmly attached to himself. To back up her efforts, her mother, Alexandra II, appealed to Cleopatra VII to beseech Mark Antony to intervene. Cleopatra had spent the winter of 37/6 BC with Antony in Syria (another son, Ptolemy XVI Philadelphus Antonius, was born to them the following year). Antony added several new Levantine territories to her realm, so that it began to take on the proportions of the old Ptolemaic kingdom.[5] Some of this came at Herod's expense. Gaza and Ashkelon had already been incorporated into her realm, and Herod was forced to cede Samaria and Jericho also. He was now leasing Ashkelon and Jericho back from her. He could ill-afford to have Mariamme and her family become independent clients of Antony and Cleopatra and then see more territory stripped from him. Herod, therefore, chose to play the diplomatic game. He removed Hananel in 35 BC and replaced him with young Aristobulus III.

The move was a serious setback for Herod's authority and ambitions, as it reinjected a viable Hasmonean descendant into a position of Jewish leadership. It was also technically illegal, for Herod had removed a living high priest from his position. He was in a no-win situation. Things became even worse for him when Aristobulus, now eighteen years old, officiated at his first festival during Sukkot in October 35 BC. He received such rousing acclaim from the pilgrims that Herod's continued authority was put on a knife's edge. Herod was not going to sit back and watch Aristobulus eclipse him with such ease. Accordingly, after the festival he brought Aristobulus and the rest of his

---

5. Richard D. Sullivan, *Near Eastern Royalty and Rome, 100–30 BC* (Toronto: University of Toronto Press, 1990), 207–208; Roller, *Cleopatra*, 92–95.

family to the royal estates in Jericho and contrived to have the lad drowned while swimming in one of the pools. To cover his part in the murder, Herod made it look like playful teenage revelry gone horribly wrong. He publicly wept for Aristobulus and held a lavish public funeral for him (*Ant.* 15.50–61; *J.W.* 1.437). But the fact was that the high priest Aristobulus III was dead, and Herod could scarcely hide his involvement. It was the second sacerdotal scalp that Herod was involved in taking.

Utterly outraged at her son's death, Alexandra II appealed once more to Cleopatra, who prevailed upon Antony to call Herod to account. Antony was back in Syria after an unsuccessful invasion of the Parthian Empire in 36/5 BC (Plutarch, *Ant.* 37.1–51.2). Herod was summoned to see both him and Cleopatra in early 34 BC. The prospect put Herod in fear for his life, especially since Cleopatra was keen to restore the traditional glory of the Ptolemaic kingdom by taking control of Judea. Herod put Mariamme in the custody of an uncle, Joseph, with the instructions that if he were executed, she was to be executed too. According to Josephus, this was because Herod was so enamored with her that he could not bear the thought of another man marrying her after his own death (*Ant.* 15.62–67). Such levels of possessiveness and paranoia were not beyond Herod, but it is difficult not to read a sense of vengeance in the situation either.

Herod came to Antony with bribes, which helped him escape repercussions for Aristobulus's death and preserved Judea from Cleopatra's clutches. Antony awarded Cleopatra control of other territories: Ptolemais-Acco, Byblos, Chalcis, Iturea, the Orontes Valley in Syria, Apamea, and perhaps even Cilicia.[6] These acquisitions appeased her, as they extended Ptolemaic sovereignty over most of Coele Syria outside Judea and gave her a foothold in the lands of the old Seleucid kingdom, of whose dynasty she was also a descendant. Herod thus returned to Judea triumphant. He was even accompanied by Cleopatra—a move that isolated his mother-in-law, Alexandra II (*Ant.* 15.62–103).

Aristobulus III was the very last Hasmonean high priest. After his death, Herod restored Hananel to the office, subordinating the high priesthood to his kingship once again. In under three years, Herod had succeeded in creating a totally new order in the Jewish aristocracy. He had set out to graft himself into the Hasmonean line and ended up grafting it into his.[7] Herod probably still hoped that a son born to him through Mariamme might reunite the royal and priestly offices. As it turned out, it was not to be (see 4.5.7 below). The high priesthood ceased to be a permanent hereditary office. Though a handful

---

6. Roller, *Cleopatra*, 92–93.
7. Adam Kolman Marshak, *The Many Faces of Herod the Great* (Grand Rapids: Eerdmans, 2015), 112–13.

of families monopolized the office (one of which was the family of Annas, mentioned in the Gospels), it was hereafter always one of external appointment, and its tenure could be terminated at the will of the ruling authority. This situation prevailed right up until the destruction of the temple in AD 70.

4.5.2 THE END OF THE SECOND TRIUMVIRATE

The personal rivalry between Mark Antony and Octavian was never going to let the Second Triumvirate last. It is ironic, then, that the fracture came through the oft-forgotten third partner, Marcus Aemilius Lepidus. He and Octavian had been working at curtailing the so-called piracy of Pompey's son, Sextus Pompey, who was operating out of Sicily. In 36 BC they finally defeated him, but a dispute arose between them over who deserved jurisdiction over Sicily. Lepidus's troops defected to Octavian, robbing him of any clout. He was subsequently convicted of insubordination and barred from Rome. Lepidus's fall from grace handed Octavian control of the entire western half of Rome's empire. Antony was still ascendant in the east and had many supporters still in Rome itself. Now that the Republic's old guard had perished, there was nothing to prevent their personal rivalry from developing into a full-scale conflict. Another Mediterranean-wide civil war was in the offing.

Octavian made the first move towards open hostilities in a surreptitious way. In 35 BC he bestowed quasi-religious honors on his wife, Livia, and his sister, Octavia, who was married to Antony (Dio Cassius, *Hist. rom.* 49.38). This made it blasphemy to speak or act against the two women—a clever move that seemed to promise continued cooperation between Antony and himself. What it actually did was amplify Antony's infidelities towards Octavia. Despite having two daughters with Octavia, Antony was clearly more interested in Cleopatra VII, who had borne him three children. Octavian chided him for the relationship, but Antony was flagrant in his disregard of Octavian's opinion, even calling Cleopatra his "wife" and accusing Octavian of maintaining paramours himself (Suetonius, *Aug.* 69.1–2).

Antony was appointed consul for 34 BC, but on the first day of his term (1 January), he resigned the office to concentrate on another invasion of Armenia and Parthia (Dio Cassius, *Hist. rom.* 39.1). This snub towards the Roman Senate showed that Antony was growing increasingly attached to ruling the east independent of Rome's formal constraints.[8] This became ever

---

8. Octavian did exactly the same thing one year later (1 January 33 BC) to concentrate on warring with the Dalmatians in Illyria (Appian, *Illyrian Wars* 28). Since he had not set the precedent, it was not viewed as a snub.

clearer when he betrothed his eldest son by Cleopatra, six-year-old Alexander Helios, to the daughter of Artavasdes of Media Atropatene as part of a mutual defense pact against Parthia. Antony was acting as a dynast whilst preparing for conflict, but not just with Parthia.

He had continued this trend when he awarded Cleopatra control of territories throughout the Levant during his negotiations with Herod (see 4.5.1 above). But he went a step further later that year (34 BC) when, after a successful campaign in Armenia, he celebrated a triumphal procession, not in Rome but in Alexandria. At the end of the festivities, he and Cleopatra distributed prospective rule of Cleopatra's Ptolemaic realm and Rome's eastern provinces (including Armenia and still-unconquered Parthian territory) among their three children. Cleopatra was named "Queen of Kings," and Caesarion, her son by Julius Caesar, was titled "King of Kings" alongside her. There were only two ways for Rome to interpret this: either Antony was giving away Roman territories to foreign monarchs, or he was making foreign monarchs part of the Roman aristocracy. Antony could have argued that these "donations of Alexandria" were no different to the way Rome ruled through client kings, such as Herod. But the appointment of Caesarion, the biological son of Julius Caesar, as co-ruler with Cleopatra was a broadside fired at Octavian, the adoptive son and heir of Julius Caesar. Antony could not have been surprised when the Roman Senate refused to ratify the arrangement (Plutarch, *Ant.* 54.1–55.2; Dio Cassius, *Hist. rom.* 49.40–41).

Thereafter, any pretense of cooperation between Antony and Octavian was dropped, even though the triumvirate was technically still in force. In 33 BC Antony formally divorced Octavia, while Octavian launched a propaganda campaign to vilify Antony. In anticipation of open conflict after the expiry of the triumvirate's powers on 31 December 33 BC, Antony and Cleopatra moved their armies and navies to the eastern Aegean (Plutarch, *Ant.* 56.1–10).

4.5.3 THE VICTORY OF OCTAVIAN (31 BC)

In 32 BC Octavian had Antony's military powers cancelled and had the Roman state declare war upon Cleopatra VII. Octavian could not thereby be charged with opening hostilities against Antony. If Antony chose to fight him anyway, then he did so in defiance of Rome and as an ally of a declared enemy of Rome.

Though some urged Antony to break with Cleopatra, it was her Ptolemaic money and forces that bulked up his own military efforts. It was with her, then, that he moved some 90,000 soldiers and 500 ships to the Greek mainland.

This, along with Octavian's propaganda campaign against Antony's relationship with Cleopatra, stoked Roman xenophobia and nationalist sentiment. The prospect of Cleopatra's forces landing in Italy, storming Rome, and Antony establishing a kind of dual empire with Alexandria was now very real.

History might have told a different story if Antony had invaded Italy with Cleopatra's aid at the end of 32 BC. Octavian was distracted dealing with discontent in Italy over taxes and would have struggled to contain an invasion. But Antony and Cleopatra's forces spent the winter in the Ambracian Gulf on the western coast of Greece. The delay handed Octavian the initiative, as it gave him time to deal with the discontent and then ferry his legions to Greece in the spring of 31 BC. He cut off Antony and Cleopatra's supply lines, hemmed in their army, and blockaded their fleet throughout the summer. On 2 September 31 BC, Antony and Cleopatra were forced into a naval confrontation at the head of the gulf, beside the town of Actium. Antony engaged Octavian's fleet, but before there was much fighting, Cleopatra escaped in her flagship back to Alexandria. This threw the battle into Octavian's favor. Antony also made good his escape, and the rest of his forces promptly surrendered to Octavian. Octavian thus became undisputed master of the Roman world (Dio Cassius, *Hist. rom.* 50.15–51.1).

Herod had sent funds and supplies to Antony (*Ant.* 15.189; *J.W.* 1.388) and would have been at Actium fighting alongside him had he not been engaged in a messy war with the Nabateans. But the outcome of Actium put Herod's political future into jeopardy since he was Antony's loyal client. Although Antony continued to live lavishly with Cleopatra in Alexandria after his defeat at Actium, Herod understood that Octavian had completely loosened Antony's grip over the eastern Mediterranean. With this seismic political shift, Herod scampered to plead for his own political future with Octavian.

One of Herod's first acts after learning of Antony's defeat was to eliminate his last potential rival so as to give Octavian as few alternatives for the Jewish throne as possible. That rival was John Hyrcanus II. Although the aged Hasmonean, now in his seventies,[9] could never again serve as high priest because of his disfigurement, he could still in theory serve as civic ruler because of his pedigree. After all, he had once been king of the Jews before resigning the position to his brother in 67 BC. A wily and paranoid Herod

---

9. *Antiquities* 15.178 puts John Hyrcanus II's age at over eighty. This is, however, impossible, since the earliest date of his birth is 103 BC, making him no more than seventy-three. Atkinson (*Queen Salome*, 96–102) argues that John Hyrcanus II was born to Alexander Jannaeus and Salome Alexandra before 103 BC, but he can only do so on the basis of the implausible suggestion that Salome Alexandra was a different person to "Salina Alexandra," who was first married to Aristobulus.

had Hyrcanus implicated in a treasonous conspiracy. In bitter irony, Herod turned him over to the Sanhedrin in deference to its authority to enact capital punishment. The Sanhedrin, now led by Shemaiah, tried Hyrcanus and put him to death (*Ant.* 15.164–82; *J.W.* 1.433–34). The only male Hasmonean descendants left alive were Herod's own three sons by Mariamme (see 4.5.7 below). Herod also replaced the high priest Hananel at about this time. Since the exact timing of this change is not known, we cannot be certain whether the change was part of Herod's attempt to eliminate rivals. However, if Herod had consulted Hyrcanus when he made Hananel's initial appointment, it stands to reason that Herod did not want Hananel influencing the Sanhedrin at Hyrcanus's trial. The man Herod chose as the new high priest was Jesus ben-Phiabi. Nothing substantive about him is known beyond the fact that his father's name was linguistically Egyptian, which suggests a connection to the Jewish community of Egypt.

With Hyrcanus out of the way, Herod travelled to Rhodes to meet with Octavian. Herod's petition to him rested on four bases. The first, perhaps counterintuitively, was that his loyalty to Antony had been unwavering. He argued that this demonstrated the kind of friend he was, and not just whom he had been friends with. Herod evidently followed the example of his father, Antipater, who had argued along the same lines in switching his allegiance from Pompey to Caesar in 47 BC (see 4.3.9 above). Second, Herod had been made king of the Jews by the whole Roman Senate, which included Octavian. His loyalty, therefore, was to Rome, and since Octavian was clearly now master of Rome, his loyalty necessarily transferred to him. Third, he claimed to have advised Antony after his defeat at Actium to kill Cleopatra. And fourth, Herod had taken the initiative to seek out Octavian. He did not play evasively with him but transparently presented himself in submission. Octavian was pleased with Herod's petition, especially since it gave him a secure frontier in Judea for his continued war against Antony and Cleopatra in Egypt. Octavian therefore confirmed Herod as king of the Jews, and a genuine friendship between them seems to have developed. The following year, Herod entertained Octavian at Ptolemais-Acco and supplied his forces on their march across the Sinai to Egypt (*Ant.* 15.183–201; *J.W.* 1.386–95).

Like his father before him, Herod's charisma and savvy made him a survivor. Antony and Cleopatra were, however, not to survive. Octavian invaded Egypt, and most of Antony's forces defected. Octavian took possession of Alexandria on 1 August 30 BC, and Antony committed suicide. Octavian permitted Cleopatra to bury him, but she also committed suicide on 10 August 30 BC, wishing to avoid becoming a trophy in Octavian's triumphal procession in Rome. Her three children by Antony did not, however, avoid being thus displayed. Ptolemy XV Caesarion, her son by Julius Caesar, attempted to escape Octavian's clutches, but he was hunted down and executed (Plutarch, *Ant.* 74.4–86.9; Dio Cassius, *Hist. rom.* 51.10–15).

4.5.4 EMPEROR CAESAR AUGUSTUS: THE ESTABLISHMENT OF THE ROMAN PRINCIPATE

With the deaths of Mark Antony and Cleopatra VII, the Ptolemaic kingdom (the Thirty-Second and final Dynasty) also died. Octavian incorporated Egypt into the Roman Empire as a province belonging to him personally. The country's perennial wealth began to flow directly to his account, making him one of the richest individuals of all time. He himself had become the Roman state and now controlled the political life of the whole Mediterranean.

Over the following years, Octavian reordered the administration of the Roman world, and by 28 BC the turmoil of the preceding decades had eased. Although dissent against Roman rule in the provinces never completely died down, least of all in Judea, the general political stability imposed by Octavian sowed the seeds for what would eventually be dubbed the *Pax Romana* ("Roman Peace"). It was a situation that would foster urban development, economic growth, travel, cultural and ideological exchange, and religious plurality. These were the conditions that fostered the spread of the Christian gospel in the first century.

By the end of 28 BC, Octavian was only thirty-five years old, but he had already been at the center of Roman political life for sixteen years and made himself the linchpin of its stability. He was ready at that point to reinstate the power of the Roman Senate. The danger, however, was that if he removed himself as the linchpin of Rome's political life, the state would degenerate into the same chaos it had experienced over the previous five decades. The Senate's power was also much reduced from the heyday of the Republic, with the Plebeian Assembly now overshadowing it. Octavian had made himself indispensable to the function of the Roman state and its provinces. Therefore, on 13 January 27 BC, the Senate and the Plebeian Assembly gave Octavian command of the Roman provinces. Three days later, the Senate bestowed on him the title *Augustus* ("Revered"), recognizing him as the restorer of Rome's constitution and the supreme patron of all senators. These two privileges mark the beginning of his life as *Imperator Caesar Divi Filius Augustus*: "Emperor Caesar, Revered Son of the God [Julius Caesar]," or "Caesar Augustus" for short.

Octavian had been given the title *Imperator* ("emperor") years before by virtue of the acclaim of his own legions. This had been a common practice towards victorious generals throughout Roman history, so the title "emperor" did not at this stage have its later connotations of exclusive supremacy. It was the title *Princeps civium Romanorum* ("First of Roman Citizens") that marked out such exclusivity. This term had been used of key figures at significant moments during the days of the Roman Republic, most notably of Pompey. But when the Plebeian Assembly granted Octavian additional powers as supreme patron of the people in 23 BC, the title was used exclusively of him. This convergence of so many political and military powers on one person marked the formal end of the Roman Republic and the dawn of the Imperial Age of the Roman Principate.[10] Caesar Augustus was lord of the entire Roman world.

4.5.5 HEROD THE KING AND BUILDER

Immediately after the demise of Mark Antony and Cleopatra VII (30 BC), Herod travelled to Alexandria to meet with Octavian. For his troubles, Octavian restored several territories to him, which Mark Antony had gifted to Cleopatra. These included Jericho, Greek cities around Lake Galilee, the *polis* of Samaria, and the coastal plain (excluding Ashkelon). This gave him several Mediterranean ports and control of key economic centers. He would later add territories immediately south of Damascus (Iturea, Gaulanitis, Batanea, Trachonitis, and Auranitis), making his sovereignty over the trade routes of Palestine complete. At the zenith of his reign, Herod's kingdom exceeded the territorial bounds of the Hasmonean kingdom at its greatest extent under Alexander Jannaeus.

These acquisitions gave Herod vast revenue streams that, along with the tax farming system he employed, made him one of the wealthiest men in the Roman world and enabled him to finance his vast resumé of works and benefactions.[11] His personal annual income was a staggering 1,000 to 2,000 talents of silver.[12] With this, he developed an enormous royal court around his person (*Ant.* 17.198–99; *J.W.* 1.671–73), in addition to the wider class

---

10. Sinnigen and Boak, *A History of Rome*, 254–58.
11. In the early part of his reign (before the Battle of Actium in 31 BC), much of Herod's income went towards maintaining his relationship with Mark Antony and Cleopatra VII. But thereafter, his revenues went into his own coffers.
12. In modern terms, this is the equivalent of between US$1.5 billion and $3 billion annually. For discussion of Herod's revenues, see Samuel Rocca, *Herod's Judaea*, Texts and Studies in Ancient Judaism 122 (Tübingen: Mohr Siebeck, 2008), 203–10.

of Herodian elite.[13] In this regard, Herod was very much in the mold of the Ptolemies (see 2.6.5 above).

More than any other single person in history, Herod left his visible imprint on the physical landscape of Palestine with his large-scale building projects.[14] Just as Augustus would later boast of having found Rome a city of brick and left it a city of marble (Suetonius, *Aug.* 29), Herod could have boasted similarly of his own realm. With the employment of architects from both the Greek and Roman traditions and the sheer scale of his projects, Herod visibly integrated his kingdom with the growing Roman Empire, giving local momentum to the notion that a new age—the international age of Augustus and the local age of Herod—had dawned.

Among his projects were several palaces, including new lavish winter quarters built over the Hasmonean estate outside Jericho, which had been damaged in an earthquake in 31 BC. He developed the stronghold of Masada, building initially a small palace, followed by an elaborate, three-tiered palace cascading over the northern face of the promontory. In 23 BC he completed a sumptuous palace on Jerusalem's Western Hill consisting of two buildings, named after Augustus and Agrippa (Augustus's closest friend). It contained room for over a hundred guests, perhaps providing the inspiration for Jesus's pronouncement, "In my father's house there are many rooms" (John 14:2). This possibility is made even more poignant by the fact that the palace was the site of Jesus's trial by Pontius Pilate, as it became the Jerusalem residence of the Roman prefect in the first century. An open plaza at the entrance to the palace should be equated with "The Pavement" (Aram. *gabbatha'*), where Pilate set up his judgment podium and delivered his verdict in the trial of Jesus (John 19:13; cf. *J.W.* 2.301). At the northern end was a defensive stronghold with three enormous towers, which Herod named after people important to him: the Phasael (42 meters tall [14 stories]), after his brother; the Hippicus (37 meters tall [12 stories]), after his bodyguard; and the Mariamme (25 meters tall [8 stories]), after his wife (*J.W.* 5.161–75).

Herod built fortresses throughout his kingdom to ensure law and order, especially along the trade routes. Some of these doubled as palatial residences, such as Machaerus, which he renovated on the Perean side of the Dead Sea,

---

13. For a detailed discussion of the shape of Herod's court, including the names of particular members, see Nikos Kokkinos, "The Royal Court of the Herods," in Kokkinos, *The World of the Herods*, 279–303.

14. For a detailed discussion of Herod's various building projects, see the excellent volume by Netzer and Laureys-Chachy, *The Architecture of Herod*.

and the circular stronghold of Herodium, southeast of Bethlehem. In addition, he developed the water infrastructure of his kingdom, especially in and around Jerusalem. Among his projects were the aqueduct system bringing water from the highlands south of Bethlehem to the temple in Jerusalem, as well as the Pool of Israel just north of the temple.[15]

Herod transformed several cities in monumental ways. For example, he developed the acropolis at Samaria, where the palace of the kings of Israel once stood, and raised a temple dedicated to his patron, Caesar Augustus, on it. He also renamed the whole city "Sebaste," this being the Greek form of Augustus's title ("Revered"), and settled 6,000 of his gentile veterans there, fueling the Jewish sense that "Samaria" was equated with "foreigner" (*Ant.* 15.296–98; *J.W.* 1.403). In Jerusalem, he constructed both a theater and an amphitheater that hosted games in honor of Augustus every five years (*Ant.* 15.268–74). When Batanea was integrated into his realm in 20 BC, Herod built a temple to Augustus at Panias beside the shrine of Pan (*Ant.* 15.363–64; *J.W.* 1.404–406). These developments reveal Herod's personal commitment to his imperial patron and how, even though he was nominally Jewish, he was perfectly comfortable with Greek and Roman values. This syncretistic attitude ingratiated him with the Roman elite, even as it offended conservative Jews. Herod was a Greco-Roman monarch in a Jewish kingdom.

In 20 BC Herod began to transform the fishing town of Strato's Tower on the Mediterranean coast into a grand new city. He renamed it Caesarea Maritima in honor of Augustus. Its crowning structure was a temple on a raised podium dedicated to Augustus and Rome. Herod also built a seaside palace, hippodrome, theater, and 16-kilometer stone aqueduct to bring fresh water to the city. But perhaps the most impressive aspect of Caesarea Maritima was its harbor. Herod had two breakwaters constructed 500 meters out into the Mediterranean, creating an enormous artificial harbor that rivalled Alexandria and Piraeus. This harbor, named "Sebastos" in honor of Augustus, allowed even the largest seagoing vessels to berth in Herod's kingdom, fostering mercantile activity. Along with the temple to Augustus, it signaled to all arrivals that they had reached a great Roman city.[16]

Herod's largesse also extended beyond the confines of his own kingdom.

---

15. Richardson, *Herod*, 190–91; Netzer and Laureys-Chachy, *The Architecture of Herod*, 136.

16. Ehud Netzer, "The Ideal City in the Eyes of Herod the Great," in Kokkinos, *The World of the Herods*, 71–91; Netzer and Laureys-Chachy, *The Architecture of Herod*, 94–118; Joseph Patrich, "Herodian Caesarea: The Urban Space," in Kokkinos, *The World of the Herods*, 93–129.

The Kingdom of Herod.

He financed gymnasia, theaters, agoras, stoas, temples, and walls in such cities as Ptolemais-Acco, Damascus, Tyre, Sidon, Byblos, Berytus, Laodicea, Antioch, Pergamum, Athens, and Sparta. In funding such projects, Herod was perhaps helping to secure goodwill towards the Jewish communities in these centers.[17] It also enhanced his own profile as a Roman-style patron with an

---

17. Richardson, *Herod*, 94.

extensive clientele. In 12 BC he also created a perpetual endowment for the Olympic Games, thereby allowing them to survive after a period of decline (*Ant.* 16.146–149; *J.W.* 1.422–28).[18] Two statues in Herod's honor were even erected on the Acropolis of Athens, describing him as "pious," "a friend of Caesar," and a man of "moral excellence."[19]

Despite his evident syncretism, Herod contributed nothing to the Samaritan community in his realm. The temple on Mount Gerizim was left in ruins. By contrast, he poured vast amounts into the religious infrastructure of Judaism. For example, he enhanced the Hasmonean shrine at the Cave of Machpelah, the traditional burial site of Israel's patriarchs near Hebron, by enclosing the site within a monumental rectangular stone wall (62 x 31 meters). He built a similar structure at nearby Mamre, the traditional location of Abraham's residence. Herod probably did this to keep fostering the unity of Idumeans and Jews, who shared Abraham as their original patriarch.[20]

In contrast to the Jews in his own kingdom, diaspora Jews were well disposed towards Herod, and he actively cultivated their goodwill. For example, he paid for added security to transfer the considerable monies raised by the half-shekel temple tax, exacted on all Jews throughout Roman territories. He also took up the cause of communal petitions when Jews found their legal concessions violated by local civic authorities. In this regard, his patronage of both Jews and gentiles made him a capable mediator. Inscriptional evidence suggests there was even a "Synagogue of the Herodians" in Rome.[21] Augustus and Agrippa were likewise honored with synagogues named after them.

4.5.6 HEROD AND THE JERUSALEM TEMPLE

Herod's biggest contribution to Judaism, and his grandest project by far, was the complete renovation of the temple complex in Jerusalem (*Ant.* 15.380–425).[22] Planning for it began in 19 BC and involved hiring Egyptian, Greek, and Roman architects, surveying the site, producing plans, securing building materials, employing the workforce, and timetabling construction around the continued operation of the sacrificial cult. It also required the training of about a thousand priests in construction labor since they alone were permit-

---

18. Richardson, *Herod*, 272–73.
19. Marshak, *Many Faces of Herod*, 155.
20. Richardson, *Herod*, 61–62; Netzer and Laureys-Chachy, *The Architecture of Herod*, 228–30.
21. Alternative suggestions for reading the relevant inscription have been offered, but these are problematic. See Richardson, *Building Jewish in the Roman East*, 120–24; Richardson, *Herod*, 266–69.
22. For an excellent survey of Herod's temple, see Netzer and Laureys-Chachy, *The Architecture of Herod*, 137–78.

ted to build the sanctuary and the court of the priests surrounding it. Actual construction began in ca. 16 BC. The first construction phase required the dismantling and replacement of the existing sanctuary. This was completed in eighteen months and dedicated with great fanfare and sacrifice (ca. 14 BC). The rest of the inner complex was completed some six years later (ca. 8 BC) by approximately 10,000 laborers, though additional work did not cease until AD 62. The site, therefore, provided lifetime employment for thousands of people, enhancing Herod's profile as a benefactor and bringer of prosperity.[23]

Herod raised and extended the roughly rectangular footprint of the precinct to 36 square acres (approximately 480 × 300 meters), almost doubling the size of the previous precinct.[24] By means of comparison, this was slightly larger than the Roman Forum combined with all the temples and buildings that lined it, all the temples on the Capitoline Hill, and the adjacent Forums of Julius Caesar and of Augustus. The entire Acropolis of Athens was just 40 percent of its size (14 square acres).

On the north side, Herod extended the complex outwards towards the recently developed Antonia Fortress, which was incorporated into its northwestern corner (*Ant.* 15.292). The southern and western portions were also extended, requiring a huge amount of earthmoving work, the construction of underground vaulting, and the erection of retaining walls up to ten stories high. These outer walls were composed of colossal limestone ashlars weighing between 2 and 300 tons each. The sheer scale of the work, undertaken without the benefit of modern machinery, is staggering, accentuated by the fact that the entire platform is still the largest retained platform on earth to this day.

The precinct was reached by bridges, tunnels, and stairways leading from various locations in and around the city. All portals led to the expansive court of the gentiles, whose vast floors were tiled with colorful, patterned mosaics. Several ritual baths (*miqvaot*) for worshippers were probably located here. This outer court was open to people of any ethnicity, which demonstrates that Judaism had gained appeal among the more philosophically and conservatively minded of Greco-Roman society. It was here, for example, that Godfearers could pray (cf. John 12:20). It also demonstrates something of Herod's own personal syncretism, as someone who had a foot in both the Jewish and gentile worlds and who brought this to bear upon the temple's architecture. What's more, the whole complex was such a marvel that it became a tourist attraction.

---

23. Marshak, *Many Faces of Herod*, 283.
24. By modern standards, Herod's temple complex was the equivalent of 24 soccer fields or 576 tennis courts. St Peter's Basilica and Square in today's Vatican is a little over 24 square acres—just two-thirds the size.

When Augustus's confidant and devoted general Marcus Vipsanius Agrippa visited Herod in 15 BC while construction was still in progress, he returned to Rome with glowing reports of how magnificent the temple was (Philo, *Gaius* 294–95).

Along the southern perimeter of the court of the gentiles, Herod built the royal stoa—a roofed colonnade of 162 marble Corinthian columns. Currency exchangers and those selling sacrificial animals operated beneath its tiered clerestory roof. This was, therefore, where Jesus caused a near riot when he overturned exchange booths and opened animal pens (Matt 21:12–13; Mark 11:15–18; Luke 19:45–46; John 2:13–17). A chamber for the Sanhedrin was built into its eastern end. Adjacent to this, along the eastern perimeter of the court of the gentiles, Herod had another roofed colonnade constructed, known as Solomon's stoa (or "portico"). Jesus taught publicly here (John 10:23), alongside other Jewish teachers and their schools. While this might have been a pragmatic choice for Jesus, the stoa's titular connection to Solomon, the Davidic temple builder, added a messianic dimension to his choice. The early church also met under the stoa's roof (Acts 3:11; 5:12). Together, Herod's two stoas projected his royal ideology (see this section below).

The sacred inner courts lay on a raised podium at the center of the court of the gentiles. A signed barrier prevented gentiles from ascending it. These inner courts were (from east to west) the court of women, the court of Israel, and the court of the priests—the latter two being raised yet higher still. The altar of burnt offering and the sanctuary of Yahweh stood inside the court of the priests. The sanctuary itself rose to a height of almost 50 meters (100 cubits [16 stories]) and was constructed of polished white marble, with the front (eastern face) decorated with gold leaf. According to Josephus, who had been an eyewitness of the temple, if one looked at the front of the sanctuary in the early morning when the sun was in the east, the gleam off the marble and gold was so intense that it was difficult to look at directly (*J.W.* 5.222).

The temple's grandeur reflected the sacredness of the place, the opulence of Herod, and his desire to integrate the Jewish nation into the Roman world.[25] The effect of the whole was so marvelous that even Herod's detractors were awestruck by it, claiming "Whoever has not seen Herod's temple has never seen a beautiful building in his life" (B. Bat. 4a). Jesus's own disciples are said to have drawn Jesus's attention to its grandeur, which prompted his prediction of its destruction (Matt 24:1–2; Mark 13:1–2; Luke 21:5–6).

---

25. Richardson, *Herod*, 249.

Perhaps one of the things that informed Jesus's opinion of Herod's temple was the ideology Herod demonstrated in rebuilding it. Herod was the founder of a new dynasty and had to fight popular Jewish opinion, which condemned him as an Idumean, a supporter of heathen Rome, a willing founder of foreign temples, a usurper, and a murderer of three high priests (Mattathias Antigonus II, Aristobulus III, and John Hyrcanus II)—hardly the resumé of a faithful Jew. To legitimize his rule in the face of such opinion, Herod had to make a contribution to Judaism that would eclipse everything that stood against him and make him the patron *par excellence* of the Jewish community. Portraying himself as the rightful heir of the Hasmonean rulers was useful but ultimately insufficient for this. Therefore, Herod turned to Davidic theology.

The parallels between Herod and the David of biblical literature are significant: both came from southerly regions in the land, served under the previous regime, married a daughter of the previous dynasty, spent time outside the country due to domestic opposition, had been in the ranks of the nation's enemies, and had taken power at the expense of the previous dynasty, being thus characterized as usurpers. But the biblical literature rehabilitated the reputation of David through the notion of an unconditional divine covenant, which elevated his dynasty to permanence (2 Sam 7). Herod could not claim a similar covenant to rescue his own reputation. Instead, he aligned his own kingship as closely as he could with that of David and his ancient dynasty. To that end, he erected an impressive marble monument to David at the site of his relocated tomb on the Western Hill (*Ant.* 7.394; 16.179–84 [see 3.7.3 above]).[26] But the temple was how he primarily cemented the association. David's son, Solomon, was the original builder of the Jerusalem temple, which symbolized the permanent covenant between the deity and the Davidic dynasty. By renovating the entire temple on a lavish scale, Herod was appropriating this legacy and billing himself as the new Solomon to legitimize his rule (*Ant.* 15.385).[27] Herod was the new king of the Jews, inaugurating a new era for the Jewish nation by recapitulating the glory of the ancient Davidic dynasty. Both the royal stoa and Solomon's stoa proclaimed this to all worshippers in the temple. Herod was aiming to capture messianic expectation and fulfil it in himself and his grand new temple. Some of his earliest coins might even depict symbols pertaining to

---

26. Josephus includes a story about Herod's attempt to rob the tomb of David, following a similar pattern to the story of John Hyrcanus I (cf. *Ant.* 7.393; 13.249). He admits that this story is missing from the records of Nicolaus of Damascus (Herod's court historian), and although Josephus rationalizes the omission, the story appears factually baseless. See Marshak, *Many Faces of Herod*, 279–81.

27. Marshak, *Many Faces of Herod*, 278–84.

an ancient Jewish anointing ceremony.[28] In previous centuries, the priesthood had expropriated Zion theology by emptying it of its royal Davidic content. Herod now seized this theology for himself and filled the Davidic void with his own royal content.

Herod's agenda helps us understand Matthew's characterization of Herod's violent response to Jesus's birth late in his reign, compounded as it was by the paranoia and familial squabbling that punctuated his final years (Matt 2:1-18; see 4.5.7 below). Herod had hijacked Davidic hopes and recreated them in his own image. For Davidic loyalists, Herod's temple might have been impressive, but it underscored the need for a new work of God to redeem the nation. This sentiment can be seen in the acclamation of Jesus as "Son of David" on his way to Jerusalem and whilst in the temple itself. The shouts of "Hosanna in the highest" that accompanied him were a call for Jesus to rise to the highest echelons of power to rescue the nation (Matt 21:9, 15; 22:42; Mark 12:35; Luke 20:41). He was being hailed as the inaugurator of a new age, the builder of a new Davidic temple in fulfilment of the classic prophetic promises. It is in this context that his demand to tear down Herod's temple must be understood (Matt 23:38; 26:61; 27:51; Mark 14:58; 15:38; Luke 23:45; John 2:19). This was not a condemnation of the temple institution per se but of the regime that had built it and the authorities who subsequently controlled it and used it as a means of oppression (cf. Mark 12:38-44; Luke 22:52-53). Those authorities certainly perceived a wide enough threat from Jesus and his followers that they sought to arrest them, and it was ultimately the reason for Jesus's execution (Matt 27:40; Mark 15:29; cf. John 11:48). The subsequent proclamation of the early church that Jesus was lord and messiah was an affirmation that God had vindicated Jesus's program of redemption and fulfilled it in a cosmic way that left Herod's temple a mere house made by human hands, akin to the golden calf made by Aaron (cf. Acts 2:29-36; 7:40-50). Despite its fabulous marble and gold facades, Herod's temple was a house built on sand, destined to fall in a storm of judgment, while his own messianic mission was to raise a new "house" founded on rock (cf. Matt 7:24-27; 16:15-20).

We do not know the attitude of the Essenes towards Herod's temple, as the Dead Sea Scrolls make no overt reference to Herod at all. He was favorably disposed towards them, to the point where he did not require them to take an oath of allegiance to him when others were so required (*Ant.* 15.368-72). Whether this was due to Herod's connection with Menahem the Essene or simply because the Essenes were politically pacifist is difficult to say.

---

28. Rocca, *Herod's Judaea*, 22-29.

The Essene site at Qumran continued to thrive during Herod's reign, despite extensive damage suffered during the earthquake of 31 BC.[29] There is, therefore, no indication that the group moved away from their apocalyptic eschatology and political withdrawal. They lived quietly under Herod's rule, even as they waited patiently for the apocalyptic overturning of his political order.

For those who no longer held to Davidic primacy, the fact that the temple had been rebuilt was seen in positive light (cf. *Ant.* 15.421; B. Bat. 4a). As the priestly party, the Sadducees who managed to avoid the Herodian purge (37 BC) found their own status renewed and elevated, tying them closely to Herod and his Herodian aristocracy. The fact that the high priest was now appointed by Herod strengthened these ties even further. Herod's regime and his new temple, therefore, returned to the Sadducees the political clout they had lost to the Pharisees in previous generations.

4.5.7 HEROD AND HIS FAMILY

Herod was besotted with the Hasmonean princess, Mariamme. After their marriage in 37 BC, the couple had five children together: Alexander III, Aristobulus IV, a third son whose name has not been preserved, and two daughters, Salome and Cypros. Notwithstanding this, the marriage became troubled after the drowning of Mariamme's brother Aristobulus III in 35 BC (see 4.5.1 above). It was strained even further after 30 BC, when Mariamme became aware that Herod had twice given instruction to have her killed if he himself were executed by Mark Antony or Octavian (*Ant.* 15.62–67). Thereafter, Mariamme was cold towards him, and the marriage became volatile. The situation was fueled by Herod's sister, Salome, who tried to convince Herod that Mariamme was conspiring to poison him. When Herod discovered that Mariamme was aware of his secret instructions concerning her, he became convinced that she was having an affair with the courtier charged with killing her. Since she probably bore the title "queen," Herod could not simply divorce her.[30] Therefore, in 29 BC Herod had her executed, along with the accused courtier. She was about thirty-five years old.

Mariamme's execution affected Herod deeply and was probably the single biggest contributor to his growing paranoia (cf. *Ant.* 15.241). Mariamme's sons

---

29. Roland de Vaux, the original excavator of Qumran, argued that Qumran was abandoned after the earthquake of 31 BC. See Roland de Vaux, *Archaeology and the Dead Sea Scrolls*, rev. ed. (Oxford: Oxford University Press, 1973), 20–24. However, Jodi Magness has demonstrated that the site continued to operate after the earthquake. See Magness, *Archaeology of Qumran*, 49–69.

30. Rocca, *Herod's Judaea*, 76.

bore a grudge towards their father for their mother's fate, and their animosity never abated. But they were in a delicate situation, as they also depended on him for their own welfare and prospects. Herod's reputation amongst ordinary people within his own kingdom also slumped. To make matters worse, 30/29 BC was a Sabbatical Year, and it was followed by years of drought, food shortages, and disease. Herod himself was struck with serious illness in 28 BC, and many interpreted his and the nation's plight as divine wrath against him. While he remained ill in Sebaste (Samaria), Mariamme's mother, Alexandra II, took measures in Jerusalem to become ruler in the event of Herod's death. Her purpose was probably to act as regent until one of her grandsons, probably Alexander III, was old enough to rule as a scion of the Hasmonean dynasty. But when Herod learned of her posturing, he immediately ordered her execution (*Ant.* 15.247–51), further embittering Mariamme's sons against him. Herod eventually recovered from his ill-health and eased the domestic crisis by procuring grain from Egypt (*Ant.* 15.243, 299–316).

After Mariamme, Herod married several women.[31] These marriages were not just expressions of his own concupiscence, for Herod had concubines, catamites, and eunuchs with whom he slept (cf. *Ant.* 16.230; 17:44; *J.W.* 1.488, 511). Rather, he developed a harem as a way of cultivating his image as a classic Judean king after the image of David and Solomon and to solidify important social connections.[32] The only reason he had divorced his first wife, Doris, was to remove her son, Antipater II, from the inheritance, to ensure that Mariamme's sons would succeed him. This embittered Antipater II towards his half-brothers and would, in time, deeply affect their relationship. Some of the children from these subsequent marriages would go on to have highly significant political careers in Judea and throughout the Greco-Roman world.

Herod's third and fourth marriages were to two of his nieces (ca. 29 BC and 28 BC), whose names have not been preserved, probably because the

---

31. The order of Herod's marriages after Mariamme I is ambiguous, since Josephus does not list them in order, *pace* Harold W. Hoehner, *Herod Antipas: A Contemporary of Jesus Christ* (Grand Rapids: Zondervan, 1980), 11–12. The only marriage whose date we have reasonable confidence in is his marriage to Mariamme II in ca. 23 BC (see VanderKam, *From Joshua to Caiaphas*, 405) and a reasonable deduction that his marriage to Malthace was earlier.

32. Richardson, *Herod*, 43–44. Rocca (*Herod's Judaea*, 76–77) argues that, as a Hellenistic monarch, Herod would not have had a harem but rather married and divorced each of his wives after Mariamme I separately. There is, however, no support for this in the sources and is undermined by the fact that, between Archelaus and Antipas (sons of Malthace), Herod sired Philip I and Philip II by two different wives.

marriages were childless (*Ant.* 17.19; *J.W.* 1.563).[33] His fifth marriage was to Malthace the Samaritan (ca. 26 BC). With her, Herod had two sons, Archelaus and Antipas, and a daughter, Olympias (*Ant.* 17.20; *J.W.* 1.562).[34] Herod's sixth wife was Cleopatra of Jerusalem (ca. 25 BC), who bore him two sons, Herod and Philip II (see this section below for Philip I).

In 24/3 BC Herod fell in love with another woman named Mariamme, who was of great physical beauty, just like her late namesake. Mariamme II was the daughter of Simon, a resident of Jerusalem whose father, Boethus, was a Jewish priest from Alexandria.[35] At the time, Jesus ben-Phiabi was high priest, having been installed by Herod after Hananel in ca. 30 BC.[36] Since the name Phiabi is Egyptian in origin and is attested at the cemetery in Leontopolis, it is tempting to connect Jesus ben-Phiabi with the Oniad temple at Leontopolis. If such a connection is permitted, Herod might have been trying to re-establish the Zadokite line in Jerusalem. However, the connection is speculative and, therefore, cannot be confirmed. In any case, Herod replaced Jesus ben-Phiabi as high priest with Simon, the father of Mariamme II. Simon's appointment was due entirely to Herod's desire to dignify the family of Mariamme II, thus bestowing greater significance upon his marriage to her.[37] She bore Herod one son, named Philip I (*Ant.* 15.319–22; 17.78), who was born before his half-brother of the same name (the son of Cleopatra). Philip I would eventually live as a private citizen in Rome and marry his own niece, Herodias (daughter of Aristobulus IV). Together they would have a daughter, Salome (*Ant.* 18.136), who danced for Antipas (Herodias's second husband) and asked for the head of John the Baptist as a reward (Matt 14:6–11; Mark 6:21–28).[38]

Herod's eighth wife, Pallas, bore him a son, Phasael, named after Herod's deceased older brother. His ninth wife, Phaedra, bore him a daughter named Roxana, and his tenth wife, Elpis, bore him a daughter named Salome. In total, Herod had fifteen children through his ten wives.

---

33. One of these nieces was his brother's daughter and the other his sister's daughter.
34. Herod married Olympias to Joseph, the son of his own brother, Joseph.
35. Josephus draws a distinction between Simon and his father, Boethus, but some modern commentators (e.g., Rocca, *Herod's Judaea*, 285) equate Simon with Boethus, mainly on the grounds that sons of Boethus were appointed to the high priesthood decades later. Yet, the chronology in no way stretches credulity, so Simon should be seen as distinct from Boethus.
36. We have no historical record to inform us whether Hananel died in office or was simply replaced.
37. VanderKam, *From Joshua to Caiaphas*, 405–408; Richardson, *Herod*, 244–45.
38. Soon after the death of John the Baptist, Salome was married to her uncle, Philip II, the tetrarch of Iturea and Trachonitis. The marriage lasted only a couple of years before Philip II's death, after which Salome was married to Aristobulus of Chalcis, alongside whom she became queen of Chalcis and Armenia Minor.

Wife	Date of Marriage	Children (date of birth)	Notes
1. Doris	ca. 49 BC	Antipater II (ca. 48 BC)	
2. Mariamme I	37 BC	Alexander III (ca. 36 BC)	
		Aristobulus IV (ca. 35 BC)	
		Son (ca. 33 BC)	Died in Rome ca. 23 BC (?)
		Salome (ca. 32 BC)	
		Cypros (ca. 31 BC)	
3. *Niece*	ca. 28 BC	—	Daughter of Herod's brother
4. *Niece*	ca. 27 BC	—	Daughter of Herod's sister
5. Malthace	ca. 26 BC	Olympias (ca. 25 BC)	Married her cousin Joseph, son of Joseph
		Archelaus (23 BC)	Ethnarch of Judea
		Antipas (ca. 19 BC)	Tetrarch of Galilee & Perea
6. Cleopatra of Jerusalem	ca. 25 BC	Herod (ca. 24 BC)	
		Philip II (ca. 21 BC)	Tetrarch of Iturea & Trachonitis
7. Mariamme II	ca. 23 BC	Philip I (ca. 22 BC)	Married Herodias (daughter of Aristobulus IV)
8. Pallas	ca. 21 BC	Phasael (ca. 19 BC)	
9. Phaedra	ca. 19 BC	Roxana (ca. 18 BC)	
10. Elpis	ca. 17 BC	Salome (ca. 16 BC)	

Despite the hatred of Mariamme I's sons towards him, Herod sent them to Rome as they entered their teenage years (ca. 23 BC) to groom them for leadership.[39] The boys were eventually welcomed into the household of Augustus himself (cf. Suetonius, *Aug.* 48). The youngest of the three, though, probably died at about this time, though the exact manner of his death is unknown.[40] The years that the older two, Alexander III and Aristobulus IV, spent in the household of the Princeps tied their loyalty to him and Romanized them. It is little surprise, then, that while the boys were in Rome, Augustus gave

---

39. In time, Herod would also send his other sons to Rome for their education.
40. Richardson, *Herod*, 231.

Herod permission to name his own heir (*Ant.* 15.342–44). Herod designated Alexander as his heir, though it is not inconceivable that his brother, Aristobulus, was also named heir in some capacity (cf. *Ant.* 16.92, 95, 129, 133; *J.W.* 1.458).[41] Herod was acting to salvage Mariamme's memory through her sons and give dignity to the Hasmonean legacy they bore—an outcome Augustus approved of.

The boys' Hasmonean heritage set them apart from Herod's other children, such that they looked down upon the others and even upon Herod himself. Such hauteur was exploited by Herod's eldest son, Antipater II (son of Doris), who was at least a decade older than them both and who actively tried to turn Herod against them after Herod fetched them from Rome in 17 BC. He appealed to Herod's legitimacy as ruler, despite his personal lack of royal heritage—an argument that worked also in Antipater's favor—and this, in turn, played upon Herod's growing paranoia (cf. *Ant.* 16.244). Antipater's efforts worked. Herod started suspecting Alexander and Aristobulus of conspiring against him and began to show favor to Antipater instead. Antipater then managed to have his mother, Doris, reconciled to Herod in 14 BC, thereby making himself a legitimate son and potential heir once again. With his paranoia running high, Herod updated his will and named Antipater his sole successor. The following year, he sent Antipater to Rome in the care of Agrippa, where he was introduced to Augustus and made "a friend of Caesar" (*Ant.* 16.66–86; *J.W.* 1.445–51).

From Rome, Antipater continued to convince an anxious Herod that Alexander and Aristobulus were guilty of conspiracy. However, Herod also knew how Augustus had grown fond of them during their time in Rome (23–17 BC). His paranoia thus combined with his anxiety not to offend Augustus and induced him to take them to Augustus in 12 BC, to let the Princeps himself determine whether they were guilty of conspiracy.[42] Augustus did not accept the charges against them. Instead, he prevailed upon Herod to reconsider the whole matter, including his current will. Herod felt the pressure of this request and so produced a new will, which named Antipater II, Alexander III, and Aristobulus IV as co-heirs (*Ant.* 16.127–35; *J.W.* 1.454–66). Such a power-sharing arrangement between hostile branches of the Herodian family was a sure recipe for disaster, but Herod felt that this was the solution Augustus had been angling for. The internecine chaos was of little concern to Augustus,

---

41. Richardson, *Herod*, 34.
42. Herod probably took his sons Archelaus and Philip I to Rome for their education at this time also.

since all three young men were now his clients anyway. But the situation was far from ideal for Herod and his sons.

By this time, the three co-heirs had all married and started their own families. Antipater married the daughter (name unknown) of Mattathias Antigonus II (*Ant.* 17.92)—the first cousin of Mariamme I and a granddaughter of Aristobulus II. The couple had at least one son, which meant Antipater's line gained Hasmonean heritage. Alexander married a Cappadocian princess named Glaphyra, and had three children with her: Tigranes (a future king of Armenia), Alexander, and a daughter (name unknown). Aristobulus IV married his first cousin, Berenice (daughter of Herod's sister, Salome), and they had five children: Mariamme III, Herod (a future king of Chalcis), Herodias (future wife of both Philip I and Antipas), Marcus Julius Agrippa (future King Herod Agrippa I of Judea), and Aristobulus V.

Despite his marriage into the Hasmonean family, Antipater continued to battle popular opinion because of his own descent (his mother, Doris, was a Nabatean) and his hostility towards the sons of the much-loved Mariamme I. To remedy this, he prevailed on Herod to betroth Aristobulus's pre-pubescent daughter, Mariamme III, to himself as a second wife (*Ant.* 17.18). Ostensibly, this made the three-way succession more viable but also boosted Antipater's claim by giving him a connection to Mariamme I's branch of the family.

Even after this betrothal, however, Antipater never let up his opposition towards Alexander and Aristobulus. Herod grew increasingly agitated by the rumors Antipater conjured, and in 10 BC he became convinced of Alexander's perfidy and had him imprisoned. Antipater's position as heir strengthened, and he gained considerable support among Herod's chief advisors (*Ant.* 16.244–60; *J.W.* 1.488–97).

Alexander might have languished in prison were it not for his father-in-law, Archelaus, king of Cappadocia, who travelled to Jerusalem and negotiated a reconciliation between Herod and Alexander (*Ant.* 16.261–70; *J.W.* 1.498–512). Yet, the rivalry between Herod's sons continued unabated. In early 9 BC Herod celebrated the completion of the Sebastos Harbor at Caesarea Maritima (*Ant.* 16.136–41). The essential works at the temple of Jerusalem were also nearing completion, making it a festive year. But this could not overcome Herod's now fully blown monomania that Mariamme's sons were intending to assassinate him. So, Herod had both Alexander and Aristobulus imprisoned in 9 BC (*Ant.* 16.320–24).

Thereafter, things soured quickly for Herod. Insurrections had broken out in Trachonitis three years earlier (12 BC), and the insurgents soon gained the support of the Nabateans, who had become clients of Rome. This escalated the insurrection into an international incident. In 9 BC a jumpy Herod defended his interests by attacking the insurgents inside Nabatean territory, just as a Nabatean delegation was meeting with Augustus in Rome. Augustus had recently lost his stepson, Drusus, who was not only the beloved son of his wife, Livia, but also one of the most gifted generals Rome had seen to date.[43] And this was three years after Augustus had lost his long-time confidante, Marcus Vipsanius Agrippa. The Princeps was, therefore, in no mood for niceties. He reprimanded Herod severely for encroaching upon the territory of another Roman client and revoked his status as a friend. Augustus also withdrew Herod's right to name his own heirs. The outcome sent Herod into a psychological tailspin (*Ant.* 16.271–99).

Herod sought to patch up his relationship with the Princeps the following year, committing the negotiations to his chief statesman, Nicolaus of Damascus.[44] Nicolaus demonstrated how the Nabatean delegation had misled Augustus in several matters, and this convinced the Princeps to reconcile with Herod and reinstate his privileges. So successful was Nicolaus in exposing Nabatean calumny that Augustus was soon of a mind to give Herod control of all Nabatean territory. Had he done so, Herod's kingdom would have practically doubled in size to encompass all habitable lands between the Lebanon and the Red Sea coast of Arabia. However, Herod was now sixty-six years of age and in a state of perpetual agitation. It is not inconceivable that he was suffering from schizophrenia or bipolar disorder. His mental state and continued struggles with his sons dissuaded Augustus from going ahead with the annexation. The Princeps also opted not to intervene in the familial squabbling. Instead, he advised Herod to discuss the supposed perfidy of Mariamme's sons, now both in their late twenties, with Saturninus, the Roman governor of Syria, and Archelaus of Cappadocia, Alexander's father-in-law (*Ant.* 16.335–58).

Despite the injection of these additional voices, Augustus's hands-off approach essentially gave Herod free reign to deal with his sons as he saw fit. Herod called for the discussions with Saturninus and Archelaus at Berytus (7 BC) but refused to let his sons even appear to defend themselves. While the general feeling was that Alexander and Aristobulus were guilty of conspiracy, the majority opinion was that they should simply remain in prison. But Herod deemed this insufficient. He journeyed back to his kingdom, which was now in turmoil over the prospective sentencing of his sons. Despite desperate

---

43. Drusus and his older brother, Tiberius, were biological sons of Livia's first husband, Tiberius Claudius Nero. Augustus's connection to them both was evident after they began living with Augustus and Livia in 33 BC. Tiberius was even to become Augustus's successor as Princeps in AD 14.

44. It is likely that Herod's twelve-year-old son, Antipas, was taken to Rome at this time for his education in the imperial capital. Cf. Hoehner, *Herod Antipas*, 14.

attempts to stay Herod's hand, he ordered Alexander and Aristobulus be taken to Sebaste, where he had them both strangled to death (*Ant.* 16.359–94; *J.W.* 1.538–51). Herod's brutality towards the sons of the beloved Mariamme caused outrage throughout the realm. It also weakened his connection to the Hasmoneans. It is perhaps for this reason that Herod took such pains to provide well for his grandchildren through Alexander and Aristobulus, who were now his only living connection to the dynasty.

Antipater, now about forty years old, was the obvious beneficiary of the executions. However, when Herod amended his will, he added a surprising new clause: if Antipater died before Philip I (the son of Mariamme II), then Philip I was to succeed Antipater on the throne (*Ant.* 17.53, 67; *J.W.* 1.573). Considering that there was an age difference of about twenty-six years between them, the likelihood of Antipater dying first was high. This additional clause potentially removed Antipater's children from the line of succession. Herod also passed over two sons who were older than Philip I: Herod (son of Cleopatra of Jerusalem) and Archelaus (son of Malthace). Part of Philip I's promotion involved his betrothal to Herodias, one of the daughters of the now dead Aristobulus IV. Philip I was about fifteen years of age at the time (7 BC), while Herodias was only five, so their actual marriage occurred several years later. Since Herodias had Hasmonean blood through her father (Aristobulus IV), Herod was clearly aiming towards integrating his family with the Hasmoneans as strongly as possible. Antipater's children also had Hasmonean blood through both of his marriages. But why Philip I was singled out for a role in this integration is unknown. What does become apparent from the sources, though, is Herod's increasingly fragile state of mind.

This was underscored over the subsequent years. In 6 BC Herod's youngest brother, Pheroras, died and suggestions soon arose that he had been poisoned. Herod became convinced that his wife, Mariamme II, had known of the plot but failed to disclose it. In 5 BC Herod divorced her and removed her son, Philip I, from the succession. Philip I was being educated in Rome at the time, and he remained there, away from any repercussions. Herod also removed Mariamme II's father, Simon, from the high priesthood after almost two decades in the role and gave the office to a priest named Matthias ben-Theophilus, who was resident in Jerusalem (*Ant.* 17.58–58; *J.W.* 1.580–600). Herod also drafted a new will in which his eldest son, Antipater, once again became his sole heir.

Antipater journeyed to Rome, presumably bearing Herod's latest will for deposit with the Vestal Virgins, the keepers of all wills for Roman citizens. He did not, however, desist from his own conniving, which included conspiracy by correspondence. He focused his attention now on turning Herod against

Archelaus and Philip II. But with the sons of Mariamme I now permanently out of the way and Philip I shunted from the succession, Antipater himself became the focal point of Herod's paranoia. By the time Antipater returned to Judea, Herod had become convinced that his eldest son was planning to do him in by poison. Antipater's arrival in Jerusalem coincided with a visit of the Roman governor of Syria, Publius Quintilius Varus (5 BC).[45] Herod instantly put Antipater on trial and invited Varus to judge the case. Antipater's own correspondence and forged letters were produced, along with a vial of poison. He was accordingly remanded into custody until Augustus could respond to official reports of the trial (*Ant.* 17.79–145; *J.W.* 1.601–45).

Despite this necessary delay in a final verdict over Antipater, Herod amended his will yet again. He removed Antipater completely from the succession and named Antipas, his youngest son by his Samaritan wife, Malthace, as his sole heir (*Ant.* 17.146; *J.W.* 1.646). Antipas, who was about fourteen years of age at the time, was in Rome for his education. His older full brother, Archelaus, and half-brother, Philip II, had been summarily passed over because, as the most recent targets of Antipater's scheming, Herod feared that they too had indeed been caught up in Antipater's web. Herod considered Antipas a candidate of lower risk. In the winter of 5/4 BC Antipas returned to Judea as the new crown prince of the Jewish kingdom—the son of an Idumean father and a Samaritan mother. Since he returned with his two supplanted brothers, Archelaus and Philip II, the journey was undoubtedly a tense one.

4.5.8 THE EAGLE AFFAIR (4 BC)

By the end of 5 BC Herod was approaching seventy years of age and was in poor mental and physical health. He was suffering from various diseases, diagnosed in modern times as either chronic kidney failure, Fournier's Gangrene, syphilis, sarcoidosis, or some combination of these.[46] It was clear that Herod would not survive much longer, and this emboldened many to contemplate life after Herod.

Among those so emboldened were two leading Pharisees, Judas and Matthias.[47] In early March 4 BC news of Herod's impending death sparked

---

45. Varus would eventually be remembered most for his notorious defeat by the Germanic tribes led by Arminius at the Teutoburg Forest in AD 9.
46. Richardson, *Herod*, 18; Jan V. Hirschman et al., "Death of Arabian Jew," *Arch. Intern. Med.* 164.8 (2004): 833–39, https://doi.org/doi:10.1001/archinte.164.8.833.
47. Josephus calls Judas "son of Sepphoris" (*J.W.* 1.648; cf. *Ant* 17.149), but this is almost certainly a reference to his place of origin. His hometown was, therefore, a short walk from Nazareth.

Judas and Matthias to call for the destruction of a golden eagle statue, which stood above one of the gateways to the temple.[48] The statue probably symbolized the connection between Herod's kingdom and Rome, for the eagle always featured on Roman military standards.[49] For Jews vehemently opposed to Roman rule, this was an emblem of hated foreign influence. For the fundamentalist Pharisees, who observed Torah with hyper-literal scruples and who created additional regulations to prevent even accidental violation, it was an iconic representation that breached their interpretation of the second commandment prohibiting idols in worship. The eagle had probably been in place for several years, and while some may have found it irritating, it evidently did not pollute the temple, and no one actually worshipped it. Thus, the call from Judas and Matthias to destroy it is best understood as an expression of populist impulses seeking to assert hyper-literal, fundamentalist Pharisaic principles. Believing Herod to be at death's door, a mob of Judas's and Matthias's disciples mounted the gateway in full public view, let some of their number down by ropes, and hacked the statue off its mounting (*Ant.* 17.149–55; *J.W.* 1.648–51).

This act of iconoclasm was a clear challenge to the status quo in Herod's client kingdom, and the plucky perpetrators knew full well it could cost them their lives. It helps put into perspective the provocative act of Jesus in overturning the stalls of the moneychangers and the pens of the animal sellers in the very same complex a few decades later. The Pharisees' vandalism was not just a gesture of religious zeal or a statement against Rome. Judas and Matthias were signaling a desire to return to the days of the Hasmonean queen, Salome Alexandra, when the fundamentalist Pharisees had controlled the Sanhedrin and wielded civic power throughout Judea. The last known Pharisaic president of the Sanhedrin was Shemaiah, who had succeeded Abtalion shortly after Herod came to power (ca. 37 BC).[50] After them, Herod gave the presidency of the Sanhedrin to his appointed high priests, so that the Sadducees and other

---

48. Richardson (*Herod*, 16–17) plausibly hypothesizes that the eagle was above the gateway of what is today known as Wilson's Arch.

49. Samuel Rocca, "The Source of Herod's Eagle on the Façade of the Temple: Eastern-Hellenistic or Roman?," *INR* 13 (2018): 85–100, points out that eagle imagery was pervasive on eastern coins and not necessarily indicative of Roman hegemony. However, the argument assumes (1) a direct connection between imagery on coins and the golden eagle over the temple gateway; and (2) popular (un)familiarity with Roman eagle imagery. Since Judea was within the Roman orbit, the Roman military eagle was well known. Furthermore, it was Herod who erected the eagle, and his response to its destruction shows that he interpreted it as a comparison of his regime (as a Roman client) with that of the Hasmoneans (under whom the Pharisees wielded power).

50. Rabbinic Judaism sees Hillel the Elder as the successor to Abtalion and Shemaiah, but while Hillel probably served on the Sanhedrin, there is no plausible indication that he attained the presidency. The same can be said for Shammai, the noted rabbi who, though younger than Hillel, is frequently cited as Hillel's theological conversation partner (and even competitor).

Herodians began to displace the Pharisees on the supreme Jewish council.[51] The Pharisees were thus receding from political life, a reality that the influential Hillel might have encouraged.[52] But evidently not all Pharisees were content to go quietly. Herod's imminent death raised the prospect of political recovery.

Herod's temple police were quickly on the scene, arresting Judas, Matthias, and some forty of their students who had participated in the vandalism. Herod, who was indeed at death's door, brought the arrested men to Jericho for a public trial. During the trial, he expressed how he was personally affronted by the incident, which he saw as an ungrateful challenge to his generous benefaction in building the temple—a feat that, he claimed, had far outweighed anything the Hasmoneans had ever achieved. Herod's response implies that the vandalism had indeed been a call for a return to the Pharisaic ascendancy of Hasmonean times. But Herod was not about to hand civic rule to the Pharisees or revive the monarchy of the high priest. The Jewish kingdom would soon see young Antipas of Idumean and Samaritan stock become their new king.

The fact that Herod conducted the trial publicly when he himself was so ill shows how passionately he felt about the affair. He was not mild in his verdict either: he sentenced Judas, Matthias, and those who hacked the eagle down to be burned alive. This was almost certainly a blatant denigration of the Pharisaic belief in the resurrection of the dead, as it prevented the bones of the condemned from being "gathered to their fathers" and kept for the putative resurrection day. The remainder of the mob were condemned as accessories and executed with the sword. By virtue of a lunar eclipse that occurred on the very night of the executions, we know that they occurred on 13 March 4 BC (*Ant.* 17.156–67; *J.W.* 1.652–55).

Immediately afterwards, Herod removed Matthias ben-Theophilus from the high priesthood. Not only had the Eagle Affair occurred on his watch, but there was to be no suggestion that the high priesthood would be anything other than an appointment made at royal whim. Matthias had been in the position only a few months and even had the unfortunate circumstance of being unable to preside at the Day of Atonement (11 October 5 BC) because a wet dream the night before the ceremony rendered him ritually unclean. A relative, Joseph ben-Ellem, filled in for him on that particular day (*Ant.* 17.166). But now, as a

---

51. This situation persisted into the first century (cf. Acts 4:5–7; 7:1).
52. Jacob Neusner, "The Rabbinic Traditions about the Pharisees Before 70 CE: An Overview," in *In Quest of the Historical Pharisees*, ed. Jacob Neusner and Bruce D. Chilton (Waco, TX: Baylor University Press, 2007), 301–2.

permanent replacement, Herod appointed a priest named Joazar, the brother of his former wife, Mariamme II, and a grandson of Boethus (*Ant.* 17.164).[53]

4.5.9 THE DEATH OF HEROD

Immediately after the trial, Herod travelled to the hot springs at Callirrhoe by the Dead Sea, hoping to alleviate the painful symptoms of his illness. It did not work, and he began to despair of recovery. He returned to his palace near Jericho and, in an unstable state of mind, ordered some of the leading citizens of the nation to be gathered and held under guard at Jericho's hippodrome to be slaughtered when he himself died, so that the nation would experience real mourning when he eventually passed (*Ant.* 17.168–81; *J.W.* 1.656–60).

While Herod awaited death, a letter arrived from Augustus with advice regarding Herod's son, Antipater II, who was still in custody in the palace at Jericho. The Princeps deferred final judgment to Herod himself, recommending either exile or execution. Herod, however, could not come to a decision, for his illness consumed him. So racked with pain was he that he even attempted to commit suicide with a knife he was using to peel an apple. He was only prevented from succeeding by a cousin who was on hand to restrain him. The incident distressed Herod's staff to such an extent that the whole palace was in emotional upheaval within moments of it happening. From his cell, Antipater thought the distressed commotion indicated that his father had finally died. He therefore tried to convince the sentry guarding him to release him, only to have the sentry report this to Herod himself. This convinced the ailing king that his son wanted him dead, so he ordered that Antipater be immediately executed (*Ant.* 17.182–87; *J.W.* 1.661–64). It was the third time Herod killed one of his own sons.

Straight after Antipater's execution, Herod amended his will yet again. He undid the marginalization of Archelaus and Philip II, which had originally been prompted by Antipater's scheming. Archelaus was now Herod's oldest surviving son,[54] so Herod named him his primary heir. He was to be given the title "king," with Samaria, Judea, and Idumea as his domain. The obvious loser in this arrangement was Archelaus's younger brother, Antipas, who

---

53. Josephus calls Joazar the "son" of Boethus, which has led some to equate Mariamme II's father, Simon, with Boethus. But Josephus makes a clear differentiation between Simon and Boethus. Josephus's point, therefore, is that Joazar was part of the priestly house of Boethus. See VanderKam, *From Joshua to Caiaphas*, 413–14.

54. This assumes that the oldest son of Cleopatra of Jerusalem, Herod, had died before this time. He disappears quickly from the historical record and never features in any of Herod's wills.

was demoted to "tetrarch" of Galilee and Perea only. Philip II was also named "tetrarch," with Iturea and Trachonitis as his domain. Furthermore, Herod granted rule of Jamnia and Ashdod (on the coast) and the balsam estates near Jericho to his sister, Salome (*Ant.* 17.188–90).

Five days after the execution of Antipater, Herod himself died in his palace near Jericho (approximately 1 April 4 BC). His new will was publicly read out in Jericho, much to the consternation of Antipas, who found himself relegated. It was Archelaus, the new primary beneficiary, therefore, who led the funerary ceremonies for Herod. The leading citizens who had been held captive in Jericho's hippodrome for slaughter were simply released. Herod's septic body was dressed in purple finery, placed inside a red limestone sarcophagus, and deposited within his mausoleum on the northeastern slope of Herodium.[55] Seven days of public mourning were then decreed throughout the Jewish kingdom (*Ant.* 17.191–99; *J.W.* 1.665–73).

4.5.10 THE AFTERMATH OF HEROD'S DEATH

Herod's last will, written days before his death, created political ambiguity in Judea, for it had not been deposited in Rome nor had it been endorsed by Augustus. Furthermore, Herod had written it while in a questionable state of mind. Thus, fifteen-year-old Antipas prepared to head to Rome to challenge its contents before Augustus and argue that Herod's previous will, which had nominated him as sole heir, was still legally binding.

This did not stop nineteen-year-old Archelaus from acting as heir presumptive in Jerusalem. He even held court in the temple during Passover (11–18 April 4 BC) barely a week after his father's interment. He carefully avoided using the term "king" for himself, since he needed Augustus to confer the title upon him. But he began to bill himself as someone who would reign differently to his father. This was welcomed by the crowds of worshippers, who were hankering for change. Calls immediately came for the easing of taxes, which had supported Herod and his elite, and the release of prisoners who had fallen victim to Herod's political whims. As a gesture of goodwill, Archelaus acquiesced to these demands.

But two further demands swiftly followed, presumably from the Pharisees. The first called for the punishment of those involved in the execution of Judas, Matthias, and their disciples after the Eagle Affair a few weeks earlier.

---

55. Ehud Netzer et al., "Preliminary Report on Herod's Mausoleum and Theatre with a Royal Box at Herodium," *JRA* 23.1 (2010): 84–108.

The second called for the removal of the new high priest, Joazar, who was seen as Herod's lackey and of questionable repute for having sided with Herod over the Eagle Affair. These demands were basically a litmus test for whether Archelaus would back the fundamentalist populist agenda of the Pharisees and work towards re-establishing their political dominance in Judea, or whether he would continue his father's approach of maintaining his own power and that of the Herodian elite. Since Archelaus had already given ground on the previous demands, he was pressured to concede on these, too. He was, however, none too happy about it, and his prevarication sparked riots in Jerusalem. Archelaus clamped down on the rioters, allegedly killing some 3,000 people during the Passover Festival (*Ant.* 17.200–18; *J.W.* 2.1–13). This violent precedent puts into perspective the fears of the Jewish authorities in Jesus's day over potential riots that might ensue from his activities (cf. Mark 11:15–18, 29–33; John 11:50; 18:14).

Archelaus left Judea for Rome to argue for the legality of Herod's final will with its power-sharing arrangement. Philip II was left in charge of Judea, with a Roman procurator, Sabinus, acting as caretaker alongside the lad (*Ant.* 17.221–23). But with Judea's political situation in flux, two of Herod's sons out of the country, and violence already simmering, the Jewish client kingdom descended into chaos. Sabinus's heavy-handedness in Jerusalem sparked violent confrontations with pilgrims at the Festival of Pentecost in early June, resulting in hundreds more deaths. Roman troops set fire to one of the stoas around the perimeter of the temple, causing the roof to collapse and kill Jewish insurgents who were hurling projectiles from it. Roman troops then loot the damage (*Ant.* 17.254–68). A portion of Herod's army also defected to the side of the uprising, but skirmishes with their former comrades did not produce any clear results (*Ant.* 17.269–70).

There were also several attempts by commoners to grab power. In Jericho, one of Herod's slaves named Simon led a slave rebellion in which he was declared king. He burned down Herod's winter palace at Jericho and a few other residences in the country before being violently stopped by Herod's loyal troops in Perea (*Ant.* 17.273–77). A similar royal pretender named Athronges also arose. He was a shepherd by profession and seems to have attempted a Maccabean-style guerilla uprising with four of his brothers. The guerilla band had some success ambushing a Roman contingent at Emmaus and evaded capture for some years. Eventually, however, its members were captured or dispersed (*Ant.* 17.278–84). In Galilee, an insurrection was led by Judas, son of the warlord Hezekiah, who had been executed by a young Herod forty years earlier (see 4.3.10 above). Judas stormed the Herodian palace at Sepphoris, a short walk from Nazareth, and set up a kind of brigand-state, which broke down the established authority structures and stirred anarchy throughout Galilee. Josephus claims that Judas was passionate for "royal honor" (*Ant.* 17.271–72). As Judas might have been of Davidic descent, his ambition takes on theological proportions. Varus, the Roman governor of Syria, dispatched troops to Galilee, and Judas's uprising was suppressed. It is, however, possible that Judas himself survived, if he is to be equated with Judas the Galilean, who led a violent rebellion ten years later (AD 6).[56] Varus then continued south and eventually gained control of Jerusalem. The chaos of multiple insurrections, damaged infrastructure, fragmented armies, and the mobilization of Roman troops from Syria underscores how volatile the Jewish client kingdom had become (*Ant.* 17.285–99).

In Rome, Augustus received the respective delegations of Antipas and Archelaus. Antipas had the backing of most of the Herodian elite, but Archelaus had Nicolaus of Damascus, his father's chief statesman, as advocate. Another delegation also arrived in Rome, probably sponsored by the Pharisees, which petitioned Augustus to dissolve Judea's client status altogether and integrate it into the Roman province of Syria. Such was the anti-Herodian feeling in Judea that many saw closer integration with Rome's provincial structures as preferable to a solution involving the Herodian dynasty. It would ostensibly involve a return to the traditional authority of the Jerusalem Sanhedrin, even as it thrust independence further away from Jewish hands. Finally, Philip II arrived in Rome, having left Judea in the custody of Varus and Sabinus, to add further strength to the case for Herod's final will and its power-sharing arrangement.

Augustus was reluctant to remove the elite of the dynasty that he himself had backed in the person of Herod. The Herodian dynasty were his clients, and he was of a mind to continue his support for them all. The case of the independent delegation, therefore, was rejected. Instead, the Princeps confirmed Herod's final will and its threefold division of the kingdom. Yet, he stopped short of naming Archelaus "king." Instead, he assigned him the title "ethnarch," with the possibility of attaining the title "king" if he showed competence in government. This told Archelaus that he had acted imprudently when he attempted to hold court in Jerusalem and had lost control of the festival pilgrims. Augustus also decreed that one-quarter of the taxes paid to Archelaus be directed straight to Rome. Antipas was confirmed as tetrarch of Galilee and Perea, with his

---

56. Equating Judas, son of Hezekiah, with Judas the Galilean is certainly plausible, but the ubiquity of the name "Judas," and the relative ages of the descendants of Judas the Galilean, who were operative during the Jewish Revolt (AD 66–73), make the equation uncertain.

territory incorporating such sites as Nazareth, Cana, Capernaum, and Magdala. He would later found the city of Tiberias on the shores of Lake Galilee as his new capital. Philip II was confirmed as tetrarch of Iturea and Trachonitis, with some of his later achievements including the foundation of Caesarea Philippi at the site of Panias and the development of Bethsaida on Lake Galilee into a *polis* named Julias. The port of Gaza and the cities of the Decapolis were trimmed off the Herodian domains and assigned directly to the Roman province of Syria (*Ant.* 17.224–49, 299–320; *J.W.* 2.80–100).

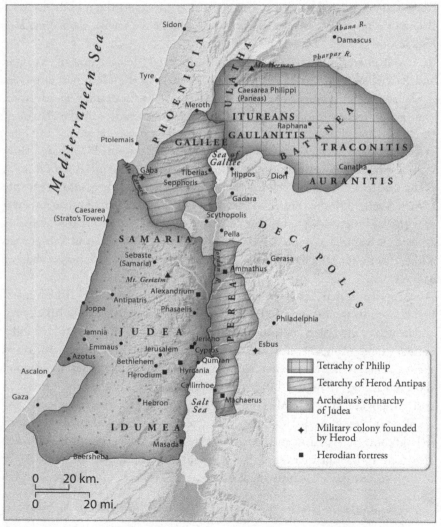

The Division of Herod's Kingdom (4 BC).

Herod's sons returned to Judea (*Ant.* 17.250).[57] Antipas and Philip II set about establishing themselves in their respective tetrarchies, while Archelaus arrived back in Jerusalem with clipped wings. He immediately removed the high priest Joazar from office, as per the earlier request of the Pharisees. Archelaus charged him with complicity in the widespread sedition that had gripped the country during his absence. But rather than giving the Pharisees any sense of victory, Archelaus stamped his own authority by simply appointing Joazar's brother, Eleazar, as high priest in his stead (*Ant.* 17.339). It was a clear signal that the Herodian dynasty and its associated elite would not give way to the fundamentalist Pharisees and their allies. It ensured that discontent continued to simmer throughout all the Herodian territories.

---

57. They probably conveyed the body of Malthace, the mother of Archelaus and Antipas, who died while in Rome. She was most likely buried in Herod's mausoleum at Herodium.

EPILOGUE

When Herod died in 4 BC, the three pieces into which his kingdom was partitioned all remained within the orbit of the Roman Empire. For Archelaus, Antipas, Philip II, and the Herodian elite that supported them, Judaism was primarily about the state. This required the political support of the Romans and a stable economic system, maintained through customs duties and exploitative tax farming. The Herodian rulers tolerated a variety of cultural and religious expressions within their domains, so long as Herodian power was upheld. The wealthy Herodian elite and the Herodian military, drawn mainly from foreign elements, buttressed this system locally.

The Sadducees cooperated with the Herodians as a means of maintaining their priestly influence in Judaism, especially through the temple institution and the Jerusalem Sanhedrin. There were, however, some conservatively minded Sadducees who were more nationalistic and critical of the Herodians and Romans, desiring less outside interference within the native Jewish establishment. For all Sadducees, though, Judaism was primarily about the cult and the Jewish ethnos as a cultural establishment under priestly leadership in the here and now.

The Pharisees pursued a populist agenda in opposition to the Herodians and Sadducees. Their decreased political influence prompted some to work purely as a lay religious movement, but there were other Pharisees still committed to political activism. For all Pharisees, Judaism was primarily about developing a pervasive religious culture that could shape the whole Jewish ethnos. In this regard, they sought to disseminate their fundamentalist brand of Judaism throughout the nation, dominated by their developing Oral Law and hyper-literal hermeneutic.

The Essenes opted for general withdrawal from the political arena in favor of pacifist piety. Many Essenes went a step further and withdrew to the monastic community at Qumran, but all of them expected the apocalyptic and eschatological intervention of God to re-establish the old order that had prevailed under the Zadokite priesthood. For them, Judaism was primarily about personal faith focused on monastic piety, mysticism, and hope for a renewed cult.

There were also the more violent elements, like Judas ben-Hezekiah, Athronges and his brothers, and Simon, the former slave of Herod. These violent figures imbibed the extremist legacy of Judas Maccabeus. For them,

Judaism was about national identity and fighting for new political and economic structures to uphold it. In this regard, they were diametrically opposed to the Herodians and their Roman backers and were prepared to take up arms in this struggle. It is possible that one of Jesus's disciples, Simon the "Cananean" (Matt 10:4; Mar 3:18), had been one such extremist.[1] The two bandits crucified beside Jesus certainly were convicted extremists.[2] Though there was little structure to these violent movements at the end of the first century BC, they would eventually spawn more organized groups, such as the Sicarii and Zealots of the first century AD.

Diaspora Jews were removed from most of these social, political, and economic currents in Judea. This is not to say they had no opinions or loyalties but rather that they operated under different conditions in which they were not the dominant ethnic group. This inevitably meant their convictions tended to be driven by the preservation of their culture as an ethnic minority. They continued to show loyalty to the temple in Jerusalem through such things as praying towards Jerusalem, paying the temple tax, and making pilgrimage when it was practicable. Some viewed Roman imperial power with great suspicion. For example, the incorporation of Egypt into the Roman provincial system in 30 BC sparked a reactionary response from some in the Jewish community of Alexandria, leading to the composition of the Wisdom of Solomon, which berated foreign rulers and idolatry. By contrast, there were others who fully embraced Roman imperial rule. One outstanding example of this was the Jewish aristocrat Alexander Lysimachus, who became financial comptroller ("alabarch") of Alexandria's ports in the first century. His family had ties to the Jewish priesthood and yet enjoyed Roman citizenship. His son, Tiberius Julius Alexander, became Roman Procurator of Judea in AD 46–48 and even served alongside Titus during the conquest of Jerusalem in AD 70. On the whole, however, most diaspora Jews were tolerant of Roman imperial power without necessarily endorsing it. Alexander Lysimachus's famous brother, Philo, was a community leader in Alexandria. He produced philosophical treatises blending Platonic philosophy and classic Jewish thought and yet participated in an embassy to petition Caligula against his radical plan to install a statue in the

---

1. This possibility depends on deriving the label "Cananean" from the Semitic root *qana'* ("to be zealous"), which was used in connection with the "Zealots." Josephus states that Judas the Galilean became the founder of the Zealots in AD 6 (*Ant.* 18.23; *J.W.* 2.117–18), but it is not clear whether Josephus was retrofitting later terminology into his account of Judas the Galilean, or whether that terminology was being used in the early first century.

2. The term "bandits" (Greek: *lēstai*) used in the Gospels to describe them is the same term Josephus uses for rebel extremists (e.g., *J.W.* 1.304). Josephus even labels Hezekiah (father of Judas) an "arch-bandit" (Greek: *archilēstēs* [*Ant.* 17.271]).

Jerusalem temple (AD 40).[3] The Caesarean Settlement, which had granted Jews significant concessions out of respect for their ancient culture, fostered this symbiosis of cultural preservation with cautious tolerance for Roman sovereignty, demonstrated chiefly by the proliferation of diaspora synagogues. This would be one of the most important factors in facilitating the spread of the early Christian movement. The largest diaspora Jewish community was located in Alexandria, where the Hebrew Scriptures had been translated into Greek. Beyond Alexandria, Rome itself had a Jewish community of considerable size, as did Antioch, but Jews were found in practically every territory under Roman hegemony. In addition, there was the diaspora community in Mesopotamia, which had taken root after the Babylonian conquest of Jerusalem in the sixth century BC. Jews were found in cities throughout the region and even seem to have become the majority in some cities, like Nehardea.

Then there were Davidic loyalists. These conservative centrists had long since left Judea's political arena and so were not an organized party as such. They were, rather, found throughout the Jewish nation in both the Levant and the diaspora. Their aspirations were political in that they desired the restoration of the Davidic kingdom under a Davidic messiah in fulfilment of the prophetic promises. For this to happen, the Herodian and Augustan order would need to be overcome. They shared much in common with the Essenes, such as the belief that their hopes could not be realized through current political and military structures but through the direct apocalyptic intervention of God. Yet, this did not produce a pacifist, mystical movement like the Essenes but a prophetic movement that sought ethical engagement with society through commitment to biblical ideals of justice and piety. Before Jesus, John the Baptist was perhaps their most outspoken proponent. They viewed the fundamentalist norms and Oral Law of the Pharisees as corrosive, even if well-intentioned, and the Sadducee agenda as breeding an institutionalist mentality that cared little for the average person or for ethical, heartfelt devotion to God. At the core of their beliefs was the conviction that God's ancient promises had not lapsed because God himself had not changed. While other quarters of Judaism also believed in a coming messiah, Davidic loyalists were convinced that such a messiah must be a descendant of David, for the Davidic covenant had established God as the eternal father figure within the Davidic dynasty. The Davidic messiah would establish the Davidic kingdom—the kingdom of God—through a wholesale transformation of the created order and the dawn of a new age.

---

3. Philo's brother, Alexander, was imprisoned by Caligula, perhaps for participating in Philo's embassy, but he was later released by Claudius (*Ant.* 19.276).

Jesus's Davidic ancestry was not contentious in early antiquity (cf. Matt 1:1; 21:9, 15; Luke 1:27; 2:4; Rom 1:3). His family was not the only one which claimed such descent either. The warlord Hezekiah and his son Judas might have alleged their descent from David. Archaeologists have also discovered an ossuary dated to this era from a tomb near Jerusalem. The inscription on the ossuary indicates that the bones inside were of someone who "belonged to the House of David."[4] Descendants of David were also known to supply wood to the temple annually on the twentieth day of Tammuz (b. Taʻan. 4:5). The assertion that Jesus was a Davidic descendant, therefore, was neither exceptional nor legendary.

Jesus was most likely born in ca. 7 BC, at a time of great intrigue and uncertainty in the Herodian dynasty.[5] That year, Herod executed his sons Alexander III and Aristobulus IV for allegedly plotting his demise. Less than three years later, he executed his eldest son, Antipater II. In addition, Herod had killed his own wife (Mariamme I) and successfully conspired to kill three high priests (Mattathias Antigonus II, John Hyrcanus II, and Aristobulus III). He also executed the warlord Hezekiah without trial, tortured many people, burned insurgents alive, took political prisoners, and arranged for the massacre of a hippodrome full of people at his own death. The account of Herod's slaughter of male infants in Bethlehem under two years of age after learning of the birth of a potential claimant to the Davidic line (Matt 2:1–18) has the hallmarks of credibility, even if Josephus never mentions it.

Luke's depiction of shepherds learning of Jesus's birth (Luke 2:8–20) not only recalls the classic shepherd imagery of the Old Testament but also contrasts with the violent movement of Athronges the shepherd and his four brothers, who were active immediately after Herod's death in 4 BC. Their belligerent campaign of terror and hate, which included the killing of Roman and

---

4. David Flusser, *Jesus* (Jerusalem: Magnes Press, Hebrew University, 1997), 180–86.

5. There is considerable debate about the date of Jesus's birth. Most indicators point to a date late in Herod's reign. Luke implies that John the Baptist was born during Herod's reign (Luke 1:5), which suggests that Jesus was also born at approximately this time. However, Luke never overtly states this. Instead, he pinpoints Jesus's birth to the time of the census in AD 6 (Luke 2:1–7). The difficulty with this is that it implies Joseph and Mary were betrothed for over a decade, unless Luke's Herod was actually Archelaus or Antipas. Either way, this poses some difficulties for Luke's assertion that Jesus was around thirty when he began his ministry, as it necessarily condenses his ministry and death into a single year, AD 35/6. From John 2:20, construction work on the temple had been going for forty-six years or been perceived to have taken a total of forty-six years when Jesus cleared the temple, and Jesus was specifically said to have been less than fifty years of age (John 8:57). Using the earliest theoretical date of AD 30 for the clearing of the temple, this puts the earliest possible date for Jesus's birth at 17 BC. It is possible that construction on the temple began that year, but it is likely that it started slightly later (see 4.5.6). Matthew's timing of the slaughter of the innocents (approximately two years after Jesus's birth), and Herod's subsequent death in 4 BC (Matt 2:16–20), gives us a more viable and precise bracket between 17 BC and 6 BC for Jesus's birth. The latter part of this period is more likely, as it better matches the intrigues around the Herodian throne.

Herodian forces (*Ant.* 17.278–84), stands in sharp contrast to the peaceable depiction of unarmed shepherds paying homage to a baby in a feeding trough and an angelic army proclaiming, "Peace on earth among men of goodwill" (Luke 2:13–14).

Luke also picks up the ongoing prophetic instinct of Davidic loyalists with the depiction of Mary, Zechariah, Simeon, and Anna. The Holy Spirit is indicative of prophetic inspiration and is seen as active in each of these figures at the start of Luke's Gospel. The Holy Spirit falls upon Mary in conceiving Jesus. She is told that her son would be called the son of God and would sit on the Davidic throne to reign over the descendants of Jacob (Luke 1:31–35). The announcement is replete with classic prophetic motifs of God ruling a united Israel through his son, the Davidic heir.[6] Mary's Magnificat (Luke 1:46–55) echoes the song of Hannah in 1 Samuel 2:1–10, which foreshadows the rise of the monarchy in Israel and forms part of the Davidic apologia that makes up both books of Samuel. Like Hannah, Mary explores the way God would reverse fortunes, including bringing down rulers from their thrones (Luke 1:52)—a statement that resonates loudly in the last years of Herod's reign. Zechariah, the father of John the Baptist, expresses similar sentiments:

> Blessed be the Lord, the God of Israel,
> for he has dealt with and worked redemption for his people.
> He has raised a horn of salvation for us
> in the house of David, his child,
> just as he had promised long ago
> through the mouth of the holy ones, his prophets. (Luke 1:69–70)

Luke depicts Simeon and Anna as standing in this roster of inspired prophetic figures when they encounter the newborn Jesus with his parents in the temple on the day of his circumcision. They confirm Jesus to be the consolation and glory of Israel, a light for revelation to the gentiles, and the redemption of Jerusalem (Luke 2:21–38). In the context of the prophetic promises, these ideas are all about the establishment of the kingdom of God under a Davidic king. In Acts, Luke portrays those who oppose this prophetic program as stiff-necked people who resist the Holy Spirit to their own detriment (Acts 7:51–53).

When John the Baptist and Jesus began their ministries some three

---

6. This identification of Jesus as "son of God" pertains to his Davidic ancestry. This is not a denial of the claim that Jesus was the incarnation of God the Son, the Second Person of the Trinity. The two ideas are integrally related, as both pertain to the direct rule of God, even though the term in the Gospels focuses on Jesus's Davidic ancestry.

decades after Herod's death, the currents pulling the Jewish nation in opposite directions had not eased. In fact, they had intensified. Their calls to repent were, to some extent, a beckoning to abandon extremism in favor of a more humane centrism that was faithful to the ethical hum of Torah and in step with the expectations of the prophets. Prophetic expectation continued to run high among those looking forward to the transformation of the age. The demands aimed at Archelaus immediately after Herod's death in 4 BC help to frame the early message of Jesus, as portrayed by Luke:

> The spirit of the Lord is upon me.
> Since he anointed me to be herald to the poor,
> he has sent me to proclaim
> > release for the captives,
> > recovery of sight for the blind;
> to let the abused go free,
> to proclaim an amnesty of the Lord. (Luke 4:18–19)

Far from platitudes or allegorical imagination, this "Nazareth Manifesto," which reiterated Isaiah 61:1–2, claimed that Jesus was the proper alternative to the power structures tearing the Jewish nation apart. It was a claim to royal prerogative—one based not on military might, political maneuver, or priestly privilege but on prophetic fulfilment, love, forgiveness, and the work of God's spirit through a Davidic descendant (cf. Zech 4:6). These ideas transcended state, cult, culture, economics, and even religion—all the arenas in which the battle for the identity and future of the people of God was taking place. Both John and Jesus were convinced that the extremes of unprincipled power and fundamentalist impulses had torn the Jewish nation apart, with a very real detrimental impact upon its people. This tenuous old order had grown too rotten to continue. It would soon be axed in a monumental eschatological work of God and replaced by a new covenant characterized not by the politics of power that proclaimed Caesar as lord; nor by the politics of pragmatism that struck bargains and compromises; nor even by the absolutizing of Torah and the hyper-regulation of human life; but by the fulfilment of God's classic prophetic promises, the expression of love for God and neighbor, and the recognition that Jesus, not Caesar, was lord. This new work demanded the repentance of God's covenant people so that they would not fall under the judgment to be enacted in bringing this new order to fruition (cf. Matt 3:7–12; Luke 3:7–14).

It was a message that revolutionized human history.

ANCIENT TEXTS INDEX

OLD TESTAMENT

Genesis
1 39
1:1. 39
1:2. 465
2:4–8. 39
3:8 39
10:4 . . . . .329, 513
11:5–7. 39
12:3 333
12:4–5. 58
14:18 143
18:18 369
22:2 143
49:10 211

Exodus
3:14 184
12:5 83
13:3 209
13:11a 142
13:3, 14. 204
19:6 . . . . . . .21, 427, 459, 468
20:2 204
20:26 183
21:10–11. 109
22:18 484
28:42–43. 183
29:4–8. 208
30:13 126
32:25–29 382

Leviticus
6:10 183
8:31–9:24. 361
10:1–2. 514
10:1–5. 381
14:10–11, 23 361
15:13–15, 29 361
16:32–33 208
17:3–4. 382
17:8–9. 382
19:1–2 185
19:5–8. 382
21 470
21:7–9. 446
21:7–15. . . . . . . 109, 110, 112
21:8 109
21:13–15. . . . . 446, 462
21:17–23. 567
23:13 469
23:33–38. 469
25:1–7. 372
27:14–21. 232
27:30 549

Numbers
18:24–28 549
22–23 495
24:17 467
25:6–15. 450
28:1–10. 335
35:25–32 208

Deuteronomy
2 61
4:2 . . . . 519, 524
4:5–8. . . . . 334, 345
4:34 342
5:6 204
5:15. 204
6:1–3, 7. 517
6:4 68
6:4–9. 342
6:8 519
6:9 520
7–11 366
11:19–21. 517
11:29 61
11:29–30 142
12 . . . . 53, 59, 61, 84
12:5 87
15 526
18:15 . . . . . 84, 429, 454, 459
21:15–17. 109
21:22–23. 475
23:3 70
23:7 451
27:4 61
27:4–7. 142
28:22–23. 493
32:4 185
34:10–12 429

Joshua
4:1–9 62
6:26 450
8:30 61

Judges
4 456
10:17 356
19:29–30 398
20:1 356

1 Samuel
2:1–10. 613
2:12–17, 34 514
2:27–36. 208
3:11–14. 208

4:4–11 514
7:5 356
9–10 459
10:17 356
17 456
17:51 . . . . 354, 398
21:9 354

2 Samuel
3:4 524
5–7 61
5:1–5 69
5:6–10 175
5:7 . . . . 178, 429
5:7, 9 . . . . 34, 437
6:12–19 175
6:16–17 34
7 589
7:10 213
7:11–14 18
7:11–16 . . . . 27, 64, 211
7:12–16 34
7:13 428
7:14 . . . . 198, 561
7:15–16 286
22:43 157

1 Kings
2:10 437
2:26–27 208
2:35 . . . . 319, 574
7:19, 22, 26 94
8:1 175
8:30 87
8:65 427
12:16 69
12:26–33 68
13:33–34 68

2 Kings
15:1–7 135
15:7 437
17:24–28 35
17:30 80
18:41–46 494
23:29–30 198

1 Chronicles
1–8 132
1–9 139
2:1–2 139
3:3 524
3:17–24 . . 132, 196, 197, 210
3:19 31
3:19–24 . . . . 31, 121
3:22 . . . . . . 53, 132, 196, 198
3:22–24 . . . . 173, 174
9 132
10 132
10–29 132
11:2 140
11:5 175
13–16 133
15:15 142
17:10–14 211
21 133
21:29 142
24:14 300
28:5 134
29:7 135
29:23 . . . . 134, 471

2 Chronicles
1–9 132
3:1 143
7:8 427
9:26 135
11:13–17 133
12:8 . . . . 133, 134, 137
18:3 132
26:16–21 135
26:20 135
26:23 437
29–31 138
30 70
30:5 . . . . 70, 138
30:11–12 70
30:13 141
30:18–20 70
31:17 458
35:20–25 198
36:22–23 . . . . 26, 134

Ezra
1–5 54
1:1–4 26
1:8–11 26
1:11 26
2:2 27
2:2, 14 75
2:64 27
3:6, 8 28
4:2 35
4:5 26
4:7–10 58
4:7–16 54
4:7–23 65
4:20 56
4:21–23 82
4:23 56
5:3–4 28
5:13–15 28
5:17 28
6:1 29
6:2 29
6:3–12 29
6:3 50
6:14–15 30
7:12 52
7:23 50
7:25 50
8:2 53
8:15–20 86
8:17 87
8:35 51
8:36 50
9:7 53
9:9 . . . . 53, 54
10 . . . . 52, 63
10:1–8 106
10:7, 9 52
10:8 52

Nehemiah
1:1 64
1:1–2 65
1:2 64
1:2–3 81

ANCIENT TEXTS INDEX

1:1–3 . . . . 56, 59
1:3–4 82
1:5–11 59
1:9 59
1:11 64
2:1–8 59
2:3, 5 64
2:7 65
2:8 49
2:9 65
2:10 . . . . 57, 59, 63, 69, 70
2:10, 19 . . . . 57, 66, 233, 364
2:11–12, 16 59
2:20 69
3:1, 20–21 43
3:16 . . . . 64, 437
3:31 67
4:2 49
4:3 66
4:3, 7 . . . . 233, 364
4:23 64
5:10, 14 64
6:1, 12, 14, 17, 19 233
6:6–7 . . . . 64, 68
6:8 68
6:9 67
6:10–13 63
6:14 . . . . 67, 69
6:15 66
7:2 . . . . 64, 81
7:7, 19 75
8:1 280
7:73b–9:5 51
9:6–37 51
9:38 75
9:38–10:39 51
10:16 75
10:32–33 126
11 132
11:10–18 59
12:2 53
12:5, 18 300
12:10 43
12:36 65
12:36–37 68

12:45 68
13:4–5 43
13:4–7 70
13:6–7 70
13:8–9 71
13:10–13 . . . . 71, 127
13:15–22 71
13:23 . . . . 70, 71
13:23–27 71
13:23–31 63
13:23, 28 63
13:26 . . . . 52, 71, 342
13:28 . . . . . 43, 57, 70, 71, 76,
. . . . 102, 103, 112

Job

26:12–13 39

Psalms

1 . . . . 121, 428
2 . . . . 121, 428, 514
2:6 . . . . 175, 429
18:42 157
33 169
33:4 286
33:8, 10–22 169
37:19–20 402
46:2 465
72:8 465
47:1–2, 7–10 333
74:12–17 39
75:10 172
79 334
79:2 333
89 . . . . 34, 39
89:10–12 39
89:19–37 286
92:10 172
96:1–3, 7–10 333
110:1–2, 4 175
113:5–6 184

Proverbs

1:6a 223
1:7 185
3:5–6 185

Ecclesiastes

1:1 . . . . 220, 241, 523
1:2 245
1:6 238
1:12–2:26 246
1:13 247
1:14 238
2:1–26 226
2:3 247
2:24–26 247
3:1 247
3:1–14 245
3:14 241
4:1, 13–16 220
4:13–16 240
5:1–7 . . . . 220, 239, 241
5:2 241
5:3 241
5:5 241
5:6 241
5:8–9 220
5:8–10, 13–17 245
5:13–17 243
6:2 220
7:11 242
8:2 241
8:2–4 220
8:2, 4–6 216
8:2–8 . . . . 243, 244
8:9–17 244
8:11 239
9:12 220
10:16, 20 241
10:17 248
11:3b 238
12:1 220
12:9 . . . . 241, 242
12:9–14 247
12:11–14 224
12:12 247
12:13–14 247

Song of Solomon

1:3 343
1:7 343

3:4 343
3:6 343
4:4 .... 343, 437
5:6–7 343
8:1 343
8:1–2 343
8:6 342
8:6–7 .... 341, 342
8:7 342

Isaiah
5:30 465
9:1–3a, 6–7 466
9:1–7 467
10:6 157
19:18 386
24:1–3, 6 199
24:1, 4, 7, 9 196
24:2 209
26:1–4 196
26:19 348
27:2–4 196
27:13 203
40–66 9
41:22–29 34
44:9–20 34
44:24–45:7 34
45:1 124
45:1–6 .... 30, 140
55:3 286
61:1a, 3–6, 9 387
63:18 199
64:1–2, 6–7 201
64:11–12 199
65:1–5, 11 283
65:17–19, 21–22a, 25 204
65:21–25 196
66:5 387

Jeremiah
3:17 333
7:12 87
7:18 33
31:31 369
31:31–34 550

32:21 204
44:1 36
44:1–30 80
44:17–19 33

Lamentations
2:3 172

Ezekiel
4:5 376
8–11 .... 62, 336
16:44 31
37:15–28 .... 104, 116
40–48 62
43:7–9 437

Daniel
1 .... 283, 344
1–6 345
1:1 22
2 .... 170, 171, 344, 346
2:31–25 344
2:34–35 170
2:37–38 170
2:40–43 170
2:44–45 170
2:47 346
3 .... 344, 345
3:16–18 .... 345, 348
3:17–18, 28 346
5:23 346
6 .... 344, 353
6:5, 10, 16, 20, 26 346
7 .... 171, 346, 347
7–12 .... 310, 344
7:2–3 465
7:4 171
7:5 171
7:6 .... 155, 171
7:7 171
7:8 171
7:11 345
7:11–27 327
7:13–14 .... 10, 347
7:13–14, 18 368

7:20–21 345
7:22 346
7:26 194
7:27 347
8 171
8:3–4, 20 171
8:5–7 171
8:5–7, 21 155
8:7–8, 22 172
8:8, 22 .... 172, 194
8:14 384
8:21 171
9 322
9:4–19 .... 322, 347
9:24–26 322
9:27 .... 309, 335, 336
10–12 .... 172, 271, 348
10:13, 21 172
10:20 172
11 .... 237, 238, 271
11:2 172
11:3 172
11:3–4 194
11:5 194
11:6–9 237
11:7 250
11:10 250
11:11 250
11:12 .... 261, 262
11:13–14 271
11:15 273
11:16–17 274
11:17 297
11:18–19 290
11:20 .... 296, 303
11:21a 303
11:21–22 322
11:24 .... 322, 324
11:24, 39 324
11:24–28 326
11:28 326
11:29–30a 329
11:29–12:1 363
11:30 .... 329, 513
11:30b–32 336

11:31 . . . . 309, 335	2:12–13. 413	9:2 123
11:33, 35 . . . . 284, 210	2:15. 382	9:3 159
11:34 310	2:17 406	9:4 157
11:35 . . . . 285, 367		9:5–6a. 159
11:39 365	**Haggai**	9:6 152
11:40 363	1:1. 59	9:8 178
11:40–44 364	1:1, 15 30	9–14. 9
11:40–12:1b 363	1:13–15. 28	9:9, 12 30
11:41 363	2:2 483	9:9–17. 128
11:42–43 364	2:10 30	9:10 160
11:44 364	2:20–23 28	10:5 157
11:45 364		11 . . . . 102, 109, 115, 116,
12:1 364	**Zechariah**	119, 138
12:2 348	1–6. 29	11:1. 122
12:2–3. 349	1–8. 42	11:1–3 . . . . 96, 104
12:3, 10. 310	1:1, 7 30	11:2 97
12:7 364	1:2–4. 215	11:2–3. 122
12:10 284	1:3. 215	11:3 125
12:11 . . . . 309, 335	1:8–11. 140	11:4, 7 123
12:11–12. 365	1:14. . . . . .175, 178	11:4–7 . . . . 102, 120
	2:1–5 . . . . 54, 55	11:4–17. . . . . 104, 112
Hosea	3:1–10 28	11:5. . . . . 113, 115, 120
2:10–12. 493	3:8 . . . . 17, 29, 427	11:6 123
4:6–9. 209	3:9 30	11:7. 104
4:6b–9. 209	4 362	11:8 . . . . .112, 115
4:16a 393	4:6 656	11:9–11a, 14. 116
	4:8 29	11:14 141
Amos	4:8–10. 427	11:15–17 115
9:11–15 . . . . 212, 213	4:9 29	12 197
	4:10 30	12:2–7. 202
Micah	5:5–11. 35	12–14. . . . 177, 178, 196, 208,
2:3 393	6:1–8. 140	211, 212
	6:9, 14 66	12:6 196
Nahum	6:9–15 . . . 28, 29, 43, 57, 174,	12:8 178
2:11b 477	178	12:9–14. 198
2:12a 477	233, 327	12:12 132
2:12b 477	6:12 17	12:13 209
3:4 485	7:1. 30	12:14 198
	7:2. 43	13:4–6 . . . . .177, 178
Habakkuk	7:5. 36	13:7 198
1:6a 513	8:20–22 333	13:8–14:4, 9, 11 203
1:6b 513	9:1–8 . . . . 123, 152, 156,	14:9 . . . . .59, 178
1:10b 513	159, 178	14:16 141
2:7–8a 405	9:1–16 30	14:16–19. 141
2:8b 406	9–10. 42	14:16–21. 178

14:17 141
14:18–19 141

Malachi
1:1 106
1:2–4 116
1:2–3 451
1:4 106
1:5 106
1:6a 107
1:8–10 116
1:10 59
1:14 37
2:1–9 110
2:8 115
2:10 . . . . 106, 116
2:11 . . . . 107, 118
2:11–12 111
2:11–13 59
2:12 . . . . 112, 124
2:13–16 114
2:14–16 111
2:17 114
3:1–4, 6–7a 119
3:6–7 214
3:8–12 127
3:8–11 128
3:11 129
3:16–18 214
3:23 494
4:2 38
4:4–6 214

NEW TESTAMENT
Matthew
1:1 612
2:1–18 . . . . 590, 612
2:16–20 612
3:1–2 478
3:7–12 614
4:17 478
5:3 234
5:17 522
5:20 . . . . 478, 518
5:45 187
6:10 190
6:12 234
7:24–27 590
9:6 347
9:9 231
9:10–11 231
10:3 231
10:4 610
10:41 . . . . 5, 8
11:12 5
11:12–13 6
11:13 5
11:19 231
11:25 520
12:1–8 526
13:24–30 574
13:54 521
14:5 8
14:6–11 593
14:13–22 570
15:1–14 519
16:2–3 186
16:6, 11–12 20
16:15–20 590
16:27–28 527
17:24 126
18:1–5 520
18:23–35 234
18:25 512
19:13–15 520
21:6–11 565
21:9, 15 . . . . 590, 612
21:12–13 . . . . 567, 588
21:21–27 8
21:23 521
21:31 231
21:33–46 234
21:35–39 234
21:45 234
22:15–16 22
22:16 573
22:17 549
22:42 590
23:1–39 527
23:4 549
23:37–24:2 567
23:38 590
24 337
24:15 337
24:27–44 527
26:31 199
26:51 567
26:55 521
26:61 . . . . 527, 590
26:63–64 348
26:64 347
26:67–68 8
27:5–8 234
27:40 590
27:51 590
28:18 10

Mark
2:1–4 520
2:14 231
3:6 22
6:2 521
6:15 8
6:21–28 593
6:30–45 570
8:15 20
8:28 8
10:45 347
11:6–11 565
11:15–17 567
11:15–18 588
11:15–18, 29–33 604
11:27–33 8
12:13 22
12:35 590
12:38–44 590
12:41–44 549
13 337
13:1–2 . . . . 567, 588
13:14 337
14:27 199
14:47 567
14:58 590
14:65 8

ANCIENT TEXTS INDEX 621

15:29 590
15:38 590
36 573

Luke
1:5 612
1:27 612
1:31–35 613
1:46–55 613
1:52 613
1:67 8
1:69–70 613
2:1–7 612
2:4 612
2:8–20 612
2:13–14 613
2:21–38 613
2:25–35 8
2:36–38 .... 8, 493
2:38 501
2:41–50 521
2:46 525
3:2 208
3:7–14 614
4:18–19 614
4:18–21 527
6:31 525
7:16 8
7:26 8
7:29 231
7:36–50 527
7:40–50 234
9:10–17 570
11:4 527
11:5–13 494
12:16–21, 42–48 574
14:28–30 574
15:1 231
15:10–16:12 574
17:16–18 110
19:1–10 231
19:7 231
19:35–40 565
19:45–46 .... 567, 588
20:1–8 8

20:6 8
20:41 590
21:1–4 549
21:5–6 .... 567, 588
22:50 567
22:51 567
22:52–53 590
22:63–64 8
23:45 590
24:19 8
24:26, 44 522

John
1:14 .... 40, 368
1:21, 25 .... 64, 429
1:24 459
2:1–11 388
2:13–17 588
2:13–22 567
2:19 .... 388, 590
2:21–22 388
3:3–8 388
3:13 347
4:19 8
4:19–26 454
4:22 454
4:23–24 388
4:25 64
5:16–18 526
6:1–15 570
6:14 .... 64, 429
7:14, 28 521
7:40 .... 64, 429
8:20 521
8:57 612
10:23 588
11:48 590
11:50 604
12:12–19 565
12:20 587
14:2 583
18:10 567
18:14 604
19:13 583
19:19–22 568
19:37 199

Acts
1:6–8 454
1:18–19 234
2:29 437
2:29–36 590
2:46 521
3:11 588
4:5–7 601
4:6 208
4:36–37 234
5:12 588
5:33–40 527
7:1 601
7:40–50 590
7:51–53 .... 7, 613
8:14–17 454
10:2, 22 528
11:27 8
13:1 8
13:26 528
15:32 8
16:13 520
17:4 528
18:2 548
21:9–10 8
22:3 527

Romans
1:3 612
1:13–16 266
1:18–32 183
3:21–26 369
13:1–5 548
15:7–8 548

1 Corinthians
5:1 480

2 Corinthians
5:17 368
6:16 389

Galatians
2:15 451
3:1–6 451

3:28–29 451	9:11–14, 23–28 190	1:22 327
4:4 .... 12, 13	10:1 75	1:29–40 330
6:15 368	10:17 75	1:33 437
	10:26–31 389	1:33–35 331
Ephesians	10:33–34 126	1:41–53 331
1:3, 20–21 190	11:10 389	1:51–53 332
1:10 10	12:22 389	1:54–59 .... 309, 335
2:11–12 389	12:24 389	1:59 335
6:12 172		1:60–61 338
	1 Peter	1:74 414
Philippians	1:1 252	2:1 350
3:4–6 518	2:5 389	2:15–28 350
	2:11 252	2:23–26 449
Colossians		2:31 437
1:15–20 .... 10, 190	**2 Peter**	2:41 396
	1:4 40	2:42 382
1 Timothy	1:21 11	2:42, 44 351
1:4 186		2:44, 47 352
3:2, 12 109	**Revelation**	2:46 352
4:7 186	1:1 187	2:48 353
6:15 37	9:1–6 561	2:50, 67–68 353
	9:13–21 565	2:70 350
2 Timothy	17:14 37	3:3–9 352
3:16 11	18:20 8	3:5 352
4:4 186	19:16 37	3:5–6 353
	21:1–4 368	3:8 353
Titus		3:10 354
1:6 109	**APOCRYPHA**	3:10–12 354
1:14 186	**Esdras**	3:13 354
	9:38 280	3:13–26 355
Hebrews		3:20–21 353
1:1–2a 5	**Judith**	3:24 355
2:5–10 .... 54, 55	9:13 176	3:38–41 357
3:1–4:11 5		3:39 357
3:2–6 389	**1 Maccabees**	3:46–56 356
3:16–4:11 389	1:1–4 309	4:1–18 357
3:20 38	1:11 450	4:19–25 357
5:6, 10 175	1:14 .... 316, 445	4:26–29 359
5:6–7:22 389	1:14–15 283	4:34 359
6:20 175	1:15 317	4:34–35 360
7:11–17 175	1:16 318	4:36–59 362
7:11–21 389	1:16–19 324	4:46 6
7:22–25 389	1:20 326	5:1–5 372
8:1–2 190	1:21–23 326	5:6–13, 24–54 373
9:1–15 389		5:21–23, 55 373

5:65–68 373	9:43–49 404	12:19–23 204
6:1–4 360	9:50–52 405	12:24–34 422
6:5–16 360	9:53 405	12:25 422
6:32–47 373	9:54 . . . . 405, 406	12:35–37 422
6:48–50 373	9:54–57 392	12:38 422
6:48–54 373	9:55 . . . . 405, 407	12:41 422
6:49 372	9:56 . . . . 406, 407	12:45 . . . . 422, 423
7:1–4 390	9:57 408	12:48 423
7:9 382	9:58–61 408	12:49–52 423
7:12 382	9:63–69 409	13:1–9 423
7:12–15 377	9:63 409	13:11–14 423
7:12–18 377	9:73 . . . . 409, 410	13:15–16 423
7:12–20 381	10:1 412	13:17–19 424
7:13 382	10:1–4 411	13:20 424
7:14 376	10:3–4 411	13:21–23 424
7:16 382	10:6–7 411	13:25–30 424
7:17 335	10:7–9 411	13:28–29 400
7:19–20 390	10:10–11 412	13:31 431
7:29–38 397	10:12–14 412	13:36–40 426
7:31 397	10:17–20 412	13:43–48 431
7:32 437	10:21–13:24 413	14:5 431
7:39–50 397	10:25–45 . . . . 414, 420	14:7, 36, 49–52 430
7:44–50 398	10:36 414	14:16–24 430
8:1–20 394	10:46–47 414	14:25 428
8:16 395	10:48–50 414	14:27, 48 428
8:21–32 394	10:51–60 415	14:36 437
9:1 398	10:61–66 415	14:41 . . . 6, 8, 428, 429, 454,
9:2 399	10:69 410	459, 499, 550
9:2–4 399	10:74–86 416	14:41–45 428
9:5 399	10:87–89 416	15:1–9 431
9:6, 9 399	11:1–3 417	15:15–24 430
9:6 399	11:4–7 417	15:25–16:10 433
9:7 399	11:9–12 419	16:1–3 431
9:10 399	11:9–19 419	16:11–20 433
9:11–18 399	11:13 417	16:16 434
9:18 400	11:15–17 419	16:19–22 434
9:19 399	11:20 419	16:23–24 . . . . 434, 450
9:19–21 399	11:21–24 420	
9:24 402	11:24–37 420	**2 Maccabees**
9:27 . . . . 6, 402	11:38 420	1:1–9 447
9:28–31 404	11:38–40 420	1:7 422
9:32–34 399	11:41–53 421	1:10–2:18 449
9:33 404	11:54–56 421	1:13–16 360
9:35–36 404	11:57–62 421	1:18–36 68
9:37–42 404	12:1–4 422	2:14 330

2:19–15:38.............449
3.....................296
3:1....................242
3:1–11................242
3:4....................300
3:5....................299
3:10–11...............300
3:11..........272, 299, 301
3:14–35................301
3:16–17................301
3:38...................303
4:4....................299
4:7–10.................314
4:9................314, 331
4:9, 12................445
4:11...................277
4:11–15................316
4:12...................316
4:13–14................316
4:18–20................318
4:21–22................319
4:23...................319
4:23–25................319
4:25...................319
4:26...................319
4:27–28, 32............320
4:29...................320
4:30–35................321
4:33...................320
4:35–38................321
4:39–42................323
4:40...................323
4:43–50................324
5:1....................326
5:5....................330
5:5–10.................330
5:11–14, 24–27.........330
5:15–21................327
5:22–23................327
5:24–26...........330, 350
5:27...................350
6–7....................353
6:1........309, 332, 335, 336
6:1a...................338
6:1b...................338

6:1–2..................337
6:2....................332
6:5....................335
6:7....................344
6:8–9..................338
6:10...................338
7:1–42.................339
7:3–5, 17..............345
7:14...................348
7:14, 23...............309
8:1....................351
8:1–4..................351
8:6....................352
8:8–11.................357
8:9....................357
8:12–25................357
8:25–29................357
9:1–28.................360
10:1–7.................362
10:13..................358
10:14–17...............358
11:16..................358
11:16–21...............358
11:18..................359
11:22–26...............370
11:27–33...............370
12:2–9.................372
12:17–28...............373
12:32–45...............373
13:3–8.................374
13:18–22...............373
14:1–2.................390
14:3..............382, 391
14:3–10................394
14:3–14................377
14:4, 7................391
14:6..............377, 383
14:10..................394
14:11–13...............394
14:13..................392
14:14–15...............394
14:16..................394
14:18..................395
14:18–29...............395
14:23–25...............396

14:26..................392
14:27..................397
14:31–36...............397
15:10..................397
15:11..................397
15:20–25...............397
15:28–36...............398
15:31..................392
15:36..................398

3 Maccabees

2:28..............229, 230
3:29...................229
4:18...................229
7:20...................229

Sirach

6:5–17.................295
7:19–31a...............294
8:1–2..................293
9:11–13a...............293
10:8...................291
13:1–26................293
13:19..................293
17:27..................350
24:10..................176
29:1–28................293
36:1–9.................292
36:1–12................292
36:1–22................284
36:10–16...............295
36:13–22...............295
36:18–19...............295
36:19..................176
39:4...................295
41:4...................350
41:5–15................295
44–49..................258
45:1–23................295
45:24–25...............295
49:4–7.................294
50:1, 4................250
50:1–4............255, 259
50:1–21......258, 295, 331
50:2..............250, 280

50:4 250
50:5–7, 11–12a,
  17 20–21 281
50:25–26 293
50:26 110

Psalms of Solomon
2:25–30 546

Wisdom of Solomon
7:27 7

OLD TESTAMENT PSEUDEPIGRAPHA

Enoch
1–36 403
72–82 378
90 310
91:1–19 403
108:1–15 403

Jubilees
6:32–38 380

Letter of Aristeas
1 227
9–10a 222
12–14 .... 199, 201
15 183
15–16 217
33 227
35 227
41 227

Psalms of Solomon
2:1–12, 22–25 511
2:25 545
5:5–8, 11–12, 18 ... 494
17:4–6, 15–26, 32–37 .. 516

Testament of Judah
21.1–4 471
21.7–8 476

Testament of Levi
14:5–8 477

SUBJECT INDEX

Abomination of Desolation, the, 329–37
Acra, 316, 318, 330–32, 343, 361, 366, 370–71, 373, 375, 391–92, 398, 405, 411–12, 414–15, 419–20, 422, 424, 430, 433, 436–37, 445
Akkabiah/Akkub, 210–11
Alexander the Great (Alexander III), 57, 88, 130
    accession of, 149–51
    Battle of Gaugamela, 162–63
    Battle of Issus, 153–54
    Book of Daniel and, 170–73
    conquest of Egypt, 155–61
    conquest of Persia, 162–64
    death of, 167–70
    eastern conquests, 164–67
    father of. *See* Philip II
    Hellenistic Era, 171
    liberation of Greek cities, 153–54
    Samaria and, 161–62
    wars of the *diadochi*, 191–95
Alexander III (son of Herod), see Herod, family of
Alexander IV (son of Alexander the Great), 168, 192
Alexander Jannaeus. *See* Hasmonean dynasty
Alexandria
    city, 160, 192–93, 220–24
    deportation of Jews to. *See* Jerusalem, siege by Ptolemy I
    Museum in, 221–24, 226, 230, 255, 296, 546
Amyrtaeus. *See* Egyptian rulers
Andromachus Affair, 16, 161–62, 217
Antioch and Jewish citizens, 313–18
Antiochene persecution, 360, 362–66
Antipas (son of Herod). *See* Herod, family of

Antipater (father and grandfather of Herod). *See also* fraternal civil war
    death of, 559–60
    dynasty of, 551–54
    political power of, 483, 531–36
Antipater (regent of Macedonia), 192
Antipater II (son of Herod), 552
Antiochus III, 276–78, 288–91
Antiochus IV Epiphanes, 313–29, 359–60
Antigonus ("One-Eyed"), 192, 193, 196, 225
Antiochus III (Antiochus the Great), 251–53
Arameans, 78–79
Archelaus (son of Herod). *See* Herod, family of
Aristobulus I. *See* Hasmonean dynasty
Aristobulus II. *See* Hasmonean dynasty
Aristobulus III. *See* high priests
Aristotle, Aristotelian philosophy, 40, 149, 186, 221, 402–3, 512
Artaxerxes I–IV. *See* Persian Dynasty
Artaxerxes V, 165
Atonement, Day of, 381–82, 389, 406, 436, 454, 460, 505, 551, 601
Augustus. *See* Octavian

Babylonian Empire, 25–27, 170–71
Bacchides, 376, 381, 390, 398–401, 404, 407–12
Bagohi. *See* Persian governors of Judah
Battle of Ipsus, 194–95. *See also* siege of Jerusalem
"Benefactor," Ptolemy III Euergetes. *See* Ptolemaic rulers
Ben Sira, 291–96
Book of the Twelve Prophets, 211–15
book of Tobit, the, 277, 278–80
"Bought," Alexander II Zabinas. *See* Seleucid rulers

627

Caesar, Gaius Julius, 21, 530–31, 536, 540, 545–59
Cambyses, 26–27, 28, 30, 36, 79
Canon
  of Torah (Law), 17–18, 51, 54, 121, 142, 448, 499, 522
  of the Prophets, 17–18, 54, 61, 64, 121, 429, 447, 499, 522
  of the Psalter, 381, 429, 522
  of the Writings, 228, 523
  Pharisaic influence over, 522–24
  vs. history, 11–14
"Chickpea," Ptolemy IX. *See* Ptolemaic rulers
Chronicler, the, 131–44
Cleopatra VII. *See also* triumvirate
  death of, 80–81
  Julius Caesar and, 546–47, 555–56
  Mark Antony and, 564–67
"Clever" Simon. *See* Hasmonean brothers
Coele Syria, 270–76, 298
"Conqueror," Demetrius II Nicator. *See* Seleucid rulers
"Conqueror," Seleucus I Nicator. *See* Seleucid rulers
Cyrus II. *See* Persian rulers

Darius I. *See* Persian rulers
Darius II. *See* Persian rulers
Darius III. *See* Persian rulers
David, House of, 178, 197–98, 202, 210–11, 220, 280, 612–13
Davidic
  descendants, 18, 64, 196–99, 210–11
  Dynasty, 132–37
  loyalists, 18–21, 177–78, 180, 287, 367, 554, 590, 611
  kingdom, 17, 53. *See also* Book of the Twelve Prophets
  priesthood, 78, 173–81
  royal family, 31
  theology, loss of, 174–77
  tombs, 437–38
Dead Sea Scrolls, 376–84
diadochi
  Jerusalem controlled by, 191–92. *See also* Ptolemy I, Antigonus ("One-Eyed")
  last of the, 224–25
  wars of, 191–95
diaspora communities, 36, 85–87, 131

early church, the, 388–90, 451–52, 581
Edomites. *See* Idumeans
Eleazar Avaran ("Pale"), 351
Elnathan, governor, 41
Egypt. *See also* Alexander the Great
  alliance with Greece, 94–95
  House of David in, 210–11
  invasion by Antiochus IV, 318–20
  priests of, 83
  reorientation in the Levant, 89–92
  revolt of Inarus, 46–48
  succession of, 88–89
  war with Persia, 92–95
  Yahwist community in, 85–87
Egyptian Dynasties
  Twenty-Ninth, 89–90, 93
  Twenty-Sixth, 89
  Thirtieth, 93
Egyptian rulers
  Amyrtaeus, 89
  Hakoris, 89, 93, 95, 104
  Nectanebo I, 93–94
  Nectanebo II, 85, 94–96, 125
  Nepherites I, 89, 95, 104
Elephantine, 36–37, 51, 58, 73, 75–76, 78–87, 89, 125, 141, 386
Essenes, 8, 401–404, 476–80, 513–17
  after Herod, 609
  response to Herod, 590–91
exile, exiles (Judeans/Jews), 1–3, 14, 26, 34–35, 39, 43, 58, 68, 102, 132, 140, 201–3, 211, 310, 335, 344
Ezra (prophet)
  Dilemma of, 53–54
  mission, 48–51
  reforms, 51–54, 63

"Father Lover," Ptolemy IV Philopater. *See* Ptolemaic rulers

"Father Lover," Seleucus IV Philopater.
See Seleucid rulers
"Fatso," Ptolemy VIII. See Ptolemaic rulers
five century overview, 16–23
"Flautist," Ptolemy XII Auletes.
See Ptolemaic rulers
fraternal civil war, 491–504. See also Pompey
Magnus

"God," Antiochus II Theos. See Seleucid
rulers
"God Made Manifest," Antiochus IV
Epiphanes. See Seleucid rulers
"God Made Manifest," Ptolemy V
Epiphanes. See Ptolemaic rulers
"Good Conqueror," Seleucus II Callinicus.
See Seleucid rulers
"Good Father," Antiochus V Eupator.
See Seleucid rulers
governor(s)
    Nehemiah. See Nehemiah
    of Judah. See Persian governors of Judah
    of Samaria. See Persian governors of Samaria
Greece
    alliance with Egypt, 94–95, 98–102
    battle in Mesopotamia, 88–89
Greek
    culture, 181–84
    ethics, 184–87
    influence, 19–20, 74–75, 187–91, 456–58.
        See also Hellenism, Judaism
    view of Macedon. See Philip II
    Xenophanes (philosopher), 39–40
gymnasium, 183, 216, 230, 295, 314, 316–18,
    445, 517

Hakoris. See Egyptian rulers
Hanani. See Nehemiah
Hannibal, 267, 273, 289–91, 537
Hanukkah, 362, 447–49, 499
Hasidim, 355, 376–84
Hasmonean brothers. See also Maccabees
    Eleazar Avaran, 351, 357, 373
    John Gaddi, 351
    Jonathan Apphus, 351, 372, 408, 410–26

Judas Maccabeus, 350–51, 354, 356–57,
    372, 394–400, 409
Simon Thassi, 351, 373, 408, 426–33.
    See also John Hyrcanus I
Hasmonean Era
    high priests' crisis during, 313–24, 374–76
    overview, 498–501
    Roman client state, 511–13
    sources for, 309–13
Hasmonean dynasty. See also Hasmonean
    brothers
    Alexander Jannaeus, 461–83
    Antigonus I, 7
    Antipater (son of Herod), 552
    Aristobulus I, 455, 458–61
    Aristobulus II, 531–36, 542–46
    Aristobulus III. See high priests
    John Hyrcanus I, 6, 9, 21, 433–40,
        450–58, 511–13, 531
    John Hyrcanus II, 483, 485, 490–91, 507,
        511, 514. See also fraternal civil war
    Judas Aristobulus I, 458–61
    Mariamme I, 563, 566, 569, 575. See also
        Herod, family of
    Mattathias (father of Hasmonean
        brothers), 350
    Mattathias Antigonus II, 564–67, 569,
        571, 573, 589, 612
    resurrection of, 569
    Salome Alexandra, 461–76, 483–91
Hasmoneans, 408–10
Heliodorus Affair, 296–304
Hellenistic Era
    beginning of. See Alexander the Great
Hellenism
    culture, 181–84
    ethics, 184–87
    Judaism and, 19, 287, 313–38
Hellenizers, Jewish, 410–11
henotheism, 33, 37, 181, 385
Herod
    building projects of, 583–86
    Davidic lineage, 589–91
    death of, 602–607, 609
    Eagle Affair, the, 599–602

family of, 591–99
flight of, 567–68
high priesthood and, 573–77
Jerusalem temple and, 586–91
"king of the Jews," 22
Mark Antony and, 563–64
Octavian and, 579–80
return of, 568–71
Rome after, 609–614
ruler of Judea, 573–77, 582–85
siege of Jerusalem, 571–73
Herodians, 573–74, 609
Hezekiah, 70, 93, 204–10
high priests
    Alcimus, 405–405
    Aristobulus I, 458–61. *See also* Hasmonean dynasty
    Aristobulus III, 458, 536, 548, 563, 566, 568–69, 574–76, 589, 591, 612
    Antigonus. *See* Hasmonean dynasty
    Eliashib, 43, 70
    Eleazar, 204–205
    Hananel, 574–76, 580, 593
    Hezekiah, 204–10
    Jaddua, 107–109, 204. *See also* Manasseh Affair
    Johanan ben-Joiada, 83, 90–93
    John Hyrcanus I. *See* Hasmonean dynasty
    John Hyrcanus II. *See* Hasmonean dynasty
    Joiada, 43, 70–71, 76
    Joiakim, 43
    Jason, 313–24, 329–37
    Joshua ben-Zehozadak, 26, 28, 31, 43
    Manasseh, 204–205
    Menelaus, 318–20
    Onias I, 204–206
    Onias II, 204–205
    Onias III, 204, 208, 242, 283, 296, 298–302, 313–15, 317–23, 336, 356, 362, 383
    Onias IV, 322, 356, 362, 370, 374–75, 377, 383–88, 390–91, 397, 442, 448
    Simon I, 204–205
    Simon II, 249–50, 254–55, 258–59, 261–63, 270–72, 278, 280–82, 287, 291, 295–96, 301, 305, 319, 331, 366

high priesthood
    crisis in the, 320–24
    Herod and, 573–77
Hillel the Elder, 10, 519, 524–27, 551, 600–1
"Hooknose," Antiochus VIII Grypus. *See* Seleucid rulers

Idumeans (Edomites)
    Artaxerxes II and, 99–102
    Herod's lineage, 573
    Israelites and, 106–107, 450–52
    occupation of southern Judah, 212–13, 293
    Qos, 33, 60, 106, 113, 450
Intellectuals (*maskilim*), 284–87, 310–11, 315, 317, 321, 323, 327, 345–46, 349, 355, 367–68, 374, 401
Ionian revolt, 48
Israelite
    ancestry, 139–40
    history of. *See* Chronicler, the
    identity, 62–63, 131–32, 187–91
    land and, 140–41
Israelite Coalition
    Malachi's critique of, 106–107, 114–19
    Manasseh Affair, 102–119
    power struggles in Levant, 98–102
    priestly problems surrounding, 109–12
    Tennes Revolt, 96–98
    theology and scribal strategy, 119–22

Jehoiachin, king of Judah, 26
Jerusalem
    Abomination of Desolation, 329–37
    city, 43–44, 62
    conquest of, 507–11
    Davidic significance, 68–69
    diadochi control of. *See diadochi*
    high priests of. *See* high priests
    rebuilding temple in, 83–85, 277–78
    renovation by Herod, 586–91
    revolt in, 54–57
    siege by Herod, 570–73
    siege by Ptolemy I, 195–204
    siege of, 195–204, 248–51, 433–38

SUBJECT INDEX

temple in, 27–31, 43, 50, 52, 57, 62–64, 68, 137–39, 280–81. *See also* Mount Gerizim
  Samarian temple, 7, 21, 57–62
  walls, 62–73
  worship in, 52–53
Jesus
  Davidic lineage and birth, 612–14
  economics and the gospel, 233–34
  John the Baptist and, 119, 234, 429, 478, 494, 593, 611–14
  messiah, 64
  teaching in temple, 588–89, 600
  threat to politics, 22
  trial of, 583
Jews, Judeans
  Caesarean settlement, 547–51
  citizens of Antioch, 313–18
  community in Egypt, 85–87, 204, 209
  after Herod, 610–11
  during siege of Jerusalem, 199–204
  government under Ptolemy, 219–20
  in Asia Minor, 251–53
  period of persecution, 338–39
  Persian politics on, 98–102
  politically and spiritually, 281–88
  rebuilding wall, 64–73
  rivalry with Samarians, 144–45
  silent era belief, 7
  taxation of, 296–97
Jewish
  apocalyptic thought, 187–91
  Civil War, 469–76
  independence, 426–98
John Hyrcanus I. *See* Hasmonean dynasty
John the Baptist. *See* Jesus
Jonathan the "Trickster." *See* Hasmonean brothers
Joseph Tobias, 237–48
Judea
  building projects of Herod, 583–86
  campaign of Crassus, 536–38
  Herod as ruler, 573–77
  incorporated into Rome, 440–45
  self-governing state, 426–33
  under Ptolemy IV, 253–62
Judean diaspora, 35, 586
Judeans. *See* Jews, Judeans
Judah
  after Nehemiah, 75–78. *See also* Nehemiah
  apocalyptic thought within, 187–90
  Davidic hopes of, 91–92, 98, 282, 402
  Egyptian influence, 89–92
  governors of. *See* Persian governors of Judah
  independence of, 104, 413–25
  prophecy of, 177–80
  Samaria and, 91–92, 98
  under Alexander the Great, 173–74
  under Antiochus III, 276–78
Judah Town, 26, 85
Judaism
  converts to, 527–28
  Hillel the Elder, 524–27
  school and synagogues, 517–22
  scripture, 522–24
Judas Aristobulus. *See* High Priests
Judas the "Hammer" (Maccabeus). *See* Hasmonean brothers
Julius Caesar. *See* Caesar, Gaius Julius
Justin Martyr, 10–11

Leontopolis (temple), 386–87, 391, 448, 593
Liberators. *See* Julius Caesar, death
"Lucky" John. *See* Hasmonean brothers
Lysias, 356–60, 370, 373–77, 381, 390

Mattathias, 350. *See also* Hasmonean brothers
Manasseh Affair. *See* Israelite Coalition
Maccabean Revolt
  Antiochene persecution, 360, 362–66
  Battle of Emmaus, 356–58
  outbreak, 349–53
  Seleucids and, 358–59
  successes, 353–56
Maccabees, 350–69, 371, 373, 392, 404–405. *See also* Hasmonean Brothers
Manasseh Affair, 102–119. *See also* Israelite Coalition

Mark Antony. *See also* triumvirate
   Cleopatra and, 564–67
   death of, 80–81
Marius, Gaius, 465, 486, 530
marriage reforms. *See* Ezra, reforms
Masoretes, 57, 156
Medes, 74, 170–71
Megabyzus, 47, 54–57, 73
Mesopotamia, 86–87
Mithridates I of Parthia, 416, 430–31, 473
Mithridates VI of Pontus, 473–74, 486–88, 490, 506–9, 547, 550
"Mother Lover," Ptolemy VI Philometor. *See* Ptolemaic rulers
Mount Gerizim temple, 57–64, 111–15. *See also* Nehemiah
   destruction of, 452–54
   rebuilding of, 254–55
   Samaritan flight to, 161–62

Nebuchadnezzar
   destruction of temple, 286
   dream of, 170–73, 346. *See also* book of Daniel
   worship of, 344–45
Nectanebo I. *See* Egyptian rulers
Nectanebo II. *See* Egyptian rulers
Nehemiah. *See also* Bagohi
   governor, 64–72
   Hanani, brother of, 65
   Judah and, 70–72, 75–78
   marriage reforms, 71
   prophet, 51
   Samarians and, 46–73
Nepherites. *See* Egyptian rulers
New Testament view, 4–6

Octavian (Augustus)
   Cleopatra VII and, 564, 581
   early years, 555–56, 558–59, 560–62
   Herod and, 567–68
   master of Rome, 578–81
   Roman Principate, 581–82
   second triumvirate, 568, 577–78
   victory of, 578–81

Olivet Discourse, 337–38
Onias the Circle-Drawer, 7, 493–96
"Opportunist," Demetrius III Eukairos. *See* Seleucid rulers
Oral Law, 4, 9–10, 21–22, 286, 446–47, 459, 468, 478, 484, 519–20, 524, 609, 611

"Pale" Eleazar. *See* Hasmonean brothers
Parthian invasion, 564–67
Passover, 70, 81–83, 138, 141, 373, 430, 434, 493, 496, 499, 510, 525, 603–4
Peace of Callias. *See* revolts, Megabyzus
Pentateuch, 51–52, 106, 121
Pentecost, 373, 435, 439, 499, 565, 604
Persia
   defeat by Alexander the Great, 162–67
   defeat in Egypt, 103
   interactions with Greece, 74–75
   reassertion of power, 122–28
   rebellion against, 73–74
   ruling of. *See* Ptolemaic kingdom
   weakening power of, 92–95, 144–45
Persian Empire, religion
   Yahwism, 33–35, 36–40,
   Yahwistic communities, 35–36, 78–85
Persian Era
   developments from the, 30–31
   Elnathan, 31
   political unrest, 27–28, 92–95, 96. *See also* revolts
   rebuilding the temple, 26, 27–31
   religion. *See* Persian Empire, religion
Persian rulers
   Artaxerxes I, 45, 46–, 73–75
   Artaxerxes I, 48–51, 54–, 73–75
   Artaxerxes II (Arsaces), 88–89, 92–95
   Artaxerxes III, 95, 128–31, 167
   Artaxerxes IV, 75, 129
   Bardiya, 28, 129
   Cambyses, 26–28, 30, 26, 37, 46, 55, 79, 129, 168, 173, 236
   Cyrus II, 25–27, 28–30, 33–34, 36
   Darius I
      effect on religion, 36–37
      empire of, 74, 88

reign, 44–45, 156, 168, 173, 177–78
Darius II, 73–75, 88
Darius III, 100, 129–30, 151, 154–55, 157–58, 162–65, 167
Sogdianus, 73
Xerxes I, 45
Xerxes II, 73–75
Persian governors of Judah
Ahiab/Ahzai, 41
Bagohi, 75–78, 81–84, 91, 126
Elnathan, 31, 41
Hananah, 41
Hezekiah, 204–10
Jaddua (the high priest). *See* high priests
Jehoezer, 41
Johanan (the high priest). *See* high priests
Joshua (the high priest). *See* high priests
Nehemiah. *See* Nehemiah
Uriah, 7, 41, 133
Zerubbabel. *See* Zerubbabel
Persian governors of Samaria
Delaiah ben-Sanballat I, 58, 77, 84, 91
Hananiah ben-Delaiah, 81–83, 91
Jeshua ben-Sanballat II, 124, 158, 161–62
Sanballat I, 17, 57–59, 76–77, 102, 453
Sanballat II, 17–18, 76, 91, 102–104, 109, 113–18, 124, 133, 136–38
Pharisees. *See also* Jewish Civil War, fraternal civil war, Oral Law
after Herod, 609
Eagle Affair, The, 599–602
Jewish sect, 401–404
schools and, 517–22
Philip II of Macedon, 149–51
Phoenicians, 96–, 216
"Pious," Antiochus X Eusebes. *See* Seleucid rulers
Plato
philosopher, philosophy, 39–40, 149, 185–89, 285, 347, 403, 517–18, 527, 610
quasi-Platonic metaphysic, 40, 188–89, 285, 306, 345–47, 363, 379, 389, 403
Pompey Magnus, Gnaeus, 505–13, 529–33, 535–45

Pompey the Great. *See* Pompey Magnus, Gnaeus
prayer houses. *See* synagogue
priesthood, 76
reforms for, 71–72
under Ptolemy, 219–20
priests. *See also* high priests
John, the father of Eupolemus, 277
Joiada, 43, 70
Zadokite. *See* Zadokites
prophecy
Israel's restoration, 20
Judah's, 177–80
silence of, 13–14
suppression of, 6–11
Prophetic History, 53–54
prophets
Anna, 2, 8, 493, 613
Essenes, 8
Ezra, 43
Hillel the Elder, 10
John Hyrcanus I, 6. *See also* John Hyrcanus
Nehemiah, 43. *See also* Nehemiah
reliable prophet, the, 6, 8, 20, 427–29, 454, 499, 550
Simeon 2, 8, 613
suppression of, 6–11
prozbul, 526
Ptolemaic rulers
Berenice I, 299, 235–36
Berenice III, 488
Berenice IV, 535
Cleopatra I, 297, 302
Cleopatra II, 325, 384, 419, 441–42
Cleopatra III, 441, 443, 463–64, 466
Cleopatra IV, 472
Cleopatra V, 479
Cleopatra VII, 226, 535
Cleopatra Selene, 480–81, 487–90
Ptolemy I Soter ("Savior"), 191–95, 210, 220–24, 283, 304
Ptolemy II Philadelphus ("Sibling Lover"), 210, 217, 221–222, 224, 225–26, 230–36

Ptolemy III Euergetes ("Benefactor"), 226, 229, 248–49
Ptolemy IV Philopater ("Father Lover"), 248–49, 251, 253–63
Ptolemy V Epiphanes ("God Made Manifest"), 242, 256, 263, 283, 271, 277, 289–90, 297
Ptolemy VI Philometor ("Mother Lover"), 230, 313, 324–29, 384
Ptolemy VIII Physcon ("Fatso"), 325, 384, 441–44
Ptolemy IX Lathyrus ("Chickpea"), 463–64
Ptolemy X Alexander I, 463–64, 480, 488
Ptolemy XI, 488
Ptolemy XII Auletes ("Flautist"), 479, 534–35
Ptolemy XIII, 544–46
Ptolemy XIV, 547
Ptolemaic
　economy, 230–33
　end of dynasty, 521
　kingdom, 215–220
　rule, 195–264
Ptolemy Menneus, 480–81, 489, 543, 565

Qoheleth, 237–47
Qumran. *See also* Dead Sea Scrolls
　during Herod's reign, 591

rebuilding Jerusalem temple, 83
resistance literature
　Daniel, book of, 344–49, 362–66
　Song of Songs, 340–44
revolt(s)
　against Persia, 73–74
　Inarus, 46–48
　Ionian, 48
　Megabyzus, 54–57
　Satraps, of the, 96
　Tennes, 96–98
Rome
　beginning of end of, 540
　Carthage and, 266–69
　civil war, 538–42, 543–46

defeat of Antiochus III, 288–91
dictators of. *See* Sulla, Pompey Magnus
expansion of, 264–66, 418, 422
incorporation of Judea, 440–45
influence of, 21, 265, 488
Pyrrhic War, 266
Second Punic War, 267–68
Roman Senate
　under Octavian, 264, 581–82

Sabbatical Year, 372, 408, 433, 435, 456, 489, 493, 496, 526, 549–50, 572, 592
Sadducees. *See also* Jewish Civil War, fraternal civil war
　after Herod, 609
　Hasmoneans and, 7
　lineage of, 349
　Seleucids and, 401–404
Salome Alexandra, 461–76, 483–91
Samaria (city), 69
　Alexander the Great and, 161–62
　siege of, 454–56
Samaria (region), 35, 44, 50, 60, 98
　Herod's contributions to, 586
　governors of. *See* Persian governors of Samaria
　independence of, 103
Samarians, Samaritans
　Arameans, 78–79
　relations with Israel, 44, 53, 61, 63, 70–71, 82, 91, 144–45
　religion of, 35, 51–52, 337
　temple of. *See* Mount Gerizim temple
Sanballat dynasty
　end of, 16, 161–62, 180, 304
　Delaiah ben-Sanballat. *See* Persian governors of Samaria
　Hananiah ben-Sanballat. *See* Persian governors of Samaria
　Sanballat I, 57–60. *See also* Persian governors of Samaria
　Sanballat II. *See* Persian governors of Samaria
　Samaria and. *See* Andromachus Affair
Shelemiah, 58, 77, 84, 91

Sanhedrin
   Pharisees. *See* Pharisees
   Sadducees. *See* Sadducees
   Senate, 220, 243, 277
   under Herod, 553–54
"Savior," Antiochus I Soter. *See* Seleucid rulers
"Savior," Demetrius I Soter. *See* Seleucid rulers
"Savior", Ptolemy I Soter. *See* Ptolemaic rulers
Second Temple Judaism
Seleucid rulers
   Alexander I Balas [alleged son of Antiochus IV], 408–20
   Alexander II Zabinas ("Bought") [alleged son of Alexander Balas], 530, 531–35, 542–43
   Antiochus I Soter ("Savior"), 225–26
   Antiochus II Theos ("God"), 235–37, 240
   Antiochus III the Great, 249, 251–53, 276–76, 288–91
   Antiochus IV Epiphanes ("God Made Manifest") [son of Antiochus III], 318, 306–10, 313, 318–20, 326–29, 359–60, 442. *See also* Abomination of Desolation
   Antiochus V Eupator ("Goodfather") [son of Antiochus IV]
   Antiochus VI Dionysus [son of Alexander I Balas], 420
   Antiochus VII Sidetes [son of Demetrius I], 431–56
   Antiochus VIII Grypus ("Hooknose") [son of Demetrius II], 443–44, 450, 472–73
   Antiochus IX Cyzicenus [son of Antiochus VII], 444, 450, 454, 472
   Antiochus X Eusebes ("Pious") [son of Antiochus IX], 436, 472
   Antiochus XI [son of Antiochus VIII], 472
   Antiochus XII Sionysus [son of Antiochus VIII], 480
   Antiochus XIII Asiaticus [son of Antiochus X], 480, 487, 506

Cleopatra Selene. *See* Ptolemaic rulers
Demetrius I Soter ("Savior") [son of Seleucus IV], 390, 419
Demetrius II Nicator ("Conqueror") [son of Demetrius I], 443
Demetrius III Eukairos ("Opportunist") [son of Antiochus VIII], 473–74
Diodotus Tryphon, 420–21
Philip II [son of Philip I], 95–97, 149–51
Seleucus I Nicator ("Conqueror"), 191–95, 419, 421
Seleucus II Callinicus ("Good Conqueror"), 474
Seleucus III Keraunos ("Thunderbolt"), 224, 248
Seleucus IV, 296–304, 390
Seleucus V [son of Demetrius II], 443
Seleucus VI [son of Antiochus VIII], 472
Seleucus VII, 487
Sennacherib, 78
Septuagint, 226–28
"Sibling Lover," Ptolemy II Philadelphus. *See* Ptolemaic rulers
Sidonians, 97–98, 122–23
Simeon (prophet). *See* prophets
Simeon ben-Shetach, 455, 459, 462, 470, 472, 476, 479, 483–85, 493–94, 517
Simon Thassi, 430–33. *See also* Hasmonean brothers
Spartacus, 506
Sukkot (festival), 362, 381, 412, 436, 459–60, 469, 499, 507, 575
Sulla, Lucius Cornelius, 486–87, 505, 530, 541
suppression of prophecy, 6–11
synagogue
   beginning of the, 228–30
   school, 517–22
Syria
   Coele Syria, 270–76, 298
   first war of, 225–26
   fifth war of, 262, 270
   fourth war of, 248–51
   second war of, 234–36
   sixth war of, 324–29
   third war of, 236–37

Teacher of Righteousness, 393–94. *See also* Dead Sea Scrolls
temple
  early church and the, 388–90
  Jerusalem. *See* Jerusalem, temple of
  Onias IV and the, 384–88
  rededication of the, 360–62, 366–69, 370
Temple of Leontopolis, 384–88
Tennes Revolt, 96–98
theological response. *See* Essenes
"Thunderbolt," Seleucus III Keraunos. *See* Seleucid rulers
Tigranes II of Armenia, 487–90, 493, 506
Tobiah the Ammonite, 57–62, 66, 69–72. *See also* Nehemiah
Tobiad family, 233, 256–62, 318–20
Tobiad Romance, 277
Tobias (character in Tobit). *See* book of Tobit, the
Tobias (father of Joseph Tobias), 233
Tobias, Joseph, 237–48
Tobit, the book of. *See* book of Tobit, the
Torah, 51–52, 61, 141–44. *See also* Abomination of Desolation, Jewish Civil War, Canon, of the Torah, Oral Law
Trans-Euphrates, power in, 92–95
Triumvirate
  first, the, 530–31
  second, the, 560–63, 577–78
Twelve Prophets, Book of, 211–15

War Scroll, 8, 355, 382–83
wars of the *diadochi*, 191–95

Xenophanes (Greek philosopher), 39–40
Xerxes I. *See* Persian rulers
Xerxes II. *See* Persian rulers

Yahweh
  communities worshipping, 35–36
  land ownership and, 52
  near Eastern religion and, 33–35. *See also* Ezra
  oldest temple to, 79
  seen under Persian reign, 36–40, 44
  Zeus and, 332–34
Yahwists, 78–85
Yehud. *See* Judah

Zadokites, 349–53. See also *Hasidim*
  crisis, 390–94
  lineage, 448–50
Zenon, 233
Zerubbabel
  Babylonian conquest, 26–35
  construction of temple, 17
  Elnathan, 41
  Shelomith, daughter of, 31
Zion, 304–305
Zoroastrianism, 37, 52

AUTHOR INDEX

Aitken, James K., 227
Albertz, Rainer, 57, 75, 91
Albright, William F., 206
Arie, Eran, 57
Athas, George, 26, 29, 79, 214, 221, 238, 244, 245, 249, 310, 321
Avigad, Nahman, 41

Babota, Pace, 309, 331, 415, 428, 450
Barag, D., 90, 101
Bar-Kochva, Bezalel, 102, 188, 206, 207, 351, 357, 359, 390, 398
Bartsiokas, Antonis, 151
Batsch, Christophe, 446
Baynham, Elizabeth, 191
Becking, Bob, 75
Berlin, Andrea M., 250, 485
Bevan, Edwyn R., 290
Binder, Donald D., 228
Blenkinsopp, Joseph, 52, 87
Boatwright, Mary T., 441, 529
Bolin, Thomas M., 37
Bourgel, Jonathan, 440
Braund, David, 537
Bremmer, Jan, 39
Briant, Pierre, 46, 94, 95, 97, 101, 124, 128, 129, 154

Cataldo, Jeremiah, 31, 42
Chaniotis, Angelos, 289
Charlesworth, James H., 61, 142, 379
Chrubasik, Boris, 172, 235, 431
Collins, John J., 478
Cotton, Hannah M., 297
Cross, Frank Moore, 76, 103
Crown, Alan D., 115
Curtis, John, 36, 125, 160

Davies, Philip R., 310
De Hulster, Izaak K., 35
Diaches, Samuel, 86
Dusek, Jan, 101, 142

Edelman, Diana Vikander, 37, 68
Eshel, Hanan, 101, 117, 118, 286, 324, 470

Fields, Weston W., 43
Fishbane, Michael, 43
Fletcher, Joann, 94
Flusser, David, 612
Frantalkin, Alexander, 101, 122, 123
Freeman, Charles, 540, 555
Frei, Peter, 49
Fried, Lisbeth S., 42, 77, 90, 207

Gaster, Moses, 142
Gitler, Haim, 108
Glay, Marcel Le, 264
Gonzalez, Herve, 12, 202
Grabbe, Lester L., 66, 70, 158, 216, 256
Grant, Michael, 216
Grainger, John D., 224, 240, 252, 272, 290, 291, 297, 409, 416, 435, 454, 460, 472, 487, 489, 507, 543, 548
Green, Peter, 152, 160
Gruen, Erich S., 227

Haag, Ernst, 296
Hall, Katherine, 168
Hezser, Catherine, 519
Holbl, Gunther, 193, 216, 217, 237, 239, 248, 251, 264, 266, 416, 465
Honigman, Sylvie, 188, 206, 211, 239, 280, 300, 381
Hoover, Oliver D., 439

Horbury, William, 210
Horrocks, Geoffrey, 149

Jeremias, Joachim, 552

Karca, Iaakov, 497
Knoppers, Gary N., 50, 70, 75, 77, 87, 91, 117, 162, 452
Koch, Klaus, 49
Kokkinos, Nikos, 583
Kolman Marshak, Adam, 576
Kratz, Reinhard G., 188, 209
Kushnir-Stein, Alla, 573

Lacocque, Andre, 365
Lane Fox, Robin J., 95, 149, 151, 153
LeCureux, Jason T., 211, 215
Leith, Mary J. W., 109
Lemaire, Andre, 60, 98, 113, 145
Lendering, Jona, 164
Leuchter, Mark, 87
Levinem Lee I., 108
Lim, Timothy H., 221
Lipschits, Oded, 27, 49, 50, 60, 66, 75, 91, 188, 211, 271, 277
Lorber, Catharine, 108, 272

Magen, Yitzhak, 57
Magness, Jodi, 591
Marshak, Adam Kolman, 589
Meleze Modrzejewski, Joseph, 210
Meshorer, Ya'akov, 93, 94, 445, 467, 492, 512
Meyers, Carol L., 42
Meyers, Eric M., 42
Misgav, Hagai, 101
Mysliwiec, Karol, 94

Neusner, Jacob, 601
Nihan, Christophe, 188, 211
Noy, David, 210

Oeming, Manfred, 27, 60

Pearce, Laurie E., 85
Pfeiffer, Stefan, 251, 254

Porten, Bezalel, 36, 79, 80, 81, 83, 98
Portier-Young, Anathea E., 188, 189
Potts, Daniel T., 416, 420

Regev, Eyal, 445, 465
Richardson, Peter, 574, 584, 592, 594
Ristau, Kenneth A., 66
Ristau, Kenneth, 66, 87
Rocca, Samuel, 582, 590
Roller, Duane W., 544
Romer, Thomas, 33, 60
Room, James, 154, 163
Root, Bradley W., 90
Rosel, Martin, 211

Sanders, Jack T., 295
Schwartz, Seth, 404
Scolnic, Benjamin, 296
Sievers, Joseph, 309, 335, 372, 428
Shatzman, Israel, 414
Shenkar, Michael, 89
Shields, Christopher, 185
Smallwood, E. Mary, 387
Sneed, Mark R., 230
Stern, Ephraim, 41, 89, 206
Stern, Menahem, 216, 217
Stoneman, Richard, 151, 154, 163
Sullivan, Richard D., 575

Tal, Oren, 101, 122, 123
Tallis, Nigel, 36, 125, 160
Tcherikover, Victor, 318
Tov, Emanuel, 227

Van der Toorn, Karel, 36, 78, 83
Vanderhooft, David S., 41
VanderKam, James C., 43, 76, 91, 204, 254, 285, 383, 390, 407, 482, 574, 593, 602
Vermes, Geza, 493, 521

Walsh, Matthew L., 172, 363
Williamson, H. G. M., 87
Wolski, Jozef, 430
Worrle, Michael, 297
Worthington, Ian, 209, 221

Wright, Benjamin G., 227
Wunsch, Cornelia, 85

Yardeni, Ada, 98

Zelinger, Yehiel, 57
Zilbersetin, Ayala, 316
Zollschan, Linda, 336, 395
Zlotnik, Yehoshua, 89